W9-BBE-427

THE POLITICS OF POSTWAR GERMANY

THE POLITICS OF POSTWAR GERMANY

Edited by Walter Stahl

With an Introduction by Norbert Muhlen

Published for Atlantik-Bruecke by
FREDERICK A. PRAEGER, *Publisher*
New York

BOOKS THAT MATTER

Published in the United States of America in 1963
by Frederick A. Praeger, Inc., Publisher
64 University Place, New York 3, N.Y.

Library of Congress Catalog Card Number: 63-9344

Printed in Germany—Hafen-Druckerei Hamburg

Preface

How firmly is democracy established in Germany? This is the question this book tries to answer. To do this, it does, in the opinion of the publishers, not suffice to describe and examine pro- and antidemocratic elements and trends existing in the German Federal Republic. It is necessary to view the democratic development within the broader framework of the political and the sociological ones. It appears also useful to view it against the background of German history. These considerations have determined the contents of this book.

Studies and reports on German youth are contained in Chapter IV. At present, almost fifty percent of the German population have not, or not consciously, experienced Hitler and the rise and fall of the Third Reich. The success of the democratic education of this youth is of decisive importance for Germany's future. Because of its importance this subject has been discussed in a volume of its own *(Education for Democracy in West Germany,* published in 1961 by Frederick A. Praeger, New York, for Atlantik-Bruecke).

The articles contained in this book were written by leading German and foreign commentators and scholars (please see List of Authors). We have asked the authors to strive for objectivity—shortcomings and failures should be neither passed over in silence nor minimized, since this book is not intended to make propaganda for Germany but to further better *understanding* of Germany.

This book is published by *Atlantik-Bruecke* (Atlantic Bridge), Hamburg, a nonpartisan group of private citizens who desire to further better understanding between the United States and Germany. We sincerely hope that this book will serve not only as an interesting source of information but will also contribute to some small degree toward this goal.

Gotthard Frhr. von Falkenhausen
Chairman

Walter Stahl
Executive Director

CONTENTS

PART II. THE HISTORICAL BACKGROUND OF THE GERMAN SITUATION

PART III. WEST GERMANY TODAY

PART IV. GERMAN ISSUES IN THE LIGHT OF PRESS REPORTS, SCHOLARLY RESEARCH, AND OFFICIAL DOCUMENTS

PART V. WEST GERMANY'S RELATIONSHIP TO THE WORLD

APPENDIX

Introduction

The lifetime of the Federal Republic of Germany already exceeds in length the lifetime of the past Third *Reich.* While Hitler's reign ended after twelve years and three months, the new Germany has now entered her fourteenth year. History rejoices in this irony: What was once in Nazi *hubris* proclaimed—and often is still mockingly referred to—as the Thousand Year *Reich* proved considerably less lasting than the Bonn republic which at its inception was considered a provisional, transitory establishment.

Although this new Germany has been remarkably stable so far, something of the initial caution toward her durability seems to survive in most present-day assessments of her nature and strength. In contrast to the short-lived Nazi Germany whose image in contemporary eyes appears clear-cut, though often simplified and sometimes distorted, the image of today's Germany tends to be veiled by doubts, uncertainties, an aura of wait-and-see among most observers. This seems rather strange in light of the fact that her open society should be easier to explore and evaluate than the previous totalitarian order with its closely kept secrets cleverly hidden behind deceptive facades.

The authors of this volume—renowned journalists, historians, sociologists—take stock of today's German political realities as they have evolved in thirteen years of democratic government. Walter Stahl, the compiler of this volume, went to great lengths to avoid one-sidedness of sources, contents, and outlook. Under his intelligent and knowledgeable editorial direction, a considerable number of researches and writers were marshalled to contribute their findings and conclusions. Varying though their backgrounds, qualifications, and viewpoints are, they have in common an intensive firsthand acquaintanceship with their fields of concentration.

Their collective inventory accounts particularly for those facets which—in the shadow of the recent past—attract our main interest. Significantly, major parts of their presentation are concerned with the question of whether this past has finally been overcome, or whether its return is possible, if not probable. After the central stress which yesterday's dictator put on "the Jewish question" (and after his crimes proved that he meant every word of it), the observers are understandably preoccupied with present-day German attitudes toward Jews and anti-Semitism. As John J. McCloy in one of his first speeches as United States High Commissioner for Germany explained in 1949, and as is still true today, these attitudes serve as the primordial test of German regeneration after Hitler's fall.

To extend the dimensions of the subject depicted here, four eminent historians paint modern Germany's background *sub specie saeculorum,* and six experts on international relations outline her foreign policy, but the second major area explored in this volume is inhabited by the Germans of tomorrow; the explorers—one being an Israeli—examine opinions and attitudes of contemporary German youth. What does this emerging generation think on a world it never made, but which it will be forced to remake tomorrow? To correct the margin of error inherent in individual observation and interpretation, the quantitative findings of reliable opinion surveys are also presented. In brief, a large amount of valuable, often original information is gathered in this book which sums up to a balance sheet of the democratic progress of the Bonn republic.

To evaluate a balance sheet, we need firm standards. To gauge the strengths and weaknesses it reveals, we must compare its facts and figures with those of other, comparable entities. As far as I see, four such bases of comparison can be used to measure the achievements and shortcomings of Germany today.

First and most frequently, we compare the German realities of our time with those prevalent in the Hitler reign. In particular, we examine whether ideas, features, adherents of that period still survive today; such an investigation, of course, does not consist in the mere enumeration of present-day Germans who have physically survived the Hitler years; their numbers and names are rather irrelevant if they have mended their ways and changed their allegiance. But the new political behavior of Germans at large, the strength of totalitarian as well as of antitotalitarian movements, the spiritual, social, international, economic, and intellectual trends of our day can be compared with the corresponding realities of yesterday. This comparison enables us to understand how far Germany has proceeded on her road toward democracy—from a starting point which denied that such progress could be made at all.

Secondly, we may consider the new Germany against the background of the Weimar Republic which also struggled to establish itself as a democracy. This period can productively serve as a basis of fair comparison.

Does Bonn share its weaknesses, which, though, often appear unduly predominant and inflated in hindsight, or has it overcome them? Has Bonn developed safeguards against its enemies which Weimar lacked, or did not dare to apply? Has Bonn—and also, of course, have forces outside its control—created spiritual, societal, intellectual, international, economic conditions different from the Weimar times, and more advantageous to the growth of a healthy order? One can better understand the Germany that succeeded Hitler when he compares it with the Germany that preceded Hitler.

Thirdly, present-time Germany, whose experience as a democracy is relatively short, if not probational, can well be confronted with one or more of the nations with an unbroken record of democracy over the past century—Switzerland, England, the United States. While we remain aware of differences that are necessitated by different historical origins and national peculiarities which cannot be eradicated (and only apostles of hopeless One-World uniformity would deem their eradication desirable), still we can employ many of their institutions, postures, achievements as yardsticks. Is Germany following these predecessors, learning their lessons, reacting to challenges with similar responses? Or, if we find marked variances, is the German way necessarily inferior? Could it be that in some instances the Germans today travel in vehicles of their own to arrive at the same destination as older democracies?

Naturally, looking at realities abroad a foreign observer is often tempted to find them almost automatically inferior to those he knows from his own country. This fallacy—based on one form of prejudice—has frequently led to erroneous judgments of Germany (as of most other countries, too). In the 1930's, Frenchmen sometimes referred to German-Jewish refugees as the *chez-nous,* the *bei-uns,* because these uprooted and homesick people liked to tell their hosts how different things had been at home—implying how much better they had been. But then, it has also and rightly been noted that, say, Frenchmen, or Britishers, or Americans abroad tend to criticize foreign countries for not being exactly like their own. Self-centered, self-righteous provincialism supplies poor standards for understanding and gauging foreign realities—including those of Germany. However, the intimate knowledge of his own country with which a foreign observer is equipped may help him to take a more accurate measure of other nations when he compares not only the strong points and successes, but also the weaknesses and shortcomings at home with those he finds abroad. For instance, information on antidemocratic groups or incidents in Germany today can be evaluated more intelligently if the observer recalls that similar groups may exist, or similar incidents occur, in his own country, too.

A certain insight can be gained also by visualizing a perfect democratic society against whose foil the young German democracy is held. More precisely, reality may be measured by utopia; for democracy—ever eager to improve itself, "indissolubly connected with the idea of amelioration" (as Alexis de Tocqueville noted after his travels in America), almost compulsively pointing to its areas of weakness—is never perfect, as little as any other organization of society, although it stresses its imperfections more. But by comparing the conditions that exist with the state that would prevail in utopia, one can discover how far reality is from its ultimate aim; more optimistically speaking, one discerns how much of this distance has been conquered. An almost absolute and generally valid standard of this kind serves as a handy heuristic instrument, but if it reveals simply that German society today differs to a high degree from a perfectly faultless and spotless democracy, we have learned little and surely are not entitled to scold the Germans for not having built utopia in these past thirteen years.

If some critics of Germany have done exactly this, though not even her friendliest observers have claimed that she is nearing the outer reaches of near-perfection, her foreign friends, and Germans themselves, tend to be more restrained than her enemies. (This, of course, has not always been so.) And a great many Germans seem sometimes almost overly critical in their views of their country—which might be one indication of the German success in the transformation to democracy. Not so long ago, the majority of their fellow countrymen rejected German self-critics as "birds who soil their own nest"; today they begin to understand that the good society needs its gadflies. But national self-criticism, whether it is to the point or overshooting its mark, tends to spoil on reaching foreign shores, where it is likely to be misinterpreted; it is no export commodity.

Whether we compare the image of the new Germany as it appears in this volume with the realities of Nazi Germany, of Weimar Germany, of other and older democracies, or even with the utopia of perfection, we find (in this reader's opinion) reason to hope. True, some ugly features of the past still survive—how could it be otherwise in a country where in this year 1962 there is hardly one city without ruins from yesterday? True, the foundations of many new achievements are still insecure; they were built in a hurry, often with makeshift means, and have not yet withstood the tests of stormy weather. Also true, Germany still suffers from the lack of a well-established democratic tradition which takes more than half a generation to grow.

But as several contributions to this volume amply demonstrate, the new Germany has resisted all totalitarian temptations—from the Berliners who defended, and still defend, their freedom against Soviet encroachments, to the statesmen who rejected offers of pacts and deals with the communist colossus of the East. While Germany tries—by no means always with complete success, yet with surprisingly great success—to clean out the rotting remnants of the Nazi past, she has made her choice in favor of the Western values of personal freedom and human dignity and a world at peace. One third of her citizens in the Eastern parts are excluded by force from this choice. As it seems, the more fortunate "West Germans" have resolved to make good use of the chance that fate has put into their hands. If they succeed in this attempt—as the material in this volume appears to indicate—it will not be only to their own benefit.

New York City, September 1, 1962 Norbert Muhlen

Part I Germany: 1945—1962

The State and the Community in Germany today

By Bernhard Vogel and Wolfgang Kralewski

A description will be given of some of the organized forces—the churches, the labor unions and the employers' associations, the refugees' organizations, the press—in the life of the German community today. In other parts of this book, mention will be made of intellectual trends which are referred to here. In the governmental sphere, the German party system and its present characteristics, the present Constitution and its actual implementation will be described.
In speaking of Germany, we will refer to the area in which a free and democratic system of government has been able to develop since the end of the last war: the Federal Republic. When the Soviet Zone, i.e. Central Germany, is meant, this will always be clearly indicated.

I. The Governmental Structure of the Federal Republic

1. The Institution of the Basic Law

The legal basis of the political structure of the German Federal Republic is the "Basic Law of the Federal Republic of Germany", passed by the Parliamentary Council on May 23, 1949. When it became evident at the London Conference of the quadripartite Council of Foreign Ministers in December 1947, that the Soviet Union would not agree to the unification of the four zones of Germany to form a free and democratic state, the three western powers took the initiative. At least in the territory of the three western zones, they wished to establish a democratic system, corresponding to principles which they had declared during the Second World War to be the peace objectives. In accordance with this decision, the Military Governors consulted with the Minister Presidents of the West German *Laender,* and instructed them to call a meeting in order to draw up a constitution. This met in Bonn on September 1, 1948, under the name of "Parliamentary Council". The *Land* parliaments of the *Laender* sent 65 delegates to this assembly.
Their task was a clear one. The three zones, composed at that time of eleven *Laender,* together with Berlin, were to be united to form a federal state, and this federation was to be given a sound, democratic constitution. The members of the Parliamentary Council did not permit their imaginations to run away with them, and fortunately they did not make the mistake—committed in 1919—of trying to construct an ideal state on paper. Quite the reverse, they were not aiming at perfection, but at a provi-

sional solution, which was to last only until German reunification had been achieved.

Even this provisional solution was undertaken with hesitation, because it was feared that a "partial German state" might be an obstacle to reunification. But at that time, every politician hoped that German reunification would ensue in a few years.

On the other hand, there were discouraging models. There was, first of all, the completely undemocratic system in the Russian zone, where the Communists, as in the other states of the eastern bloc, pursued their own interests without any consideration for the population. If free Germany were to be given a new order, then it must at all costs be very different from what the Communists had established in their zone.

Apart from the dark shadows from the East which fell across the meeting of the Parliamentary Council, all politicians and also the people themselves were still under the sway of the reign of terror by Hitler and his party, a reign which had ended in a horrifying catastrophe only three years previously. Respect for law and for human dignity, which had been trodden underfoot for twelve years by the National Socialists, had to form the foundations of the new Germany. All politicians—with the exception of the Communists—shared the common aim that a system must be established which would never again offer opportunity for development of a totalitarian movement. With this in mind, the mistakes of the Weimar Constitution were very carefully analyzed, and changes were made in all those provisions which were thought to have aided Hitler to seize power in 1933.

Aside from the efforts to avoid the mistakes of the past, there was another factor. Of the 65 members of the Parliamentary Council, 27 belonged to each of the two main political parties, the Christian Democratic Union and the Social Democratic Party. Both parties entertained serious hopes of winning the next election and forming the first federal government. The spokesmen of the two parties, Dr. Adenauer and Dr. Schumacher, also both saw themselves as the future chancellor. Thus both parties worked at the constitution in the belief that it was their constitution, according to which they would have to govern in the future.

On this basis, the Parliamentary Council was able to create a useful constitution for the free part of the German nation; the Bonn Basic Law. It has now been in force for thirteen years, and during this time has proved highly successful. No voice which might be taken seriously has as yet been raised to demand any important amendment to the Basic Law.

Some things have, however, taken a different course from that intended by the lawmakers. This is only natural. The political life of a country cannot be pinned to a text forever. The constitution of a country also continues to live and develop, since politics are made by human beings.

2. Parliament and Government

The fathers of the Constitution in the Parliamentary Council were more or less in agreement on one point, namely that the Weimar democracy had become frayed for two reasons. In the first place, because there had been too many political parties; and secondly, because these parties had never been able to form a strong government which could direct the country with a steady hand in times of difficulty. Both reasons are closely interconnected and are, in fact, only two sides of the same question. The Parliamentary Council, therefore, attacked the problem from both sides at once and adopted measures which would simultaneously reduce the number of political parties and strengthen the government.

Past experience had shown that even a democratic system of government could not exist without strong leadership. Democracy and authority are not antagonistic, but belong together. From this it may be understood that a noticeable characteristic of the German Constitution is that, although the head of government is chosen by Parliament, it is only with difficulty that he can be dismissed from office after his election. In this way a close link is established between the head of government and Parliament on the one hand, but on the other, the latter holds a clearly established position of leadership.

The head of government, who according to an old tradition in Germany, holds the title of Chancellor, is elected by a majority of the *Bundestag*. It is true that the Federal President has the right to suggest a candidate, but the *Bundestag* can elect anyone it chooses as Chancellor. The candidate who wins the votes of half the members of the House is elected. Should no one receive this majority, the candidate who obtains the most votes is elected.

The Federal Ministers, who form the Cabinet, are nominated at the suggestion of the Chancellor. Since a Chancellor who has once been elected has practically a free hand in the choice of his Ministers, the majority of the *Bundestag* is, as a rule, not inclined to elect him before he has submitted a list of Ministers. In these preliminary negotiations, the Chancellor must take the wishes of his parliamentary delegation and those of his coalition partner into account. It has always been found that the Chancellor enjoys considerable freedom whenever he has to deal with several coalition partners. If his own party has an absolute majority, as was the case in 1953 and 1957, the Chancellor is severely limited in his choice. Formally, therefore, the Ministers are not elected by Parliament, and the individual Minister does not require the confidence of the *Bundestag* to perform his office, as long as the Chancellor is prepared to work with him. Nor does the Basic Law rule that the Ministers must be members of the *Bundestag*.

In actual fact, however, no one can now become a Minister who has not been elected as deputy to Parliament. (In Adenauer's first Cabinet in 1949 there were four Ministers who were not at the same time deputies, in the second Cabinet, in 1953, there was only one, and the third and fourth Cabinets, in 1957 and 1961, consist only of deputies.)

The Federal Chancellor, once elected by the *Bundestag*, can be overthrown during his period of office, which normally lasts four years, only by a new Chancellor having previously been elected by a majority. This has not yet occurred. According to the text of the Constitution, the *Bundestag* has no influence upon the removal of Ministers from office. Practice has shown, however, that the deputies are able to exert such a strong influence upon the Federal Chancellor that he is forced to dismiss a Minister. The most remarkable case of this kind was the dismissal of the Minister for Expellees, Professor Oberlaender, against whom such severe charges were made in public that the Opposition attacked him in Parliament and the Government party was unable to ignore the situation. Legally, the Chancellor was not obliged to dismiss him, but was forced to yield to political pressure.

3. The German Bundestag

According to old German constitutional tradition, the legislative consists of two houses. One represents the entire population of the Federal Republic by means of deputies chosen in direct election; this is the *Bundestag*. The other house represents the German Federal *Laender* through their Governments; this is the *Bundesrat* (Federal Council).

The *Bundestag* is by far the more powerful house, if only for the reason that the Cabinet is appointed from its midst. In legislation, however, the *Laender* Chamber, the *Bundesrat,* is also of considerable importance. More will be said of this later.

The fourth *Bundestag* is composed of 516 deputies. Twenty-two of these come from West Berlin and have a very unusual status; they are deputies without voting rights, and may exert only an advisory function in debates. Furthermore, they may not be elected directly by the population of West Berlin; they must be sent to the *Bundestag* by the Parliament of the *Land* Berlin. This provision goes back to 1949, when the western allies did not permit the Basic Law to apply in full to the territory of West Berlin.

The remaining deputies are elected by the population of the Federal Republic in direct election; half of them according to a system of majority votes in the election districts, the other half by proportional system by means of party lists.

The fourth *Bundestag* was elected on September 17, 1961. It has 251 deputies of the Christian Democratic Union, 203 deputies of the Social Democratic Party, and 67 deputies of the Free Democratic Party. (The Berlin deputies are not included.)

In addition to the task of choosing the Chancellor, thereby forming the government of the country, the *Bundestag* is entrusted with legislation and the supervision of the government.

The *Bundestag* holds an absolute legislative monopoly. No other body can pass laws, although most bills are introduced by the Government, whose officials have drawn them up. The deputies themselves seldom take the initiative in introducing a bill. For this reason, Parliament has only a relatively small staff at its disposal, which deputies may employ in their work. But no matter by whom the bills are introduced, they must be discussed and passed by the *Bundestag* before they can become law. This legislative competence cannot be transferred to the Cabinet; it is accorded only to the plenary meeting of the *Bundestag,* and not to any of its committees. Only in certain definite cases is the Cabinet authorized to issue decrees for the implementation of laws; these, however, require the approval of the *Bundesrat.*

The budget laws are a particular type, discussed and passed by the *Bundestag* every year. All expenditure which the Government intends to undertake must first be sanctioned by Parliament. The *Bundestag* has the right to keep constant watch over the budget, and at the end of the fiscal year, to examine whether the money has been spent sensibly and economically. In its supervision of financial matters, it is supported by an independent and very powerful control authority, the *Bundesrechnungshof* (Federal Accounting Office).

These activities are part of the work of supervising the Government. But in addition to this, the *Bundestag* has other means of keeping permanent check upon the Government. One of these is the Question Hour. As in the English House of Commons, every deputy has the right to put questions to the Ministers at all times. This arrangement is not based upon any tradition in Germany; it was first introduced into the standing orders of the *Bundestag* in 1951. It soon became evident that the deputies were making increasing use of this opportunity, and now no session is held that does not open with a question hour.

In addition to this, several deputies may join together in addressing written questions to the Government. If these are what are called "major questions", members even have the possibility of opening a general debate on the question after the Government has replied.

In individual matters, the most effective instrument of control may be an investigation committee. The *Bundestag* has the right to appoint special committees for all matters which it considers worth investigation. These committees have wide powers. However, use is seldom made of these rights. The committee which was appointed in the spring of 1962 to examine whether or not the Federal Minister of Defense had behaved correctly in allocating building contracts was the 18th investigation committee since 1949.

Of all these control instruments, it may be said that they may be employed by the decision of a minority; no majority vote is required. This provision is very important, since it takes into consideration the special circumstances of the parliamentary method of government. Wherever a cabinet is formed by a parliamentary majority, it does not mean that this majority is always interested in keeping a check upon it. This task is carried out to a large extent by the opposition, which of course is always in the minority, and for this reason must be able to make use of the instruments of control.

In order to be able to handle its many tasks efficiently, especially those of legislation, the *Bundestag* has formed a large number of standing committees, of which there are 26 at present. In general, there is a standing committee for each Ministry. They meet far more often than does the *Bundestag* itself, and deal with quantities of work. All the deputies are proud of their hard work in the committees, where they gain wide experience in their special fields. During the course of negotiations, they often prove their superiority over the officials from the Ministries, and are able to boast that they are quite well informed of what is going on in "their" Ministry.

However advantageous this specialization may be, it has two drawbacks to which critical observers constantly draw attention. For one thing, the standing committees offer a favorable field of activity for lobbyists. Pres-

sure groups are particularly eager to exert their influence on Parliament not just from the outside, but to get their representatives elected as deputies to the *Bundestag.* Those deputies who also belong to a pressure group naturally make an effort to be appointed to the standing committee which deals with their interests.
Secondly, the specialized work blinds some of the deputies, perhaps the majority of them, to general political problems. This state of affairs was once hinted at by the remark that the Federal Chancellor had no special ministry which submitted bills and consequently no special committee. Therefore, the Bundestag first noticed matters of actual politics when it was too late.
The two points described here as drawbacks are not a German problem alone. All Parliaments have to face it and seek some practical solution. Efforts are also being made in the Federal Republic to find more appropriate methods of procedure.

4. The Federal Government

The Chancellor and the Ministers form the Cabinet, which is officially known as the Federal Government. Normally all Ministers are head of a Ministry. Of the 21 Ministers in the present Cabinet, only one has no department under him. The Ministries and the areas of their competence vary in size. The smallest Ministry is that of *Bundesrat* and *Laender* Affairs with approximately 50 officials. The four largest are the Federal Ministries of Foreign Affairs, of the Interior, of Finance and of Defense, each of which employs many more than 1,000 officials.
A Federal Minister, therefore, unites three functions in one person. He plays a leading role within his political party, he is head of a federal department, and he is a member of the supreme governing body, the Cabinet.
Cabinet decisions may be reached in two ways. Either the chairman decides what shall be done and the members must obey his orders, or all issues are discussed together and a joint resolution is then reached. In the latter case, the only function of the chairman is to preside over the Cabinet. A solution has been found in the Federal Republic which lies half-way between these two possibilities. This approach was already indicated in the Basic Law. Under the chancellorship of Dr. Adenauer, usage has shaped this system and made it highly effective. Many issues must be discussed and decided upon in the Cabinet in a community spirit. These include all bills which are to be submitted to Parliament, as well as matters upon which differences of opinion have arisen among the Ministers. In such cases and in many others, which are not specified in detail, the Cabinet first debates and then votes. In order to deal with this large mass of work, the Ministers meet at least once every week.
Nonetheless, the Federal Chancellor is more than just a chairman. His stronger position is based legally upon the provision in the Basic Law that he shall determine general policy. In important cases, therefore, he may issue directives to the Cabinet or to individual Ministers. The Chancellor has seldom made use of this power. But since the Ministers must always count upon the possibility of receiving such instructions from the Chancellor, his expression of opinion has considerable weight in a general debate.

These legal provisions induced the Federal Chancellor to build up a smoothly functioning personal administrative staff, the Federal Chancellery. The activities of this office, which since 1953 has been under the direction of Under Secretary Dr. Globke, a much disputed figure, today form a secure foundation for the ascendancy of the Chancellor in the Cabinet. In the name of the Federal Chancellor it exerts a certain amount of control over the entire organization of all the Ministries, in order to secure a uniformity of administrative method. Many questions of dispute between the Ministries, therefore, need not be decided by the Cabinet at all, since the officials concerned generally come to an agreement when they receive advice from Chancellery officials by order of the Chancellor. In this manner, the Federal Chancellor was not only able to strengthen his own position considerably, but a way was also found to coordinate the activities of the governmental machine which continually expanded to cover new fields. The fact that there are two chief coordinating agencies, namely the Cabinet and the Chancellery, has, up to now, not been found to be detrimental.

The Administration

The most striking characteristic of the administrative organization is the absence of subordinate agencies of the Federal Government. Almost all Ministries are concerned solely with preparing legislation and coordinating the implementation of the laws by the *Laender*. Subordinate agencies of their own, in the sense of a link between the supreme authorities and the people, are an exception. As a rule, these functions are exercised by the administrative agencies of the *Laender*. Exceptions to this rule are the federal army, the frontier and customs authorities and the postal authorities.

Many new administrative problems arise from the ever increasing sphere of competence of the international organizations. The Federal Republic is a member of all European institutions, and has transferred part of its sovereign rights to supranational organizations. In many fields, therefore, the Ministries no longer work under the orders of the German Federal Government, but follow a European policy. This shift of competence to the international level affects chiefly the Ministries of Defense, Economics, Agriculture and Nuclear Energy, but all others are also affected.

The system of professional civil servants who are nonpartisan in the execution of their duties is adhered to in the Federal Republic. Thus when a change of government takes place, relatively few officials need to give up their positions. All the same, the political parties try to acquire adherents among the civil service, in order to exert political influence in this way, too. Another problem which causes the officials much trouble is the activities of the pressure groups. These matters should be taken seriously, but there is no need for greater concern here than elsewhere.

The question is often raised as to whether the German civil service does not suffer from the fact that before 1945 many of its members belonged to Hitler's party. It is true that during the Hitler period almost every civil servant had to become a member of the party, and after the war it was not possible to do without a large number of these persons.

Repeated and vehement disputes have, of course, taken place in Germany as to whether this or that official who held a high position during Nazi times is suitable for government service now. But even the most critical observers must admit that up to now no groups of former National Socialists have emerged within the civil service, nor has the Government been influenced or hindered by the activities of such persons.

The Armed Forces

Within the scope of the executive power, the armed forces hold a special position. The German *Bundeswehr* has been in existence since 1955 and now comprises some 375,000 soldiers. It is divided into the three traditional services, the army, the navy and the air force.

Every precaution has been taken to ensure that the entire military system is clearly subordinate to the political leadership. All military matters—insofar as these fall at all under the competence of the Federal Republic—are responsible to the *Bundeswehrfuehrungsstab* executive staff, which is composed of the Inspectors of the three forces and the Inspector General of the *Bundeswehr.* All Inspectors are directly attached to the Ministry, where they hold the posts of division heads. The supreme command rests in the hands of the Minister of Defense who must hand it over to the Chancellor in time of war.

In order to afford the *Bundestag* an opportunity of keeping a constant check on the huge organization of the armed forces, the special office of the *Wehrbeauftragte des deutschen Bundestages* (representative of the armed forces in the *Bundestag*) has been created. Regulations concerning the supreme command have only limited application to the *Bundeswehr.* All active forces, that is, all divisions, units of the air force and the navy, are under the command of SHAPE. The *Bundeswehr* has no General Staff of its own.

When the decision was taken in 1955 to build up the federal army, it was necessary to proceed in a great hurry. Serious difficulties had to be overcome in forming the officer corps. There were still no young officers, and the old officers had become estranged from their profession in the ten intervening years. Naturally, it was not possible to employ all those who had once been professional soldiers.

5. The Federal Laender and the Bundesrat

Modern Germany came into existence in the second half of the 19th century through the union of the separate German states. Nonetheless, it remained —apart from the Hitler period—a federation. Thus, apart from the *Reich* capital of Berlin, there were the numerous capitals of the *Laender,* some of which—such as Munich—retained their independent character and have always continued to be flourishing centers of cultural life. The federal system, however, formerly labored under one difficulty: one of the *Laender,* namely Prussia, had more inhabitants than all the others put together.

By once again becoming a federation, the Federal Republic is continuing a German tradition. It is, however, also the outcome of measures taken by the occupation powers, who brought the German *Laender* back into existence again after 1945. But they were not just reconstituted within their former boundaries; a completely new territorial arrangement of Germany was sought. The most important part of this plan was the dissolution of the old Prussia, in order to achieve some balance between the sizes of the individual *Laender*. Thus some completely new *Laender* were established, for example, North Rhine-Westphalia, while other *Laender*, such as Bavaria, retained their traditional territories. The motive of the occupation powers in reviving the *Laender* was the wish to decentralize state authority. This was no longer to be concentrated in one single capital. The new federally organized nation does, it is true, labor under certain difficulties—such as the egoism of the *Laender* in financial matters—but on the whole, it has proved successful. Its chief advantage is that government administration is better adapted to local conditions and greater opportunities are offered to regional political forces to play a role in shaping public life.

For the same reasons, there is room for considerable independent activity within the *Laender*—the *Staedte* and *Gemeinde* (cities and counties). Their councils are elected by their citizens and are entrusted with the autonomous government of their own local affairs. Communal autonomy is an old tradition here and even in Napoleonic times was adapted to the new needs (in Prussia through the reforms of Freiherr vom Stein). A democratic sphere of life existed (in the towns) long before Germany became a republic in 1918. This is the breeding place of democracy, and even today the ranks of the city mayors continue to provide a number of Ministers and Heads of Government. Dr. Adenauer was for many years *Buergermeister* of Cologne, Willy Brandt is Mayor of Berlin.

The German Federal Laender

Listed in geographical order from North to South.

	Capital	No. of inhabitants in millions	Area in thousand sq. meters	Strongest Party in the *Land*
Schleswig-Holstein	Kiel	2,3	15,7	CDU
Hamburg	City state	1,8	0,7	SPD
Bremen	City state	0,7	0,4	SPD
Lower Saxony	Hanover	6,6	47,4	SPD
North Rhine-Westphalia	Duesseldorf	15,7	34,0	CDU
Hesse	Wiesbaden	4,8	21,1	SPD
Rhineland Palatinate	Mainz	3,4	20,0	CDU
Saarland	Saarbruecken	1,1	2,6	CDU
Baden-Wurttemberg	Stuttgart	7,6	35,8	CDU
Bavaria	Munich	9,4	70,5	CSU
With special status:				
Berlin (West)	City state	2,2	0,5	SPD

Each *Land* has its own government, headed by a Minister President. (In the city states of Berlin, Hamburg and Bremen the official titles are somewhat different.) The constitutional arrangements correspond largely to those of the Federation, with the exception, however, that the *Laender* do not have a President and (apart from Bavaria) no second house.

The Bundesrat (Federal Council)

Cooperation between the Federation and the *Laender* is regulated by the Basic Law. The most important spheres of federal legislation are foreign affairs and defense, currency, trade, customs, postal services and federal

railroads. The most important fields in which the *Laender* are competent are cultural affairs and the greater part of the administration.
Cooperation between the *Laender* at the federal level takes place in the *Bundesrat*. Every *Laender* government is represented here through members of its cabinet. According to the number of its inhabitants, each *Land* sends three, four or five representatives. Altogether, the *Bundesrat* has 41 members with voting rights, in addition to four representatives from Berlin without voting rights.
The *Bundesrat* discusses every bill introduced by the Cabinet before it is brought before the *Bundestag*. It may itself take the initiative of introducing a bill. After a resolution has been passed by the *Bundestag*, the *Bundesrat* must debate upon the bill in a second passage. Insofar as the *Laender* are affected by its content and sphere of application—which is the case in about half of the bills—the approval of the *Land* parliaments is required before a law comes into force. The *Bundesrat* must also give its approval to the decrees of the Federal Government. Differences of opinion between the two Chambers are adjusted through a special Joint Conference Committee.
The *Laender* take yearly turns at providing the President of the *Bundesrat*. The President in office is Vice Federal President.

6. The Judicial System

Following the example of many democratic constitutions, the Basic Law opens with a list of basic rights, which constitute directly applicable law. Should a citizen feel that his basic rights have been violated, he may appeal to the courts. The courts are in every case obliged to protect citizens from all encroachments by the government.
Compliance with these provisions has been taken very seriously, since it was a question of proving that, contrary to Hitler's state of tyranny, the Federal Republic was a nation governed by law and order, a state in which law is the supreme authority. This claim means that government action may be taken only within the limits of law and justice. In order to guarantee this, powerful courts are needed, courts which, if necessary, are able to assert themselves against the government.
With unrivaled thoroughness, many new courts and appellate instances were established, but unfortunately no uniform court system. For all civil and criminal proceedings there are regular courts. Administrative courts are competent for disputes with administrative agencies. But should a citizen feel that his rights have been infringed by the Finance Department, he must appeal to the Finance Courts. Social security matters are judged by the Social Courts, and disputes between employer and employees by the Labor Courts. In the lower instances at least, the courts are composed of professional judges and laymen; some criminal proceedings are judged by a jury.
All courts with their higher courts come under the competence of the *Laender*. In order to coordinate court decisions, however, there are Federal Courts for all judiciary branches. Added together, the number of courts runs to over 1,200, at which some 12,000 judges are employed. The judges are professional civil servants, trained in law, enjoy complete independence and may not be dismissed from office.

For the political development of the Federal Republic, the institution of the *Bundesverfassungsgericht* (Federal Constitutional Court) has been of far-reaching importance. This is a supreme federal court on an equal footing with the Government and Parliament. It is organized on the lines of a court, and follows the procedure usual in Germany. The close link with political life is emphasized by the fact that the judges are elected with a two-thirds majority by the political organs, namely one half by the *Bundestag,* and one half by the *Bundesrat.* One third of the judges holds office for life, two thirds retire after eight years. The tasks of the Federal Constitutional Court include the interpretation of the Constitution when differences of opinion arise between the Federation and the *Laender* or between different *Laender.* Another important field of competence derives from the fact that every citizen is entitled to appeal to the Constitutional Court in an action concerning civil liberties. To a certain extent, it can restrict democratic liberties considerably, since upon the demand of the President it may rule that a political party shall be prohibited on the grounds that its methods and aims endanger the Constitution. The Court has twice availed itself of this possibility when it prohibited an extreme rightist party and later, the Communist Party.

In reaching their decisions, the judges of the Constitutional Court dispense with the quibbling over legal subtleties, usually so popular in Germany. Instead, they aim at formulating political maxims which may be generally understood. They enjoy universal respect, since it is generally recognized that they play an effective role as guardians of the Constitution and of democracy.

7. The Federal President

The head of state of the Federal Republic is the Federal President. Whereas Parliament and the Cabinet are determined by the majority party or a coalition of parties, the President is the symbol of national unity. He is not elected by the *Bundestag,* nor is he entrusted with his office through direct election by the people. (Under the Weimar Republic the President was elected by the people; this did not prove satisfactory.) For his election, a special assembly is convoked—the *Bundesversammlung* (Federal Convention). This is composed of the deputies of the *Bundestag* and an equal number of members sent by the *Land* Parliaments. Altogether it numbers more than 1,000 persons.

The political powers of the President are restricted, in order to avoid the danger of a rival government to the Chancellor. He represents the Federal Republic as Chief of State at home and abroad. He receives foreign envoys and appoints federal civil servants and federal judges. The federal Ministers nominated by the Chancellor also require his approval. Finally, international treaties and federal laws do not become valid until the President, after they have been passed by the two Chambers, has signed them.

As was shown in 1961, the Federal President may influence the forming of the government, should the elections not have produced a clear majority. Although his right of proposal does not enable him to force a Chancellor upon the *Bundestag,* he is still able to accelerate the process of the election of a Chancellor.

The office of Federal President should not be judged according to its limited powers. It has been of importance for the development of democracy in Germany because of the exemplary way in which the two previous incumbents, Professor Theodor Heuss (1949—1959) and Heinrich Luebke (since 1959), have administered their office. Both were entirely different personalities. Theodor Heuss, a Protestant from Wuerttemberg, a clever journalist and professor of political science, was a left-wing liberal. His marked unmilitary, civilian demeanor lent a new style to the young Federal Republic. Heinrich Luebke comes from a Catholic farmer family in Westphalia. He had made a name for himself as an agricultural expert, and is said to have no enemies, but many friends, who respect him highly for his integrity.

Both Presidents have, through their discreet behavior, strengthened confidence in state management at home, while abroad they are considered convincing symbols of the new German democracy.

II. The German Political Parties

1. Development up to 1945

Political parties do not enjoy a good reputation in Germany now and did not even in the last century during the Empire. At that time they were regarded as specific groups—especially of Socialists and Catholics—which would not subordinate themselves to the masses, did not recognize the authority of the State (at least not without reservation), and maintained suspicious relations with the outside world, whether with the Pope in Rome or with the Socialist International in London. They were considered disturbers of the peace and grumblers. When the German Kaiser, Wilhelm II, exclaimed upon the war credits approval by the *Reichstag,* "I no longer recognize any parties; I only recognize Germans!", he was expressing the opinion of many people, and his remarks met with general agreement.

The Weimar period in particular did not improve the parties' reputation. When the war was lost in 1918, and the German Kaiser and all the princes abdicated, Germany was, it is true, left with nothing but the previously defamed. The difficult task of making a new beginning fell particularly to the *Zentrum* and the Social Democrats. When as a result of the obligatory introduction of proportionate representation at all levels, the door was opened for party splits, there was much talk of party squabbles and disputes. In the *Reichstag,* many parties were represented, some of them by no more than two or three deputies. More decisive was probably the fact that to the man on the street, the parties did not seem equal to their tasks. No wonder that because of this, the man who promised to end this situation and to replace talk and discussion with actions and deeds found many followers. But even he—even Hitler—appeared first as the leader of a party, the National Socialist German Workers' Party, which soon did not want to be *a* party but *the* Party, the only one allowed to exist under a law it promulgated.

Subsequently, in 1945, when National Socialism had collapsed, and those Germans who had belonged to its party were brought to court and for the most part convicted for being members, many swore never again to join a party, regardless of its name. Under no circumstances did they want to have the same thing happen again. It is therefore not surprising that in 1945 the new parties had to cope with a great many prejudices, often old ones. So it is no wonder that even today, 17 years later, aversion to parties, uneasiness and reserve about them have not disappeared and our major parties have comparatively few members (SPD: 600,000; CDU: 300,000; and FDP: 80,000).

The first important political groupings formed as early as 1848 in *Paulskirche* in Frankfurt, where for the first time freely elected representatives of the people from the entire then-existing German territory met to work out a German constitution. But that attempt failed.

In the Empire after 1871, the character of the *Reichstag* was influenced decisively by the Conservatives, the Liberals (split since 1862), the *Zentrum,* and the Social Democrats. However, the effectiveness of these parties was in fact very slight, since the *Reichstag* of that time was invested only with consultative functions, being almost devoid of influence on the policy of the *Reich* and particularly on the personalities who guided it.

At any rate, two of these parties—the *Zentrum* and the Social Democrats—at that time developed the characteristic traits still influential in German politics today. Both represented minorities: on the one hand, the Catholics, and on the other the Socialist-minded workers. Both were harshly oppressed by Bismarck and at first critically hampered in their development. Nonetheless, in this very "period of struggle", both of them gained the strength to become well-organized, firmly led parties backed up by reliable supporters. Both were bound together in some things but separated by more. Putting it simply, it can be said that what they had in common became the basis for collaboration in 1918, and what separated them became the starting point for the antithesis of 1949.

When in 1918 someone had to assume responsibility for the collapsing *Reich,* it was natural for the *Zentrum* and the Social Democrats—the two strongest caucuses of the last *Reichstag*—to go about this task, though neither did so without considerable reservations. In order to avert the threatening Communist revolution, which had already engulfed the territory of their eastern neighbor, and to prevent complete governmental collapse, both were sufficiently farsighted to defer their own objectives temporarily for the sake of the whole and to collaborate despite all differences. Especially the leader of the German Social Democrats, Friedrich Ebert, developed from a party leader and Socialist deputy of the *Reichstag* into a statesman and first President of the *Reich* and at least until his death (1925) lent a certain cohesion to the young democracy, pressed from within and without.

These two parties were joined by the German Democratic Party, newly established on the liberal wing. In the first constituent *Reichstag,* these three parties had a strong footing, and it seemed possible to lend the new State its characteristic form under this coalition. In fact, the constitution worked out in Weimar was largely their doing.

At the very next elections the majority dissipated never to materialize again. The Democratic Party, especially, lost so many votes that it soon played the part of a small splinter party.

In contrast, the *Zentrum*—as the actual middle-of-the-road party and the one with a limited but dependable reservoir of voters—was at virtually no time during these years able to evade the responsibility of participating in the Government. For the sake of compromise, it consistently had to defer substantial portions of its basic program in order to secure for Germany a functioning Government at all. For a good seven of these 14 years, the Chancellor came from the *Zentrum* Party.

On the other hand, the Social Democratic Party—originally the savior of the country—slipped more and more into the unhappy role of the silent partner. Only on very rare occasions could it decide to participate in the Government. It was too afraid, and not without reason, that the workers would definitely turn to the German Communist Party—which was gaining ground anyway—if it entered a Government with rightist parties. But neither was it able to take energetic action in opposition. Its feeling of responsibility for this State it had helped to establish and its loyalty to the constitution preponderated. Hence, for years at declined active collaboration, particularly in the field of domestic policies, but frequently tolerated the respective coalition Cabinets tacitly, in order, as it said, to prevent anything worse.

When Hitler was appointed Chancellor in January, 1933, his powerful and vociferous movement in the *Reichstag* actually faced only three serious opponents: the *Communists,* who hoped after all to achieve the revolution which had been anticipated so long and missed out so often in the years before at Hitler's expense; the *Zentrum,* which for years had tried to salvage whatever was still salvageable and was now beginning to have self-doubts; and the *Social Democrats.* All other parties were long since in process of dissolution. Hitler promised everything to everyone and through tricks obtained agreement to the Enabling Act against which only the Social Democrats voted. As early as July, 1933, he banned all parties except the National Socialists.

But the nuclei of the parties continued to exist. Although banned, persecuted, partly emigrated, and sent to concentration camps, they never died out. On the contrary, there began a great process of reflection, meditation and discussion. What the party system now amounts to in the Federal Republic is the fruit of this reflection. Nonetheless, these years took a heavy toll; many of the best did not survive this period and are lacking today in the tasks of development.

The Communists recognized only too soon that their expectations had deceived them. Their hope that Hitler would only be their forerunner did not come true. Consequently, they took a new tack. In place of keenest contradistinction to and uncompromising rejection of the Social Democrats, there now came the demand for collaboration, destined to become a reality in one part of Germany. The pressure of the Russian occupation forced unification of the SPD (Social Democratic Party of Germany) and KPD (Communist Party of Germany) into the SED (Socialist Unity Party of Germany).

The Social Democrats were firmly determined to reject this request. But they, too, realized that only a transformation from a workers' party to a people's party would open the path to joint responsibility for them, if any chance at all should remain after Hitler. Still, there was no doubt but that after the collapse, the SPD would immediately revive.

The most pronounced transformation took place in the ranks of the *Zentrum* leaders. In spite of many attempts to reach other groups of voters, the party had always remained a Catholic one which, it is true, was able to rely on its voters almost without condition; but which, being a specifically Catholic party, seemed to be irrevocably limited to the Catholic minority. "We have to get out of the tower," a *Zentrum* deputy had written as early as 1906; but that had not been accomplished even in 1933.

As great and as old as denominational differences in Germany may have been, the only way of seriously surmounting these barriers was through an alliance with Protestant Christians. Although there had always been attempts in Protestant quarters to become politically active, all initiatives bogged down in regional or completely insignificant splinter groups which were not able to develop into a united party of any importance. German history provides many reasons for this but this does not alter the facts. National Socialism first led the way in placing more emphasis on common ground than on differences and effected a great change.

It is probably no exaggeration to consider the fruit of this process the conquest of an antithesis, existent in Germany for centuries at least in the political field: the rise of a Catholic and Protestant union. At the same time, one cannot overlook that not all Christians by far, and particularly not all Protestants, joined this union or even approved of it. Moreover, one should appreciate that this, at first, ideologically imbued union signified one of the conclusive steps away from the classical "ideological" parties of the kind characteristic of Germany for almost a century.

Of course, this trend also affected the liberals. The divided forces tried once more to attain cohesion.

The nationalist-conservative groups, last of all, remained silent. After 1945, there was no longer any place for ideas of a new but democratized monarchy or for nationalistic feelings. It may be that some officers who numbered among Hitler's most resolute opponents considered such ideas as late as 1938 and 1939, but they came to an end at the latest after the unsuccessful coup of 1944.

2. The New Start in 1945

Therefore, diverse as it was in individual sections of Germany, the new beginning after 1945 was not really surprising.

The Communist Party (KPD) was the quickest and best organized to appear on the scene again. It was actually the only group which had never completely ceased to exist and whose cadres and underground organizations had continued to function even in concentration camps.

The Social Democratic Party (SPD) did not lose a day, either, in beginning again with its old name and, for the time being, with its old platform. It also had an executive committee which had remained at least partly intact and which returned from Britain.

The *Zentrum,* however, did not revive, at least not in its old form. Although some adherents remained loyal to the old name, this little group quickly receded into insignificance, soon to disappear entirely from the political scene.

On the other hand, simultaneously and independent of one another in Berlin, in Cologne, in Frankfurt, and with slight differences in Munich, the Christian Democratic Union (CDU) arose, which styles itself Christian Social Union (CSU) in Bavaria to the present day.

Very diverse regionally and under various names, the liberals finally rallied as the Free Democratic Party (FDP) at federal level.

The newly founded parties were limited to these four only for a short time. When the Allied licensing provisions relaxed and finally lapsed altogether, a large number of additional political groups arose in this spring climate. There were parties, membership cards, organizations, and platforms long before there were once more parliaments to which the parties could have sent trusted men and women. It took a long time before the first preparations for drawing up a new, democratic constitution began in the three zones of the Americans, British and French. At first political activity was restricted to the Commune (Gemeinde); later to the *Land*. It was also these *Laender* parliaments which provided the deputies to the Parliamentary Council (Constituent Assembly), in which the CDU and SPD were represented in equal strength—important for further development of the German party system.

Another factor which became important was that this Parliamentary Council drew up an election law, in essence still in force with certain amendments. Although in principle the system of proportional representation was retained, it was nonetheless modified substantially on the basis of unfavorable experiences undergone previous to 1933. It tends toward certain advantages of the majority system which favors a concentration of the electorate in only a few parties.

When in August 1949, the German people again elected a Central Parliament for the first time in 16 years, the results did not seem to differ from earlier ones: Deputies from 11 different parties took their seats in the new *Bundestag*.

3. Movement towards concentration

However, one of the first and most important acts of this Parliament, the election of the Federal Chancellor and in connection with it, the formation of a Government, led to a decision which—as we are aware today—was to become of momentous importance in regard to the further development of the German party system and in regard to political conditions in the Federal Republic. The two largest parties, the CDU and the SPD, did not unite but instead separated. The first, the CDU, became the main bearer of governmental responsibility; the other, the SPD, became the nucleus of the parliamentary opposition. Therefore, on each side of Parliament stood a large and powerful party which, from the outset (although not so perceptibly at first), was potentially capable of relieving the other in office; and which together drew everything else into their spell.

In fact, the history of the parties since 1949 is the record of progressive concentration.

The share of the two major parties in the number of eligible votes was as follows:

	CDU	SPD	Total
1949	31.0 %	29.2 %	60.2 %
1953	45.2 %	28.8 %	74.0 %
1957	50.2 %	31.8 %	82.0 %
1961	45.4 %	36.2 %	81.6 %

All parties which joined with the CDU in the Government dissolved sooner or later. All parties which shared the opposition with the SPD also exhausted themselves and vanished from the *Bundestag* with the exception only of the FDP.

Even in 1953, no more than six parties returned to Parliament. Four of them formed the Government; the SPD once more became the opposition.

In 1957, besides the CDU and the SPD, only the FDP and the *Deutsche Partei* (the latter, however, only with the help of the CDU) managed the jump over the hurdle of the election law, which had been raised higher once again. In 1961, the number of parties represented in Parliament dropped to three; no other party came anywhere near satisfying the 5 % minimum clause. This development, which is surprising in the light of the history of German parties, was not followed to such an extent in the *Laender*. The situation in regard to elections to their parliaments is a little different. Nevertheless, the development led to a fundamental change in the party system.

It has often been said that in postwar Germany there are no longer any ideological parties, and that the party system has become highly similar to the Anglo-Saxon one. This is at least partly true. After 1945, the two parties which now dominate were doubtlessly established by groups with strong ideological ties. The SPD revivers felt pledged to Socialism and considered Karl Marx and August Bebel their intellectual forefathers. In the same way, the founders of the CDU were predominantly devout and practicing Catholics and Protestants who on the basis of their Christian responsibility felt an urge to establish an emphatically Christian party. Even now, these two groups constitute the cores of the two parties, but other forces have joined them. Although party conventions and rallies point out the significance of the C (Christian) in CDU again and again, the party has also opened its membership rolls and ballots to those who do not follow the party because of its Christian creed primarily. Quite naturally, the success of its election campaigns of 1953 and 1957 was mainly due to the fact that it attracted voters outside the ranks of the actual church-going Christian population, who were satisfied with the foreign and economic policies of the party in Government during the preceding years. In the case of the SPD, this transformation from an ideological party to a people's party stands out more clearly. It has not only found new groups of voters apart from the workers who traditionally adhere to it, but has also quite consciously and openly repudiated its forefathers, especially Karl Marx, as well as its previously proclaimed goals, particularly the nationalization of large portions of the economy. Especially during the past election campaign, it devoted a great deal of effort to making that fact understandable to its potential electors.

Hence, one must say that both parties have changed from ideological parties to people's parties in the measure that they increasingly divided the electorate between themselves, and the voters adhering to them spread beyond the group originally associated with them ideologically. The more the two-party system came to predominate in Germany after World War II, the more the two rivals became alternatives; the more the voter had to decide in favor of the "lesser evil" and the more the actual *weltanschauliche* components probably receded into the background.

Of course, this process is not yet by any means concluded, and no one can say whether or not it will continue and finally lead to a system approximating Anglo-Saxon conditions. No final verdicts can be delivered in the light of the election results in 1961 alone. In broad sections of the population, the CDU is still regarded as the ecclesiastical, clerical party; and in the minds of many, the Social Democrats are still the "Reds", who aim at overthrow and only camouflage their traditional Marxism for the sake of clever tactics. This line of argument is amply fomented, especially by the respective opponent, simply for propaganda reasons. However, the two ideological groups still, in fact, constitute the actual foundations of the parties, especially in the CDU.

Accordingly it seems appropriate to speak of the direction in which the party system is moving and at the same time to emphasize how very much this development is still in motion. Whether the two-party system can permanently predominate will depend conclusively on whether in the future the two parties continue to succeed on a larger scale in winning over voters in numbers far exeeding that of their traditional supporters. Whether both parties continue to be spared division will depend conclusively on their success in retaining their traditional ideological supporters.

4. Differences Between the Parties

The CDU resulted from a movement to rally Christians of both major denominations. The Catholic Christians, who were more united anyway as a result of the political tradition of the *Zentrum,* the common experience in the Diaspora, and not least their greater church discipline, adhered to it in far greater numbers than the Protestants, who are still much more broadly politically distributed. Nevertheless, the party makes deliberate provision for consideration of both denominations on the basis of parity, since especially the Catholic section knows from experience how much it depends on its partner's support.

The fundamental profession of Christian faith is nowhere as evident as in the field of educational policy. The most apparent and distinct difference from the other *two* parties is without doubt to be found in this realm. In no other question of domestic policy do the antitheses and persuasions collide so frequently and harshly as in this one. In the field of educational policy—chiefly a matter for the *Laender*—the tie between churches and party is also the firmest. In this regard, the hottest issues are efforts for the recognition of parents' rights—and the topics growing out of this: the organization of school systems and teacher training. Also, the creation of a special Federal Ministry for Family Questions and the policy on the family which it represents have their foundations in Christian doctrine.

The CDU has achieved its most significant successes in two fields which at first do not seem to be of specifically Christian character: in foreign and economic policy. Since the establishment of the Federal Republic, the CDU and especially its leader Konrad Adenauer, has pursued a clear and unambiguous conception in foreign policy and maintained it to the present against all objections from without and particularly from within. Its policy is based on the two pillars of an unconditional alliance with the West and an equally unconditional unification of the countries of the European continent, including Britain, if possible. Although this policy was at first developed in the light of total collapse and under the influence of the Western Allies, over the years it met with steadily growing approval in all quarters of the population, especially young people. But as a result of this very policy, the Federal Government placed itself in ever more marked opposition to the efforts of the Soviet Union. Although diplomatic relations were established with the Soviet Union in 1955 as a means of ransoming German prisoners of war still being detained, the political figures of the CDU in particular showed an emphatically uncompromising attitude.

Again and again they had to face the reproach that by tying the Federal Republic progressively more closely to the West, they were obviously losing sight of the real goal of any German policy: reunification. Yet the Federal Chancellor's personality resolutely restored Germany's credibility and credit in the Western world.

The CDU achieved equally great successes in the field of economic policy. Here, free market economy, which was created by Ludwig Erhard, especially not only helped to overcome the catastrophe of World War II and develop a new German economy, but gradually placed the Federal Republic in a position to render a substantial contribution to the common Western defense and to aid developing countries.

At no time has the CDU had a large membership. It is estimated that only between 2 and 3 % of its voters are also members; that means that it probably has barely 300,000 enrolled members. However, even they represent more of a loose following surrounded by a very large number of persons associated with the party, whose support it can count on with certainty, but who still do not want to become more closely tied to it.

In the case of the CDU, the membership dues cover only an insignificant fraction of its expenditures; during election periods especially, the party is very dependent on contributions. The apprehension often expressed that the party thus becomes dependent on contributors does not take into account that, particularly in such a large party, the influences inevitably immunize one another, and that whereas a one-sided orientation to a certain pressure group is conceivable in small parties, such a group is bound to come upon distinct limits very quickly in the CDU, just because it includes nearly all sectors of the population.

At the time of its re-establishment in 1945, the SPD at first relied on its former following, which for the most part was still Marxist-minded and had the extensive support of part of the workers. However, the idea of renouncing the use of force and revolution had long since become common coin. It was intended to work for a free Socialism by democratic means. In continuation of the development of these ideas, the party adopted after lengthy, tough discussions, a party platform interlaced far less with Marxist ideas than with liberal ones at Bad Godesberg in November 1959.

Its tight and disciplined organization still links this party very firmly with its tradition, the effect of which is evident, among other things, in its comparatively large number of members.

It has by far the largest party organization with over 600,000 members. Their cohesion is often very marked, and it is quite possible to use the term "party community" in this regard. They also defray a considerable portion of the costs of their federal organization (estimated at about 3 million marks annually) out of dues.

In addition to the traditional ideological antitheses to the CDU, which are evident particularly in educational policy, there has from the beginning been an embittered struggle concerning foreign, economic and defense policy.

In view of the indisputable successes of the party in power, it became obviously more difficult from the economic policy standpoint for the SPD to maintain its traditional demands for nationalization of major industries and greater planning for the economic process. Here again, a distinct transformation can be discerned which, however, never abandoned the fundamental demand for a larger share for the workers of the profits attained and of co-determination with industry.

When it was founded in 1945, the FDP resumed old liberal traditions. In this regard, the obviously predominating idea was to appeal to those groups who were oriented neither to the Christian Democrats nor to the Social Democrats. During the subsequent period this consistently led to the question of whether or not the party should have its place "between" SPD and CDU or "to the right" of the latter. North of the Main, there was a greater inclination to orient the party towards the right, and south of it, the party has always had its home more in left-wing liberal traditions.

The 10 theses of its Berlin platform of 1957 stress the freedom of the responsible individual. In practice, this resulted in an especially marked activity in the field of economic policy. The goal was an economy as unhampered as possible and largely immune from governmental intervention. Social reforms contradicting such objectives do not meet with any favor from the FDP; the "welfare State" is dreaded.

In actual practice, the party has cooperated both with the CDU and with the SPD. In matters of educational policy, its position was closer to the SPD, because of a certain basically anticlerical attitude. On the other hand, in matters of economic policy, it had more than a passing fancy for Ludwig Erhard's free market economy. However, it was very often compelled to make clever alliances to avoid further curtailment of its somewhat narrow base. Its actual membership is as limited as that of the CDU. It is estimated at about 80,000.

5. The Adherents of the Parties

Repeated attempts have been made to study which population groups have a special inclination towards which parties. More and more use has been made of American population research methods, but political science institutions have also carried out extensive investigations.

It is found that as a rule—and always in *Bundestag* elections—the percentage of voters going to the polls is extraordinarily high in Germany. Rarely do less than 80 % appear at the polls on election day. As in democratic communities everywhere, the young people, especially the women, go to the polls in smaller percentages than do the older age groups. Curiously, the rural population is especially far above the average in voting interest.

The CDU's following is most solid in purely Catholic rural areas where it not infrequently ranges up to 80 % and more of all voters. In the cities, which have a greater mixture of denominations in Germany, and in rural areas with a mixture of denominations, it is far less popular. Its success does not increase again until we come to the predominantly Protestant North, where it is no longer considered a Catholic party. The areas of concentration of the SPD are, conversely, located in the larger communities, especially the large cities and industrial centers.

The FDP also to some extent has its adherents concentrated in the cities, especially in medium-sized ones. However, it also has a dependable reservoir of voters among Protestant farmers in certain districts. Liberal quarters of the Protestant Church are in general very receptive to it.

In 1957, 40 % of the Protestants voted for the CDU and 37 % for the SPD. Of the Catholics, 64 % voted for the CDU and 24 % for the SPD. It is a familiar fact that more women—who numerically preponderate in Germany as a result of the two wars—than men vote for the CDU. This observation is explained on the basis of the generally more conservative basic attitude of women, but also on the basis of the great attraction the patriarchally severe personality of Dr. Adenauer holds for women voters. In addition, there is also the women's stronger attachment to the church; they are more willing to follow the clergy's advice. In the other parties, including especially the SPD, men are usually in the majority.

Among occupational categories, the majority of workers still incline towards the SPD. 53 % of them voted for the SPD in 1957, in contrast to 35 % who followed the CDU. The CDU on the other hand dominates farmers (61 % : 11 %) and the self-employed (51 % : 9%), but also has a great many adherents among salaried employees (56 % : 27 %) and civil service officers (55 % : 25 %). Self-employed and civil service officers also make up a large share of the FDP's voters.

6. The Bundestag Elections

Buttressed particularly by these realizations, the election campaign is becoming more and more of a tough struggle to swing the so-called "floating vote", groups of voters who perhaps can be reached. An ever-increasing effort is devoted to attempts to canvass certain sectors of the population and influence their political decisions.

Above all, elections to the *Bundestag*, which take place every four years, develop into major battles of this kind. The elections to the *Laender* parliaments and the local elections, scattered over the intervening years as they are, do not attain anywhere near such popularity.

The first preparations for *Bundestag* elections begin virtually on the morning after the preceding election when the parties go about taking up

their positions. Of course, the election campaign proper does not start until about six to eight months in advance of election day.
In past years, the parties have changed over more and more noticeably to the practice of putting their leading personalities in the forefront. Originally, only the CDU did so. In 1953, it pushed its candidate for chancellorship with a markedly plain but effective poster showing the Chancellor's picture and bearing the caption "Germany votes for Adenauer". In 1961, the SPD followed this example. It presented an alternative candidate in the person of Willy Brandt, Mayor of Berlin, who is popular *a priori* because of his office, and matched the CDU "team" with its own leading personalities. The small parties, who would only have aroused smirks with chancellorship candidates of their own, were compelled to follow this example and post the most photogenic portraits possible. The question of who would become the new Federal Chancellor—which would actually not be decided by the people at all on election day—came to the fore much more than the question of who should represent the constituency in the *Bundestag* during the next four years. This troubled political scientists more than it did party electioneers.
Many observers say that in the past few years the German election campaign has increasingly resembled the American one, and that serious discussion and debate are receding more and more in favor of a great propaganda hubbub. Even if it seems questionable if this is really the case in the United States, certainly at least the 1961 election campaign showed that these apprehensions did not apply to Germany.
The fact is, that when August 13, 1961, suddenly struck the smoothly running election campaign—when a wall cutting through the city was set up over night in Berlin and everyone instantaneously became aware of what a powder keg the Federal Republic is sitting on—it was shown that, although the parties' election campaign machinery could hardly be stopped at that late point, the voters suddenly became meditative.
They were startled out of their political complacency and wanted to have discussions and talk about the ominous situation. Most of all, the voters wanted to know if a way out could now be found. It took the parties a few days to adapt accordingly. The SPD was the quickest to succeed in doing so, especially its chancellorship candidate. who now suddenly stood in the center of events.
By September 17, election day, the general excitement had hardly settled down and the public opinion pollers reported that the proportion of those still undecided was not dropping, as is customarily the case, but was mounting constantly. Nonetheless, these facts were not reflected in poor activity at the polls; as many votes were cast as four years before (almost 88 %). But they voted somewhat differently. The CDU could not continue its success series. The momentary political thunderstorm had some negative results for the responsible party in power. The Chancellor's age and the as yet unsettled question of a successor contributed, too. The CDU's losses, it is true, were not catastrophic, but they were clear and extended through the entire Federal Republic.
However, the SPD was not satisfied either. Although it gained votes, even on a very considerable scale, it did not win. The SPD did not achieve its goal of making it impossible to form a Government without it. It broke

out of the 30 % ghetto, but it is still separated from its big rival by over nine percentage points.
As a matter of fact, neither of the two major parties was any longer able to determine upon the formation of a Government alone. The two-party system seemed interrupted. Too many voters, who were urged to the polls by current political events and had been estranged from the CDU by the vehement criticism of the party in power and its leaders, were still unable to decide in favor of Willy Brandt as an alternative and sought another possibility instead, a third course of action.
They had a choice of other parties, from the Communist-influenced German Peace Union to the right-wing German Reich Party. However, the voters followed none of these splinter groups, but concentrated on the third party which had always had a voice in matters, though behind the scenes; they voted for the FDP.
Consequently, this party quite unexpectedly gained the real victory; it climbed from 7 % to more than 12 %.

7. Financing the Parties

The work of the Parties costs a great deal of money. For example, the SPD (the only party for which we have fairly precise data, submitted annually to the party convention), expends approximately 3 million DM annually for the activities of its federal organization. In addition to these regular costs, there are the enormous sums that must be raised for an election campaign. In 1957 and 1961 respectively, about 60 million DM in cash were spent by all parties together.
It is not always easy for the parties to raise these sums. Three principal sources can be listed for the funds: the regular dues paid by members; individual donations by members, persons friendly to the party, firms and organizations; and allocations from tax proceeds.

Membership Dues

The membership dues are uniformly fixed for the entire federal organization only in the case of the SPD. They amount to between 1.20 DM and 36 DM monthly (for a gross income of more than 1,200 DM). The other parties have foregone uniform fixed membership dues.

Donations

All parties are dependent on donations to defray their expenses. The smaller the receipts from membership dues, the more dependent the party is on donations. These donations come mostly from firms whose management is on friendly terms with the party concerned or from organizations with which it has friendly relations. The two sources cannot be separated from one another, since there are certain organizations devoted only to financing one or more parties, gathering donations from private individuals and firms for this purpose.
For various reasons, the donors frequently wish to remain anonymous. The parties are happy to comply with this requirement. Unfortunately, the provision of the Basic Law to the effect that the parties must render public account as to the source of their finances has not yet been put into practice.

Financing by the State

Heretofore, only the activities of the party caucuses in the parliaments have been paid for out of public tax proceeds. However, these funds do not always cover the expenses of the caucuses, and it is therefore customary for the individual deputies to pay a portion of their daily allowances into the caucus' common treasury. It is also known that SPD deputies are also obliged to pay part of their salaries into the caucus' treasury.

Recently, it has been becoming more and more a habit for parties to request subsidies from tax proceeds. For example, a sum of 20 million marks is contained in the federal budget for activities of the parties. Some of the *Laender* have followed this example. Moreover, some party spokesmen advocate that the State should finance the parties entirely.

III. Organized Forces in Society

1. The Churches

For almost 1500 years, Germany has been a Christian country. Its history and its entire culture are imbued with this spirit, and even today 96 % of Germans profess Christianity. As in the past, by far the majority of German children are baptized, marriages are contracted in church, and a clergyman pronounces the blessing at the grave.

Germany is the homeland of the Reformation, and it has been split into denominations since the days of Luther and the counter-reformers. Catholics predominate in the South and West, Protestants in the North and East. Until 1945, the Catholics in the German *Reich* were definitely in the minority, and they still are in the Russian-occupied area. Within the territory of the Federal Republic, however, the situation is much more balanced: There are about 50 % Protestants to about 47 % Catholics. This change in favor of Catholics has met with a great deal of attention in the past 15 years. Many critics feared that this shift in ratio would lead to Catholic domination and possibly even to a clericalization of the State and society. In reality, the denominational ratio does not cut uniformly through all classes of society. Starting as early as the secondary school, Catholics attend in a percentage smaller than that corresponding to their ratio in the population. At the university level, the number of Catholic students drops to 38 %.

Their ratio is above the average among workers, small farmers, and lower ranks of civil service officials, while Protestants predominate among the entrepreneurs, the salaried employees, and the higher civil service officers.

Nonetheless, in many fields, the Catholic Church wields far more powerful influence than does the Protestant.

It has a comparatively tight network of organizations in which the Catholic faithful are joined together.

Without a doubt, both churches in the Federal Republic are among the organized forces which have a determining influence on the image of society.

During the period of resistance to Hitler, they provided one of the few islands of refuge. A considerable portion of the German resistance movement rallied around the Confessional Church and its leading figures, like Niemoeller and Barth, and around the Catholic episcopate, especially Cardinals Galen and Faulhauber. Following the smashing of National Socialism, they took a prominent part in reconstruction, and today they are important buttresses of German society.

In the initial post-war years—when the churches were still filled to overflowing and it was quite apparent that people were turning to Christianity—they exerted a direct influence. Now they take more of their action indirectly, through their organizations and societies.

The Catholic Church first had to travel the long path from fundamental toleration of democracy as a form of government and way of life to positive affirmation of it. It first required such a pro-church constitution as the Basic Law and such a powerful and successful party as the CDU in order really to activate and develop its organizations politically. Particularly Catholic laymen discarded gradually their reservations against everything having to do with politics, which for a long time seemed to them to be an all too worldly matter. Even today there are groups who without doubt are more closely associated with the governing Christian party than with the State it governs.

In the Protestant Church, the relationship to the State has been a different one ever since Luther's time, less complicated and more unconditional. Obedience was due the ruler, the governmental authority. For the German Protestants, the head of the State was at the same time the supreme church authority. The Protestant Church had to accustom itself to an elected governmental leadership which expected its active cooperation as early as 1918.

According to the legal system of the Federal Republic there is no established church, and fundamentally separation of church and State prevails. The major denominations enjoy the privilege of being corporate bodies under public law. In practice, the churches are not only completely unhindered by the state, indeed they are assisted by the State in every manner. It collects the church taxes, and on the basis of an old commitment, it pays clergymen and religious educators. Never has the church in Germany enjoyed so many liberties as today. At the same time, it must be taken into consideration that not all church figures regard the situation as ideal. They are too well aware of how much devoutness and trust in God permeate the Germans living in oppression in the Soviet Zone and how much satiation and indifference prevail in the Federal Republic.

In any case, the large number of registered members of the two churches must not lead to misconceptions. It is considered good form in Germany to be Protestant or Catholic, but this devulges nothing about the degree of piety. Church membership is not canceled when one no longer attends Sunday services. The percentage of Protestants who actually take part in congregational activities is extremely small; it is estimated at 15—20 %. In the case of the Catholics, it is higher, but probably does not exceed 50 %.

The practicing Catholics in particular are generally well organized. There are many so-called "status organizations", which are devoted to social and cultural tasks in addition to their religious concerns and definitely pursue political aims as well. The most important organizations of this kind are probably the Labor Movement, the Catholic Men's League, the Catholic Women's Federation, the Federation of German Catholic Youth, the League of Catholic German Graduate Professional Men, the Kolping Family, the Catholic Rural Folk, and the Federation of Catholic Businessmen. There are also organizations of this kind in the Protestant sphere, although their drive is not so strong. They, too, run a Protestant Labor Movement, a Men's League, a Women's League, and a Union of the Protestant Youth of Germany.

These organizations probably make themselves felt most effectively in the field of cultural policy, where particularly the Catholic societies wage a traditional and often embittered struggle with the State because of their demand for Catholic schooling. Since the German *Volksschule* (primary) school) is a matter for the State (and specifically for the *Laender*), the question of whether to have denominational or common *Volksschule* leads directly to the political realm.

The question of whether or not churches should state a position on the pending decisions consistently leads to vehement controversies at election time. No one contests their right to admonish the faithful to fulfill their duty to vote. But as a rule, particularly the pastoral letters of the Catholic bishops go substantially farther and—in a manner intelligible to everyone, though never explicitly—recommend voting for the candidates of the CDU. It has not yet been proved whether such appeals win more loyal Catholics for the CDU or estrange larger groups of liberals from it.

Seen as a whole, a weakening of church leaders' influence on political life in the Federal Republic seems to be setting in, despite all fears to the contrary.

2. The Trade Unions

The trade unions can look back upon at least a hundred year tradition, and next to the churches, they surpass all other organizations in membership. The German Trade Union Federation (GTUF), by far the mightiest organization of employees, numbers greatly in excess of 6 million members. In addition, there is the German Salaried Employees' Union with less than a half million members. The professional organization of the civil service officers, the German Federation of Civil Service Officers, should not be mentioned in this connection, since its members take a dim view of being classified as a trade union. All of these organizations are nonpartisan and nondenominational. However, there is also a Christian trade union (CGD), which because of its limited membership (less than 50,000) does not carry any weight.

The GTUF is actually only an association of 12 trade unions which comprise the employees of individual occupations (shop unions). A total of about one third of German workers and salaried employees are organized in unions. In individual occupations, however, the proportion of union members is very much higher. For instance, about four fifths of the miners, two thirds of the railroadmen, and one half of the metalworkers are members of a GTUF union. The unions of these occupational groups naturally play a leading part in the trade union federation.

The German labor union movement has not always been so uniformly organized. Since in the second half of the 19th century it emerged from two different labor movements, the Socialist and the Christian, it was for a long time divided into two powerful, ideologically oriented organizations. These two tendencies were joined by still a third, a liberal one, in which primarily salaried employees united.

In the period prior to World War I, these organizations pursued the aim of improving the social security of the workers. During World War I, especially near the end, trade unions assumed more and more a political role. The wartime economy could not have been organized without their participation. The increase in membership indicates how greatly their importance developed: in 1918, they had about three times as many members as in 1914 (the Socialist trade union alone had over 8 million). At the time of the collapse, when the army disintegrated and the parties, unaccustomed to power, took over the Government, the trade unions played a very important part in maintaining order. It is no coincidence that precisely the three parties which assumed responsibility for the Government (SPD, *Zentrum,* and Democrats) were the ones which were backed by trade union movements of their own. The major mass organizations of the workers were the ones who prevented a revolution on the Leningrad model and paved the way for reform. Of course, they were now able to implement many of their social demands. Their most important victory was the right to negotiate autonomously with the employers on collective wage agreements. Thus, a great responsibility for orderly economic development was also conferred on the trade unions.

Occupied with these important tasks, the trade unions once more qradually turned their attention away from general political affairs after 1918. Although they perceived the danger of the Hitler movement in 1932, they were not able to decide in favor of unified political action. Almost before they noticed it, Hitler had taken over the Government and dissolved their organizations. Soon after Hitler took power, trade unionists of all tendencies began to organize a resistance movement against the brown-shirt dictatorship. When the anti-Hitler officers sought contact with this resistance center, it was too late; and these efforts were, therefore, doomed to failure. However, during the period of persecution the realization came that after the war there must be only one united trade union movement and that it must collaborate on political problems. The Occupation powers, who no longer wanted the former partisan trade unions, therefore met with great willingness on the part of German trade unionists. Consequently, the establishment of the GTUF came about in 1949.

Nonetheless, the work of unification was not completely successful and not without difficulties. Within the GTUF, those members who also belong to the SPD—about 10 %—constituted the largest group. At the same time it was well organized and was able to take over almost all leading positions. This development alone led to tensions, for the Christian trade unionists sensed a curtailment of opportunities to exert influence. The conflict became even more acute when the GTUF raised social demands which were leveled against the CDU Government. Foremost among these was the demand by employees in large plants for co-management. A general national crisis loomed when the GTUF threatened that if necessary, it would enforce its demands by means of a general strike (1952). In the end, the Federal Chancellor and the Chairman of the GTUF, Hans Boeckler, negotiated a compromise in which both sides yielded. Public reaction clearly opposed the GTUF, so that it has not undertaken any similar drives since then. Some Christian workers did not want to tolerate the obvious neglect of their interests any longer and therefore in 1955 established an organization of their own, the CGD.

The GTUF accepted this loss because it does not want to forego political activity. The trade union leaders cannot do so either, for the more all attractive demands in the social field are met, the more they have to prove their continuing *raison d'etre*. They believe that the best way of achieving this is by turning to political questions. Hence, many congresses of the shop unions are mainly devoted to political topics. For example, many meetings have dealt, among other things, with the question of atomic armament of the German armed forces, advocating a negative standpoint which has never been shared by the CDU and since 1960 has no longer been shared by the SPD.

On the other hand, wage negotiations with employers are conducted as though it were not necessary to make any allowance for the Federal Republic's economic policy. For the general welfare, a curtailment of collective bargaining autonomy will certainly be demanded of the unions and employers soon.

3. The Employers' Associations

The employers' associations provide a counterpart to the trade unions. They were originally associations of entrepreneurs for defense against strikes. Since 1912, they have formed the Union of Employers' Associations. After World War I, they became "wage partners" with the trade unions when the unions achieved the right of negotiating autonomously with the employers on collective wage agreements. Even now, they and the trade unions negotiate wages, thus influencing prices. They dominate an important sector of the economic system over which the government has hardly any influence.

The employers are now united in the Federal Union of German Employers' Associations, a collective organization composed of 13 intertrade *Land* associations and 36 trade associations oriented to occupations. The federal organization represents nearly 90 % of all private enterprises in industry, handicrafts, commerce, agriculture, banking, insurance, and transport. In this connection, it considers itself the partner or opponent of the trade unions, but also approaches parliaments and governments on questions of social policy of common interest to all employers.

In addition, there are entrepreneurs' associations which have a far greater influence on policies than do the employers' associations. They are more tightly organized and focus their attention on a small number of items. In order to give their influence on policies the most effective form possible, these associations devote more and more effort to proposing political candidates, particularly to the CDU and FDP. As the following table shows, these efforts have had considerable success:

4th **Bundestag,** 1961	CDU	SPD	FDP
Independent entrepreneurs of industry and commerce	32	9	18
Leading business employees	9	5	3
Retail merchants and tradesmen	20	8	4
Farmers	47	3	12

However, the trade unions were no less adept:

	CDU	SPD	FDP
Wage earners and salaried employees, especially union members	29	47	2

The influence of the entrepreneurs' associations on policies is not confined to recommending candidates. Another activity is financial backing of parties. Here again, they give preference to the CDU and FDP.

Of all entrepreneurs' associations, the most powerful is the Federation of German Industry. It is the main institution engaged in financing parties.

The political influence of the Federation of German Industry is considerable but by no means so powerful that it could lay down all policies, or even the economic policy, of the Federal Government, as its chairman has at times believed. For example, it was decided to raise the exchange value of the mark despite the express opposition of the Federation. The threatened suspension of donations to the CDU failed to materialize.

Another powerful organization—though not a typical entrepreneurs' association—is the German Farmers' Association. Its strength is based chiefly on the fact that the CDU has its greatest reservoirs of voters in the rural (Catholic) areas. An oft-repeated threat by the Farmers' Association to the effect that it might perhaps be no longer able to advise its members to vote CDU, has rarely met with a deaf ear. For a long time the German farmers have been so much accustomed to State assistance that it appears a matter of course to them now. At the same time, many of them fear the European Common Market, because the prices of German agricultural products are the highest in Europe. In order to safeguard the economic basis of agriculture for the future, the Government is carrying out a reform program and expending large sums on structural improvement. However, the farmers' associations—with a large representation in the *Bundestag* (see Table) —hope to obtain a large part of the funds in the form of direct subsidies.

4. The Refugees' Associations

The catastrophe at war's end produced the Federal Republic's largest welfare problem: the integration of refugees. This term includes two categogies. In one group are the people who at the end of the war were expelled from German areas east of the Oder and Neisse or from other Central and Eastern European areas. More than 8 million of them came to the *Laender* of the Federal Republic. The other group are those Germans who have left the Russian zone since 1945 (about 3 million). Expressed in approximate numbers, out of 13 inhabitants of the Federal Republic, three are refugees.

Expellees and refugees soon united in organizations in order to satisfy their social demands through combined efforts.

At the time when the task of representing welfare interests was the dominant one, the refugees first united to form regional organizations in their new home areas. Simultaneously, another kind of organization arose, that is, the association of persons of the same origin: associations of Silesians, Pomeranians, East Prussians, Sudeten Germans, etc. Both organizations existed for a long time side by side, and they are still not completely amalgamated.

The political tendency in the *Land* associations is, of course, different from that of the regional expellees' associations. In the former, every effort is made to keep awake the recollection of the traditional homeland and to strengthen the feeling of common allegiance. Connected with this is the wish to return to the land of their fathers, regardless whether it was formerly part of Germany, such as Silesia, Pomerania, and East Prussia, or whether it was the area of settlement of a German minority in a foreign country. The major theme of all meetings of the *Land* associations therefore is the right to the homeland, which is regarded as one of the elementary human rights.

The expellees' associations vigorously oppose attempts to discuss the question of the frontier between Germany and Poland, because they fear that even an impartial discussion of the subject might detract from their right to their homeland. The more the social demands of the refugees are now fulfilled, the more the leaders of these associations turn to foreign policy problems, following the course just implied. A social-oriented group has transformed itself into a foreign policy pressure group.

To many Germans, the activities of the refugees' associations are unwelcome. However, these critics must admit that the expellees have repeatedly declared solemnly that they never want to implement their right to the homeland by force or war. In view of the present international pattern of power, a declaration of this kind is virtually tantamount to renunciation.

Moreover, the activities of the refugees' associations meet with less and less support among the refugees themselves. Even if the membership stated by the organizations are accurate, only about one fourth of the expellees living in the Federal Republic belong to them. The refugees' integration among the original population is steadily progressing. As early as 1955, ten times as many marriages were contracted between refugees and original inhabitants as between refugee couples. Finally, the party which declared itself the special spokesman of refugee interests, the All-German Party, received less than 800,000 votes (2.8 %) in the 1961 elections.

5. The Press

Sometimes the question is asked if the press in the Federal Republic has so much influence and power at its command that it could be termed the fourth power, next to the Parliament, the Government, and the courts.

Without a doubt, it has a great influence on the population and on its cultural and political conceptions, but since the degree to which it interlocks is only limited, it lacks the really typical feature of an organized force. Since earliest times, the press in Germany has been decentralized and Berlin has never had London's or Paris' power in this field. The Berlin papers never surpassed the *Koelnische Zeitung* or the *Frankfurter Zeitung* in significance and influence. Even now there are a dozen major cities in the Federal Republic with ranking daily newspapers. Chiefly, papers in the *Laender* capitals play independent rolls—another sign of deeply rooted German federalism.

The press in Germany claims to be independent and in many cases non-partisan—and the party press actually has little importance. Nevertheless, certain tendencies and certain party preferences do come to view.

Among the newspapers, the *Axel Springer Verlag* stands out distinctly. With 10 newspapers—including the daily newspaper, *Die Welt* and the tabloid, *Die Bildzeitung*—it publishes about 10 million copies.

The economic association press has many influential publications, but they only rarely receive attention outside the limited group of interested persons. The agricultural organizations have almost 40 papers with a total circulation of more than 1,500,000. The German Trade Union Federation and its unions have 70 newspapers with a circulation totaling 5 million.

The church papers also merit attention, because of their readers' generally firm belief in the news they contain. On the Protestant side, there are more than 300 publications totaling over 5 million copies, and on the Catholic side, more than 250 with a total circulation of over 10 million. In this regard, the church newspapers, especially at diocesan level, play quite an important role.

However, the local papers, which are read or at least scanned at the breakfast table in more or less every German household, have the largest and most regular reading public. They appear daily in more than 17 million copies. Although they have as a rule only a small editorial staff and in many cases exchange whole sections of their issues through a "matrix service", it still cannot be denied that they have a certain degree of seriousness. They all devote a great deal of space to political items, which always appear on the first pages. The top headlines usually concern foreign policy. In these newspapers, the local news, which assuredly receives most attention from the readers, is of special importance.

Truly supraregional significance can probably be attributed to only three daily newspapers. Although they also have local editions, their readers are distributed widely over the entire Federal Republic. These readers usually take one of them as a "second newspaper", that is, through a subscription in addition to the local daily newspaper.

Published in the South, in Munich, is the *Sueddeutsche Zeitung,* which reputedly inclines more in favor of the Social Democratic opposition and is said to be characterized by a very liberal spirit. Published in the North, *Die Welt,* too, leans toward the opposition (but not so much toward the SPD simply on that account), and is somewhat aggressive. It devotes a great deal of space to the problem of partitioned Germany. Published in Frankfurt-on-Main is the *Frankfurter Allgemeine Zeitung,* of the three papers the most loyal to the Government and the most peaceable. It devotes much effort to recovering the former reputation of the respected *Frankfurter Zeitung.* It is proud of having the widest distribution in Germany, whereas the *Sueddeutsche Zeitung* has difficulty in crossing the Main northwards and *Die Welt* has hard work to find readers in Bavaria and Southern Germany.

The highest circulation is attained by *Die Bildzeitung.* It boasts of a daily circulation of 3,200,000 copies. It is a tabloid whose sensational reports on murders, catastrophes, bribery, and sex crimes are devoured on the commuting trains and streetcars. This newspaper, which is sold almost exclusively on the street, devotes little space to political information. On the other hand, it must not be overlooked, for it reaches a large class of readers who never used to pick up a newspaper.

Political weeklies do not have a very high circulation in Germany, and of all of those which have tried to attain greater importance, only *Die Zeit* and *Christ und Welt* have finally been able to secure a large group of readers.

Conversely, another publication also appearing weekly receives very great attention from its opponents as well as its friends. *Der Spiegel,* a German news magazine, as it styles itself, in any case probably numbers among the most controversial press publications in Germany. In breezy and seemingly objective reports it takes up every conceivable subject. However, clever agitation, whose influence is beneficial and detrimental at the same time, lurks in the background.

This array of publications is supplemented by the spoken press: radio and television. The radio stations, which are not governmental but are corporate bodies under public law, are scattered over the entire country, conforming roughly to the *Laender boundaries.* Through their dissemination of news without comment, they contribute a great deal toward informing the population, and ample use is made of this service. In contrast, the relatively infrequent commentaries, which are usually presented in a very moderate manner, probably reach a substantially smaller number of listeners. The television system has so far been operated jointly by the radio networks. In the future, it will be joined by a second channel under the jurisdiction of the *Laender.*

Concluding Remarks

Friendly critics, well—acquainted with the Federal Republic, say that the difficulties with which Germany now has to struggle are neither greater nor smaller than those with which any free country always has to deal. German problems are restoration of peace, security, relations with the other countries of the world, maintenance of economic prosperity, the smoothing out and settling of social differences, domestic political controversies of all kinds, and, finally, preservation of the free democratic State. But do they not overlook that this same basically liberal system has only a very short history in Germany? Did not the first such attempt, made between 1918 and 1933 in the period of the Weimar Republic, end in an immeasurable catastrophe? Do not many responsible Germans repeatedly ask how matters stand in regard to democratic mindedness on the part of the population, if a definite change has occurred, and particularly if German youth is democratic minded not only for opportunistic reasons but through conviction? If one then reads the results of the frequent public-opinion polls intended to find out the situation with respect to political interest and political knowledge, gloomy prognoses never lack. They say that the majority of the people are politically uninformed and, in fact, uninterested and indifferent; that they forget the common welfare over their own everyday worries; and that they have only very blurred conceptions as to how Germany is governed and what major decisions are in the offing.

In this connection, remedies are demanded again and again. It is asserted that a better democratic education should arouse more appreciation and more love of the State, that the individual citizen must grasp what responsibility and what rights and duties he has under democracy. Of course, these tasks are primarily left to the schools, *Volksschule* and secondary school. But almost in greater measure, they are the responsibility of adult education and hence the educational realm which deals with citizens already eligible to vote.

After World War II, adult education and one of its most important branches, political education, at first came into severe discredit. In Hitler's *Reich,* people had had to go through so much political indoctrination that they simply had had enough of it for a while. Moreover, even before there was anywhere near enough bread and butter again, the occupying Powers began to refer a great deal to democratic re-education, often in a manner that did not appeal to the German mentality. Both reasons tended to diminish political interest instead of strengthening it. The deep wounds of war first had to heal; a certain degree of normalization had to come about. Subsequently, the Germans noticed that it was necessary to take sides in the great new conflict looming up between East and West and, besides providing for protection through the new Federal Defense Forces, to develop a political system superior to that of the East. It was at this point that determined efforts initiated political education on a major scale. During this period, starting roughly in 1950, there was a rapid expansion in adult education in general and political education in particular. Everywhere there arose new and supplementary educational establishments of the German Association of Public Evening Colleges, a nonpartisan, interdenominational educational organization supported or fostered mainly by local communities. In the most diverse forms—in evening lectures, weekend programs, seminars, conferences, discussions, and forums—new approaches to political education were sought, and some of them were followed resolutely. Academies devoted exclusively to relatively long courses in political education were also established, some of them by governmental authorities and some by the large parties, the trade unions, and the churches. The two major denominations joined in with a great deal of initiative and founded adult education establishments everywhere.

Through financial assistance, the State lent support to such institutions most willingly, in some cases perhaps too willingly under the false impression that more money would make up for the long-neglected work rapidly.

On the other hand, the State was compelled to become active itself in order to counter the wave of propaganda from the territory of the Soviet Zone which threatened to inundate the Federal Republic. Year after year, agents and political propaganda specialists streamed into the industrial areas in particular. This infiltration was bound to be dangerous in the long run and had to be opposed in some way. Consequently, the Federal Government also developed programs of its own and put the Ministry for Youth and Family Questions, the Ministry of the Interior and the Ministry for All-German Questions in charge of implementing them. Among other things, many trips to Berlin were organized to demonstrate the contradictory governmental systems to West Germans, using this divided city as an example, and to familiarize the visitors with Communism in a manner more impressive than some lectures. Since August 13, 1961, however, about the only illustrative material left concerning the system prevailing in Central Germany is the wall cutting through the city.

All those responsible for political education pay special attention to the political education of the younger generation. Many educational opportunities are offered in addition to instruction at school, where, of course, civics has been made a regular school subject.

Inquiring as to the success of all these efforts, one meets with the difficulty of finding appropriate standards. Should they be judged by the degree of participation in voting, by the attendance at political meetings, by the numbers of party members, or by the size of printings of political literature? In any event, it is certain that the results of political education in the Federal Republic should, of course, not be overestimated, although a great deal of money has been expended on it. Too many resentments remain to be eliminated, and so far there has been too little time. However, unless all signs deceive, there is, nonetheless, a gradual increase in the section of the population which takes an interest in political affairs and in the further development of the Federal Republic. The effort is beginning to bear fruit. On the other hand, meditation has begun concerning new forms of political education which with perhaps less expenditure but more special knowledge would help to develop active minorities.

In the last analysis, probably everything depends on whether there is adequate time to complete the unfinished business in calm and peace and to strengthen friendship with the nations of the western world in such a way that it continues to be of lasting character.

The Developments in Domestics Politics

By Kurt Becker

The Federal Republic is not a State founded by the Germans. It even met with some resistance from them. There was very widespread apprehension that a semistate, then a provisional entity, might come to represent something with a final character, complicating the organization of a unified State including all Germany. But against this objection was the realization that prospects of establishing an all-German government seemed to be becoming more and more remote due to Soviet resistance. For that reason, even the critics deferred to the request by the three Western Powers to establish the foundations for a free, democratic State in the zones they occupied. The founders of the Federal Republic were, therefore, the three Western Powers. However, starting with this State's inception in 1949, it was Dr. Konrad Adenauer—already 73 years old at that time—who as Federal Chancellor shaped the State in accordance with his will. More than anyone else, he shaped the Federal Republic through his personality. He consolidated the Western Powers' experiment. The three features of the Federal Republic which stand out today—stable democracy, security, and prosperity—are mainly due to his efforts. The rapid return of the free part of Germany to the community of free peoples and its admission to the Western Alliance as an equal member were, to be sure, favored in large measure by antagonism between the two World Powers, especially after the war in Korea. Nonetheless, it was Konrad Adenauer who from the beginning seized the historical opportunity. Often relying only on his own determination and facing powerful opposition at home, he put the Federal Republic in the position it now occupies in the West.

He went about that task with the natural and confident authority of a patriarch. His way of governing satisfied the desire for energetic leadership which is widespread in Germany. He did away with the preconception that democracy and authority are mutually exclusive, thus contributing to the stabilization of democracy. His vigorous leadership impressed his political opponents as well. At the same time, his policies stung them to ardent fervor, and they launched all-out attacks on his "lone decisions", which often came as a surprise even to Adenauer's closest associates. With this firm style, the Chancellor has frequently violated the democratic niceties, but he has very seldom come in conflict with the Constitution.

He exploited to the limit the opportunities the Constitution offered him. That is what makes his success what it is and at the same time explains why Adenauer has made so many people his opponents in domestic politics.

A cumulative effect of two factors make the full extent of Adenauer's authority understandable. The first is the Constitution: it is in all respects centered on the institution of the office of Chancellor; it makes the head of Government the strongest figure in the State, practically precludes Government crises, and only permits him to be replaced if an absolute majority in the Parliament decides on a successor. The second and equally important factor is that this letter of the Constitution assumed living form as a result of Adenauer's confident personality, which pushed the meaning of the Constitution to the limit of what a democratic State can bear. The members of the Cabinet have nonetheless reconciled themselves to the Chancellor's dominating position, as have both the Parliament and, surprisingly, even his opponents. That can perhaps be seen from the fact that this political leader, who is now 86 years old, is quite generally, and by no means disparagingly, called "the old man".

Adenauer's instinct for situations in which a quick decision assures leadership is illustrated by a little episode which took place in 1946. Leading Christian Democrats were gathering in order to unite their party into an organization for the British Zone. After the politicians had been standing about in conversation for some time, Adenauer sat down at the table without further ado and, pointing out his age, assumed the chair. No one contradicted him. Everyone sat down in astonishment, and within a short time Adenauer was chairman of the CDU.

At the time he was president of the constituent assembly, he was already regarded as the future Chancellor. When the first *Bundestag* elections in 1949 ended in victory for the CDU, Adenauer invited the party's leading figures to his home in Rhoendorf-on-Rhine. He was host and consequently chairman of the gathering. He was the spokesman, and the meeting ended with the decision—by no means a foregone conclusion before that—that Adenauer was the candidate for the chancellorship. By the scantest conceivable majority, one vote, he was elected Chancellor by the *Bundestag* in September, 1949.

At his home in Rhoendorf, another decision had been taken which has determined domestic political developments to the present day. It was the decision to form the first Federal Government against the Social Democrats. It meant that the political battle was begun, and an agitated decade passed before this struggle between the two major parties gradually diminished in harshness as a result of an outside influence: Soviet pressure on West Berlin.

Adenauer had to summon all his powers of persuasion in 1949 to win support of his party associates for this plan. At that time, there was not yet a part chairman at federal level, and he was, therefore, unable to bring any pressure to bear. In contrast to Adenauer, many Christian Democrats coming from the Catholic labor movement were unable to conceive of inaugurating a democratic State except in close cooperation with the Social Democrats. They rallied around a man whose name was Jacob Kaiser. After the war this upright democrat had at first been chairman of the CDU in the Soviet Zone until the Soviet military administration dismissed him from his post. When Jakob Kaiser submitted to Adenauer's demand for a Government without the Social Democrats, he and his associates thereby lost a dominating influence. From that time on, the party's left wing with its nationalization ideas was paralyzed and Kaiser was only a figure on the periphery of events.

However, Adenauer needed allies for his Government. The election victory had not been decisive enough to provide an absolute majority. He therefore approached the Free Democrats, a liberal party of the middle class. Their common ground was Professor Ludwig Erhard's liberal economic policy, which in 1949 was crowned with impressive successes and provided grounds for the most exhilerating expectations. This economic upsurge was the main attraction for German voters and determined the outcome of the first elections to the *Bundestag.* Under their party leader, Dr. Kurt Schumacher, the Social Democrats fought for nationalization, but to the public, after years of privation, objectives of that kind were synonymous with economic distress, empty shopwindows, and food rationing. Schumacher and his party were stunned by the results of the election. Victory had seemed certain to be theirs. Contrary to its tradition, under Schumacher the party had taken on markedly national-minded features, because he, as party leader, believed it was the only way of stabilizing democracy. There is no doubt that many people belonging to the middle classes, who till then had been cool to the labor party, now sided with it. Because of its campaign against liberal economic policy, there was not sufficient support to bring about victory.

Schumacher was willing to enter into a joint Government if his party were permitted to provide the Minister of Economic Affairs, but by naming this specific condition he made it easy for Adenauer to decline the offer. Of course, this circumstance was just what Adenauer had been hoping for. An alliance with the Social Democrats would have rendered his candidacy for the chancellorship doubtful. Apart from the material differences from the Social Democrats, Adenauer is also a pugnacious individual by nature.

He does not think much of joint internal political points of view that are attained only by means of permanent compromise. He has always been convinced that only clear distinctions from other parties lead to success for one's own. He has proved to be right, and he has not hesitated to create differences even where they hardly existed. From one election to the next, his thoughts have always been dominated by considerations of electoral strategy.

The differences between Government and opposition, which degenerated into hostility, began with the policy of prosperity. but the struggle did not flare up in full force until Adenauer was elected Chancellor and outlined his foreign policy program. This policy, which aimed at a close alliance with the victorious Western Powers, became a domestic political conflict of the first order. It was not until 11 years later, in 1960, that this phase gradually drew to a close.

Together with the Free Democrats and the German Party, a rather amorphous conservative group which has disbanded in the meanwhile, Adenauer formed his first Cabinet. The opposition forces were the Social Democrats, a number of small splinter parties, and the Communists, who had come out of the election with only slight success. The Government's freedom of action was still restricted by an occupation statute: The laws required the consent of the High Commissioners, and the Federal Republic was not yet allowed to establish relations with foreign countries. Dismantling of industries was still in progress and decartelization of concerns continued. Although all the parties except the Communists were basically in agreement with the orientation to the West which was now being ushered in, the views as to methods collided with full force. In the stricter sense, a political duel was developing between Adenauer and Schumacher, and because of their incompatible personalities it mounted to dramatic climaxes which went far beyond the material justification.

Consequently, the Federal Republic revealed a scene of domestic political strife from the very beginning. However, since all of the important parties adhered to the Constitution and allowed no doubts to arise on this point either by statements or by actions, the situation was, in fact, fundamentally different from the turmoil during the period of the Weimar Republic, when the forces of the center were slowly crushed by the radicals of the left and right.

The first major clash in Bonn took place after only a few weeks when the Federal Chancellor concluded the so-called Petersberg Agreement with the three High Commissioners without consulting the Parliament. In it, the Chancellor committed the Federal Republic to integration in the Western community. The Western Powers stopped nearly all dismantling activity, relaxed some industrial restrictions, and expected German accession to the international Ruhr authority, which was intended to maintain inspection of West Germany's industrial potential, and to the Council of Europe. The result was a tumult in the *Bundestag,* the first of many. In the terms of the agreement, the opposition said it detected dangerous German advance payments which did not bring about equality with the victors but would prejudice some elements of the peace treaty.

Unpleasant recollections of the self-destructiveness of policies during the Weimar era are attached to the terms *Vorleistung* (advance payment) and *Verzichtpolitik* (policy of forfeit) in Germany. At that time, it was the national-minded right wing that used these terms to defame Foreign Minister Stresemann, who was striving for an understanding and accommodation with the West. Therefore, during the *Bundestag* debate (which lasted until the early morning), when Schumacher in his excitement hurled the epithet "the Federal Chancellor of the Allies", it became clear that the struggle over German foreign policy would from then on be waged with an implacable harshness.

The Chancellor meanwhile held fast to his fundamental course. He wanted Germany to regain its sovereignty step by step, and he was willing to pay a price. On the European scene, he sought an accommodation with France; on this basis the Chancellor wanted to integrate the Federal Republic into the West. It was hence only logical for Adenauer and Schumacher to become the great antagonists whose differences of opinion over foreign policy determined domestic political developments. It may be assumed that Adenauer had foreseen this struggle and, therefore, wanted to govern without the Social Democrats from the outset, in order to be all the more unhampered in following his own course. Later on he thoroughly exploited this situation.

Relations with foreign countries were still denied the Federal Republic at that time, but Adenauer was not willing to do without a foreign policy. He took recourse to the medium of the press interview, carrying on foreign policy in this unusual manner. It was not long before he set off the next political bombshell: in an interview with an American newspaper, he declared for the first time that Germany was willing to share in the military defense of the West. Then came the negotiations on the Coal and Steel Community, the first economic association of the six Western European States. The scene was always the same: a vehement and often unbridled struggle between Government and opposition. Yet when Adenauer became more and more specific about making a German defense contribution the subject of international consideration, he laid himself open to criticism even in his own ranks. His associates had long since become accustomed to his "lone decisions," but his position threatened for the first time to collapse when Adenauer communicated a memorandum on the problem of German rearmament to the Western Powers without informing his Cabinet, to say nothing of consulting it. The Minister of the Interior, Dr. Heinemann, resigned in protest. In the early Fifties, when negotiations were carried on with the Western Powers on German rearmament, it was seen how little the population—whose thinking was still completely overshadowed by the defeat of 1945—was prepared for such a total change in the Allies' postwar policy. Adenauer faced a powerful and constantly mounting opposition and had to go through hard battles in convincing the public that the creation of a German army was intended to further the security of the West and not the preparation of any aggressive policy. A number of elections to *Land* parliaments revealed the setback Adenauer's party had suffered. The election returns were tantamount to a heavy defeat. The Social Democrats and trade unions were the most influential opponents of rearmament and accession to the Western Alliance. They feared that the Federal Republic would in any case become only a second-rank State in the alliance and that the Soviets would never concede national unity to Germany, if it had become strong militarily and was closely aligned with the West. However, Adenauer placed the main emphasis of his objectives on the consolidation and security of the Federal Republic. Moreover, a united Germany did not seem attainable to him unless it were the goal not only of the Federal Republic but of the entire Western Alliance.

In May, 1952, the treaties between the Western Powers and the Federal Republic were signed. Bonn pledged to join the European Defense Community and received sovereignty at the same time. Another two years went by before these treaties were dealt with in the Parliament. The tide slowly turned. The public seemed gradually to become accustomed to the idea that the Federal Republic could not leave its own security to the Western Powers alone. Relations with the Western Powers, which were becoming closer all the time and now retained only a few features recalling their status as Occupying Powers, confirmed the views of a constantly increasing portion of the population that a historical chance was being offered—alliance for the first time with all the great Western Powers. This current was stronger than that of the neutralists, who believed that the path to national unity must necessarily go by way of nonalignment.

In September, 1952, the opposition party was struck by a blow of fate from which it did not recover for a long time: the death of its chairman, Dr. Kurt Schumacher. It is certain that his death changed the direction of internal political developments, for Schumacher was one of the most significant figures in postwar Germany. His ardent patriotism, talent for leadership, and great determination made him Adenauer's only equal among his adversaries. Without Schumacher, the Social Democrats were engaging in a struggle which seemed almost futile.

As the *Bundestag* election approached in 1953, the Chancellor had overcome his low point. Under Erich Ollenhauer, the Social Democrats did not fight with less fire than under his predecessor, Dr. Kurt Schumacher; but the voters lent their favor more and more to the men heading the parties and not so much to the parties themselves. A legend slowly grew up around Adenauer: the legend of the great old man who succeeded in setting Germany free from the consequences of defeat and in winning confidence abroad. Relying on these factors, Adenauer was able to face the coming election with optimism. In addition, there was another important event: In the spring of 1953, Adenauer for the first time visited the United States, where President Eisenhower and the public gave him a reception whose heartiness was a demonstration. More clearly than any declarations, this success confirmed that the Federal Republic had not only undergone an economic upsurge but had again also built up a noteworthy political and moral position. On his return, the Chancellor was received with a jubilation which no German politician had enjoyed since the war. The election in the fall took the form of a triumphal success for Adenauer. For the first time in German history, one party succeeded in entering Parliament with an absolute majority. Not even Adolf Hitler succeeded in doing so in the last relatively free election of that period in 1933.

In spite of his absolute majority, Adenauer formed his second Government, like the first one, in cooperation with other parties. He has always made a point of giving his policies a broad basis in Parliament. This time he even succeeded in combining in the coalition a two-thirds majority, by means of which he could amend the Constitution at any time. The opposition was thus deprived of any chance of thwarting the policy of alliance and the organization of a German army by resorting to a complaint to the Federal Constitutional Court. Besides the Free Democrats and the German Party, the refugees' party also entered the Government. Although the *Bundestag* debate on the treaties, which was held soon after the formation of the Government, developed into a battle waged with unusual firmness, its outcome was nevertheless clear from the very beginning. The debate lasted for several days and was broadcast by radio from morning till late at night. To everyone's surprise, the population took interest on a scale that was in striking contradiction to the general assumption that the public had a closed mind in regard to politics. This assumption has also been refuted by the high attendance at the polls during all four *Bundestag* elections (more than 80 %).

The debate itself was of hardly any consequence in the years that followed. Really lasting importance must be attributed to the controversy in 1952 over the Soviet note of March 10 of that year, in which Stalin offered reunification through free elections, probably in order to prevent German rearmament. The Chancellor believed he was unable to see in this offer any real chance, and he applied his influence among the Western Powers in accordance with this view. Yet even today, 10 years later, many political figures of all party affiliations believe that at that time there was possibly the last tangible chance for national unity, or at least for purposeful negotiations. The criticism that is raised against the Chancellor's action in this connection alleges that Adenauer devoted his efforts primarily to the Federal Republic's integration with the West and to a policy of security, and pursued the objective of reunification only in second line.

Following the major debate on the treaties in 1954, the Federal Government suffered a heavy setback since the bill concerning the European Defense Community failed in the French Chamber of Deputies. This delivered the deathblow to the project. Adenauer's policy, to which he had pinned his entire prestige, threatened to topple all of the Chancellor's conceptions. That was the case chiefly because the treaty package foundered, of all things, on the French, on whom Adenauer has always relied in particular to support his policy. However, only a short time later, at a Nine Power Conference in London, a modified form of the treaties was worked out which even yielded more favorable conditions for the Federal Republic: admission to NATO and the Western European Union and a more liberal wording of the Bonn Treaties, which restored sovereignty.

It was nonetheless coupled with an agreement on the Europeanization of the Saar, which was under French political and economic control. The domestic political scene was once more completely dominated by this set of treaties. The *Bundestag* debated with undiminished ardor and the public again listened in on the radio. The material differences persisted. The Government had to fight not only against the opposition but also against the feelings of a large portion of the population based on many resentments and emotions. These sentiments were summed up in the term *ohne mich* (count me out), which was virtually an abbreviation for a vague type of nihilism which was a typical result of the dictatorial system under Hitler and the loss of the war. Adenauer, a great admirer of Dulles, merged with the "policy of strength" as one conception since this debate. One of his most striking statements during the debate was that only the might of the Atlantic Alliance would make reunification possible, whereas the Social Democrats continued to regard this alliance as the paramount obstacle to national unity. However, the Saar Agreement, which France had made a condition, was considered even by the treaties' advocates to be a high, distressing price for the French concession, membership in NATO. Although they belonged to the Government, the Free Democrats voted against the Saar Agreement. It was the first deep rift in the coalition and later led to the Free Democrats' resignation from the Government.

On May 5, 1955, all of the treaties came into force. Federal Chancellor Adenauer had consummated his major undertaking. The bitterness of the parliamentary contests nonetheless continued to make itself felt. The day on which the Federal Republic received its sovereignty was passed without much outward display. In the company only of his closest collaborators, Konrad Adenauer held a ceremony in observance of the occasion.

In October of the same year, the referendum of the Saar population on the projected Europeanization ended with an impressive rejection. Since the Chancellor had not only concluded this treaty but recommended its adoption just before the referendum, his prestige also suffered a blow. That was all the more the case since the French themselves now declared they were willing to have the Saar area integrated into the Federal Republic by stages.

The controversy between Adenauer and the Free Democrats over the Saar issue, which was taken as a test case in regard to the Chancellor's attitude towards reunification, soon led to a critical climax and a serious rift. The Saar issue only accelerated this process. However, the background was an uneasiness on the part of the Free Democrats which had been growing for a long time. Although they were in basic agreement with the Chancellor's policy of alliance, they advocated a more active policy vis-à-vis the East at the same time. They were disappointed that the diplomatic relations with Moscow established in the fall of 1955 had not been utilized for a solution of the problem of Germany. On this point, the Free Democrats, under their chairman, Thomas Dehler, came close to the views of the Social Democrats. In doing so, they manifested an attitude which was spreading in the Federal Republic, especially in intellectual circles. On the other hand, Dehler and his party also had the feeling of being stifled in the Government by Adenauer's much larger party. They found that they could hardly realize their objectives. More and more, the Chancellor regarded them as a sort of satellite party of the CDU. In the spring of 1956, when Adenauer advocated an election law that possibly would hardly have allowed the Free Democrats to continue to be represented in the Parliament, they initiated an open fight. With the aid of the Social Democrats, they ousted the Government of the largest *Land* in the federation, North Rhine-Westphalia, in which they had cooperated with the CDU. Thus they headed for an open breach in Bonn. A wing loyal to the Government fell away, but the majority dropped out of the coalition with Adenauer's party.

These occurrences were more of a symptom than a development of practical significance. They reflected a mood, but there was no possibility of ousting the Chancellor. Moreover, Adenauer was able to forego the two-thirds majority in the Parliament since no conflict over the Constitution was to be expected. On the contrary, even the Social Democrats, although continuing to be determined opponents of rearmament, stated their willingness to collaborate on amending the Constitution so as to settle the specific questions of supreme command and of the incorporation of the armed forces in the democratic polity under constitutional law. The Social Democratic leaders believed they would be able to implement a part of their conceptions by adopting this ambivalent attitude. This assumption proved correct, but for a long time the party's adherents did not forgive their leadership for acting on it.

In conjunction with the preparations for building up the armed forces (the Federal Defense Forces), it became evident that even the policy makers of the parties in the Government had not fully appreciated the domestic political consequences of the treaties, which were a foreign policy concern. Work on the amendment of the Constitution nonetheless proceeded smoothly because all the parties were in agreement that by structure and character, the Federal Defense Forces must be an instrument of public policy and must not occupy a special position as though the army were a State within the State, as was so often the case in the history of Germany. There probably was no longer any trace of this danger, but it was in any case eliminated by the constitutional provisions on the armed forces.

However, when the Government had to decide whether it intended to introduce selective service, a severe conflict flared up once more between Government and opposition. Whereas in previous years the domestic political battle had raged chiefly over foreign policy, it was now continued in the realm of defense policy. The build-up of the Federal Defense Forces also met with great difficulty, and within a short time the Government had to concede that it was not in a position to activate 500,000 men in three years. The period was prolonged by several years. (By 1962, there were nine divisions and 380,000 men.)

During this period, the public mood was subject to marked fluctuations. In the fall of 1956, the Government was benefited by an event on which it had no influence at all: the uprising in Hungary. The Soviet intervention, which beat down this uprising by force, revived memories of the uprising in the Soviet Zone on June 17, 1953, and the Chancellor's defense policy seemed more convincing than during the previous months. From this time on, it became clear that the Social Democrats were conducting their opposition to membership in NATO and to German rearmament from a hopeless position. Although *ohne mich* was still a factor in politics, it was losing momentum and the urge for security was growing.

This trend and the continuing economic rise decided the outcome of the 1957 *Bundestag* elections. Supported by his successes, which completely eclipsed his setbacks, the Chancellor this time won an even larger majority in the *Bundestag* than four years earlier. Only a few deputies of the German Party remained to join the third Government under Adenauer. The refugees' party was almost shattered and was no longer represented in the *Bundestag*. The Free Democrats had taken up a position in distinct opposition to Adenauer, which netted them many losses.

Shortly thereafter, internal policy was heading for the most acute controversy the Federal Republic has seen since its establishment. Animated by immense fervor, the parties fought over the question whether the Federal Defense Forces should be armed with atomic weapons. Assisted by Defense Minister Franz Josef Strauss, a controversial figure, but one with great political talent, Adenauer had a hard battle with the opposition, which by means of an unparalleled campaign mobilized the public against atomic armament. A referendum, the goal of the Social Democrats, was nonetheless termed incompatible with the Constitution by the Federal Constitutional Court. If it had taken place, it would assuredly have caused a heavy defeat for the Government.

The vehemence of the dispute over atomic armament would certainly not have been conceivable unless the background had been the fundamental problem of foreign policy: what appeared at that time to be the indissoluble contradiction between the defense policy championed by the Government and the thesis, as asserted by the opposition, that the policy of reunification must have absolute priority, even if it includes a risk in regard to defense policy. However, the public also reconciled itself to the decision on the atomic armament of the Federal Defense Forces much sooner than had been presumed. The opposition found a great deal of sympathetic support for its arguments; notwithstanding, the demand for effective protection against a Soviet aggression was stronger, and the policy of the Social Democrats made only little allowance for these specific feelings.

Up to that time, the Christian Democrats and the Social Democrats had opposed one another irreconcilably for eight years, and it seemed impossible for the two parties to develop a uniform conception in regard to the major national issues, except in the form of purely rhetorical declarations. Domestic politics was completely dominated by that fact. The Chancellor's goal of completely integrating the Federal Republic with the West stood in contrast to the demand by the Social Democrats and to some extent by the Free Democrats, not to regard these ties as indissoluble until the Soviets' political price for German reunification had been ascertained. There were also differences of opinion concerning the extent to which German policy should draw practical conclusions from the Soviet thesis that there are two sovereign German States which must come to terms with one another concerning the ways and means of reunification. The Social Democrats were willing to be more accommodating on this matter than the party in power, although both parties officially termed the Federal Republic the only legitimate German State.

In November, 1958, a change gradually began to take shape. In the form of an ultimatum, the Soviet Prime Minister demanded that West Berlin be transformed into a demilitarized free city and that the Western troops be withdrawn. Only a few months later, Moscow submitted a peace treaty which met with unanimous rejection. However, the Government and the opposition were unable to agree on a German plan in answer to this Soviet draft. In the spring, two leading Social Democrats, Professor Carlo Schmid and Fritz Erler, went to Moscow in order to sound out the possibilities for a solution of the problem of Germany in conversations with Khrushchev. They were depressed when they returned. Nevertheless, the party shortly thereafter published a phased plan for reunification which in some elements followed the Soviet two-State theory and envisaged appointing commissions including representatives of both parts of Germany on a basis of parity.

Profound distrust accumulated and the Social Democrats had to face severe attacks. The opposition leaders now seemed to realize that their contradiction of the Government on foreign policy, defense matters, and economic policy would never offer the party an opportunity to gain the majority and form a Government. With great self-denial, the party had just a short time earlier approved the principle of home defense, at long last. Now it seemed determined to part with its Marxist tradition and set out on the path to becoming a people's party for which all groups and classes could vote, along the lines of the CDU. It drew up a new basic platform, and under the leadership of its most vigorous personage, Deputy Chairman Herbert Wehner, it turned into a party that now bore only very few socialistic features.

A year later, it also dropped its German reunification plan, which had so greatly increased the number of its opponents. It abandoned the fight against atomic armament. After the striking failure of the summit conference of 1960 in Paris, which was terminated before it had actually begun, the party declared its unqualified assent to the Western Alliance in the *Bundestag*. It was a sensational change in course which a small group of leaders had carried through despite resistance within the party.

Under the impression of the Chancellor's outstanding personality, the elections in Germany had developed more and more into a plebiscite for or against him, and the party was of only secondary importance. The Social Democrats, therefore, decided to present a man of growing appeal as an alternative to the 85-year-old Konrad Adenauer. This man was Willy Brandt, Mayor of Berlin, who had always been an exponent of the moderate right wing of the Social Democrats. Long before the party officially decided to do so, Willy Brandt inclined more to the Government standpoint than to that of his party associates in regard to the alliance with the West and defense policy. In the 1961 election, he did not, however, succeed in casting the victory of Adenauer's party in doubt; yet the Chancellor was likewise unable to repeat the great successes of 1953 and 1957. He lost the absolute majority.

These shifts were in considerable part a sequel to August 13, 1961, when the Communists built a wall cutting through Berlin in order to check the mass exodus from the Soviet Zone to the West. This event was the greatest shock in recent years. The inactivity of the Western Powers and the vacillating attitude of the Chancellor—who hesitated for a long time before visiting the city, which yearned for moral reinforcement— gave rise to serious doubts as to whether Adenauer's brusque attitude towards the East had not contributed to permitting developments to become so aggravated. On account of Adenauer's advanced age, many people wondered whether the time was not ripe for a replacement. His manner of governing, completely attuned to his own person, created an uneasiness from which the Social Democrats profited in part but not so much as the Free Democrats, who were able to double their voting power. Following the election, Adenauer was in a major crisis since it seemed for several days uncertain whether he would become Chancellor for the fourth time at all.

It was the third crisis Adenauer had been through in recent years. The first occurred in 1956. Because of resentment, political differences in regard to foreign policy, and vexation at the Chancellor's authoritarian attitude, the Free Democrats, who had left the coalition at that time, took the lead in a general anti-Adenauer sentiment. In this way, they moved closer to the Social Democrats, which cost them heavy losses in the elections. Reserve toward the Chancellor also spread to quarters within his own party, but this involved only a resistance which was not supported by the majority of the people. It therefore collapsed before it had fully developed.

The second crisis came in 1959. To the unprecedented surprise of the public, the Chancellor announced his candidacy for the office of Federal President. Obviously Adenauer wanted to remain at the helm even as President. He soon sensed that the Constitution offered him only limited opportunities in this regard. When he was faced with the unmistakable fact that his own party had different ideas concerning the choice of a successor than he himself had, he announced his withdrawal from the candidacy. A wave of indignation surged even through his own party, which wanted the successful Minister of Economic Affairs, Ludwig Erhard, as successor, contrary to Adenauer's obvious wishes. When the Chancellor adhered with determination to his intention of remaining in office, the majority of the CDU deferred to him, and to the disappointment of his friends, Erhard himself maintained a pronounced reserve. The Chancellor's manipulations with the highest offices of the State nonetheless undermined his authority. At that time, a gradual decline in his prestige signaled its approach.

The third crisis took place following the 1961 *Bundestag* election. After the loss of the absolute majority, the question of a coalition partner was only one of those which arose. Another which was of much more incisive significance was whether or not Adenauer would be able to remain head of Government under such a coalition. On the one hand, the Social Democrats assuredly would have been willing to enter into an alliance without making an issue of Adenauer as a partner. Their party had already conducted its election campaign with the demand that the situation in international relations, and particularly the threat to Berlin, required a Government of all the parties. For his own part, Adenauer would not lend his support to this idea. Since 1949, he had always made it a point of avoiding joint action with the Social Democrats and instead to carry on the fight against them.

For many years, this attitude had been politically logical, but since 1961 there were no longer any grounds for it. The Social Democrats not only practiced great restraint, but they had also gone so far towards correlating their policies with those of the Government that hardly any fundamental differences were now evident in regard to the important issues. However, Adenauer decided in favor of a pact with the Free Democrats. Although they had at first insisted on Erhard becoming Chancellor instead of Adenauer, they had to abandon this demand because they did not find the necessary support in the Chancellor's party. In the end, a compromise was found to the effect that Adenauer would continue to head the Government for only a limited time, until about 1963, and would then resign.

Now as before, the opposition anticipates entering the Government after Adenauer's resignation. The stormy times in domestic politics during the Fifties are therefore a thing of the past. All three parties are very close to one another and act almost as though they were in one Government together. Foreign policy alone does not explain this situation, although the broad parliamentary majority which Foreign Minister Schroeder has found for his unimaginative policy is remarkable. However, the parties are also guided by tactical considerations in their reserve. They are preparing for the day when Adenauer resigns. When that time comes, no party would like to forego joining the Government, because in the course of 13 years it has been seen that the crowning success in politics is apparently unattainable for a party as long as it remains in the opposition.

The question of who will someday succeed Konrad Adenauer in his office has been discussed for years in Germany with great interest. Ludwig

Erhard is regarded as the CDU's "crown prince". Still, it is one of the Chancellor's weaknesses that he has not been able to take the step of breaking in a successor in good season, in order to preserve continuity in policies. This has given rise to increasing tension within the Chancellor's party, but it does not affect the respect and veneration felt for this great old man and his historical achievements.

The Status of Berlin

The desire and the attempt to give West Berlin the status of a *Land* of the Federal Republic failed in 1949 as a result of the veto of the Western Powers, and they put a special arrangement into effect on account of the four-power status of the city. But in actual practice, in administration and in the application of laws, there is no appreciable difference between Berlin and the other *Laender* of the Federation. Berlin deputies have seats in Parliament, although without a vote. The viability of the city is based on an annual subsidy of about a billion marks from the Federal budget.

Berlin, the old German capital, is more than a problem in constitutional law, economics, or finance. Berlin is the symbol for determination to unite Germany. That is what it continues to be even today, although since 1961 it has been stated in the official declarations that it is impossible to discern any feasible chance for the restoration of national unity.

Attempts during the Fifties to transfer a portion of the Government to Berlin were unsuccessful, but a large number of high governmental offices of the Federation now have their headquarters in Berlin. Until 1958, the *Bundestag* also convened once a year in the city, and as recently as 1959, the Federal Assembly elected the President in Berlin. Since that time, the Government and the Parliament have foregone demonstrative functions and meetings in the threatened city in order to avoid heightening the tension. This decision was at first highly disputed, because it could not be denied that the Federal Republic had thus retreated in the face of Khrushchev's threats. All political figures were clearly aware that Bonn had by its action abandoned a right gained by custom which might to a certain extent establish precedents for political solutions in regard to West Berlin.

Until 1961, Berlin had another function of incalculable importance. It was a fascinating magnet for the Germans who live under Communist domination in the Soviet Zone. In 10 years more than three million Germans fled from the Soviet Zone to the West, the great majority of them choosing the Berlin route. However, this stream of refugees, which was mounting immensely, was stopped on August 13, 1961, by a hitherto inconceivable measure: under the military protection of the Warsaw Pact States, the East German Communists built a wall cutting across Berlin. The political determination to prevent the Communist strangulation measures from crippling the free portion of the city has since that time increased rather than decreased the large-scale programs of support and assistance intended to maintain the viability of the city.

The Power of the Highest Offices

No high public office in the Federal Republic has been given its new form under such a profound influence of recent historical experiences as that of the head of State, the Federal President. The powerful position of the *Reich* President under the Weimar Republic, who was at that time the most important figure in the conduct of the State, had done much to paralyse democracy's ability to function. For example, the *Reich* President could maintain a Chancellor in office who did not have the support of the majority in Parliament. He was permitted to dissolve Parliament on relatively simple grounds. His extraordinary powers, which originally were intended for an actual national emergency but could be invoked more or less according to his own discretion, lent him almost the authority of a temporary dictator. Moreover, as commander-in-chief of the armed forces, he had at his disposal an instrument whose very existence was alone sufficient to break potential political resistance.

Another reason why the office of *Reich* President, held by Field Marshal von Hindenburg from 1925 to 1934, is marred by a serious historical blemish, is because it was he who appointed Adolf Hitler Chancellor of the *Reich* and permitted a dictatorship to install itself in Germany while formally maintaining the democratic Constitution.

The intention was to prevent that from ever happening again. In order to provide an almost absolute safeguard against recurrence, the office of Federal President, which is not subject to parliamentary scrutiny, was purposely invested with only very little significant authority, most of his official acts even requiring the Federal Chancellor's countersignature.

The Federal President now has the right only to propose a Federal Chancellor to the Parliament. The Parliament is not, however, bound by this proposal. If a majority so desires, it may elect a Chancellor of its own choice who must then be appointed. The President accordingly is more like a broker, invested only with the natural authority that is inherent in such a high office by its very nature.

Only the historical background lends meaning to the weak position of the Federal President, who has hardly any other way of wielding an influence on practical policymaking, even on major decisions, than by consultation. The real power in the conduct of the State is now in the hands of the Chancellor.

In the main, the role of the Federal President is purely that of a dignitary. The possibilities of taking part in molding the State are not to be found in his powers, but only in his personality. Whether he will be able to persuade the political leaders of specific views depends on his personality alone. Supreme command over the armed forces is no longer vested in him, either, but in the Minister of Defense (in time of peace) or the Federal Chancellor (in time of war).

In complete contrast to German tradition, the State is headed by a figure whose position is politically neutralized. Moreover, in order to avoid leaving the selection of a President (as was the case under the Weimar Republic) directly up to the people—who might possibly decide in favor of a dangerous demagogue—the President is elected by the Federal Assembly. It is made up of all the deputies of the *Bundestag* and an equal number of deputies of the *Laender* parliaments.

When the first Federal President was elected late in the summer of 1949, the man chosen conformed completely in character and personality to the image the constituent assembly had projected for a Federal President. The man selected was Professor Theodor Heuss, who until that time had been party leader of the Free Democrats (liberals). He enjoyed a high reputation among political figures of all leanings, but probably would have had little chance of being chosen by the people in a direct election. Theodor Heuss was a scholar and journalist. In the fullest sense he embodied a synthesis between a professor and a man of politics, and thus a type which has always had a high reputation in Germany but had never been able to advance to the highest offices.

Through his conduct in this office, Heuss created an entirely new sphere. His intellectual personality, his liberal persuasion, and his outward bearing —which did not at all conform to the international conception of the top man in a German State—contributed a great deal to making it possible for the Federal Republic gradually to gain the confidence of the Free World.

In office, Heuss observed pronounced restraint in regard to everyday politics, and certainly more than had been expected of him. He probably established extensive precedents in this way as to his successors' opportunities and freedom of action. It is certain that a man of Konrad Adenauer's temperament would have imparted much greater political weight to this office in spite of any fetters of constitutional law. Theodor Heuss's restraint *vis-à-vis* the political leaders probably did a great deal to heighten the Chancellor's power and authority beyond the measure intended for him by the Constitution.

Only once has the Federal President placed himself in open contradiction to the Chancellor: in 1952, when a domestic political struggle of incomparable harshness flared up over the Government's goal of rearmament. At that time, the Social Democratic opposition believed it had found in a complaint to the Federal Constitutional Court the most effectual resource in its apparently futile fight against rearmament. The fact was that the Constitution did not foresee an army and the sphere of defense at all. It was, therefore, a disputed issue whether the Government had a right to enter into a military alliance and establish armed forces without amending the Constitution. If it had been necessary to amend the Constitution, it would not have been possible without the agreement of the opposition. Nevertheless, the bill concerning the establishment of an army would have had to be signed by the Federal President. Under these circumstances, the Federal President's decision at that time to request an expert opinion from the Constitutional Court in regard to the legal aspects revealed that he also had doubts concerning them. Heuss's action was of moral benefit to the opposition, whereas the party in power, and particularly the Chancellor, considered it an unexpected setback for their own position.

Heuss subsequently withdrew his request for an expert opinion. It is assumed that he did so at Adenauer's urging. Within a short time, this question no longer had any practical significance, because the Constitutional Court sanctioned the Government's action. However, this single highly political episode occurring in relations between Federal President and Chancellor gave rise to a great deal of ill-feeling, as was demonstrated shortly thereafter when Parliament decided by a majority to curtail the Federal President's rights further in order to preclude the occurrence of any similar incident in the future. Since that time, the Federal President has no longer been free to request an expert opinion from the Constitutional Court.

The storm soon died down. In 1954, the Federal President's term had expired, but all the parties agreed unanimously to elect Theodor Heuss for another five years. This time he also received the votes of the Social Democrats, who only five years earlier had demonstratively sent their party leader, Dr. Kurt Schumacher, into the election battle in full anticipation of defeat. In 1959, after 10-years' tenure of office, another re-election was not possible. A general embarrassment set in. A personage like Theodor Heuss, who had risen to high honors, was nowhere to be seen. Being the strongest party, the Christian Democrats now claimed the right to present the candidate. In this way, they introduced a new element into the scheme of the presidential election, but that was entirely in keeping with the character of the Federal Republic, which during its 10 years of existence had developed more and more distinctly into a State based on parties. After several unsuccessful starts, in which Ludwig Erhard was also considered a candidate for a few days, Konrad Adenauer, 83 years old at the time, surprised the public throughout the world with his decision to relinquish the chancellorship and run for the presidency.

Adenauer had quite obviously overestimated the chances of being able to retain control of foreign policy from the Federal President's mansion. For this reason, he shortly afterward gave the public, and particularly his own party—which was already completely absorbed in the struggle over a successor for Chancellor—another shock by renouncing his candidacy for the presidency. A "presidential crisis" set in. The highest office of State, even though not the most powerful one, whose future development under Adenauer promised to become unusually interesting, had now been subjected to considerable strain in terms of public esteem. No one in high political quarters cared to step in as a stop-gap.

Because of these developments, the prospect that Adenauer's party would propose a candidate whom the other parties would also accept was dissipated. The candidate finally chosen was Dr. Heinrich Luebke, for many years Minister of Agriculture in Adenauer's Cabinet. In protest against the preceding occurrences, the Social Democrats had presented as their candidate an important political figure who is held in high respect far beyond the confines of his own party: Professor Carlo Schmid. From the very first day on, they were among those who respected Luebke's personality fully.

In Heinrich Luebke, a man moved into the presidential mansion who, in contrast to his predecessor, wanted to heighten the political significance of this office. It is an open secret that the period during which he belonged to the Cabinet as a Minister under Adenauer did not create any precedent as to the Federal President's relationship towards the Federal Chancellor. Luebke maintains close contact with all leading political figures, and his relations with Konrad Adenauer are much cooler than those of his predecessor. For instance, following the last *Bundestag* election in September, 1961, he was for a long time reluctant concerning whether to propose Adenauer to the *Bundestag* again as Chancellor in view of the altered conditions for securing a majority. He did not decide in favor of doing so until after having failed to find sufficient support for any other solution.

The Federal States

The Federal Republic is, as its name reveals, a federal State. Ten *Laender* (not including West Berlin) are united in it. Many of them, however, are arbitrary configurations, with the exception of Bavaria and the two city-states, Hamburg and Bremen; the historical demarcation of boundaries between the German *Laender* was not restored following the war. The 10 *Laender* came into being on the drawing boards of the Allied commanders, and the lines of demarcation between the various zones of occupation were taken as the basis. In this regard, only secondary consideration was given to whether the individual *Laender*—which, in fact, were supposed to have a considerable degree of autonomy—were viable from the economic point of view, or to whether the population had a sense of community which had developed in the course of history.

Even on these grounds alone, the idea of federalism met with extensive opposition at that time, although it was able to draw support from a sound tradition in Germany, especially in the southern areas, which had never been part of Prussia, once the largest German State.

During the first few years after the establishment of the Federal Republic there was a powerful trend that favored the reapportionment of the territory and wanted to revise the decisions of the Allies. However, the only thing that came about was the consolidation of three *Laender* in southwestern Germany to form the *Land* of Baden-Wurttemberg. Other demands were ignored by the Federal Government. Moreover, the majority reconciled itself to that situation. Once they had been created, the existence of the *Laender* developed a legislative independence which could not be disrupted any more by sentimental demands.

The federal structure of the State was not an invention of the constituent assembly, although it included many advocates of federalism, such as the Christian Democrats: the deciding factor was the instruction of the occupying Powers. They made this one of their conditions for creating the projected State. The *Laender* heads of Government at that time, who played a special part in collaborating on the work in preparing the Constitution, did not view this requirement with displeasure. They no longer wanted to have their autonomy curtailed, now that they had achieved it, in favor of a Federal Government. However, not much of this self-assertion can be detected at the present time.

The Allies' motive was declared clearly: they were in agreement among themselves not to give their permission for a German central Government again having all power in its own hands. In the same way, in economics, the major concerns in heavy industry were to be decartelized and decentralized in order to eliminate the political danger of the concentration of power in their hands—an effort to disperse political control of Germany. Accordingly, there was no question of undermining the federal structure. The centralists, including particularly the Social Democrats, also deferred on this point. However, their interest was in the distribution of powers between the Federation and the *Laender.* They wanted to preclude the Federation's becoming the suckling calf of the *Laender.* Therefore, they fought for extensive rights for the Federation and for its financial strength, based on their view that the distribution of revenues is at the same time the distribution of power. The Christian Democrats, headed by Konrad Adenauer, took a cool attitude toward this effort on the part of the Social Democrats. The then chairman of the Social Democratic Party, Dr. Kurt Schumacher, finally presented the three Allied party control officers with an ultimatum. He stated that his large party's collaboration on the Constitution was contingent on the Federation's becoming viable in the political sense. He carried this demand to victory, thus achieving a great gain in prestige.

Seen in retrospect, this episode was somewhat ironic, for the Federal Government, headed by Konrad Adenauer, owes thanks for the extensive authority now at its command to the implacable fight by the Social Democrats, who at that time were firmly convinced that the first Federal Chancellor would come from their ranks.

Since the establishment of the State, the Federal Government has with every passing year developed a greater preponderance *vis-à-vis* the *Laender.* In point of fact, Federation and *Laender* no longer are factors of like value. The *Laender* are falling more and more to the level of administrative provinces, although with Governments and Parliaments of their own. All really important political decisions are made in Bonn. Almost the only domain remaining under *Laender* control is that of educational and cultural policy.

This development has assuredly been influenced very greatly by Konrad Adenauer, but even if he were followed by a weaker figure, the wheels of history could no longer be turned back. Moreover, it has proved more and more true that many of the tasks in the field of science and research far exceed the resources of any individual *Land* of the Federation. The problems of the 20th century make integration mandatory and favor the accretion of power in the central establishment.

However, there is still a third reason that has provided a basis for the priority of the Federation: in far greater measure than was foreseen, the Federal Republic has developed by character into a State based on parties. Consolidation into parties has become the most important feature of the driving political forces, in comparison to which the natural conflict of interest between Federation and *Laender* pales to insignificance. Except in regard to certain measures, the policymakers in the Parliaments of the *Laender* and at the head of the *Laender* Governments act in conformity with their party affiliation, even when this involves taking up a position in contradiction to the interests of their *Land.* Besides, no matter how federal the scheme of the parties' organization may be, the party leadership at federal level determines the guiding political principles. Therefore, in regard to important political issues, the decentralization in the organization of the State is neutralized by the power of the parties' headquarters.

Every regional election reveals what an extensive influence the political differences among the parties in Bonn have on politics in the individual *Laender*. The election campaigns are dominated by topics of federal policy and not by problems of policy at the *Land* level. It is not surprising that in this manner the structure of the Federal Republic assumes increasingly centralistic features without the Constitution having been changed. Even the most populous *Land* in the Federal Republic, North Rhine-Westphalia, with its concentration of industry in the Ruhr area, has not aspired to any dominating position among the *Laender*. The assumption that old Prussia might rise again out of this *Land* proved very soon to be erroneous. Karl Arnold, who was for many years Minister President of this *Land*, intentionally followed a path of his own for many years, but even he progressively adopted his policies to the more forceful personality of Chancellor Adenauer.

The self-assertiveness of the Minister Presidents, the heads of Government in the *Laender*, has receded steadily. Besides, the more energetic personalities in the parties are attracted in increasing measure by Bonn, because they want to collaborate there on the major decisions. As a result, the *Laender* are suffering a manifest loss of vigorous political figures, a phenomenon which has done a great deal to undermine the federal system.

The constantly decreasing political importance of the Federal Council reflects this process distinctly. This second chamber of the Federal Parliament, in which only members of the *Laender* Cabinets have seats, embodies the instrument of the *Laender* in federal policymaking and has a salient significance in legislative procedure. It is a fact that numerous details of bills have been struck because of the Federal Council's veto; but in most cases only details were involved. With very few exceptions, the important political elements were not affected. The reason for this harmony is because the majority in the Federal Council is made up of *Laender* Ministers who belong to Adenauer's party. The cohesive force emanating from this common party affiliation is more powerful than the differences that might arise from the diverging interests of Federation and *Laender*. Even the Bavarians, the component population of Germany who are most insistent on their autonomy, hardly represent an exception in this respect any longer.

This condition is becoming more and more evident. Only seven years ago, the Federal Council was frequently a rather dangerous hurdle for the Government. At that time, the issue was the controversial combination of treaties stipulating the Federal Republic's accession to NATO and the restoration of German sovereignty. On account of the existence of several coalition Governments in the *Laender*, the conditions for securing a majority in the Federal Council were unclear, and for a long time it appeared completely uncertain if the treaties would be passed by it.

Since that time the *Laender* have imposed their will on the Federation in only two decisive cases.

The first was in the summer of 1955, when the Government wanted to initiate the build-up of the armed forces with a law comprising only a few lines of text. The Federal Council's objection compelled the Government to announce its plans in detail and make provision for the existence of the armed forces in a comprehensive amendment to the Constitution. By their action, the *Laender,* however, only anticipated what would otherwise have been done by the *Bundestag,* whose majority was of the same view.

The *Laender* prevailed over the Federal Government a second time when they launched an all-out attack on the plans for a television network dependent on the Government to cover the entire territory of the Federal Republic. The *Laender* considered this a violation of their competencies. Following a complaint to the Federal Constitutional Court, the decision turned out in their favor.

Although the federal system in Germany has taken a different direction than was projected under the design of the Constitution, it is nonetheless an effectual factor, especially with respect to decentralization of administration. The articulation into Federation and *Laender* is now accepted as a matter of course. No one publicly advocates a modification, which furthermore would not be at all possible under the Constitution. On the contrary, a large majority considers this structure an effective weapon—in case of more unstable times, which the Federal Republic has been spared so far—against an authoritarian central Government that might lead the country down a disastrous path.

The Shadow of Weimar

The dispute over the Public Emergency Law is one of the many controversies in which Government and opposition have confronted one another irreconcilably and full of mistrust. From 1958 to 1961, the Government endeavored in vain to have special powers conferred on it in the event of a state of public or national emergency. The attempt failed because the Social Democrats withheld their assent, and the Constitution could not be amended without their cooperation, since the parties in power did not possess the necessary two-thirds majority.

The Social Democrats feared that the Government would not use extraordinary powers of this kind to combat assaults on the democratic State and its Constitution in an emergency or in case of riots, but might someday try, on shabby pretexts, to declare a state of emergency and establish a quasi-dictatorial regime. They met with the full backing of the trade unions, with whom they have very close relations, or were even urged by them to state this refusal.

On account of the domestic political stability and because the forces of the extreme right and left, such as the Communists, either were banned or had declined to insignificance, many Social Democrats believed that the Government only wanted to forge an instrument with which to quell even nonpolitical strikes and thus purely labor disputes. A conclusive factor in this dispute was the concern that the Government wanted gradually to eliminate all opposition forces and work towards a one-party State by abusing the emergency powers. In reality, the Government provided no grounds for these suppositions. Perhaps the pronounced sense of *raison d'état* demonstrated repeatedly by Konrad Adenauer and some of his Ministers inspired the imagination of his opponents. However, the vehemence of this dispute can be understood only on the basis of experiences under the Weimar Republic. During that period, *Reich* President von Hindenburg made use uncounted times and very often without compelling reasons, of the extraordinary powers conferred on him by the Constitution. In this manner, Parliament's rights were curtailed or even paralysed. These were the first authoritarian encroachments on democracy which did a great deal to undermine it during the Weimar period. Any similar suspension of the free constitutional system in case of extreme emergency, even though for only a limited time, is a constant nightmare to many Social Democrats, because on the basis of experiences under the Weimar Republic they regard it as the preliminary stage of a dictatorship of the kind established under Hitler. This trauma in the minds of the Social Democrats has in recent years even stifled realistic appraisal of the dangers which, though not at the present time, might perhaps menace the Federal Republic in times of crisis as a result of infiltration from Communist East Germany and actions steered by the Communists, or in fact as a result of developments similar to a civil war in a divided Germany. The Government wants to be prepared for such an eventuality and would like to close the gap in the Constitution which remained open in 1949. At that time, when the Constitution was drawn up, this was still done entirely under the impression of National Socialist domination and the decline of the Weimar Republic. It was only natural that policymakers of all shades of opinion wanted to concede as little power as possible to the State and its leaders. The obvious reaction to an excessively powerful Government was the demand for a Government tamed by the provisions of the Constitution. Another factor was that this Constitution was worked out at a time when no one believed in such a rapid elimination of Allied privileges and the occupation regime in Germany as subsequently occurred.

However, emergency control is technically still in the hands of the three Western Powers—as laid down in the so-called Bonn Treaty, which established the sovereignty of the Federal Republic—so long as no German laws regarding a state of national emergency have been promulgated.

Consequently, the dispute over the emergency laws involved their material contents only superficially. The necessity for them has always been acknowledged even by some important Social Democrats, though only unofficially. In reality, these controversies simply reflected the contradiction in thinking between Government and opposition, which for a long time seemed indissoluble. The Government was firmly determined to lend the leadership of State all the attributes of sovereignty in order to be fully prepared even in times of crisis and in case of any threat from without or within, maintaining the Government's ability to take action. Conversely, the Social Democrats for a long time not only opposed all efforts for defense against an aggression from without, but they also projected this attitude on the internal structure of the State and resisted granting the Government more power with extreme severity.

One of the things to which it may be possible to ascribe their reserved attitude is that they had been in opposition from the beginning, since 1949, and often equated the party in power to the State, just as the Government, vice versa, frequently was inclined to regard its political opponents as adversaries of the State at the same time. Moreover, it is in keeping with the tradition of the Social Democrats—a party nearly a hundred years old which in the course of its history had to endure several periods of suppression—for them to look upon the authority of a Government with the greatest suspicion, as though in reality even now this power could, as so often in past decades, only be leveled against them or against the workers. For this reason, the party has to its own detriment often had to submit to the reproach that its suspicions concerning the Government's loyalty to the Constitution are greater than their concern over the concrete danger involved in the Communist threat.

Therefore, one of the many evidences of great changes in the Social Democratic Party is its revised attitude towards legislation for an emergency. Following the *Bundestag* election in 1961, the first talks between Government and opposition on an amendment to the Constitution were arranged very quickly, and they were free of the onus of distrust.

The Radicals

The radical groups in the Federal Republic have actually played no more than a peripheral part at any time. Nevertheless, their existence both on the left wing and on the right has always had an influence on central developments due to concern that the history of the Weimar Republic might repeat itself. Numerous newly founded parties, mainly of the extreme right, attracted particular attention—much more than the size these cults justified. Yet postwar Germany studied Hitler's vestiges very conscientiously.

These groups never attained really alarming size. Still, local election victories by the extreme right-wing Socialist *Reich* Party under General Remer caused apprehension. As a major, Remer had taken a prominent part in the supression of the uprising of July 20, 1944, in Berlin and was consequently promoted to general by Hitler. In Wolfsburg, the city where the Volkswagen plant is located, he succeeded in obtaining the most votes in a municipal election and extended his successful campaign to other towns in northern Germany. Because of this sudden upsurge and the indisputably neo-fascist character of this party, the Federal Government successfully applied to the Federal Constitutional Court for its prohibition.

The radical left wing manifested itself through the Communists. In the 1949 *Bundestag* election, they won 5.7 % of the votes and 15 seats. Yet the frightening suppression of all freedoms in the Soviet Zone and the horrifying experiences that were stamped into the minds of uncounted East German refugees when the Red Army marched in, placed narrow limits on the development of Communism in West Germany from the start. The rejection of Communism goes much deeper than might be explained on political grounds alone. Four years later, in the *Bundestag* elections in 1953—shortly after the uprising of June 17, 1953, against Ulbricht in the Soviet Zone—the Communists lost more than half of their support. They no longer received any more than 2.2 % of the votes. The Parliament was thus barred to them because they had failed to achieve the minimum requirement, 5 % of the votes.

Since that time, no groups of either the extreme right or the extreme left have belonged to the *Bundestag.*

After the ban on the extreme rightists, it was a matter of logical consequence to apply for a prohibition of the Communists, who were also opposed to the Constitution. On application by the Government, the Federal Constitutional Court pronounced the ban in 1956. Although this was generally considered logical and completely incontestable from the legal point of view, many persons still doubted the expediency of the ban, or to put it more precisely, the expediency of the Government's application for the ban, since, of course, the Court itself only was competent to decide on the legal issue. The critics believed it was wrong to force the Communists underground, where surveillance was impossible. In addition, they considered it a mistake to ban the Communist Party, which was insignificant in terms of political effectiveness, instead of completely destroying its prestige (which was hard-hit anyway)—together with the prestige of the Soviet Zone, which claimed leadership of all of Germany—in open battle through annihilating election defeats. This was done in an impressive manner in Berlin, where the Communists received only 1 % of the votes.

Economy

In no field does German postwar policy have a more brilliant success to show than in that of economy. In only a few years, the Federal Republic surmounted the destructive consequences of war and of dismantling in the years afterward. The depression of the years 1945 to 1948, when German industry languished hopelessly and almost inanimately, was overcome in a breathtakingly short time.

A second period of the founders, comparable to that of the 19th century, began. The Federal Republic developed a flourishing economic activity, and as early as the beginning of the Fifties the expression "German economic miracle" was coined. The Federal Republic now ranks third among the industrial States of the world, following the United States and the Soviet Union, and the standard of living of the population has risen to a level never attained before.

The personality of the Federal Minister of Economic Affairs, Professor Ludwig Erhard, the creator of the free market economy, is symbolic of this economic success. His energy and his courageous decisions during the transition from a rigorously controlled economy with socialistic features to a maximum of free enterprise made Erhard one of the most popular political figures in Germany. However, the basis for this upsurge was laid by the policy of Adenauer through his efforts for an accommodation with the victorious Western Powers. Just a few months after the establishment of the Federal Republic, it was possible as a result of the so-called Petersberg Agreement with the three Western Powers to bring about a general abandonment of the dismantling activity on the part of the Allies and to have them relieve the economy of the fetters imposed by numerous limitations on industrial production. In the course of the subsequent six years, this path was followed consistently. With the Federal Republic's accession to NATO and the restoration of German sovereignty in 1955, this chapter was on the whole concluded. The bans on production which have continued in effect since that time relate chiefly to items of armament and war material, especially nuclear weapons. However, such limitations as those on steel production, shipbuilding, and aeronautics were dropped as long ago as the early Fifties.

Moreover, the Government gradually cancelled the measures introduced by the three Western Powers for the decartelization of concerns in the basic industries—coal, steel, and chemicals—and of the major banks, which had been an important component of Allied occupation policy and at first had even been continued after the establishment of the Federal Republic. However, the former concentration of economic power was not restored in every instance.

As grotesque as it may sound, there is no doubt that dismantling had a beneficial effect in many respects. In no other way would the modernization of industry and shipping have ever been compelled on such a thorough-going basis. Without this modern plant for industry, it would, of course, not have been possible in such a short time to attain a competitive position in foreign trade, which together with the construction trade is the most important pillar of economic upswing.

Here again, the decisive premise was of a political nature: it was the American decision to rescue Germany from the economic debility of the initial postwar years with the aid of the Marshall Plan. Without this assistance through the Marshall Plan it would never have been possible to overcome the damage of war and dismantling so quickly and thus to re-enter the world economic scene. It was the decisive initial aid.

Notwithstanding his successes, which very soon were visible even at a glance, Erhard's policy of free market economy was hotly contested at first. It was not compatible either with the policy of nationalization still being championed by the Social Democrats at the beginning of the Fifties or with their inclination towards a controlled economy. This resistance diminished from year to year and is now as good as eliminated. The only connection in which it can still be appraised as a factor is in the matter of political scrutiny over the concentration of economic power.

Another important element in the powerful upward trend of the economy was the influx of more than 10 million refugees from the German eastern areas and the Soviet Zone. Their presence confronted West Germany with a great many problems. There was at first a great fear of mass unemployment, and no one knew how it would be possible to create so many new jobs and build so much housing. On the other hand, it was very quickly seen that the political and human tragedy of mass expulsion from the eastern areas and of the exodus of refugees from the Soviet Zone also had its reverse side in economic terms: a considerable reservoir of manpower from all branches of industry accumulated. Moreover, the refugees were people who had come to the West almost completely divested of personal property and often without the bare necessities for daily existence. They were, therefore, especially eager to work, and they wanted to regain what had been lost as quickly as possible. Consequently, the refugees were not only additional manpower, but at the same time additional consumers who lent immense impulse to the production and sales of consumer goods.

The benefits of an economic policy that encourages all the initiative of private enterprise may be made evident by stating some figures and comparisons that illustrate in outline what development has been achieved in the period from 1949 to 1962. In 1950, there were 15 million employed. Twelve years later, employment stood at 21 million. The great fear of mass unemployment was still a concrete factor on the political scene at the time when the Federal Republic was established. As early as the mid-Fifties, full employment had virtually been achieved, and since that time the shortage of qualified manpower has been a persistent problem. Twelve years ago, the number of unemployed was more than two million, and at the present time, it is barely over 100,000. Even this low number is misleading, since there are actually more unfilled positions in industry than unemployed persons all together.

In 1950, industrial production had already reattained almost 90 % of the 1936 level, but by the end of 1961 it had soared to 262 %. During the same period, the value of German exports increased from 8.4 billion marks (1950) to 51 billion marks (1961). That was the case even though trade with the East, which was rather considerable in former times, is no longer of any real consequence, amounting to only 3.7 % of total exports at the present time.

The increase in income is in keeping with this comparison. The average income of employed persons has more than doubled in 12 years, although many items required for everyday living have, of course, become appreciably more expensive during the same period. In point of wages, the workers in German industry are now at the top of the European scale, and they have at the same time the shortest working hours. The trade unions fought for this status in many tension-filled rounds of negotiation with management, during which strikes were very often threatened but only rarely carried out. In the Federal Republic, strikes have up to the present time not played remotely the same part as an instrument of dispute as in other European countries. They have practically never disturbed the development of the economy.

The Federal Republic's membership in the Coal and Steel Community of the six Western European States and in the European Economic Community has so far not influenced the structure of the economy. Some changes are expected in the course of time as a result of the gradual elimination of customs tariffs. They will involve those branches of the economy in which the Federal Republic has less favorable conditions for production than other member States. In this respect, the adverse aspect of high wages will make itself felt particularly in branches of industry whose production costs include a high wage component.

Moreover, constantly increasing prosperity has assuredly contributed decisively to domestic political stability in the Federal Republic. Since one of the most important features of German economic policy is the element of freedom, economic upswing and the prosperity of the great masses have from the beginning sent out the powerful rays of a brilliant example to Communist-dominated East Germany. The flourishing economy of a free country stood in contrast to the permanent economic crisis of an area plundered by the Soviets where Communist functionaries, following the precept of Moscow's five-year plans, plunged the economy into one crisis after another and have to the present day not proved to be in a position to provide adequate food for the population and to supply them with the consumer goods of everyday life.

In no field is the Federal Republic's political superiority to the Soviet Zone sensed more distinctly by the West Germans than in that of the economy. The concept of the affluent society has become a political attraction of the first order. It plays a salient part in the contest with the Soviet-occupied part of Germany. In the Federal Republic itself, a great many phenomena derive their substance from the "economic miracle." They include first of all Konrad Adenauer's four election victories. They would never have been conceivable on their actual scale without Ludwig Erhard.

The Social Democrats' opposition to this economic policy, which was manifest for a long time, is still surmised to exist by large segments of public opinion, although it has long since become a thing of the past. In the elections, the Social Democrats had no success with their attempts to storm this fortress of Erhard's economic policy with its firm upward trend.

The fact that no noteworthy extremist groups were able to develop on the outer wings of the left and right can probably be attributed to prosperity. They require the hotbed of economic crisis, as was evidenced very clearly during the Twenties in Germany. A prosperity that did not accord an equal share in the upswing to all segments of the population naturally gave rise to domestic political complications. Along with the growing opportunities for individual advance, new, hitherto completely unknown, demands have come about and the desire for possessions has also grown. A considerable amount of German criticism concerning the domestic scene is leveled against signs of attempts to restore the old social order which were a direct concomitant of prosperity. At the same time, Ludwig Erhard, when he speaks of welfare through free market economy, is always the first to lay special stress on the social function of this system, which is intended to serve the common welfare and not as a relapse into the early days of unbridled economic liberalism.

German domestic criticism also deplores the fact that the irresistible concentration of economic power is associated with names figuring among the leading economic group under Hitler; regardless of whether they were convinced National Socialists or not and whether they served that system only reluctantly or lent it their whole-hearted support, they had contributed to the consolidation of the Nazi regime.

A problem that is acknowledged even by the most ardent adherents of Erhard's economic policy is whether the concept of the affluent society has not to an excessive extent become the focal political idea and done too much to foster materialistic thinking, thus becoming a substitute for other major goals of national policy, such as the reunification of Germany. From the time of unconditional surrender in 1945 and the partition of Germany immediately afterwards, there seems to have been a lapse in the people's will to work for nonmaterialistic political goals with the same energy as for economic success. In comparison with the fascination of prosperity, there has so far been only a feeble development of the citizen's obligations to the State or to a concept of the State situated in the realm of politics and generally acknowledged as binding. In appeals to the public, political figures of all leanings, therefore, consistently deplore this state of affairs, in which the part of the German people living in liberty does not display the features of a nation to the same extent as it resembles an economic society organized as a State.

Social Policy

During the first years of the Federal Republic's existence, social policy took as its primary goal a rectification of the material effects of war. It was intended to provide compensation to more than eight million refugees from the eastern areas (not counting the refugees from the Soviet Zone) and to several million persons who had lost their homes, property, or businesses during the war as a result of air raids or whose savings and old-age pensions had been wiped out during the war and the subsequent period of inflation.

The State was not able to do so. It is true that its coffers were not empty and that on the contrary the increasing prosperity led to constantly rising revenue receipts. However, even an attempt to satisfy German domestic war damages through governmental compensation alone would have been doomed to failure. For that reason, the Government decided to take an unusual step which probably was feasible on the projected blanket basis only immediately following such an enormous catastrophe and sweeping revolution as was represented by the war and the complete collapse of the German *Reich*. That step was the idea of an equalization of burdens.

A favorable fortune had spared the property of companies, entrepreneurs, farmers, and landowners who retained their factories, farms, and buildings; and under a long-term plan covering several decades, it was intended to impose levies on this intact property in order to raise the billions which during the same period were to benefit those who had suffered damage or loss of property. Of course, only a token compensation could be paid in many cases.

When it became law as early as 1952, this gigantic scheme was applied chiefly according to how the aid could best be turned to the purpose of activating the initiative of refugees and bombed-out persons, encouraging them to establish the basis for a new livelihood and to create new jobs. Accordingly, businessmen and farmers who had fled from the East received in many instances noteworthy credit assistance to enable them to build up replacements for their lost establishments. Quite a number of industrial plants that once were located in the East rose once more in the West and climbed to unimagined prosperity. Old people received pensions to save them from the direst distress. So far, a total of about 40 billion marks have been allocated for all categories of assistance.

With respect to its effect, the economic aspect of Equalization of Burdens might be regarded as an internal German parallel to the external assistance which was received through the American Marshall Plan. Equalization of Burdens was among the factors that played an important part in the "economic miracle," since the initial assistance it provided offered notable incentives for intensive efforts on the part of the recipients. It was accompanied by tax relief which in effect often assumed the character of compensation.

It was only after this revolutionary law on Equalization of Burdens was put into operation that social policy devoted itself in an increasing measure to uncounted improvements in social insurance and pensions for persons disabled as a result of the war.

An incisive decision in this respect was the adoption of the so-called "dynamic" old-age pension. Under this system, the pension is increased on a blanket basis at regular intervals in accordance with the indexes for the overall rise in prices and for national income, which so far has risen constantly. In this way it is intended to prevent the pensioneers from possibly becoming the victims of diminishing purchasing power, a form of creeping inflation.

In 1954, an allowance for children was also introduced and has been extended continually since that time. Starting with the third child, an allowance of 40 marks per month is generally paid, the funds for this purpose being raised out of revenues and through payments by the employers.

The election slogan "Property for Everyone", which was introduced by the Christian Democrats, has long since been seconded by all of the parties. This conception is of focal significance in social policy, because it is presented as an alternative to the Communist idea of collectivization. This principle is applied primarily to the construction of individual homes, through tax relief, governmental subsidies, and premiums.

The practical aspect of these measures is, of course, also the effort to overcome the housing shortage. Although 500,000 dwellings are being built annually with governmental assistance in recent years, totaling six million during the past 12 years, the need has not yet been met. War damage has not yet been made up for, and new demand has also come about in the course of 17 years, generated by the increase in population as a result of a surplus of births over deaths, by heightened demands resulting from the constantly rising standard of living, and particularly by the three million refugees from the Soviet Zone who have streamed into the West in addition to the eight million expellees from the eastern areas.

These considerable achievements in housing construction, promoted intensively by governmental assistance, have (together with all the effects accompanying them) also become a principal factor in the economic trend. Social policy is assuming more and more importance in domestic politics. The major differences among the parties are, on the surface, fought out in the conflict over the size of social benefits. However, the underlying issue is the much more decisive fundamental question whether social policy does not contribute in an ever increasing measure to paralyzing the liberal concept of the personal responsibility of the citizen and to transforming the Federal Republic from a State based on social justice into a perfected welfare State in which the State safeguards the citizen against all risks and takes precautions against all eventualities. In the view of the conservatives and liberals, this development is bound to lead to State Socialism by default.

Through their successful social policy, the Christian Democrats under Adenauer have, of course, taken a great deal of wind out of the Social Democrats' sails. As recently as the early Fifties, the Social Democrats based their campaign against the Government on the theory of the impoverishment of the great masses. They asserted that it could not be overcome under a liberal economic system, but only under a Socialist State. However, constantly growing prosperity caused the collapse of this theory. Another reason why the opposition had a hard fight on its hands was because Adenauer went much farther in his social policy than the Social Democrats had anticipated.

Within Adenauer's party, groups representing industry are faced with a powerful influence of chiefly Catholic trade unionists, which is referred to as the so-called left wing, and liberal tendencies also make themselves felt. There is hence a great deal of tension concerning establishment of the boundary between the State based on social justice and the total welfare State. Very often, the trade unionists of the left wing, whose position complies with the Catholic social doctrine, are in very close proximity to the Social Democrats, even though there is a considerable difference in their theoretical premises. On more than one occasion in the past, that fact has led to joint action by the two groups in the Parliament and blurred the dividing line between the parties in power and the opposition.

COMPOSITION OF THE GERMAN BUNDESTAG

PARTY	PERCENT OF TOTAL VOTE				BUNDESTAG SEATS			
	1961	1957	1953	1949	1961	1957	1953	1949
Christian Democrats	45,4	50,2	45,2	31,0	251	277	244	141
Social Democrats	36,2	31,8	28,8	29,2	203	181	150	130
Free Democrats	12,8	7,7	9,5	11,9	67	43	48	53
German Party	—	3,4	3,2	4,0	—	17	15	17

The Trend in Foreign Policy from 1945 to the Present

By Hermann Proebst

After the outbreak of World War II and before German foreign policy became possible again, the Allies had no uniform policy on Germany. They had only one war objective towards which all of the forces fighting against Hitler were bending their efforts. This objective was: destruction of the Third *Reich.* The arrogance of the National Socialist leadership, which had taken the word "total" as its favorite watchword, provoked in the minds of the attacked and offended nations a desire to retaliate which was also total. The one uniting desire which held together the alliance of unlike partners was that of completely eradicating any German inclination towards domination and preventing the future development of German power once and for all. Only a few of the men who had to labor under the burden of highest responsibility to win the murderous war were thinking beyond the aspired day of victory. Aside from Churchill, hardly any of them flinched at the prospect that a most dangerous vacuum would grow in the place where the Germans once had taken a part, for better or worse, in preserving a tolerably reliable balance in the heart of Europa. It appears that no one imagined at that time how much trouble it would cost to protect this area from the covetousness of the Eastern victor once Germany had been divested of power.

It was by no means as though nothing had been said about the future which would be in store for conquered Germany. The general prescription first came to light during discussions between the Allied statesman. After Churchill and Roosevelt met in December, 1941, the indications became more clearly in favor of breaking up the territories of the *Reich.* Also, during an early visit by Eden to Moscow, Stalin had intimated that he would not be satisfied with the Sudeten area being returned to Czechoslovakia. Besides the restoration of Austria's independence, he seemed to have in mind the cession of East Prussia to Poland and the creation of an autonomous Rhine State and an independent Bavaria. From the notes of Hopkins, who was considered Roosevelt's most influential adviser for a time, we know that the President, during the first official negotiations with British Foreign Secretary Eden in March, 1943, held the view that the errors of the peacemakers of Versailles should not be repeated, but that this would not preclude the victors from taking advantage of separatist currents within Germany. He said that at any rate Germany should be split up into several States. His predominant motive was to deprive Prussia of any possibility of exercising a hegemony in future.

At the first Quebec Conference in August, 1943, Eden let it be known that Great Britain would make agreement by the population a prerequisite for any type of partition. Nevertheless, specialists continued to be called upon to advise the Governments on this delicate matter. There were even unsolicited suggestions by "experts" who were suddenly inspired by ideas. As a characteristic anecdote, it may be recalled that a British political figure from Scotland suggested to his Government to bring considerable areas of Northwest Germany back under the British crown, invoking ancient connections between Great Britain and the Electorate of Hanover. Churchill, however, was more inclined to include Bavaria in a Danubian Federation; but Stalin, on the other hand, was not at all in favor of any such "pan-German" notions. The scene was haunted for a while by the idea of placing the area adjacent to the Kiel Canal under international trusteeship. At the Quebec Conference, Secretary of State Hull cautiously summarized the result of all studies in the following manner: the top American administration circles did, in fact, consider the plans for partition with sympathy in principle, but the specialists, in contrast, were very much in doubt as to their expediency. He said that they had one particular misgiving: that is, whether the democratic way of living would strike deeper roots on the soil of a dismembered Germany. Eden and Molotov reported that there was the same controversy between Government and experts in their countries.

Although all deliberations remained very vague, the problem still did not disappear from the agenda. The first conference of the Big Three took place in Teheran at the end of November, 1943. There, President Roosevelt proposed splitting up Germany in five autonomous States and three international territories. The State Department was subsequently authorized to study the pertinent problems thoroughly. In the memorandum prepared by the top officials under the chairmanship of Stettinius, detailed arguments were presented for rejecting the partition plan. Nonetheless, the subject reached the second Quebec Conference by way of Treasury Secretary Morgenthau's plan. Under this plan, the expanded internationalized Ruhr area, the Saar and the Rhine Palatinate would be separated from Germany. The remaining Germany would be divided along the line of the Main River. This proposal was declared the official policy of the United States of America. Although Hull and Stimson, supported by McCloy, did bring about the abandonment of the Morgenthau Plan, the ghost of the partition idea still hovered over the Yalta Conference in February, 1945. And in the secret protocol of the so-called Crimea Conference, we read under Article III, Division of Germany: "It was agreed that Article 12a of the conditions for the capitulation of Germany be supplemented as follows: The United Kingdom, the United States of America and the Union of Soviet Socialist Republics will be in supreme authority in regard to Germany. In exercise of this authority, they will undertake those steps—including the complete disarmament, demilitarization and division of Germany—which they deem necessary for future peace and security. Study of the procedure for the division of Germany was placed in the hands of a committee consisting of Mr. Eden (chairman), Mr. Winant and Mr. Guzev. This body will consider whether it is desirable to include a French representative."

We are as well informed on the secret consultations of this committee (meeting in London) by Professor Mosely, who at that time was attached to Ambassador Winant, as the confusing subject permits. At that time, the committee was ready with two drafts for a document of surrender, of which one, renewed in Yalta, was kept secret from the French, whereas the older one had already been approved by them. However, in the end, the London committee was not able to put through either of the two, because the headquarters of Commander-in-Chief Eisenhower went over its heads to Churchill with a proposal which differed substantially both from the old draft and from the version adopted in Yalta. In the name of the military leaders, who were surprised by the unexpectedly early date of surrender, General Bedell Smith stressed that the document should contain nothing which might provoke the German military leaders to resume battle and resist to the utmost. Accordingly, for reasons of expediency, the express mention of an intention to divide Germany was left out of the document of surrender. Although the London committee had worked in vain for inclusion of this intention, the course taken by the committee's consultations is highly noteworthy. The fact is that in these discussions, there occurred the first signs of the change Stalin was preparing to carry out in his policy on Germany. Whereas Molotov had formerly nodded zealously to the Allies' partition plans, his delegate Guzev now intimated more and more distinctly that his superior no longer thought very much of the idea of tearing a nation apart. Towards the end of the negotiations, Guzev showed his complete lack of interest. In fact, he said that Moscow had not considered the intention discussed in Yalta to be a firm plan, but instead an extreme resource to be used in an emergency to put appropriate pressure on the Germans. On May 9, Stalin himself stated in a public speech that the Soviet Union did not intend to dismember Germany. He had even anticipated the American military leaders by a small margin. While the most effectual type of division of the *Reich* was still being theorized about indefinitely and generally in London, Stalin was already heading methodically towards a *de facto* partition, perhaps aiming for the demarcation line along the Elbe which had already emerged as a possible boundary of the Soviet-Slavic sphere of influence in the agreement he had concluded with Benes in the midst of the war.

It was in this manner that it came about—as George Kennan said in a lecture in London in 1957—that "the armies of the Soviet Union and the Western democracies were permitted to meet in the middle and take control of this area before it was possible to achieve a corresponding agreement on its future permanent status." But at least no partition was effected, for the demarcation of occupation zones could not be understood as such. Actually, the unity of Germany was at that time not cast in doubt by any of the victorious powers in any agreement or action having the force of international law. The Allied Control Council was only the temporary custodian of a German State which had become incapable of functioning and was without a Government of its own. The only thing left over of all the partition plans drafted with so much imagination was the statute for the establishment of a Ruhr Authority to supervise exports as an inspection agency. It fulfilled this office for a short time, until the Stuttgart speech of American Secretary of State Byrnes brought about a new departure in this respect as well. The Western Powers also understood very soon what was really involved in the forceful Soviet desire to intervene in the inspection of the Ruhr area. Molotov was unable to prevent the resistance he put up against French claims to the Saar area from frightening even Bidault back into the camp of the Anglo-Saxon Powers.

This background has almost been forgotten today. But it is useful to call it to mind, because everything that has been done and achieved in the years since 1945 can be appreciated properly only if it is measured by the depth of the abyss into which Germany threatened to plunge at that time. Perhaps it was of a significance that will be conclusive for all future time that the Berlin Declaration of June 5, 1945, by which the four occupying Powers took over supreme governmental authority "in view of the defeat of Germany," no longer contained a word about a specific plan of division. The same applies equally to the Potsdam Agreement of August 2, which mentioned the desirability of maintaining economic unity. The only thing still under discussion was the right of the Allies to establish the frontiers at a later date. The gradual disappearance of the most terrible of all the conditions planned by the victors will at least shore up the thesis of those savants of public and international law who since that time have asserted that unconditional surrender was a purely military procedure affecting only the *Wehrmacht,* and that it by no means effected the eradication of the legal identity of the *Reich.* The expression "unconditional", according to this view, refers only to the inability of the vanquished to negotiate any further conditions in favor of the defeated troops or the prisoners of war. This view states further that the addressee for all obligations arising out of the June declaration "in view of the defeat" was in any event a unified Germany.

At any rate, this question also caused a stir in Germany itself. As recently as the constitutional convention at Herrenchiemsee, where experts on public law from the *Laender* labored for a first draft of a Basic Law for the Federal State to be constituted of the Western zones of occupation, contradictory opinions collided with one another. It is true that the majority of the legal experts advecated the view that the defeated *Reich* continued to exist of the people on the territory it still possessed. At the same time, a minority was of the opinion that the *Reich* was irretrievably lost through *debellatio,* and that consequently only the *Laender,* which had emerged from the collapse, could be considered as serviceable building blocks. So it was now up to the *Laender* to create a completely new polity out of a free association. It was possible to conserve this latter view as a secret reservation in some *Laender* parties, but the political practice of the Federal Republic subsequently passed over it. Whether this involved the Federal Government's claim to be recognized as the only legal representative of the German people, or whether the subject was war obligations, pensions and restitution, the assertion of a legal succession was always substantiated to an increasing degree. This has not always been successful, as the vain efforts to bring about the return of German assets in foreign countries proves from time to time.

This daring grasp at the legal succession entailed a predecision as to the foreign policy to be pursued by the new Federation. A no less significant predecision was taken by the Parliamentary Council when it prescribed the restitution of German unity in the Basic Law as an objective ordered by the Constitution and binding upon any future Federal Government. It must be kept in mind that at the time this was done, it was not possible to speak of an independent foreign policy any more than of rearmament. The conception of supreme authority was conceived very thoroughly by the occupying Powers and was strictly carried out by them. Even in regard to domestic affairs coming under the authorized German administration, there were weighty interventions by the Military Government. This was true not only of the decentralization of industry, which was a touchy point especially for the British, but also of marriage laws. In a situation characterized by impotent German agencies and a politically naive and suffering population, self-confidence and optimism were required to keep in mind and realize the distant objective which lay beyond the provisional or, as Theodor Heuss preferred to say, transitory, entity.

It was pointed out that the Parliamentary Council had to adopt its decisions in "total lack of responsibility." In the midst of an exhausted people which was intent only on getting along and considered the vacation from high-level policy a permanent condition, and in the face of occupying Powers who gave priority to re-education, it was said that the Parliamentary Council lodged a demand for unity which was incompatible with the defect in sovereignty still attached to the Federal Republic as well. In the meantime, we have come to realize that the lack of sovereignty caused by the presence of the Allied armed forces was a boon from heaven, for it was the basis of our security and our freedom. It was not the least gifted who warned against insisting on sovereignty and feared the moment when the occupying Powers would remove the supporting trellis on which the German administration twined upwards. Since we were in any case dependent on assistance from outside, especially from America, and since our relations with this protecting Power were characterized largely by the limitations of our sovereignty, it was in the interest of German policy to postpone, if possible, the elimination of the "defect". More precisely, at the outset of German foreign policy, the difficult task was to balance steps being taken to rewin certain sovereign rights with efforts to durably bind the protecting powers to the German fate.

Men of insight soberly recognized this state of affairs early. After the Paris Foreign Ministers' Conference had adjourned without success in May, 1946, Erik Reger wrote in the *Tagesspiegel* that the number of conferences necessary was of secondary importance as long as interruptions and postponements did not remain merely dead spaces but confirm the view "that the political stability and economic recovery of Europe are influenced by *agreement or disagreement* on the German problem, though not by the future of Germany—we do not think in such arrogant terms." As early as September of the same year, there occurred an event which suddenly thrust the Paris Conference and even the discussion about the time for the meeting of the General Assembly of the United Nations into the background: the speech by Secretary of State Byrnes in Stuttgart. It conveyed the impression that the world could no longer evade the subject of Germany. His main emphasis was on the questions broached in regard to the future governmental structure and the frontiers. Here, constructive solutions were proposed at long last. A new phase of American policy on Europa had begun. France showed disappointment at what seemed to many to be American wooing for the favor of a people which no longer represented a factor worth wooing. At the same time, Byrnes had stated unmistakably that the Germans had Hitler and Hitler alone to thank for all present distress. Moreover, the assurance given by him to the effect that Germany would be kept viable and would be assimilated approximately to the standard of its neighbors was attached to two conditions intended to calm the former victims of Hitler's war. The first referred to the integration of the Saar into the French economic zone, the other signified permanent demilitarization.

It is not superfluous to recall, too, that Warsaw immediately reacted with extreme indignation to the declaration by the American Secretary of State concerning the provisional character of the Polish western boundary. Poland said this was a matter of life and death and that America was touching a *casus belli*. For a long time, Moscow wrapped itself in silence, thus allowing the impression to arise that in any case there was agreement on the goal of an economic and political unity of Germany to be created in the end. However, as far as implementation was concerned, it was naturally insinuated that the views still diverged greatly. It was assumed that Moscow would give preference to a centralized organization, whereas Washington desired a decentralized Germany with a federal structure. It was known that London considered the prerequisites for unification of the zones to be already fulfilled. The attitude of the Labor Government and the political possibilities it granted the German parties (especially the Social Democrats), sometimes to the annoyance of the Soviets, at that time prompted a Swiss observer to provide his article, tuned to the key of "Who would have thought it?", with the title: "Are the Germans Back in World Politics?"

However, such observations anticipated the actual events. In December of this significant year 1946, the Council of Foreign Ministers had fixed the time and place for the first peace talks with Germany. They were to begin on March 10 in Moscow. It was felt that for the first time since unconditional surrender, a faint outline of the future all-German destiny was taking shape. In the meantime, the agreement on the unification of the American and British zones had taken effect on January 1. Aside from a statement concerning the eastern frontier, the Soviets had not yet stated their attitude precisely. In Germany, there was a great deal of apprehension as to the new year, which some thought might bring peace; and most feared that it would be a harsh peace paid for at a high price. A widespread opinion was that peace for Germany presumed that the Great Powers knew what they wanted from Germany. Of course, every Power had its particular intentions; but how would they find a common course? For the time being, it was considered a masterpiece that Byrnes had even been able to bring the Four Powers to one conference table.

The Moscow Conference, far from finding any firm basis, only accelerated the disintegration of the wartime alliance which probably had already begun in Potsdam. There, Truman felt both tricked and at the same time repelled by Stalin; and for his own part, Stalin became suspicious that America only wanted to use the atomic bomb to deprive him of the spoils of his victory in Asia. This time it was Secretary of State Marshall's turn to lose his patience; some say he lost it too soon. But Bevin also tore his hair in desperation. In response to Bidault's biting remark that God alone knew any longer where anyone stood at this conference, Bevin said that he had no idea that even God Almighty was attending this meeting. Molotow had driven the game of cat and mouse to the extreme. The others felt disgusted and went home without having accomplished anything. It was a shock for everyone. In Germany, no one at that time consciously dared to speculate on disagreement among the Allies. It was said ominously that this would mean lasting partition. The prevailing opinion was that a provisional arrangement based on division would be not only be dangerous but unviable. A leading newspaper wrote: "If even the Bizonal Agreement, the attempt to initiate only economic unity, has been met with great reserve by the other two Powers (France and the Soviet Union), it must unfortunately be anticipated that any reorganization of Germany going beyond that will meet with much greater difficulties."

In his commentary on the failure of the Moscow Conference, however, Walter Lippmann said in an appeasing tone that some of the differences arising among the Big Three were to be attributed only to psychological misunderstandings. He said that it was, therefore, vital to have a "productive continuation of their Teheran and Yalta talks" (thus without France). This sounded just as though Truman had not already been sobered in Potsdam. Meantime, the official policy of the American Administration drew other conclusions from the failure of the conference. It now chose, with determination and without wavering, the path which was to lead to the recovery of the community of European States left in the zone of freedom. For the Germans, the time for a foreign policy in the sense of independent participation in international life had not yet come, but it was not as far off as some sceptics thought. The London decisions of the Western Foreign Ministers faced the Governments in the zones of occupation with the task of constituting a West German State of a federal type. How heavily the Minister-Presidents felt the burden of this responsibility-fraught authorization weighing on their shoulders was revealed when the Bavarian Minister-President undertook a final attempt to bring all the *Laender* heads (including those of the Soviet Zone, which was still organized federally at that time) to the conference table in Munich. After the Soviet order to withdraw arrived from Karlshorst, everyone knew that the dies had been cast. The reciprocal interaction of *faits accomplis* began on both sides of the demarcation line.

When the status under international law underwent the first decisive change upon the establishment of the Federation, an enormous step had been taken in comparison to the year 1945, when the last remnant of German governmental authority seemed eradicated. Now there was once more a central authority provided with a modest measure of power to act under international law. Nonetheless, the limitations still dominated, so that no one would have been justified in speaking of German foreign policy. It is true that the other countries were already disputing over the part Germany would some time have to play: for example, in the British House of Commons, where Churchill, with his daringly improvised proposal to convert Great Britain, France and Germany into a firmly crystallized European nucleus, came into sharp conflict with Foreign Secretary Bevin, who wanted to adhere irrevocably to the existing institutions, the Council of Europe and the Atlantic Treaty. From the time of Churchill's stirring speeches in Metz and Zurich, Germany was already present in all debates on a united Europe, as an unknown quantity, so to speak. Indeed, it might be said that in its plunge, Germany had been spared the most direful impact, because it was caught up by a benevolent readiness to respond to all of the sufferings and atrocities of the recent past by achieving a united Europe. Those wise, brave men, who kept alive the spirit which was the basis for the great plans of Robert Schuman should always be remembered in gratitude. Among them was Albert Camus, who anticipated the program for a reconciliation between the two nations already in April, 1944, before Hitler was defeated. In his third letter to a German friend, Camus said, "During this entire period while we have been serving only our country stubbornly and silently, we have never lost sight of one idea and one hope and have always kept it alive in ourselves: Europe. And in the last analysis, I am also aware *that not everything will have been accomplished with your defeat.* Europe must then first be created. It must always be created."

Konrad Adenauer built on this kind of willingness when he circumspectly began to lay the basis—with patient soliciting for the confidence of the erstwhile "hereditary enemy"—for a foreign policy which first of all had to be European unification policy. In March, 1951, the Chancellor, at that time Foreign Minister as well, formulated a foreign policy program for the first time in an interview. Since that time, but not before, it has been possible to speak of a German foreign policy at all. Adenauer stated that he did not believe in a power of powerlessness, but in the strength of confidence. He said that German foreign policy must be free of any concealed motives or any possible duplicity and must not veer between East and West. He said that an honest foreign policy was at the same time the most realistic policy. He warned against considering everything a defeat which did not seem unambiguously to be a victory. He said that in reality, foreign policy was an art of balancing, a process of give and take. "Victories" were to be expected neither from power nor from powerlessness. Every result, even the slightest, was valuable. Even so-called "prepayments" sometimes had to be taken in the bargain and were in fact necessary for a post-Hitler Germany. Here, the Chancellor anticipated his reply to the reproaches the opposition was later to lodge against his policy on the Saar question. Adenauer added that in a stage of German quasi-sovereignty which represented only a temporary solution, it was possible to make any step forward seem ridiculous if it were measured against the objective. Seen from the zero point, it was, nevertheless, a step forward. Naturally, the job was not finished with revision of the occupation statute; and naturally Germany could not remain a State with diminished rights forever. He said that with the tough patience he felt he had at his disposal, he would continue to work towards the objective of equal rights and duties, but that he would most prefer it if Germany did not have to become a fully sovereign State at all again, and if it could make a common sacrifice of sovereignty together with the other States of Europe. He said that the age of European national States had expired, that the federation of Europe must be created, and that he hoped to live to see it. All of this was stated by the first Foreign Minister of the Federal Republic just a few days before the initialing of the Schuman Plan, at a time when he still had to drive up to the *Petersberg* to discuss the most important questions of foreign policy with the three High Commissioners.

The Federal Republic was destined not to pursue this reasonable program with the reserve which seemed appropriate in view of the situation at the time of its establishment and in view of the continuing distrust of Germany throughout the world. Already in the previous summer, the outbreak of the Korean War had caused even more general shock than the Berlin Blockade. The peoples of the West felt themselves to be directly threatened more strongly than before. The Soviet attack, which Krushchev was later to attribute to an erroneous appreciation of the world situation by his predecessor in his destalinization speech, invigorated the will of the European nations to unite more closely, just as the Communist *coup-d'état* in Prague had called forth the Atlantic Alliance. Following a period which had been dominated by ideas on disarmament and demilitarization, a desire for appropriate means of defense became overwhelming. The conversation turned to armament, and the Germans were also to make their contribution to defending the freedom in favor of which they had decided.

A people which meanwhile had not been unhappy to bow to the decision of the victorious powers that it should never again take weapons in hand, found itself faced over night with the necessity to comprehend as a new duty the thing that had only yesterday been strictly forbidden. The old balance in world politics was destroyed, and it was necessary to work for a new one. A dispute began about the question of whether the Western Powers could or should bank on cooperation by the Germans, and if so, to what extent. In this connection, it may be said that the controversy over the course of German foreign policy is as old as the policy itself. It arose from the discussion on the expediency not so much of German rearmament itself, whose psychological problems were assuredly felt to be severe by everyone. The actual issue was rather whether the Western Powers—who were responsible for the domestic order and outward security of their zones and who controlled the most important sovereign rights—should go so far as to allow the mere impression that they were dependent on a few German divisions in the creation and consolidation of a new balance to arise in the mind of their wartime Soviet ally, with whom they disagreed. In the main, the impassioned controversy brought three opinions to light. One said definitely: *ohne mich* (without me). Another advocated a modest national army just sufficient to maintain armed neutrality. The third was inclined to favor the plan for a European army "including German armed forces."

For well-considered reasons, Adenauer decided from the outset in favor of the plan for an integrated European army. In his mind, dispensing with armed forces was out of the question because of foreign policy considerations. The Western Powers should recognize that the Federal Republic was willing to serve the common cause and to incur sacrifices as well. On the other hand, a national army seemed to him to be dangerous from the point of view of domestic policy. He was frightened by the thought of the temptation into which some future, nationalistic generation might be led by the mere existence of an army without international connections. Not a word need be said about the fact that allowance for French sensitivities confirmed him in this view. After all, it had been his experience that even after the shock of Korea, France had sounded Moscow out in the hope of avoiding German rearmament by diplomatic means. In this regard, it was certainly the most bitter disappointment for Adenauer that the French idea for a European army (Pleven), which was nearly carried out as a result of his accommodating attitude, finally came to nothing because of the negative vote in the National Assembly in Paris.

Mendés-France had even gained his investiture majority only on the basis of having handled the treaty on a European Defense Community as ranking second to Indo-China and of having stated that the EDC Treaty was moreover in need of revision and thus unacceptable in the existing form. The blow to the Paris Treaties, which were now denied ratification after a waiting period of 25 months, was softened by Eden. The British statesman courageously sprang into the breach and ventured to act against British tradition, which recommends avoiding treaty ties with Continental Powers except when endangered by war. He was able to win France over relatively quickly through adequate British guarantees against undesirable German growth in power. Accordingly, on the basis of an agreement made in London, there came about on October 23, 1954, those treaties which opened the path to independent responsibility by cancelling the occupation statute. The following were signed in Paris on that day: the Saar Agreement; the protocol on termination of the occupation regime in the Federal Republic, including an exchange of 10 communications between the Foreign Ministers or High Commissioners and the Federal Chancellor; the Status of Forces Convention containing reserved Allied rights; the Three-Power Declaration on Berlin; the declaration on the invitation to the Federal Republic and Italy to join the Brussels Pact; and the protocol on the invitation to join the North Atlantic Treaty.

State Secretary Hallstein judged that Bonn had achieved three essential prerequisites for its foreign policy by concluding the treaties: the recovery of sovereignty, security in the face of the Soviet Union, and remedies against any danger of isolation. The remark concerning the first point calls for a qualification in so far as the Federal Republic was not and is not by any means sovereign in the classical sense—that is, in regard to the decision on war and peace. As far as the fourth task—the achievement of unity—is concerned, Hallstein said the Federal Republic was now fortified and in a better position to seize an initiative of its own. It was just this point that was cast in doubt by the opposition. In those quarters, it was regretted that Adenauer had given priority to rearmament and ratification. The question was raised whether it would not have been preferable to work for a Four-Power Conference and to attempt to place rearmament on the conference table, in exchange, so to speak, for reunification. This was similar to what used to be said of the Chancellor: that he had, somewhat prematurely, traded the defense contribution to obtain sovereignty.

Since the Soviet note of 1952, which has already become legendary, the complaint had never died out to the effect that there had been a failure to find out the true intentions of Soviet policy and, as was said, to "sound out" all possibilities. Unfortunately, the Soviet Government has never given such reserved confidence even the slightest chance, nor has it ever given the slightest encouragement to any alternative to the official foreign policy. The note mentioned previously, which was moreover sent to the three Western Powers and not to the Federal Government, had in the last analysis been aimed very precisely against the establishment of the European Defense Community.

If Moscow had meant the proposal seriously, as many patriots hoped, Molotov would certainly have committed an inexcusable error when he failed to stir a finger after the demise of EDC in August, 1954. For Adenauer's concern for the maintenance of credit ability always stood in the forefront. To him, it naturally meant an alarm signal when, for example, he had to read in the London "Times" that public opinion in Germany was sliding away from the Western alliance, although reunification was at the time unattainable at any price—a fact which Dulles termed brutal and unnatural.

On the world political scene, there was meanwhile a new, unalterable factor, namely, the hydrogen bomb; and the Soviet Union gloried in stating that it also possessed the secret of how to produce it. It could be considered improbable that the Soviet Union would now be more open to suggestions than during the 10 years when it had to exert itself to break the atomic monopoly of the Americans. Instead, it had to be assumed that as a result of its significant advances in arms technology, the self- confidence of the Soviet Government would rise to become immeasurable. It was after the death of Stalin and during Malenkov's short term of office that Churchill, as though in a premonition of the stiffening of attitude to be feared, delivered that nearly visionary House of Commons speech in which he called upon the statesmen to open talks on world policy "on the highest level" for the sake of the destiny of mankind. Since that time, there has been much talk of the summit. When Krushchev came to power, he began to favor this idea, which may have been flattering to his conception of equality among the world Powers. He liked to jibe at the conferences of Foreign Ministers and other "incompetent" assistants who could not decide anything anyway unless the supreme heads were in favor. In fact, even the Berlin Conference had served no purpose other than to allow Molotow to twist it into an introduction to the Indo-China Conference.

The first conference at the summit in Geneva did not by any means gain its true significance from the negotiations on what was termed the connection between European security and the German question, that is, reunification. More important was that the seeming result of the conference gave the final impetus for the Soviets' decision to let the curtain fall for good and for them to say distinctly that reunification was not a subject which they intended to discuss any longer. The ink was not even dry on the paper with the directives to the Foreign Ministers pointing out the connection (which Eisenhower had pushed through with some pressure) when Krushchev made a stop in East Berlin on his return trip, where he held a speech in the *Lustgarten* in order to tear up the newly signed agreement in public. Never, he said in vehement words, would the Soviet Union leave the "German Workers' and Peasants' State" with its Socialist achievements in the lurch. Consequently, in Geneva the responsibility of the Four Powers for restoring German unity was fixed for the last time. In East Berlin, however, Krushchev harshly and irreconcilably defined for the first time the so-called principle of the existence of two German States and proclaimed it as a component of Soviet Russian policy.

Since that time, the West has had to do with this two-state principle proclaimed by Krushchev, and nothing seems to indicate that any concessions could induce Moscow to relinquish it. If there had ever been a two-tier policy of the Soviets on Germany, as some think, it has become completely one-tier since 1955. It may be that Colonel Tulpanov in Karlshorst once stood for the one policy—that of developing the Communist regime in the Soviet Zone without compromise and proof against crises, without regard for the reaction in the West—while Minister Semyonov at that time held the other policy in readiness—that of soliciting support through liberalization and thus speculating on all-German emotions in the Federal Republic. Now, however, this was over and done with. Ulbricht not only enjoyed an increasing support on the part of the Soviet Union, but he was permitted to even go so far as to occasionally spur Moscow on to greater zeal in the interest of his regime. In the light of such background, it is necessary to evaluate the Chancellor's decision not to continue rejecting the Soviets' invitation to negotiate on resumption of diplomatic relations.

As early as the Berlin Conference, Molotov had made the sensational-sounding statement that the then nonexistent diplomatic relations between the Soviet Union and the Federal Republic did not mean that resumed relations were not possible in the near future. That was before Geneva. After Krushchev's repudiation of the summit conference results, the establishment of official relations was a realistic alignment with the existing situation, although the relative advantage of being able to represent the interests of the Federal Republic directly in Moscow had to be paid for by putting the Western Allies at a disadvantage, for, according to Hallstein's Doctrine, they were forced to concede to the Soviet Union the privilege of being the only former victorious Power able to maintain legal relations with two German Governments. As a result, the Federal Government was prompted to even stricter observation of loyalty to treaties *vis-à-vis* the Western Powers, which sometimes prevented it from using the Moscow connection in the manner Ambassador Kroll may have wished.

During a confidential conversation with a visitor, Krushchev once said that no one should believe he was afraid of the Germans, and that not even atomic weapons in their hands would fill him with apprehension. What really disturbed him was the Bonn Government's possible influence on American policy. His observation that neither the unification of Europe could be blocked nor the strengthening of the Atlantic Community be hindered probably nourished Krushchev's suspicion that the policy of the West, urging towards a revision of the situation arising in 1945, had not yet been discouraged by his brusque reply to the Geneva connection. In order to make it completely clear that there were worse things than the *status quo* the Western Powers desired to improve in Germany, he increased the pressure on West Berlin. In Leipzig, he then said frankly what he hoped to be able to extort: a treaty agreement fixing the results of World War II, thus legalizing the Soviet Union's acquisitions and sphere of influence and thus making any attempted revision in favor of the West illegal. What he intends is to convert the booty resulting from the wartime rights of the victor into possessions under international law. Since November, 1958, all efforts undertaken in Geneva or in exploratory talks consistently come up against the Berlin ultimatum, which continues its threatening existence in spite of postponed deadlines. After all, there are few points on earth where Krushchev would find a more convenient opportunity to put pressure on the opposing alliance, to split it temporarily, or at least to isolate the Federal Republic.

When Eisenhower talked to Krushchev in Camp David, it was still believed in the West that it would be possible to terminate the Cold War without having won it. It was thought that it would be possible to do away with the issues individually and in succession. Since the time when President Kennedy began trying to develop a strategy adapted to the flexible tactics of the Soviets, it has become increasingly clear that what is involved is a global controversy in which all sources of conflict and issues are indissolubly connected. On assuming office, the new President found himself confronted with the unresolved situation in Laos. The mishap with the unsuccessful attempted invasion on Cuba was an additional factor. The worst disappointment came with Krushchev's rude interruption of negotiations on terminating atomic tests. This very Geneva conference on an atomic moratorium had been regarded by Kennedy as the effort offering the greatest propects of reaching the long-term *modus vivendi* with the Soviets which is dictated by the continuing stalemate in the arms proportion between the world Powers. An additional aggravation was the fact that in the attempted exploration in Moscow, America was finally thrust off into the Berlin problem, which naturally offers the least room for free political play. After his meeting with Krushchev in Vienna (where he wanted to sound out his opposite number), the President knew that the Soviet boss remained unerring in the pursuit of his objective of seeing the results of World War II fixed and in his decision not to believe (at least seemingly) the assurance by the Americans that they were also determined to risk all. At that time, the world was very close to the brink of war, and since then, Kennedy has been trying to embed the acute German source of danger into the total theater of the present Cold War. In this way, he wants to expand the area for maneuvering, gain tactical freedom of movement and relativize the individual case.

The responsibility America has assumed, against its will at first, as a world Power will always have to be kept in mind in Germany. Our wishes, our successes and our disappointments in regard to national questions can only be measured against this absolute quantity and the risk which the guarantee pledged to the Federal Republic includes. In this respect, impatience is just as improper as premature distrust. We have to resign ourselves to the fact that "the roads of national destiny are paved with the rubble of foundered negotiations." Even when he was dangerously ill, Dulles said of such unsatisfying negotiations that "the result was that the statesmen can now apply diplomacy without having to live constantly in fear of war." This was backed up by the realization that no individual conflict, taken by itself, would be worth the risk of war. The upward revaluation of this risk through arms technology, together with downward revaluation of the individual matters of dispute, simply leads to a situation in which all of us must become accustomed to *living with unsolved problems,* perhaps for a long time. The only important thing is that we must never falter in cases where matters can be changed for the better through our own efforts, by consolidating European unity and in securing the Atlantic Community.

Rapallo: Myth and Reality*)

By Fritz René Allemann

Forty years ago (on April 16, 1922) in a small seaside resort on the Gulf of Genoa, a treaty was concluded which—unlike most of the diplomatic instruments of that already remote era—is still capable of rousing strong emotions: the Treaty of Rapallo. For the first time since the end of World War I, the representatives of the Weimar Republic and the Russian Socialist Federal Soviet Republic (which later developed into the Soviet Union) signed a formal agreement which caused a sensation at the time and, like a mythical force, has never ceased to haunt men's minds. Even today, forty years later, the words "Rapallo policy" still arouse secret hopes and uncanny fears; at this very moment, indeed, the catchword appears to have acquired a renewed topicality, attracting some, depressing others.

Hardly any other event in diplomatic history is capable, at such a distance of time, of arousing such contradictory feelings. For some, "Rapallo" represents an event as catastrophic as the fall of man, a disastrous aberration, an evil deed which was bound to bring forth evil, if not a downright pact with the Devil himself. Yet for others the document would appear in retrospect to have been a diplomatic masterpiece, the result of great constructive statesmanship, an example of *Realpolitik* which might well serve the politicians of today as a model and guide (and would do so if these men had not got themselves entangled in "doctrinaire" conceptions).

In the negative and hostile attitude to the Treaty, it is still possible to sense the shock which it produced at the time in the Western world, the depth of which may be measured by the intensity of the condemnation which it still arouses. On the other hand, it is possible to feel, even now, in the positive enthusiasm for the Treaty the pride felt at the time in the achievement of a brilliant coup and also the conviction that the coup was going to influence the whole future of mankind.

On both sides, there was and is the conviction that Rapallo was more than the answer to the challenge of a particular passing moment, that it was rather the fulfillment of a constant possibility in German-Soviet relations which may become topical again at any time—the possibility of German-Soviet cooperation beyond the differences of social systems and political attitudes.

There is, in fact, nothing in the treaty itself to justify either the bitterness of its enemies or the enthusiasm of its champions. When the effect it had

*) From *Encounter*, published in London

is measured against its actual content, the misunderstanding must seem quite grotesque. On closer examination and viewed from the distance of forty years, the document which agitated so many minds, sowed so many suspicions, and aroused so many hopes turns out to have been quite unsensational. Indeed, it might be called strikingly harmless. On the surface, at least, it was merely an attempt to settle the "conflict between Germany and Russia" by mutual agreement. Since the defeat of the *Reich* in World War I had rendered the separate Russo-German Peace of Brest-Litovsk meaningless, and since the Soviet Government had never signed the Treaty of Versailles, it was not surprising that the two powers should have decided to come to an understanding. They achieved it by a mutual renunciation of their claims for war damage and war costs. Germany even went further and waived all claims for compensation for damages by German citizens arising from the Revolution, provided that the Russian Government did not "satisfy similar claims of other States." At the same time, it was agreed to resume diplomatic and consular relationships and, finally, the two governments affirmed their desire to meet the economic needs of the other party "with mutual feelings of goodwill"—a deliberately vague formulation of a readiness to cooperate in the economic sphere.

That was all—and there was quite certainly nothing world-shattering about it. Neither of the two powers had made a one-sided or irrevocable political choice. Rapallo did not establish an alliance or a political bloc. Fundamentally, it was a straightforward "normalization" of the relationship between the German *Reich* and the Soviet Republic. Only the financial clauses went any further than that and they, too, were simply intended to make a clean sweep by the mutual cancellation of all claims (which were in any case problematical and would have been difficult to fulfill). Since Germany had not the slightest hope of collecting war compensation from the Soviets, while, according to the Versailles Treaty, Russia was able to claim German reparations, it was the *Reich* that benefited most from Article I (renunciation of claims for war damage and war costs). It made up for this advantage by acknowledging the Soviets' right to expropriate German nationals without compensation. Since the Russians were only able to collect German reparations in agreement with the Allied Powers (and such agreement was dependent on a Russian acknowledgment of Tsarist prewar debts), the Western powers and not the Russians would have been the real beneficiaries of any German "reparations" paid to the Soviet Republic; for this, if for no other reason, it was not difficult for the Russians to waive their legal claims on the Germans. They also thereby gained the assurance that Berlin would keep out of any international association which attempted to enforce claims for compensation for foreign capital that had been "socialized" by the Russians. Each of the contracting parties, therefore, gave to some extent a guarantee that it would not participate in a "united front of creditors" directed against the other State. This in itself shows how advantageous the arrangement was for the two parties. It banished the German nightmare of having to pay the costs of an understanding between the Soviets and the victors of World War I; at the same time, it dispersed Soviet fears that victors and vanquished might unite in an imperialistic phalanx against the young and isolated Soviet power which was still rather uncertain of itself.

As one looks back on Rapallo, however, it is impossible to dispute that, leaving all the ulterior motives on one side, the content of the agreement was eminently reasonable. It was certainly more in accord with the realities of the situation than most of the schemes put up by the diplomats and financiers at that time. It is now generally agreed that the demand for reparations, in accordance with the wartime slogan *le boche payera,* was not only politically unwise but also economically senseless and disastrous and impeded the recovery of economic life throughout the world. Even in 1922, it must have been clear to any alert observer that the elemental event of the Russian Revolution could no longer be revoked by external pressure. It was not the actual text of the treaty which caused the "Rapallo shock". "The fact of the signing was more important than the formal content," as has been said by one of the historians of German-Soviet relationships.[1]) What excited world opinion was the political pattern traced out by this attempt at a *rapprochement* between Berlin and Moscow: the beginning of cooperation between the Outsiders. The Allied Powers had entirely failed to reckon with the possibility that Germany and Russia, who were both excluded from the "family of nations", treated as outcasts, and deliberately isolated by the victors, might come together despite all the differences in their social and political organizations. That this event took place on the periphery of the first great post-war international conference to which the two hitherto ostracised powers had, by way of exception, been invited, was regarded as a manifestation of base ingratitude and malevolent cunning, the more so as no one had been prepared for the explosion of this diplomatic bomb.

The Western Powers had only themselves to blame for thus being caught entirely unawares. It is a well-known fact that all the efforts of the German delegation in Genoa to make contact with the leading British representatives before the conclusion of the treaty had been in vain. It is also a fact that the German Foreign Minister, Walter Rathenau, had hesistated for a long time before signing the document. This was not because he had any misgivings about one or other of the clauses, but because he was afraid that a sudden coup of this nature might break up the Genoa Conference (his fears turned out to be perfectly justified), and because he saw that it might endanger the chances of at any rate a partial understanding with the victors (though, in view of Poincaré's rigidly hostile attitude, he doubted whether such chances in fact existed at all). Rathenau only yielded reluctantly to the pressure of Chicherin, who claimed that the Soviet negotiations with the Western Powers had been far more successful than was actually the case, and who was eagerly supported by the "Eastern politicians" in the German delegation (who, in addition to *Reichskanzler* Wirth, included the later Secretary of State for Foreign Affairs, Ago von Maltzan). It may well be argued that the undoubted concrete results of the agreement were largely invalidated by the unprecedented psychological effect which the "bomb" caused in the West. Unexceptionable though the treaty itself may appear to have been, the diplomatic *coup de main* with which it was presented to an angry and astonished world may well be regarded as highly

---

1) Edward Hallett Carr,
1952.

questionable. Be that as it may, it does not alter the fact that a certain measure of German-Soviet cooperation was inherent in the logic of the current international situation. Forgetting all the side issues, it does seem almost inevitable that two isolated powers, which were practically excluded from all international communications, should have tended to seek for a mutual understanding and even to enter into a close union with one another. When a nation has a large number of enemies, it naturally tries to make contact with others in a similar position. There is no sense in applying abstract ideological criteria to the politics of a State which is forced to operate under such unusual and oppressive conditions, or to get morally worked up about it; and it would be equally absurd to project the utterly different world pattern of today into the past and blame the statesmen of that age for only following "narrow national interests". Since the victors of World War I had neglected to create any common interests with the vanquished, there was nothing for the latter to do but exploit to the utmost the modest opportunities of independent action which still remained open to them.

Let us be quite frank about it—Rapallo was the receipt for Versailles: the spirit that ruled in the Versailles Treaty (the spirit of unrestrained national egoism, with no commitment to any international ideas) was bound to produce the "spirit of Rapallo". One cannot defend Versailles and also condemn Rapallo. The fruit plucked on the Gulf of Genoa had grown on the tree which the victors planted three years before. This is not an excuse for the treaty but it is a judgment on the policy which made a German-Soviet *rapprochement* unavoidable.

By thus recalling the circumstances surrounding the Rapallo treaty, we should be saved from the temptation of distilling from this event and from the widespread collaboration between the Weimar Republic and the Soviet Union which followed a supratemporal principle of German diplomacy to be applied in all circumstances and in every situation. The positive Rapallo myth is just as contrary to historical fact as the negative one and infinitely more dangerous in the present situation. The agreements of 1922 were quite definitely not a *Suendenfall* which it was necessary subsequently to disown. Still less, however, were they a model to be followed at will in the future. They were rather the product of a unique political situation which, as far as it is humanly possible to judge, will never recur and which has meanwhile become part of history. It is quite possible to believe that they accorded with this unique situation, that they were realistic and to that extent justifiable and right from the standpoint of the parties concerned. But this has no bearing whatsoever on the question whether a new Rapallo would be equally justifiable or even feasible in the radically different world of today, that is, within a completely different set of international relationships.

On the contrary: when one recalls what was really behind the German-Soviet *rapprochement* of 40 years ago, what caused the two parties to make this move, what they hoped or were entitled to hope from it, and then compares the picture with the situation as it is in 1962, the irrelevance of any model derived from the situation of that time to the current problems of German politics leaps to the eye at once.

The decisive factor is the radical displacement of political power and influence which has taken place since 1922. At that period the *Reich* and the Soviet Republic, albeit for different reasons, were not only in a similar state of international isolation; their acting in unison was also facilitated by the fact that they were completely equal partners. Potentially, they were both still great powers, but for the time being both were weakened and strictly limited in their freedom of maneuver. Germany and Russia were both suffering from the consequences of an exhausting war and a heavy defeat which had thrown them, for the moment, into a position of inferiority. The advantageous geographical situation of the Soviet Republic, in the "heartland of the Euro-Asiatic land mass", its incomparably greater area and larger population, were offset by its technical backwardness and by the devastations caused by the Revolution and civil war and by the German partner's incomparably greater industrial power. Furthermore, the *cordon sanitaire* of young national states which the victors had drawn right across Central Europe from the Baltic to the Black Sea separated the two states from one another and spared them the problems which arise from immediate proximity. Both states were equally interested in preventing the political consolidation of this mid-European Zone. Both were pursuing, in particular towards Poland, a "revisionist" policy (or what the Soviets now call "revanchist"). This, too, brought Berlin and Moscow closer together, though it was obvious that they would not need to be afraid of one another only so long as the situation created in Eastern Europe by Versailles and Trianon persisted—a situation which they were jointly endeavoring to undermine. As soon as the barrier between them was removed, their friendship would also threaten to fall to pieces, since they would then meet as rivals in the intervening zone. (This inevitably happened in the new phase of the German-Russian entente at the time of the Ribbentrop-Molotov pact.)

Their relationship was, therefore, by no means free of mistrust (and even mutually justified mistrust). There was altogether a piquantly paradoxical element in the friendship which began in Rapallo. The *Reichsregierung* knew perfectly well that the Kremlin was planning to carry the "proletarian revolution" into Germany and secretly promoting with all the means at its disposal the German Communists' plans for a *putsch*. For its part, the Soviet Government had no illusions about the ulterior motives which were behind the flirtation of the German middle classes with Communist Russia: it was perfectly aware that the supreme concern of the Germans was to secure for themselves a modicum of independence in foreign policy. It also realized that, with increasing stabilization, German capitalism was bound to succumb to almost irresistible pressure from the West. This, in fact, happened only a few years later with the Locarno Pact and the entry of the German *Reich* into the League of Nations, though Stresemann took the precaution of offsetting these westward moves by concluding the German-Soviet "Berlin Treaty" of 1926.

For these reasons, if for no others, it was impossible for the relationships which had been created in Rapallo and which were subsequently intensified by trade agreements and secret military cooperation between the *Reichswehr* and the Red Army, ever to be crystallized in the policy of a real bloc.

Even at the time of the Versailles Treaty, Germany's economic and political connections with the West were too close for it to be able to enter an intimate association with the Russians. Thus, the friendship of Rapallo was always a very partial one, hemmed in by various reservations, and, despite the secret military agreements, it really boiled down more to a mutual neutralization (with an admittedly, for a time, very benevolent interpretation of neutrality) than even a potential alliance. Each of the parties knew that the long-term interests and intentions of the other ran counter to his own. There was no reason why this should necessarily prevent them traveling for some part of the way together, and so long as their respective forces were more or less equally balanced, they were able to afford a temporary association.

Today, none of these presuppositions exists any longer. On the contrary, not merely the long-term but also the intermediate interests of the Rapallo partners are so utterly antithetical that an understanding between them is well-nigh inconceivable. Since the Soviet Union has used its victory in World War II to advance its military perimeter to the very gates of Lübeck, into the Harz mountains and as far as the Werra, and also to incorporate a third of Germany politically and socially into its own domain, there is simply no longer any basis for a Rapallo type of agreement. If in the early twenties the Versailles policy of the Western Powers drove the *Reich* almost irresistibly (at any rate, for a time and with certain reservations) into the arms of Russia, Soviet policy since 1945 has led even more inevitably to the Federal Republic being driven into the arms of the Western Powers. As long as Moscow insists on the *status quo,* this situation is unalterable, because it is inherent in the logic of the distribution of power in Europe even more than was the Rapallo Treaty.

Now it may be asked—and this seems to be at the bottom of the recently revived talk about "Rapallo"—whether their possession of the Eastern Zone of Germany as a mortgage does not offer the Soviets an opportunity of drawing the Germans as a whole on to their side. If one day they were to be weary of the everlasting crises in the Russian Zone of Germany, and the pressure on Berlin seemed too risky, might it not occur to them to take the opposite direction and by making concessions at the expense of the "German Democratic Republic" entice the Federal Republic to leave the Atlantic Alliance since they are unable to compel her to do so? Is it really impossible that some Government in Bonn might be tempted by such an offer to change course and turn Eastwards?

It may, of course, be objected that the argument is entirely speculative, since there is at present not the slightest indication that a *reversement* of this kind is even under consideration in Moscow. The much disputed memorandum of 27 December can certainly not be construed in this sense; however unwonted its tone of studious wooing and however interesting some of the hints in the text might seem, it did not contain the remotest suggestion that Moscow might be envisaging the surrender of her Zone. On the contrary, the whole document was a skillful, though unsubstantial, attempt to render a German-Russian reconciliation on the basis of the *status quo* palatable to the recipient. The memorandum was concerned not with offering a deal on the basis of common interests, but with sweetening the prospect of capitulation to a superior power.

It is, however, still an open, albeit for the time being, purely hypothetical question, what the reaction would be if Moscow were one day to decide on tangible and more concrete offers. The hypothesis may be thought extremely improbable—and in my own opinion, it quite definitely is so—on practical grounds alone (since Moscow cannot "write off" the Eastern Zone of Germany without seriously endangering the whole cohesion of the Eastern bloc) and, above all, on ideological grounds. But this does not absolve us from envisaging such an eventuality.

In so doing, we must try to visualize the nature of a possible Russo-German partnership under present conditions. In Rapallo, the powers that met were of equal standing. In the meantime, however, the then Soviet Republic which territorially had been cast back almost to its eighteenth century condition, has become a world power, whereas the German *Reich* is now reduced, geographically, to the Federal Republic and, politically, to the condition of a third-class power. Under these circumstances a "new Rapallo" would be an agreement between extremely unequal parties.

Even in 1939, it was still possible for Germany and the Soviet Union to meet as equals (in the Ribbentrop-Molotov pact) and divide up central Europe *(Zwischeneuropa)* between themselves. But today (and tomorrow and the day after tomorrow) any cooperation between them would be determined from the outset by Russia's obvious and unchangeable preponderance.

There may well be something attractive for the Soviets in the idea that the Federal Republic might one day turn its back on the Western camp and join with Moscow in a *tete-à-tete*. But what on earth would ever induce Bonn—no matter who happened to be in power—to meddle in such a dangerous enterprise? The prospect of German reunification? Ten years ago, most of the Germans shrank even from the adventure (likewise hypothetical) of making an international agreement on the neutralization of Germany as a whole the subject of negotiations! Their reasons for resisting such a move were doubtlessly good and compelling ones (though that is an arguable question). But compared with a "new Rapallo" which, under present conditions, would mean Germany's leaning for support on Russia's superior forces, an acceptance of the Stalin proposals of March, 1952, would have been a perfectly harmless venture. (Whether the proposals were meant to be taken seriously or were merely a tactical maneuver is immaterial in the present context.) At that time, the idea of keeping a united Germany out of all one-sided military commitments was still based on the conception of a European system of security and of a Four-Power guarantee. However problematical such a project may have appeared, it cannot be denied that, compared with an isolated German-Soviet arrangement which would be attainable only by a wanton breach of the Western Alliance, it was bound to seem infinitely more "realistic". No German politician in his right mind will ever be prepared to play the part of junior partner (and suicide candidate) in a *societas leonina* with Moscow.

Of course, there are people—and not only Dr. Dehler and Ambassador Kroll—who regard an agreement with Moscow as quite feasible, even at the price of heavy sacrifices. But the important thing is that, unlike the open and secret adherents of the German *Friedensunion,* they would not dream of undertaking such an operation on their own responsibility and behind the Allies' back. An arrangement reached without the consent of the Western Powers could be anything at all, but it could certainly not be another Rapallo. And there is really no sense, from the German or from the Western point of view, in burdening one's thoughts about all this with historical parallels which are not real parallels at all, or to summon up ghosts which are resting peacefully in their graves.

There is, however, one quite different and very topical question: whether, under what conditions, on what basis and with what ultimate purpose a bilateral German-Soviet conversation or even, maybe, a German "initiative" *(nach Osten)* might be possible and meaningful, what might be hoped from it in the most favorable circumstances, and what dangers might lurk therein. One cannot, however, discuss *this* question rationally without first clearing away the rubble of a past which has nothing whatever to do with the problems, opportunities, and dangers of the present and which can only distort one's vision of the future.

Berlin

By Kurt L. Shell

I — From "Point Zero" to the Blockade

The situation in which Berlin finds itself today as the symbol of the West's defense against totalitarian encroachments does not lack a certain irony. It expresses most poignantly both the disappointment of the hopes held in the West of the "one world" emerging from the war against Hitler as well as the success of American policy born from the shattering disillusion of the post-war period. If we wish to appreciate the paradox of the phenomenon Berlin, we must briefly turn back to the last war years and attempt to recapture the atmosphere, preoccupations, and apprehensions in which the decisions were made which created the pattern and problems for decades after.

In 1945, when the capital of the defeated *Reich* was occupied by the Red Army, Berlin was described as "the world's biggest heap of rubble." Almost 20 % of its buildings were either totally destroyed or damaged beyond repair and another 50 % required some repair from the ravages inflicted by bombs and gun fire. The services supplying gas, electricity and water were not functioning, the subway tunnels had been flooded and all public transportation had ceased. The population of the capital had declined from 4.4 million to 3 million. So vast did the task of clearing away the rubble and restoring the seemingly irreparably shattered structure of Berlin appear that it was suggested—not entirely flippantly—as the more efficient and rational course to evacuate the entire population and resettle it in a new location. In 1945, this proposal might have found some support—even among Berliners (though this is doubtful, given the tough loyalty of their attachment to their city); but when a similar suggestion was made 15 years later in the pages of the *Manchester Guardian* as a means to solve what had then become the "Berlin Problem", it could not be taken seriously; for by then, Berlin had come back to full, energetic life, however "abnormal" and problematical its political position was.

In the last phases of the war, Berlin—and the Berliners—apparently did not appear very important to the men of power who directed the Allied war effort; except, perhaps, as the symbolic center of Hitler's realm, the occupation of which would demonstrate the complete and irreversible defeat of Germany. Unlike 1918, the victors would march through the Brandenburg Gate and thereby prevent the emergence of any "stab-in-the-back" legend. The implications for the future of Germany of the occupation zones and sectors drafted and settled prior to the armistice were not seriously considered, for winning the war and maintaining Allied unity were obviously considered much more important objectives. Given the assumptions—widely held at that time—that most Germans were deeply infected by the Nazi bacillus, that the job of "democratizing" the German nation would be a slow and difficult one, and that one of the foremost tasks of the post-war period would be to prevent the re-emergence of the "German menace"—a common interest of the Western Powers and the Soviet Union—it is understandable that the questions of zonal divisions and Allied access rights to Berlin were treated as of secondary importance; though retrospectively, it may seem preposterous that of the various alternative drafts for the division of Germany into occupation zones—some of which either placed Berlin into a Western zone or gave it direct connection with it (by having the zones radiate from Berlin or by providing broad land corridors from the city to the West)—the one chosen placed the former German capital 110 miles inside the occupation zone assigned to the Soviet Union. The proposal which originated with a British cabinet committee in 1943 before the Western armies even had set foot on the Continent seemed then not unfair in the light of the military effort and sufferings on the part of the Red Army. Thus, it was never seriously challenged and apparently accepted without searching discussion. In the frequently quoted words of the Allied Protocol of Sept. 12, 1944, Germany was to be "divided into three zones, one of which will be allotted to each of the three Powers, and a special Berlin area which will be under joint occupation by the three Powers." The question of Western access rights to the city was treated even more cavalierly. Satisfied with Russian assurances that the presence of Western occupation troops in Berlin "of course" implied rights of access through the Soviet-occupied zone, Western leaders were willing to leave the precise working out of these rights to the military commanders; and they, in turn, deferred the question till the end of hostilities. Another indication of the small significance attached to Berlin was the decision to leave its conquest to Soviet troops (Eisenhower: "Berlin is no longer a particularly important objective"), although the pattern of German defense during the final phase of the war was to offer to the Western troops considerably less resistance than to the Red Army.

Thus, the Soviet troops took the city of Berlin and for two months ruled it as its sole masters. This two-months' period of exclusive Soviet rule had far-reaching consequences: most important, the Soviets alienated a large part of the city's population by the wave of indiscriminate looting and raping and created a lasting identification (reinforcing that created by Nazi propaganda) of "Russian" with "barbaric." Furthermore, they proceeded at once to re-establish Berlin city and borough administrations, packing them—behind a facade of democratic politicians—with handpicked Communists, (particularly in such sensitive organizations as the police force) stubborn roadblocks in the effort to unify and democratize the government of the city. Thus, while the first Lord Mayor of Berlin, appointed by the Soviets, was a non-Communist, the deputy mayor was an old-time Party member, and the head of the police a thoroughly indoctrinated and Moscow-trained Communist. The Soviet authorities had also insisted that all central governmental bodies be located in what was designated as the Russian sector of occupation—this was not entirely unnatural, as the former government center of Berlin was located in their sector. Thus, the Berlin legislature and executive ("Magistrat") remained —until the splitting of the city in 1948—under the sole physical "protection" of the Soviet military command and the Communist-controlled East sector police force.

It would be a mistake, however, to project the mood and insights of a later period into the first phase of post-war existence in Berlin. While the relation between the Western Allies and the Soviet Union was by no means free of frictions and increasing tensions, it can be said that till 1948, they made genuine efforts at solving common problems and tried to avoid the appearance of "quarrelling in front of the maid" (i.e. airing in public Allied differences and "wooing" the Germans). The Allies cooperated in restoring city-wide services, established common ration scales and agreed that—on a live-and-let-live basis—each military Commander could remove borough officials in his sector of occupation.

Similarly, it should not be assumed that the Berlin population—and particularly Berlin politicians—were then clearly and wholeheartedly committed to cooperation with the Western Powers: How could they? For a prolonged period, they were treated with cool distance or supercilious contempt (regardless of their record under the Nazi regime); they believed (rightly, as it turned out) that only through working with all the occupying powers—and this included very definitely the Russians—could a deepening of the division within their city and Germany as a whole be avoided. As yet, the depth of the abyss which separated the meanings given to the concept of "democracy" by the West and by the East had not become fully apparent.

Thus, it is understandable that initially a large percentage of the politically active Berliners also favored close cooperation of all the "anti-fascist" political parties which had been licensed by the occupying powers. In June, 1945, four parties (originally authorized by the Soviet Command) had been re-established—the Social Democratic Party (SPD) the Communist Party (KPD), the newly founded Christian Democratic Union (CDU), and the German Liberal Party (LDP). The Social Democrats —dominant in Berlin until their suppression by Hitler—initiated an attempt to merge with the Communists in order to avoid the fateful division of the German working class which had facilitated the triumph of Nazism. At that time (summer 1945), the Communists, however, opposed such outright merger. When, by December, the Communists had changed their views under Russian prodding and now argued for a merger of the two parties, the majority of Social Democrats had had second thoughts. The appeal of "proletarian unity" was indeed strong and was backed by the chairman of the SPD Central Committee, Grotewohl. But the growing unwillingness to be publicly identified with the "Russian" and Stalinist-Communist Party proved stronger. The opponents of the merger were able to force the holding of a plebiscite among all enrolled SPD members. This plebiscite, held on March 31, 1946, revealed for the first time in a nutshell the coming pattern of East-West division and with it the glory and tragedy of Berlin. Faced with the possibility of defeat for "their" conception and "their" candidates, the Soviet Command interrupted the vote on polling day and prevented its completion in the Russian-controlled Sector of Berlin; in the three Western Sectors, the decision was unequivocal in its opposition to fusion with the Communist Party:

1. For immediate merger: 2,937 votes
2. For an agreement between SPD and KPD "assuring common work and outlawing fratricidal struggle": 14,763
3. Opposed to merger and agreement: 5,559

Thus, the first major step of splitting the city politically was taken. For in the Soviet Sector (as in the Soviet occupation zone), the two parties were—under Russian pressure—merged into the new "unity party," the SED (Sozialistische Einheitspartei Deutschlands); while in the three West Sectors, the SPD remained an independent and powerful party organization.[1] Which of these parties proved the more attractive to the population of Berlin was shown with exceptional clarity at the first and unfortunately only city-wide election held under essentially free conditions on Oct. 20, 1946. Berlin had always been a "left" city (which the Nazis had found a particularly tough nut to crack), and the first post-war vote did not change this fact. But of the almost 70 % which the SPD and SED polled when added together, the SED only received 19.8 % and the SPD 48.7 %; though, as could be expected, the SED did better in the Soviet Sector than in the three others.[2]

The tug-of-war within the SPD, the ruthless interventions of the Soviet occupiers on the side of the Communist and pro-merger forces, the election campaign which had largely been fought as a struggle over "totalitarianism" and, finally, the outcome of the election with its clear endorsement of Western political ideals, had done much to establish more sympathetic ties between the Western occupation authorities and the democratic population and politicians of Berlin. The process which was to transform the "occupyers" into protectors" was under way. The warborn stereotypes were shifting as the "Cold War"—in Berlin as elsewhere—began to gather force. The Soviets, faced with a vote which gave proof of the widespread popular hostility to their political goals, entered on a course which might be described as "defend split and consolidate." They could no longer hope to extend their control into areas outside their occupation sphere by means of (however manipulated) democratic-parliamentary processes. But, by utilizing every legal-technical lever and, where this proved insufficient, by the application of brutal pressure, they could try to prevent militant anti-Communists from gaining power in the Western

[1]) Because of the special occupation status of Berlin, the SPD remained a legal party in East Berlin, but not in the rest of the Soviet Zone. The branches in East Berlin were dissolved by decision of the leadership in August, 1961 after all communication with the West had been blocked. The SED remains a legal party in West Berlin although the German Communist Party is forbidden in West Germany. After August, 1961, the SED party offices in West Berlin were closed by order of the police, but the party was not suppressed.

[2]) Expressed in percentages of the valid votes cast, the results in the four sectors were the following:

	SPD	CDU	LDP	SED
American Sector	51.9	24.8	10.6	12.7
British Sector	50.8	27.1	11.8	10.3
French Sector	52.6	19.0	9.1	21.2
Russian Sector	43.7	18.7	7.8	29.8

sectors and assure simultaneously the complete control by "their" SED of the East Sector. The abyss between the concepts and methods of Stalinist totalitarianism and Western parliamentary democracy *(not* one between "socialism" and "capitalism"), briefly and superficially obscured by the warborn alliance, was opening up wider than ever—and it ran right through the center of Berlin and Germany; and the Germans were being enlisted—occasionally enthusiastically, occasionally reluctantly—in the struggle. From the election of 1946 till the blockade of 1948, the political situation in Berlin reflected schizophrenically the attempt to combine the two incompatible principles of democracy and dictatorship within one city. Those political personalities — outstanding among them Ernst Reuter—who were chosen by the democratic parties as their leaders were *personae non gratae* to the Russians; and, vice versa, politicians sponsored or accepted by the Soviet authorities were viewed askance and frequently disavowed by their own party members. In this period, Berlin remained nominally one political unit under a single, freely elected House of Representatives and *Magistrat.* But through the provisions of the Temporary Constitution which gave each occupying power full control over personnel and execution of policies in its sector, the Soviet authorities possessed the means to wreck unified administration and to sell every concession at a heavy political price. To maintain a single administration for the whole city it was, therefore, necessary to deal and compromise with the Soviet authorities (and their local German agents, the SED). But to do so inevitably led to charges of "weakness" in the struggle against totalitarian Communism and to agreements which failed to obtain legitimizing popular support. Some Berlin politicians (e.g. the SPD-mayor Dr. Ostrowski and the CDU-deputy mayor Dr. Friedensburg) desperately attempted to avoid complete, one-sided identification with Western policies which, in their view, would hasten the division of the city. But their attempts were bound to fail, particularly as the choice increasingly became one—Berlin mirroring the German situation as a whole—between rebuilding a viable administration in the West Sectors (at the price of splitting the city) or accepting the existing chaotic condition of authorities and officials at cross-purposes. It was a continuous choice between two evils—and each encumbered with potentially fateful consequences for the future of the city. For over a year, the Soviet authorities succeeded in blocking Ernst Reuter, the Lord Mayor selected by the majority of the City Parliament, from assuming his office.[3] In November, 1947, the SED organized a "German People's Congress for Unity and a just Peace" which was designed as the nucleus for a future nonelected assembly within a "People's Democracy." Arbitrary arrests and kidnappings (an estimated 1,600 by March 1948) continued in the Soviet-controlled Sector (and occasionally outside as well); while the Western Allies found it impossible to obtain redress or explanations from their Russian "partners" in the Berlin Command.

[3]) Ernst Reuter had been a prominent Communist party functionary after World War I, but had soon broken with the party and turned strongly against it. He returned to Berlin from exile in Turkey after Hitler's defeat and soon made his mark in the city administration and the Social Democratic Party by his firmness, expertness and efficiency.

II — Blockade and Split

The developments inside Berlin merely registered dramatically the deepening crisis in East-West relations which marked the year 1947. The attempt to carry on effective Four-Power control over Germany had broken down and the Western Allies had taken steps to organize their zones—independent of Soviet approval or disapproval—into a viable unit which began to show the outline of a future (West) German state. The breakdown was made manifest by the withdrawal of the Soviet representative from the Allied Control Council in March, 1948. The Soviet Union's rejection of participation in the Marshall Plan and the Communist coup in Czechoslovakia had destroyed the still-existing bridges of cooperation between East and West. The hopes of reaching agreement even in subordinate areas were correspondingly small. For Berlin, the most immediately acute question was the city's place in the developing system of two rival currencies on German soil. Western and Russian experts had been carrying on protracted negotiations, attempting to achieve agreement on a much-needed currency reform for all of Germany. When this was seen to be out of reach, the Western Allies proceeded to prepare currency reform for their zones alone, once again opting for stabilization of the area under their control at the price of formally deepening the division within Germany. Initially, it was not seriously considered to include Berlin (much less three of its four sectors) in the West German currency area. On the other hand, inclusion of Berlin in the Soviet currency bloc would have been viewed as tantamount to abandonment of the city by the West. Heated discussions raged in Berlin over the alternatives: West Mark, East Mark, or a third Berlin (Bear) Mark? Ernst Reuter argued for full integration into the West-currency area, Dr. Friedensburg for a Berlin Mark which would allow Berlin to act as economic (and political) bridge between the two parts of Germany. The Western Allies wavered indecisively. Their first announcement (June 18) exempted Berlin from the West German currency reform; the Soviets replied three days later with a currency reform in the East zone which they attempted to force on all four Sectors of Berlin; and this, in turn, led the Western Allies to extend their own currency to the three West Sectors of the city where West Marks and East Marks were declared valid on a one-to-one basis. By Soviet order, only East Marks were considered valid in the East Sector of Berlin. And when subsequently and inevitably the impossible situation of two concurrent currencies (of nominally equal but de facto vastly disparate market value) existing side by side in the three Western sectors was ended and only the West Mark was generally accepted, a major step toward the establishment of West Berlin as a separate entity had been taken.

Early in 1948, the Soviets had begun to probe Western readiness to hold the Berlin position by harrassing actions against Allied traffic to and from Berlin. As previously indicated, Western access rights rested on implicit assurances rather than explicitely formulated rights, particularly as far as the traffic by land and supplies for the civilian population were concerned. The opportunities for the Soviets to delay or interrupt this traffic—arising out of Berlin's geographic position deep in the Russian zone of occupation—were numerous and of such a nature as to force upon the Western Powers the decision whether to be the first to use military means or not. It is, therefore, not surprising that Allied counsels were strongly divided on the possibility of holding Berlin against a full-scale Soviet blockade and on the measures to be employed to maintain the Western position in the city if it was decided to do so. In the background there loomed—then as now—the risk of another major war. In the face of obvious Western doubts and lack of resolution—talk of evacuating Allied garrisons was rife and faith in the ability of overcoming the Russian blockade almost nonexistent—the West Berlin population initially had little confidence in the West's will or ability to protect it against Soviet pressure. Only as a result of the quite unexpected and dramatic success of the Western "airlift" was this doubt largely dispelled and the lasting and tight link between the Western democracies (foremost the United States) and "our Berliners" forged.

When the West German currency reform was extended to West Berlin on June 23, the Soviets first attempted to force the Berlin Assembly through SED-directed riots to reject the reform. When the democratic representatives remained firm, the Soviet Union cut off all overland access to West Berlin from the West (June 24). After several days of hesitation, with rumors of abandonment flying, President Truman decided "to stay in Berlin" and authorized organization of the "air lift." For the Berliners in the West sectors, the answer to the question whether to throw in their lot with the Americans was by no means an obvious one. The success of a prolonged attempt to supply West Berlin by air was far from assured; in case of abandonment by the West, it would have been wise not to antagonize the Communists; and even in the short run, deciding for the West meant accepting obvious risks and disadvantages.

The Soviets were tempting West Berliners by promising to supply them with all necessities, if only they registered for rations in the East sector. But under the leadership of politicians who were determined to rely fully on Western support—and by such loyal behavior also to tie the West more fully to its commitments—the initially hesitant West Berliners gained a feeling of confidence and solidarity. At first preoccupied with the uncertainties brought about by the confused currency reform and subsequently with the problems created by acute shortages of fuel, power and food stuffs, they came to accept—and in a strange way even to enjoy—their unexpected position as "beleaguered outpost of Western democracy". They gained pride in their role as they felt themselves identified with the "strong West", the roar of whose airplanes they could hear overhead day and night. For the first time, they saw themselves accepted and appreciated as Allies in the fight for a good cause after years of pariah existence. At the heart of their option for the West was undoubtedly their rejection of Russian Communist totalitarianism, not so much as an abstract theory, but because they had experienced it and observed its operation close up since the arrival of the Red Army in 1945. In this mood, they simply decided to "hold out", cope ingeniously with the innumerable problems and inconveniences besetting them during the dreary blockade winter and follow the cues which they received from their own trusted political leadership. Thus—in spite of the hardship it involved—the vast majority refused to register for food rations in the East Sector; participated in the vast mass meetings called by Mayor Reuter to demonstrate and boost morale, refused to participate in Communist-led demonstrations, worked overtime when necessary, trudged long distances to work and cooked meals at odd hours without too much grumbling; in sum, tried to live as normally as the extraordinary circumstances permitted.

While the splendid organization of the airlift—effective well beyond the hopes initially put into it—as well as the hardihood of the West Berliners succeeded in foiling the Soviet goal of forcing the entire city into the Communist camp, they could not prevent the fatal and permanent division of the city itself. The process of splitting the city, under way ever since the election of 1946, now reached its climax. In the Soviet Sector the working of the freely elected city officials was gradually rendered impossible; non-Communist city employees were dismissed in large numbers, the activities of the non-Communist parties and trade unions hampered and circumscribed. In August and September, the Communists succeeded in preventing the City Assembly from holding its meetings in the accustomed place by packing the hall with shouting bullies and staging violent demonstrations—unchecked by the Communist-controlled police of the East Sector.[4] Thus, the Assembly was forced to call its next meeting in the Western part of the city—from where it has not returned to this day. The *Magistrat* remained in the East Sector a while longer (Dr. Friedensburg being determined to stick to his post as Mayor of an *undivided* city). But its work was being undermined by the refusal of SED officials to execute orders of their legitimate superiors who had to establish branch offices in the Western sectors and transfer their files to them in order to carry on some sort of orderly administration. On November 30, the Communists called an "extraordinary meeting of the city assembly" to which only the SED and Communist-controlled mass and plant organizations sent delegates.

This meeting voted removal of the freely elected *Magistrat* and appointed a new, Communist one which was recognized two days later by the Soviet Commander as "the only legitimate city executive." The regularly scheduled elections were held a few days later, but only in the West Sectors—in the Eastern Part, the Soviet authorities had forbidden them. The result of this "blockade" election held in the face of a long, tough winter was unequivocal in its endorsement of those men and parties pledged to resist the totalitarian threats and blandishments.

Though the SED had called for a boycott of the election and attempted to intimidate the population of West Berlin, 83.9 % of all registered voters cast their ballot for one of the three democratic parties, showing

---

[4]) The Soviet military commander, when requested by the President of the Assembly, Dr. Suhr, to assure the physical safety of the elected representatives, blandly replied: "Does he (Dr. Suhr) desire that the Soviet Commander . . . interfere with the relations between the Magistrat and Berlin workers and employees who are dissatisfied with the present policy of the Magistrat and Assembly? . . . Why doesn't he turn in this matter to the German police of the district?"

that the SED following had been reduced to only approximately 5 or 6 percent.[5] Ernst Reuter's Social Democratic Party received almost two thirds of the votes cast (64.5 %)—a tremendous tribute to the man who had become the symbol for West Berlin's stubborn spirit of resistance.

III — Decade of Reconstruction

With the termination of the blockade in May, 1949, a new chapter began for Berlin. It marked the end of Soviet hopes to incorporate the entire city into the Soviet power bloc and was thus a serious and well-publicized defeat of its offensive policy. But this over-all Western success was severely tempered for Berlin by the fact that the city was now —as it had not been before—split into two (unequal) halves with separate (and hostile) political, administrative and economic systems. From then on, the ever more hardening line dividing Germany ran through the city itself.

In order to dispel mistaken notions, it must, however, be pointed out that this dividing line in Berlin was—until August, 1961—by no means an "iron curtain." The public transportation network (subway and elevated trains) continued to connect both parts of the city and communication between them remained essentially unhindered. Though more and more Berliners moved their residence into that part of the city where they were employed, tens of thousands, the so-called *Grenzgaenger* continued to live in one part and work in the other. (These were mostly, though by no means exclusively, residents of the East Sector who held on to jobs in the West Sectors.) Relatives visited each other freely, friendships and romantic relationships were maintained and initiated, ministers preached sermons in churches in East and West sectors. As the economic gap between the two parts began to widen, East Berliners (and East Germans) went for frequent shopping trips to West Berlin to acquire goods which they could either not obtain at all or which were of much poorer quality in the East Sector. These purchases were both risky and expensive, for they were in theory forbidden by the Communist authorities and, besides, the value of the two currencies had established itself at a ratio of roughly one West Mark to four East Marks, so that the visitors from East Berlin had to pay, in fact, for the goods they bought four times as much as they cost customers from the West. To facilitate visits to theaters, concerts, movies and other entertainment for residents of East Berlin and thus maintain a maximum of contacts, the West Berlin authorities initiated a scheme whereby for these purposes a one-to-one ratio of East to West Marks was accepted. It is estimated that about a quarter of all visitors to West Berlin's movie

---

[5]) The SED refused to put up candidates in this election. The percentage figure here given is therefore somewhat speculative, based on comparison with the number of nonvoters at previous and subsequent elections.

houses came from East Berlin; 25,000 subscription members of the *Volksbuehne theaterring* were East Berliners; fairs, circuses, exhibitions counted on and depended for their margin of profit on the Eastern half of the city population. The traffic from West to East was naturally far thinner, as purchases in the East Sector for visitors from the West were impossible or unattractive.[6]) But certain East Berlin institutions of culture and entertainment—the rebuilt State Opera, the fascinating *Komische Oper,* Bert Brecht's famous *Berliner Ensemble*—attracted large numbers of visitors from the West. Yet, though communication between the halves of the city was possible and easy, there developed, nevertheless, a certain feeling of separation. Thousands of West Berliners thought it too risky to enter the East Sector because they had at one time got embroiled in anti-Communist arguments or activities or, because they had "come over" (illegally) from East Germany or East Berlin as refugees; and many more simply felt it to be "depressing" or "threatening" to visit a power realm where "one never knew what could happen to one." Thus, a subtle and insidious process of "writing off" the other half of the city — not officially, not openly, but as an inward development—of saying "Berlin" and meaning "West Berlin" began.

This process was furthered by the decade of rapid economic development for West Berlin following the end of the blockade. In 1949, Berlin —in both halves—was still largely the "rubble heap" it had been when the fighting ceased. The economy functioned at a bare subsistence level, the unemployment figure stood (during the blockade) at 113,000. It increased catastrophically for the next few years as a consequence of currency reform, economic isolation, and structural weaknesses. But after 1953 with the incorporation of West Berlin into the flourishing West German economic and financial system, the number of unemployed began to decline drastically. By summer 1955, it had fallen from 300,000 (in 1952) to roughly 100,000, by summer 1959, to approximately 40,000, and by 1961, the problem of unemployment had given way to one of finding a sufficient supply of workers.

West Berlin's economic upward development—which lagged behind that in West Germany by several years—is further reflected by the production index which had dropped to a miserable 23 in 1950 (1936 = 100), had risen by 1953 to 67, in 1955 equaled that of 1936, and by 1960 stood at 153. Wholesale trade doubled between 1950 and 1960, retail trade tripled. Turnover of industry (foremost of the electrical industry) in West Berlin rose from 1,79 billion DM in 1950 to almost 10 billion in 1960; exports from West Berlin, which were less than 100 million DM in 1950, reached nearly 400 million DM in 1953 and over one billion DM by 1960. And average saving deposits rose from 18 DM per capita in 1950 to 842 DM in 1960.

While before, during, and for a few years after the blockade the West Berlin economy had subsisted almost exclusively on American aid, the

[6]) A large number of West Berliners, however, regularly went to barbers and hairdressers in East Berlin whose services they could obtain for one quarter of the price they would have had to pay in the West.

economic progress beginning 1952 was due largely to the accelerating integration of West Berlin into the rapidly expanding West German economy. It was further stimulated by a spate of government measures designed to facilitate investments and growth in Berlin. The German Federal Republic also made outright financial contributions to such projects as extensive housing and public building programs, extension of the subway network and construction of an intracity *Autobahn* to anticipate the rise of motorized traffic.

The growth of economic and financial ties between West Berlin and the Federal Republic occurred in spite of the highly ambiguous legal position occupied by West Berlin in the German constitutional system. In the "Basic Law" of 1949, establishing the German Federal Republic, Berlin was listed as one of the *Laender* making up the Federation. But the Western Allies insisted on "suspending" this provision and repeatedly declared that Berlin "could not be governed by the German Federal Government." This they did presumably to underpin their claim that Berlin was *not* part of any of the four occupation zones and thus not "on" the territory of the Soviet zone; and that their own military presence was in no way affected by the grant of sovereignty to the German Federal Republic. In spite of this insistence on Berlin's "independent" status, the Western Allies nevertheless permitted a sweeping application of German federal law to West Berlin. While the West Berlin Constitution of 1950 had provided on their demand that each federal law, to be valid in Berlin, had to be separately voted by the city parliament, this was altered subsequently to permit the wholesale and automatic "reception" of such laws by the method of a "comprehensive act" *(Mantelgesetz)*. With some exceptions (such as laws relating to re-establishment of German military forces), West Berlin's status has thus been de facto assimilated to that of other German *Laender*. But striking abnormalities and ambiguities persisted and persist. Thus, the decisions of the Federal Constitutional Court, for instance, were held not to apply to West Berlin, while federal ministries maintain branch offices in West Berlin to supervise administration of federal laws; West Berliners are not permitted to vote in elections for the German parliament and are only allowed to send a nonvoting delegation (selected by the West Berlin assembly) to Bonn. On the other hand, the *Bundestag* and many of its committees hold occasional meetings in Berlin; and the election of the German President in 1954 and 1959 took place in West Berlin. For the West Berliners, the claim to be part of the Federal Republic and the future capital of a (yet to be) reunited Germany is an important part of their political faith, an assurance that West Berlin—physically divided and geographically isolated—is not destined to remain permanently an island-half-city floating in a twilight zone undefined by international law.

In the decade following the blockade, life in West Berlin became "normalized." But the feeling of "normalcy" rested on a thin crust of (necessary) illusion, and on the fact that West Berliners like most people most of the time once more returned to their circumscribed private sphere and became unaware—or accustomed—to the extraordinary aspects of their situation. They got used to not being able to walk or row through the lake-filled countryside surrounding Berlin; they got used to *Vopos*[7] checking their papers when they drove over the *Autobahn* to West Germany. And, if for some reason they feared the Communist wrath, those who could afford it used the airplane to hop over the 100 miles of Communist territory separating their city from its "hinterland." They got used to the presence of foreign soldiers—and came to depend on them for their feeling of security. For they accepted the fact that Berlin (West Berlin to be accurate) was a "ward of the West", existing "normally" precariously balanced on the edge of the East-West conflict.

The relative quiet of this "normalization" process had been shattered once during this decade: On 17 June, 1953—shortly after Stalin's death, a strike called by building workers in East Berlin had turned into a riot and that into an uprising which—for a breathless moment—seemed to succeed in overthrowing the Soviet-imposed Communist regime. But—as in Hungary three years later—Soviet tanks broke the uncoordinated uprising; and West Berliners were prevented by their own police and Allied troops from rushing over into the Eastern part of their city to join their fellows in the fight. Although 17 June was henceforth declared to be a special day of commemoration, the lesson learned by Berliners on both sides of the sector division was bitter and —as 13 August, 1961 showed—lasting: that it was useless to take their fate into their own hands, to be rebellious and heroic, and that the Western Powers would not run risks (in spite of the rhetoric of "roll back") in order to change the *"status quo"*, a *"status quo"* which decreed the division of their city. June 17 was thus not a turning point in the postwar history of Berlin but a milestone in its process of "consolidation by division." For it confirmed the fundamental decision which had been made by the Western Allies and by German politicians like Dr. Adenauer and Ernst Reuter: that successful reconstruction of the "free part" of Germany was only possible at the price of (temporarily, as it was hoped) deepening the split. The feeling of "normalcy" rested on yet another tacit assumption which turned out to be shaky: that the Communist leadership would allow the West Berlin "show window" permanently to throw its bright and attractive light into the East Sector and—beyond—into the "GDR", further undermining the attempt of these Communist leaders to transform and consolidate *their* territory as the Western democracies obviously had succeeded in consolidating theirs.

IV — From Khrushchev's Ultimatum to "the Wall"

In the winter of 1958, the period of relative quiet came to an end and the "Berlin problem" turned once again into an acute "Berlin crisis". For reasons at which we may only guess, Premier Khrushchev and his German "governor", Ulbricht, decided that the time had come to force the pace, to settle the problem of West Berlin which Khrushchev had once described as "a bone in our throat". The draft of a "peace treaty" presented by

[7]) Short for "Volkspolizei", the so-called "People's Police" in the Soviet Zone.

Khrushchev contained primarily two demands which proved totally unacceptable to the West Berliners, West Germans, and also their allies: the formal recognition of the "GDR"—thus the *de jure* legitimization of the division of Germany and the rule of a Russian-imposed dictatorship over one of its parts; and the transformation of West Berlin into a so-called "free city" deprived of the legal, military and political ties with West Germany and the Western democracies and of the presence of American or other forces ready to defend the city against surprise attack or infiltration.[8]) With the city's routes of access by air, water, and land completely under the control of the "sovereign GDR", no one could have entered or left the city without Communist permissions. This "offer" was put forth by Khrushchev with a time limit of six months, at the end of which—he threatened—Western occupation and access rights in and to West Berlin would be considered null and void, thus permitting the "GDR" authorities to impede or interrupt traffic—military as well as civilian, by air as well as by land—to the city. In December, 1958, elections to the city parliament were held in West Berlin. The vote of the SED which campaigned for the Communist "free city plan" shrank to less than 2 percent. Participation in this election reached an—even for Berlin unprecedented—high of 92,8 percent of all eligible voters. Behind this defiant attitude, however, a certain feeling of insecurity made itself felt. Share values dropped and for several months the balance of saving deposits showed a deficit. But when spring came and with it the tacit withdrawal of the time-limit set by Khrushchev, the curves moved upwards once more. In fact, the years 1959 and 1960 were for West Berlin economically the most successful of the entire post-war period. With prolonged negotiations in the offing, an "era of good feeling" in US-Soviet relations in the air (reaching a climax in the "spirit of Camp David"), the fears of the winter seemed once more remote, and the "normally abnormal" situation of West Berlin once again assured its precarious stability. The negotiations at Geneva in which the Western Allies had appeared willing to make concessions in order to obtain an interim agreement (particularly with regard to the removal of so-called "irritants") ended in failure to the relief of many West Berliners. Once more it seemed possible to sit back and relax. But the periods of calm were growing shorter. When Khrushchev aborted the Paris Summit Conference in May, 1960, the immediate apprehension in West Berlin was that he would now make good his threat to sign a unilateral peace treaty with the "GDR" thereby confronting the West with a most dangerous *fait accompli.* But when the Soviet leader stopped over in East Berlin on his return flight from Paris, he once more seemed in no hurry and expressed his willingness to wait in order to settle the problem of West Berlin with President Eisenhower's successor.

Early in 1961, he set out to do so in the most determined effort to date. At the Vienna meeting with newly elected President Kennedy, he repeated without significant changes his demands of 1958 and stressed his determination to push them through at any price. In East Berlin and the East

---

[8]) West Berliners clearly understand that the function of the Western military presence in Berlin is that of a deterrent, a "trip-wire" which the Soviet or East German forces cannot cross without involving the United States (as well as the other NATO powers) at once in military action.

Zone, word was spread that, come what may, a peace treaty confirming the existence of the "GDR" as a sovereign state and transforming West Berlin into a "free city" would be signed by the end of the year. This threat with its implication of tightened control over movement in and out of the "GDR" in combination with the newly resumed ruthless push for complete collectivization of East German agriculture led to a further rise in the already vast stream of East Zone inhabitants making their way via West Berlin to West Germany. Repeated appeals to the population in the East Zone not to abandon their land or their jobs and not to depopulate their part of Germany availed little. The description of the "Golden West" as an economic and political paradise, the newspapers' gloating references to the rising number of escapees, and the favorable treatment which these escapees received from the labor-scarce West German economy did little to stem the tide of those leaving the East Zone for good.

Occasionally, Berliners had vaguely discussed the nightmarish idea that some day the Communists would make the intracity border "tight." But it was generally assumed that they would wait with such a measure till the signing of a "peace treaty." And even then, it was thought this could hardly take the form of hermetically closing off one part of the city from the other. Even the highest officials in West Berlin had refused to take seriously the possibility of a "wall" through the city. At what point in time the East German Communists began to consider it is unknown.[9])

In July, 1961, Communist authorities launched a violent campaign against what they called the Western "kidnappers", "headhunters" and "seducers" of the citizens of the "GDR." By controls on trains and roads, they attempted to intercept everyone who traveled without valid excuse from the East Zone into East Berlin. And still the men and women "came over" in thousands and registered in West Berlin's refugee camps.[10]) President Kennedy mobilized reserves and repeated somberly his determination to defend American rights in Berlin and protect the free Berliners. In Paris, during the first days of August, the foreign ministers of the Western Allies conferred and worked out plans "to meet all threats to Berlin." But although there was an air of apprehension in Berlin and Western radio commentators were uncertain whether in good conscience they could continue to advise Germans in the Communist Zone against leaving their homes, normal life went on during these summer days, as friends and family members visited each other across the sector line and Berliners from the East Sector mingled with the crowds window-shopping on *Kurfuerstendam*. Then, on the night from Saturday to Sunday, from the 12th to the 13th of August, the Ulbricht regime (carrying out a decision of the Warsaw-Pact Nations, as it claimed), closed off the East Sector along its whole length by barbed wire, behind

---

[9]) On June 16, Ulbricht was reported as having replied at a press conference:

> "I understand your question to mean that in West Germany some persons wish that we mobilize the building workers of the capital of the GDR to erect a wall. The building workers of our capital are mainly occupied with the construction of housing . . . No one intends to erect a wall."

It is not clear whether this was a feint or expressed his genuine conviction at the time.

[10]) In the period from January 1 to August 15, 1961, the number of refugees from the "GDR" registered in West Berlin and West Germany was 159,730. This compares with 199,188 for the entire year 1960 and 143,917 for 1959. July 1691 was the first month since 1953 in which the figure reached 30,000. After 1957, Berlin became the foremost exit point as the Communist regime tightened its controls over the traffic between the East Zone and West Germany.

which its armed forces and "plant defense groups" took up position. Fear of a violent uprising on the part of the East Berliners, as well as apprehension of possible Western efforts to remove the barbed wire by force were undoubtedly strong among the Communist leadership. But this fear turned out to be unfounded on both counts. The East Berliners, remembering June 17th and Hungary, suppressed their anger and desperation. The Western Allies—and the West Berlin authorities dependent on them for protection—were equally afraid of a repetition of a Budapest-type uprising. Their reaction to Ulbricht's stroke was one of exasperatingly slow deliberation; except that West Berlin police immediately received orders to keep people well away from the sector border to prevent any incidents which might set off an uncontrollable explosion.

V — Life in the shadow of the Wall

The immediate impact of "the Wall" (it became that, technically speaking, only a few weeks after the August 13th) on West Berlin was traumatic. The shock administered by the Communists and the absence of a forceful response by the West led many to the anxious question: "Will we, too, be abandoned? Will America stand by her guarantees should the Communist move further?" For, latent under the sometimes forced air of optimism, lies for many West Berliners the doubt that Berlin—of all places—should be thought worth the risk of war. Given the almost universal conviction that the only language which Communists (or Russians—the two are usually identified) understand is that of forceful action, any exhibition of weakness by the West such as Ulbricht's unhindered violation of the free communication in Berlin, was seen as inevitably leading to further aggressive steps and eventually to the total conquest of the Western position. Deeply shaken by Ulbricht's open show of force, the West Berliners were not ready to accept the subtle distinction between Allied rights in West Berlin as contrasted to those in the East Sector. The fact which President Kennedy subsequently restated, that the gradual annexation of East Berlin into the Communist sphere of power and authority had been proceeding for more than a decade and that the Western Allies had never attempted forcefully to counter this development—had, de facto, tacitly accepted it—was widely overlooked in the shock of what was felt to be "another serious defeat" for the West.

The deep scepticism and apprehension regarding the reliability of Western guarantees for the "free" part of Berlin probably lasted no more than a week. When, by the week-end following August 13th, Vice-President Johnson and General Clay arrived from the U.S., followed by the demonstrative reinforcement of the U.S. Berlin garrison, the jubilation of the population which greeted them was a measure of the relief felt at this outward sign that the United States had not forgotten or abandoned West Berlin. The exuberance of the welcome was not dimmed by the awareness that the arrival of these soldiers and politicians represented in no way effective countermeasures designed to restore the situation in Berlin to what it had been prior to August 13th. For the moment it was enough to know that Ulbricht's troops would march no further and that Berlin was still safe.

In spite of the feeling of relief and reassurance which grew in the weeks following those crisis-laden August days, the division of Berlin through the erection of "the Wall" had a profound impact on the life of the city quite apart from that on the lives of those who suffered great personal sadness and even tragedy through separation from friends and relatives. In the first place, it dramatized the "abnormality" of the West Berlin situation in a unique and obvious manner; and thereby tended to reopen the question as to the long-range future of the city. Secondly, by depriving the city of its functions as "shopwindow", "light tower", "symbol of reunification", and "haven for refugees", it created doubts as to the worth-whileness and even possibility of holding this exposed position. Thirdly, by cutting off the stream of escapees "the Wall" also deprived West Berlin of the influx of the men and women needed to maintain its level of population in spite of an unfavorable age structure and the inevitable loss through normal migration.[11])

With the erection of "the Wall" the problem of "morale" became the decisive element for the future of West Berlin. The situation since August 13th differs significantly from that of the blockade period in the demands it makes on the city's population and leadership. Then, they were faced with what was essentially a combat situation of limited duration. The effort required of each Berliner in meeting the challenge was obvious. The visible threat forged solidarity among the people; and it created ties of confidence and affection between the inhabitants, the political leadership, and the foreign occupyers. Today, it is much less clear to the individual what is expected of him. There is no end in sight to the latent threat. And the indefiniteness of the crisis tends to create a feeling of weariness, a longing for relaxation. Also, the higher living standard of West Berlin and the close integration of its economy with that of the Federal Republic make the city more, not less, vulnerable to crisis. During the blockade it existed at a subsistence level artificially maintained. Now, it is part of a market system in which "viability" depends on the inclination—which can not be forced—of investors and workers to pursue their activities in West Berlin rather than some other easily accessible and equally pleasant or profitable location. In such a situation it does not help much to operate with appeals to "duty" and "service". To "dramatize" the Berlin situation may create the opposite effect of the one desired: namely, by presenting the picture of a "heroic front line city" to frighten those whom one wishes to reassure and attract. On the other hand, it is imperative to maintain the interest of foreign powers and even the West German Government in the fate of West Berlin, and this can only be done by underlining its role in the Cold War, its tragic division by "the Wall." Is it defensible to live normally in the face of "the Wall"? Put differently: how does one organize

---

[11]) The number of "border crossers" (Grenzgaenger) who lived in East Berlin but worked in West Berlin is estimated at more than 50,000. The population structure of West Berlin is such that mortalities exceed births by an average of 14.000 per year, a figure which is expected to rise to 20,000 in a few years.

everyday life—which requires routinization gaiety, acceptance—without allowing the suffering of one's fellowmen on the other side of "the Wall" to be forgotten and without becoming numb to its monstrous existence? In this conflict between "normalcy" and "crisis", between "learning to live with the Wall" and maintaining moral indignation at its brutal existence the forces making for stabilization and lessening tension have been gaining ground. The average West Berliner is encouraged by the political leadership as well as by his instinct for survival to "accentuate the positive", not to give in to despondency, to work, to found a family in spite of the Wall. Visitors, workers and business men are to be attracted not because of the thrills offered by "living dangerously" or by appeals to their "national duty", but because (West) Berlin remains a bright, spacious, growing city in which one can live pleasantly and make money generously. It is with these assumptions in mind that the West Berlin authorities have been active in developing plans to assure the future of their city. The physical security against Communist aggression (guaranteed by the presence of protecting Allied troops) is a prerequisite for the realization of all such plans; and so is the maintenance of at least one access route entirely free of Communist control—as the airways are at present—so that no one need fear traveling to and from the city. But, in addition, a "climate of confidence" is required which will keep those presently living in West Berlin there and create attractions for "immigration" to it from the West. This is, perhaps, most easily achieved in the area of business enterprise, for it is feasible to influence market conditions in such a way as to make capital investment in West Berlin more profitable and less risky than in other parts of Germany; which is being done (by tax preferences, accellerated write-off provisions, etc.) in enlarged measure since the summer of 1961. It is more difficult to induce persons of working age to move from West Germany to Berlin as long as over-full employment is maintained in the German economy. While it is possible to offer certain advantages (e.g. a special housing program for such workers has been started and practically interest-free loans are given to newly-weds), Berlin employers cannot be expected to raise wages above the average level prevailing in West Germany[12]) and the possibility of subsidizing wages from Government funds is severely limited.[13]) It must be assumed that the prosperous economy of West Germany (as long as it remains prosperous) with the opportunities of unhampered movement will always prove, on balance, more attractive than the necessarily special and more restricted conditions offered by West Berlin.

One of the most widely discussed plans is the one of making of West Berlin a large-scale "center of culture and learning", an "Athens-by-the-Spree" attracting students, scholars and artists in large numbers; to make it the "intellectual capital" of Germany, even if—for the foreseeable future—it cannot be the political capital. Funds are being made available to expand

---

[12]) At present, wages in West Berlin are, on the average, slightly below those in comparable West German cities, a factor which gives West Berlin producers a certain competitive advantage.

[13]) An elaborate scheme of improving wage and income levels in West Berlin through a program of graduated tax reductions has been worked out between the German Federal Government and the Berlin authorities. After August 13th, the Federal Government, as an immediate "shot-in-the-arm" for the economy and morale of West Berlin voted a one-time grant of DM 50 million, a large part of which was handed out as "vacation aid" — DM 100 for every West Berliner. The wisdom of this payment — promptly dubbed "trembling money" ("Zitterpraemie") was widely questioned.

the existing universities and to create various additional scientific and pedagogic institutions. It is as yet an open question whether creative cultural and scientific effort is capable of being harnessed into a particular direction by the expenditure of ample funds; or whether it follows inherent dynamic pulls which radiate from gravitational fields to which material efforts are essentially subsidiary. It is, perhaps, just in the sphere of the intellect that the loss which Berlin suffered when it ceased to be a meeting place between East and West is hardest to compensate.

It is not my task to describe in any detail the events which have taken place in the months since the erection of "the Wall"; fundamentally the situation has remained unchanged since then. The trauma, the apprehension and suspicion have been covered by a thickening crust of assurance. While in the first period of shock—from August till roughly October—the number of families moving out of Berlin had risen drastically, the curve of outward migration had returned almost to normal by the end of the year. Similarly, the rate of savings and withdrawals returned—more rapidly than during the previous crisis in 1958—to its previous favorable balance. And thus it might be said with some justification that West Berlin is—in a way—back to where it was before August, 1961. It cannot be stated with certitude whether "the Wall" has strengthened or weakened the spirit of the people in this city. As it was not followed by further communist "victories", it may have even reinforced the feeling of "we have been through so much, we can face whatever else they may try". But it also has clearly revealed the volcano—ever ready to erupt—at the edge of which Berlin has rebuilt its life. Ironically, the "status quo" which the Western Powers are pledged to maintain in Berlin now includes "the Wall". Being realists, most West Berliners know that for the foreseeable future they will have to live with this absurd, monstrous creation and yet must not cease to raise their voices against it. But, long accustomed to live with uncertainty and paradox, they face with a certain nonchalance the continuation of the "permanent temporariness" which has characterized the fate of their city since the end of the war and for which in our divided globe there is no end in sight.

Part II The Historical Background of the German Situation

Concise German History

By Michael Freund

The history of the German people began to take shape in the melting pot in which the Teutons, the Roman Empire and Christendom had been thrown together—the Christendom which at the same time incorporated the Rome that was dying and the Rome that was destined to survive. The effect of this ferment of secular and spiritual Rome on the Teutons was to produce new peoples, among these the Germans.

The Teutons themselves lacked the capacity to lay the foundations of a political state, with the result that when they invaded the Roman Empire they did not take over the government but merely formed its army. Rome needed their strength for its own protection; they needed the Roman genius for administration, without which their supplies of corn and reinforcements could not be assured.

In the period between 500 and 800 A. D. the Roman Empire passed through a serious crisis. The conquest of North Africa by the East Romans and by Islam destroyed the unity of the Mediterranean area which had been the keystone of Roman power. It seemed as if the end of Rome and of Christianity had come. That would have meant the end of the Germans, too, so that German history might have ended almost before it began. The Slavs were pressing westwards as far as the Saale and the Elbe; they had even penetrated deep into Thuringia.

If the Roman Empire had actually ceased to exist, it is possible that the Teutons would have been employed as mercenaries by all the great powers of those times—the Mohammedans, the Huns and the Mongols. With the exception of the Franks, they had adopted Christianity only in the degenerate form of Arianism with its national churches. Most of the Teutons in Italy, Gaul and Spain eventually fused with the local populations to form the new Latin peoples, the Spaniards, the French and the Italians.

Then the Frankish king, Chlodwig, built an empire which stretched from the Limes Germanicus, Rome's old boundary in Germany, down to the Pyrenees. The fact that Chlodwig became a Catholic was a decisive factor in helping him to extend his domain; by identifying himself with the Church of Rome he paid tribute to the universal principle of the Roman Empire and was thus qualified to become a universal leader.

Charlemagne

In 768 Charles the Great, or Charlemagne as he is better known in Western countries, succeeded to the Frankish Throne. He represented the medieval ideal of majesty and greatness. He compelled the Saxons to come into his kingdom and into the Christian fold, an operation which was necessary though cruel in its execution.

Charlemagne also made a thrust forward into the Slav territories and through this conquest and penetration he wrote the first chapter in the millennial struggle between Slav and Teuton, which has provided the Germans either with a historical mission or an arena for their annihilation.

Within Charlemagne's kingdom two great Western peoples, the Germans and the French, were germinating. When, after his death, this kingdom was partitioned, the parts that remained were called "France", the "regnum teutorum" (the German Kingdom) and the Burgundian-Netherland area. The German people had now entered the stage of history.

Already Charlemagne's predecessors had begun to base their title to legitimacy, not on their dignity as kings, but on the blessing of the Church. In 800 Charlemagne went to Rome, where he was crowned "Emperor" by the Pope. This was the beginning of the "Holy Roman Empire", a spiritual and temporal power, comparable almost to the Mohammedan Caliphate, in which "spiritual" and "temporal" forces were very closely linked.

Strangely enough it was the Germans, and not the French, who first grasped the imperial scepter. The first, memorable royal family to occupy the throne in the new "German Kingdom" were the Saxons, of whom Otto the Great stands out as the most famous. His victory over the Huns represents one of the great turning points of history because, after the Huns had been defeated, they settled down—as if by a miracle—and adopted Christianity; from then on they ceased to be a threat to the Germans.

The kings of those times had to base their power not on the territorial princes, who were too rich and too important to be able to obey but on the bishops who—being "men without a family or property"—were free to serve the community; moreover they were the only people who had mastered the art of reading and writing and were thus the successors to the officials of the Roman Empire, whose garb they wear even up to the present time. But the king believed that he could not rely on his episcopal "prefects" unless he was in a position to give orders to the Pope, who commanded the souls and the consciences of the clergy. What is more, the domination of Italy meant the control over the great European trade routes as well as over the famous Curia, which comprised the only financial system of those times. So in 962 Otto the Great took Rome by storm, to the accompaniment of indescribable atrocities, and had himself crowned as Emperor by a not too reputable Pope, whom he himself had installed. Thus the events which attended the inception of the Holy Roman Empire of the German Nation were anything but glorious.

Otto's son, Otto II, who married a Byzantine princess Theophano, and his son Otto III, for whom his mother acted for many years as regent, thought of themselves only as Romans, and knew hardly anything about Germany. Germany had to suffer for the fact that these Emperors had succumbed to Rome; meanwhile the Danes and the Slavs were exerting strong pressure on the *Reich* from the north and the east.

In the West, around 1000 A. D., the frontier between the Latin and the Teuton languages areas began to take definite shape. Until then, the French language had been gradually pressing eastward, and it was still uncertain whether it would reach the "Limes".

At that time France appeared to be the spiritual and religious center of the Western world. It was in the French monastery of Cluny that the ideas of ecclesiastical reform originated, which were to excite the attention of the Western world for more than a hundred years. At first, all that the reform movement wanted was to correct the abuse under which the nobility —who had sometimes not even taken religious orders and seldom possessed any religious education—were allowed to occupy well-endowed ecclesiastical offices.

For a time the Emperors gave their support to this movement because, after all, bishops who could not write were of no use for secular administration. But Cluny raised its demands. It wished to deprive the Emperor of his right to appoint bishops and to ensure that clergy must always be invested in their office by other clergy, in order to give the Church secular powers to assert its authority in the world, since a large part of the population had to be governed through the Church.

Thus the Emperors had to build up an organization of secular officials. In this work the Salian or Franconian Emperors were especially conspicuous. They raised a body of men, who were able to carry out all that the ecclesiastical bureaucracy had been able to do: to write records of government proceedings, to calculate and generally to carry on the work of administration. They had on their side the lesser nobility who were responsible "directly to the *Reich*" and were made independent from the princes by becoming hereditary owners of their lended property. It was from these lower orders of nobility that the Emperors recruited their first secular officials, the so-called "Ministerialen".

Meanwhile the Church was making claims to temporal power. It was the "Monk Hildebrand", administrator of the finances of the Curia and its dominant personality, who now struck a deadly blow against the secular power of the Empire. In opposition to the dazzling glory of the Church, which would not yield to the Monk, he appealed particularly to the mendicant friars (now a respectable order), to those who had pledged themselves to "holy poverty", to the lower classes in general and to all who were living in poverty. The real clash came under Henry IV. Both Emperor and Pope chose the humble and those who were dependent on high authority in preference to the mighty and those rich enough to indulge in disobedience and treachery. A contemporary chronicler writes of Henry IV that he had "kept down the mighty and raised up all of low degree".

Henry IV, who is famous because of his undignified submission to the Pope at Canossa, was in fact a strong, active and cunning ruler. By building a network of castles and forts, he sought to strengthen his position in relation to the great nobles, who made a business of rebellion and treachery. The nobles, however, did not intend to wait until they had been made powerless and the only effect of this enterprise of Henry's was to provoke them to rebellion.

In the midst of these disturbances in Germany came the startling news that the Pope had excommunicated the Emperor and relieved all his subjects from their obligation to obey the imperial authority. It was then that Henry IV made his pilgrimage to Canossa where the Pope awaited him, fearing the worst; there he prostrated himself before the Pope, confessed his sins and begged for mercy and readmission into the Church. The Pope had not been inclined to show any mercy, but it was difficult for him to reject Henry's plea, so he gave absolution. When the Emperor returned, however, he found that he had gained nothing by his submission; the German princes had decided to depose Henry, and they did not consider the absolution of Henry by the Pope a sufficient reason to revoke their decision.

In 1048 Henry IV marched against Rome, taking "his own" Pope with him. The latter, in return for the tiara, crowned Henry as Emperor. Gregory invoked the aid of the Norman Princes who commanded a terrible foreign legion consisting of Saracens, Normans and the Italian rabble. They were quartered in Rome and, as a result of the destruction they caused, Rome was more like a city of the dead. Gregory did not dare to show his face there again. He died in exile in 1085.

Henry remained powerless in Northern Italy; the inglorious death of his great enemy was of no avail to him; he returned to Germany and allowed his son Henry to be crowned as king. Henry V, however, placed himself at the head of an insurrection of the princes, had his father cast into prison and afterwards brought him to trial. The old Emperor saw clearly that he was faced by the choice between abdication and execution; he therefore confessed everything which was demanded of him. Why, after all, should he have a better conscience than his executioner?

Civil war raged throughout the Empire; the Western world seemed to be in the process of dissolution. In 1095, in order to rouse the West from its state of decay and to provide wealth for starving Christendom, Pope Urban II announced a Crusade for the conquest of the Holy Land. "Any of you who until now has been a robber, shall be made a knight."

On their way southwards the Crusades made indeed robbers into knights and beggars into kings. In various German towns through which they passed, they were responsible for frightful slaughter among the Jews. Many became rich without regard for the Cross.

In 1099 Jerusalem was captured to the accompaniment of unspeakable atrocities. Beggars were made into princes and robbers into knights, but there were also some knights who degenerated into robbers. It was the first exuberant blossoming forth of Colonialism. Germany was in the throes of a social revolution: "God will now enrich those who were poor at home." The Crusaders were dazzled by visions of plunder; unbelievers —the Moslems, the Jews and after them the heretics—were systematically persecuted, murdered and plundered. Often the victims had first to be made into unbelievers, so that the process of putting them to death as heretics and then robbing them of their wealth could be justified; the forfeiture of their lives was made an excuse for the forfeiture of their property. This campaign against heretics, which occurred toward the end of the 12th century, was a sordid outgrowth of the Crusades.

Henry V was soon called upon to face the same problems as his father; he could not renounce the right to appoint bishops and other clerical dignitaries who administered his kingdom; at the same time it was certainly contrary to the spirit of the Church that its servants should be chosen by any other than ecclesiastical considerations. These controversies led Henry to make two expeditions to Rome.

Finally, in 1122, agreement was reached in the so-called Concordat of Worms. The king had to renounce his traditional right of investing bishops and abbots without control of the Church.

The death of Henry V was followed first by the usual series of intrigues by rival candidates to the throne. Then there developed the historic feud between the two leading German families, the Guelfs and the Hohenstaufen. The Saxon dukes were called the Guelfs, while the Hohenstaufen were known as the Waiblinger after their castle at Waiblingen. For eighty years, civil war was waged between these two families. Through a hundred years of German history resounded the cry of "Hie Welf, hie Waiblingen". These names were also adopted by the rival families in the Italian Civil War (Guelfs and Ghibellines).

The Hohenstaufen were still inspired by dreams of Rome and the Crusades; the Guelfs wanted to colonize Eastern Europe, although they still lacked the means to really Germanize the Slav countries.

When Conrad III was succeeded in 1152 by Frederick I of Swabia, the second Hohenstaufen king (whom the Italians called "Barbarossa" because of his red beard), it seemed as if a new era had dawned. Frederick was praised by his contemporaries for his mental keenness and strength of purpose, his courage and energy and joy in battle, his candor, geniality and eloquence, and his unerring sense of justice. It was, however, not long before Frederick Barbarossa became involved in a murderous struggle with the Lombard communes, which made it difficult for him to display these qualities. Under Barbarossa's instructions, Milan, as the major Lombard city, was razed as is said in the words of Isaiah: "Thorns shall come up in her palaces, nettles and brambles in the fortress thereof; and it shall be a habitation of dragons." All that remained of Milan was an expanse of scorched earth; a few years later it was rebuilt and became a more beautiful city than ever. Cities and nations are not easily exterminated—a consoling thought which recurs throughout German history.

During Frederick Barbarossa's reign the feudal system became more rigid. The Emperor insisted that his feudal lords must all have been born of knightly rank, so that in effect a barrier was placed in the way of the promotion of a citizen or a farmer and it was not possible for a person of lowly birth to be rewarded—however brave he might have proved himself to be.

The day of German world-dominion came to a close in a blaze of evening sunshine. A Pope had already begun to ask "who has made the Germans the judges of this world?" But through the marriage of his son Henry to the heiress of the Sicilian kingdoms, Barbarossa seemed to have reached the height of Hohenstaufen power. It looked as if this union would result in the creation of a great Mediterranean empire. Normans and Saracens encompassed a wide area in the Mediterranean; they controlled a chain of islands which formed a base for their raids on ships and on men. It was a great empire, indeed, but no longer a German one.

Frederick II, the son of Henry VI, eventually became Emperor after he had promised the Pope to retire to Germany. However, he held fast to Sicily and began to shape it into a compact military and administrative unit. But Palermo was no better suited than Damascus to become the capital of a German Empire. Like most tyrants, Frederick was a great patron of architecture and building; he encouraged the development of the natural sciences and founded the University of Naples. He kept a hold over his meanly estated officials and mercenaries by means of his money, on which they were entirely dependent. His taxation system ran like a machine.

Frederick had promised the Pope to lead another Crusade but there were delays which the Pope believed were due to bad faith. Finally, in spite of having been excommunicated, he set sail for the Holy Land, and later Emperor Frederick made his triumphal entry into Jerusalem.

Colonization of Eastern Europe

At this point German history reached a turning-point which was destined to affect its course for centuries to come. It was decided that the Crusaders should not go again to the Holy Land, which had witnessed so many scenes that were anything but holy; instead, it should conquer, colonize and christianize Eastern Europe.

In 1216 a patent was granted to the Teutonic Order of Knighthood under which its Grand Master was given the status of prince and it was commissioned "to raise the glory of the Emperor above that of all the kingdoms of the world" by subjugating and converting the "Pruzzen" (hence the later name Prussians).

At the same time Germany was threatened by a danger of unusually destructive force—the Mongol invasion. One man, the Mongol prince Genghis Khan, had, by modern methods of government and war-making, created out of nothing the most powerful empire which had yet been known in the history of mankind.

On April 9, 1241, after Breslau had been burned by the Mongols, a battle was fought near Liegnitz, which was one of the decisive, though one of the most terrible, battles in German and European history. The invading Mongols were confronted by an army made up of Poles, Moravians, Silesians and German volunteers, conscripts and Crusaders. The wild and barbaric Asiatic forces prevailed, but the castle of Liegnitz stood firm and the Mongols were shy of laying siege to it and taking it by storm, so the danger was averted.

These inroads by the Mongols finally heartened the German idea of directing a crusade toward the East; but the peoples in Eastern Europe were no match for the German knights as had been the technically superior Moslems. The various tribes which had remained behind in their wake had, in the eyes of the Germans, about as much importance as had the Red Indians for the first white settlers in North America.

At the same time, through the work of the German pioneers in colonizing and founding cities in the East, something of dignity and permanence was created which the blood-stained futility of the Crusades had lacked.

In the Empire, Henry VII, son of Frederick II of Sicily, tried to create a state after the Sicilian pattern, though without its cruelty or its glory. He had neither Saracens nor Normans at his disposal, like his father in Sicily and, therefore, he had to rely on his *Ministerialen* (Imperial officials) and on the cities and their money. But the princes were growing wealthy too, and their power was too great for the cities.

At the Court Council they forced the young king Henry VII to agree to a law under which citizens of towns were not allowed to form any fraternities, confederations or alliances, either between their cities or among themselves, and in 1231 the important *"Statutum in favorem principum"* was enacted, under which the king renounced the exercise of his sovereign powers over justice, roads, coinage and customs, cities and castles within the domains of the territorial princes; he was thus deprived of all sources of revenue on which he might have been able to build up any power.

Furthermore, the cities were not to be allowed to assimilate any of the serfs or bondsmen belonging to the princes or the Church as *"Pfahlbuerger"* (that is, citizens who lived outside the city wall, but within the scope of its jurisdiction). This meant that such persons could no longer secure their freedom by becoming citizens of a town. All the same, money remained money and the cities exercised through their financial capacity still a powerful influence.

The Diet at Ravenna forbade cities to appoint on their own authority town councils or mayors and councillors; in some cases they were even forbidden to build town halls—which were, after all, one of the glories of Germany. The first association of German cities was dissolved; but in the long run all these attempts against German cities did not succeed. The Diet of Ravenna might as well have tried to prevent water from flowing downhill.

Frederick II died in Sicily. He had been a demonic genius, a magician and, in the eyes of many, the forerunner of the Age of Enlightenment. After his death bestial methods were employed by the Pope, the French who were at that time penetrating into Sicily and what are sometimes called "the people", to exterminate the Hohenstaufen in Sicily. For a time the Empire was without an Emperor—though the Germans were hardly conscious of the fact.

Eventually Rudolf of Habsburg was chosen as German Emperor. He was a ruler of the modern type who looked after his personal and state possessions in an accurate and business-like manner. Out of the chaos he succeeded in creating something which, for want of a better name, we shall have to call Germany.

Rudolf of Habsburg's great opponent was Ottokar of Bohemia. The question at issue between Rudolf and Ottokar was the place which the Slavs were to take in the German Empire, whether Slavs and Germans could be brought together under one regime and, if so, how. The struggle ended with Ottokar's defeat at the battle of Duernkrut in 1278, where he was treacherously murdered by his personal enemies.

In the German East, large-scale colonization was taking place—mostly without the assistance of the Empire or the princes; the organizers formed closely integrated communities before they set out on their missions, so that they were almost able to set up "prefabricated" cities and villages in the country which they occupied.

In the 12th century Eastern Holstein, Mecklenburg and Pomerania were brought substantially under German rule; German settlements were founded over large parts of Brandenburg and the Slav territories to the south.

It was principally in the 13th century that the Teutonic Order was engaged in the subjugation of the Prussian Baltic area. The city of Kulm was founded in 1231; Elbing in 1237 and Koenigsberg in 1255. There were now, in fact, two Germanies—"Colonial Germany" east of the Elbe, a Teuton-Slav country with a social and authoritative order of its own, which stood out in strong contrast to the "Germania romana", the Western and Teuton-Roman Germany.

These German cities associated themselves with the Teutonic Order and, in the middle of the 13th century, joined to form a league which stretched right across Germany and was afterwards known as the Hanseatic League. This Hanseatic League was a state within a state; it created its own fleet and carried on its own wars.

However, the Scandinavian states soon succeeded to block the outlet from the Baltic, while the Turkish conquest of Constantinople cut the great trade route to the East. Since the prosperity of the German cities depended on their long distance trade, Germany and its cities became poor as the result of being cut off from the overseas world.

At this point, German history is overshadowed by the rise of the Western national states, meaning the decline of Central Europe and the Empire.

It was not possible for the Empire to develop into a modern state because the territorial princes could not be made subjects ot a superior power. These new-style rulers—"the magicians of power" as Bacon called them—based their rule on the power of money, the systematic taxation of their subjects, and a body of officials and an army paid by the state and dependent on it. This policy, however, was only possible for the princes, not for the *Reich.* Endowed with such instruments of government, Philip the Fair was able to extend the power of France, without regard to the weakening *Reich,* eastwards beyond Toul and Verdun as far as the Rhine. The Bishops of Cologne, Mainz and Trier opened their ecclesiastical principalities to French influence and their hands to French money. A sort of Rhine Federation came into being. Whereas France was developing into a powerful state, the German princes always chose the weakest and "most charitable" of their number to be their king, so that if he became too greedy or too powerful he could be overthrown just as easily as Governments in France were upset between 1918 and 1939.

In 1308 a Luxemburger, Henry VII, became King of Germany. In 1310 he set out on an Italian campaign in the old tradition, and he was effusively welcomed by Dante. He reached Rome by way of the usual blood bath, and on July 29, 1312 he received the Imperial crown at the hands of a Pope, whom he himself had chosen. This was one of the last Italian campaigns to win power over Rome and the Pope; the German rulers came to rely more on their own strength than on the virtue of the papal anointment.

Yet under Ludwig the Bavarian the ghost of the Roman campaigns made another brief appearance. He supported the Minorite (or Franciscan) Order, which had been condemned by the Curia and, in the old-fashioned violent method, he made a Franciscan Pope.

Charles IV of the House of Luxemburg had a happier experience. He had received a French education and had mastered the modern art of governing through his money, his officials and his military; he succeeded in bringing to an end the war of the German kings against the Papacy without capitulating; he founded the first German university in Bohemia, which country he regarded as the cornerstone of his power—and he was not the last German king to do this.

By means of the Golden Bull of 1356 an oligarchy of the more important princes seized for themselves, as a "College of Electors", the right to choose the king. The object of this new arrangement was to ensure that the Pope should not exercise any influence on the election. The German kings should hold office in their own right; from Maximilian I onwards, the German kings—although they had not been anointed by the Pope—called themselves Emperors. The Empire had ceased to be holy, Roman, and an Empire.

The Electoral College consisted of three ecclesiastical princes, the Archbishops of Trier, Cologne and Mainz, and four secular ones, the King of Bohemia, the rulers of the Rhine Palatinate, Saxony and Brandenburg.

Meanwhile in Bohemia a Reformation was taking place, which turned out to have more of the character of a revolution—that of Jan Hus. King Wenzel, who at heart sympathized with Hus, but was too cowardly and profligate to support the revolution.

His successor Sigismund, however, put an end to it. The last hopes of the Germans for a united Empire were centered on this highly educated and enlightened German Emperor. The pamphlet "Reformatio Sigismundi"—a fake—was the slogan which expressed the hopes of the idealists of that time. But the power of the German princes was too strong for them. Because of the spiritual crisis by which Christianity was threatened, a Council was held at Constance (1414—18). The Curia, however, soon took the reins into its own hands, and Jan Hus was sent to the stake—a world-shaking event. The Council deposed a Pope by means of a decree written in the language of Jan Hus, and condemned the latter to death as a heretic. The flames which burnt Hus at the stake in Constance spread rapidly to the Hussites of Bohemia. From the castle at Prague, which has played such an important part in world history, a Hussite army commanded by the Captain of the Castle Ziska, invaded the Empire spreading fire and terror, and it was only with difficulty that they were checked. Although for a time it seemed as if they were going to drench the whole of Western Europe in blood, the Hussites eventually agreed to a peace which gave them only apparently unimportant concessions—that the laity should receive Communion in both kinds, the chalice as well as the paten.

Sigismund's Empire had collapsed into ruins. Just at this time (1417) the Hohenzollern family had been entrusted with the Mark of Brandenburg.

The Habsburgs were noted for their good luck in exchanges and purchases of territories—due to their policy of arranging marriages to their advantage. Frederick III in particular was skilled in accumulating territories by purchase, by cunning, by the exercise of power or by exploiting the exigencies of the moment: the arrangement of marriages between princes and princesses, irrespective of whether they loved, hated or were quite indifferent, was in his case merely incidental to his policy. "Alii bella gerant, tu felix Austria nube." (May others wage wars, but you, fortunate Austria, go on marrying.)

Maximilian I, "the last of the knights" and the creator of a modern German army, appeared only to "inherit" what was almost a world empire.

The Renaissance, which believed that it was able to bring about a rebirth of mankind, if not its deification, reached its climax under Maximilian—at least in Italy. The Renaissance appeared to be the forerunner of the Reformation, but it believed that man was the image of God, that his spirit was a reflection of the divine wisdom, whereas in the eyes of the Reformation, mortal men, nature and the world were deprived almost entirely of participation in the word and spirit of God.

In 1453, the Byzantine Empire collapsed, and it seemed as though a pillar of Western power had gone. The Turks captured Constantinople, but could not gain complete control of the Mediterranean because they suffered a crushing naval defeat at Lepanto in 1571.

Maximilian attempted, by the use of a regular income, to build up a standing Imperial army. No one disputed that the Empire ought to be united: Maximilian thought that this unity could be achieved only through the creation of an army, but the princes thought that this could be brought about through their regular conferences and talks.

The Reformation

When the storm of the Reformation broke over Germany there was no longer any central authority strong enough to give uniform direction to the spiritual forces behind the religious reforms, nor powerful enough either to carry through the Reformation in its entirety or to suppress it completely. Thus Germany became religiously divided.

The original cause of the Reformation was unimportant—the issue of indulgences. The Church has never taught that a sinner can buy himself free from the consequences of his sins, though that is what the Dominican monk Tetzel preached at various places in the Bishopric of Magdeburg. The sale of indulgences formed a part of the financial system of the Church of that time. (Abuses were subsequently removed by the Council of Trent.) The proceeds from the sale of indulgences, which Tetzel peddled, were divided in equal shares between the Curia and the outstanding German banker Fugger. The latter had provided the 23-year-old Archbishop of Magdeburg, a Hohenzollern, with the money, by means of which he had been able to buy the consent of Rome to his becoming simultaneously—in contradiction to canon law—Archbishop (Elector) of Mainz. Fugger considered his share in the profits from the sale of indulgences, which the Archbishop of Magdeburg had extended to his North German diocese contrary to custom as his security.

The great revolution, which destroyed the Empire and which gave it a new spiritual cohesion only through the power of the spoken and the written word, started, when in 1517 Luther nailed his 95 theses to the door of the castle church at Wittenberg.

Luther knew hardly anything about the special "business" which Tetzel had been carrying on by preaching the sale of indulgences. At first it was a case of one monk against the other. Investigations and disputations only resulted in a widening of the breach. When, during one of these arguments, Luther declared that even the Ecclesiastical Council was not infallible, the Duke of Saxony exclaimed, "Heaven help us. It's the plague."

In the midst of this religious dispute came the election of a new Emperor in 1519. The Spaniard Charles V, who had been brought up in the spirit of Burgundy, was chosen in preference to the French candidate Francis I, with the result that the powerful influence of France made itself felt in Germany. Charles V was not susceptible to the primitive forces of the Church for the very reason that he had an open-minded and universal outlook.

From Luther's point of view, on the other hand, reason was a prostitute; he believed that mankind and the world were so deeply sunk in the depravity of original sin that all the works of the human spirit—culture, science and indeed every manifestation of higher activity—represented no more than a screen over his wretchedness.

At the Diet of Worms in 1521, Luther, who had been summoned by the Emperor to attend, declared that he could not retract what he had said. He had already been excommunicated; now he was formally outlawed from the Empire. But the Empire had reached such a state of disintegration that none of the princes carried out the decree. On the way home from Worms Luther was captured by mounted men in the service of the Elector of Saxony, ostensibly to be put into prison. In fact, he lived for many years in safety as "Junker Joerg" in the castle of the Wartburg at Eisenach. It was while he was at the Wartburg that Luther translated the Bible into his own language and thus created a standard of written German with lasting influence.

What the Empire needed at this time was a leader, a reformer, intent also on the rebuilding of state and society—a kind of "armed prophet". The common people, Anabaptist groups, peasants and knights, were in a state of revolt. Luther merely denounced them and went on looking for the right words for his German translation of the Bible. If the Germans had only had a Cromwell who, out of the anarchy which followed the religious upheaval, had been able to organize an army, Germany would have been as wax in the hands of such a "Messiah with a sword".

The Emperor also—like Luther—left Germany to look after its own troubles; he was preoccupied with his war against France. So it came about that Protestantism was too weak to spread over the whole of Germany but was at the same time too strong to be entirely subdued.

In 1526 the Diet promulgated a decree providing that each prince should order the ecclesiastical affairs of his own state in accordance with his responsibility to "God and his Imperial Majesty"—in other words, as he liked.

Meanwhile, important social movements were in progress and these threatened to overshadow the Reformation; they culminated in the Peasants' War, which was the last link in a chain of unrest and revolt stretching back into the Middle Ages. The peasants as a class were however not ripe to exercise any authority; perhaps a man like Wallenstein could have moulded them with great effort into an army. But they had neither leader nor organization, and therefore their revolt was easily crushed.

The *Reichsritter* (Knights of the Empire), equally in revolt against the social order and trying to exploit the Reformation for their purposes, were also a class obviously on the decline, because the Empire was no longer able to keep them occupied with feats of war, nor could it confer knightly honor and knightly rewards.

The various forms of social revolt were accompanied by the emergence of extreme and passionately assertive religious sects. Most of these believed that mankind could reach such a stage of intellectual perfection, if not of deification, that law and authority, power and property would become superfluous. They provided the breeding-ground for European dreams of progress and for Utopias of every sort. Luther spoke in very scathing terms of these "Anabaptist mobs".

When the Emperor returned from the war, it was too late to suppress the Protestant movement. The reforming princes replied to a *Reichstag* decree of 1529 with a formal "protest" (hence the name Protestant), and force was not invoked against them. The new faith had begun to organize itself; its followers had already seized Church property, and, if this had had to be restored, thousands of those who had embraced the new faith would have been affected. Moreover it was the princes themselves who were mainly responsible for despoiling the Church; it would have been as difficult to extract the booty from their clutches as to release a lamb from an eagle's claws.

The Religious Peace of Nuremberg in 1532 was another example of this mixture of recognition and reservation—though the latter was largely disregarded. It would not have been possible to turn Protestant princes into

Catholics without deposing them as princes. The cause of Protestantism therefore became identified with particularism. That was why France—as the patron of German disunity—entered into an alliance with the German princes. In the monastery of Schleyern the freedom of the German princes (that is, their right to be disloyal to the Empire) was formally placed under the protection of France.

A long period of confusion and indecision led up to the Schmalkalden War of 1546/47, the first of the religious wars, named after the League between the Protestant princes which had been concluded at Schmalkalden. The Emperor gained an overwhelming victory in the battle of Muehlberg. The Electorate of Saxony was transferred to Maurice of Saxony, who belonged to another line of the Saxon royal family.

The way now seemed clear for Charles to proceed. Titian painted him in all his dignity and glory "riding on the battlefield of Muehlberg". Charles planned to carry on with Maximilian's reforms, to create a genuine Empire by establishing Imperial estates, an Imperial administration and an Imperial army.

His efforts were checked by the "Princes' Revolution" of 1552, led by Maurice of Saxony. The princes frustrated the Imperial reform plans and, in return for the French king's support, presented him with the bishoprics of Toul, Verdun and Metz, which up to then had been regarded as among the most valuable possessions of the Empire. The princes did not consider this too big a price to pay for the French help.

The Reformation had won—if continued existence can be reckoned as a victory—but Protestantism had not yet obtained control of the Empire. The religious Peace of Augsburg allowed the princes to determine the religious faith of their subjects. The Empire, as such, had no longer any religious faith of its own, and had even less right than a minor prince to dictate the faith of its subjects. An important feature of this religious peace was that it recognized the tremendous transfer of property which had been carried out in Germany. The Church had lost territories of the size of whole provinces. The secularization of Church possessions, by means of which the territories of the German princes had been rounded off, had just as far-reaching effects on the map and the political development of the German Empire as the great territorial adjustments of Napoleon's time. It was the princes who profited by these changes. What they had left for the maintenance of their churches and their pastors and for the support of their schools and the needy varied very much from one principality to another.

It is true that the Empire and the Catholics had made the "*geistlichen Vorbehalt*" (ecclesiastical reservation) according to which an ecclesiastical prince, if he accepted the Protestant faith, was required to resign. The effect of this provision would have been to perpetuate Catholic rule in the ecclesiastical principalities, but there were only very few princes who possessed sovereign rights in the true sense. Although the rulers of the North German monasteries, bishoprics and the large ecclesiastical bodies exercised secular authority over their subjects, they did not have the status of ruling princes, and they, therefore, denied that the ecclesiastical reservation applied to them.

One after the other, Magdeburg, Halberstadt, Merseburg, Meissen, Naumburg and Luebeck fell into the hands of Protestant princes, who regarded themselves as entitled to exercise full authority. Almost every dispute about such Church possessions led the Empire to the brink of war, just as did the struggle for the possession of Cologne, Strassburg, Aachen and Donauwoerth, in which four towns the Catholics prevailed.

Germany was in the throes of a cold war. Each of the rival religious bodies had formed a military association. In the case of the Protestants, it was the "Union"; on the Catholic side, the "League".

In 1609, Henry IV of France, who had adopted Catholicism for political reasons although he remained at heart a Protestant, was watching for the opportunity to invade the Empire and, with the assistance of the Protestant states, to break up the Habsburg dominion. But Catholicism was now inspired by a new spirit of resistance. The Council of Trent, held between 1545 and 1563, was not like the reforming council of Charles V's time; its mood was not one of reconciliation but of preparation for war. Luther had thought at one time that his only enemy was unbelief; now the Protestants had another faith to grapple with.

The Jesuit Order, which was organized on military lines, controlled by iron discipline and characterized by its unquestioning obedience, became the backbone of the Catholic resistance against the Protestant attack. In many of the Catholic states, this Order formed a general staff for the reorganization of spiritual and cultural life.

On the other hand a new militant opponent of the Catholic Church, Calvinism, was gathering strength, particularly in the area of the Netherlands and Burgundy and in the Anglo-Saxon countries. In the eyes of the Lutherans, the Empire still remained the legitimate authority *("Obrigkeit")*, established by the will of God—even though that authority might be now no more than a symbol. For the Calvinists it was otherwise; they dared to rise against it—and it soon seemed as if their opportunity had come. The Habsburg *Reich* was being drowned in the Protestant flood. The insurrection was headed by the "historic aristocratic nations"; in Bohemia the Catholics were in a negligible minority; in Upper Austria hardly a Mass was celebrated; in Vienna, it was difficult even to find a Corpus Christi procession.

Then came a family squabble between the two Habsburg princes, Rudolf II and Matthias. Both were ready to invoke the powers of hell to assist them in winning the struggle for power. Under these circumstances the Bohemians obtained their "Letter of Majesty", which they interpreted—probably erroneously—as conferring the right to choose their own king.

Matthias was succeeded by the Jesuit King Ferdinand II—the Emperor of the Counter Reformation. He was prepared to sacrifice many of his territories for the sake of a Mass. In return for a promise of help, the Habsburg Empire was divided into a Spanish and an Austrian part. Spain received Naples, the principality of Milan, the "free county" of Burgundy and the Netherlands—the Northern part of which had been engaged since 1578 in a war of liberation against Spain, in consequence of which it became detached from the Empire. The effect of these territorial changes was to leave France in the merciless grip of Spain.

In 1619 the Bohemians elected Frederick, the Elector Palatine of the Rhine, as their king—the Emperor's emissaries having previously been thrown out of a window into the castle moat. This famous "Defenestration of Prague" dragged Europe into a war which lasted for 30 years. The weak Habsburg Emperor appealed to the Catholic League and princes for help, and in particular to Duke Maximilian of Bavaria. Maximilian demanded as the price of his assistance the Palatine territory and Electorate—a demand which was bound to upset the German states system, and when the Imperial ban was placed on the Elector Frederick, this had the effect of opening the doors to the Spaniards. The League marched in support of the Emperor, but not a single Protestant prince came to the aid of the new king of Bohemia. In November, 1620, the Bohemian army was defeated in a few hours at the battle of the White Hill near Prague; the Elector Frederick fled and incidentally was nicknamed the "Winter King". Frightful punishment was meted out to the Bohemians. The Hussite nobles, whether of Czech or German race, were outlawed, executed and robbed of their property. A new Bohemia and a new ruling class had to be created.

The Bavarian prince claimed his promised reward; the Elector Palatine was outlawed; the legions of Spain, who had been waiting for their chance, marched into the Palatinate. No one knew exactly what England would do—least of all King James I of England, father-in-law of the Winter King. Spain would not have attempted to go into action against the British fleet, but James—condemning his son-in-law's policy in Bohemia and fighting only for his legitimate principality—hesiated too long and was successfully deluded by the Spaniards. So Germany was delivered over to war and destruction. The Catholic League and Spain now pursued Frederick, who fled to North Germany.

Now, fear made the Protestant princes of Lower Saxony valiant; they took up arms and placed themselves under the leadership of the King of Denmark. Germany was becoming the battlefield on which this war was to be fought.

In the confusion and the distress of war, the Emperor raised an army of his own—a measure which the German princes had hitherto not permitted. Wallenstein, one of the most puzzling figures in German history, who had made a great fortune out of the plunder which had followed the proscription of the Hussite nobles, offered to raise an army. Like a great Condottiere, he paid the army out of his own pocket or out of the spoils of war. In the territories which he conquered he introduced an elaborate system of taxation and levies, which was a new thing in German history. Wallenstein revived the old plans of Maximilian and Charles V. With his army behind him, he wanted to establish the Imperial authority over the independent princes. He repeated Charles V's saying: "I want the Empire to have not many leaders, but one only." The great historian Ranke holds that the introduction of Wallenstein's system meant the greatest break in the constitution of the Empire for hundreds of years. Wallenstein also wanted to extend the Empire until it reached from the Baltic to the Golden Horn, and he was the first to think of building a German fleet. However, at the Diet of Regensburg in 1630 the German princes proved strong enough to bring about Wallenstein's downfall.

Nevertheless the Emperor tried to carry out in his dominions something which could not have been achieved without Wallenstein's system—a far-reaching religious restoration. All Church property that had been acquired since 1552, the date of the Peace of Augsburg, was to be restored. The Restitution Edict of 1629 would have once again revolutionized the territorial and political system of Germany; certain principalities would have been torn asunder if they were to restitute the spoil they had gained by religious zeal. The German Empire would have become a predominantly Catholic country; Protestantism would have been pushed to the border of German national life and it might perhaps have become—in the words of a historian—a denominational curiosity.

Perhaps the Lutheran states would have fought rather than become a curiosity. But, above all, Sweden and France did not want to see German Protestantism perish. Above all they did not want their voice in Germany to be smothered. German Protestantism was a force on which the Swedish King relied, although the mass of German Protestants dreaded the idea of becoming a base for either Sweden or France. But Sweden felt her position to be threatened when Wallenstein penetrated in 1629 the Southern coast of the Baltic Sea. In 1630 Gustavus Adolphus—one of Sweden's greatest Kings—landed with an army in Pomerania. His campaign was supported by English money and French diplomacy, and Brandenburg and Saxony were compelled to join him. Under a treaty, made in 1631, France agreed to finance him. Magdeburg was taken by storm by the Imperial General Tilly, to the accompaniment of atrocities, and a fire—not caused by Tilly—consumed nearly the whole city. Gustavus Adolphus won a victory over the hitherto unbeaten Tilly at Breitenfeld and pressed on into South Germany, until he reached Munich. In 1632 the Protestant armies won the battle of Luetzen, but Gustavus Adolphus was among the slain.

At this time, when the Empire and Catholicism were in great danger, the Emperor recalled his General Wallenstein. Wallenstein was successful in holding up the Swedish forces, but he conducted the campaign entirely in his own arbitrary way, entering into negotiations with rival parties and upsetting whole nations—again solely at his own discretion. His aims were always ambitions; whether he wanted to become a Cromwell or simply to build up a great empire for his monarch is uncertain. Ferdinand could, of course, not agree to the former and obviously he did not even want to be made great. On January 24, 1634, Ferdinand II, the man whom Wallenstein wanted to make "Monarch of the World", signed an order that Wallenstein was to be taken into custody, dead or alive. On February 25, 1634, Wallenstein was murdered.

After Wallenstein's death his ideas of religious peace and of a Germany free from foreign troops seemed to take root. The Peace of Prague, between the Emperor on the one side and Electoral Saxony, Brandenburg and the most important Protestant states on the other side, appeared to have brought peace to the Germans. It is true that in the hereditary Habsburg territories and in South Germany, Protestantism was abandoned by the German Protestants. It was agreed that the Emperor and all the princes of the Empire would join in expelling foreign troops from German soil. The Swedes were to be bought off.

Whether the Empire and the Lutheran princes would have had the strength and the courage to carry on this war of liberation is doubtful. But the consequence of the Peace of Prague was that Richelieu the "Cardinal of France" decided to make an open attack on Germany. He concluded an alliance with Bernhard of Weimar, one of the most capable military leaders of the Protestants in Germany. Bernhard von Weimar proved himself useful by achieving considerable success on the Rhine, and equally useful by his early death, as a result of which all his conquests passed to France. The fleur-de-lys flag now flew over the fortress of Breisach which lay on the line of communication between Spain and the Netherlands. The ring of Habsburg power, which had at one time encompassed France and threatened to choke it, had now been loosened—and indeed broken; moreover France saw an opportunity of cutting the vital lines of communication between the different parts of the Habsburg Empire.

After the French invasion there could no longer be any question of restoring Catholicism or the Catholic Imperial family to the Empire. The Emperor Frederick III (1637—1657) had none of his predecessors' mania for counter-reformation. After Germany had suffered untold damage and devastation as the result of thirty years of war, peace was concluded in the Treaty of Westphalia signed at Osnabrueck and Muenster in 1648.

Under this treaty, Brandenburg lost the important area of Hither Pomerania together with Stettin, the better part of Farther Pomerania, Bremen and Verden to Sweden, which henceforth acquired the rights of a German state. The German Empire was cut off from the Baltic, but Sweden's power had passed its prime. In the long run it was impossible for Sweden to retain a kind of Viking empire on the farther side of the Baltic. In the case of the territories which the French gained under the Westphalian Peace it was a different matter. These were to form jumping-off points in France's long-term offensive—the beginning of a titanic struggle which reached from Louis XIV's wars of conquest, the war of the Spanish Succession to Napoleon's campaigns, and which left its mark on European history. France received the fortress of Breisach and territories in Upper and Lower Alsace. The cession of Metz, Toul and Verdun was finally confirmed. France had finally burst the bonds of the Spanish encirclement which had at one time seemed to give the Habsburgs mastery of the Western world.

The Peace of Westphalia also formed a part of the constitution of the Empire. Foreign princes were among its guarantors and they became members of the Empire. On the other hand large parts of Germany (East Prussia and Habsburg possessions) did not belong to the Empire. In the words of the contemporary international lawyer Pufendorf, the constitution of the Empire had become a monstrosity.

After 1648, France began to push forward in the direction of the Rhine and the Netherlands. The sea powers supported the resistance to France's conquests. Their vital interests were threatened and to Louis XIV and Napoleon, England was Public Enemy No. 1. If the French had carried the day they would have created a barrier across the North Sea beyond Amsterdam, cutting England's communications with the Continent. Europe would then have fallen a willing and an easy prey to France. England fought doggedly against this by all means in her power and her fleet was the decisive factor in this war—as in all other modern wars. The French did not hesitate to stab their enemies in the back. They egged on Sweden to fight against Brandenburg, when the latter came to the help of the Netherlands. It is true that the Great Elector defeated the Swedes at Fehrbellin, but when it came to making peace—having been deprived by the Emperor and the Netherlands of the fruits of his victory—he turned to the French.

Now it was possible for France—in alliance with Brandenburg and owing to the cowardice of the Empire—to continue its conquests in peace time. France made a claim to all areas which had at any time been subject to those territories which she had conquered in 1552, 1648, 1668 and 1679. "Chambers of Reunion", made up of first class lawyers, were appointed to give the proceedings an appearance of legality, and they dug out of the murky past evidence of any areas which had ever been attached to France's recently acquired possessions. Piece after piece was torn from the decaying body of the Empire. In 1681, on the grounds that it had at one time been attached to an insignificant French possession, France succeeded in seizing Strassburg. As the Empire was so weak, considerable parts of it fell into French hands like ripe plums, and, with the help of vague legalistic memoranda, they acquired what otherwise they could only have won by the sword.

This was possible because France had no great power on its borders. The two German great powers had turned their faces eastwards. Prussia had great powers along its Eastern boundaries, Sweden in Hither Pomerania, the Habsburg Empire in Moravia, and Poland. East Prussia still formed an island in a Slav sea.

The Habsburgs were in an even worse position. France had egged on the Ottoman Empire against the Austrians. Sometimes there seemed to be a danger that the Empire might be crushed between the pressure of the Ottoman Empire on one side and France on the other.

Two years after the occupation of Strassburg by the French, the Turks, having surrounded Vienna, stood at its gates. If the Sultan had been able to take Vienna by storm, as he had once taken Byzantium, the whole of our traditional Western civilization would have broken down. But finally a united German-Polish army appeared; the Turks were beaten and afterwards gradually pushed back from Vienna by troops of the Habsburg realm until at the beginning of the 18th century a frontier was established which lasted until 1908.

All leaders of the Habsburg Empire, from Maria Theresa to Victor Adler, the leader of the Austrian Socialists who died in 1918, were convinced that if their multiracial Empire were to be held together, only the Germans and especially the German language could do it. The Habsburg Empire was neither a German state nor a non-German state; it was half in and half out of the German Empire.

The Rise of Prussia

Nor was Brandenburg-Prussia in a different position. East Prussia, on which the state of the Hohenzollern was largely founded, did not belong to the *Reich,* and the Hohenzollern did not wish it to belong to the *Reich* because they aspired to a sovereignty not subject to the Imperial Authority.

The first foundations of Prussian power were laid by the Great Elector (1640—1688). He created the groundwork for Prussia's standing army and, in spite of opposition from his nobles, proceeded to build up a strong centralized administration. The Great Elector succeeded to free Prussia from Polish suzerainty. Although he defeated the Swedes, he was foiled by the Emperor when he attempted to gather the fruits of victory, and—seeing in France the coming power— he felt that it was wiser to march with her than against her. Then, however, a fundamental change in France's attitude became apparent. She was clearly aiming at becoming the leading Catholic power succeeding Spain as protector of European Catholicism, but wanted to spread the Catholic faith in all directions and to bring England back into the Catholic fold.

In 1685 the French king revoked the Edict of Nantes, under which toleration had been extended to the French Protestants (Huguenots). Although the Brandenburg Elector was not in the habit of restricting his political alliances to princes of the same religious faith, he saw that the France of Louis XIV was no partner for him. He encouraged the Huguenot refugees to settle in Brandenburg-Prussia and particularly in Berlin, which owes very much to the Huguenot leaven. In 1688 France made another attempt to push forward into the Burgundian-Netherland area, but this time it showed signs of weakness; instead of gaining a victory it merely laid waste the countryside.

The Rhine Palatinate was devastated by Louis XIV's generals with a technique which would have done credit to more modern times; the castle at Heidelberg bears witness to this. The decisive breakthrough which Louis XIV attempted was not to be achieved until the days of the French Revolution and its lord and servant Napoleon.

In 1701 the Spanish royal family died out. The Spanish king had appointed as his successor the heir to the French throne. The merger of these two royal houses would have put France into the position of a world power, and world power is not something which can be inherited; it has to be fought for. France was not strong enough to pursue such a far-reaching aim in opposition to the major part of Europe. The Emperor's son was a rival candidate and a coalition between him and the sea powers fought the War of the Spanish Succession against France (1701—1714). In 1704 the Emperor's general, the Prince Eugene, and the English army under the Duke of Marlborough won a victory over the combined French and Bavarian armies at Blenheim (Hochstaedt) near Donauwoerth. Although the offensive power of France was broken, it showed a remarkably tough defense. The real turning-point of the war came with the death of the Emperor Joseph I (1705—1711). His brother Charles VI (1705—1740), who succeeded him as Emperor, was also the heir to the Spanish throne. Great Britain saw the danger of a Habsburg Spanish-Austrian Empire dominating Europe and, in accordance with its traditional policy of the balance of power, gave its support to the opposite side. After the rage of the extreme anti-Spanish party in England and the rancor of the Emperor had died down, peace was concluded. Philip, the son of the French king, remained King of Spain; the Habsburgs retained Naples, Milan and the Spanish Netherlands (Belgium) and thus finally established themselves as a great European power. The French kept Strassburg, Alsace and the Free County. The weakest party, the Empire, had had to foot the bill.

Almost simultaneously with the war of the Spanish Succession, the Nordic War was fought (1701—1721). France had hoped that the result of this war would be to help Sweden back to its old position of power and thus to restore the old encirclement of the Empire by France and Sweden, but in fact it worked out quite differently. Meanwhile in the East the star of a great Empire was rising, which for a long time was a German ally but eventually became Germany's great adversary—Russia.

Under Charles XII, Sweden, feeling itself on the point of decline, spurred itself on to strenuous effort. Having forced the Saxon Elector Augustus (August der Starke) to renounce the crown of Poland, Charles XII thought he could just as easily dispose of the Tsar of Russia; he suffered under an illusion to which the Germans have often succumbed—that he would be able to win the support of the Russian people. When he reached the country of his Cossack allies, he found that it was nothing but a desert. At Poltava, in the depths of the Ukraine, Charles XII's army was annihilated; the parallel with Stalingrad is a striking one.

Charles XII then fled to the Sultan of Turkey and begged him—in vain—to join in the war against Russia. Finally he returned and took part in the heroic defense of Stralsund. Brandenburg had meanwhile grown stronger; it was able to gather the fruits of victory; the important territory of Higher Pomerania was assigned to it, but Sweden was allowed to retain a few possessions on the Baltic coast of Germany down to Napoleonic times.

Meanwhile Prussia made her independence of the *Reich* evident by proclaiming herself a kingdom. On January 18, 1701, the Elector Frederick III crowned himself as King Frederick I of Prussia at Koenigsberg. His kingdom consisted only of the old state of the Teutonic Knights, Prussia, and not of Brandenburg. Frederick had crowned himself King in order to show that he was under no obligation of obedience either to the Empire or to the Emperor. One part of the Hohenzollern domain was now a sovereign European state.

The foundations of the power of the Prussian kings were laid by Frederick William I (1714—1740). He created Prussia's standing army and compelled the nobles to enter the service of the monarchy, whose power he built up into a "rocher de bronze" (rock of steel). Nevertheless the alliance between the Prussian monarchy and the Prussian nobles began to take shape, under which the career of army officer was reserved for members of noble families. Frederick William I was not without a touch of greatness, though he cannot be regarded as one of the outstanding personalities of German history, because he lacked intellectual force and superiority.

Frederick the Great

It was his general lack of human understanding which led to the tragic conflict between him and his son Frederick II, known as Frederick the Great (1740—1786). To begin with there was a severe clash between the Calvinist father, who looked down on art and culture as useless trash and the enlightened son who thought and spoke in French and was fond of writing and philosophizing. But eventually the spirit of the father prevailed in the son. Frederick the Great overcame what was trivial, frivolous and superficial in the French culture of that time, but his education and outlook remained French. He became the hero of a nation whose language he did not speak. His father had torn him away from his youthful preoccupation of playing with estheticism—but he was broken in the process.

At the same time as Frederick the Great, his great antagonist Maria Theresa (1740—1780) came to the throne of the Habsburgs. She too is one of the great figures of German history. Like Frederick in Prussia, Maria Theresa carried out in the Habsburg Empire a policy of enlightened absolutism. She introduced unity throughout her empire, created a compact customs area, founded the administrative system and the elementary schools of Austria; she prepared the way for the liberation of the peasants from feudalism and unified the legal system throughout the Habsburg dominions. Nor did the pious Empress hesitate, when necessary, to assert the authority of the State against that of the Church. She was not a freethinker, but a believer; for this reason she hated Frederick's freethinking proclivities and his "rebellion" against the Empire; he seemed to her to be the demon of power politics. She had yet to live to see the day when her own son, Joseph II, would be regarded as the embodiment of the "crowned revolution".

When Maria Theresa succeeded to power, the Habsburg Empire was threatening to fall to pieces. The various princes throughout Europe were waiting only for the opportunity of dividing the spoils. The Bavarian Electoral Prince raised a claim to the Habsburg Empire. Frederick the Great invaded Silesia, and France laid hands on Belgium. The Bavarian Prince was elected Emperor as Charles VII. Frederick the Great mistrusted Bavarian-French intentions but was anxious above all to secure what he had gained, so he retired from the struggle. The important transfer of territory, which changed the balance of power within the German Empire, seemed to have been confirmed.

But it proved to be only a temporary armistice, as was bound to have been the case. The conflict spread until it became a world war in the truest sense. England launched what may be described as its second "Hundred Years' War" against France, which extended from the War of the Spanish Succession to the Napoleonic Wars. As soon as it became evident that the Habsburg Empire was not going to collapse, it began to win more allies than Frederick. The scales turned dangerously in favor of Austria. Could Frederick have been expected to look on while Austria gained the superiority, which it would then undoubtedly have used to reconquer Silesia?

Thus it came about that Frederick II renewed his attack on Austria and the second Silesian War began (1744—1745). This led to the formation of an overpowering coalition against Prussia, consisting of Saxony, Poland, Austria and England. Frederick was a versatile man but diplomatic finesse was not among his gifts. His opponents were dangerous because they were backed by England's money. It was only by the luck of war that the prince who—in the words of Goethe—"delighted in the impossible" escaped annihilation. The Peace of Dresden, signed in 1745, left Prussia in possession of its power and of Silesia.

In the following 12 years of peace, there was a far-reaching rearrangement of alliances, destined to mark history.

For centuries Austria had been engaged in its "hereditary struggle" against France. England, now struggling with France for world dominion, had at one time been bound to Austria by the "time-honored alliance", with which the name of the famous Queen Elizabeth is still associated. All this was now to be reversed. Austria entered into an alliance with France and thus surrendered its old function as the protector of the Rhine. In the later treaties of alliance with France, Austria conceded the Netherlands as a reward for France's assistance, so that that country became in effect France's Rhine boundary. On the other hand, Prussia now formed an alliance with Great Britain.

Austria, Russia, France and Saxony seemed to be about to conclude an alliance against Prussia. Frederick II thought he could see the writing on the wall wherever he looked, and so—after the manner of the Schlieffen Plan of the 20th Century—he launched an attack against his enemies in spite of their greatly superior forces, with the hope of detaching some of the states from the enemy coalition before it had mustered its full strength. The two offensives clashed, but Frederick failed in his attempt to overpower the enemy before they had had time to fight a decisive battle. Time worked against him. In such plans as these, which are designed to counterbalance the disadvantage of inferior numbers, victory or defeat depend on a few hours—and in such cases Fate is usually not kind. Was it not Frederick himself who said that "God is always on the side of the bigger battalions."

In 1759 Frederick's armies were decisively beaten by the Austrians and the Russians and it looked as if all was lost, but it was then that the "Miracle of the House of Brandenburg" occurred. Frederick's enemies did not follow up their victory, with the result that he obtained breathing-space. Nevertheless, if numbers counted, Frederick was bound to lose. Then the second miracle in the history of the House of Brandenburg happened: in 1762 the Tsarina Elizabeth died. Her successor, Peter III, was a warm admirer of Frederick the Great and at once made peace—and indeed concluded an alliance—with him. This alliance however lasted only a few days, because Catherine (the Great) had her husband murdered by her lover. But Catherine was not going to renew the war; she knew that there were better things than fighting.

In 1763, the Seven Years' War was brought to an end with the Treaty of Hubertusburg which, by maintaining the status quo, brought Frederick the reward for his persistence. This war of conquest, which Frederick had launched in 1740—in his own words, without proper consideration—proved to be an epoch-making one. It had changed the map of the old "Empire" and a new power had been created—but one which was encompassed by two great powers. It is true that the king of Prussia was—according to Voltaire—a king over frontiers and its Eastern possessions in particular were wedged in between the various Eastern races. The partition of the crumbling Polish Republic however provided Prussia with an opportunity for filling in the gaps between the different parts of its kingdom, although the absorption of considerable numbers of Poles made it more vulnerable. (At the beginning of the 19th Century only about 60 % of the population was German.) As a result of the first Partition, Prussia received West Prussia without Danzig and Thorn; from the second in 1793, Danzig, Thorn and almost the whole of the heart of Poland; from the third Partition in 1795, Masovia with Warsaw.

Parallel with the partitions of Poland, the dissolution of the Ottoman Empire was proceeding. Russia and Austria were engaged in a life or death struggle for the Balkans. Germany was not directly concerned in this, but Russia's path to Constantinople lay across the dead body of Austria, and the abandonment of Austria would expose all Central Europe to Russian power. Karl Marx wrote at a later date: "Russia's aims cannot be realized unless Hungary, Turkey and a part of Germany are wiped off the map." Thus Germany—if it did not want to be wiped off the map—had to be prepared to fight in the Danube region and in the Balkans, if necessary against Russia.

The French Revolution

Three years after the death of Frederick the Great, the great French Revolution broke out. At first this was regarded in Germany as merely an internal crisis and revolt which concerned France alone. Between the years 1789 and 1850, however, there was a complete revolution in Germany's national life, too.

The era of the French Revolution began in Germany with a serious crisis within the Habsburg Empire, which seemed to afford an unprecedented opportunity for Prussia. Once more—as in 1618 and 1740—it seemed as if the Habsburg Empire was breaking up. Maria Theresa had been succeeded by Joseph II (1780—1790). Like Frederick II, the son had rebelled against his parent, in this case his mother. Joseph wanted to force a uniform German-speaking administration on all the Habsburg possessions; he wanted to abolish the special privileges of the nobility and the Church, to dissolve monasteries which were opposed to his progressive ideas, to abolish the existing form of provincial self-government and to replace the historical boundaries by the introduction of artificial divisions after the manner of the French departments.

But the Habsburgs lacked the revolutionary force which would have been required to carry through such far-reaching schemes. At the time of the French Revolution, the Austrian Netherlands, Hungary and Bohemia were seething with revolutionary ferment, partly due to a revolt of the nobles and partly a result of general unrest. In spite of this, Frederick William II of Prussia (1786—1798) was not the sort of man to exploit the internal difficulties of the Habsburgs. All the same, Prussian agents were active in the Netherlands, Hungary and Bohemia, and a war was contemplated against Austria, with Poland and Turkey as allies. This, however, was soon brought to an end with the Treaty of Reichenbach, which brought Austria humiliation and for Prussia nothing. The new Emperor Leopold II (1790—92), through a mixture of wisdom and flexibility, managed to obtain mastery over the revolutionary movement in his own country.

Now, however, the old countries of Europe had to contend with frequent —and often unavoidable—conflicts with the new revolutionary France, which was developing new, dynamic forms of internal and external policy. As regards foreign policy, revolutionary France still followed the familiar lines of the old French regime: encouragement of German disunion, pressure forward to the "natural boundaries" of the Rhine and the Netherlands—this "alluvial deposit of French rivers". Prussia and Austria, for their part, cherished dreams that they could easily disperse the revolution in France. In their deliberations at Pillnitz, Prussia and Austria had drawn up a program of intervention, to which all Europe was to be asked to agree, and which was therefore no more than an impotent challenge. France answered by resorting to desperate measures—the mustering of the whole nation by means of terror, which produced victims in large numbers. In April 1792 began the war which was destined to change the face of all Europe.

The intervention armies however entered into the war feebly and at an old-fashioned jog-trot pace, while at the same time they issued threats that Paris would be reduced to dust and ashes. The sight of an army which displayed such genteel cowardice instilled in the French the courage of despair. At Valmy on September 20, 1792 the interventionist army was repelled by a mere cannonade or, as Carlyle expressed it, "a whiff of grapeshot". Goethe remarked that this marked the beginning of a new era in world history. The vast rabble of the French armies inspired the anxious with terror and soon succeeded in breaking through to the Rhine. There they set up an occupation which lasted for 25 years, and which was at the same time oppressive and beneficial.

One reason why the two great German powers were so halfhearted in their conduct of the war, was that they were always looking back over their shoulder. Russia had made use of the engagement of Prussia and Austria to prepare to incorporate all Poland. So long as the threat from the East remained, a serious war in the West was not possible. It required the Atlantic Alliance to dispel the German fear of an attack from the rear. From 1795 onwards, when Prussia concluded the separate peace of Basle, in order to "be able to play its part" in Poland, Germany has had to face the historic problem: the choice between an alliance with the West or the East, or the alternative of a war on two fronts.

Prussia recognized the French occupation of the Rhineland "until the conclusion of a permanent peace" (which never came) and at the same time undertook to bring about the neutralization of North Germany.

Napoleonic Wars

Meanwhile the man who overcame—and at the same time inherited—the French Revolution had led the French armies against the First Coalition and, after a highly successful campaign in Italy, had pressed on to the gates of Vienna, where the Habsburgs had been compelled to agree to the Treaty of Campo Formio. Under this settlement they received Venice but surrendered the whole of Northern Italy and the Netherlands; they were being pushed eastwards. For many years negotiations were carried on at Rastatt with the Empire—which was now little more than a shadow, although there was never any prospect of peace. Napoleon's war of 1799 to 1801 against the Coalition also brought him success and by the Treaty of Lunéville Austria was pushed still further back in Italy.

The years that follow are almost the strangest period in German history—if one does not include the present. The Treaty of Lunéville laid down that the rulers who suffered losses of territory on the left bank of the Rhine should receive compensation in the form of territories on the right bank, in particular ecclesiastical ones. A largescale reallocation of German territories now took place under the supervision of France and Russia, who had joined in a secret treaty to form a protectorate over the German Empire. A committee of the rulers, (the *Reichsdeputation*) working in co-operation with the French and Russian trustees, disposed of the various claims like a syndicate of real estate agents. Germany was put up for sale: its money and its women (often the daughters of the princes, who were greedy to acquire new territory) were at the disposal of Napoleon's marshals (some of whom had been stableboys and coachmen); in such ways some of the German states enlarged their territories. Three million Germans had to change their allegiance. The Holy Roman Empire ceased to exist and the ruler of the Habsburg realm, who had been Emperor of the Holy Roman Empire, assumed the title "Emperor of Austria". The ecclesiastical domains, which had been in existence since the days of Otto I, disappeared from the map of Germany; the Imperial free cities, with few exceptions, shared the fate of the Empire, and most of the smaller German rulers lost their pocket principalities. Those who gained from this redistribution were the medium-sized German states; every one of these is Napoleon's creation and most of the German *'Laender'* as they existed in the 20th century descend from the satellites of Napoleon.

In this repartitioning of Germany, Prussia was left somewhat out in the cold. At that time the King of Prussia was Frederick William III, an honest but weak monarch, completely lacking in initiative, who viewed the tremendous changes in Germany and Europe which were taking place during his reign with uncomprehending and incredulous amazement. In the course of these events Napoleon had offered Prussia as bait the electorate of Hanover on the throne of which sat George III, at the same time king of England. The acquisition of this territory would have enabled Prussia to round off its dominions and to become a very powerful force in North Germany, though obviously at the cost of a war against England. For Prussia, however, war against England held as little attraction as war against France. It chose, therefore, to share the privileges of the neutral countries—to be the last to be devoured.

When in 1805, the Great Coalition declared war on Napoleon, Prussia remained neutral toward him—although at that time there was some prospect that a war might have been successful. On the other hand Prussia refused to fight for Napoleon in spite of the reward which he offered. In the end Napoleon gained a brilliant victory at Austerlitz over the Austrians and the Russians.

Now 16 German princes seceded from the Empire (which had practically ceased to exist) and formed a Confederation of the Rhine under the leadership of France; practically with the sole purpose to recruit the population of these territories for Napoleon's wars.

The most important thing for Prussia was now to avoid war against Napoleon at all costs. But Prussia now put forward demands which might have been considered reasonable before the Austrians had been knocked out at Austerlitz. Only Russia and England were now left to carry on the struggle, but England could not help in a land war and Russia's troops were too far away. Prussia just drifted into war. Its conduct of the war was just as clumsy as its diplomacy and the result was that there was a general lack of morale throughout the army. The defeats at Jena and Auerstaedt, therefore, led to a complete collapse of the Prussian state. Napoleon entered Berlin in triumph and proclaimed from there his "continental system" which forbade all trade with England, hoping in this way to force the island empire to its knees. However, in 1807 Prussia pulled itself together and continued to fight side by side with Russian troops. But Napoleon was in all respects superior; he marched triumphantly into Koenigsberg, while the Prussian royal family fled eastwards to Memel.

The worst part of all this was that Russia left Prussia to its fate. The Emperor of the French and the Tsar of Russia met on a raft on the River Memel near Tilsit with the object of dividing the world between them. Yet Napoleon had not won his war until he had conquered England. And until England had been defeated there was still hope for the nations of Europe. But Russia did not want to be drawn into a war against England. Napoleon was left with the choice either of invading England or of attacking Russia; whereupon Germany's only hope of a turn in the tide was founded.

The rest of the Germans were, however, forced to look on while Prussia, which had become a European power, was crushed and left with an army of a limited size and not allowed an independent foreign policy. As a result of the treaty of Tilsit, Prussia had to surrender most of its gains from the Partitions of Poland and all territory left of the Elbe. Prussia had become what it had seldom been in the course of its history—merely a country "east of the Elbe".

Out of the Polish territories which were ceded by Prussia under the Treaty of Tilsit, Napoleon created the Duchy of Warsaw, at the head of which he placed the King of Saxony. Under Russian pressure, Napoleon refrained from carrying out his original plan of wiping Prussia entirely off the map or of breaking it into pieces by taking away West Prussia; but the French Emperor left for Prussia no more than a torso—a fan-shaped state consisting of Silesia, Brandenburg and Pomerania, West Prussia and

East Prussia; greater Poland had no outlet to the sea but formed a sort of "cordon sanitaire" which separated Russia from Prussia; the Saxon King obtained a Polish crown, while Poland was still divided from Saxony by Prussian Silesia. There were signs that the various divided peoples might rise in rebellion. The national uprising in Spain in 1809 had rather dimmed the glory of Napoleon's reputation for invincibility. But seldom can a successful war be carried through by a popular uprising; it must have the power of an organized state and an army behind it.

In 1809 Austria launched an attack against Napoleon, hoping thereby to stimulate national risings; but the powers—Russia and Prussia— held back, and national uprisings proved no sufficient substitute for the help of the world powers. Neither the people nor the powers responded and Austria was beaten.

But Germany's cause was by no means hopeless because, in spite of all his glorious victories, Napoleon had still not won. His greatest enemy had hardly been affected by his victories. This enemy, Great Britain, had backed all these coalitions against France; its money had seemed always to be able to conjure up new enemies against France; and its mastery of the seas was hardly disputed. If Napoleon's continental blockade of England was to be effective, Russia must be either persuaded or compelled by war to take part. In this way it was England's "little storm-beaten ships" (Churchill) which drove Napoleon into the wide open spaces of Russia and ultimately led to Germany's liberation from French domination. The army which Napoleon assembled for his invasion of Russia was drawn from all over Europe; 200,000 of its 600,000 men were German, but the greater part of his "grande armée" perished in the snows of the Russian winter. Only the Prussian General von Yorck managed to rescue something of the Prussian army from the murderous war against "General Winter, General Hunger and General Darkness". On December 30, 1812, Yorck, acting on his own responsibility, concluded the Convention of Tauroggen with his Russian opposite number. Eventually the King, too, reluctantly acquiesced. In an appeal "To my People" he went so far as to promise that the whole German Reich would be shaped according to the wishes of the German nation.

In the years 1807 to 1812 wide-reaching reforms had been carried through in Prussia. Stein was responsible for the municipal reforms of 1808 and the abolition of serfdom in 1807. This last reform caused, however, great losses to many German peasants. The property rights of the large landowners were to be redeemed by the peasants by the transfer of portions of their land; this was fatal for the weaker members of the peasantry east of the Elbe. Thus the liberation of the peasants meant very largely that the peasants were "liberated" from the soil. This resulted in the creation of a class of land workers—an agricultural proletariat—and led at a later date to a migration of Germans from the East to the West and their replacement by Poles, who were engaged by the large landowners because they represented cheaper labor. At the same time during the "Reform Years", compulsory military service was introduced; to serve as a soldier ceased to mean a loss of "respectability"; the army was no longer a "horde held together by the whip" *("zusammengepruegelte Horde")*.

In spite of the disaster which he had suffered in Russia, Napoleon managed to create yet another army. If he had been content to accept France's boundaries as they had been before the Revolution, he could have saved his dynasty. Indeed Napoleon's cause was not yet lost; this was illustrated by the fact that the states of the Rhine Confederation still held out for him; if his prospects had been hopeless they would hardly have remained loyal to him.

The fate of Napoleon, of Germany and of Europe was decided in a three-day "battle of the nations" at Leipzig, which lasted from October 16 to 18, 1813. By the end of that year the Rhine provinces had been liberated and in 1814 the allies were able to follow up their victories by carrying the war into France. Napoleon put up a stubborn defense but finally his power collapsed. He was first sent to Elba, but escaped from there, landed in France and seized power again, so that Europe had once again to take up arms against him. His campaign lasted only 100 days, and he was finally defeated at the battle of Waterloo in 1815. The man who had redrawn the map of Germany and who, in the eyes of many Germans, was their Emperor in the long line of succession from Charlemagne, died in exile on the rocky island of St. Helena.

Congress of Vienna

France, which had been heartless in victory, was granted easy peace terms. She was allowed to retain her territories within the frontiers of 1792, including Alsace and Strassburg. Germany's sun had set; its voice at the Congress of Vienna was only that of a ghost. Negotiations were conducted with the German princes; the task of reconstructing Germany—so far as there was to be a Germany and it was not regarded merely as a subject for hatred and abhorrence—was left to the princes.

The various German states however profited by the dissolution of the Empire and emerged with many gains. Prussia was able to weld its scattered Eastern territories into a coherent whole, although in some parts of it the German language was by no means predominant.

What was more important was that from then on Prussia owned territories in the Rhineland and Westphalia. Prussia and "east of the Elbe" were no longer synonymous, although the order of society which had been typical of its Eastern territories, made its impact on the whole new state. The two parts of Prussia were separated by a "corridor" consisting of the two states of Hanover and Hesse; both these states were to pay the penalty of their geographical position in 1866, when they were incorporated in Prussia.

The "German Confederation" which was created at the Congress of Vienna made a mockery of Germany. "Don't let's talk about Germany. It just doesn't exist." These words of Schwarzenberg's typify Germany's position after 1819. The new German federal constitution was an unbridled triumph for what Bismarck called at a later date the "ungodly humbug of the sovereignty of the German princes";—yet the Germans had believed, with the Frenchman Renan, that their War of Liberation was unique in its epic character and in the loftiness of its aims.

But after 1815, these German dreamers discovered that their "Wars of Liberation" had only liberated them from Germany. The "German Confederation" was an alliance, its members being subject to the law of nations and not to the public law of a united state; and was as able to make decisions as an East-West-Disarmament Conference. The majority required for decisions of importance was so large that, thanks to the confusion of conflicting interests, a negative decision could always be assured.

The German Confederation proved to be a monstrosity in that its membership included foreign princes (Denmark representing Holstein, England Hanover and the Netherlands Luxemburg), and also because the great German Powers were members in respect to a portion of their dominions only. (East Prussia, West Prussia, Posen; Hungary, Venice, Milan and the other Italian territories which were under Habsburg rule, formed no part of the German Confederation—and they included some of the most German province (the whole of genuine "Prussia")—although Bohemia did.) If this Confederation had exercised real power, and if some of the subjects of Prussia and the Habsburgs had had to obey it and the others not, the two great German powers would have been torn asunder. On January 1, 1834, the disorderly collection of states which called itself the "German Confederation" did at least, under the leadership of Prussia, form a customs union, from which the Habsburg realm was excluded. Prussia was vitally interested in breaking down the Hanover-Hessian customs barriers which separated its two constituent parts. Frederick List once said that railways and custom unions, and not diplomats and Parliaments, would bring about German unity but he was not quite correct, because in 1866 members of the customs union went to war against one another.

National Assembly at Frankfort

The political unity of Germany was something which had still to be realized. In March, 1848, it seemed that at last the German people themselves had the opportunity of solving this problem. The February Revolution in France had caused the fall of all the German Governments; the horror which the great French Revolution had left in its wake, seemed to have created in Germany a political vacuum in which the future was waiting to be shaped.

A preliminary Parliament of liberal politicians summoned a German National Assembly which met in St. Paul's Church *(Paulskirche)* at Frankfort in May and in the same month appointed an executive head of the *Reich (Reichsverweser).*

It soon, however, became apparent to the delegates at St. Paul's Church that what was needed was the help of a German Power which could impose its will on the others; many did not appreciate this, others did not want to, and no one dared to say so. Thus arose the strange plan of crowning the work of the St. Paul's Church Assembly by electing an Emperor. The election of an Emperor proved to be the Parliament's deathbed performance; the defenseless delegates offered the Imperial crown to the man who, they hoped, would complete the revolution for them. The first Frankfort plan had provided that no head of a foreign state (the Emperor of Austria was considered as such) should be allowed to govern Germans. But within the old Empire a "narrower circle" should be formed. The German territories should be welded together into a real state, which would incorporate the German nation; this would include the whole of Brandenburg-Prussia from the Rhine to Koenigsberg, Posen, West Prussia, the Sudeten territories, German Austria and all other states in the Confederation, to the extent that they were German.

The Dahlmann Plan would thus have separated the Habsburg Empire into two parts, one of which would really have been ruled over by the Austrian Emperor, while in the other part he would be no more than a symbol and a decoration. The reply of the Government in Vienna was very simple: If you want to subject Habsburg territories to the upstart authority of a "German Empire", and if you are hankering after reigning where we rule, come and fetch these territories yourselves, and try to drive away the divisions which are stationed there to protect them. The Habsburgs had large armies at their disposal, whereas the delegates at Frankfort had only a few stage soldiers on policeman's duty.

Prince Schwarzenberg, the master of Austria-Hungary, went even further. He said that the Habsburgs would regard the formation of a union between all non-Habsburg parts of the German Confederation as a casus belli. Thus it was not possible to form a closer association between the German states—even if German Austria and the Sudeten territories were excluded.

The Frankfort delegates then proposed to enter the lists with an "Hereditary Emperor" whom Schwarzenberg would perhaps permit to rule over "little Germany". In this way the so-called "Constitution of Renunciation" was evolved in March 1849; this provided for the union of all the German states outside the Habsburg dominions, instead of having a divided Habsburg Empire and a schizophrenic Emperor, one half of whom would be a man to govern and give orders, while the other half would just wear a dazzling uniform.

On the basis of this constitution, which apparently left the Habsburgs in peace (but in fact deprived them of any influence in the proposed "little" German Empire), the King of Prussia was chosen by the first popular democratic assembly as German Emperor, to the accompaniment of church bells and gunfire. Prince Schwarzenberg had, however, always said that the acceptance of this crown would mean a war, but in any case it was not a crown which a King of Prussia could accept. The constitution had been framed on very democratic lines, in order to win the support of the republican left wing for the idea of an Emperor. Nor had the delegates provided for the King of Prussia to be consulted in drawing up the constitution, for which he must be prepared to go to war. The King of Prussia had not been asked to say in what political uniform he would like to fight. Even another king than the eccentric Frederick Willian IV would have rejected this imperial crown, of which Schwarzenberg remarked that he would not wish his bitterest enemy to be compelled to wear it.

When the Prussian King declined to accept the Imperial crown on these terms, the Frankfort Assembly was dead. The Austrian and Prussian Governments withdrew their representatives from the German National Assembly. The rump of the Parliament allowed itself to be dispersed by Wuerttemberg soldiers without offering any resistance.

The King of Prussia regretted all the same that the revolution had not led to a unification of the *Reich* outside the Habsburg realm under Prussian leadership. He put the blame on the popular origins of the proposed constitution; to him, it smelled too much of the people. He proposed that the German princes should voluntarily join together to form a confederation under the leadership of Prussia. This was the so-called *"Union Plan"* as the Frankfort Parliament had suggested, but deprived of its democratic teeth. Those who responded to this proposal were essentially the states which were within the range of Prussian guns or whose princes were afraid of popular movements. Some of the middle-sized states secretly informed the Tsar that they were not prepared to keep the oath of allegiance which they had taken to the King of Prussia. This *Union Plan* was merely a small and spoiled edition of Frankfort. Schwarzenberg let it be known that even this *Union Plan* would be regarded by him as a casus belli; he objected to the union as union, whether brought about by parliaments or kings. In anv case this *"Union"* meant war against Prussia.

Prussia was thus faced by the question: should it go to war for the sake of half an empire after it had refused to strike for a real empire? What turned the scale was a declaration by the Tsar of Russia saying that he could not permit either of the great German powers to be destroyed. Thus Prussia might win a victory over Austria or the Habsburgs over Prussia and either of them might reward itself by making minor territorial adjustments or by claiming reparations, but neither state—Prussia or Austria—could really win the war. Basically the Austrians were quite keen to make war if only to remove that cheeky upstart Prussia, and in the event of a full-scale war Prussia would have tried to realize its old dream of splitting up the Habsburg Empire into various national entities. But the Tsar did not—any more than Khruschev—want Germany to cease being a double-headed monster.

By the Convention of Olmuetz in 1850 the "Union" was given a decent burial. There would be no fratricidal war—nor would there be any Germany. The "German Confederation" rose out of the grave with the odor of Lazarus about it.

By the Convention of Olmuetz in 1850, the "Union" was given a decent burial. There would be no fratricidal war—nor would there be any Germany. The "German Confederation" rose out of the grave with the odor of Lazarus about it.

Bismarck

Otto von Bismarck, as Prussian delegate to the *Bundestag,* had learnt to detest the pompous impotence and the superiority of the Habsburgs. Finally, as the result of a particularly absurd dispute about the Prussian Constitution, he was made Chief Minister of Prussia; he managed to maneuver his king into three successful wars, as a result of which he brought the German Empire into being

The liberal house of parliament took exception to the fact that in the new army (which was basically the same as the old one), the "standing army" (the real soldiers) was given greater prominence than the "militia" (the *"Landwehr")*. In the face of the King's decision to resign, Otto von Bismarck was on September 24, 1862, appointed Prussian Chief Minister. He was prepared to act contrary to the wishes of Parliament if need be; moreover he repeatedly persuaded the King to do what he did not want to, and finally Bismarck made him German Emperor—something he had never wanted to become.

As early as 1862 Bismarck's ultimate aim was the "German Empire", although he was always sceptical about long-distance political aims and because of this he never felt sure that he would be able to reach his goal. He dared not confess that he had such an aim in view; the only reason that his policy was successful was because, at the various stages which led up to his final achievement, he was able to convince his partner that an Empire was not what he had in mind.

There was no chance of creating the Empire until its enemies were divided. The individual states fought for their self-glorification, which made it impossible for them to be true Germans. The Habsburgs protested against the loss of their privileged position in the Empire. Napoleon III was not prepared to agree to German unity unless he was given huge "compensation"—which ultimately worked out to mean the annexation of the Rhineland. The foreign princes who were members of the German Confederation did not want to allow themselves to be squeezed out of the Empire, nor did they want it to be divided into two parts—German and non-German.

The opportunity of isolating the various Powers and of swallowing them one after another—like the leaves of an artichoke—came in 1863 when Denmark, by the issue of a new constitution, attempted to incorporate practically the duchies of Schleswig and Holstein in its own political system. Napoleon III encouraged Prussia to annex the Duchies; naturally he expected a rake-off in the form of Rhineland territory. Bismarck gave him no explicit promise; he did not refuse but just remained silent. But his lies were always on the fringe of truth. So he was able to convince Napoleon that he had been promised something.

Napoleon knew quite well that the action against Denmark could only lead to Prussia's—with her vital interests in Schleswig-Holstein—taking possession of her booty.

By what seemed a miracle, Bismarck managed to persuade Austria to join in taking action to obtain something that Prussia—and only Prussia—wanted.

Legal heir of the Duchies was a prince of Augustenburg. The clever politicians who directed foreign policy in Vienna thought that they could create on Prussia's flank a medium-sized state, which Vienna could not have obtained without a major war and which had nothing to protect it but the talkative impotence of the "German Confederation".

When, therefore, it came to the point, the threat to Prussia's flank, about which Vienna had dreamed, proved to be nothing more than a damp squib. An attempt to divide up the Duchies into "occupation zones" having failed, the Austrian Governor of Holstein called upon the princes to proclaim the new Duke, but the Prussian troops marched in as if on parade. No one was prepared to resist, because resistance would be hopeless. It was all over in a day.

Denmark had now seceded from the German Confederation. Prussia had established a footing on the Baltic. A long step forward had been taken towards the realization of the Empire about which the delegates at Frankfort had dreamed. Austria had shed its blood and had paved the way for the formation of the Empire from which it was to be excluded. Napoleon had given "encouragements" all round.

Bismarck could now see the way clear for the war against the Habsburgs, which he regarded as inevitable. After he had concluded an alliance with Italy, who delivered the first blow, Bismarck—the "reactionary" in the German *Bundestag*—made a proposal to convene a German *Reichstag* based on universal suffrage. After 16 years Prussia had after all accepted the Frankfort constitution and the crown—this time not in spite of, but because, it meant war. This war against Austria was decided on the field of Koeniggraetz in Bohemia.

Now that Denmark and the Habsburgs had been disposed of, it was the turn of Bismarck's third opponent, the France of Napoleon III. The North German Confederation, which had been formed in 1866, had become a strong power north of the Main; but it was obvious that any attempt to extend its domain beyond the Main would be answered by Napoleon III with war.

Bismarck wanted to make peace with the Habsburgs on terms which, in the event of a war against France, would ensure that the Habsburg realm at least remained neutral. Therefore he demanded from Austria little more than that it should retire from the German Empire. Hanover, Electoral Hesse, Nassau, Frankfort, and Schleswig-Holstein were incorporated in Prussia. Thus, at the same time as the new Empire was formed, a Greater Prussia was also created. By entering into defensive-offensive alliances, the Southern German states aligned themselves along the North-German Confederation. Yet the Southern German states would not have followed Bismarck in an aggressive war. An attack from France was necessary for the creation of the German *Reich.*

It was for this reason that Bismarck staged the so-called Hohenzollern candidature for the Spanish throne. France began to talk about Charles V, and "encirclement"—which in fact was nothing more than a net of cobwebs. France's reaction was more splendidly foolish than Bismarck in his fondest dreams had dared to hope.

On the slenderest of grounds, France now declared war in support of something which she had for centuries regarded as her vital interest—the prevention of German unification.

France's military leadership was no better than her diplomacy. She was quickly beaten and Napoleon III was taken prisoner at Sedan. France's Third Republic came into existence. France was still a great Power; it had only to reconcile itself to the existence of a united Germany and the German *Reich* which on January 18, 1871, was proclaimed—rather tactlessly—in the Hall of Mirrors at Versailles.

Bismarck had said when the *Reich* was formed: "We have only to put Germany in the saddle; she will know how to ride"—and, in fact, Germany did not ride at all badly. The new *Reich* was not a dictatorship: it was a state like all the others. The rule of law prevailed in Germany and, the new *Reich* had also what was, in practice, a form of parliamentary government because, although all the important measures which were introduced were not determined in detail by the *Reichstag,* by virtue of the Budgetary Law they had in effect to receive Parliament's approval. If, for instance, the *Reichstag* had liked to withhold its consent, there could have been no army or navy. The Chancellor governed with the support of a parliamentary majority. The weakness of the *Reich* was due to the political inexperience of its Chancellors. They were not recruited from the field of politics; according to the constitution, a member of parliament could not become a minister. Nearly all the Chancellors were unknown men; they seldom had the real confidence of the Emperor; most of them had been merely recommended to him. These Chancellors had never had to expose themselves to the glare of publicity; they had never had to prove their worth by fighting political battles.

It is true that Germany knew how to ride—but it was already riding in the direction of war. Bismarck was always plagued by the "nightmare of coalitions". France soon emerged again as a European Power. The Congress of Berlin convinced Bismarck that Russia's aims were still directed against the Balkans and Constantinople, and that her plans could only be realized over the dead body of the Habsburgs. And if that happened, Russia would have been standing at all Germany's frontiers—as she is today. So in 1879 Bismarck entered into an alliance with Austria-Hungary. The result of this was that Germany was dragged into the struggle between the two Great Powers in the Balkans for what remained of the Ottoman Empire. From now onwards the issue of peace or war for Germany depended on the relationship between the Habsburg Empire, distracted by racial enmities and the fear of dissolution, and the Greater Serbian movement, protected by Russia and employing means of every sort—even criminal ones—in support of its aims.

Bismarck thought it unlikely that either Russia or the Habsburg Empire would risk destruction "for the sake of a few stinking tribes of the Balkans," because neither of these empires was capable of carrying on a major war. But in fact even the least important peoples were of value to Russia and the Habsburgs, as a jumping-off base for their expansionist plans.

Meanwhile France had entered into an alliance with Russia, not solely for reasons of revenge, but because she was genuinely afraid of the power of the *Reich.* A war between the *Reich* and the Habsburgs on the one side and Russia and France on the other side might at any time have broken out overnight but for any of these states it was sheer madness and certain destruction to go to war without the assistance of Great Britain.

Admiral Tirpitz had, however, the very foolish idea of building a German battlefleet that should make it impossible for Great Britain to go to war against Germany without a risk. The decision of the *Reich* to challenge the British Empire by building up a fleet was one of the most incomprehensible and disastrous acts in German—and indeed European—history. The *Reich* was essentially a land power, and not intended to be a seapower, and the seas were open to it only as long as England kept them open.

This "plaything of the Emperor's", the German battlefleet, never constituted any actual danger for England, but it would have called for superhuman qualities to have been able to overlook the German challenge. Churchill expressed it in moving terms: "The ships of our fleet were all that we had. . . On them . . floated the might, majesty, dominion and power of the British Empire. All our long history, built up century after century . . . depended upon them. Open the sea-cocks and let them sink beneath the surface, and in a few minutes—half an hour at the most—the whole outlook of the world would be changed." *

What is more, the German fleet was worthless. The hostility of England had been incurred to no purpose. Admiral Tirpitz based his calculations on the old rules of naval strategy, according to which a blockade meant the formation of a narrow ring around the port that was being blockaded. Thus the British fleet would have to form a close ring around the German North Sea ports if it wanted to blockade Germany. This being the case, it would naturally be possible, by means of a German battlefleet, to break through this ring and to win the war in the course of an afternoon.

However under Winston Churchill, the British adopted the policy of the so-called "distant blockade". Churchill realized that they needed only to seal up the English Channel and the north-west passage near the Orkneys; the Germans would then never bring their fleet as far afield as that, so that they would remain tied up in their ports and would in effect still be blockaded. By a single stroke of the pen, the British Admiralty converted the great German battlefleet into a miserable heap of scrap iron.

First World War

In August 1914 the *Reich* started the war, without knowing how it was going to provide its population with bread and its army with munitions. The war was eventually decided by "General Hunger". From the very first Germany had been attempting the impossible.

The primary impulse for the war was the Habsburg belief that only a successful war could save their Empire from dissolution—it was in this sense a desperate gamble with destruction. They had already resolved on

---

*) Winston Churchill: *The World Crises 1911—18*, p. 119.

the war against Serbia in order to stamp out the Greater Serbian agitation at its center, even before the Austrian Crown Prince was assassinated. But after the murder of the Austrian Crown Prince it was easier to believe that Russia would not intervene to protect its pawn, Serbia. But Russia was not deterred by dynastic considerations. Thus the whole machinery of the alliances was set in motion: Russia assisted Serbia, the *Reich*, Austria, France, Russia.

Only Great Britain declared that it was uncommitted. The British people would never have entered the war for the sake of purely national interests. The Government relied on the German plan to march through Belgium, which was known to Sir Edward Grey, and which clearly placed England under an obligation to take action.

The German general staff had worked out a plan which was to make it possible for Germany to win the war, even against superior forces, contrary to all probability and in spite of inferior numbers. Count Schlieffen had evolved the plan of making a wide flank movement through Belgium, thus forcing France to its knees before the Russian steam-roller appeared. The success of this plan depended on a few hours; it "nearly" succeeded but, as Churchill once said, for Germany, everything short of complete victory meant defeat; while for the Allies, everything short of mortal defeat meant a victory. If only France could remain staggering on its feet, the war was lost for Germany. France did remain on its feet. It was in vain that England had been challenged by the building of the fleet; the march through Belgium had also been in vain.

Anyhow, the *Reich* managed—it looked like a miracle—to hold out against five continents for four years and in the end the whole world had to be mustered before the Germans could be finally defeated.

The tremendous effort which had been used up in the war, left the world so exhausted that the victors found it impossible to impose a true peace and to create a united world with a political unity. The new German Republic which was founded in 1918 did not grow up in a world of democracy. It had not been a complete victory for democracy; for democracy too, anything short of complete victory meant defeat.

The Untrue Myth

By Alfred Rapp

In the small town of Leonberg near Stuttgart in Wuerttemberg, the little building where the first parliament in Germany convened five hundred years ago still stands. Half a millennium ago, during the Middle Ages, there was such a thing as a parliament in Germany. The English House of Commons is the "mother of all parliaments". But the Germans also had public representation at the same time. Of course, it is true that in most cases only the nobility, the high clergy, and the townsmen met together, but this was also the case in the British House of Commons. Among this number neither a peasant or a journeyman was to be found. The members of the "Commons" were well-to-do people, just as for many centuries in the American Congress where no poor man would sit. But the rulers in the townshalls of such free towns as Strassburg, Ulm, and Augsburg were simple artisans. These free towns were the first citizen-states of Europe and the first parliamentary republics of European history, although they were under the nominal rule of the emperor. Neither England nor France had anything of the like.

The government in the Strassburg townhall was more parliamentary, more republican, and more democratic than that in the House of Commons in London. No king had to call this body to meeting and no king could dissolve it. No lord or nobleman had any say in it. The citizens of these German towns governed themselves. No English or French town knew this freedom of the bourgeoisie in these free towns. Moreover, it was in this old Germany that Alemannic peasants from the Alpine valleys round the Lake of Lucerne formed the confederation which was the kernel of what was to become Switzerland and thereby the first peasant state in Europe.

The Peasants' War in the era of the Reformation was the greatest battle for freedom in Europe. France and England also experienced peasants' revolts; but the German peasants kindled the great revolution of the "common man". The history of democracy in Europe does not begin with the English revolution of the seventeenth century or the French of the eighteenth, but with the German revolution of the sixteenth century. This revolution has been forgotten because it failed and history takes little notice of those who are defeated. But Jos Fritz, the peasant from the Rhine, and the "father of the Peasants' War", stands at the head of the geneological tree of the history of European democracy. This German revolutionary remained up into the nineteenth century the only champion of democracy who had come from the people itself. The leaders of the "Glorious Revolution" in England were lords and rich citizens. At the head of the

French Revolution stood counts and barristers. But the old German democratic revolution was directed by peasants; and until the nineteenth century in Europe, the peasants constituted nine tenths of the population. They were the people.

European history has no other democratic revolution than the German Peasants' War. Some four hundred years ago, the German peasants posed the question, "When Adam delved and Eve span, who was then the gentleman?". This is the proto-question of every democracy. It was asked directly for the first time in Europe by the Germans—and nobody who has read the documents of the German Peasants' War can deny it. Long previous to the "Glorious Revolution" in England which turned England into a monarchy of the nobility, and prior to the French Revolution which changed France into a citizens' republic, these German peasants of an earlier age had striven to found a people's government, an empire of the people.

Of course, it is a sign of revolutionary extravagance when peasant hordes want to tear down castles because no house ought to be larger than a farmhouse and in the same way when the French revolutionaries wanted to dismantle church towers because they rose above the roofs of the citizens. But it is a great historical step when the aristocracy was done away with so that everyone could be a "common man". These peasant warriors founded an "Evangelical Community". They asked for nothing more than the justice of God and the ancient rights and privileges. The peasant's council was to rule the empire. The rebellious peasants with pikes and scythes swarmed over half of Germany, fought in great battles against princes and knights. More fighters for democracy died in the Germany of this time than later in England and France.

Had these peasants won their revolution, Germany would have become the first and would have been the oldest democracy in Europe. This did not come about because knights and foot soldiers broke up the hordes of peasants and defeated them. But this unsuccessful revolution was a testimony against the historical legend that the Germans are born as submissive subjects. On the contrary, they have been known in history as being stubborn. It was first through the catastrophy of the Thirty Years' War in the seventeenth century that the submissive German character came into being. For a whole generation the Germans had fought against each other and the French, Spanish, and the Swedes had carried out their campaigns amongst themselves on German soil. The hamlets were continually in flame and epidemics raged within the townwalls. All commerce came to a standstill. All Germany lived in misery, and when the peace was signed, Germany had lost one third of its population, its wealth, and its vigor.

It was during this time of want, of poverty and difficulties, of gloom and penury, that the submissive serf came to light in Germany—he who would perish before the majesty of his sovereign. The model of the German despots, however, was the French king Louis XIV's much praised France; command and obedience were just like those in Germany under the rule of the despotic princes. And when the "philosophers of freedom" like Montesquieu, Diderot, and Voltaire lived and taught in France, they did not praise the French kings, but venerated the Prussian king, Frederick II, as the *"roi des philosophes"*.

Whoever sees in these *philosophes* of the Enlightenment the forerunners of freedom in Europe should not forget that they regarded Frederick the Great as their patron. To praise Voltaire and to condemn Frederick would be an offence against historical truth. Frederick's Prussia, it is true, is one of the examples of the "untrue myth" in German history. His Prussia serves as the prototype of German reactionariness, of traditional German despotism, of lack of freedom in Germany at a time when freedom's spirit was awakening in France. But the "fathers of freedom" in France viewed this very Prussia quite differently.

They knew that the French marquis in their own country was no less arrogant than the Prussian Junker and that the exclusiveness of the English nobility was unequaled in Europe. The barbaric discipline of the Prussian army found its counterpart in the English navy; and to be a sailor on an English battleship might well have been even worse in the eighteenth century than to be a grenadier in the Prussian army. But it was in this very Prussia that all were equal before the law and its justice, something which was unknown in Voltaire's France. Prussia was the first European state to abolish torture. And tolerance in questions of faith was already a royal law in Germany, while in England Catholic citizens were underprivileged.

Thus the Prussia of Frederick II was regarded by contemporaries in Europe as the most progressive state among the reactionaries. The French revolutionaries of 1789 offered the supreme command of the army to a Prussian general, reared in the Frederickan school, because they saw in revolutionary France and Frederick's Prussia the two most modern states of Europe. The English liberal, Fox, said that there was only one constitution in Europe aside from that of England, namely that of Wuerttemberg, and that in this Swabian land, parliament's legal advisor spoke of the "innate, ancient freedom of the Germans". It was during the years of the American War of Independence that Friedrich Schiller wrote his drama *In Tyrannos,* Against the Tyrants.

During the early years of the French Revolution, Friedrich Schiller became an honorary citizen of France. But 1789 is not a date in German history. Germany did not experience a storming of the Bastille. No peasant in Germany plundered a castle and only a few citizens in the Rhineland planted a liberty tree. But even the French obeyed the commands of the dictator Napoleon a few years after the Revolution. He is, of course, the "Robespierre on horseback", the dictator with democratic traits. But the democratic elements of Napoleonic France spread to the West and South of Germany as well. The liberation of the peasants was proclaimed and the freedom of the towns established. The latter was still unknown in France itself.

Prussia, too, had its revolutionaries for freedom: vom Stein, Scharnhorst, and Gneisenau. The Prussian general, Scharnhorst, broke the hold of the aristocracy on the supplying of material for the officer corps. This was a similar revolution for the Prussian army to the one that was brought about in the French army; therefore, Scharnhorst is called the "Prussian Jacobite". His close advisor, Gneisenau, said openly that he wanted to reach into the "arsenal of the revolution" and did so. Baron vom Stein, at times a sort of Prussian prime minister, did not advocate a "blind admiration of the French Revolution's methods". His opponents, however, said, "Unfortunately for us, this man has been in England and has brought back all of his political wisdom from there."

In Napoleon's age, Prussia had a liberal of the English sort, who reminded his people of Montesquieu's words that freedom had its origin in the German woods and who desired that the "nation take part in the management of its own affairs". Napoleon outlawed him and declared him an enemy of France. Stein left office prematurely. But the Prussian reformers became revolutionaries in 1813 when they wanted to declare war against Napoleon's hegemony in Germany. "The king must arm the people so that people don't arm themselves against the king," a minister in Berlin declared. Another said, "I see no means by which we can restrain the violence of the mob."

The state chancellor, Prince Metternich, in Vienna, spoke openly of the Prussian revolutionaries, commenting, "The spirit, which was awakened through the general resistance against the French government in Germany and increased through Stein's proclamations, had grown to such a degree, especially in Prussia, that the war for liberation did not differ greatly from a war for liberty."

Stein referred to the "riffraff of German princes". His friend Arndt wanted to call for a general uprising, and Stein and Gneisenau demanded a "free constitution". These Prussian reformers have their place in the history of democracy in Europe. In Germany, their aims and their work did not perish, as is often said. It is, however, true that Germany was to be ruled by Metternich after the defeat of Napoleon and not by Stein. This Germany of the "Biedermeier" period was no idyll, but, however, not any different from the France of the same period, a symptom of a revolution.

It was not the French, but the German students on the Wartburg who in the years after Napoleon protested against the absolute rule of the princes, and it was not Paris alone in 1830 that experienced a revolution. There were also uprisings in Frankfort, Saxony, and in Kassel. And in Southern Germany, the bell of new parliaments tolled. Already more than a hundred years ago, the representatives of the people in Munich, Stuttgart, Karlsruhe, and Darmstadt convened. The parliamentary tradition in Germany was not shorter than that of France. The French parliament of the "Bourgeoise-King" was, however, more powerful, but it was representative of the rich. In a German parliament of the period, complaints were heard, "that soon there will be nothing left but on the one hand accumulated wealth and on the other the rags of misery. The contrast between rich and poor, insolence of the former and greed of the latter and the resulting hatred and envy will bring the most dangerous inflammable elements into society."

This Germany of a hundred years ago was neither a garrison nor the model of a submissive and subordinate nation. The German revolution of 1848 may well be compared with the famous French revolution of the same year. In March of 1848, an eyewitness wrote from Berlin, "For twelve hours the city resounded with the thundering of cannon fire and shooting of guns. Today the people have been victorious. Berlin celebrates its revolution, a revolution that has been more hard fought for than that of Paris." Barricades were erected in Berlin just as they were in Paris. Ministers of the king fell in Berlin just as in Paris. The rights of the people were proclaimed all over Germany; and the first freely chosen parliament met at Frankfurt in the Church of Paul in order to frame a German constitution.

However, this parliament failed, and whoever loses will later be blamed. But even the much-praised French parliament of 1848 was short-lived and succumbed to the new dictator, Napoleon III. But the people's rights proclaimed in the Church of Paul lived on for all Germans.

It is also a part of the myth of undemocratic Germany that the Church of Paul conference was only a fleeting episode—a breath of fresh air in the vacuum of reaction. Many of the fighters for the German revolution went into exile. Like Karl Schurz, who was later Secretary for the Interior in the United States, the revolutionaries emigrated to America. "If I cannot be a citizen of a free Germany," replied Karl Schurz, "then I want at least to be a citizen of a free America." A German democrat of 1848 became a general in the War between the States, a soldier in the Battle of Gettysburg. But German democracy did not go into exile with him.

While a dictator ruled in France, Prussia was close to becoming a parliamentary monarchy. King William of Prussia is supposed to have commented to his minister, Bismarck, that he could already anticipate, in light of the Berlin parliament, that he would end up like Charles I of England, who lost his head by decree of Parliament. Otto von Bismarck brought about the founding of a republic in France through his victory over Napoleon's army. This republic would probably not have come about without the defeat of the emperor by Bismarck, who, however, preserved the monarchy in Germany where the parliament would not reign. But he did not, as is reported, stamp upon German democracy with his riding boots.

As a soldier, Bismarck gained only the rank of lieutenant in the reserves. The Junker Bismarck was the son of a bourgeois mother and was considered by the older aristocracy as a revolutionary. As prime minister, Bismarck dethroned kings and expressed himself frankly on the subject of his own king. He was no lackey. When he was chancellor of the empire, he permitted the German parliament to vote with equality, a phenomenon that the English parliament would experience only later. He was characterized by others with his words, "It is not through speeches and majority decisions that the great questions of the day will be answered but through iron and blood." Here, he meant the achievement of German unity. It was during these very years that President Lincoln in America had to protect the Union against secession through iron and blood. The American Civil War cost more blood and iron than Bismarck's wars for German unity.

This unity was the so-called Bismarck-Empire and this German Empire in the American view of Europe was the place of middle class dissatisfaction and monarchal despotism during the years in liberal Europe before the First World War. This was also the view of Germany that President Wilson held. But this view is historically false. Ever since the American Revolution many American citizens have identified monarchy with tyranny. Of course, these existed "by the grace of God". However,the German Kaiser had fewer rights in accordance with the constitution than the President of the United States and the Kaiser also had a parliament without whose ratification no law could be passed.

The government did not originate from the parliament as in England or France. But the government of the Kaiser could not rule without a majority in congress. Bismarck was neither a Richelieu nor a Metternich. What Bismarck wanted was "that the monarchal power would be controlled by independent representation of the *Laender*". He felt this was necessary, "for even the most ideal monarch, if he is not to become dangerous to the public weal, needs criticism and this criticism can be best provided by a free press and through parliament." Even Bismarck, appointed by monarchs and not voted into office by parliament, had to gain, just like any French or English governmental chief, a parliamentary majority. This parliament was elected in such freedom and broadness that the Social Democrats, who wanted to upset the monarchy and the empire both, had the strongest representation in the congress of 1913.

Bismarck wanted to fight them every bit as much as they wanted to attack the reigning house. But in this very period in which all citizens in Europe considered the "Reds" to be the destroyers of the general welfare, Bismarck commented that, "The Social Democracy is at any rate a considerably strong indication to the propertied classes that things are not altogether as they should be." And it was this Germany that experienced a social legislation unparalleled in such liberal countries as France and England. The allegedly great reactionary of the bourgeois era of Europe was called a revolutionary by the liberals of his day because he insisted that all citizens be allowed to vote at a time when general suffrage was slowly gaining ground in England and France. Amused, Bismarck once repeated the cry of a Prussian aristocrat, "You are not a royalist but a red-spotted revolutionary." The German congress of 1900 had a more democratic foundation than that of the English House of Commons.

The German Empire, republican France, and the constitutional monarchy of England were not worlds apart at the beginning of the twentieth century. The Germans of the Empire lived much like the French and the English in a constitutional state. They were also equal before the law and its courts. The German state had like the others independent judges, a free press, a parliament, and the German cities had their own governments and policies —unknown in French local government. In the government of the empire there were more ministers who had "come from below" than in the English government under Edward VII, which was more like an aristocrats' club And for all the exclusiveness of the Prussian aristocracy, the English nobility had more power within the state and the government.

The gulf between the middle class and the working class was large. But it was not larger than that in France and England before the First World War. With regard to the middle class, Germany resembled Western Europe more and more. Not a middle-class power, the German Empire was, however, characterized by bourgeois freedom. A few years before World War I, Kaiser William II abdicated *de facto* as a result of the protest of parliament to his over-hasty remarks. The Germans were well on the way to a constitutional monarchy. They did not erupt out of the boiling pot of despotism into liberty during their revolution of 1918 as suddenly as the French did in 1789—as beautiful as this phrase still rings. Exactly the complaint that this was no revolution in the fullest sense of the word is proof for the fact that no revolution was necessary in order for Germany to take the step from a constitutional monarchy to a democratic republic.

Had there been no war and defeat Germany would have naturally developed into a constitutional monarchy. Due to the defeat and the consequences of the devaluation of all that existed, the impoverishment of the broad masses of the population, and their protest against the conditions, the Weimar Republic was too heavily burdened with the mortgage of poverty and need to effect the freedom it wished. When the French became republicans after the defeat of 1870, no Frenchman was any the poorer. As the Germans became republicans after the lost war of 1918, very many were poorer. They were not advocates of the republic. But those who blame the German right wing in the Weimar Republic should not forget that the French republic, whose beginning was much more favorable, had had a strong and hostile right wing for about a generation. In the Weimar Republic, however, this right wing was tamed after the end of the great inflation, the great social revolution, within a few years. It is another of the sometimes forgotten truths about democracy in Germany that this first German republic did survive years of heavy pressure from right and left. The English, American, and French democracies are based on the rise of the middle class. The German, on the other hand, had to be founded upon the defeat and decline of the bourgeoisie. This republic's task was much more difficult. It overcame the fact that many had lost their property, but it could not overcome the fact that millions of its people had no work.

If it were true that the Germans are born submissive subjects and favored an authoritarian sort of government by nature, they would have enthusiastically voted for Hitler's party after the fall of the empire. But only twelve deputies from the Nazi party had seats in the German parliament in 1928, although Hitler had been agitating already for some twelve years. Much has been written about the roots of National Socialism in the very German character itself and in the undemocratic nature of German history. In view of this, it is very simple to parallel the growing number of unemployed with the number of mandates of the Nazi party in the last years of the Weimar Republic. And this leads us to the truth.

It opens our eyes when we realize that a democracy can be undermined when fathers lose their property, sons lose their incomes, and millions do not know whether they will have to starve tomorrow. The fall of the Weimar Republic was the result of desperation. Millions in need listened to the demogogues, the nature and character of whom they knew nothing, since this dictatorship was a new thing in German history. Neither Frederick II nor Bismarck nor William II was a tyrant and only Frederick was a despot. He saw many of his kind on the thrones of Europe; he was not a special German appearance and German history is not the speciality of the submissiveness of a people.

In the Middle Ages, the Germans lived just as freely as the French and the British. During the Reformation they even became the first great revolutionaries for the liberty of the European peoples. They freed themselves from Absolutism later and more slowly than others because the German citizens remained weaker due to their torn and impoverished country after the Thirty Years' War than the French. The *Untertan* lived longer in Germany than in Western Europe. He lived in the Germany of the twentieth century. But he was already dying out as a type when Heinrich Mann characterized him. For, in these years, the strongest democratic labor movement of Europe came into being in Germany and freedom of spirit, of research and science, of literature and the press in the German Empire was no less great than in other Western democracies.

It is true that the Germans realized a republic later than others. It is, however, wrong to declare that German democracy has no roots in German history and is only a phenomenon of the present day. The German Federal Republic and the Weimar Republic before it do not break with the German past. They have their roots in a development that began a hundred years ago and which at that time renewed something that had already existed before Germany fell under the yoke of Absolutism. The Germans then did not discover freedom only a few years before and then again several years after Hitler.

How was Hitler Possible?

By Michael Freund

Many must have asked the Almighty, how He could have created such a monster in human form as Hitler to perpetrate his evil works. Indeed, it was precisely that utter negation in him of all normal human instincts, his flair for the fantastically unexpected, his disregard of all moral boundaries which made possible his incredible rise to power.

It would be superfluous to state that "National Socialism" was a tribulation peculiar to Germany and that other countries were not exposed to the same hazards and blandishments. Had it not been for the adventitious appearance of this extraordinary individual ,"National Socialism" would never have soared into the ascendancy—a system in which as Hitler always expressed it: "*I* am the party; *I* am National Socialism."

That Hitler contrived to insiduously reach heights of personal power unparalleled in German history was due to the mask initially donned by this machiavellian freak. Satan made his debut as a small-time German citizen. Hindenburg believed that Hitler starting as Postmaster General would perhaps in the course of time make his way up. In their 1933 plans, the wielders of power in Germany imagined that they could snare him by pandering to his vanity and appease him through the glow and shimmer of power and possession, as Shakespeare might have put it.

For Hermann Goering, these sops would have sufficed. Power, military and public prominence, landed estates and castles satiated his ego. For all other prominent Nazi personalities, the triumphant statement of von Papen was true: "We have got the national socialist Chancellor hemmed in, since the number of national socialist representatives in the cabinet was but small on January 30, 1933." Hitler proved insusceptible to the designs for his psychological "neutralization". He was convinced that he possessed an extraordinary inner power and a mission which fitted his post World War I statement: "Then I resolved to be a politician..." He claimed that an inner light illumined his erstwhile alleged physical blindness which was to be a torch for blind human groping. He was convinced that he was destined to lead his disciples to ascendancy over others. This version of seeing a "light" and the call to a mystic mission paralleled the miraculous spiritual enlightenment of such saints as Ignatius de Loyola.

In the fulfillment of his mission, Hitler was obsessed with the urge to acquire Power for military conquest to revenge German defeat in World War I—which he felt was due to errors and shortcomings. He was equally obsessed with the aim of creating a new territorial Germany through major war in the east to secure oil, wheat and the essentials for real economic independence.

Hitler's objectives were furthered by the scepticism of Germans and the rest of the world about such preposterous schemes being feasible. Although in the National Socialist party program the Jew was declared to be alien to the German people, the nature and extent of his anti-Semitism were not realized.

At a time when Germans had ceased to take any political program seriously, Hitler's program was taken with a grain of salt. Somewhere, there seemed to be a false note, but where? His announced policy objectives were so radical as to seem impracticable. So the anti-Semitic program was interpreted at the most as possibly depriving Jewry of civic rights (in the German legal sense). Whatever might be the ethics or expediency of such a measure, there was no suspicion of lurking moral monstrosity and the depravity of being made accessories to mass murder.

Napoleon once said: "The Germans are no revolutionaries; they are not sufficiently bloodthirsty and murderous." Then there appeared a German politician on the scene with the requisite murderous make-up to effect the only revolution in German history. But who could believe that in the 20th century a legally appointed Chancellor of a nation commanding universal esteem for its outstanding cultural contributions and status could be a mass murderer? On his appointment as Chancellor, many probably had misgivings; but out and out infamy could not be foreseen.

In his monumental *Mein Kampf*, Hitler stated that if a statesman perpetrates a crime, it should be on such an incredible scale that no one would give it credence. Few ever read this work and those few who had, did not believe that the patently diabolical inhumanity would be installed as a permanent political system.

An American attending a conference of the *"Evangelische Akademie"* in Tutzing (Bavaria) stated that the anti-Hitler movement in the U.S.A. had stalled owing to the sheer disbelief with which accounts of the Third Reich had been received.

The late Vice-President of the Federal Constitutional Court, Herr Katz, who was a member of the editorial staff of the *New Yorker Staatszeitung & Herold,* once told me that a detailed account was once received of the gassing in the Auschwitz concentration camp. The chief editor, in agreement with the entire editorial staff, declared he would not make himself a laughing stock by publishing such a preposterous item. It reeked of the exaggerated atrocity stories of World War I—of the corpses from which Germans were alleged to have made soap—of nuns with severed breasts—of infant's hands cut off—of priests hung up alive as clappers in belfries.

The *New Yorker Staatszeitung & Herold,* though a vigorous opponent of Hitler, declined to give this account publicity. In the 20th century, it was just not conceivable. And for just that reason it was possible.

In *Mein Kampf*, Hitler had indeed detailed beforehand how he would rise to power and how he would use that power. Today, when reading this book, one sees the blueprint prepared for a colossal war and a continental scale of organized inhuman cruelty. Of the 16 millions who freely elected Hitler to power, hardly a hundred had read *Mein Kampf*. Unfortunately for the German people, the book was heavy reading and too obscure for its content to be readily grasped. Those who did read it, or learned its contents, rejected both the book and its author. One needs only to read the reports of foreign embassies in Berlin shortly before or after Hitler's seizure of power to recognize this reaction. All the excesses and bizarre objectives of Hitler's adherents were indulgently regarded as the immature manifestations of mushroom growth. The reports of ambassadors, at times were extremely critical; at times they foresaw war, but at the worst a war on the lines of 1914, never the diabolical and unconventional war which Hitler had in mind.

Reason and good sense cannot comprehend unreasonableness; good meets the same difficulties with evil. Diplomats probably had not read *Mein Kampf*. Their press and publicity offices obtained material for their reports from public announcements and meetings. What they so gleaned seemed too fantastic, too confused and, at times, too diabolical for any reputable diplomat to take seriously. By dismissing as impossible what was announced, conditions were created for its realization.

Hitler was a past master in the unprincipled arts of lying and masked deceit. He adapted his declared policies to appeal to the majority of the German people. In external affairs, he did what this majority considered right and possible. At times, he even accomplished what wise minds considered impossible.

In Germany, the impossible piled on the impossible. As ruler of a helpless nation, Hitler arbitrarily violated the Versailles Treaty which most people believed could only be achieved by war and victory. In this, he was just lucky. While raving against the crushing terms of the Versailles Treaty, he was quick to exploit the failure of that Treaty to really cripple German potential.

A shrewd French publicist once wrote in regard to the Versailles Treaty that it was too mild for such hard peace terms. By this he meant that such conditions can only be imposed on a people if it is possible to break their backs. Potentially, however, Germany's economy was unimpaired. Within Germany, there had been no destruction. On the east, Germany was now bounded by a number of powerless buffer states. The two major powers in the east had been broken up into small and moderate sized states torn by social and nationalist unrest.

Hitler appeared to be able to achieve the impossible and the credulity of the Germans increased regarding his ability to do so. In fact, Hitler only exploited opportunities as they presented themselves. The terms of the

Versailles Treaty were too severe for a German democracy to survive, but mild enough to permit a Hitler to come to power. The Western Powers legitimatized Hitler in view of the creation of an air force—though it was founded on planes borrowed from the commercial airline *(Lufthansa)*—when they had resolutely turned down every such request by the Weimar Republic. This conciliatory behavior by the Western Powers was interpreted as weakness and made the Germans feel their defeat by the Allies was a mysterious riddle and not merited when Germany had collapsed while her armies were still on every front deep in enemy territory. It seemed as though Germany had been struck down by some sinister phantom power. The German civilian population had not witnessed the defeat. (Viewed realistically, victory for Germany would have been a miracle.) What they did know was that for four years, lacking oil, raw materials and the essentials with which to wage modern warfare, Germany had battled against five continents.

Churchill summed up the situation in these glowing terms:

"For four years Germany fought and defied the five continents of the world by land and sea and air. The German armies upheld her tottering confederates, intervened in every theatre with success, stood everywhere on conquered territory, and inflicted on their enemies more than twice the bloodshed they suffered themselves. To break their strength and science and curb their fury, it was necessary to bring all the greatest nations of mankind into the field against them. Overwhelming populations, unlimited resources, measureless sacrifice, the Sea Blockade, could not prevail for fifty months. Small states were trampled down in the struggle; a mighty Empire was battered into unrecognizable fragments; and nearly twenty million men perished or shed their blood before the sword was wrested from that terrible hand. Surely, Germans, for history it is enough!"*)

In the Hitler era, the general feeling of the German people—not to be equated with the stupid "stab in the back" legend—was that there was something odd about the events of 1918 and that Germany had suffered and lost too much. This feeling covertly gave impetus to National Socialism.

The possibility of a major war against their former victors was an idea which the Germans could not so readily accept. From the very outset, there was no enthusiasm for the war triggered by Hitler. The shock of World War I was still as profound with the Germans as with the French, whose collapse was attributable not so much to German military might, but dread of another insensate holocaust in battle.

Hitler administered the repugnant medicine of willingness to wage war in homeopathic doses—with minor campaigns and little sacrifice of German lives. Thus, he raised confidence in his strategy of a war of swift movement and lightning successes instead of the prolonged "hell of blood and mire" associated with the positional strategy of World War I. The miracle of Germany's struggle in 1914—18 against a host of enemies and

---

*) The Rt. Hon. Winston S. Churchill: *The World Crisis 1911—1918*. 2 vols., London: Odhams Press Limited, n. d.—vol. II, p. 1402.

the dismay at her collapse was overshadowed by the new miracle of the Hitler regime and accepted without protest.

Hitler succeeded by defeating his opponents of the Weimar Republic with their own weapon— the ballot box. Hitler did not come to power through civil war, force, or an advance dictator to pave the way for him. Paradoxically, this dictator became one through the very distaste of the ruling classes for civil war, force and the ruthless operations of a dictator. To every suggestion for a *coup-d'etat* to end Hitler's soaring ascent, the aged President von Hindenburg invariably replied, "I am too old to conduct a civil war." At the beginning of 1933, there was no legal way out of the governmental crisis but through introducing Hitler into the government—a participation he accepted only to get a foothold for a later chance to seize full power.

The government of January 30, 1933, was formed quite normally. President von Hindenburg conformed to convention. He asked all parties and almost all answered that only a Hitler government would be possible. It was not clause 48 (the dictatorship clause) of the Weimar Constitution which brought Hitler to power, but the extreme unwillingness of the President to invoke this clause against Hitler.

On December 1, 1932, Chancellor von Papen had evolved a scheme for provisional government without the *Reichstag* (i.e., without Hitler). It was felt that the situation was so serious that the President had the right and moral obligation to place the welfare of the nation above his constitutional oath of office. Parliamentary government without Hitler was no longer possible since no majority could be otherwise secured. On the night of December 1, von Hindenburg was even prepared to override the constitution; but General von Schleicher attacked von Papen from the rear by canvassing the "expert" views of the General Staff. In Germany, the "Expert" was—and is—almost idolized. To such an "expert", cabinet and President now bowed their heads. The General Staff had weighed in advance the pros and cons of civil war. General von Schleicher took over the cabinet, bringing with him a Major Ott—who later with the rank of General was posted as Ambassador to Tokyo. Major Ott had almost apocalyptic visions if a state of emergency under martial law were proclaimed. In East Prussia, possibly the Poles would invade. In Hamburg, a dock labor strike could cripple food imports and hunger would trigger off civil commotion and bloodshed. In the Ruhr district, mines and iron/steel works would be paralyzed. Traffic on the Rhine would cease with a risk of the Rhineland reviving its separatist ambitions.

All these forecasts were socio-political matters which the Army did not understand. A similar *coup-d'etat* was staged by von Papen's government to oust Braun in Prussia on June 20, 1932. A similar *coup-d'etat* was later staged by Hitler's government by the Enabling Act—perhaps more legally, but much more fatal to democratic freedom. Yet, none of Ott's ominous predictions transpired.

In Germany, millions were unemployed and hungered. Dissolution of the *Reichstag* for an extended period was not of the least importance to these millions. But, the cabinet recoiled from the specter of civil war because the generals dreaded it. The majority in the cabinet concurred in the attitude of the Defense Minister who recoiled from the use of force and whose ambition was to outdo the civilians in pusillanimity and fear of bloodshed.

The ruling classes were dazed by the revolutionary wave as if it were a supernatural phenomenon and seemed paralyzed like the victim of a snake's hypnotic gaze. The comatose minds of the tired ruling class were impressed by the "brown battalions" of the S.A. hordes—recruited by the lure of personal gain or the pressure of necessity—as a reflection of real power.

Grotesque as it may seem, Hitler came to power because he represented an escape route from civil war, from constitutional violation and the only legal solution of a crisis in German politics. In January, 1933, Hitler personified legality!

Hitler's movement sparked into flame late; it flared up at a time when the German people felt their existence threatened by an economic crisis for the third time—following on the Versailles Treaty and then by currency inflation. It got its first boost from these last named two crises after the termination of World War I, and in 1923, Hitler almost managed to seize power in Bavaria.

The bulk of public opinion believed the Versailles Treaty was aimed at breaking the back of the German nation. The currency inflation which followed this treaty did indeed break the once comfortable situated middle class who had possessed substantial cash savings and it brought in its wake a major social crisis. The impoverished middle class withdrew with dignity into aloof and profound bitterness—not actively hostile to the Weimar Republic but distrustful of all that was new and strange which now prevailed.

If the Versailles Treaty and the currency inflation had given the N.S.D.A.P*) impetus, it had still not given it enough vigor to survive the chaos following World War I as a major political party. After 1923, the Party's representation in the *Reichstag* dropped to a miserable figure of 12 members, making it merely another splinter political group. In an editorial office of an influential journal, much amusement was caused when a staff member suggested the national socialist movement should be watched. Then came an economic crisis and the German people again felt themselves being strangled. Germany had seen the currency inflation reduce former millionaires to poverty and wide sectors of society ravaged as by an evil blight. In 1930, economic anxiety was deeply rooted in the minds of the people. And now, Hitler's program with an alluring offer of rescue from sinister forces found appeal. In the election of September 1930, the N.S.D.A.P. leaped ahead, doubling its parliamentary representation and reaching the status of a real political factor. The existing government ex-

*) N.S.D.A.P. = German National Socialist Labor Party.

ecutive—so far as one could judge—seemed bereft of purposeful activity. What Hitler later accomplished could equally well have been done earlier. A nation with an intact production potential could have organized a public credit scheme such as that with which Hitler later financed the country's economy.

It is not true that the first economic impetus to the Third *Reich* came from rearmament—that came much later—but from a normal labor employment scheme (on no gigantic scale) which Hitler initiated and which the rising global economic recovery favored.

Minor factors and fortuitous circumstances operated to Hitler's advantage. In itself, National Socialism had no irresistable appeal. As a party, it had no traditions; no roots in German history; it was only since 1930 that it experienced a powerful and unhealthy upsurge. It had its "forerunners" both in Germany and elsewhere abroad. But, behind any successful movement, march a legion of more or less similarly oriented aspirations and, even before the Third *Reich,* there was a disgraceful extent of anti-Semitism. The overbearing Junker, who sweepingly ascribed all evils to "half-baked government clerks, primary school teachers and Jews", did not belong to the background of the national socialist movement. (So wrote Stein, correspondent of the *"Frankfurter Zeitung",* who even somewhat lamented the passing of this gnarled old type.) To be an anti-Semite in the Hitler sense required the character of a murderer. The notorious *"Endloesung"* (Hitler's slogan for the final solution of the Jewish problem) was carried out by a handful with the intent (at least) to do so clandestinely.

Hitler's outstanding talent was to parade in any costume to suit his purpose. At times, he posed as a conservative; at times, he was typically Prussian; at times, he was the nationalist; and at times he strutted as a soldier. Offering no excuse for anti-Semitism in the Germany of that period, Hitler had to conceal his brand of "gas chamber" anti-Semitism from the people.

It was not the Versailles Treaty itself which catapulted Hitler into prominence. He came up when the worst sequelae to that treaty were over. Even in his *"Mein Kampf",* Hitler stated that revision of the Versailles Treaty could be neither a foreign policy nor military objective. However, from 1933—39, Hitler had a great following of people in pursuit of his objectives of creating a "Greater Germany" and a revisionist policy to overcome the Versailles Treaty with the sentimental appeal of uniting all German speaking peoples. Referring to these policies, the British Ambassador in Berlin stated the objectives in themselves were not unworthy but that the methods employed to achieve these objectives were reprehensible.

Between 1933 and 1939, Hitler carried out schemes which were listed in the programs of all German political parties, viz., the liberation of the Rhineland; equality of status in diplomatic and military spheres; the union of Germany and Austria; liberation of the Sudetenland Germans (the German populations in sectors of the former provinces of Bohemia and Moravia); abolition of the Polish Corridor; the reunion of Danzig with

Germany. Thus, at first, Hitler succeeded by refraining from any hint in his declared policy of intolerable and diabolical intentions. His satanic power of later years was acquired by setting objectives which were not his alone but shared by the German people in general and not regarded as reprehensible. Nothing diabolical could be impugned in ending unemployment; in building the Autobahn highways; in seeking union with Austria—which the Austrian General Assembly had enthusiastically welcomed in 1918, which the Austrian President, Karl Renner, termed the realization of a life's dream; and which the Archbishop of Vienna, on March 13, 1938, greeted with *"Heil Hitler"*.

It could not be regarded as sinister in principle to campaign for the independence of the Germans in the former Sudetenland (Sudetes Mountains) since, as Hitler put it, it could not be ordained by the Almighty that three million Germans as a majority in the Sudetes Mountains should be subject to an overall Czech majority numbering seven million.

Likewise, the clearing up of the disputed issues of the Polish Corridor and Danzig separation could not be condemned. Nor could one cavil at the Germans seeking to be and act like the great powers.

Even the victorious Allies had receded from their status as victors and only defended some of the conditions of the Versailles Treaty with an uneasy conscience. It was not just the German people who elevated Hitler to power but all Europe; the German people thought no longer of their defeat, but a man was welcomed who had overcome intolerable economic conditions. If the German people did not look too closely at the means employed—not so very much removed from those common to world politics—they saw in Hitler's achievements of 1933—39 a realization of their own hopes in external affairs. What would have been an end objective for a democratic Germany became for Hitler merely a means to an end.

These targets—the union with Austria, the liberation of the Germanic areas of Czechoslovakia (Sudetenland), the settlement of the Corridor question and the re-incorporation of Danzig in Germany—were objectives which a democratic Germany would have pursued on their own merits.

Hitler conducted his campaign against the Versailles Treaty only as a preparation for a major war. He wanted to prepare for this "major war" by stages—as he took over Austria, he prepared to surround Czechoslovakia; when he overran Czechoslovakia, he held Poland in a vice; finally, he attacked Poland in order to have a springboard from which to pounce on the Soviet Union. He then turned and neutralized the West up to the Atlantic in order to crusade against the East with his rear protected. By the time the German people realized that Hitler had overreached himself, they could hardly offer any resistance. They had given a politician complete and sole power when he seemed to merit such trust. Hitler's executive program, which he used to secure passage of the Enabling Bill, did not seem unreasonable on the whole, however much objection to details might have been raised. In approving a seemingly feasible policy, the German nation endowed their Chancellor Adolf Hitler with far wider powers than were actually necessary.

Thereafter, the German people were compelled to helplessly witness the onward march of the impossible and unable to comprehend the worsening situation because of their shackles and blinkers.

Until 1939, Hitler seemed to be pursuing purely power politics as practiced by the Western Powers in conformity with their position as of 1918. What the Western Powers seemed to have forgotten was that Power as a real force is inalienable from power politics and that victory and supremacy can only be maintained by those live forces which had won the victory. Vis-à-vis Hitler, they had adopted a conciliatory avoidance of facing issues even toward a mere display of his power. A venomous snake can exist only because it is not destroyed when seen!

The German people saw in France and England two great powers—not the victors of 1918—but as they were in the pre-1914 era. Hitler, by contrast, viewed them like a hyena watching their "declining vitality" and the approaching end of these States. The seasoned diplomatic and military experts, however, regarded the flouting of important clauses of the Versailles Treaty as a grave and risky venture which, according to conventional ideas, only war could resolve and for which Germany was far from adequately prepared.

During these years, Hitler skated recklessly on thin ice. He gambled and achieved what seemed impossible. Gradually, the Germans thereby lost their sense of judgment and discrimination between sound and reckless enterprises. Very slowly, they slipped into the clutches of the demon in Hitler, until 13 years later, the ignominious defeat of World War II broke the evil spell. The demoniacal element in Hitler was as Goethe described:

> "All that seems to us limited, has no limits for it; it seems to toy arbitrarily with the essential elements of our existence; it annihilates time and space . . .
>
> This demoniacal element is at its worst when it becomes a ruling passion in any human being. In my lifetime, I have encountered many—some close up, some from afar . . .
>
> Such types can command an amazing power and exert an incredibly compelling force over all mortals . . . and who can say how far-reaching is this effect? All decent moral forces combined are helpless against them; to no effective purpose is it if human beings suspect them to be deceivers or deceived, the masses still will be drawn to them."

Summarizing, it may be said that the Hitler episode could only have occurred because, at first, he accomplished what was reasonable and necessary; he later succeeded in doing what seemed to lie way beyond the realm of possibility.

The German Resistance Movement

By Hans Rothfels

Shortly after the end of the war, the subject of this article became more or less taboo in the United States and the other Western countries. Increasing casualties in the final battles and the horrors which came to light when the concentration camps in Germany were captured caused passions to mount. Propaganda identified the Germans completely with the National Socialists. The Hitler regime itself had naturally maintained that it had the German people behind it, body and soul, in a kind of monolithic solidarity.

It is, however, pertinent that generally—Germany was no isolated example—no system of government has the absolute support which it claims. A regime may make resistance extremely difficult and dangerous, as the Hitler regime certainly did, but it cannot close all openings and loopholes. For one thing, the rivalries and struggles for power within the governing class make that impossible; for instance, the jealousy that existed between Goebbels and Rosenberg in cultural affairs allowed a measure of freedom from time to time. Even the opposition found ways of getting their views into the government censored middle-class press. If rivalries at the top enabled intellectual opponents to make use of such loopholes, limitations of totalitarian power also emerged in the middle and lower sectors of public life. They resulted from the overlapping of authority in an inflated bureaucracy, the conflict between sections of the Party, and especially between the Party and the State, enabling remnants of the old Civil Service outlook and professional objectivity to survive. Without doubt, all levels of the administrative machine felt the pressure of the party line, especially in the technical departments. There were groups of people, however, who consistently formed a tacit but effective opposition and took every opportunity to sabotage the execution of penal measures and facilitate the escape through underground channels of people marked out as victims. Anyone who was close to such events, whether personally or through the experience of friends and relatives, will recall striking examples. The "United States Strategic Bombing Survey" (1947) confirms this: "It was known to 'insiders' that there were quite active cells of this nature in government agencies, such as the Ministry of the Interior, the Ministry of Justice, the Ministry of Labor, and certain courts and prosecutors' offices, not to mention local legal services. Such persons could, and sometimes did, effectively sabotage Nazi law enforcement."

Actually, however, the Allied leaders and the Western intelligence services knew of very much more and of very much stronger opposition than such individual acts of sabotage, and, at least, in the attempt on Hitler's life on 20 July, 1944, it could not be publicly passed over. To explain an event which did not in the least fit the picture of monolithic solidarity, the Allies used the version which Hitler himself put out over the radio that it was the work of a small clique of ambitious and degenerate officers. For the rest of the resistance, the Allies held a conspiracy of silence as far as possible. American intelligence officers were the first to break it down. They were honest enough to report on the many contacts which they had had during the war with German resistance circles. After Alexander B. Maley and Franklin L. Ford, the book written by the former head of the OSS in Switzerland, Allen W. Dulles, entitled *Germany's Underground* appeared in 1947.

Much has been written about the German resistance movement in the fifteen years since that date and a wealth of material has been published[1]); even in English, there is no lack of information easily available. Nevertheless, myths and misunderstandings have survived. While in Soviet literature and writings under Soviet influence it is claimed that the only resistance to Hitler came from the communist camp, Western interest has been largely focused on the military sphere. It is argued that the senior military men willingly accepted the regime as long as rearmament offered them enticing professional prospects and victory followed victory or there was still a prospect of final victory; that signs of resistance first appeared or took concrete shape during the war and then only when the coming disaster cast its shadow before it. Resistance it was said was, therefore, only an attempt of certain classes to emerge from the catastrophe as blue-eyed boys, or as it has been epigrammatically put, an attempt to save the General Staff for the third world war.

To draw up a balance sheet which, being neither prosecution nor defense, attempts to arrive at the truth, we must go back to the years before 1939. Also we should examine the circumstances in which resistance developed during the war, as well as its composition, motivation and aims in both these periods.

First of all, regarding the actual seizure of power, we should note that as long as there were free elections in Germany the National Socialist Party (NSDAP) never obtained more than 37 % of the votes (in July 1932). Even in March, 1933, in the rigged and hysterical elections that followed the burning of the *Reichstag,* it only reached 44 %. Also the question arises as to what extent the terror and various pressures applied to force people into line succeeded—apart from the loopholes and underground channels already mentioned.

---

[1]) The present writer published his book *The German Opposition to Hitler* in 1948 (Henry Regnery Co.). It is now out of print. A revised German edition appeared in 1958 (Fischer Buecherei, Frankfurt a. M.). It has been retranslated into English and published by Oswald Wolff (London, 1961). In the United States it can be obtained from the Henry Regnery Co. A special study on *The German Resistance in its International Aspects* has appeared in "Studies in Diplomatic History . . . in Honor of G. P. Gooch" (London, 1961), pp. 348—63. Mention should also be made of the English translation of the biography of Goerdeler by Gerhard Ritter.

Of course, no statistical basis can answer this question. The plebiscites which Hitler organized with their almost 100 % votes in his favor are no evidence, nor are the questionnaires and white-washing certificates produced in the years after 1945, which showed how many people claimed to have been "in the resistance". A conclusion reached by the American Military Government is more interesting and fruitful: after examining a million applicants for employment in the U.S. Zone, it found that in 50 % of cases "there was no evidence of Nazi activity". Even if all conceivable causes of error are taken into account, the percentage of those classified as non-Nazis remains surprisingly high. A more detailed critical analysis would doubtless show that they merge by imperceptible degrees into the classes of those who were Nazis only in name, the so-called "followers", and those who conformed. However, in many cases the distinction between non-Nazi and anti-Nazi is clear and tangible. When Count Moltke, during Mussolini's visit in 1937, refused to put out the customary flags from the windows of his Berlin house in *Unter den Linden* and persuaded the other tenants to adopt the same attitude, the front of his house certainly revealed something more than "no evidence of Nazi activity".

Abstention, public refusal to conform from the beginning or at least after the blood bath of June, 1934 had fully revealed the criminal course on which the regime was bent, was in itself a form of resistance, and must be appreciated. It was easier for unknown men and women than for those who were in any way in the limelight. It was risky even for people who would not normally attract attention, and it was undoubtedly a significant sign of the regime's failure to permeate large classes of the population. It shows that there was a reservoir of strength on which the active political resistance movement could count, and did count, once power was struck from the oppressor's hands. These were people who were not prepared to accept the regime as something that could last, even if they could not rise up against the Gestapo with their bare hands. Many of them made the bare minimum of concessions, but in the ordinary things of daily life, they did not wish to depart from what common decency required.

It was often only a step from the moral aloofness of tacit disapproval to more active opposition even if this did not as yet take the form of actual political resistance. Simple human feelings and the irrepressible call of humanity led a good many to give help to the persecuted. There are many well-authenticated cases of courageous men and women who supported their Jewish friends and neighbors by hiding them or obtaining food and false papers for them. In Berlin, an organized group of this kind went under the code name of "Uncle Emil". There were both Protestant and Catholic bodies which were active in giving extensive help. Among the small number who despite everything were not afraid of making a public protest, the Dean of Berlin Cathedral, Monsignor Bernhard Lichtenberg, should be mentioned; after the pogroms of November, 1938, he himself used to pray, and he asked his flock to pray "for Jews and the inmates of concentration camps."

This brings us to the part which intellectuals, the clergy, and the Church played in early forms of resistance. Undeniably, most academics succumbed although there were from the beginning notable exceptions among scholars, artists, and writers. Nothing need be said here about those who were driven abroad or emigrated; their flaming protests against the misdeeds of the regime reached a section of the German public, too. Among the men and women who belonged to the so-called "internal emigration", by which was meant those who stood aside, were many who knew how to use the means of escape already described. A technique of "indirect attack" was devised, as for instance in the periodical *Die deutsche Rundschau,* in which articles appeared about a South American dictator or past atrocities which clearly resembled events nearer home. The great literary success of Reinhold Schneider's book *Las Casas vor Karl V* is a striking example. In it a Dominican friar, a contemporary of Columbus, implored the Emperor to put an end to the sufferings of the Indians: "Your Majesty, your people are sick. Heal them. Have done with the unrighteousness from which they suffocate." In Werner Bergengruen's *Der Grosstyrann und das Gericht,* the thoughtful reader could also see, as early as 1935, the writing on the wall. In the same year, Ernst Wiechert gave an address to German youth at Munich University in which he pleaded with them "not to remain silent when conscience bids them to speak, for there is absolutely nothing which so saps a man's spirit as cowardice."

Resistance dictated by conscience, such as he demanded, was first and foremost the concern of religious people. Members of sects such as the Quakers, the Mennonites and "Jehova's Witnesses" were among the first to adopt an unequivocal attitude of passive resistance. At the beginning, a number of factors persuaded the organized churches, both Protestant and Catholic to compromise. But the increasing pressure of the regime soon turned the underground struggle into public conflict. To the need to resist individual attacks and acts of interference was added a fundamental conflict of principle with the cross and the swastika as its symbols. Thus, the Catholic bishops and the Protestant *Bekenntniskirche* raised their voices. They protested against the Gestapo's interference and attempts to undermine the Church from within. They also attacked the substance and character of the National Socialist system itself, its totalitarian claims made in complete disregard of the sanctity of the life of the individual, its mockery of the most elementary concepts of justice, its racial dogma with its travesty of Christian beliefs, its deification of Hitler and its glorification of a community of German blood in the chosen people.

There was no possibility of avoiding this fundamental antagonism once it had clearly come to light. It was not avoided. It can be traced directly from the first appeal of the Emergency Alliance of Parish Priests *(Pfarrernotbund)* in September, 1933 to the Confessional synods in Barmen and Dahlem in the spring and autumn of 1934; on the Catholic side, to Cardinal Faulhaber's sermons on the Old Testament and the pastoral letters of the German bishops on the Papal encyclical of March, 1937. As events succeeded one another, the tone grew sharper. In March, 1935, a manifesto against racial mysticism was read from all Protestant pulpits. It resulted in the arrest of 700 clergy. The *Bekenntniskirche's* memorandum of Whitsun 1936 went even further: it said "if blood, race, nation and honor are to be raised to the rank of eternal virtues, the Protestant christian will be compelled by the First Commandment to reject such an assessment. If the Aryan is glorified, God's word testifies on the other hand to the sinfulness of all men. If anti-Semitism is forced upon Christians as part of the National Socialist philosophy, enjoining hatred of the Jews, the Christian command to love thy neighbor stands in contradiction to it." Pointing in the same way to the fundamental question for mankind, a pastoral letter of the German bishops declared: "We would like to make it absolutely clear that we are not taking a stand merely for religious and canonical rights, but also for human rights as such . . . Unless these are respected, the whole structure of Western civilization must collapse."

All this was not only preached and passed around. It sometimes led to waves of popular protest, as for instance in 1936 in the Catholic province of Muenster where crucifixes were successfully restored to the schools. Above all, hundreds of clergy and church officials suffered for their resistance and were turned out of their pulpits or offices, imprisoned or confined in concentration camps. In Dachau alone, 800 Catholic priests and 300 or 400 Protestant clergy met their death. One characteristic example is the martyrdom of Paul Schneider, a Protestant pastor. He had already come into violent conflict with the "German Christians" in 1933 and 1934, was arrested, set free and then expelled, but nevertheless returned in 1937 to his still loyal parish; that meant his sentence to Buchenwald concentration camp. There he became a heroic figure. Despite terrible ill-treament, he kept appealing, as a Catholic priest has reported, to the conscience of the S.S. guards and the Camp Commandant, shouting "I accuse you before God's throne of judgment. I accuse you of the murder of these prisoners."

It may be argued that all this did not amount to political resistance and that it did not really endanger the regime. No less a man than Martin Niemoeller, himself one of the most determined fighters, has subsequently accused the Church of not having tried earlier and more purposefully to overthrow the regime. Others, however, may see it in a rather different light. It lay in the nature of things and should not be a cause for regret that they concentrated, by spiritual protests and insistence on the Gospels, on defending their own sphere. The only way in which Christians could deliver a frontal assault on the very core of National Socialism was by complete opposition to its worldly totalitarian pretentions and its claim to control all public and private life, rather than by setting themselves against individual abuses of public power. As the Bishop of Berlin, Count von Preysing, put it in the summer of 1937: "The question is whether there is a Power, that of God, which transcends all earthly power, and whose Commandments are to be obeyed irrespective of time and place, country or race; of whether every human being has his own rights, of which no community or State can deprive him; of whether, in the last resort, man is free and is allowed to be free, or whether his freedom of conscience can be limited or denied by the State." Those words clearly pointed the way to direct political resistance, which churchmen such as Bonhoeffer and Gerstenmaier or Jesuits like Roesch and Delp followed. Outward rebellion by the Church could not have been based on religion in the same way as religion provided the moral and spiritual inspiration for the political revival.

Moreover, in the early years, there was certainly no lack of other active and independent opposition which used more direct methods and sometimes had its own philosophical background. In the first place, it is symptomatic that the number of executions, which numbered only eight in 1930—32, rose to 534 in the period between 1934 and 1939; that in the year 1936 alone 11,687 people were arrested for illegal socialist activity. According to a Gestapo report of April, 1939—before the outbreak of war and before action against foreigners was started on a massive scale—there were 162,734 persons in protective custody, and 27,369 charged with and 112,432 sentenced for political offences. These figures conceal a vast human tragedy, though it should, of course, be borne in mind that persecution does not always prove the existence of opposition and that it is not necessarily the result of opposition. The regime persecuted entire classes of people who had no political views, but it also knew where to find its most active enemies. The Communists suffered the first and hardest blows, for they lost nearly all their 4,000 officials at one swoop. They had, however, the advantage of training in revolutionary methods and produced the model for the organization of opposition cells, groups of five, which were to operate independently and did not know each other. But in addition to those formed on party lines, groups also sprang up spontaneously. In Berlin, as early as 1933, students and young working people formed one. It called itself the "Red Spearhead" *(Roter Stosstrupp)* and distributed, until it was discovered at the end of the year, thousands of copies of a mimeographed weekly under that name. Another opposition organization, which also drew its support mainly from young people, was the "International Socialist Fighters' Association" *(Internationaler Sozialistischer Kampfbund)* which was brought to trial in 1936. But the middle-of-the-road parties and those of the left, the Democrats, the Center and the Majority Social Democrats, who had been the real defenders of the Republic down to 1933, continued the struggle. Of course, their leaders had to go into exile sooner or later. The Social Democrats moved their headquarters to Prague, and then to Paris, London, and Washington. Their supporters within Germany set up an organization consisting once again mainly of young people which called itself "The New Beginners" *(Neubeginner)*. It rejected the belief, which was still widely held and was in line with Marxist hopes of a comeback, that the dictatorship must necessarily disintegrate; its aim was to form hand-picked units into a closely knit secret organization in touch with the workers in important sectors of industry. This underground work was certainly not ineffective. The result of the shopsteward elections in the spring of 1935 was still far from what the National Socialists had hoped and demanded. In Saxony, trade union circles estimated that only 50 to 60 % voted "Yes", while 20 to 25 % voted "No" and the same proportion spoiled their ballot-papers. But in the meantime, the underground workers went through bitter experiences. With few exceptions, the "New Beginners" also had to go into exile.

Despite these setbacks, secret activities greatly increased in the first years of the Hitler regime. Germany was flooded with pamphlets and leaflets. Every possible device was used to disguise this propaganda campaign and keep the distributors anonymous. But the Gestapo improved its methods and drew its net closer and closer. The working classes had to bear the brunt of its counteroffensive. The losses were heavy. In 1934, the *Manchester Guardian* spoke of the "ten thousand unknown heroes". In the following year, there was a new wave of terrorism. Observers with first hand knowledge of the work of underground parties agreed that there was too much rather than too little opposition activity in Germany. Could mass propaganda really threaten the Nazi regime, or the theft and concealment of a few weapons change the situation in a way which could justify the losses incurred? It was all very well to rub the Gestapo's nose in the mud, but such methods proved in the end suicidal. It became clear that it was more important to preserve the cells of resistance in the working classes, especially in the socialist and Christian trade unions, and to systematically train new members. Thus, a change of strategy took place from 1935 onwards, which led to a lessening of overt agitation.

The determination to resist found, however, channels which transcended the political parties and the churches, and it also took root in the middle classes. The exceptionally critical address which von Papen made to students at Marburg on 17 June, 1934, was a significant pointer. It was written by Edgar J. Jung, a lawyer and young conservative from Munich, whose associates had definite plans for overthrowing the regime, and among whom there also appear to have been men on the right wing of the Center Party and members of the People's Conservative Party like Bruening and Treviranus. Jung himself was a victim of the "Night of the long knives" on 30 June, 1934, which not only disposed of the radical wing of the S.A. but also of all possible opponents of the regime. Bruening and Treviranus managed with difficulty to escape abroad. Among those who survived was an old-style Prussian *Junker,* Ewald von Kleist. He was safely looked after by Ernst Niekisch, a National Revolutionary, just as von Kleist had earlier freed this determined opponent of Hitler from an S.A. cellar. Such relationships, which cut across all ordinary affiliations, were characteristic of the new situation. In cells active in both trade union groups and in the white-collar workers' organization, Leuschner, Jacob Kaiser and Habermann became known as leaders. Other resistance groups grew up composed of men and women from very different camps, drawn together on a regional basis or around some person like Beppo Roemer, a stalwart of the Oberland Volunteers, who early proclaimed the need to murder Hitler. Through contacts at Berlin police headquarters and the Foreign Ministry, this group received regular information on Hitler's daily movements, but their plans for an attempt on his life never came to anything. Roemer's circle included Niklaus von Halem, the industrialist, who recognized after June 30th, 1934 that only force could be of any use against the "apostles of chaos". Many other people who were later connected with the attempt on Hitler's life on July 20th, 1944 were active in these early resistance centers. When Schlabrendorff, who had very wide contacts, returned to Berlin from the country in 1938, he rightly observed that while the opposition had previously been generally copied from the forces which had existed before 1933, there was no longer any firm organization but a sort of cooperative action in which various forces were developing. There were a great many groups which overlapped with one another. The bond which held such different elements together was clearly more the unity of their moral convictions than that of particular social aims. This was true of the founding of the German Freedom Party *(Deutsche Freiheitspartei)* in 1937—38. Its first leaflet emphasized the dignity of man as the rallying point for all opponents of the Nazi regime.

Carl Friedrich Goerdeler played an especially important part in drawing together these overlapping groups. He had resigned his office as Lord Mayor of Leipzig in 1936 because he had failed to prevent the removal of a public monument to a Jewish philosopher. The industrialist, Robert Bosch of Stuttgart, then employed him and provided not only the money but—more important—the cover he needed for his travels and his extensive operations against the regime. His contacts extended to practically all the non-Communist resistance groups, and he served as contact for many of them. He was in close touch with the socialist and trade union leaders, with retired civil servants and business men, but also with officials of the Foreign Ministry, where a determined opposition group was gathering around State Secretary von Weizsaecker. He was in contact with churchmen and university professors, with foreign statesmen and foreign friends, and in particular with high German army officers, the one social group which the National Socialist Party had not found it easy to penetrate. At least von Hammerstein-Equord, Chief of Staff until February, 1934, known as the "Red General", firmly opposed all the Party's attempts. Whatever importance may be ascribed to other forms of resistance, an uprising not backed by arms stood no chance of success under the Nazi system, whether it started on the barricades or took some other form of popular rebellion; nor was there any hope for a revolution from above, whether set on foot by a conspiracy within the regime itself or by leading figures in society and the civil service. The chains of the S.S. and the Gestapo first had to be broken. That could only be done by the nation's armed forces; and there could be no question of another *Kapp Putsch.* When General Beck was first approached and asked whether he was prepared to proceed against Hitler, he replied that a change in the regime was a matter for civilians, but that if the civilian opposition took the initiative, the Army would not be found wanting.

In the light of the events of 1938, the military changed its mind, and the year before the outbreak of war saw the first real effort at military and political cooperation; it was on a much larger scale than all previous attempts. The decisive cause was the realization that Hitler was bent on war: this became crystal clear to the High Command and the Foreign Minister in November, 1937 and was confirmed by the Czechoslovakian crisis in the summer of 1938. In a series of memoranda to the Commander-in-Chief, the Chief of Staff, General Beck, expressed his opposition to the "unalterable decision" to engage in an aggressive war, which Hitler had put on paper. The following words occur in one of these memoranda: "It would show a lack of stature and understanding of his task if in such times a soldier of the highest rank only looked at his duties and responsibilities within the limited framework of his military orders and without recognizing his overwhelming responsibility to the entire nation. Exceptional times call for exceptional deeds."

General Beck urged not only technical criticism and military obstruction. The Chief of Staff also envisaged resistance in the form of a concerted refusal by the leading figures on the General Staff to cooperate in the war plan. The notes for a talk which Beck gave on July 16th show that he also expected that there would be political tension at home, and a few days later, he put it more explicitly: the Army must be prepared not only for the possibility of war, but for an internal struggle which might be confined to Berlin. Appropriate instructions were to be sent to such people as von Witzleben, the Military Commandant there, and Count Helldorf, the Chief of Police.

Here, we have beyond any question the first seeds of an organized *coup d'état,* which Beck's successor, Halder, fostered. The General Staff's military intelligence advisers believed that if the German people were made aware of the disastrous prospect of war, which was every day becoming easier to see, the intoxicating effect which Hitler's series of external successes—freedom to rearm, the reoccupation of the Rhineland and the *Anschluss* with Austria—had had on so many Germans would wear off. If it were clear beyond doubt that the regime's policy must lead to war, the Government could be overthrown. The various resistance groups which had drawn together since 1937 shared these conclusions. They not only decided to do everything to prevent a war, but they also considered the threat to peace, which was clear and must be made clear to all, as a unique opportunity of ensuring wide support for a *coup d'état.*

There is no doubt that this analysis of public opinion was correct. In September, the German people, inclined to wishful thinking and without any real knowledge of the facts or their background, enthusiastically fêted Mr. Chamberlain as the man of "peace in our time" whenever they saw him. There were other remarkable events. Hitler's decision on September 27th, as a threatening gesture but also no doubt in order to test or raise morale, to march one of the new *panzer* divisions through the streets of Berlin, was greeted with icy silence. Hitler himself experienced a similar reception when he appeared on the balcony of the Chancellery; there was none of the accustomed homage. At the height of the international crisis there were unmistakable signs of deep mistrust of the regime.

Whether the conspirators had foreseen all this does not matter. At any rate, they counted on a Nazi set back. This could, they reasoned, perhaps lead to the dictator's submission and decline. Or, if he continued on his catastrophic course, which seemed likely, they hoped to bring him to justice as a war monger. Besides von Witzleben and Count Helldorf, the two men already named by Beck who held key positions in Berlin, the Military Governor of Potsdam was won over to the conspiracy. Further, there was a *panzer* division in Thuringia under General Hoepner ready to counter any attempt by Hitler's Munich bodyguard to relieve Berlin. The technical preparations for the *putsch* would thus seem to have been sufficient to ensure its success. Its weakness lay in the assumption that the Western democracies would oppose Hitler's action against Czechoslovakia and thus reveal the increasing threat of a general war. At any rate, everything conceivable was done to persuade Britain, at least, to oppose his actions.

This brings us to the political side of the movement. As far as this existed at all, it stemmed partly from military intelligence officers and partly from the resistance circle in the Foreign Ministry. First of all, Ewald von Kleist, who has already been mentioned, went to London on August 18th on a mission for the military intelligence department. He had talks with important Englishmen and in particular with Churchill. He emphasized that Hitler had decided on war. The Generals who opposed him must, however, have support from abroad; he suggested that Britain should make a firm public declaration; if war could be avoided it would be the beginning of the end of the regime. In this talk with Churchill, Kleist went further: he said that if the Generals stood firm for peace, a new Government could be formed within forty-eight hours. The fact that Churchill, who was out of office, was prepared to accept the proposal that Britain should follow von Kleist's advice did not help much. The Prime Minister's ideas on the best way to preserve peace were different, and he made none of the statements that had been asked for.

Next came another and even more unusual step, for which von Weizsaecker, State Secretary at the Foreign Ministry, took the initiative in agreement with Beck. On verbal instructions, the German Chargé d'Affaires in London, Theo Kordt, asked for a secret interview with Lord Halifax, the British Foreign Secretary. It took place on the night of September 7th, and he entered by the back door of 10 Downing Street. Kordt made a prepared statement in the name of political and military circles in Berlin which were seeking by every means in their power to prevent a war. Its substance was that if Hitler were allowed to go on and plunge Europe into war there would be no hope of a return to honesty and decent conduct among the European nations—the door would be finally closed. If on the other hand Britain made a public declaration, war could be avoided, and the National Socialist regime would not survive such a diplomatic defeat. Kordt said he was in a position to give an assurance that if then Hitler still stuck to his present course, the political and military circles for whom he was speaking were determined on a *coup d'état.* His message ended with the unequivocal promise: "If the statement which we ask for is made, the leaders of the Army are prepared to oppose Hitler's policy with force."

While the declaration that had been asked for was awaited in Berlin, the Army continued its preparations. Chamberlain's decision to fly to Berchtesgaden on a peace mission naturally caused a setback. But in the critical days of Godesberg, when Hitler's increased demands again precipitated a crisis in the negotiations, the general feeling once more seemed to be that action would be taken. In the meantime Beck had been relieved of his post, but his successor, Halder, showed himself fully prepared to follow the course which had been set and to strike. Orders had been prepared for a *coup d'état* to begin on September 29th, which was to include the seizure of the Chancellery in Berlin. On the afternoon of the day before, the 28th, news was received that the British and French Prime Ministers had accepted the invitation to a meeting in Munich. This sensational news, we are assured, produced a shock effect on all the conspirators, and the result was that the plot collapsed.

Whatever its chances of success may have been, it certainly contradicts, as does all the other evidence of early opposition movements, the suggestion that the Germans were docile and servile and only began to resist under the pressure of coming defeat. The scope of the *coup d'état* went far beyond military considerations: its aim was not merely to prevent a general blood bath being started by German aggression; it was rather part of a determined attempt to pacify Europe and to restore understanding and decent behavior in international relations and within Germany itself. Army officers and civilian officials undertook it with conviction in sharp opposition to their own Government. The appeal for support from abroad could not have been made if a definite moral urge had not overcome all the inhibitions caused by the influence of convention and social tradition.

Similar unorthodox efforts continued until September, 1939. Warnings of Hitler's and Ribbentrop's intentions continued to be backed by plans for a military rebellion, but the most important thing was to make desperate efforts to prevent the outbreak of war. To this end men of the resistance movement made private visits to London, and secret information was also sent to the Foreign Office. Thus, von Weizsaecker warned the Foreign Office of the coming Ribbentrop-Molotov pact, which was to make war inevitable. If in the autumn of 1938 there was some hope of an agreement on a general European settlement, the opposition movement in the German diplomatic service was now driven into urging the British to successfully conclude their own negotiations in Moscow. A diplomatic defeat for Germany seemed the only way in which the catastrophe could still be prevented.

The dilemma which this brings out so clearly and which must have made the difficulties of the German opposition very much greater than those of resistance movements in occupied countries, grew more acute with the outbreak of war. Could one help to bring about the defeat of one's own country? Should one stand aside from the national war effort and overthrow a Government, however criminal it might be, when one had sworn allegiance to its head? The answer was found on different levels and in very many different ways. There were groups like that around Count Moltke composed of Catholic and Protestant clergy and extending from left-wing socialists to right-wing conservatives who were convinced that the evil must run its course, and that force, or even political assassination could not, as things were, do any good. They spent all their moral energy on planning how human rights could be restored by far-reaching political and social reforms in Germany and in a federal Europe, once National Socialism had disappeared. Even Goerdeler and those of the senior civil servants who surrounded him were busy with drafts of a new constitution and social reforms which assumed that the end of the war was approaching. This preparatory intellectual work and the consequent undermining of the regime should not be underestimated, although it did not lead to even rudimentary outbreaks. In the eyes of the Nazi court, the mere "thinking" of Graf Moltke was a capital offence.

There were, however, violent outbursts and spontaneous actions which occurred despite obvious grounds for caution. Among them was the attempted uprising of Munich students in February, 1943 by the Scholls and their friends. They could not have supposed that the pamphlets they distributed and their appeal to all university students could have altered the march of events in any way, but they were convinced that it was their duty to bear witness to the power of decency and to clear Germany's name of the crimes with which it had been besmirched, and also to help, through their sacrifices, in rebuilding Europe on new spiritual foundations. The indignation over crimes committed in Germany's name, the theme of purification and atonement, can be found again and again in the moving words of witnesses. A senior officer joined the ranks of the conspirators, confessing in a letter about the crimes of the S.S. in Poland that he was ashamed to be a German. Dietrich Bonhoeffer, a parish priest, said "I pray for the defeat of my country—it is the only way we can atone for our sins." Army officers with deep moral conviction were prepared to work for their country's defeat. Thus, General Oster, a member of Admiral Canaris's intelligence staff, gave a warning through the Dutch Military Attaché of the intention and exact dates of the invasion of the neutral countries—Denmark, Norway, Belgium, and Holland.

In other cases, it took longer before minds were fully made up. Nevertheless, the opposition in the Army was ready with plans even in times of triumph. Immediately after the Polish campaign, General von Hammerstein wanted to arrest Hitler and bring him to justice when he was on the Western front. But Hitler had his suspicions and cancelled the visit, and Hammerstein was removed. The High Command's resistance to Hitler's plans for an offensive on the Western front may have been largely based on logistics, but it was also the result of political and moral objections to further aggression. We now know that an attempt to murder Hitler figured among the designs of the resistance: the seizure of the Chancellery in Berlin in November, 1939 was thwarted by an unexpected move. On the other hand, the plan for Hitler's assassination in March, 1943 came nearer to success when a time-bomb was successfully smuggled on board his aircraft by von Schlabrendorff; it was intended to spark off a rising, but the charge failed to explode. After that a number of accidental circumstances and increasingly sharp measures to give Hitler protection thwarted several further attempts on his life, the most important being Stauffenberg's action of 20 July, 1944, which also failed because of an accident. It was unsuccessful in that Hitler remained alive and thus many people were not freed from an oath which they found it so hard to break. If these and other scruples of conscience are appreciated, it is all the more impressive that many did follow the absolute demands of morality.

While these attempts on Hitler's life were being made, the General Staff went ahead with detailed plans to take power including a provisional Government under Beck, the suppression of the S.S., the arrest of the party leaders and Gestapo chiefs and the freeing of the prisoners in the concentration camps. The necessary orders, which went under the code name of *Walkuere,* were drawn up in the Ministry of Defense and were ready at the end of February, 1943, shortly before the attempt on Hitler's aircraft. On July 20th, 1944 they were, owing to the speed of the counterblow, only partly carried out. They were most fully implemented in Paris, where the key military leaders had early been brought into the conspiracy and were masters of the situation.

From the beginning of the war, and in continuation of the efforts which had been made earlier, the many different contacts of the resistance groups with the Western Allies continued. Their common purpose was to make known the extent and the aims of the opposition within Germany and so to destroy the false picture of a monolithic Germany, sometimes by means of very detailed and accurate information. Another purpose was to obtain assurances that any government which overthrew the Nazi regime would be given the chance of negotiating a moderate peace. In this way, the wind would be taken out of the sails of Hitler's and Goebbels' propaganda that it was a war aimed at the complete destruction of Germany, and it was hoped thereby to win over to the conspiracy some of the military leaders whose attitude was still uncertain. There were without doubt still illusions on the German side about some things. Von Hassel and also Goerdeler believed for a time that the *Anschluss* with Austria and the Sudetenland could be preserved, i.e., those of Hitler's conquests which were supposed to have been justified by "self-determination". But the attempts to sound out the Allies soon became more modest and aimed at maintaining the status quo of the Weimar period. At the same time, far-reaching guarantees were to be given on the limiting of German sovereignty and in particular, its right to wage war. These approaches were made to Britain through the Vatican, through Switzerland, and Sweden. In the winter of 1939—40, they were followed up in the United States, which was still neutral, through a member of the resistance group in the Foreign Ministry, Adam von Trott, and they provoked detailed discussion in the State Department. Approaches were also made through two German Protestant clergymen, well briefed for a meeting with the Bishop of Chichester in Stockholm, who in turn passed on his information to Anthony Eden in very great detail. The correspondent of the Associated Press, Louis P. Lochner, also gave President Roosevelt direct information on the German resistance movement through a sort of "steering committee" of which high military officers, senior civil servants, and labor leaders were members. He was also given a secret radio code for use between the President and the conspirators. But the reply which Lochner received in Washington was to the effect that it would be "most embarrassing" to take any cognizance within the framework of official policy of the existence of a German opposition.

All other soundings also came to nothing. Stalin used very different tactics when he set up the so-called "National Committee of German Officers" and drew a clear distinction between the Germans and the National Socialists. On the Western side, no attempt was made to encourage the resistance movement, which was ready for an uprising and was working for one. In the end, principally because of the Soviet attitude, the Casablanca Conference decided upon the formula of "unconditional surrender" and so closed the door.

The Allies' responsibility for delays and hesitations cannot be passed over. It was their refusal to extend any hope of a more bearable, rather than a punitive peace after Hitler's fall which firmly placed the burden on the shoulders of the resistance movement itself, for better or for worse. As General von Tresckow put it, it was now a matter of risking their lives in an all-out attempt to justify themselves in the eyes of the world and before the bar of history. One of the civilians who was sacrificed following the assassination attempt on Hitler's life on July 20th, 1944, the former State Secretary Planck, son of the famous physicist, said: "The attempt must be made if only for the sake of Germany's moral rehabilitation, even if it should not result in any direct improvement in Germany's prospects in the field of foreign policy." The reply to "unconditional surrender" was an "unconditional attitude" of opposition to a regime which had brought such shame upon Germany, irrespective of the chances of success. It held out nothing beyond the hope of shortening the war and of so saving countless lives and of preventing the whole of Europe and Western civilization from sinking into the abyss which lay ahead.

This hope was also disappointed. Failure led to the liquidation of leaders whose disappearance, added to that of so many others, made irreparable gaps among those who were prepared to play their part in building up the resistance movement. But the convictions which spring from a desperate situation, the defense of humanity and the struggle against inhumanity have their own logic. Their aim is not limited to the struggle against the Nazis and is not attained when tyranny is overthrown in one country alone. In their own way, the men of the German opposition were among the pioneers in a Europe which was overthrowing national divisions and reaching out to supranational values, for which many suffered and gave their lives. It is welcome that these men should be so widely recognized by the youth of today and by the army in Federal Germany, as pioneers not only of a new Germany but also of a new human order. But it is also to be hoped that through a better understanding of their work, discussed here briefly, the world at large will be able to judge them fairly.

Part III West Germany Today

Have the Germans Changed?*

By Walter Jacobsen

Psychological assessments of the broad, postwar, political attitudes in the Federal Republic of Germany as of 1952 and 1959 (with a 1962 supplementary review).

Prefatory Note: (The approach to a collective assessment)

No scientifically precise procedure has yet been devised to arrive at a psychological assessment of political attitudes in a nation. In this context, strictly considered, "basic attitude" is a misnomer. Diverse *individual* scales of values, temperaments and opinions can be collected, which could be typed as a "group viewpoint" or a "group attitude", but a uniform basic political-psychological attitude as such just does not exist in any advanced society.

Any science dealing with precisely measurable or computable factors would reject such an unitary notion as a "national character" as nonexistent, conceding only the existence of a multiplicity of individual characters. Even such a term as "group character" would be regarded as inadmissible.**)

And yet, in political spheres, one hears so much talk of the German "national character", "mentality", "basic attitudes" (and, indeed, incorrigibility as a race) that it would be shirking responsibility for any serious mind to indefinitely turn a blind eye to such ill-founded assertions and their consequences.

This diagnostic problem should be tackled even if it appears to use "unscientific" methods—since no scientifically exact methods exists. In order to gain an intregrated totality of impressions, of necessity, reliance, then, must be placed on personal experience (including the exchange of views at conferences held on this topic); on a cross section of voluminous published material both in Germany and abroad; on a study of sociologic and psychologic studies (both equally inexact!); and on numerous discussions with political and nonpolitical personalities.

The political-psychologist—trained to correlate human beings and social trends to their conditioning psychic foundations and backgrounds—should seek to arrive at a totality of analytical results *("Ganzheitserfassung")* even though fully aware that psychology can never supply a complete answer without the risk of flirting with "psychologism". In order to reach such a totality of analytic results, the psychic factors in a political climate

*)Preprint from a new publication series on political psychology currently appearing in Germany.

**) Here, the concept of "character" as an unchangeable hereditary endowment will be excluded from consideration.

must be singled out and individually studied to assess their influential values.

The concepts "totality of impression" *("Ganzheitseindruck")* and "totality of analytical results" *("Ganzheitserfassung")* are still important evaluative criteria in individual total personality assessment, despite set psychological test questionnaires and scales. No practising psychologist would dispute that in any individual character analysis there is invariably operative an unascertainable element of subjective residuals. He can only strive to whittle down this element to the minimum using personal diagnostic experience and the accepted instruments of his profession. Even in individual analyses, the principle of judgment must be based on a complex of criteria, so that the totality of impression cannot be eliminated from consideration as one of the legitimate criteria in a collective study. With unobjectionable methodology still to be developed for collective analysis, it should be permissible to form an "overall" impression—even with hazy outlines—from a multiplicity of observations and individualized studies. Generally, it is then possible to differentiate and classify such impressions into groups according to the prominent features which appear, since neither *"Ganzheitseindruck"* nor *"Ganzheitserfassung"* imply that all observations can be reduced to one common denominator.

Collective analysis no longer lacks somewhat more precise techniques. There is the probing of representative sectors of public opinion (public opinion polls); the "group experiment" (group discussion on a controlled experimental basis); the case method of individual exploration according to definite empirical rules applied to a large number of representative subjects. One needs to very clearly appreciate that these somewhat more exact methods *alone* still fall far short of reaching what can be termed *the* dominant (or any differentially selected) basic attitude of a whole people. The results so obtained still represent only a partial aspect on which attention becomes riveted. In consequence, such a result can produce a distorted focus on certain marked traits, or a selective judgment of individuals or groups. This inherent limitation may be likened to the analysis of an individual's intellectual potential by scrupulous check against reliable tests which yield results possibly instructive in themselves but which offer little information about the total personality.

A. An Assessment of the Collective Aspects of Political Thinking (1952)

1. Inhibitions and Self-deception

The apparent public reluctance in the Federal Republic of Germany to retrospectively probe and study the psychic factors underlying political appraisal and behavior in the recent past and present possibly is traumatic in origin. Even the intelligentsia appear to have been affected by a similar psychological inhibition. The reason for the prevalence of these inhibitions is fairly obvious. In no field is the axiom of "unbiased detachment" more difficult to fulfill than in that of social psychological studies—more so since any psychological assessment is bedeviled by political factors. It is only human to avoid dwelling on painful, distressing disappointments and frustrations; on inept moves and mistaken judgments—except possibly in defensive, collective self-vindication.

If, however, a psychic trauma and its conflicts are to be resolved, then the heroic measures prescribed in psychotherapy must be adopted. Unpleasant buried traumatic material must be disinterred and squarely faced if an abiding, unhealthy "complex" is to be avoided.

What applies to the healing of psychic trauma in the individual is indicated even more imperatively in a social aggregate of national proportions. Self-vindicative arguments tend to consolidate and ramify without awareness of their dwindling objectivity. The more unrealistic such arguments become, the more extreme is the reaction likely to be when ultimately fact and fantasy collide. Politically affect-laden group thinking has triggered many a crisis. Feelings of wounded personal dignity—not merely of the individual but collectively—build tensions which sometimes find heightened expression in collective attitudes and behavior bereft of calm, objective thinking.

In 1952, it could be observed that many an emotional complex stemming from nationalist aspirations and National Socialistic propaganda—the effective potential of which is unquestionable—still smoldered. Here and there, a flare-up occurred much to the consternation of those circles which either never had succumbed to these meretricious blandishments, or had since fully realized the crass stupidity of the Nazi way of thinking. Such a renewed flare-up has more than a political significance. It has psychological interest. One needs to appreciate the psychological factors at work which will reject proven fact and seeks to surrogate worthy motives to bolster an imperiled ego. One must also concede that unsparing self-criticism of ingrained and long-prized behavioral patterns constitutes an unusually difficult problem.

2. Lost Opportunities

Conditions immediately following the collapse of the Hitler regime did not favor rigorous self-examination. Everyone was too preoccupied with pressing problems of "self"—of how to maintain the most primitive standards of life and overcome dire need. Notwithstanding these priority preoccupations, in all strata of society, an urge was recognizable to seek a reckoning with the "golden pheasants" (so-called because of the golden brown uniforms worn by Nazi functionaries). For many a misled and partially disillusioned follower, such a swift settlement with former Nazi executives might have hastened a more profound awakening. There was a general feeling that a "cleansing cloudburst" would have been salutary for morale. Possibly, had this occurred, former values would have been earlier ensconced in the political consciousness. Much protracted confused thinking might well have been forthwith and permanently corrected. Instead, confusional thinking crystallized into conflict complexes.

Retrospectively, no one can affirm with certainty whether or not Germany would have experienced a real revolution from within were it not for the presence and rigid discipline of the Occupation Forces in the crucial weeks immediately following cessation of hostilities. With very few exceptions, their absolutely impartial treatment of *all* Germans also tended to dissipate this explosive potential.

Just what psychological effect these circumstances alone had on various sectors of the population has not been studied—the effect on those former more or less staunch adherents of the collapsed regime (which claimed to have conducted a purely defensive war)—on those who had been in active resistance, or passive opposition, or hounded by the former governmental system—on those who for long had wandered in the pathless wilderness of doubt and distrust.

The multiplicity of conflicts and political effects could not be purged at that time. Probably only a sudden, profound and sustained revolutionary experience could have had this salutary effect. But this was not feasible since those held culpable and against whom such a revolution would have been directed were out of reach—mostly in Allied custody. Thus, pent up resentments found no outlet. In the main, even the misled and deluded did not realize their error and delusion. A countermovement was needed to partially compensate the crushing experience of disaster and exploitation of credulity as well as to restore emotional equilibrium. But this was not to be. These unresolved conflicts and lingering effects remained in suspense for a much later and much more complicated resolution by a purely intellectual approach. In successful psychotherapy, both mental and emotional elements are important. Here, the emotional element was missing. The "unresolved residuals" in outlook, appraisals, and ethics remained a latent virus.*)

3. Emotional Confusion

In 1945, instead of a general sense of relief associated with the overthrow of a tyrant and a resolute, unified effort to build anew, there arose a wall of mutual distrust and smoldering ill-humor concealing normal reactions. This phase can be explained partly by the specter of hunger that for many months stalked the whole country; and partly by the dire need for housing. A few months later, winter ushered in fresh trials to an exhausted people with neither adequate heating nor clothing. To these factors was added a certain repugnance felt by many Germans for the victors' occupational policies, soon to be followed by a renewal of mutual distrust arising from an individually directed denazification campaign. Nevertheless, many indefatigable workers selflessly strove for rehabilitation on a free democratic basis. Many more were discouraged by the continued absence of any beckoning prospect in spite of liberation. The persistent hostile croakings of former supporters of National Socialism seemed to be confirmed. For yet others, the long cherished hope of creating a radically New Order was dampened by the aggravating impositions which permitted only piece-meal reforms.

This phase of widespread national negativity did pass gradually but was marked by a widely prevalent shibboleth: "Politics? Count me out!"—an

---

*) Author's note—Apparently, abroad some manifestation of a spontaneous resurgence was *expected*. For instance, such a sentiment may be found in the following excerpts from the Preface for the German edition of *Hostages of Civilization* by Eva Reichmann (listed as no. 36 in the bibliography).

"... I am aware of all the reasons why a spontaneous outcry of indignation was stifled ... I am aware of the disruption of the material essentials for existence prevailing in those post-war years; I am aware of the psychological mechanisms of self-protection which are evoked when unsparing self-criticism would inevitably crush morale. Despite so much understanding, there remains an element of sorrow and disappointment. Should indifference and moral inertia—the very weaknesses which plunged the Germans into collective guilt—again taint a new Germany?"

The Preface closes on this note:

"Unhealthy factors cannot be corrected by being silently burried. To awaken awareness and to neutralize the causes were the aims of this book."

eloquent and succinct reflection of the jettisoning of ideals and pre-occupation with self and personal interests.
The direct shock effects of the overthrow of the Hitlerian military and political systems were past, and many former Hitler supporters then imagined that they could now view the past and present with aloof detachment. The manifest misdeeds of the former regime were pushed aside. The individual generally—and quite legitimately—did not feel culpable. His personal integrity seemed redeemed, particularly when he recalled many personal reservations he had had against the excesses of the National Socialists. Consequently, he rejected all the more vehemently imputations of collective and universal guilt. Still harking along the road of individualism, he resented the day-to-day hardships which he felt "others"—not he!—had deserved.
For some considerable time, the "other Germany"—which had consistently opposed the Hitler regime—had been irritated by the indiscriminate policies of the "enemy forces". Only very gradually did the Allied Powers relinquish the heedless notion of universal guilt. Good will began to concede to the German democratic forces scope for expression.

No doubt some dissatisfaction was felt by the Allied Powers because they considered the Germans were "dragging their feet" over "denazification" in the administrative services and restitutive measures for victims of past persecution. All in all, in 1952, the picture presented was one of dearth in psychological and ethical sublimation. Even at that time no *unanimously* acceptable and clear cut constitutional foundation for democratic growth seemed to exist. Whether the new constitution, framed in 1949, would have a consolidating and unifying effect on public opinion, only time would tell. At that time, notwithstanding much informative publicity, for many Germans, Democracy continued to be by no means a convincingly attractive constitutional concept.

Civic alienism and apathy predominated. The younger generation pursued an attitude of civic and political scorn. It was said at the time that they "drifted without any ideological rudder". As various random public opinion probes showed, here and there, a sprinkling of even neo-fascist and anti-Semitic elements were uncovered with a measure of public support which could not be ignored. Reactions to "Resistance", or more specifically to the abortive attempt of "July 20, 1944", were characteristic of the conflicting indecisions in judgment of a still too recent event.

"Democracy—its pros and cons—its differing constitutional patterns" and the like were subjects of lively debate approached with more confidence and objectivity. This was a feature by no means inconsistent, for it would be very fallacious to assume that democratic ideals are alien to the German mind. With the restoration of former traditional values: freedom, truth, justice, humanity, tolerance, and recognition of human dignity find general acceptance and even some enthusiasm in Germany. (Admittedly, as always "other gods"—yet to be mentioned—overshadowed these ideals.) Liberation from tyranny brought Germans nearer to the free democratic peoples of the West, and right from this juncture German willingness to cooperate with the West was widespread. The real snag lay in the emotional confusion with its conflicts and unrest which was and remained a product of 25 years' systematic nurture in the German mind. No imposed form of democracy could readily eradicate these elements of unrest and bring about equilibrium.

4. Political Party Formation to Prescription

After the collapse of the Hitler regime, the Allied Powers prematurely pressed for the formation of political parties to operate a conventional democratic system. Psychologically, the German people were just not in the position at the time to form clear-cut, well integrated party organizations. Universal fermentative thinking prevailed, but dissension did not arise so much from clash of political ideas as from a sudden complete swing from the ruins and dismay of a shattered authoritarian system to a far-reaching, new, free democratic order. As a practical issue, this pressure to form new democratic parties came much too early in the transitional stage for the civic body to orientate itself. Individual citizens were confused with the sense of compulsion and now confronted by a "*military* government", disciplinary alignment to the new authoritarianism was in itself undemocratic in essence. Instead of concentrating on the abstract formulation of ideological aims and party organization, controversy not unnaturally centered around the more fundamental survival problems, such as the policies of the Occupation Powers in dealing with dire needs, food rationing in terms of austere calorie intake, the dismantling and immobilization of important industries, and the repercussions of incipient friction between the Allied Powers; above all, the burning general problem of ensuring even an austere subsistence level. Many a politician looking ahead for a sound foundation for a future German democratic government deplored precipitate haste and would have preferred to see political parties take shape naturally. Instead, the new imported wine of democracy was filled into hastily adapted wineskins. Political orientation of the people was oversimplified. Survivors of parties defunct for a quarter of a century proceeded to retrieve and refurbish old signposts from the junk heaps and from these the population had to make their choice. These party groupings took the form of a bourgeois block having a conservative right and more liberal left wings; opposing this block was the socialist proletariat also with two wings—a moderate right and a radical left. The pattern was of course essentially democratic and eventually ready-made political "reach-me-downs" came to be accepted. The situation might be likened to a natural gushing fountain from which the waters did not flow in natural but prepared channels.

5. Outer Calm—Inner Conflicts

In the course of time, even the mixed feelings in regard to the presence of the Occupation Powers faded. Prejudice and generalizations withered for lack of sustenance. Then came the Stuttgart speech of U.S. Secretary of State Byrnes, followed by the Marshall Plan and the Berlin Airlift, all of which impressed even those nursing resentment over military defeat. Nevertheless, deep-rooted nationalist sentiments are slow to disappear and may be the explanation for the "true" motives ascribed to the former enemies. Slowly, the realization was borne out that a supranational necessity ordained a defensive pact between all those nations which prized the tenets of human freedom. For many years, however, dissension and conflicting inconsistencies continued to be the main characteristics of the West German political attitude. The reasons lay in the past saturation with National Socialism, incomplete personal readjustment even in 1952 and the psychological aftermath of a lost war.

At this stage, while catastrophic blunders were generally conceded, forthright moral condemnation of those responsible for the disaster was slow to come. Sentimental regrets at the military defeat were still keenly felt. Only reluctantly, was it now conceded that the resistance movement had justifiable grounds. Serial novels in the popular pictorial magazines reflected the urge for national self-vindication as well as the dawn of self-criticism. Some circles sought to bruit abroad the "stab-in-the-back" hardy perennial in an unfavorable, chary public mood. With little support from the radio networks, the films and publications of this time sought to assuage the deluded who had in good faith loyally backed their credulous beliefs in defense of a Germany with "her back to the wall" against a surrounding host of enemies. The moment still had not arrived to state and have accepted unvarnished facts, e.g., that the German soldier had been exploited and sacrificed to further evil designs. Even the ethics of the ill-starred coup of "July 20, 1944" were viewed from two opposing standpoints by the majority of the population. Equally conflicting were the reactions to the activities of the new Federal Republic of Germany, towards Israel, the reinstatement of government personnel released from service under section 131 of the Constitution and other issues. These conflicts all seemed to be rooted in deep resentments. They often created a war within the individual but any position taken managed to sidestep a clear decision by escape into the noncommittal.

Here again, one sees the difficulty of accurately correlating collective analytical results from external signs with causative factors. Individual conversations not confined to superficialities disclosed typical character reactions familiar to the psychoanalyst seeking to establish motivation. The individual appraisal of basic attitudes particularly in the political sphere, which the subject himself is unable to do, often can only be grasped and indirectly assessed by probing the unconscious. Proneness to lack of clarity and awareness of a basic personal attitude is marked when a nation as a collective aggregate is afflicted with a form of neurosis resulting from a calamitous course of events and culpable personal involvement. Analogous conditions prevailed after World War I, which were studied by the English psychologist W. Brown and to which reference was made at the 1947 Psychologists' Congress in Bonn in the comprehensive address by Walter Beck entitled *"Massenpsychologie"* thus:

> "Following deep depression, Germany passed into a manic phase manifested by dissociation and regression. It is necessary, therefore, that the unconscious should be reached in every individual and a sort of psychocatharsis produced which can only be accomplished by the individual himself from within."

Whereas the task of the historian and sociologist is to analyze broad currents and developments, the attention of the political psychologist should be directed at the conscious and unconscious spheres of the individual in the sum totality of events.

B. 1959 Assessment of Collective Political Thinking (with a supplemental commentary on political reorientative dynamics)

1. Psychological Ambivalency

Between the years 1952 and 1959, much evolutionary change occurred in the predominant West German group mind. The demoralized political attitudes of early 1952 had largely subsided. In 1952, the leitmotiv in political thinking appeared to be escapism from psychalgic experiences and deferment of any critical introspection to a more convenient later date for more mature historical evaluation. Seven years later, it became clear that this comforting escapism could not be pursued indefinitely although the thinking of 1952 still flourished. Incontestable documented facts, quickly given historical treatment by the press, just could not be ignored nor accepted with equanimity. Again conflict! The better self increasingly revolted at the inexcusable crimes to which National Socialism had led and the morally indefensible war policies dictated by Hitler. Yet, personal and individual culpability deriving from collective guilt was too bitter a pill to swallow. For the majority, to equate misplaced good faith and misused credulity with collective guilt, smelled too unpleasantly of disloyalty, unprincipled escape and national untrustworthiness.

Under an exterior mask of conformity, inner conflicts built up. The democratic "good neighbor" policy in human relations was quite earnestly and assiduously pursued. Material well-being improved and with it came the opportunity to entrench the Self more firmly against the unwelcome intrusion of introspection and retrospection. There were two facets to this conflict. In the one, there was sought encapsulation; qualms of conscience jarred against the sense of national solidarity. In the other, organized publicity stirred awareness of the past to contend with the ugly exhumation of symstematically interred material.

No matter how the ego sought sanctuary from the encapsulated thought-by-immersion in the day-to-day affairs of life, inner tranquility was variously and subjectively disrupted.

In many cases, it may be that the conflict persisted owing to the deep sense of disciplined decency instilled into every average German from childhood on. A revulsion of shame was felt at the realization of having slithered into utterly amoral political ventures. Tradition and upbringing had built up an almost allergic sensitivity to aspersions on the national honor. Of those, whose unquestioned alignment with established Authority anesthetized inbred values with no subsequent twinges of remorse, no analysis will be made here.

Owing to this affective clash of dual thinking, the psychological disjunction worsened. Partly, objectivity and self-examination was lacking; partly, an irresistible urge prevailed to bypass serious reflection and take the easier route of conditioned association. In a broad sense, "the easy way" lay in moving with the herd sufficiently to avoid becoming conspicuous as a nonconformist suspect. Depth psychology continued to play truant in political consciousness. In such circumstances, it is difficult to fight the urge to escape from personal associative culpability.

2. Orientation and Adjustment

At this stage, the motivation of that sector seduced by the insidious and overwhelming Nazi propaganda techniques might be considered. Despite their complexes and bifurcated psychology, with some exceptions, this sector seemingly had more or less adapted to the new democratic order. How can one explain this behavior in psychological terms?

a) Was it the Compulsion of Subordination?

Superficially viewed, external compulsions were operative. These covered certain administrative control measures, such as denazification, mass regulation, "probity" grading, restrictive promulgations and other social pressures of varying degree. No one relished social ostracism on account of allegiance to an outlawed system especially when the average German by nature is law-abiding, conformist and deferential to authority—even when it goes against the grain. Even official factual exposures failed to completely disillusion, in that they carried the weight of authority which had to be accepted rather than make it too evident that regrets were felt for allegiance to a former "official" social pattern. The old style nationalism with its hierarchical authoritarian system might be taboo. Vindicative slogans, such as the revived "stab in the back" legend were felt to be out of tune with the times. Secretly, however, some compromise between the old and new orders was not excluded.

However, such a readjustment purely from unquestioning obedience to authority is an inadequate explanation. That would be an exaggerated reflection of resignation, of a deeply resented capitulation. This resentment could well be assumed from the reactions and reservations one often heard expressed in regard to the complete surrender of rooted ideals. The nationally conscious German does not so readily abandon old "gods" in whom his forefathers believed and which had become essential elements of his world. Fatherland, duty, obedience, discipline and order, national honor and prestige, sacrifice and heroism, faith and fidelity, "the German way of life and thought", sentimental conviction (now looked upon somewhat askance abroad even though not unworthy in themselves) were to be "traded in" for freedom of human rights, democratic sense of duty, humanity, equality of status and human dignity, right to co-determination, civic sense, sense of joint responsibility, furtherance of peace, freedom from bias and recognition of national aspirations, tolerance, good neighborly relations, readiness to cooperate in partnership, civil courage and vigilance of social conscience. Halfhearted acceptance of compromise being easier than total rejection, a certain illusory character was ushered into the political sphere—which abroad was construed as inherent in the German character. Yet, in this compromise acceptance, there was enough good practical sense to make the most of any given and seemingly unchangeable situation without vengeful, chauvinistic or revolutionary thoughts.

Consistent with this attitude, came economic adjustment to altered conditions in order to build security for the future on rational bases. Following a more secure economy came somewhat tardily the cultural development on the principles of a free society.

Still later and more slowly, followed awakening to the democratic ideologies underlying state and society. While formal acceptance was generalized, deep conviction and faith was still lacking. For one sector of the people, this democratic ideology remained an acceptable solution with no better alternative—an imposed system rather than a hard won prize of faith and conviction. The acceptance of such a compromise was appreciably promoted by unfavorable comparison with constitutional/political developments behind the Iron Curtain.

Summed up, this political-psychological orientation had the character of gradual acclimatization—a transitional phase never free of adaptive difficulties. A psychological "hang-over" from the past is liable to arise with ambivalent manifestations. Rearmament—heavily discouraged for 7 years—was a subject that chafed many such sore spots and raised debatable ethic issues. The complex reparations and restitution issues and the reinstatement policies of former officials also raised fundamental political clashes of internal rather than external origin.

These chafing points since seem to have lost their sensitivity, but it would be rash to predict that they are permanently healed and that psychological splits are dead. It is difficult to eradicate such catastrophic, deep-rooted rankling in those of a generation who have had these experiences directly; but, looking back, the West German realizes how successfully and resiliently he has survived the crushing moral and material effects of military defeat and unconditional surrender, with worldwide unsparing moral condemnation. Today, West Germany has a world status rated so high that residual wounded nationalist sentiment has been assuaged.

b) Reorientation

Despite unquestionable gains in new stimuli and experience from the 1945 planned psychological campaign—mainly from the U.S.A.—the impact on Germany was not altogether happy. In part, perhaps this was due to a lack of psychological adaptive preparedness, but heavily influenced by the not unnatural psychological resistance by a people with internationally esteemed cultural and scientific attainments, nationally humiliated and subjected to a "foreign educator". Notwithstanding this inner resistance to the unpopular "re-education", no one can claim that the American effort to orientate the German mind towards prevailing democratic sociologic and psychologic ideals completely failed in its purpose.

3. Impulses for Slow but Genuine Change

Factual Confrontation

There were a number of factors which took much of the wind out of the sails of lingering staunch disciples of the "Hitler Mission". More and more incontestable testimony accumulated from eyewitness accounts of the notorious concentration (extermination) camps at Auschwitz, Buchenwald, Belsen, etc. Secret ministerial directives of the Third Reich appeared in published form in bookstalls. Broadcasting networks ran serial programs on parallel lines. Illustrated magazines featured similar themes in serial version. Film producers brought out a series of films with purposive motifs such as *Duell mit dem Tode, Canaris, Des Teufels General, Fuenf Minuten vor Zwoelf, Der Zwanzigste Juli,* etc. In many West German schools, the *Diary of Anne Frank* was read to pupils by teaching staff; others visited the theatrical production of this book. The Press gave prominence to such judicial trials as those of the sadist executioners of the Era of Secret Horror—Schubert and Sorge. Against such a mass of overwhelming and incontestable testimony neither condonation, circumstantial extenuation nor any brand of sophistic counterarguments could stand up.

Fractional Rebellion

Both from the psychological and political angles, it is interesting to speculate on the background of the scattered stubborn citizens who risked secret meetings, issued leaflets, etc., in allegiance to rooted beliefs. The psychic aspect is difficult to generalize with certainty. Politically, despite its very limited existence, such resistance cannot be so lightly dismissed because of its inherent psychologic "virulence". This attitude was not confined to the few who manifested resentment. It affected many who subconsciously still clung to traditional ideals of "discipline and order, blind obedience, national prestige, etc.", as essential elements of true patriotism.

The transition from nostalgic retrospective and illusional thinking to realistic current patterns of responsible democratic thought was very fluid indeed. It was difficult to assess how many converts to the new way of thinking were stable and how many unstable.

With so much assiduously concealed and much else instinctively left unspoken, it is difficult at any time to probe the subliminal consciousness and as difficult indirectly to evaluate. Possibly, deep psychological analytic methods could delve into the subconscious and uncover some criteria for the ethical bases conditioning the broad political attitude. What has been termed a "Group Experiment"*) is a useful step in this direction.

Pressure of Public Opinion

To a great extent, what can be regarded as the general attitude reflects the prevailing publicized patterns of thought and evaluation with only minor deviations in shading. These prevailing patterns were influenced by current political and economic factors as much as by their interpretation by publicity media. What the individual personally felt or desired, generally, was overlaid by the force of public opinion, so often presented as ethically justified. Even in the most liberal democracies, the twin forces of authority and majority are not easy to oppose.

How these twin forces influence public opinion in the Federal Republic of Germany can be gauged by studying a cross-section of various sectors of the press, political party literature and even official releases.

Socialogical Aspects

These external pressures operated not merely as an approved public norm but also as a compulsive corollary to altered sociological conditions. These

---

*) See Bibliography No. 35.

sociological conditions prevail in all highly industrialized countries and might be succinctly termed the "impact of the masses". Two publications*) are particularly apt in this context.

"The old order changeth yielding place to new." Family ties loosened; the sheltered security of rooted traditions and foreseeable workings of less complicated patterns of life were crumbling; urbanization and industrialization were advancing apace. More than ever in this increasingly regimented economic order, the individual was thrown upon his own devices while exposed to higher socio-economic standards and pressures than ever before from a de-personalized environment which goaded him with diverse urges and compulsions. To swim with the stream; to keep pace with others generally; to escape the disgruntled sense of ostracism—these became priority values. Conformity and personal realignment even invaded leisure time with new technical diversion media; "to keep up with the Joneses", automobile excursions became a widely cherished objective. Under these influences, extroverted preoccupation crowded out introspection and independent ethical evaluation. All of this combined with the constantly increasing tempo of the drive to build a conventional pattern of democracy in postwar Germany as then outlined by the most influential molders of thought.

This socio-economic trend prevails in all industrialized countries but its politico-psychological repercussions in Federal Germany were somewhat more complex than elsewhere. In Federal Germany, these effects were traceable to the profound influence—notwithstanding a mixed reception—of liberation from totalitarianism.

Until 1945—and for a few years to follow in milder form under the Allied Military Government regime—a dictatorial bureaucratic system had kept the people on tight reins. Under such conditions, no natural sociological evolution has ever occurred in a democracy. The enforced conformity over years reached so far into personal lives that even forms of verbal expression were subject to monitoring. After liberation, freedom for independent personal ethical decision brought a radical change from the former uniform pattern of external attitudes. With the new slogan "Dictatorship is out" came an expectant attitude as to what democracy would really mean. In this confused psychological state, there was a burning desire for freedom of self-expression and the right to call a spade a spade. With this constant yearning, the failure to better utilize the freedom for self-assertive aspirations has been commented on as remarkable by German sociologists. The self-surrender to prevailing political and economic policies, the lack of manifest initiative in the cultural field and the adverse effect thereon of commercial and conformist considerations—all these features have been criticized. The great initial enthusiasm with which freedom of free individual thought was greeted now seemed to find expression in the direc-

---

*) Walter Ehrenstein's book (No. 9 of the bibliography), published in German as *Daemon Masse*, might well have carried an English title—"The Herd Demon". It deals with the "fellow traveler" problem of the Nazi era.

David Riesmann's *The Lonely Crowd* is based on an extensive demographic-sociologic-psychologic study of rising populations and the impact of advancing technology on economic life.

Hofstaetter, in his *Gruppendynamik*, expressed the view that instead of the directly translated title, for the German reader "The Uneasy Masses" would have been a more apt translation.

tion of personal welfare and not in political or ideological channels. The feeling of the man in the street was that he had no real voice in affairs or policies—which, perhaps, was a residual hesitancy from the dictatorial regime and a reluctance to personally venture into politics. When one is to a considerable extent materially secure after much widespread privation, there is an understandable unwillingness to take chances. The average man in the street preferred to let evolution take its own course. He was more inclined to make any necessary personal adjustment but leave the direction of affairs to their freely elected representatives with the right of expression and to the influential democratic agencies. So long as the economy flourished, why worry?

This distant attitude did not exclude some who felt scepticism and exercised some inner self-criticism, but it had no positive or tangible effect. Many Germans felt dissatisfied with the compulsive conformist influences which affected practically everyone. Secret resentment was felt at the reappearance of externally enforced alignment—even if now manifested without force. In these, there was a wish that the citizens would show more political consciousness, engage more actively in politics and generally manifest more political maturity.

There were others who were nonconformist for other reasons, who rarely gave expression to their views. Their opposition was based on the "weakness" of democracy in comparison to their preferred more forceful authoritarian system.

Both the elements mentioned in the previous two paragraphs, if they could, would have altered the seemingly inevitable direction of sociological evolution. Their comparative potential force was hard to assess since it was not merely a matter of tangibly existent quantitative and effective strength but the uncertain extent of subliminal and suppressed factors.

Characteristic of this evolutionary stage of the young democracy in 1959 was the considerable degree of general conformity with changing times and sociological conditions. After what has been perpetrated politically in Germany and beyond its frontiers, it might be inferred that the urge to come to terms with oneself was weakened in step with this trend.

"Reappraisal and Reorientation" as Self-educative Factors

That complex stated in the subheading above and so vaguely expressed in German as *Aufarbeitung*—which became reduced almost to a degrading slogan—needs the consideration which now follows. At this point, what is decisive is not whether such a personal stock-taking was seriously pursued; what is decisive is whether or not sufficient opposition was shown to the attempts at doctrinal revival by hardened disciples of an erstwhile antidemocratic system.

Many pedagogues, politicians and journalists endeavored as much as possible to impress on the German mind the complex concept of "Reappraisal and Reorientation" of past happenings. Certainly, in many cases, this endeavor bore fruit. Here, one needs to differentiate between an older generation with personal recollections and experience of the past two decades and a rising generation who were to judge analytically and evaluate past events from hearsay knowledge. Viewed overall, the willingness of the German citizen—quite apart from inherent capacity to do so—to unsparingly and dispassionately review all that transpired in the name of Germany has not been particularly marked. The Hitler regime and the World War II were regarded as nightmares of the past and—like such ugly dreams—mostly not analyzed. The distaste for a rigorous "reappraisal and reorientation" as well as the urge to seek personal sanctuary, or to regard the issue as one of fundamentally individual vindication predominated. Shirking this issue cannot be dismissed as a mere willful avoidance of facing a painful personal or national "conscience court". There were three potent motivations. First, the human tendency, in itself healthy, of erasing depressing recollections from the memory—and here, a distinction must be made from a deliberate, secret thought burial with which forgetfulness later can also be associated. Second, the immediate postwar period was one when personal survival and material rehabilitation were far too pressing to leave time for reflection. Third, there prevailed the feeling that it was pointless to look backwards, to shed tears over spilt milk; what was done had been done and could not be undone; to work out a sounder future seemed more important—particularly with new political problems to face. Critical politicians, however, feared where no honest will to confront facts and come to terms with oneself about the past existed, some doubt must linger as to a possible relapse in basic political attitudes. Expressed in psychological and psycho-therapeutic terms, it would be termed a latent susceptibility to any dangerous stimuli—including political seduction by a demagogue, arising not *from* but *on account* of widespread political indifference. Only a few of the naive Nazi "fellow travelers" could appreciate that it was just their political inertia and blindness that had helped to put National Socialism into the saddle, by succumbing to the most primitive sophistry, even if skillfully couched.

In itself, the mere silence of those who regarded the forceful talking of Hitler and the authoritarian principle as the salvation of Germany and the cessation of hostilities merely as a German military defeat was no guaranty of the permanent permeation of democratic thinking. But, it can be regarded as a welcome indication of gradual maturation. Political maturity is known to be a slow process!

"Reappraisal and Reorientation"—Its Connotation?

The German term is *Aufarbeitung* and no excuses are offered for this rendition. (If a better rendering comes to the mind of the reader who understands the implications and workings of this expression, it can be freely substituted.)

This concept had no uniform connotation in Germany*). Some understood the term as a rational cognitive process of scrupulously factually reviewing past events of what transpired prior to and during the Hitler regime. In conformity with this interpretation, it was felt that if happenings of this period were viewed with sufficient objectivity, valid assessment and

*) See No. 2 of the bibliography.

assimilation would follow. In this process, good and evil were to be allotted their rightful places with an unsparing presentation of individual and collective involvement. From such an objective recapitulation of facts, an inner "reconditioning" would follow which would make a new beginning possible with an easier mind. The disingenuous attitude of "Let's forget it all" without an honest self-appraisal was banned. It was believed that once having met the moral obligation of a spiritual stock-taking and being satisfied that all had been done that could have been done by way of restitution, then the past could be finally and justifiably forgotten.

Another school of thought gave this term a more extensive and divergent interpretation. In their view, the rational cognitive process and factual recapitulation were only an obligatory preliminary stage. The *essential* element of the process was that having reached a corrected perspective, it be constantly held in mind what had transpired in Germany and what had been perpetrated by Germans. This view implied that assimilated material far from being erased should be consciously kept alive in the memory. It could be said that this attitude met an emotional conscience urge and also paved the way to a rational discernment of practical politics.

To try to express the emotional element in words, one must refer to the sense of overwhelming helplessness in the knowledge that no adequate amends could ever be made and the humiliating thought that history would record that it was in the name of the German people that such organized, massive scale crimes had been perpetrated. Not to be omitted from this context was the oppressive thought that other nations could never forget the chronicles of history; that as human beings a "cultured, well-bred" people had failed in a fundamental moral obligation by tacit consent, or turning a blind eye to the evil works and instincts of an oligarchy.

In practical politics, to bear in mind the lesson learned from the past had the virtue that an awakened national consciousness would sound a timely warning against any future, smooth-talking political demagogue and the subtle techniques of misrepresentation and suggestion. This was as necessary for the older as for the coming generations. Even in 1959, one heard references to "the Specter of Manipulation from above".

If the second more comprehensive view was not particularly marked nor widespread, the cause lay in a number of simultaneously operative "resistance" factors. These could be enumerated as: deliberate escapism—natural blunting of the memory—readaptation to a new political environment—orientation towards the future rather than the past—the lure of tranquility—a pace of life which left no time for reflective thought—the affective repugnance for anything depressing and the pragmatic pointlessness of retrospective thinking.

Escapism in Two Phases

In the first phase, facts as presented were rejected on the ground that they were utterly inconceivable and incredible. Such an acceptance would have struck at the very foundations of the whole edifice of faith and cherished beliefs.

When the revelations proved too overwhelming to discredit, then came the second phase when the individual sought to personally alienate himself from the machiavellian activities of the former regime. The "fellow traveler" sought to whitewash himself by disclaiming any personal responsibility for what had transpired.

This autosuggestion of disclaiming any personal responsibility was not always subjectively quite convincing. Such deliberate escapism often left residual doubts which were very deleterious and carried an inherent risk of neuroses in individuals with a sensitive conscience.

Between these two phases of escapism, recourse was frequently had to familiar dialectic vindicative or circumventive arguments to still the inner conflicts of ambivalence, to justify Self, or even to shift responsibility elsewhere. Some examples were: "Where wood is hewn, chips must fall" (a German proverb)—"That is certainly boundless exaggeration"—"Our critics are no better . . ."—"It was a matter of Germany's very survival"—"Intentions were good, but resources failed and sabotage was at work"—"Abnormal situations call for abnormal measures"—"Excesses and abuses exist everywhere"—"Those who were 'persecuted' had themselves to blame", etc.

Those who were content with such conscience salves shirked any real confrontation with conscience. The conflict with moral issues offered the choice either of accepting a share in collective responsibility and renunciation of any evasive maneuver; or, to resolutely suppress all thoughts touching this unpleasant theme.

It is perhaps characteristic of this two-phase escapism that in the years immediately following the cessation of hostilities, it was remarkable how seldom one heard reference in conversation to National Socialism, the Third Reich, a lost war or persecution of Jewry. If mentioned at all, the topic would be hastily changed. These moot points were subjects more suitable for public addresses, the press and radio. Quiet reflection is more profitable than disingenuous social interchanges.

Analytic Evaluation of Escapism

As a rule, pulling a shroud over awareness of the recent past did not lead to neuroses, partly for the reason that a certain supportive comfort was gained from the widespread incidence of this condition and, partly, of the very gradual acceptance of truth and facts.

Escapism stemming from fear of disillusionment and the demolition of cherished ideals could be due quite as readily to a hypersensitive as a blunted conscience. This differentiation is important in any true evaluation. It is the hypersensitive who, when profoundly shaken, least manifest their inner abasement. Their reaction is much more likely to take a diametrically opposite direction manifested by unapproachableness or indefensible opposition and factual contradiction. It is this factor which caused many an emotional storm when children questioned their fathers too closely about the past. Another factor in evaluation is that during the course of the 15—20 postwar years, the pace of spiritual and psychological maturation had so quickened that it was honestly difficult in many cases for the individual to recognize and identify his wartime self. This was not just a matter of natural or "convenient" forgetfulness, but rather in the nature of a psychological "blackout". Years later, to these individuals, the whole wartime scene was as unreal as the paralyzing termination of war in unconditional capitulation.

These factors supported those who sought escape and hampered the process of "reappraisal and reorientation" in those more accessible to this approach.

The Angle of Political Education

The preceding paragraph brings out certain inferences affecting political education.

The first phase of escapism, i.e., of rejection of facts, was successfully combated by the unsparing publicity campaign. The mission of disillusionment might well be said to have been fulfilled. But, with the escape mechanisms of the second phase well advanced, there lay a certain hazard of defeating the purpose of "reappraisal and reorientation" by excessive dosage of "disclosures".

Once having conveyed conviction of factual material, the chronicler of history is no longer competent to deal with the situation. At this stage, an experienced psychologist of political maturity is needed to ease the inner conflicts of the "convert" and assist him in reaching a rational poise without loss of human dignity.

The sequel to *Aufarbeitung* was a general tendency to seek an explanation for the course taken by events. While such a "probe" into the past is a very reasonable course, it mostly tended to seek *material* causes and miss the element of contributory negligence in ethical evalution of *personal* motivation, behavior and attitudes. This self-examination should have had a prominent place if political awakening were the objective. Had it been extended to the entire people, not merely to old supporters of National Socialism, possibly the psychological results would have been more gratifying.

Here, only the psychological aspect is of interest in providing a key to motivation and decisions of the individual as a unit of society—be they of autonomous or heteronomous origin. Psychology is not concerned with politics—which is the interest of political science and sociology. Thus, the Versailles Treaty, the German unemployment crisis of the 30's and similar political events are only factors for consideration insofar as they influence behavioral patterns. The same limitation applies to the unorthodox and nonconformist intellectual trends prevailing during the existence of the Weimar Republic.

b) The Irrepressible Adolescent

(Resurrection of Psychologically Interred Material)

In the last few years (preceding 1959), a second factor exerted an increasing influence on the attitudes and behavior of the West German. This was the gradual approach to adulthood of a rising generation with no personal experience of that which had brought Germany into so much discredit. Their search for knowledge and understanding constantly exhumed interred thoughts in the older generation. It is not suggested that this searching and agonizing catechism of fathers, uncles, and teachers by the rising generation found uniform expression. Studies carried out*) showed that all shades and angles of enquiry stirred the adolescent—serious political interest in the past, present, and future in a genuinely democratic ideological sense—a stirring of responsive interest sometimes superficial with only formal democratic adaptation—diametric extremes of utter indifference—blunted conscience—apathy—irresponsiveness or sheer mental inertia—up to deliberate rejection of anything having to do with politics. The background to these attitudes can be studied from special studies made. The adolescent attitudes gaining ever more vocal manifestation were not just lacking in uniformity but actually conflicting. On the extent, slant and impressiveness in school treatment of recent history and the approachability of adult relatives depended the effect and trend of enquiry as to adult personal involvement.

"Resurrection" had one common feature which press and radio campaigns did not disclose. The radio could be turned off; printed matter could be put aside; but the personal approach could not be evaded successfully forever. Youth sought to reach a personal assessment. This search by youth directed at parents and teachers sparked conflicts and discussions which had long been absent. But, the insistence of youth in no way corrected adult ambivalent thinking—perhaps, only hardened it.

Here, it should be noted that, in general, the adolescent curiosity was not directed at "fellow traveling" but, knowledge of Nazi tactics gained from press and films, prompted the blunt query "How on earth could you be taken in and accept such charlatans?" It was less downright reproach and condemnation of intimate cooperation with the Nazis and far more a silent rebuke for lack of resistance. Sons and daughters were torn between natural bonds of affection and a critical alienation from their elders. Not surprisingly, some—not great numbers—took up arms in defense of National Socialism and opposed current ideals or even formed groups with romanticized concepts of national socialist ideals.

What Can We Expect of The Younger Generation?

Broadly, the younger generation claimed to be free of all shackles; politically, they were convinced they would not be so easily misled as their elders appeared to have been. A touch of supremely confident omniscience perhaps belongs to this age. They have no personal experience nor conception of the manifold subtleties of political subversion and can only recognize certain familiar set patterns from the past. Nevertheless, they are better equipped basically than their forbears with an awakened democratic consciousness. The will and endeavor to adopt a healthy practical approach should be the decisive factor in meeting any future political perils.

---

*) See Nos. 14 and 27 of the bibliography

Psychologists who have made studies of youth have conflicting views of their future political leanings. It might be wisest to remark that despite this conflict of reactions, a diagnosis cannot guarantee a prognosis.

c) Prosperity Overshadows Political Consciousness

The rapid growth of self-awareness in the mentality of the German people since the cessation of hostilities was promoted by two major external influences.

The proverbial industry and skill of the German ushered in economic recovery within an unexpectedly short time—an achievement of collective effort of which the citizen could be justly proud. Those who thought more profoundly qualified this achievement by recognizing the unquestionable forward thrust given by Marshall Aid.

The country's prosperity was shared by practically every citizen so that material anxieties for self and family were banished. The individual was stimulated to yet greater personal achievement, leaving apparently little time for abstract ideals. Even interest in their fellow countrymen across the border in the German Democratic Republic and the reunion of divided Germany was one of detached sympathy but concern. East-West tensions were viewed with apprehension. Some criticized this generalized attitude as "materialistic", "sybaritic", "superficial", "boom complex", etc. Such pejorative labels imply a moribund desire for higher values, but such appraisals are much too facile to be valid.

Making the most of prevailing prosperity does not affect the philosophy of life. It does tend to inhibit, in some degree, all urges not activated by sheer necessity and lying dormant in some incalculable measure. The problem with which political psychologists and pedagogues are faced is not how to counteract the seemingly materialistic philosophy of life but, rather, the discovery of what political ideals are hidden behind the facade of apparent pragmatism; whether these ideals still conform to the aims set out in the Federal German Constitution, whether the much contested worldliness now invading religious life really represents an hedonistic apotheosis of Mammon or a serious spiritual quest for a more approachable anchorage than those which frustration and confusion cannot negotiate.

The common characteristic of external behavioral patterns in West Germans is to seek what seems comprehensible and attainable. In grandiosely couched programs, fair promises, noble but impractical objectives, as measures for creating an utopian world, there is no interest. The West German is more realistic and in tune with the times—indeed, if one is so disposed, this can be termed more extroverted.

The foreigner visiting the Federal Republic of Germany would observe an externally conformist behavioral pattern which does not match the deeper lying political attitudes. Traditional German basic attitudes are not altogether effaced, but that economic prosperity has contributed largely to a change in the mentality of the people is a point which cannot be omitted.

d) Prosperity in Jeopardy Revives Political Consciousness

Self-awareness, politically, has also grown in Federal Germany, compensating for some inferiority feelings stemming from the time of the capitulation. The present firm political position and self-awareness which came almost overnight was a surprise for the Germans themselves. To be in alliance on equal footing with a former enemy so quickly was never expected. Here was a nation forced into unconditional surrender, its machiavellian leaders brought to justice by the law courts of the victors, within a decade or so welcomed as an important ally and ranged in the front rank against an adversary termed by the Nazis "Enemy No. 1". To achieve this position, to even be financed by former adversaries, makes it clear that Germany must have made adequate amends and won great confidence.

Still less was it expected that West Germany would hold a key position geographically in the Cold War and that Federal German reactions—whether official or merely popular feeling—would carry international weight.

The universal condemnation abroad of the German people collectively soon became silenced. No longer was there any pressing need for self-vindication. The alliance with former adversaries was not based on sentimental affinity or natural bonds, but, on the expedient necessity of uniting against a common danger. It is no wonder, then, that despite close political, economic and military association, from time to time press and unofficial utterances abroad indicated that residual reservations about the Germans remained. Such situations particularly chafed those Germans who had given the least thought to the causes of such misgivings.

Aside from those factors adversely affecting Self, what could jeopardize practical action and political viewpoints was the continuing problem of divided Germany. It was a problem of ever increasing importance with a new and growing political and sentimental content. The carving up of the *Vaterland,* the increasing alienation from close relatives still across the border was a festering sore. Admittedly, there was still a lag in democratic purposful techniques. In regard to the profound stirring, one saw relatively little active political participation or demonstration, because it was generally felt that politics remained the field of the politician. A progressive democratic orientation in this respect can be awaited from the next generation since more thorough grounding is being given in the schools for civic and political consciousness. In the older generation, a certain indifference to positive action and a preference for conformity to public opinion remained. There was also a feeling that no serious risk of any communist propaganda infiltration existed. Almost every West German citizen felt, at the moment, a democratic system was preferable to another dictatorship—this time from the left. In the Eastern Zone, the dictatorship regime was an educative experience for many who were not otherwise politically-minded.

e) Memory and Blacking Out

It has been said that oblivion from oppressive memories is a natural human protective mechanism which is regenerative and helpful for further healthy psychological continuance. But, the coin has a reverse, politically negative side. Oblivion assumed that outside Germany similar thought processes and motivations were operative,—in countries and nations which had suffered from former German aggression. There, a certain dread lingers. The German is tagged as "sinister" and "dangerous", and he seemed all too soon to have forgotten the past. Against this irrational apprehension comes the rational argument that such anxiety is now unfounded. When with foreigners, the German is rather apt to forget that what he has long put behind him (and reciprocally expects), is liable to create a false impression in the foreigner.

Brief Supplement as of 1962

Confrontation with unpleasant truth has continued since 1959. Such films as the Swedish production *Mein Kampf,* the Eichmann Trial in Israel, intensified follow-up of accessories to Nazi crimes, circulating exhibitions such as *"Die Vergangenheit mahnt"* (Reminder from the Past), and *"Das Dritte Reich"* (The Third *Reich*) as well as more historical publications were contributory factors. Even the adolescent "inquisition" had progressed, triggered partly by films, judicial trials, radio and television programs and other publicity media, partly by intensified history teaching policies in schools.

Lapse of time promotes nonaffective thinking but suppresses the duty urge to critical self-examination. Current external hazards assumed more importance and since 1959 have been an important factor in the awakening of political awareness in the West German. At the same time, internal incidents in Federal Germany caused much upheaval. For example, around 1959/60, there appeared to be a sporadic revival of anti-Semitism which—though not confined to Germany—caused considerable alarm everywhere.

These incidents were thoroughly investigated[1] and assessed[2] as unorganized, sporadic egotistic excesses of immature youth designed to excite a psychological point in Germans. This was not a very false judgment of a sensitive spot, but proved to be a complete failure in reawakening race hatred as inculcated by the Nazis. These incidents did at least show that if the racial problem be not completely eradicated, any attempt to incite the people failed miserably.

The effect of these isolated demonstrations was that the Association of German Students held a one-week conference early in 1960 in which competent authorities were requested to furnish still further clarification about Jewry for the political evolution of the people.[3]

There remains much to be desired in the firm plantation of the free democratic attitude in the population to meet future contingent crises. For a deep conviction, not only systematic political education but more initiative is required. And this applies equally to a sector of the university/professional student. As the Frankfurt/Main Sociological Research Institute states[4], the "authoritarian potential" is quite marked in the strong governmental system appealing to the people.

---

[1] See No. 41 of the bibliography.
[2] See No. 23 of the bibliography.
[3] See No. 44 of the bibliography.
[4] See No. 14 of the bibliography.

That, in general, a desire for peace exists in the West German is hardly necessary to stress, since no one could have a deeper dread of a third World War. In this context, one hears too often—"rather suicide". No illusions exist about the survival of the German people if a clash between East and West should really occur. The German seems to have become a pacifist of the type that will not permit himself to be steam-rollered and has a horror of subjection once again to a compulsory totalitarian indoctrination.

Anti-Semitism in Germany

By Erich Lueth

The history of the sufferings of the Jewish people in the Third Reich cannot be understood unless German anti-Semitism is traced back to its roots. The story of persecution during the short-lived Hitler regime is without doubt one of the most terrible tragedies in the history of man, but what happened from 1933 to 1945 is no more than the end, the final act, of a long passion.

The dread warning of the gas chambers and crematoria is written in fire and smoke into the skies stretching over all nations and all continents. It is a caution to all who are prey to prejudice or false doctrines, to individual or collective arrogance.

But, as the somber experience gained in the Hitler era shows, those who have fallen most deeply into error are the least susceptible to warnings or enlightenment.

There have been anti-Semites and Jew baiters as long as there has been a Jewish nation. Israel quarreled with the one God who revealed Himself to them. The Jews' possession of the invisible and only God's revelation was a challenge to all the man-made idols worshipped by the nations surrounding Israel and was a challenge also to those who believed in the bird-headed god or the beautiful gods made of marble.

As the possessors of a divine secret, the Jews have from the very beginning caused those who could not or would not share the faith of Israel to look upon them with uneasiness. As the people of The Book—which the Jews have remained to this day—they have again and again aroused distrust, fear, and jealousy in those whose relationship with the written word, the law, wisdom, and the existence of the spirit has remained sterile. Many anti-Semites—though certainly not all—are primitive and more or less illiterate. The intellectual level of these *Primitiven* is revealed by a study of the files of the two most recent court hearings dealing with anti-Semitic activities in the Federal Republic of Germany. The proceedings concerned the defiling of the synagogue in Cologne and the desecration of the Jewish cemetery at Salzgitter-Jammerthal.

In both cases, the culprits were youths whose hatred of Jews can hardly have been based on personal experience in relations with Jewish fellow citizens.

The "Jewish enemy" whom these young people wished to hurt by daubing swastikas on to the walls of the new synagogue in Cologne or by smearing slogans of hatred on the cemetery of Jewish concentration camp victims near Salzgitter was, therefore, not a real enemy but some chimera, some phantom—a fiction of ignorant muddleheads.

Yet, these young primitives repeated what they had heard others say, and these again did not necessarily know any Jews or anything about Jewish history, the Jewish character or the Jewish religion. Any such knowledge, had they had it, might have immunized them against the bacillus of anti-Semitism and made them unfit to carry anti-Semitic infection. It is much more probable that, as indeed the files of the hearings seem to indicate, the teachers of these young Jew-haters are to be sought amongst the Hitlers, Goebbels, Rosenbergs, Streichers, and Himmlers of this world. And so "the Jew" became Enemy No. 1 to these young people. The Aryan supermen of the Greater German *Reich* had succumbed to his cunning. and revenge must now be sought for that defeat. Since there are but few survivors of the Jewish minority in Germany, the symbols of their existence were attacked: a house of God, a monument, and the tombstones of the dead.

It may be asked why these sons of incorrigible Nazis did not vent their wrath at the defeat of their fathers on the real victors, the British, the French, the Americans, and the Russians? But maybe these former enemies have long ceased to be phantoms and have taken on sober reality, have turned into human beings like the rest of us—outwardly not even so very unlike these young Jew-baiters.

The Jews, however, are no longer there, save for a few exceptions. Traditional prejudice can draw new and unbridled inspiration from the absent, the refugees and, alas, also from the murdered. It is, therefore, true to say that whatever virulent anti-Semitism still exists in Germany is a macaber anti-Semitism without Jews.

Psychological tests and carefully prepared public opinion polls bear out that even after Hitler the strongest anti-Jewish prejudices are revealed in places where before Hitler there were few or no Jews, whereas anti-Semitic feelings are much less frequent in areas where relatively many Jews had lived. In other words: the presence of Jews reduces anti-Semitism while their absence renders prejudice against them the more virulent This fully justifies the answer given by a well-known rabbi from the USA to a young German student of theology. In his deep dismay at the fate of the Jews in Germany the latter had asked his guest, "How do you explain the disease of anti-Semitism?"

The rabbi replied: "I have two answers. The first is that many people cannot understand why we have always remained what we are—Jews—, and bear us a grudge for it. And secondly: if anti-Semitism is a disease, then it is not a disease of the Jews but of the gentiles, and not least a disease of the Christians. To many of them, the fact that we will not be converted gives offense. It sometimes causes men of good will to think about us, and some of them respect us as a result. Zealots say we are obdurate or infamous. The *Primitiven,* however, come to hate us. Some of them have turned this hatred into a doctrine and even—where they had power to do so—into a death sentence."

The rabbi's lapidary answer shows that it is not enough merely to study the final, and at the same time most brutal, phase of anti-Semitism—what one might call biological anti-Semitism.

Critics of National Socialism have contemptuously referred to this sort of biological anti-Semitism as a "veterinary philosophy"; they have described it as confused, full of contradiction and unacademic, in no way different from all other National Socialist pseudoprograms. While according to the Nazis, the Jews were an inferior race, they accepted the Arabs—their Semitic cousins—as a noble or at least as a good and valuable race. They honored the Grand Mufti of Jerusalem and made him an ally in their struggle against the British—which of course may have been due to wartime opportunism. After all, Hitler was prepared to make an alliance with the devil—whose name at that time was Stalin—against the Anglo-Saxons. Nevertheless, the Nazis' liking for the Grand Mufti was genuine enough because he had set himself against Jewish immigration to Palestine.

To him these immigrants were not repatriates, returning to the land of their Jewish forefathers, nor Semitic cousins, members of one and the same family, but infidels, rivals and Europeans—enemies of his own patriarchal system.

Among the louts who desecrated the Salzgitter cemetery there was a Syrian Arab. It was enough for his Neo-Nazi German accomplices to have his approval of their hatred of the Jews and of Israel which is receiving reparation from the Federal Republic of Germany under the Luxembourg Treaty. We may draw some comfort from the fact that neither the *"Freikorps Grossdeutschland"* (Free Corps "Greater Germany") nor the further attacks on German "spittle-lickers of the Jews" planned by the ringleader, a certain Sonnemann, ever materialized. Beyond those immediately involved in the desecration of the Salzgitter-Jammerthal cemetery, Sonnemann found some four or five others who sympathized with his cause but not one of them was prepared to risk his skin in any further operations. They feared the results of breaking the law.

If we look into the early beginnings of anti-Judaism, we will very soon find that it had nothing to do with anti-Semitism. It was not racial hatred. It could not be, because the first antagonism against Israel meant enmity and war amongst Semitic peoples; not racial hatred, but a kind of fratricidal war, a war within one family of nations, war amongst neighbors— not unlike the tribal wars known to us from the past history of all continents. And yet, this hostility towards Israel was marked by one particular feature: resistance to Judaism, or attack on it; it was anti-Judaism, opposition to a religious idea which would not fit into its surroundings. It was through this religious idea that the Jews stood out from all their neighbors. For this idea they were prepared to suffer and to suffer more than nations are generally prepared to do.

Many regarded as uncanny the unwillingness of the Jews to submit, and their spiritual strength which enabled them, even after physical subjection, to retain their religion and thereby their spiritual individuality. And since no one likes to identify himself with the uncanny—and, in fact, it is very difficult to do so until the mystery has been revealed—the Jews have remained alien to other peoples, including their neighbors.

It has always been difficult to grasp this Jewish power to accept suffering, and it has remained so to this day. Jewish self-preservation has been considerable in the Egyptian and Babylonian exiles, under the menace of the Romans and the Christians, in the diaspora, in the face of threats coming from the Arabs or the Russian Zsars, and even under the torture of Hitler's thugs.

Some of these persecutors, torturers and bullies were purged by the sight of their Jewish victims' greatness and capacity to accept suffering, others were driven insane by it. Only the stone-hearted remained untouched. Today, however, those *Primitiven* are the most dangerous whom a kindly fate has spared from becoming accomplices or henchmen of the murderers, although their hatred is unbridled. These people evidently lack sufficient power of imagination to conjure up before their minds the institutions of Hell. To this day, they believe the gas chambers and crematoria of the annihilation camps to be the devilish products of Jewish imagination rather than the work of their own fellows. In talks with young Germans deeply shaken at what was done to the Jews, they frequently refuse to condemn the murderers of the Jews and maintain that all this is propaganda made for the one and only purpose of sullying the memory of good National Socialist heroes and upright Germans. In their unconcern, stubbornness, and self-satisfaction these blind admirers of blond Nazi giants are not unlike Narcissus. To them, Hitler's concentration camps were not more than centers for criminal elements whom the orderly minded guards were obliged to keep in iron discipline with their submachine guns. I heard one of these young muddleheads say, "Possibly, a few hundred thousand Communists, gipsies, criminals, and Jews may have been killed. The camp commandants and their guards were hard, but just." They also quite blandly ask, "Did not the Jews themselves provoke their fate?"

They even brush aside the evidence of documentary films made in the concentration camps. This is easy once you decide to close your mind. But it is very difficult indeed to make these unteachables see truths which militant anti-Semites refuse to recognize to this day. They reject the truth because they hate it or because deep down in their subconscious they fear it—as indeed they must in the face of its enormity. Therefore, adamant anti-Semites avoid film performances in which concentration camp scenes are shown. Broadcasts of the Eichmann trial, which deeply moved millions of Germans who followed them by radio or on television, were simply switched off by this minority of unteachable anti-Semites. Newspaper reports on this unhappy subject are read by millions of people of good will, amongst them many who are in no need of this reminder. But those who ought to read them avoid such literature because they do not wish to be ashamed.

In this way, the problem of vicarious responsibility arises for many Germans. This is indeed a noble Christian principle. If the culprit does not own up to his guilt, then those who have feeling must stand in for the unfeeling, and those who understand must take the place of the obdurate.

For guilt must be recognized and expiated if it is not to propagate itself. Since many Germans want to go forward with this process of self-purification—not only so as to regain their good national name in the eyes of other peoples, but also in order to free themselves of their complex—they often find themselves in a particularly awkward position. Objective Jewish observers of this process have spoken of a hypertrophy of German guilt complexes. A Jewish paper discussed some books recently published in Germany under the headline "New German Flagellantism".

We see, therefore, that it is not simple to convince those who survived persecution of the sincerity of the change that has come over the Germans. Some do not wish the innocent to take upon their own souls the burden of guilt. Others expect a general admission of guilt. They confuse person and nation, historical liability and individual complicity in the deed.

Truth, which has many facets, forces us to admit that the number of Germans who had no need to change after the fall of Hitler is by no means small. There are probably also many in whom remorse has brought about change. The only difficulty is with the indifferent, who do not feel concerned and even refuse to bow before the victims. The most difficult of all, however, is to solve the problems of the primitive, the ingrained fanatics of anti-Semitism. We might well ask to what extent the primitive members of a nation represent it

Since Hitler was borne to power on the shoulders of many of the *Primitiven* and since this meant the rule of insanity and barbarity, we must, after this bitter experience, beware of giving these *Primitiven* any chance of ever again becoming representative. Unhappily they have only too frequently reached this stage in the course of history—and not only in our most recent past. For reasons of self-protection alone, the *Primitiven* must not be allowed any political fool's license. Nor may we grant any mitigating circumstances for "minor offenses of race-hatred" to those who have a "reduced sense of political responsibility" because experience has shown that such minor offenses are only too quickly followed by atrocious crimes.

It is part and parcel of the psychology of latent anti-Semitism that the alleged Jewish archenemy is of no human interest whatever. Anti-Semites wish for nothing but bad Jews. A good and just Jew would be a source of irritation to them.

Where anti-Semitism is a disease which regards itself not as a weakness but on the contrary as a kind of herostratic strength, it is impervious to cure. Anti-Semites never have any aptitude for establishing human contact with anything that is Jewish. Being profoundly egocentric, they believe in the necessity of their hatred, which is the reflection of their own character. They will not allow this character to be shaken by Jews. They require the Jew not as a person but as fiction, something on which they can vent all their dissatisfaction with themselves. To them, the Jew is a welcome, even essential, lightning conductor for all their wrath. He provides them with easy explanations of all their self-caused failures. But Peguy was right when he wrote, as far back as in 1910, "The anti-Semites speak of the Jews, but I would rather say that they do not even know Jews."

However stupid and scientifically untenable biological anti-Semitism may have been and may still be, it has been a deadly dangerous political weapon in the hands of unscrupulous enemies of humanity. In individual cases and for inexplicable reasons, even these monsters have in time of merciless persecution been prepared to give protection to individual Jewish citizens.

When they did so, they very simply abstracted from the concerned person the fictitious Jewish characteristics, which in any case never fitted. It was really a renewal of the unsavory institution of "protected Jews" who from the Middle Ages until well into modern times "enjoyed" the safety granted them by temporal and even ecclesiastic princes in Germany.

The whim of a Nazi was sufficient to allow a privileged Jew to survive. "I say who is a Jew (or who is not)" was a maxim applied not only by the despotic Goering; other nazi grandees and commanders used it too. But those who had the misfortune to be and to remain Jews—and of course they were the vast majority—were outlawed and had no right to live under the nazi regime. They were the helpless victims of a blind and ferocious hatred. To destroy them was regarded not as a crime but as a service to the State.

All these horrors could happen only because those who perpetrated them were neither prepared to understand who it was they persecuted, nor to realize that their victims did not in any way correspond to the picture which those suffering from criminal anti-Semitism had fixed in their minds. May these victims forgive me when I say that the alleged subhuman characteristics of the Jews were in fact a projected self-portrayal of their inhuman persecutors. In the terms of depth psychology, therefore, the crimes of the persecutors were an act of self-destruction.

Now that all these horrors have happened, one may ask whether there are in the history of the German nation, or of others, any examples on which the great prosecution in nazi-Germany could have been modeled.

Of course, there is no previous example of the "industrialization of mass murder" of persecution brought to such technical perfection. Nevertheless, there have been similar manifestations and synonymous philosophies which have led to attempts to subject the Jews intellectually, religiously and morally, or even to destroy them. In his excellent essay on the origins of and changes in anti-Semitism which appeared in 1939, Erich Kahler (USA), points to the first State-ordered attack on the Jews which the Seleucid Antiochus Epiphanes undertook from 175 to 164 B.C.

It was the intention of Antiochus to Hellenize Judea by force; when its people resisted, he attempted to annihilate them. Kahler describes the methods of the totalitarian Antiochus. Under his rule of terror, the Law was set aside, temple services and ritual were forbidden on pain of death, the Tora Rolls were burned and desecrated, the Greek cults had to be observed, the Jews were forced to eat pork and—worst humiliation of all—to take part in the Dionysian orgies: murder, torture and martyrdom—the beginning of a millennial pattern.

At that stage, the Jews defended themselves by force of arms and with great obstinacy. With their God, they defended their country, their city, their Temple, and they did not yet face a closed and hostile world as they were to do later in the Christian era. The despotism of Antiochus was followed by the rebellion of the Maccabeans and the autonomous rule of the Hasmonaean priests. In answer to the Roman subjection of Judea, which was more or less ferocious according to the personal character of whoever was the dictator, emperor or viceroy at the time, there was a constant series of rebellions. Roman hostility to the Jews was marked by one additional specific feature which was absent from Greek anti-Semitism: anger at the spiritual toughness of this little nation which so obstinately resisted the power of the Roman Empire, not only in the province of Judea itself but also beyond it, through the unfathomable firmness of its religious ideas which spread further and further throughout the Empire and were especially attractive to the enlightened among its people. (Erich Kahler)

We find that already at this early stage political and religious rulers—the Roman Emperor was a god—feared Israel which, in their own spiritual uncertainty, they looked upon as a threat to their power. They, too, were less afraid of the Jew as a man than of the mysterious idea of Judaism. The Roman philosopher Seneca said, "The customs of this criminal people are spreading to such an extent that already they have followers in all countries, so that the vanquished are imposing their laws upon the conquerors."

As the idea behind the Jewish people is the Law, a law different from that of the Romans or later from that of the Church and still later different from the law or rather the lawlessness of the Third Reich, and since this Jewish Law glows with the power of the spirit and the majesty of direct revelation, the rulers of this earth and those who were of another turn of mind must indeed fear for their doctrines. And so it was that these rulers, even though they were not primitive men, took recourse to the sword and legalized the killing of Jews for which they hired primitive helots and assassins.

Thus, there were persecutions in Spain from which only enforced baptism offered an escape. Under Pope Innocent III, a decision was taken in 1215 against the "infidels", meaning the Jews. They were ordered to wear a special costume so that they should be immediately recognizable; it was a wide coat and a pointed hat with a yellow pompon. There is, of course, here a parallel with the disgraceful star which Jews had to wear during the terrible days of the Third Reich. Altogether there are parallels between the self-deification of the Roman emperors and the hubris of the national socialist *Fuehrer*.

Political and religious zeal have made a large psychological contribution to anti-Semitism. Christian zealots were offended because the Jews, among whom Christ had appeared, would not recognize the Savior as other nations had done. The crusaders attacked not only the pagans who had come to power in Palestine, but also the infidel "perfidious" Jews. It was then that, from the Christian angle, the unity or at least the living link between the Old and the New Testament was broken. Christian zealotism had struck a blow at the root of its own faith. For how could the Jews be perfidious and infidels when Christ Himself had said, "Think not that I am come to destroy the Law and the prophets, I am not come to destroy but to fulfill." He was, after all, a Jewish prophet.

Other evil examples and precursors of anti-Semitism can also be found in the Holy Roman Empire of the German Nation. The Christians no longer saw in their Jewish brethren their neighbors, their "elder brethren in God", but, because they would not recognize the Messiah, they were looked upon as less than strangers and, in accordance with the claims of the church militant, they were placed under a special law. In other words, they were excluded from the general laws and regulations applicable in the Empire and to the subjects of the German princes. In exceptional cases, they were appointed "protected Jews"—servants of these princes—because in contrast to the large majority of the people, including even courtiers and citizens, they were able to read and write and to do accounts.

Unfortunately, it is only too clear why the Germans citizens of the early Middle Ages could not obtain a just picture of their Jewish fellow men. The Jews were outcasts from society. They were excluded from land ownership and the exercise of most crafts. Only in exceptional cases could there develop any man-to-man relationship based on human confidence. In addition, the Jews bore the stigma of clinging to a faith which was not that of their fellow men, a faith which was not the only true and saving faith.

Despite the very close religious affinities between Jewry and Christendom, a chasm was torn up and a whole world of antagonisms created. In critical times of disease and pestilence, the „outsider" then became the incarnation of evil, the cause of all misfortune. Who but the Jews—who were sure to have poisoned the wells—could have brought the Black Death upon mankind?

Anti-Judaism on the part of religious zealots, or even a lack of self-reliance in political philosophers, need not be primitive; to "know all" is frequently a vice of the clever. Not all intelligent men are at the same time wise. Not all teachers are mild and gentle enough to include the possibility of error in their own teachings. Few are prepared to give to the teaching of others the serious thought it deserves or as they expect to be given to their own. Nathan would never have been called the Wise had his tolerance not risen above the intolerance of his fellow men.

Pogroms occurred not only in Russia but also in Germany. It was not always disease or pestilence which caused a mass psychosis and a rising of the primitive against the innocent victims of mass insanity: the Jews. Witch-hunting is another constantly recurring manifestation of the need felt by the emotionalized masses to personify the invisible source of evil and thereby to make evil visible and tangible. Witches can be seen and touched: so can Jews and gypsies.

It is not without interest to note that one of the hooligans accused of desecrating the cemetery at Salzgitter-Jammerthal spoke of witch-hunting. Only, he described the whole world's indignation at the Hitlerite crimes as a witch-hunt organized by bad Germans and anti-German foreigners against

National Socialists and their lofty teachings. What a short-circuit of logic, what confusion of the mind!

Objective historians have put on record that though the anti-Jewish pogroms in Germany and in other European countries were carried out with complete abandon by *Primitiven* they were very frequently instigated and organized by men coolly calculating their power-political chances.

Nothing is more open to doubt than any allegedly spontaneous indignation of "the people". Rarely are demagogues the direct spokesmen of their nation. But very often they are willing tools in the hands of those whose aim it is to distract attention from their own guilt or failure and to make a whipping boy of someone else.

The ways of anti-Semitism in Germany became more confused than in other countries. This may be largely due to the fact that dynastic developments were splitting the country more and more apart and exposing it to a series of internal crises; this development was more confused and more full of inherent contradictions in Germany than in other parts of Europe. Religious divisions played their part in this. As Gamm puts it in his very meritorious *History of Judaism* (1960), "Martin Luther cherished the great hope that one of the most glorious results of his work would consist of converting the House of Israel to the true faith. The reformer was deeply disappointed when he found that the Jews remained adamant in the face of even his purified doctrine and that therefore his 'Dear Day of Judgment' was still far off. Thus, we find a vast difference between what Luther wrote in 1523 in his pamphlet to show that Jesus has been born a Jew, and in 1543 when he wrote about the Jews and their lies. These writings are characteristic of Protestantism's trend from spiritual tolerance towards acute anti-Judaism, on which point there was hardly any difference between Protestant and Catholic Europe after Luther's death."

Gamm continues, "The strongest source of anti-Judaism is, however, to be found in Christian hubris towards Israel. The promises made to the chosen people were interpreted as relating to Christendom as the 'true Israel'; Christianity was considered to be in the right and St. Paul's pained reflections on his people (Romans 9: 1—5) were forgotten. Thus, we find that the presumptuousness with which Christians dispute the Jews' title to their heritage is the real root of anti-Semitism. National Socialist racial pride is the distorted ideological fruit of religious pride and a presumptuous sense of superiority vis-à-vis the Jews."

Right up to the present day we hear the allegation that the Jews "murdered Christ"; and this statement—which is fraught with danger even on theological grounds—is not refuted on the basis of both theological and legal understanding, nor is any constant attempt being made truthfully to depict the "trial of Jesus of Nazareth". When we fail to do so, we give in to the same cheap generalizations and distortions of history which we note and rightly censure in the biological or political anti-Semitism of the Nazis.

All zealots are alike. The Christian concept of the Jews as the "children of darkness" or as "descendants of the devil" does not differ in its essentials from the biological contempt in which National Socialism held them.

For what could "descendants of the devil" be if not subhumans, so different from the Aryan master-race or the shining teutonic heroes towering above them?

Whenever we study the psychology of anti-Semitism, we find identical or similar manifestations of the contempt in which the Jews are held. There is a Christian attitude of fear towards the Jews, and Gamm still regards this as "a source of emotional anti-Semitism".

The Nazis' hatred of the Jews was really nothing but fear of the Jews, a cramped expression of their own non-Jewish inferiority. This Aryan inferiority complex, which they endeavored to compensate by presumptuousness, may have been the result of countless defeats, undigested in the consciousness of the Germans.

As close as the affinity may be between German and Jewish intellectuals—and the indestructible love of many Jews for Germany and her intellectual development is evidence of that love—the difference between Jews and Germans in another field is astonishing. The Torah, the Five Books of Moses, bear living witness to the fact that both in their national and in their religious history the Jews have recognized their defeats as well as their errors and shortcomings. The Germans are incomparably less apt to own up to their own defeats, shortcomings and weaknesses. Only reluctantly will they seek in themselves the cause of their misfortunes or their failures. The Germans do not understand themselves, and those among them who adore the ideal of the master-man or the superman understand themselves least of all. Their hubris collides harshly with the greater self-assurance of the Jews, which is grounded on self-criticism. Thus, we see that just because the hated Jew has that spiritual bearing which the Jew-baiter lacks, the latter hates him all the more.

We often hear National Socialism described as a pagan movement and Hitler as Anti-Christ. To many of its adherents, this heresy had become a kind of hectic pseudoreligion or substitute for religion. In the case of many Nazis, the adoration of Hitler became hypertrophied until it was something of a myth. In the homes of some of his enraptured adorers, there was even something like an altar with a picture of Hitler, surrounded by candles. Awkwardness and some residue of pious awe saved these people from actually praying to the *"Fuehrer"*, although many of them adored him ecstatically.

Since National Socialism did not evolve any ideas of its own but borrowed and plagiarized from others its program, its dialectics and its tactics, the anti-Semitic ideologists, fantasts, and hysteric persons felt no inhibition in recasting the ideas of zealous anti-Judaism into those of zealous anti-Semitism. In so doing, they carried out a truly shocking process of intellectual forgery. Even Christ was Aryanized, his murderers turned into demons; in the minds of pagan National Socialists, the Jewish Passover wine became the blood of murdered Christian children.

Ideas which were rampant in the era of witch-hunting, such as the horrible invention of Jewish "ritual murder" were revived in order to stamp the Jews as the embodiment of evil, of all that is criminal and sinister. The

National Socialists unscrupulously dragged even Luther down and made him into a Crown witness for anti-Semitism. None of these falsifiers and misinterpreters of history realized, or was prepared to realize, that Luther's anger was no more than the expression of the unrequited love of a reformer who had firmly believed that by reforming the Church he could at long last win over God's chosen people.

The age of enlightenment brought new hope for the Jews in Germany too. Moses Mendelssohn earned the admiration and respect of his gentile fellow citizens. They regarded him not only as a great Jew but also as a worthy representative of the German mind. A few years later, French absolutism was swept away by the Great Revolution. Even before that, in 1782, Joseph II had issued his Edict of Tolerance in Vienna. 1812 saw the emancipation of the Jews in Prussia, but reverses after the defeat of Napoleon brought in their wake a renewed discrimination against the Jews; many of the freedoms granted them on paper were withdrawn even before they had come in force. In 1819, there were tumultuous excesses in Baden and Bavaria and in a number of major towns elsewhere. Jewish homes were ransacked and synagogues burned down. Yet, the struggle for the basic civic rights of all Germans, including the Jews, had begun and could not be halted. The days of reaction and despotism were numbered.

Gabriel Riesser was elected to the Parliament which met in St. Paul's Church in Frankfurt, where he represented the Duchy of Lauenburg. A few years earlier he, as a Jew, would not even have been allowed to spend a night in an inn in the constituency he now represented. However, the same year in which Jewish representatives were allowed into the German National Assembly witnessed unseemly outrages against "mansions, landlords, rent collecting offices, vicarages and Jews" alike.

This kind of indiscriminate rebellion is a characteristic feature of confusion in a situation of political transition. The thirst for liberty which was abroad at that time was quenched with fermenting spirits. The oppressed attacked not only their oppressors, but their fellow sufferers as well.

In that restless age, German Jewry produced in Riesser a champion of its rights, who was endowed with outstanding qualities. This man's personal career, his rapid rise, the mass of difficulties which he had to surmount before he became Vice-President of the Frankfort National Assembly and then Vice-President of the Hamburg Senate, notary public, and finally a Chief Justice, impressively reflects the conditions under which the Jewish minority lived in Germany.

Riesser, who was born in Hamburg on April 2, 1806, as the son of a secretary to the Jewish Court at Altona, took his doctor of law degree at Heidelberg University "summa cum laude". Soon afterwards, Heidelberg University refused him the coveted post of private lecturer. Though his Jewish faith was not given as the reason for his being rejected, the allegation that there were already too many applications for private lecturerships was a cheap and easily refutable excuse. Those who had taught Gabriel Riesser law had aroused in him the passionate desire to play his part in the struggle for the great legal and constitutional reform of Germany. The ideals of law pointed to the future. The statutes and legal systems still in force in the States of Germany were rooted in a long obsolete past and threatened to perpetuate injustice.

Thus, young Gabriel Riesser was faced with the decision of either taking up an unloved profession or following the vocation of a reformer. Belonging to an underprivileged group himself, he would fight for his own rehabilitation in the wider context of the struggle for the civic liberties of all Germans. Riesser took up this challenge and burned himself out prematurely in the 57 years of his life. In his youth and early manhood his health seemed robust; he was indefatigable. His legal ability was generally admired. His literary knowledge was no less exceptional, and as an orator, he was considered a second Demosthenes. His gift of languages was so phenomenal that he was able to give a rousing farewell address in classical Greek to the Johanneum in Hamburg. He read the Thora in Hebrew and studied French and Anglo-Saxon literature in the original texts.

So convinced was young Gabriel Riesser that the early establishment of general human rights and civic liberties for all throughout Germany was necessary and self-evident, that in contrast to former Jewish spokesmen, he did not continue the struggle for more rights for the disinherited, but with bold self-assurance demanded the establishment of justice as such He claimed not a part of freedom, but all of it.

Some of his intimidated coreligionists took fright. They feared that by asking too much even an effort to obtain minor improvements would be doomed to failure. Riesser remained undaunted. He was not prepared to engage in tactics, nor was he interested in compromises which would mean that he would have to waive claims in one respect in order to obtain concession in another. To his mind, the dignity of man required that the law should be based on an indivisible principle. He felt he would be betraying that principle if he compromised even part of it.

So Gabriel Riesser became the center of a struggle which lasted for many years. The chronicle of this struggle, from which Riesser emerged victorious as a German patriot, gives us a detailed picture of the social, legal, and political effects of anti-Judaism in Germany.

Gabriel Riesser's very first pamphlet was a manifesto. Its title was *On the Condition of the Members of the Jewish Faith in Germany, Addressed to the Germans of all Faiths* and was published in 1831. Dr. M. Isler, the editor of the *Collected Writings of Gabriel Riesser,* describes as follows the conditions under which German Jews lived at that time:

> "In 1830 the condition of the Jews in Germany was still very depressed. Legislation in the various States reflected all degrees of exclusion from civic rights. There were cities and States which adamantly refused entry to Jews . . . The activities of the Jews gave rise to all kinds of anxiety, competition in trade, the manufacture of cheaper clothes and shoes, problems of conscience in taking oaths, uncalled for defense in Court, and so on."

The German-Jewish poet, Ludwig Boerne, who belonged to the *Junges Deutschland* movement in literature had, it is true, attempted to bring about a change by his polemic treatise *The Wandering Jew* published in

1821. He was vituperated or passed over in silence. His work was talked about in intellectual circles, but the princes and their ministers did nothing. While Boerne was a writer, Riesser was a born politician. What he said appealed to politicians, and he scored a bull's eye every time.

"I will have nothing of justification or concessions," he called. "You have no right to accuse us of a lack of ability or dignity while it is you yourselves who unlawfully prevent us from giving proof of our ability and dignity."

With the rousing enthusiasm of youth and the full *élan* of a just cause, Riesser continued, "I will have nothing of concessions or individual rights. They would but renew the old shame and prolong it by new humiliations." And even if force were employed to deny the Jews their human rights, nothing could rob them of their human dignity, pride, and culture.

Isler says, "This pamphlet electrified wide circles. Some of the older Jews were frightened because they feared that such bold language would immediately entail evil. But the younger generation felt a sense of relief that one of their number had dared to express so ruthlessly, so truthfully, and so beautifully what each of them believed he had himself thought."

The echo in non-Jewish quarters was strong and positive, too. There was no lack of joyful recognition. The progressive, those who had been infected by the spirit of the French Revolution or German idealism, made this 25-year-old political author their champion. Hardly more than a youth, this David had become a pioneer in the vanguard, or even a brilliant young commander in the coming battle for democracy.

His success certainly helped to make his enemies prepare for battle. One of them. Dominie Dr. H. E. G. Paulus, of Heidelberg, got ready for the counterattack. His literary reply, which also appeared in 1831, was called *Jewish National Segregation; its Origin, Results, and How it May be Mitigated.* This attack was unexpected, because Paulus had been numbered among the advocates of religious liberalism. But politically, he was "intolerant". To his mind, human rights in no way included civic rights. According to him, citizens without civic rights—that is to say, the Jews among others—were fully in possession of their human rights; but they were to be denied any share in the State. He rejected any Jewish claim to civic rights for the reason that they were "a separate nation", and themselves wished to remain so, considering their aloofness from others as a "religious duty".

In the opinion of the then septuagenarian Paulus, the Jews could pronounce themselves Germans by one act only: acceptance of the Christian religion. They would have to abandon their original faith, the Law, circumcision, and the Sabbath.

The immediate force of these arguments was not very great. Nevertheless governments and politicians were impressed by the personality of their author. In particular, all those who hated Jews were grateful to the respected Heidelberg theologian for his paper and used it as a weapon against emancipation.

Paulus' pamphlet caused Riesser many a sleepless night. Then he sat down and wrote an answer, entitled, *In Defense of Equal Civic Rights for Jews, and in Reply to the Arguments of Dr. H. E. G. Paulus. Dedicated to the Constituant Assemblies of Germany,* by Gabriel Riesser. He wrote this in six days and placed it under the motto "We have one Father in Heaven, God, Who is the Father of all, and we have one mother, Germany, here below". It was the outcry of a patriot—emotional in language, but brilliant and irrefutable in its logic.

This Jewish Winkelried*) contradicted Paulus' opinion that it was the Jews' ambition to govern the gentiles. Also, Paulus had alleged that the Jews now had access everywhere to the crafts and to farming. Riesser proved that in many German States they were still explicitly excluded by law from these activities.

Regarding the reproach that the Jews constituted a separate nation within the German people, Riesser said, "Only he is an alien who was not born in the country, who has come in from abroad." The Jews, however, were born in Germany and if legislation deprived them of their German nationality, then the law could not be directed against them as a people but only against their religion. He proclaimed, "We want to belong to our German fatherland, and we shall belong to it everywhere."

This was an entirely new kind of language, a firm logic and an interpretation of law which raised enthusiasm among many supporters of progress; but it was also language calculated to incite the enemies of the Jews to prepare even more determined counterattacks. As Luther and many others, including a number of Popes, Paulus believed that the Jewish problem could be solved by the Sacrament of Baptism. But when Ludwig Boerne and Heinrich Heine, both of whom had become Christians, continued to attack and criticize governments, Christians and Jews alike where they stood in the way of progress, the anti-Semites blamed the Jews for all Boerne's and Heine's invective and satire. Baptism or no baptism, they said, both had remained Jews in their lack of respect toward the Christian community and the established order.

Here, we clearly see the beginning of "biological anti-Semitism" long before Gobineau and Houston Stewart Chamberlain. The enemies of the Jews declared them to be Asiatics.

The intellectual battle was now joined on a broad front. Gabriel Riesser had set his aim very high, and he was well prepared. He knew the history of all the great nations, not only of his own continent. At one stage he put the ironical question, "Did not the Germanic tribes themselves set out one day from the East, and did it not take them an age of migration to reach Europe?"

Riesser knew that the first Jews settled in Germany in the 4th century A.D., so that they had incomparably senior residential rights than the members of many other tribes who had time and again fought against the Germans but had now become absorbed in the German nation, although they were by no means of Teutonic origin. Why should they enjoy all rights but not the Jews, who for had centuries tied themselves to the German people in language and spirit?

*) Swiss national hero, who in 1326 drew the attack of an enemy force upon himself and thus enabled his countrymen to win the decisive battle of Sempach.

Riesser's love of Germany, which shone through all his writings and speeches, was moving and made many friends for him among rich and poor, among the educated and the simple. It spoke for him in government circles, in the Christian camp, and even among well-meaning conservatives circles, the members of the liberal professions and in upper ranks of the bourgeoisie. It also made his adversaries all the more obdurate.

But as the general trend of events led irresistibly to the establishment of civic rights, and as Gabriel Riesser was able time and again skillfully and with success to show that law and freedom are indivisible, the emancipation of the Jews became part and parcel of general emancipation, despite anything the anti-Semites could do.

As far back as in August 1948, Gabriel Riesser had come to one of the culminating points of his struggle in the Frankfort National Assembly. That Assembly had proposed to guarantee active and passive franchise under the constitution to all Jewish citizens. However, one of the members, Moritz Wohl, made an attempt to keep Jewish rights restricted; not so much the franchise as the other civic rights. The first sentence of his motion read, "The particular circumstances of the people of Israel shall form the subject of special legislation which may be decreed by the *Reich*."

This would have opened the door wide to arbitrary action and restriction, especially in the field of material progress. Riesser asked for the floor and walked up to the rostrum. He said, "I claim the right to speak to you on behalf of a class which has been oppressed for thousands of years and to which I belong by birth."

From the first moment of this debate, the House was electrified by the passion of Riesser's oratory. He refused to discuss his religion, because Parliament was not the forum to air personal religious beliefs. He simply pointed out that he had refused and would go on refusing to change his religion so that he might acquire rights which had been shamefully withheld from him.

He gave a masterly description of the legal situation of his Jewish co-citizens and again defended the claims of the German Jews to be relieved from special legislation and to be accorded equal political rights. He touched his audience deeply when he said, "I myself have lived under conditions of profound humiliation and until quite recently, I could not have been entrusted in my own home town with the office of night watchman. I regard it a feat of justice and freedom—a miracle almost—that I am now authorized to speak here for the cause of justice and equality without having been converted to Christianity."

His peroration was rousing, "Do not believe that you can decree special legislation of this kind without causing the whole system of freedom to crack. You will never cast out part of the German nation to intolerance and hatred."

It was the same Gabriel Riesser who delivered the famous "Emperor address" in St. Paul's Church in Frankfort. He was part of the delegation of deputies who offered the King of Prussia election to be Emperor of the Germans. Gabriel Riesser was recognized throughout as one of Germany's leading patriots. But the King of Prussia refused to accept the Imperial

Crown from the hands of the people. Much later his brother received it in Versailles from the hands of the princes. The Parliament in St. Paul's Church failed; it never became the Parliament of all Germany. It never reached the objectives it had set for itself. The assembly came to nothing because the German princes did not wish it to succeed. Nevertheless, the points had been set, even though such great men as Carl Schurz had to flee and seek a second home for themselves in free America. Riesser and his friends remained behind and in ceaseless local struggles endeavored to translate into practice, at least at the regional level, what the National Assembly in the Church of St. Paul had failed to achieve.

How much the citizens of Hamburg regarded Riesser as one of their finest representatives is shown by the fact that he was invited to deliver the Schiller Centenary Memorial Address (in 1859) on behalf of all the city's patriotic associations. In the same year, Riesser entered the new Hamburg Parliament as a deputy. Somewhat later, the city appointed him Chief Justice, making him the first German judge of Jewish faith. This appointment heralded a new era, although there was no shortage of reverses.

To this day, the violence of the struggle which the labor movement in Germany had to carry on in order to have the fourth estate recognized is not properly understood in the USA. It was only after this struggle had been successfully concluded that real parliaments could evolve in Germany and especially in the minor principalities. However, there were frequent relapses into class franchise. As late as in 1905, there occurred a deterioration of the electoral law in Hamburg. The weight of a vote depended on income and anyone earning less than 1200 marks per annum was entirely disenfranchised. Small wonder then that the political history of Germany was filled for decades with constitutional and electoral struggles.

Jewish lawyers scholars, and writers fought in the ranks of the labor movement. From this, there necessarily resulted considerable political hostility to Jews and Socialists alike on the part of the conservatives and reactionaries. Much of the historical failure of the German bourgeoisie in the cities and in the rural areas can be traced to the lack of understanding with which the prosperous looked upon their economically weaker fellow citizens. They simply did not measure up to the social obligations which the industrial revolution brought in its wake.

Violent demagogic means of anti-Semitism were not infrequently employed in the struggle for political power in the young German parliaments. Once again, we witness an overlapping of political anti-Semitism, racial discrimination, and religious intolerance. While France had its Dreyfuss case and pogroms occured in Russia and Roumania, an anti-Semitic movement was unleashed in Prussia and Germany by the Hohenzollern Court preacher, Stoecker. It is now 60 years ago that in liberal Hamburg men put themselves up as candidates for elections who openly set themselves down as anti-Semites—as if that in itself was a political program.

Theodor Herzl's Zionist Movement and his idea of a Jewish State were an answer to the many anti-Semitic phenomena in Europe. Time and again, the most sensitive among the Jewish citizens were disappointed. They so dearly wished to be part of the national community of all Germans but found themselves brusquely repelled so that some of them began to dream of their ancient and yet new Jewish home, of a new national State of their own.

Twenty-two years after the first Zionist Congress was opened in Basle, ten years after the birth of Tel-Aviv, the first Jewish city to be founded in Palestine, one year after the proclamation of the Balfour Declaration which promised the Jews British help in building their new national home, parliamentary democracy was established in Germany on the ruins of the Hohenzollern *Reich*. At long last, the Germans, too, had put into practice all civic rights, including universal suffrage for men and women.

One of the fathers of the Weimar Constitution for the German *Reich* was Hugo Preuss. Walter Rathenau and Hilfferding were appointed Ministers, one charged with Foreign Affairs and the other with Finance. But the Weimar democracy was born under the ill star of Imperial disaster. Many Germans felt a nostalgia for the past and had no love for their new State or the new political order, though it had given them the right to have their share in government and responsibility, and though it held out equal chances to all.

Democracy had been called in when the *Reich* was in mortal peril and a new beginning was to be made. Since, however, the heavy burdens of the Versailles Treaty cast their shadow over this beginning, the fire brigade, as it were, and not the real incendiaries were held responsible for the 1914/19 conflagration. Both Rathenau and Erzberger were assassinated; the latter because he was alleged to be subservient to the victorious Allies, and the former because he was a Jew into the bargain. Their murderers belonged to a small clique of misguided nationalist fanatics, but there were many who sympathized with that clique.

In the German universities, the small groups of democratic, catholic or Social Democrat students were not by any means as influential as the dueling organizations whose statutes contained the ill-famed clause excluding "non-Aryans" from membership.

No Jew could belong to any of these associations. Although the Weimar Constitution guaranteed the emancipation of all groups and minorities, the new State was being undermined from within. It soon turned into a "democracy without democrats" since the adherents of dictatorship—both on the extreme right and the extreme left—began step by step to get the better of the democratic parties.

This process received a boost from the economic crisis of unhappy memory and the resultant high degree of unemployment. Hitler, the most fanatical of all demagogues, was racing to power. The misery of the lost war and the inflation, only briefly interrupted by a few years of prosperity, finally led to unparalleled mass-unemployment for which the "democratic lackeys of the Allies" and the Jews were held responsible. The founders of the Weimar Republic were reviled as "November criminals", although in the years of the Weimar Republic the Social Democrats had taken part in the government for a relatively short time only. With an untroubled conscience and in sovereign contempt of historical truth some people said, "The Jews are our misfortune. It is all the fault of the Jews." The sequel, the "Thousand Years' *Reich*" which lasted but a meager twelve years, is well known.

The first victims of the concentrations camps which were set up after Hitler came to power were Democrats, Socialists, Communists, and Pacifists. In the early stages, attacks against the Jews were limited to their removal from the civil service and from cultural life. In 1935, the Nuremberg Laws prohibited mixed marriages. Jewish shops were boycotted, although during the Berlin Olympic Games of 1936 an effort was made to save appearances, and the boycott notices were temporarily removed so as not to shock foreign visitors.

From 1938 onwards, all Jewish Germans had to add "Israel" or "Sarah" to their first names and in the same year, Jewish physicians were no longer, allowed to practice. In November, 1938, the synagogues were burned in reply to Grynspan's attack on the German diplomat v. Rath and the mass deportations of Jewish citizens began. Now the concentration camps were filled to bursting point with Jewish victims. Their number grew beyond measure. Herman Goering gave instructions that the "final solution" of the Jewish problem be prepared. Those hapless victims of persecution who remained alive and had to do forced labor were compelled to wear a Star of David to proclaim that they were Jews. Then came the mass annihilation of millions which reached its macaber culmination from 1942 to the fall of 1944. Men, women, and children were murdered; it was a war of annihilation against defenseless prey.

Those who survived the great persecution at long last again enjoy full civic rights in the Federal Republic of Germany. The Constitution explicitly gives complete protection to all ethnic and religious minorities. It is an entirely different matter whether Germany, which through Bergen-Belsen, Oranienburg and Dachau has become a Golgatha, is really habitable again for the survivors, and whether it can one day mean home to them again. There are some twenty-five or thirty thousand Jews left in Germany and the number of elderly people is predominant in their communities.

All non-Jewish Germans of good will felt a sense of deep shame, helplessness, and even despair.

There can be no doubt that there were more than seven "just men" even amongst the Germans. Tens of thousands of non-Jewish, anti-Nazis had suffered the same death in the concentration camps as their Jewish friends. In Berlin alone, a few thousand persecuted Jews managed to hide with non-Jewish families. They were saved. If, however, the *Gestapo* found them it meant torture and a horrible death for them as well as for their protectors. It is not part of my subject to speak of restitution and of the comprehensive reparation legislation in the Federal Republic. Nor is this the place to discuss the operation "Peace with Israel" which was inaugurated on August 31, 1951, or to refer to Konrad Adenauer's Government Declaration of September 27, 1951, in which the Federal Republic stated its desire to enter into negotiations with Israel and the Jewish World Organizations. These negotiations ended in the well-known Luxembourg Agreements under which goods to the value of 3.5 thousand million DM are shipped to Israel. What I have, however, set out to do is to probe into the condition of the German people and to find out whether the poison of anti-Semitism which from 1933 to 1945 had been made the State philosophy of the Third Reich is still effective or whether the German people has rid itself of it.

Obviously, a few cases of recidivism, a relatively small number of outrages by unteachable anti-Semites, are sufficient to tear open old wounds in the memories of surviving victims and to reactivate the latent distrust of the civilized world. A few thousand hardhearted anti-Semites, daubers of swastikas, demagogues, and apostles of hatred can create the impression that there has been no change in Germany or the soul of the German people after the horrors of the Third Reich. Nevertheless the malignant anti-Semites in the Federal Republic of Germany are certainly a minority and very likely a relatively weak one. However, it is unfortunately true that the militant humanitarians are also no more than a minority in Germany, although I think it to be a much stronger one than that of the vicious anti-Semites.

The position in the old democracies is not so very different; there, too, the fence-sitters, the undecided, the colorless are in the majority. It is the great task of the humanitarians to win over the undecided and the indifferent to their side. Over the past fifteen years, the democratic parties in the Federal Republic have been fairly successful in this respect. Successful enough, at any rate, to make it possible for the latest supplement to the Federal Act for the Compensation of Victims of the Nazi Regime to be unanimously adopted in the Federal Parliament.

But, now that indivisible justice has been restored, one of the most important challenges facing humanitarians of all political shades in Germany is the restoration of a fair image of the Jew as a man. It is only because so few Germans have ever found out what Jews are really like and how worthy of admiration is the history of their religion and their suffering, that such an unfair and ugly distortion of that image could develop.

There are today in Germany many individuals and groups endeavoring to rectify this. There are thirty German associations for Christian-Jewish cooperation. In German universities and adult education centers, countless lectures are being delivered on Jewish history and Judaism. In broadcasting and television, there are many reports on the contribution made by Jews to the intellectual and economic history of Germany. Books by German Jewish authors and books from and about Israel are published in great numbers and reach impressive editions.

But personal contact, the restoration of partnership between Germans and Jews, is far more important than any theoretical study; what is needed is a revival of direct and manifold meetings between Germans and Jews—especially of the younger generation.

There has once been an astonishingly fruitful German-Jewish symbiosis. Despite this, the emancipation of the Jews with the German community came very late, if not too late even. The more precious to Germany are the few Jewish communities that have been saved, and the more important it is to intensify the relations between Germany, the Germans, and Israel. It is no less important that the Jewish Communities throughout the world, into which many Jewish emigrants from Germany have moved, should keep close human and intellectual contact with one another.

Nobody is better able than the Jew himself to dispel the unrealistic and distorted image of the Jews. This produces a delicate situation because the injured has no cause to visit the house of his deprecator. Therefore, those Germans who are of good will must again and again take the first step. They should also ask their Jewish friends to speak to the young people of Germany.

Let me quote an example: in Minden, a town of 50 000 inhabitants, 20 surviving Jews have rebuilt their destroyed synagogue. Some Torah Rolls had been saved. That synagogue and the neighboring assembly room of the Jewish community have become a place where hundreds of young people meet the survivors of persecution.

Another opportunity is opened by the thousands of young students and trade unionists who visit Israel. All this is but a beginning. But, thank God, it is a good beginning. We all should help to ensure its success.

Ideologies of Extreme Rightists in Postwar Germany*

A Study of the Aftereffects of National Socialism

By Hans-Helmuth Knuetter

The Extreme Rightists and the Social Conditions Between 1945—1948

The capitulation of the German *Reich* in 1945 must not be evaluated as a military and political event alone. The entire German population was struck by the collapse of those values that had up to then been valid and above all by the social consequences of the catastrophe. Its results are more important for the period preceding the postwar rightist radical development than the political and military aspect of the collapse.

The social degradation of a considerable portion of the population, the denazification, the influx of refugees from the East, the effects of the dismantling of industry upon the labor market and on the mentality of those who were hit by it, prolonged the period of collapse until the year 1948, when the economic recovery began with the currency reform. The political revaluation of defeated Germany, caused by the ever-growing disparity between the Soviet Union and the Western powers, was outlined as early as the fall of 1946 in the address of the American Secretary of State, James Byrnes, in Stuttgart, and entered the stage of realization in July, 1948, when the Allies outlined a plan to form a German nation out of the *Laender* in the Western Zone.

The denazification undoubtedly strongly influenced the ideals of the later extreme rightists. In the territories of the three Western zones, a total number of 6,083,694 persons were involved, in all of the four occupation zones approximately 245,000 former National Socialists were interned, of which until January, 1947, approximately 100,000 were again set free.[1]) This deprivation of freedom resulted in the diminishing of the previous social status of many, if not most of those involved. This is especially true of those engaged in the free-lance professions. A social degradation likewise befell the full-time collaborators of the NSDAP (National Socialist Party) and its related organizations, as well as the professional soldiers.

---

*) This study, which was written in the Department of Political Science of the University of Bonn, first appeared there as a doctoral dissertation under the title, *The Image of National Socialism as found in the writings of Extreme Rightists since 1945. A study of the problem of continuity and accommodation of political ideas.* Excerpts are reprinted here with the kind permission of the publisher, Ludwig Roehrscheid Verlag, Bonn. The original title is *Ideologien des Rechtsradikalismus im Nachkriegsdeutschland — Eine Studie über die Nachwirkungen des Nationalsozialismus.*

1) Justus Fuerstenau: *Die Entnazifizierung in der deutschen Nachkriegspolitik* (Denazification in German Postwar Politics). Philosophical Dissertation (typewritten), Frankfort 1955, Appendix 3. "Entnazifizierung" (Denazification), *Staatslexikon*, 6th Edition, Freiburg, 1958, Volume 2, pp. 1195. The following statements are also based on Fuerstenau's information.

In the American Occupation Zone, where the denazification was most severely carried out, those concerned were put under a ban not to exercise their professions until their cases came to trial, which had a similar degrading effect.

To be sure, the denazification left little resentment behind among the large masses of those concerned; where it exists, its effect has been negligible. One reason for this probably consists in the fact that the denazification was gradually carried out in an ever milder fashion, and that all of the restrictions under which those involved were placed were lifted one by one. The chief reason, however, can be found in the economic recovery which, since 1948, has gradually done away with the social degradation.

Only among a minority of those involved did the resentment of the disenfranchised become virulent. On April 4, 1954 four smaller organizations, which contained at the most 50,000 members (that is only a small fraction of those who were denazified or interned), merged into the *Bundesverband ehemaliger Internierter und Entnazifizierungsgeschaedigter* (The Federal Association of Aggrieved Former Internees and Denazified Persons).

If the denazification did not unleash any recognizable resentment among the masses of those concerned, so much the more clearly was it discernible among the extreme rightists. The experiences of internment, the embitterment over the loss of former influence, the hatred of those who took over the reconstruction of the country, provide an inexhaustible source of material for writings filled with resentment.

* * *

In addition to denazification and internment, the economic situation, the catastrophic food situation in the three Western zones, also played an important, if lesser role, with regard to the resentment of the extreme rightists. Such resentment broke into print, if only in individual cases, as, for example, in the following:

> All Germany is an immense concentration camp—this sounds like an inflammatory exaggeration. Let us compare sober figures. The prisoners in the concentration camps of the Third *Reich* received 1,675 calories daily in the worst periods of the war—if we disregard the period of the final collapse. But after the capitulation, the daily calory count for all of Germany dropped from 1,550 to 825—in the French Zone to 805 calories at the beginning of the year 1948. In the French Zone of Occupation, the German population, when all is said and done, received only 200 grams (less than 7 ounces) of meat a month, while the personnel of the French occupation received—from German live stock—225 grams of meat daily. This hunger ration is not the undesired consequence of a catastrophe. It is systematically and forcefully maintained by blocking the frontiers. In Holland and Denmark, provisions are piling up which are not allowed to be delivered to Germany and therefore must be sold in England below cost. . . . German property worth more than 20 billion gold marks is available throughout the world in good dollars, pounds, francs, and kroners, but not one pfennig is returned, for "the German people have begun to suffer for their terrible crimes . . ."

> For the second time in its history, the German *Volk* is experiencing democracy as the consequence of a lost war, for the second time it is experiencing "freedom" in the form of an enforced "democracy"...
>
> National Socialism is dead, it is so dead in these first months after the defeat that even the most soured party member of yesterday is honestly prepared to accept any solution that is offered to him. Only slowly do the German people recognize that what is at stake is not the destruction of National Socialism, not the punishment of criminals, but the crushing of the strength of the German people.[2])

Here we have lined up all of the arguments which served as a basis for self-justification of the extreme rightists after 1945. In addition to denazification and social degradation there was the pressing economic want. Neither failed to exercise influence on the political attitude of the population.

Observers of political developments in Germany are in agreement that the rejection of National Socialism by the German people after the collapse was complete and genuine, but they also agree that the plight of the first postwar years, together with the charge of collective guilt, evoked a hardening against the incipient willingness to change:

> Two years have passed since Germany, having been bled to death, tossed every vestige of belief in Hitler overboard and greeted the Allied troops as their liberators in the hope that peaceful conditions might speedily be obtained. But in these two years hunger, frost, and pestilence have taught us the meaning of bitter need and the vultures of the black market. The requirements of this peace will be hard and bitter ones and most difficult of all to fulfill will be perhaps those of which the least is spoken in the daily misery: Proof of our change of heart...
>
> Truly the choking fist of hunger is strangling the German people. It stifles all feeling of responsibility, and the screams of despairing masses drown out the voices of hope and of demanding rights.
>
> But just as this new misery rejects the sacrifices of the past to the former demands, so does the bitter disappointment of those who are reduced to such miserable straits deepen the dissension. And instead of one unified people that presents a picture of good will to the present situation, the daily papers of East and West once again report the desecration of Jewish cemeteries by cowardly riffraff which is ready to take possession of its Nazi inheritance and which distributes circulars in some places announcing that Hitler is not dead but that a new Barbarossa will return in good time.[3])

---

2) Peter Kleist, *Auch Du Warst Dabei* (You, Too, Were Involved), p. 395 ff; *Die Deutsche Gemeinschaft* (The German Community), May, 1956, page 3, claims that in the Belsen concentration camp 800 calories were given prisoners daily; the same amount was permitted for Germans by the English in 1945. With regard to the nutrition situation, cf. Dr. Hans Schlange-Schoeningen: *Im Schatten des Hungers (In the Shadow of Hunger)*, Hamburg, 1955, p. 15 ff and the table on p. 302 f. According to this, the calory count actually did contain more than 2,000 in the spring of 1945; in 1946—47 the official compositions in the bizonal areas of the British and American occupation was 1,400 calories, but sank to some 800 to 900 calories from time to time and from place to place (for example in June and in September, 1945 and in June, 1946). For the French Zone, the composition was about 200 calories less than the official composition of the bizonal areas. All in all, Kleist generalizes from regional and temporary occurrences.

3) Walter Baron, "Deutscher Spaetsommer" (Late German Summer), *Deutsche Rundschau* 70, 1947, Heft 9, pp. 195,199. Also J. Emyln Williams, "Wohin fuehrt der Weg?", (Where does the Way lead?), *Das ist Germany*, edited by A. Settel, Frankfurt, 1950, p. 73.

Against the background of this economic plight, all efforts of a "re-education", a democratizing, seemed to be doomed to failure. The term "democracy" was interpreted as an empty catchword behind which the despotism of the occupation powers was solely and simply concealed. To be sure, the particulars about a new National Socialistic activity could not be verified, as legal organizing possibilities for the radical rightists hardly existed as yet. All observers were of the opinion, however, that a hardening out of spite could be ascertained among a greater portion of the population. It was attempted a number of times to determine the extent of this group of the population by means of a poll of opinion. On May 4, 1947 the results of an inquiry by the U.S. *Nachrichtenkontrollabteilung* (U.S. Intelligence Division, Office of Information Control) were released, which, however, covered only the U.S. Zone and the American Sector of Berlin. Thus, the North German areas, where during the early postwar years the strongest extreme-rightist tendencies were found, were not taken into account. According to this survey, 19 % of the respondents admitted that they were National Socialists, 22 % that they were adherents of the Nazi race theory, and 20 % that they were anti-Semites, 6 % declared themselves opponents, and 33 % indicated indifference. These results occasioned one newspaper to draw the grotesque conclusion that 94 % of the German people had failed to grasp the meaning of what had happened. One year later, 65 % of former Nazi party members and 49 % of nonparty members declared that National Socialism was a good thing.[4])

That the alleged Nazi impenitence on this scale did not square with the facts follows from the election results of the years 1946 to 1948. Since 1945, political parties with strong extreme-rightist tendencies—even though still limited regionally—were in existence, though they were unable to show any kind of success worth mentioning. This could in no way be attributed only to the confining impositions of the occupation powers which at the most could hinder a supra-regional amalgamation but not the possibility of taking part in elections. At state elections the new rightist extremist parties were never able to obtain more than 3.1 % of the total vote.[5])

Although the success of the new rightist parties probably would have been greater without the limitations imposed by the occupation powers, the number of votes they received, even in areas where they were located, would still have remained far below the results that they should have had if the pessimistic statements of the far-reaching comeback of Nazi ideas were true. Even though the new rightist parties did condemn National Socialism throughout, they should have had a more appealing effect on dis-

---

4) Erich Peter Naumann and Elisabeth Noelle, *Antworten* (Answers), Allensbach, 1954, p. 24 f.

5) The new extreme rightist parties obtained the following results at state elections held before the currency reform:

	Votes	Percentage
Deutsche Konservative Partei (DKP), Hamburg, October 13, 1946	9,625	0.3 %
Deutsche Rechtspartei (DRP), Niedersachsen (Lower Saxony), April 20, 1947	7,245	0.3 %
DKP/DRP, Nordrhein-Westfalen, April 20, 1947	24,879	0.5 %
DKP/DRP, Schleswig-Holstein, April 20, 1947	32,000	3.1 %
Nationaldemokratische Partei, Hessen, April 25, 1948	2,484	0.2 %

Municipal elections, which are politically less significant, and in which the parties also take part—in isolated cases with better success—are not included here. (Compilation according to: Richard Schachtner: *Die deutschen Nachkriegswahlen* (The German Postwar Elections), Munich, 1956, pp. 22—68.)

guised Nazis than the other parties—if for no other reason than their appeal to national pride and traditional values. An attempt has been made to explain the favorable remarks about National Socialism in the above-mentioned survey as being based not on the ideas of Nazism or its methods of domination, but rather Nazism's claim to establish discipline and order after the collapse of the Weimar Republic, which was universally regarded as chaotic. But this explanation cannot entirely satisfy us, for the new rightist parties likewise appealed to security and order, but still were not elected.

The real reason for those favorable remarks can much more likely be found in the fact that the horrors of the Nazi past dissipated in the face of the catastrophic economic development from 1945 to 1948. As a result, therefore, we find that:

1. Denazification and its consequences and economic distress led to a mounting distrust of the new democracy. Incipient readiness toward active cooperation floundered under the pressure of social conditions.
2. The extent of the alleged retrogression to National Socialism was just as much overestimated by observers of the time as was the depth effect of resentment produced. Political and economic reconstruction have in time done away with them both.
3. Resentment of disenfranchisement continued to rankle a comparatively small group of former internees.

The Revival of the Rightists, 1948—1952

From 1945 until 1948, the efforts of extreme rightists to organize into a concentrated group were strongly confined. A large number of Nazi underground organizations were uncovered in 1945—46. Among the rightist parties that sprang up and possessed an Allied license was the *Deutsche Konservative Partei,* which was founded in Wuppertal in November, 1945, and in Westphalia, the *Deutsche Aufbaupartei* (German Reconstruction Party) came into being around the same time. The two parties merged in 1946. Under the name *Deutsche Rechtspartei* (German Rightist Party) they took part in the *Bundestag* election campaign of 1949. In January, 1950, the party split into the *Nationale Rechte* and the *Deutsche Reichspartei.*

These parties, which at first were composed almost exclusively of former nationalists, proceeded with the greatest of caution. They emphasized their opposition to National Socialism and designated themselves as associations of conservatives and monarchists. Their criticism of the *gemeinschaftszersetzenden Wirkung* (communal disintegrating effect) of the political parties and the stress on reviving national feeling made it attractive also for those rightist radicals who first began to take an interest in founding their own parties after compulsory licensing was abolished. Foremost among them was the *Sozialistische Reichspartei.*

The activities of these parties in the British Zone were limited to individual counties of the states of Lower Saxony, Schleswig-Holstein, and North-Rhine Westphalia. (Some weak adjuncts existed in Hamburg.) Since 1948, the *Nationaldemokratische Partei* has been in existence in the U.S.

Zone in Hesse, since the fall of 1947 the *Deutsche Block* and, since 1948, the *Vaterlaendische Union* have existed in Bavaria.

Since 1946, these parties have taken part in nearly all of the state and municipal elections. While they were able to send some of their representatives to the municipal parliament, they were unsuccessful in making inroads in the state legislature. In spite of organizational weaknesses, the arrival of these groups on the scene aroused attention at home and abroad and was interpreted as proof of a resuscitation of German nationalism.

Actually, the new rightist organizations first experienced an impetus after 1949. The chief reason lies surely in the abolishment of compulsory licensing: thereby the most essential obstacle for organizational development was removed. Moreover the political importance of West Germany grew in proportion to the intensification of disparity between East and West. A heightening of national self-consciousness was the result. The increase of social differences also played a not insignificant role: while before the currency reform nearly everyone had to suffer economic want equally, now, after the reform, part of the population enjoyed an economic advancement, while others—such as unemployed or displaced persons, who were massed mostly in Northern Germany under unpleasant conditions—were cut off from such prosperity. If one takes the election results as a basis, one finds that the rightist radicals reached the height of postwar success in the years 1949 to 1951:

In the *Bundestag* election on August 14, 1949, the DRP *(Deutsche Reichspartei)* was able to win 273,129 votes (8.1 %) and 5 mandates in Lower Saxony. On May 6, 1951, the *Sozialistische Reichspartei* received 366,793 votes (11 %) in Lower Saxony and 16 mandates. On October 7, 1951, it obtained 25,813 votes (7.7 %) in Bremen and 8 mandates. Except for the modest success of the *Deutsche Reichspartei* in the Rhineland-Palatinate in April, 1959, in which it obtained 87,222 votes (5.1 %) and one mandate in the state election, no extreme rightist party has succeeded since then in reaching the required 5 % minimum in any state election. A tabulation of the extreme rightist political parties gives the following picture:[6])

Year:	No. of Rightist Parties:
1945	2
1946	1
1947	2
1948	4
1949	6
1950	11
1951	12
1952	74[7])

6) Compiled according to documents of the *BVN-Archiv* as well as those based on my own investigations. In spite of the best efforts to include also the splinter parties, these figures are sometimes questionable. It is, for example, often impossible to ascertain whether and when a group discontinued its activities. If there is no official disbandment, fusion or prohibition, a party sometimes disbands on its own and quietly disappears from the scene. Consequently it is possible that some of the figures are not quite accurate. Equivalently, the same can be said for figures of associations, youth and cultural organizations.

7) This sudden increase can be explained by the new formation of successor organizations of the SRP, which was outlawed in October, 1952. Most of the successor organizations were soon in turn outlawed. It is hard to tell whether these organizations were only traditional societies or political parties. As they nonetheless tried to take part in the Lower Saxony elections of November 9, 1952, they are regarded here as parties.

1953	14
1954	16
1955	11
1956	11
1957	8
1958	8
1959	7

During this time period, these parties had a total membership of about 35,000.

More important than the political parties, which have lost their significance since 1952, are, therefore, the associations, youth organizations, societies for cultural purposes, publishers and book clubs, as well as periodicals.

Among the associations that fall under an extreme rightist category are:

1) Associations serving a special purpose, such as those of aggrieved denazified persons, employees, and soldiers' organizations;
2) Associations with general political aims which are differentiated from political parties only inasmuch as they do not take part in elections.

The first group, especially, should be designated as rightist radical only with qualifications. These associations continually emphasize their loyalty to the Federal Republic, yet extreme rightist tendencies among their members are unmistakably discernible beneath the surface. Taking the moderate official course of these groups into consideration, one is nonetheless justified in classifying them under the heading "rightist radical".[8]) The following table shows how the associations of this category developed from 1945 to 1959:

Year:	No. of Associations:
1945	0
1946	0
1947	0
1948	0
1949	4
1950	8
1951	16
1952	28
1953	13
1954	22
1955	16
1956	16
1957	17
1958	14
1959	15

Taken together, the associations embraced a membership of 49,000 persons minimum, 112,000 persons maximum during the period from 1949 to 1959.

In regard to associations with cultural or religious aims, the picture looks like this:

---

8) This is made evident by the example which the "Stahlhelm" makes. Its official organ, which bears the same name, painfully avoids every form of extremism. But in its internal information letter (bimonthly since 1954) the extreme rightist tendencies are unmistakable. Personal reports affirm the impression of an official course of loyalty and unofficial radicalism.

Year:	No. of Associations:
1945	0
1946	0
1947	2
1948	2
1949	4
1950	5
1951	5
1952	5
1953	5
1954	5
1955	5
1956	7
1957	6
1958	6
1959	6

Included in these groups are associations like the *Bund fuer Gotterkenntnis* (Alliance for the Cognition of God—Ludendorff) or *Das Deutsche Kulturwerk Europaeischen Geistes* (The German Cultural Association for a European Spirit). The number of constituents in these groups is about 30,000.

The data with regard to the youth organizations is not very reliable, due to very strong fluctuations. Splitting, disbanding, founding of new groups occur so frequently that the changes take place faster than they can be registered. Consequently, material published about extreme rightist youth groups until now differs considerably. It is certain, however, that the report that there are 70,000 rightist radical youths in the Federal Republic is grossly exaggerated, as is the figure of 30,000 to 40,000, which was released later. The strongest youth organizations in this category are the *Jugendbund Adler* with 1,500 to 2,000 members and the *Deutsche Jugendbund der Kyffhaeuser* with an alleged 4,600 members. On June 24, 1954, the *Kameradschaftsring nationaler Jugendbuende* (KNJ) was founded in Hamburg. In the beginning of 1955, nineteen rightist radical youth groups met in Cologne, some of which joined the *"Kameradschaftsring"*. In May, 1958, nine groups belonged to the KNJ. In 1959, due to internal tensions, the parent organization disintegrated, the *Jugendbund Adler* remaining, as we have said, the strongest group. All other associations had considerably fewer members. On January 6, 1960, the Ministry of the Interior announced that fifteen to eighteen rightist radical youth groups existed in the Federal Republic with the high estimate of 2300 members. A compilation of DGB in March, 1960 cited fifteen extreme rightist youth groups (highest estimate 2,950 members) and five military youth groups (highest estimate 2,750). With regard to the first estimate, there was a fully grotesque overexaggeration.

Essential to the bearing of these youth organizations is the fact that their leaders are mostly older men who belonged to the Nazi party, or the SA (*Sturm Abteilung*—Storm Troopers) or SS (*Schutz Staffel*—Elite Guard) and for the most part were members of extreme rightist parties after 1945. These youth leaders try unequivocally to influence the members of their groups along Nazi lines.

More important than the organizations, however, is the journalistic production of the rightist radicals. The following tables show the development of publishing houses, book clubs, and magazines:

Year:	No. of Publishing Houses and Book Clubs:
1945	0
1946	0
1947	0
1948	0
1949	0
1950	2
1951	6
1952	11
1953	16
1954	17
1955	17
1956	22
1957	18
1958	15
1959	15

Year:	No. of House Organs:	No. of Non-Organizational Magazines:	Total:
1945	0	0	0
1946	0	0	0
1947	2	0	2
1948	2	0	2
1949	4	1 (?)	5 (?)
1950	11	2	13
1951	22	7	29
1952	19	7	26
1953	12	10	22
1954	15	7	22
1955	14	8	22[9])
1956	15	8	23
1957	13	7	20
1958	13	7	20
1959	12	8	20

Although here, too, every effort has been made to include every group, even the smallest publishing house, book club, and magazine, it is likely that some internal bulletins and the like were overlooked. Among the book clubs as well, it is sometimes extremely difficult to ascertain whether or not they still exist.

Circulation figures of these magazines are for the most part rather low. The *Deutsche Nationalzeitung,* which made its appearance in 1953—54 with its alleged more than 30,000 copies, held the lead. Since then the

9) At variance with this estimate is the report of the *Bundesamt fuer Verfassungsschutz* (Federal Office for the Protection of the Constitution): *Feinde der Demokratie* (Enemies of Democracy), March-April, 1956, p. 6. According to it, there were 27 magazines, of which 15 where party organs and 12 independent.

Deutsche Soldatenzeitung alone has more than a circulation of 30,000. Thus, the circulation figures exceed the 10,000 limit only in exceptional cases. To the extent that they can be determined at all, they lie in most cases between 2,000 and 6,000 copies, while a considerable number of hectographed bulletin sheets and the like remain far below this number.

From the four tables above, one can deduce that the upswing of radical rightists began in 1949 and, since 1952—53, has begun to stagnate or decline slightly.

As a matter of fact, the remarks of the extreme rightist publications from 1949 to 1952 show a strong optimism. They proceed from the firm conviction that democracy, the "system of defeat", will soon again have "managed" itself out of existence and the inheritance will accrue to them. The image of democracy that these rightists hold is apparently determined by their experiences in the years 1929 to 1933. Unemployment and foreign policy weaknesses appear to them as characteristics of the democratic state and awaken the expectation that the Federal Republic will soon share the fate of the Weimar Republic. Certain groups actually expected, in all seriousness, shortly to be able to "take over" political power:

> From 1953 on, the Federal Republic will have an SPD government. This government will, by around 1955, have mismanaged itself out of existence. There follow the struggles for political power between Right and Left. The entire political development is preparing the ground for the *Freikorps Deutschland* to take over political power, which will occur around 1957.[10])

The radical rightists were so sure of themselves that they openly demanded that former emigrants be dismissed from political positions and that former resistance fighters be punished:[11])

> The year 1951 has brought us successes which will fill the profiteers of the collapse and the jackals of the Allies with a panicky terror and make them realize that the year 1945 cannot protect them forever, and that the day of reckoning may strike sooner than they deem possible.[12])

The rightist radicals directed their hopes on the *Bundestag* election of 1953:

> When the *Bundestag* convenes again, the second period of the government will have begun. Many symptoms indicate that the current Christian-bourgois majority will suffer the same fate that they did in the first period.
>
> Since the Federal Government became conscious of the fact that a serious opposition exists among the people, it began an energetic

10) From an internal circular letter of the *Freikorps Deutschland*, which was outlawed in February, 1953. Here quoted according to: *Und morgen die ganze Welt!* (And Tomorrow the Whole World), Frankfort, 1952), p. 15.

11) Speech by Richard Etzel at a conference of the *Deutscher Block* in Hamburg, March 19, 1951. All members of the government should be investigated to determine what they did before 1945. Emigrants should be punished. Also Heinrich Sanden, "Landesverrat trifft das ganze Volk" (Treason Concerns, Everybody), *Nation* Europa 1, 1951, Heft 8, p. 48.

12) FR-Brief 35-36/1951, p.l.; quoted according to: *Das Urteil des Bundesverfassungsgerichts vom 23. Oktober 1952 betr. Feststellung der Verfassungswidrigkeit der Sozialistischen Reichspartei.* (The Verdict of the Federal Constitutional Court of Oct. 23, 1952 re.: Determining Whether the SRP is Unconstitutional.) Tuebingen, 1952, p. 69.

struggle that sometimes looked like a desperate one for public opinion.[13]) In point of fact there did exist general dissatisfaction with the Federal Republic in 1951-52. Unemployment figures rose steadily since the currency reform,[14]) and opinion polls showed that the institutions and leading persons of the Federal Republic enjoyed merely slight esteem.[15])

However, the optimism of the rightist radicals was dampened at the turn of the year 1952-53.

The outlawing of the *Sozialistische Reichspartei* in October, 1952, did not, to be sure, have much of a deterrent effect at first, as the rightist radicals apparently believed that they could carry on the activities of their organizations underground. Up till January of 1953, however, sixty-one successor organizations and the *Freikorps Deutschland,* as well as the regional associations of the *Deutsche Gemeinschaft* and the *Arbeitsgemeinschaft Nation Europa* were outlawed in Berlin. A further heavy blow against the radical right was the arrest, at the behest of the British High Commission on January 15, 1953, of the former state secretary in the ministry of propaganda, Werner Naumann, and a group of ex-Nazis. They were accused of having attempted to infiltrate the FDP and by subversive means to use it as a point of departure for a seizure of power. Immediately thereafter, speculations arose as to the underlying reasons for these measures, nor were suspicions lacking that the English had had only made the arrests in order to injure the Federal Republic's foreign policy or to upset her trade relations. Since the outlawing of the SRP, the foreign press once more concerned itself to a growing degree with the problems of German rightist radicalism, which by this time—in spite of various prohibitions—was regarded as a greater danger than in the period in which it thrived. A great deal of attention was also raised by a published report of the American High Commission. On January 23, 1953, it revealed the results of an opinion poll in regard to the attitude of Germans to National Socialism: 44 % of the respondents thought that it contained more good than bad.

Thus, Naumann's group was arrested at a time when the reputation of the Federal Republic's foreign policy was truly in jeopardy. But all speculation of the underlying reasons for the action is untenable, for Naumann himself permitted a portion of his papers to be published. These papers clearly showed that Naumann's group did actually make plans to exploit the FDP for their own aims. The English were greatly concerned that the German officials, though able to resist a direct attack of rightist radicalism in the

---

13) Gerd Walleiser: *"Halbzeit"* (Halftime), In: *Nation Europa* 1 (1951) H. 8, p. 63—According to a remark of the executive head of the SRP, Heller, the party in 1953 expected 40 to 50 mandates in the Bundestag to upset the scales in such a way that neither the CDU nor the SPD could govern. *(Und Morgen die ganze Welt.* Frankfort, 1952, p. 80.)

14) Unemployment Figures:

1947	595,200
1948	603,900
1949	1,263,000
3. 12. 1951	1,653,600 (peak)
31. 3. 1952	1,579,600
30. 9. 1952	1,050,600

Stat. Jahrbuch fuer die Bundesrepublik Deutschland. Stuttgart, 1958, p. 117; Statistical Yearbook 1949/50 (published by the United Nations) New York, 1950, p. 91.

15) *Jahrbuch der oeffentlichen Meinung* (Yearbook of Public Opinion), 1947—1955. By Elisabeth Noelle and Erich Peter Neumann. Allensbach 1956, pp. 162, 163, 167, 170 & esp. pp. 172, 179. With interesting possibilities for comparing how public opinion changed along positive lines from 1953 on.

form of the SRP and similar groups, would only be able to defend themselves against a secret infiltration with great difficulty (which at the same time would have signified an action against one of the parties of the government coalition). This induced the English to take action; trade jealousy or intentions to disrupt foreign policy had nothing to do with it. The arrest of Naumann and his group in any case made it clear to the extreme rightist that they could not hope to succeed in their aims whether by means of direct attack or by infiltration.

The results of the *Bundestag* election of September 6, 1953, finally, constituted the last link of that chain of events which shattered the rightist radicals' hopes of victory. From the time of the outlawing of the SRP on, they experienced only setbacks and defeat. Economic consolidation and the quiet development of domestic politics meanwhile led to a strengthening of state consciousness, which did not give rightist radicalism a chance to take root. The recognition that democracy need not be identical with unemployment, want, domestic chaos, and a weak foreign policy, prevented rightist radicalism from winning a mass following.

After the press, domestic and foreign, referred alarmingly to the German rightist radicalism at the turn of the year in 1948-49, and again in 1952-53, similar anxious remarks once again became frequent at the turn of the year 1955-56. This time, however, the concern was not with organizations, but was directed rather toward the subversion of the administrative and judiciary branches of government.

Among the rightist radicals the weight of their activity since 1953 shifted more and more to journalistic efforts. Except for the *Deutsche Reichspartei,* which likewise was unable to achieve any greater victories, the rightist parties deteriorated into thoroughly insignificant sectarian groups. The recognition of their own insignificance apparently has led to an ideological hardening. The optimism of the years 1949-1952 has been transplanted by a cramped adherence to the Nazi past. While in 1951 critical remarks about the personality of Hitler were possible in the *Nation Europa* and Hans Grimm in 1950 still made a distinction between "insane Hitlerism" and the positive content of National Socialism, by 1954 and 1955 only the glorification of Hitler remains.

To be sure, the remarks about National Socialism before 1953 do not differ basically, except in degree, from those made in later years. The positive basic attitude in both spans of time is the same. But embitterment over their own lack of success hardened their judgment.

Rightist Radicalism Between Continuity and Accommodation*

One result of this paper is that there actually is such a thing as a continuity of National Socialistic and to a certain extent even pre-Nazi

*) EDITOR'S NOTE:
Due to space limitations we must unfortunately skip over a number of chapters in the author's dissertation. Among other things, the author discusses:
The image of National Socialism in the writings of the radical rightists; judgment of Hitler and other Nazi personalities in the eyes of the extremists; evaluation of nazi persecution measures; the question of guilt and the war; resistance and collapse; dictatorship, democracy, parliamentarianism, and political parties in the eyes of the rightist radicals; and the mentality and methods of the radical rightists.
In the following pages the translation of the author's dissertation is continued with the concluding chapter, which actually in summarizing the entire study includes a brief treatment of the more important points discussed in the untranslated chapters.

extreme rightest ideas. The reasons for and the nature of this continuity are presented here briefly in summation.

One important basis for this continuity can be seen in the rightists' identity or association with certain types of individuals or groups. The largest portion of rightist radical publicists and of members of extreme rightist associations are persons who even before 1945 were actively involved either with Nazi organizations and publications or with the corresponding institutions of non-Nazi extreme rightists. The basis of the ideological continuity is, therefore, the personal indentity with rightist extremist groups or individuals. With regard to the *Sozialistische Reichspartei,* for example, the most unequivocal judgment is possible because, as a result of the confiscation of their records—by order of the Federal Constitutional Court in connection with the trial—all essential personal documents were available.[16]) The records clearly showed that the SRP had tried to recruit former Nazis just because of their former membership in the party. As for other organizations like the *Waffen-SS-Traditionsgemeinschaft HIAG,* the personal continuity was just as evident as with the Ludendorff adherents or the *Stahlhelm.*

This personal identity explains why the rightist extremists of today are not in the least prepared to break away their own past. This inertia is interpreted by them as steadfastness of character, as loyalty, while those who departed from National Socialism after the collapse are regarded as characterless. Holding fast to the National Socialist train of thought appears, therefore, as moral stability (as strength of character in a time devoid of character) and heroic stamina (since the strength of character is persecuted and ridiculed). That anyone can change his convictions because of better understanding—without losing his conscience—appears to the rightist radicals as totally unthinkable. But, of course, if somebody changes his opinion in the interests of National Socialism, that is another matter! In this case there can be no talk of lost conscience.

While the ideological continuity of the National Socialists who emigrated after the war's end is the least unbroken, [17]) the radical rightists who remained in Germany exert themselves to make certain adjustment to the postwar political concepts. This accommodation is characterized by a highly veiled language. By no means do the rightist radicals admit to being extremists and defenders of National Socialism, but claim that they are likewise democrats and adherents of freedom. It is necessary from time to time to investigate in detail what the rightist radicals mean by these terms—their interpretation in most cases differs from the meaning given these words in common usage. Similarly the rightist extremists tend, to be sure, to vindicate Nazi persons and procedure, but at the same time to deny that it has anything to do with vindication. Thus, for example, Arthur Ehrhardt and Hans Grimm in their glorification of Hitler emphasize that they never belonged to the close admirers of Hitler, that

---

16) The decision of the Federal Constitutional Court on October 29, 1952, pp. 37—44, especially p. 43 f.

17) As expressed in a publication, *Deutsche Ehre* (German Honor), cited in *Feinde der Demokratie* (Enemies of Democracy), December 1952-January 1953, p. 35. "National Socialism alone can lead Germany to world importance. The bourgeois national parties must open their doors wide, if they want to justify themselves before the future." The periodical, *Der Weg* (The Way), which appeared from about 1947 to 1957 in Buenos Aires, wrote in the same vein.

is to say that they did not approve of the personality of Hitler, though they did sanction his "historical appearance". The contrast between official concealment of Nazism, while in point of fact actually endorsing it, is especially striking in some of the remarks of the SRP which were quoted in the verdict against this party.

It is, however, by no means the case that the rightist radicals accommodate themselves for reasons of opportunism—rather and above all in fear of punishment. No matter how much this reason also may contribute, the decisive factor remains the loss of unlimited faith in the future, which characterized the rightist radicals before 1933. Among rightist radicals today there is a more or less clear recognition that a simple restoration of the Third *Reich* is impossible. Since they have no concrete idea how a modification might be possible, they swing aimlessly between the desire for retaining individual aspects of a system that once gave them personal prestige and self-confidence and the vague awareness that this desire has no chances for success at all. In compromise, they submit to a large extent to an outward accommodation to the views of their opponents. At the same time, the ideological continuity remains strong enough as to enable those on the outside to see through this apparent accommodation.

The question as to the future outlook of rightist radicalism must also be answered accordingly. Since the extreme rightists of today are preponderantly identical with the adherents of Nazism and the pre-Nazi rightists, and since their views are designated by this identity, there are many indications that the problem in its present-day form will take care of itself—by the dying out of the generation which consciously accepted and experienced National Socialism. Of course, there will still be persons and groups even then who feel uneasy in modern society, for whom the pluralism of modern democracy is uncanny and the stress on responsibility for making one's own decisions is uncomfortable. This strata will always seek authoritarian solutions, so that the basic problem of rightist extremism remains, even if presumably the selection of its arguments changes.

Overcoming Rightist Radicalism

Thus remains the additional question whether rightist extremism actually is a present danger—even if only potentially—and if so how can one cope with it?

First of all it can be ascertained that the designation "rightist radicalism" as well as the catchwords "neo-Facism" or "neo-Nazism" are used now and again as means of warfare in domestic political disputes for the purpose of defaming opponents. Communists, especially, use every means of propaganda to "prove" that the Federal Republic is a "Fascist-dominated" State. Thereby the reactions abroad raise speculations as to whether the accusations in question cause more responsive reactions in foreign countries than among the West German public. By trying to create foreign policy difficulties for the Federal Republic they hope to serve their own Communist aims. From an endless sea of printed material, including newspaper articles, books, pamphlets, documents, and movies, we can mention only a couple of grotesque examples here. In the movie, *"Unternehmen Teutonenschwert"* (Project Teutonenschwert), it is "proven"—contrary to the actual facts of the situation—that General Hans Speidel, the present NATO Chief of the Allied Land Forces in Central Europe, had King Alexander of Jugoslavia and the French Foreign Minister Barthou murdered in Marseille in 1934. Similarly, in his book *Kriegswahlen in Westberlin* (War Elections in West Berlin), Otto Nuschke, the former chairman of the Soviet Zone CDU, pointed out that Ernst Reuter, the late Lord Mayor of West Berlin, lived in Turkey during the war by means of a passport extended from time to time by the Ambassador von Papen. From that Nuschke concludes that Reuter was a "turncoat and confidence man of the Nazis". In this connection precisely the SPD is designated as a neo-Fascist party, which desires a "hot war".[18]) Such attacks are, of course, not to be taken seriously. They give the extreme rightists only a welcome pretext for the claim that everyone who speaks out against rightist radicalism is helping himself to a catchword coined in Moscow. These remarks uttered with a definite intent, which in milder form are occasionally advanced in the Federal Republic itself, are totally useless as a way of evaluating the significance and possible overcoming of extreme rightist appearances.

Any serious assessment must proceed from the awareness that rightist extremists can be divided into three groups:

1. To the most comprehensive group belong the voters of the extreme rightist parties, who on account of their fluctuation can hardly be counted. While in 1951 in Lower Saxony over 300,000 voters cast their ballots for the SRP, this figure was subsequently reached only at the *Bundestag* elections, but never again in smaller elections. The core of extreme rightist voters then is very unstable.
2. To the second group belong the subscribers and readers of extreme rightist publications. In contrast to the first group, whose ignorance or sudden awakening of sympathy could evoke a turning to rightist radicalism for a short period, here we are concerned with conscious adherents who, however, remain passive and, except for the purchase of the publications, do nothing for the extension of rightist radicalism.
3. To the third group belong, finally, the members and functionaries of parties and associations, publishers and co-workers of publications, in short those rightist radicals who are not only conscious, but also active champions of their views.

Every attempt to cope with and overcome political radicalism by means of instruction and awakening of a democratic consciousness will have to start from the fact that in the third group will actually be found the uneducable who are persistent in their prejudices and are immune to factual arguments. On the other hand, a skillful political education program could most likely wield a great deal of influence among the members of the first group, who mostly seek authoritarian solutions for their wel-

18) Otto Nuschke, "Kriegswahlen in Westberlin" (War Elections in West Berlin), *Neue Zeit,* December 3, 1950. Printed in the author's *Reden und Aufsaetze* 1919 bis 1950 (Speeches and Essays, 1919 to 1950), Berlin, o.J., 1957, p. 255.

fare only in specific concrete situations. Political education can especially have, as its goal, the prevention of these emotional fear reactions at the outset by enlightened instructions. In all probability, such efforts will also reach a portion of those who belong to the second group, even though there is a constant change-over to the activists—in fact, overlapping occurs in practice generally in all three groups.

The impression should not be aroused here that political education is regarded as a utopian panacea. It is only a preventive measure, behind which the "negative" methods of combating extremism by the police and by justice still retain their significance. It can, however, hardly be disputed that the outlook of rightist radicalism for the future is not only dependent on an economic or a political crisis, which could drive greater masses into the structure that is already present, but that political education could also exercise at least a certain softening effect on the more intelligent portion of its potential students. If it cannot exclude emotional reactions of fear, it can at least intercept them.

"Rightism Lacks Attraction" *

An Empirical Report on Rightism by the Federal Ministry of the Interior

The rightism encountered in the Federal Republic is weak and disunited, contradictory and unattractive. This is the conclusion reached by the Federal Ministry of the Interior in a comprehensive empirical report on rightist organizations. Just published, it is based on findings by the Federal Office for the Protection of the Constitution.

This report says that in recent years rightism has been unable to exert any influence on the formation of political intent among our people or to win over any considerable groups of the population. The rightist parties have been unsuccessful in every election campaign they participated in, the report points out, and the population has been just as determined in rejecting the arguments of the rightists regarding the important events and problems of day-to-day politics.

The Federal Ministry of the Interior states that "rightism has become isolated", with a consequent membership loss for rightist groups, while a certain radicalization in word and deed has at the same time developed among remaining adherents. Under certain circumstances this might lead to political radicalization if internal political tensions were to develop or if economic conditions were to deteriorate. The Ministry affirmed that the Federal Office for the Protection of the Constitution is therefore keeping rightism under incessant supervision and is combating it with all constitutional means.

The Federal Ministry of the Interior is of the opinion that the strength of rightism in the Federal Republic is often assessed wrongly both at home and abroad, and that undeserved significance is attached to it. This mistaken view, the Ministry points out, is due mainly to erroneous figures, which have given the impression that rightism is supported by a widely ramified organization and growing membership.

According to the inquiries of the Federal Office for the Protection of the Constitution, a total of 86 rightist organizations and publishing houses with about 35,400 members and adherents existed in the area of the Federal Republic in 1961, while 85 such organizations with 54,200 members and adherents had been in existence two years previously. Rightist organizations have therefore lost 33 % of their adherents within two years. The actual membership of rightist parties amounted to 12,300 at the end of 1961

*) From *Allgemeine Wochenzeitung der Juden in Deutschland,* April 27, 1962. This report brings the foregoing study up-to-date. Knuetter's manuscript was finished in the fall of 1959.

(as compared with 17,200 at the end of 1959), and that of rightist youth organizations to 2,100 (the democratic youth associations comprising about 4.5 million).

The report states that the followers of the rightist organizations are predominantly lower middle class, people who cling to the idea of a corporative state because of a certain class consciousness. So far, the German manual worker has generally kept aloof from rightist groups, the report notes.

All efforts of rightist organizations to rally their forces have, according to the Ministry's report, so far failed because of competition for leadership among the groups and lack of a suitable "leader". After the complete failure of the "Deutsche Sammlungsbewegung" in 1961, only one further attempt at unification has been made, the aim of which was to form an association of expediency of all nationalist and neutralist groups.

The Federal Ministry of the Interior is not unaware of the fact that, apart from an unknown number of nonorganized rightist lone wolves, there are "latent rightist tendencies in the area of the Federal Republic which cannot be expressed in precise figures".

Rightist organizations are financed chiefly by membership fees, contribution drives, subsidies by wealthy friends at home and abroad, and profits from the sale of published matter. There are all in all 46 publications with an edition of 160,300 copies, which comes to about 30,000 more than in 1959. Twelve publishing houses and six distribution agencies figured as the publishers of books or pamphlets (about 100 titles) with rightist tendencies.

The report goes on to say that nonorganized adherents to rightist views express themselves mainly as free-lance journalists, authors of books, or pamphleteers, by "scrawling" activities or by creating disturbances. The number of lone wolves holding nationalist views and engaged in the journalistic field is estimated at about 225 in the whole of the Federal Republic. The number of those caught as the originators of "scrawling" activities or disturbances for political reasons is about the same.

According to the report there are, in addition, some organizations of immigrants from the Eastern Bloc in the Federal Republic which are rightist in view, often engage in anti-Semitic activities, and harm the reputation of the Federal Republic abroad. As a rule, these organizations are scattered not only throughout the Federal Republic but also in various countries of the free world; they do not, however, have many members. Among them are some groups of the former Hungarian *Pfeilkreuz* Party, the Croatian *Ustaschi,* as well as RONND, a Great Russian, anti-Semitic and nationalist organization, and the Ukrainian OUN.

The report says that there have been hardly any comments on the Eichmann case by rightist organizations in the Federal Republic, whereas international Fascism abroad used the case to glorify nationalist ideology openly and to defame the Jewish people as the "worst war criminals and mass murderers of all time". It is recalled that newspapers, pamphlets and leaflets of this kind were introduced into the Federal Republic from Sweden, Great Britain, the United States, Egypt, Spain, and Argentina, and disseminated in rightist circles.

Several thousand copies of a rousing pamphlet published in Cairo—"Israel's nuclear rearmament against the Arab Nations is to be financed by the Eichmann case"—reached the Federal Republic, and some consignments of this pamphlet were intercepted successfully. Equally large editions of three other foreign papers containing inflammatory anti-Semitic articles on the Eichmann trial were distributed among rightist circles in the Federal Republic.

According to the report, the Federal Office for the Protection of the Constitution registered a total of 389 National Socialist or anti-Semitic incidents in 1961. These took place, as in the previous year, mainly in Berlin, North Rhine-Westphalia, and Lower Saxony. It is stated that of offenders and accessories to these acts, 303 persons—among them 30 women—have so far been discovered, and 79 final judgments for criminal offenses committed by reason of National Socialist motives were pronounced in the past year. (There were more than 200 in 1960.) The offenders were punished as follows: 45 with imprisonment, 26 with fines, 3 according to the discretion of the Juvenile Court Act. Of the sentenced offenders, 12.7 % belonged to the 16—20 age group, 42.5 % to the 21—35 age group, and 44.8 % were over 35.

In addition, the report continues, 1,083 offenders who participated in the "scrawling" activities of the previous year were discovered. Half of these were below the age of 30. The report says that 44 % acted from motives hostile to the constitution, that in 28 % of the cases the criminal offenses committed spontaneously on impulse or under the influence of alcohol were due to "subliminal political motives", and that the actions of another 28 % were due—"with the utmost probability"—to nonpolitical motives.

According to the report, no indications of any central direction of such incidents by groups of organized rightists have been found. The authorities for protection of the constitution have, however, established that the German Soviet Zone not only is making use of the anti-Semitic and National Socialist incidents for a world-wide campaign of defamation of the Federal Government, but has actually launched activities of this kind in the Federal Republic. Several inflammatory pamphlets from Eastern Germany are reproduced in the report as evidence of this.

The Federal Ministry of the Interior goes on to say that the Federal Office for the Protection of the Constitution knows of about 450 foreign parties, organizations, and publishing houses that are connected with international Fascism through nationalist, anti-Semitic, or racially discriminatory aims.

Among the groups of foreign Fascists working on an obviously supranational level, the following tried to gain an organizational foothold in the Federal Republic: the *Europaeische Neu-Ordnung* of Gaston Armand Amaudruz (Swiss) and its youth organization *Jeune Legion Européenne;* the *Europaeische Soziale Bewegung* of Per Engdahl (Swedish) of Malmoe; the *Mouvement d'Action Civique* of Jan Thiriart (Belgian), in the form of its international organization *Jeune Europe;* the *Northern European*

Ring in Coventry, with its organ *The Northern European;* the *Nordbund,* with its headquarters in Thun (Switzerland); off-shoots of the *American Nazi Party,* as well as anti-Semitic individuals abroad, such as Einar Aberg (Swedish), Savitri Devi Makherij, an Indian woman, Professor Albert Conrad Leemann (Swiss), Friedrich Wilhelm Kuhfuss of Barcelona, and Professor von Leers of Cairo. The West German police have repeatedly seized publications by the last two authors.

Apart from the influence of non-German Western Fascism, obscure contacts of rightist circles with the East have also on occasion been discovered, says the Ministry report. The *Kongress fuer Entspannung und Neutralitaet in Europa* (Congress for Neutrality and Easing of Tension in Europe), which came to an end in May 1961, can be regarded as an example of this. Its manager, who supported rightist catchwords in the Federal Republic, at the same time supplied agitatorial broadcasting material directed against the Federal Republic to the East Berlin television service.

Former National Socialists Today

By Manfred Jenke

Anyone who frequently encounters foreign visitors to the Federal Republic and has talks with them on German politics is consistently impressed that these visitors have one question of quite special importance to them. Yet many do not ask this question because of exaggerated tact or for fear of offending their German host. This question should, however, be asked and discussed again and again. Not by remaining silent but by speaking frankly will it be possible to remove the misunderstandings and the distrust between the Germans and their partners in the free world, and in the East Bloc countries as well.

But now, let us pose the question in all preciseness. Let us put it just as directly as the author of an American book on Germany phrased it in 1961: "People often wonder where the millions of Nazis have disappeared to, all those who once hailed and faithfully served the Fuehrer. What has happened to those thousands of top Nazis in Hitler's Third *Reich*—the high officials in the administration, the Brown-Shirt bullies and the SS guard officers who once strutted in snappy uniforms and riding boots, with their chests covered with "lametta"? Where are the Nazi diplomats, the geopolitical strategists, and the advocates of a master race and *Lebensraum?* Where are the thousands of judges and prosecutors who, year after year, sent countless "enemies of the state" to the gallows and tens of thousands to lifelong hard labor, starvation, and death? What has happened to the thousands of brutes who committed the daily massacres and tortures in the concentration camps? Where are those who supervised the extermination of millions—including women and children—in the gas chambers? Finally, where are the tens of thousands of Nazi teachers, the millions of fanatical Hitler youths, and the thousands of highly indoctrinated youth leaders who are today in the age group between thirty-five and forty-five?"

"Are all of these people now convinced democrats?" asks the American author; and in his book, from the introduction of which these questions are taken, he tries to prove that even today, 17 years after the end of the Third *Reich,* the Nazis are in power in Germany—or have regained power after it was denied them for a brief period in 1945.

These assertions elicited surprise in Germany. Quite a lot was explained by the fact that the author, by his own admission, wrote his book without having been in Germany himself and without speaking with German political figures or writers about their answers to his questions. If he had, he would have been able to learn that all the events and developments he describes have for a long time been known and subject to lively discussion in Germany itself.

The first statement that must be made in connection with the appearance of "revealing" books on alleged neo-Nazism in the Federal Republic is: National Socialism is not taboo in Germany. It is subject to lively discussion with a greater or lesser degree of objectivity and thoroughness, but in a very large number of different places. From political science to publicity in newspapers, periodicals, books, movies, radio and television, and to instruction in elementary schools, "digesting the past" is at the present time a subject which most profoundly occupies people mentally and emotionally in Germany. Every day, books and reports appear with new facts, presented consistently in a very informative and objective manner, concerning the Third *Reich,* National Socialism, Hitler, and his adherents. These publications are cited and discussed daily in countless newspapers, periodicals, radio and television broadcasts, and even in school instruction. Almost every weekend, there are conferences at which qualified lecturers present the latest findings of research on the history of National Socialism to adolescent and adult listeners and explain where the dangerous and criminal aspects of this system were to be found. During the first postwar years, the Germans often enough received Allied re-education negatively and without understanding. During the period of the "economic miracle", they were almost exclusively interested in their own material well-being and in building up their private livelihoods. However, the phase of profound inner occupation with the Nazi past seems to have begun during the past three years. Since this past had a very large part in influencing and shaping the lives of all Germans, the presumption is that the controversies about this past cannot be concluded for a long time to come. Also, many young people who were not of an age to be acquainted with the Third *Reich* from their own experience are now beginning to ask very pointed questions. They ask not only their teachers but their parents why they followed a dictator like Hitler blindly; and the replies given and the resulting discussions are often impressively ruthless and honest. Of course, they are sometimes revealing as well in cases where older people do not have the courage to admit openly that they were Nazis and, thus, in part guilty of the German catastrophe.

The noteworthy aspect of these discussions is that Germans are attempting by mental occupation with the subject to make up for the revolution that failed to materialize in 1945. When the German troops surrendered unconditionally to the Allies on May 8, 1945, National Socialism as a politically effective force in Germany was as good as crippled. "Total war" had simply mentally exhausted the majority of Germans. War-weariness was prevalent everywhere, hardly surprising after five-and-a-half years of war. There was a marked yearning for peace and quiet and for termination of the constant air raid alarms—and a perceptible desperation among the many people whose relatives had died or were missing—all this in addition to the consequences of material deprivations and losses. In the eyes of most Germans, National Socialism was thoroughly compromised; not so much, however, as the result of a critical discussion of its ideas or their effects, but rather because of the elementary experience of the "movement's" collapse under the burdens of "total war". It was also the result of an evident grotesque disproportion between the pathetic claim of the official appeals to "stick it out" during the final months of war on the one hand and the contemptible dodging of responsibility on the part of their authors on the other. It was with satisfaction and not without scorn that many Germans noticed in 1945 how the former "Golden Pheasants" of the National Socialist Party cringed into the background and were at eager pains to have their past forgotten.

Quite a few Americans and Britons who at that time set foot on German soil again for the first time wondered in surprise how it was possible to meet so many people who professed never to have been National Socialists or to have been "against it from the very beginning". In many cases, such statements were felt to be hypocrisy or clumsy attempts to curry favor. They soon gave rise to the distrust from which the image of Germany is still suffering throughout the world. It was actually true that in 1945 the National Socialists had shrunk to a tiny group of incorrigible fanatics. The mere facts of the final war years had convinced the majority of Germans that National Socialism had not offered a way out of the difficult economic and political situation of the Twenties and Thirties, but instead had led into a dead-end street.

How clearly even former prominent National Socialists realized that a concluding line had been drawn is demonstrated by a quotation from a work[1]) written by Dr. Werner Naumann, the former State Secretary in Goebbels' Ministry for "Popular Enlightenment and Propaganda". He, too, had to admit that the National Socialist Party was finished, and he gave the following reasons: "The National Socialist Party was an accumulation of the most diverse forces, which were all trying to wield an influence in shaping the Third *Reich.* Their capacity ranged from Schacht to Ley. Idealists and opportunists, loyal officials and convinced Socialists, enterprising captains of industry and artists of a pronounced individualistic character, representatives of liberalism and adherents of collectivist views, were kept together in it by strong leadership. From the first day of its existence, the most diverse groupings struggled within this party for the implementation of their wishes. The period of its activity was too short for a typifying force to carry the day. Therefore, with the downfall of leadership in the year 1945, the bond that held all of them together also snapped. From that day on, there has never again been an organization like the National Socialist movement, and there will never be one again." Naumann's presentation, given not as an excuse but as an explanation, is given too little attention abroad when the subject is the Nazi movement. It is true that the Third Reich was ushered in by the far-reaching agreement of millions of Germans, and even of prominent representatives of the democratic parties, to Hitler's policy. But in the course of the mere 12 years that the "Thousand-Year *Reich*" lasted, ever increasing numbers of these original adherents turned their backs on Hitler. At first, it was a large group of adherents from the "period of struggle": the assassination of the

---

[1]) Werner Naumann *"Wo stehen die ehemaligen Nationalsozialisten?"* in F. Grimm (Ed.) *Unrecht im Rechtsstaat:* Tuebingen 1957, p 242.

SA Chief of Staff, *Roehm,* in June, 1934, induced hundreds of his "Veterans" to turn away from Hitler. The measures initiated in 1935 against the German Jews elicited not only disapproval and disgust, but fear as well, in large sectors of the middle class who had until then sympathized with Hitler. The provocative policy towards Austria, Czechoslovakia, and finally Poland led to ever-increasing opposition and resistance in military circles. When the National Socialist opportunists gradually moved into the forefront in the civil service, growing bitterness spread among the old, loyal public servants. But to the same degree that the National Socialists caused opposition by their measures, they succeeded in containing or suppressing these oppositional moods and currents through fear and terror. Parades and demonstrations, of course offered the outside world a picture of a fanaticized people who trusted and obeyed implicitly according to the motto "One People, One Reich, One Leader". This picture, as everyone in Germany knew even then, was false. Yet it is one of the features of a totalitarian regime that a small group of determined and fanatical lèaders in the top positions of power is completely capable of harnessing and exploiting an entire people, no matter how highly civilized and well-educated, through unlimited terror and propaganda. Today, we are aware that, for example, the majority of people in the European countries bordering on the Soviet Union—in Poland, Hungary, Rumania and Bulgaria—are by no means Communist in their thinking. But we also know that a relatively small group of Communist functionaries possess all the resources of the State and all control levers of society to make these people defenseless prisoners of a system they inwardly reject. What was going on in Germany under the National Socialist régime is entirely comparable in its final phase to the Communist dictatorships. It must always be kept in mind that between 1933 and 1945 the true face of National Socialism did not become apparent to many Germans until after they had naively applauded Hitler on January 30, 1933. But the same Germans were able to condemn this system completely—on the basis of bitter experience—on May 8, 1945.

Let us recall once more the results of the investigations which the American authorities conducted in Germany after 1945 to determine which Germans had been Nazis and which had not. In a cross section covering more than a million Germans it was found then that there was a small group of about one percent who had been genuine and proven members of the resistance. They had therefore lost their positions or had been put in penitentiaries or concentration camps. About 30 percent had in one way or another expressed their disapproval or their disagreement with Nazi methods. Later, in the denazification hearings, they were able to present witnesses who testified that they had already taken up a position contrary to Hitler in conversations during the war years—or they were able to prove that they had taken an active part in church life, a thoroughly suspect attitude during the National Socialist period.

About 50 percent of those interviewed had not worked actively for the party, although some of them were members of the National Socialist Party. They were mainly small merchants, salaried employees, or civil servants who for the sake of their career had joined the National Socialist

Party or one of its organizations—more of a conformistic decision without actual political commitment. They had behaved passively in the National Socialist Party; of course, they had thus tacitly declared their agreement with the views advocated by the party. These 50 percent were evaluated in general as fellow travelers who should be given the chance to make amends for their political mistake. After a short time, they were able to return to their positions, from which they had often enough been removed soon after the surrender.

The picture in regard to the remaining approximately 18 percent was more difficult. They had, in the view of the American authorities, been the real Nazis, by having made their ideological, organizational, and propaganda contribution to the National Socialist Party. Among these roughly 18 percent were those cited in the introductory remarks: the fanatical Hitler Youth and SS leaders; the high National Socialist administrative officials, judges and scientists; the concentration camp guards; and the large number of "officeholders" of the National Socialist Party who had represented the far-reaching National Socialist Party apparatus of control throughout Germany, down to every dwelling house. All of them were also removed from their positions during the summer of 1945, unless they "went underground" on their own or emigrated to Spain or Argentina. However, a large number of high administrative officials, diplomats, judges, teachers, and writers, as well as economists and artists, were dismissed together with them and calculated among the 18 percent of "true Nazis" only because they had finally become members of the National Socialist Party in their positions—which they had often occupied long before 1933. Although these men had never been National Socialists inwardly but conservatives, liberals, Catholics, or Socialists, they were numbered among the top Nazis because they had not been removed from their positions during the period of the Third *Reich*. At the same time, in spite of their membership in the National Socialist Party these men were often not even "fellow travelers" in the sense of having identified themselves more or less superficially with the ideas of the National Socialist Party. Many of them actually used the membership badge of the National Socialist Party so that they could carry on resistance against the excessively lunatic measures of National Socialist policy without being disturbed. This was especially so since the style in which the top Nazis carried on policy was inwardly alien and disgusting to them.

Of course, the great tragedy of the years between 1933 and 1945 is that these persons, who carried some weight and would have been able to wield influence, did not go beyond individual acts of resistance and were not in a position to bring about a serious turn of events during the war years. There is a report elsewhere in this book on the German resistance movement, which included men and women from all walks of life, and on the reasons for its tragic failure (cf. Rothfels, *"The German Resistance"*, p. 156).

Seen from abroad, the invisible struggle going on in the minds of many Germans, from which many of them suffered deeply inwardly, was of course bound to appear as lack of determination, incomprehensible passivity, and in fact indifferent toleration of Nazi atrocities. Without wanting to excuse this attitude—after all, millions of people fell victim to Hitler's war and extermination machinery—an attempt must nevertheless be made to explain this postion; for only by comprehending it is it possible to understand how these same people thought and acted after 1945.

At first, they were removed from their positions. Later on, however, with the relaxation of the Allied denazification provisions and with the increasing economic and administrative recovery of the Federal Republic, they gradually came back into leading positions. These were, let it be well understood, not the National Socialist criminals, concentration camp bullies, and convinced high leaders of the Hitler Youth, SS and National Socialist Party. The latter usually of their own free will avoided working for a State they did not inwardly respect, because it had been established on the foundations of an alleged "occupation regime". The few National Socialists still convinced after 1945 gathered in some extreme right-wing and neo-Nazi groups. The most important one, the Socialist *Reich* Party, was declared unconstitutional by a judgment of the Federal Constitutional Court after only four years of existence and was thus prohibited. During the period of development of administrative units in the Federation and the *Laender,* very great care was taken to exclude candidates for civil service offices who had participated in National Socialist crimes. For a long time their Allied denazification certificates were called in for checking. In the Federal Defense Forces there was a special "personnel examination committee" which investigated the past of each applicant for higher officer ranks thoroughly. It excluded from the outset those applicants who during their period of service in the Third *Reich* had participated in any way in war crimes, as far as the Committee could determine. All this was done even though it was very difficult to examine and evaluate systematically the extensive dossiers, since some were in Soviet hands, some in American, some in French, and some in British. This made it possible in isolated cases for persons to obtain rather high positions in administration, in public life, or in the Federal Defense Forces, who did not actually satisfy the requirements for political impeccability. Numerous court cases initiated since 1959 have detected more and more such persons. They have been and still are being removed from public service. After the former special courts and special units of the *Waffen-SS* and police files, which the Allies had controlled, were returned to the Federal Republic, a Central Investigation Bureau of the judiciary authorities in Ludwigsburg began to process this material. As a result of its activities, additional judges, public prosecutors, police officials, and other administrative officials, who had disqualified themselves by participation in National Socialist war crimes, had to leave public service. All of these cases, some of which yielded hitherto unknown factual information on atrocities committed in the occupied areas of Poland and other East European countries, were given great attention in the German press. They, in turn, had an effect on the mental preoccupation with the past, which is taking place in schools, adult education centers and mass communication media.

Our final question is: What about those public officials in the Federal Republic who are consistently cited as examples to show that high and top positions in the Federal Republic are filled by former National Socialists? To mention some names: Federal Foreign Minister Gerhard Schroeder, State Secretary Hans Globke, and former Federal Minister for Expellees Theodor Oberlaender. These three men, whose relationship to National Socialism was quite different in each case, are cited again and again as outstanding examples of the Federal Republic being on the way to re-nazification. We can answer concisely by stating the facts: Federal Foreign Minister Schroeder, born in 1910, made an application in 1934 to be accepted as a member of the National Socialist Party and the SA. He was at that time 23 years old. But as early as 1938, at the age of 27, he decided upon active collaboration in the "Professing Church", a church brotherhood whose director, Pastor Niemoeller, had shortly before been committed to a concentration camp. A short time later, Schroeder, a young lawyer, married a woman who was not a "pure Aryan" under the "Nuremberg Laws". Thereupon, he was—as he had foreseen—excluded from the National Socialist Party. He never was an active member of the National Socialist Party, a fact which has been testified to by numerous prominent democrats.

The case of Globke is more complicated. Dr. Hans Globke worked in the *Reich* Ministry of the Interior even before 1933. As a convinced Catholic, he regarded it as his duty to continue working in the Ministry after Hitler's seizure of power. After Hitler had promulgated the "Nuremberg Laws", Globke wrote a commentary in which he attempted to somewhat modify these provisions against the German Jews. Many persons in the Federal Republic now reproach Globke for having agreed to do this work and demand that Globke should not be allowed to work as a civil servant. Others disagree, saying that there is proof of resistance activity on Globke's part in the interest of the Catholic bishops. Globke's tragedy is that he "took part in order to prevent something worse", thus becoming to some extent an accomplice of the Third *Reich*. On the other hand Globke has repeatedly proved his anti-Nazi attitude during his period of activity for the Federal Government.

The case of Oberlaender has a political and a moral aspect. The former specialist on ethnic questions, who worked for the colonization of the Eastern areas in the *"Bund deutscher Osten"*, was charged on the basis of Soviet documents with having participated in mass executions following the occupation of the Polish city of Lvov. In reality, it developed that Oberlaender had not been in Lvov at that time. Accordingly, he had to be rehabilitated. Nevertheless, many people in Germany consider it wrong that a man like Oberlaender, who regards the far right as his political home, was allowed to play a leading part in the Federal Republic. The fact that this question can now be discussed openly in the Federal Republic shows that there is certainly no claim to power on the part of former National Socialists, and at the very most a tolerance which occasionally goes too far. In this connection and in conclusion, it must be remembered that about one third of the present German population is too young—to have consciously experienced National Socialism. These young people are growing up in a democratic State. And growing up in this democracy shapes their consciousness more markedly than some older persons' memories of the National Socialistic era.

The Nazis in the Judiciary

By Theo Sommer

Has the German judiciary been offering too comfortable a refuge to unreconstructed Nazis? Two recent events have underlined the pertinence as well as the urgency of this question. The first one was the voluntary—involuntary retirement of nearly 150 judges and prosecutors who feared that documentary evidence of their nefarious administration of the law under the Hitler regime might yet be produced against them. The second one was the *cause célebre* of Dr. Wolfgang Fraenkel, newly appointed Prosecutor General of the Federal Republic, who was forced out of office by amply and seemingly incontestably documented East German charges that he had been an "executioner-judge" in 34 cases between 1936 and 1943.

Neither of these events, I am afraid to say, has supplied a comforting answer to the many anxious questions about the integrity of the West German judiciary. The wholesale retirement of incriminated former Nazi officeholders in midsummer 1962 obviously diminished the number of those disgracing the legal branch of the Federal Republic. But it is equally obvious that a good many others, hardly less involved and no less a disgrace, adroitly slipped through the meshes of the official review boards or through the built-in escape hatches of their own individual consciences. At any rate, the Fraenkel scandal—which came into the open only after expiration of the June 30 deadline for voluntary retirement—would seem to indicate that the Damocles sword of still more unpleasant revelations, still more unexpected discoveries and still more disgraceful charges involving other men now serving in legal posts continues to hang above the head of the Germans. No one concerned with—and concerned about—the viability of West Germany's democratic institutions can view this prospect with equanimity.

It is hard to be objective about this situation, but it is also necessary. For neither is the picture as dark as Communist East Germany elects to paint it for the benefit of the outside world; nor is it as bright as some West Germans care to see it for the benefit of their own peace of mind. In this context, complacency and dramatization are equally harmful. Both tend to obscure the facts and obfuscate public opinion.

Three questions must be raised and answered if we want to get to the heart of the matter. First of all: how many lawyers who served as judges and prosecutors during the Nazi era are back in office today; were they Nazis then and are they Nazis now? Secondly: how can it be explained that many a judge or prosecutor who excelled in subservience to the Nazi regime was sacked only recently or not at all; what efforts have the Federal Government and the *Laender* administrations made to ferret them out and get rid of them? And thirdly: has the German judicial corps overcome the corrupting influences of Germany's thirteen years under the swastika; has the terrible lesson of the past been thoroughly learned?

I.

Some time ago, Martin Sommer, one of the most brutal and sadistic torturers among the concentration camp guards of the SS, was tried and convicted in Southern Germany. At his trial, the presiding judge was one *Landgerichtsdirektor* Adolf Paulus. No sooner had he meted out a life sentence to Sommer, than it was learned that his own record was highly dubious. Thus, when handling clemency petitions in 1943, he turned down the supplication of a Ukrainian who had been sentenced to death for no graver an offense than a trivial brawl in the stables of his employing farmer. Paulus is still in office, and who knows how many similar, as yet undetected cases there may be? It is hard to tell. No one should be surprised if, in the series of war crimes trials now being held in Germany, one of the indicted executioners arose and put the embarassing question to the judge: "And what were *you* doing at that time, Your Honor?"

It is, unfortunately, an indisputable fact that more "Paulusses" have been wearing the black robe again than is beneficial for the reputation of the judiciary and for the moral health of the nation. Nor can it be denied that the profession as a whole emerged from the Nazi era with its moral spine broken and its prestige—although not its authority—severely undermined.

To be sure, the judges, prosecutors, and lawyers probably behaved no worse under the rule of the swastika than the rest of the Germans. The corrupting influences of those dark years did not stop short of any group. They spared neither the university professors and teachers nor the writers and journalists, neither the scientists nor the businessmen, neither the military nor the medical profession. But recognition of this fact, of the universality of corruption and the omnipresence of weakness, does not extenuate the jurists. As Dr. Max Guede, the irreprochable predecessor of Fraenkel in the post of Prosecutor General, ably put it four years ago: "We jurists, we public prosecutors and judges above all must accept our share of the blame. We cannot but acknowledge our special responsibility for justice and admit our failure and guilt. We must acknowledge our special responsibility, because to us, more than to anyone else, the guardianship of justice is entrusted; we must admit our failure because we were not strong enough, and above all, not courageous enough, to fight for justice and, if necessary, to make sacrifices for it; and we must confess our guilt because justice perished whereas we survived."

Indeed, a great number survived and are now back in office. There are 15,000 judges and prosecutors in the Federal Republic today. As no reliable statistics are available, one can only estimate how many of them already served in legal posts between 1933 and 1945. According to Fritz Bauer, Prosecutor General, of Hesse, the figure must be put at two thirds to three fourths of the total; according to Dr. Paul Arnsberg, writing in *Rheinischer Merkur,* it is "above 5000". Need all of them be removed from office?

I should not think so. The concept of collective guilt, whether applied to a nation, a family or a profession, is a totalitarian concept; the fact that it was preached and practiced, under particular postwar circumstances, by the victorious democracies does not make it any less totalitarian. We should not and must not condemn those who have survived because they were weak only, who were terrorized but did not terrorize themselves. They are guilty, but only in the sense that all of us are guilty who lived and acted in those years.

Certainly we must make sure that they have seen the error of their former ways, that torturous self-questioning and the honest recognition of their previous shortcomings has changed them and hardened them in their determination henceforth to defend what is right, rather than merely administer what is law. But we should not make a few thousand pay for the turpitude of many millions. Nothing should be demanded of them but a straightforward and convincing answer to Guede's question: "How do you feel today about the events of yesterday? How would you act tomorrow if the situation of yesterday recurred?" And we must be satisfied with their explanation that the experience of having failed once has made them sadder and wiser men and has immunized them against new temptations.

I do, then, draw a distinction between those lawyers whose sole crime was their unability to muster enough courage for open resistance and martyrdom, who tried to serve justice even in a framework of General lawlessness, and those others who actively abetted the regime of injustice. The former failed only as we all failed, but the latter made themselves willing—and often eager—tools of terror. For them there can be no lenience. Once we deny the concept of collective guilt, we are forced to look for guilt in the individuals—that is the inevitable corollary of our proposition, if it is to be more than a threadbare excuse for doing nothing at all.

There were heinous cases of judicial terror. During the First World War, only 141 death sentences were meted out in Germany; during the Second World War the figure skyrocketed to 16,000, not counting another 10,000 death sentences pronounced by military courts (the comparable figure for Great Britain stands at 159). These statistics alone would suffice to indicate the widely prevalent corruption of the judiciary; they offer a faithful reflection of its servile self-abasement. But it is not only the numbers that are appalling. Even more appalling is the spirit underlying a great majority of the judgments. The judgments go a long way to justify the remark by the prosecution at the Nuremberg War Crimes Trials: that all too frequently the murderer's dagger was hidden under the robe of the jurist.

Take the following cases:

- In Kassel, a woman who had stolen 37 parcels addressed to soldiers was sentenced to death.
- An old man, after an air raid, took some horse reins from a bombed-out lot and made himself a pair of suspenders from them. He was sentenced to death on account of pillage.

- One German was sentenced to death for having given six cigarettes to a British prisoner of war.
- A young Polish girl, four months pregnant, was sentenced to death because she had stolen some clothes during an air raid. Another Polish girl received the same sentence for slapping a German shopowner in the face during a petty quarrel; the judgment said that she had "damaged the reputation of the German *Reich*".
- A Pole was executed because he had allegedly stabbed the dog of a German customs officer. The core of the evidence produced against him: the dog angrily barked at the accused when confronted with him in court. The incredible charge was that by stabbing a German shepherd the Pole had "violated Germany's national honor".

These are not, I fear, isolated instances. They are not drastic exceptions but rather examples standing for thousands of similar verdicts. And tens of thousands of other judgments not involving the death sentence, although no less a travesty of law, could likewise be adduced here in evidence against Germany's judiciary.

How many judges and prosecutors participated in these travesties of justice? In 1959, the East German Communists started their first violent attack upon the Nazis in the judiciary of the Federal Republic. "A total of 1,000 Nazi blood judges are now working for Bonn," proclaimed their party paper at that time, and 1,000 names of judges, prosecutors, and attorneys still (or again) in office were listed on the famous-infamous roster published by the Communist "Committee for German Unity".

I have always felt that this total was simply too round and neat a figure to be correct. Nevertheless, one could hear prominent jurists in the Federal Republic say that the West German judiciary had cause to dismiss one in ten of the men included in the East German list. There was wide agreement that a hundred judges of injustice was a hundred too many. They compromised the remaining German lawyers; they tainted the whole legal system of the new Germany; and they undermined the belief in law and justice in general.

Meanwhile, the Communist roster has swelled to include nearly 2,000 names. And meanwhile, it has also turned out an illusion that a mere hundred jurists need be removed from office to clear the name of the profession. This summer, 149 took advantage of the government's retirement offer. But a good many incriminated men—presumably far more than the officially admitted twelve—are still in office. Adolf Paulus continues to preside over juries. In Hamburg, the judges who condemned the pregnant Polish girl to death still pronounce justice "in the name of the people", and the prosecutor who demanded the sentence is now president of a *Grosse Strafkammer*. Elsewhere, the situation seems to be much the same. And new documentary evidence is continually coming to light. How many more judicial scandals must we expect? And why is it that in the middle of 1962, seventeen years after the end of the war and the downfall of the Third *Reich*, the dark shadows of the brown past continue to hover thickly over our legal branch?

II.

It has been critically remarked that only insufficient efforts were made after the war to purge the judiciary's ranks of the Nazi judges. No doubt there is more than just a kernel of truth to this allegation. "Indeed, we have taken it too easy," Dr. Guede warned even in 1958. "Now we shall have to face everything anew, and the bitter issues will be even more bitter, a difficult problem even more difficult." His statement had the ring of prophecy—a prophecy which has since come true. But Guede has also repeatedly pointed out the objective factors that stood in the way of a thorough weeding-out among West Germany's lawyers.

First of all, there is no denying the fact that initial errors were committed by the Allied occupation authorities in permitting former Nazi judges and prosecutors to start again in the West German service. Denazification failed dismally in this respect, as it barely scratched the surface. The question put to the lawyers was merely: "Were you a member of the Nazi party?" Nobody was asked the really relevant question: "Did you serve with a Special Court—and if so, what is your record?" Thus, quite a few got away with half-truths. Once denazified, they were hard to impeach a second time. Anyway, persecution of Nazi crimes was a province which the Allies reserved to themselves for many years. Even after the Germans again took charge of their own affairs, documents concerning the activities of the Nazi courts remained in Allied hands for a long time.

Then the East German communists, for their own specious reasons, stepped into the breach. They were lucky, too, luckier than the West Germans: it so happened that a large part of the pertinent legal documents was found in the Soviet Zone and has been generally inaccessible to the Bonn authorities. East Berlin's prized possessions include the files of the Leipzig Supreme Court as well as those of the military courts. But even Ulbricht's henchmen find it a tedious and time-consuming task to process those files. This explains why they have been able to divulge their incriminating information only piecemeal, and why further revelations must still be expected. The Poles and the Czechs are likewise busy processing the legal files captured by them at the end of the war, and so are the Soviets. In fact, many documents concerning German jurisdiction in occupied Czechoslovakia were turned over to Prague by the Kremlin as late as 1958.

There was, in the beginning, some inclination in the Federal Republic to dismiss the Communist revelations as tendentious propaganda lies. In the face of mounting evidence to the contrary, this attitude was not sustained for long. Certainly the element of hypocrisy which lies at the base of the relentless East German campaign cannot escape anyone; Ulbricht's regime is founded on terror and injustice as much as that of Hitler. Also, it is probably true that some of the documents have been falsified or "fixed". And it is incontestable that many of the accusations rest on superficial evidence such as the mere fact that a judge was a member of a Special Court—because it is well-known that most of these courts included judges who had been charged with, not volunteered for, the task of administering Nazi special legislation, and many who were determined to do all they could to spare the victims at least some of the consequences that these laws threatened them with. But soon it was generally agreed that a document is a document, no matter where it is kept, even when taken from Communist archives—just as truth remains truth even when it comes from the lips of a murderer. Thus, the painful process of screening the judiciary finally did get underway in West Germany.

However, it ran into numerous legal obstacles as soon as it started. For how does one get rid of a judge?

In Germany, as in all democratic states, judges enjoy special constitutional privileges which serve to safeguard their judicial independence. Judges are irremovable; they cannot normally be relegated from the bench. In this manner, it is hoped, they will be impervious to the pressures, claims, interferences, and encroachments of the political powers that be. No judge, therefore, can be convicted under German law unless a *dolus directus* is proved—a deliberate warping of justice *(Rechtsbeugung)*. A simple miscarriage of law is not sufficient for conviction, not even a *dolus eventualis*. "Intent," as Supreme Court Justice Douglas once said, "often makes the difference in law. An act otherwise excusable or carrying minor penalties may grow to an abhorrent thing if the evil intent is present." *(Dennis* v. *United States)*. Intent makes all the difference in this context, too. But how do you prove it?

Actually, there is only one way: an admission of the incriminated judges that they were intentionally and deliberately warping justice and abetting injustice. Such an admission, however, is a most unlikely thing. In fact, even Fraenkel, when asked to explain the legal opinions he had rendered at the Leipzig Supreme Court, avowed that "subjectively" he was at no time conscious of doing wrong. And so say practically all the others concerned; all of them claim that they never overstepped the boundaries of law and justice.

This rule of the *dolus directus,* then, is the first and foremost obstacle to a thorough purge of the German courts. To be true, the idea strikes one as rather grotesque that those judges who thought nothing of giving up their independence to an inhuman totalitarian system should now insist on their constitutionally guaranteed independence, thus evading the punishment they deserve. But legal retribution at the price of once more violating basic principles of law—can we really afford that? There is many a reasonable and liberal man in Germany who would abhor the mere idea. And it would indeed appear to be a moot point whether, in attempting to establish the principles of "equal justice under law" and "due process of law", one would act wisely if one started by first upsetting these basic principles.

There are other obstacles. The deliberations of the judges are secret; any one who served on a three-man panel can fairly safely claim that he was outvoted. Another factor operating against prosecution of judicial misdeeds is presented by the limitations of action. "Warping justice" should have been prosecuted within ten years; manslaughter cannot be prosecuted any more after 15 years; the limitation in the case of murder is twenty years. Even if blatant terror verdicts were considered manslaughter or murder in the guise of justice, hardly anything could be done about it now.

So is there nothing at all we can do? Two years ago, when first writing about this subject, I thought there was one promising avenue of approach. At that time, I suggested that the *Deutscher Richterbund,* the Judges' Professional Association, speedily take the matter in hand. "We keep hearing the argument that neither Federal nor *Laender* authorities could officially commission anyone to evaluate the East German files as this would imply a *de facto* recognition of Ulbricht's regime. Isn't it, for that reason, the special duty of the German jurists to take upon themselves this painful but necessary task?"

Whatever hopes I may have had in this respect in 1960—I was disillusioned. The *Richterbund,* after some feeble attempts, relapsed into indolence. It did, as far as is known, try to bring its influence to bear upon some tainted judges and prosecutors, but not to much avail, and it shirked the challenge of a comprehensive self-purge. In the end, the *Bundestag* threw its weight behind the efforts to remove the blot upon the West German judiciary. In 1961, a new *Richtergesetz* was passed, Article 116 of which said: "Any judge or prosecutor who has been active as a judge or prosecutor between September 1, 1939, and May 9, 1945, can be pensioned at his request. The request can only be filed until June 30, 1962."

This article offered an emergency exit to all those members of the judicial corps who had reasons to fear that they might still be enmeshed in legal proceedings on account of the verdicts they pronounced during the war. It involved neither punishment nor moral stigmatization, and it was, by way of commentary, narrowed down to be directed only at those who had been responsible or co-responsible for "inhuman death sentences". The result was the voluntary retirement of 143 judges and prosecutors—quite a remarkable result, although only a partial result. Frankly, I do not consider it satisfactory yet. It leaves much to be desired and can only be a beginning. Fourteen "blood judges" are officially admitted still to be in office, but inofficially there is talk about a far larger number. Also it is realized that quite a few incriminated men have meanwhile found a refuge in the social and administrative courts.

Four things must now be done: First: an independent body must finally be commissioned to screen the documents kept in East Germany—either a body of eminent German jurists or, as an alternative, a council of Swiss or Austrian lawyers. Second: a central authority must speedily be entrusted with the task of appraising the remaining dubious cases in order to assure that legal misdemeanor is measured with the same yardstick in all the *Laender.* Why not establish a review board similar to the one that so successfully screened the officers for the new German Army? Third: pointed recommendations must once more go out to incriminated judges with the object of forcing them into retirement. Fourth: if such recommendations were to avail nothing, the *Bundestag* ought to give serious consideration to amending the constitution, thereby designating as removable all judges and prosecutors who held office during the war—and follow this up with drastic action against those with a tarnished record.

I know all the arguments against such special legislation, yet I do no longer see any other way. Apparently the Federal Ministry of Justice has now reached the same conclusion. Another period of grace will be extended to the incriminated judges. Those who refuse to take advantage of it will then be forced out of office. But even with the aid of a constitutional amendment it will be impossible to oust *all* the tainted judges; we should be grateful if the most monstrous cases were got rid of. I, for one, have resigned myself to the realization that there cannot be any "final solution" to the problem. No cut-and-dried formula exists, no neat answers suggest themselves. The mortgage of the brown past is still heavily weighing upon us. The mortgage is difficult to settle, and the past is hard to live down. Tragic as we may find it, we are condemned to exist under the shadows of yesteryear; condemned to suffer a tantalizing situation in which no *absolution* can be given and no *solution* can be achieved.

What is needed in such a situation is the virtue of *resolution,* lest new doubts about the future arise from the unredeemed and unredeemable failures of the past. Does the German judiciary evince such resolution?

III.

This is not a political question; it is one touching the realm of judicial ethics and legal morality—and that, really, is the core of the matter. For the failure of the German judiciary during the Third *Reich* was not a political failure as much as it was a moral failure. The seeds for this were planted long before Hitler came to power; the moral decay of the judiciary had set in decades earlier. "There were few aspects of German life," it has rightly been said, "where the stage for the advent of Nazism was better set than in the German judiciary."

The judges failed because they easily soothed their consciences with the traditional formula that an order is an order, and a law is a law. Judicial positivism was the bane of the whole profession: what was legal was also considered legitimate, and what was law was, by dint of a comfortable equation, automatically regarded as the embodiment of justice. The sense of right and wrong withered away; the judges became mere legal engineers—specialists applying paragraphs with narrow-minded skill, unable to distinguish between justice and injustice and oblivious of the fact that their independence, to be real, must be anchored in greater depths than those of formalized law. Thus, they tended to forget that there is a core of justice which must not be violated by any ordinance or authority, and that behind any legal system lie supralegal principles and values that provide the yardstick by which injustice remains injustice even if it is cloaked in the garb of law.

Gustav Radbruch, the great legal philosopher, never tired after the war to expound this view. His preaching was not in vain, for his ideas were reflected in many a court decision—at least for a while. Recently, however, there has been a notable recurrence of positivism in several instances. In 1961, the Supreme Court postulated that opposition to an unlawful regime could be regarded as justified only if it had any chance of success—certainly a highly contestable postulate. No less controversial was another judgment rendered by the same Court in July, 1962. A farmer who was mistakenly sterilized in 1940 was denied damages because he had been sterilized by virtue of a legal, if erroneous, decision "which only independent judges, subject only to the law, could have arrived at and actually have arrived at." The law these judges were subject to, *nota bene,* was the Nazi Hereditary Hygiene Law!

So there are, undeniably, some dubious trends back toward blind obedience to whatever is codified law. Also, evidence of an impermissible degree of *camaraderie* amongst the judiciary has recently come to light, especially in the Fraenkel scandal—a kind of *camaraderie* that is only too willing to cover up for a member of the group. These signs will have to be watched; they do give cause for concern. But there are many encouraging signs, too. And they, rather than the questionable ones, would seem to indicate the prevailing current of the time.

One is the lively debate conducted within the legal profession itself, and especially the unequivocal stand taken on these matters by its younger members. Another, even more important one, is the vivid and articulate interest the great public is taking in all cases involving the integrity of the judiciary. The papers—from the popular illustrated magazines to the sophisticated opinion weeklies—are inevitably on the right side of the debate. They have made short shrift of Fraenkel, and they are clamoring ever more impatiently for the removal of the Nazi judges. Not only is there a wide consensus, but also something like a public conscience has emerged—and that conscience is extremely sensitive. It is this climate of opinion which, together with the agonizing reappraisal going on within the legal branch, justifies our best hopes for the future.

Militarism in the Federal Republic?

By Wolfgang Sauer

There is no doubt that many people in the Western world and above all in the United States would very much like to know what effect the rearming of Germany has had on the political and social life of the country, and if there is any danger of a resurgence of militarism or not. Naturally one can first ask the question: should one not begin by agreeing on the meaning of the word "militarism". However convinced many Americans are that the old Germany was militaristic, there are nevertheless others, such as the historian of the *Reichswehr,* Harold J. Gordon, who disputes this, at least for certain periods of history, and many Germans would completely reject this classification.

It would, therefore, appear profitable to clarify this point of definition. However, this can obviously not be attempted, let alone solved, within the framework of this study. On the contrary it would appear to lead us away from the actual problem we are discussing. The point that interests us is not so much the question of whether or not a scientifically defined conception of the word "militarism" is applicable to present-day circumstances in Western Germany, but rather another question, that of whether or not the civil-military relations in the Federal Republic will develop as unsatisfactorily as they did, at least at times, during German history between 1871 and 1945. In order to look into this problem, it is sufficient to review briefly the historical facts, a task which is unavoidable within the framework of the present theme. Only such a historical review of some of the serious troubles can help one to understand the difficulties with which the rearmament policy in the Federal Republic has had, and still has, to cope.

Historical Background

The special role which the armed forces played in the political and social life of the modern German state can only be understood from looking at the special way in which this state came into being. Usually one speaks about civil-military relations in connection with foreign policy. German political science, for instance, traditionally deals with the theme under the title "Policy and Warfare". But especially in Germany, this role of the armed forces in foreign policy was of secondary importance. Despite the serious conflicts in this field, such as the controversy between Moltke and Bismarck about the continuation of the war against France in 1871, the points at issue of the *Schlieffenplan* of 1914 and the adventurous collaboration of the *Reichswehr* with Russia's Red Army from 1920-21, the decisive problem was on the home political front. This problem was that the basic crisis which affected the state and social order in Germany in the 19th century was mainly solved or covered up by military means. During the unsuccessful revolution of 1848, the German liberals and democrats tried in vain, by compromise, to unify the approximately 30 separate states into which Germany had been split in those days. At the same time, they tried to bring into force a free political constitution. The impotent stagnation which followed this fiasco was brought to an end by Bismarck, who unified Germany by military action with the help of the Prussian army. With masterly astuteness he took advantage of the opportunities that presented themselves to exploit war in its two social functions in order to form the German state: first against Austria in 1866 to separate, and then against France in 1870/71 to integrate.

In this way, a united German state came into being. But it lacked a constitutional compromise which would have given it a stable and lasting basis, and this defect could not be made good until the disintegration of this state in 1945. It is a characteristic of the German nation's history, that the nation knew only a few short periods in which it was not necessary to proclaim at least a partial state of emergency—namely between 1890 and 1914 and again between 1924 and 1930. At other times, the Catholic Church, the Social Democrats, the first World War, the revolutionary disorders after the war, and finally, the economic slump of 1929, in this order, gave cause to suspend, completely or partially, whatever formal constitution was in force. When Hitler came to power, the state of emergency became permanent; the National Socialist "Third *Reich*" never had a formal constitution. The roots for the special political role of the German army are found in these basic social and political crises. The German nation, which came into being with the outstanding assistance of the armed forces, could never completely dispense with military support; the army was not only an instrument for foreign policy, as in other countries, but to a great extent also an *"Ordnungsfaktor"* on the home front or, as it used to call itself proudly, "the iron clamp of the *Reich*". For this reason, the army was deeply involved in the various changes in government. The option of military leadership in the transition to a new regime always played a decisive role, not only at the founding of the German *Reich* during the years 1860 to 1871, but also at the founding of the Weimar Republic and in Hitler's bid for power.

It is undeniable that the structure of the modern German nation has a certain similarity with the way in which some overseas countries were formed; in this connection one could mention, above all, the South American States; also present-day Turkey, Egypt, and Iraq. In contrast to these countries, however, the German army as a rule did not participate openly in political controversy or attempt to gain power directly; the *Kapp Putsch* of 1920 and the attempted *coup d'état* of the 20th of July, 1944, are exceptions, and their justification was strongly disputed in the army both beforehand and afterwards. The armed forces also seldom came to the fore in political leadership. Between 1871 and 1945, 29 different Chancellors headed the Government, but only two of them came from the officers' corps, and both of these were appointed against their will. They were General von Caprivi (1890—1894), who was ordered to fill this post by the Kaiser and then ruled more liberally than did Bismarck; and General von Schleicher (November 1932 to January 1933), who was only forced by circumstances to come out from behind the scenes where he had been politically active before. Of the six heads of state, who during the same period represented the German nation, only one was an officer: Field Marshal von Hindenburg *(Reichs* President from 1925-1934). However, at the time when he assumed his appointment he was, like Eisenhower, a retired officer and was elected and supported by civilian elements outside the army.

This relatively "normal" picture, however, does not tell the whole story. It becomes complete only when one takes into consideration the strong political influence that was exercised informally and indirectly by the leaders of the German armed forces. At the same time, a whole gamut of procedures and methods were developing; they reached from the political influencing of conscripts to veiled military dictatorship, but they all resulted in a limitation or even suppression of democratic development. The former dominated in the Empire from 1871-1914, when the army, with it compulsory military service, functioned as the "School of the Nation", in which young citizens were not only trained militarily but were also politically formed, which meant above all a disciplining of the rising middle and working classes in the interests of the ruling conservative monarchy. The molding—and at the same time disturbing—effect of this relatively inconspicuous but intensive "national education" can hardly be overestimated. Another form of indirect influence was the formation of collateral military governments. Since the revolution of 1848, they had periodically existed in Prussia during the various crises. The best example is the "silent" dictatorship of General Ludendorff during the first World War. Ludendorff operated from far behind the scenes; the then constitution of the *Reich* with all its institutions was not only formally maintained, but Ludendorff himself was by no means the supreme military leader but functioned officially only as assistant to the Chief of the General Staff, von Hindenburg.

A third variation developed during the period of the Weimar Republic. True, the army had then lost its influence as an institution able to train citizens, since conscription had been abolished by the Treaty of Versailles, and the army was also officially under civilian control within the framework of the democratic parliamentary constitution. But the army rose to a semiautonomous political power which during the serious conflict between the democratic and antidemocratic forces that went on during almost the entire existence of the republic intervened on its own initiative or under the force of circumstances on a number of occasions to settle political disputes. In 1930, the *Reichs* Minister of War, Groener, proudly stated that the *Reichswehr* had become a factor in Germany which nobody could ignore any longer in making political decisions. The traditional concealment of the political influence of the armed forces was not always possible, but on the whole it was achieved in large measure. The best example for this is the role of General von Schleicher, who from 1918-19 had a great, and from 1925-26 onwards, a decisive influence on the policy of the *Reichswehr,* but who until 1932 did not hold any leading military or civilian appointment in the Republic.

Under the totalitarian regime of the National Socialists, the leadership of the armed forces also attempted to achieve a key position in domestic affairs, a sort of "dictatorship within a dictatorship". The armed forces supported Hitler's seizure of power with this objective in view, but the attempt failed. Through his influence over the masses and by exploiting the rivalries between the different branches of the armed forces, Hitler was able to subject the proud Prussian-German officers' corps to his plebeian domination. The National Socialist regime, for the first time in the history of modern Germany, showed the surprising picture of the armed forces completely under political control. However—and this is the other side of the picture—the National Socialist movement itself was controlled by an extreme radical militarism. This movement was, indeed, the distorted caricature of what the military leaders had wanted. This explains the initial expectations and subsequent disappointments which the National Socialist movement evoked in the officers' corps and also explains the initial cooperation and subsequent opposition of the armed forces under Hitler.

The peculiarity of the German system of government consisted therefore—both in the Empire as well as in the Republic—of two clearly separated elements, namely, the then existing institutions based on law and order but politically weak, and under or behind these, a concealed military "State within the State", as a hard core or stabilizing factor of the whole system. It is without doubt a proof of the cautiousness and intelligence of the German generals that they renounced making forthright bids for power. Only thus was it possible for the dual system to survive for such a long time. But undoubtedly this created a society too full of pretense and illusion to overcome the German crises; the reaffirmation of this system at all turning points of modern German history slowly undermined both the civil as well as the military institutions and made them ready for Hitler's coming to power.

The Policy of Rearmament

Turning now to the question of whether or not and how far the historical problems of civil-military relations will repeat themselves in the Federal Republic, it should first be pointed out that the time for a final answer has not yet come. The build-up of the *Bundeswehr* started at scratch six years ago. From the purely technical and organizational points of view, this build-up is now nearing its conclusion, but it is obvious that neither the formation of the internal structure of the new armed forces nor their assimilation into the West German social system is yet completely accomplished. The following description can therefore only be in the nature of an interim report; the time has not yet come for clear, well-founded answers.

It has been pointed out[1]) that the military-political situation in the Federal Republic differs fundamentally from that of the Weimar Republic, because today, as opposed to 1918-19, the state came into being before the army.

1) Fritz René Allemann, "Die Nemesis der Ohnmacht: Wiederbewaffnung als politische Aufgabe", in: Der Monat, vol. 7, May 1955, pp. 99—105.

Whereas the armed forces played a decisive role in the founding of the Weimar Republic, they played no part in the establishment of the Federal Republic. The Federal Republic was founded in 1949; the *Bundeswehr* in 1955. One can carry this observation even further if one follows the thesis of a German professor for constitutional law.[2]) According to this thesis, in the case of the Federal Republic, the economy was set up even before the state. The economic reconstruction after 1945 was carried out largely without governmental assistance, by private and institutional initiative, with employers and employees cooperating in a surprisingly smooth way. The state—not to mention the armed forces—proved to be superfluous as a regulating authority. The assertion is that in this manner the new West German society has acquired an independence and stability which the state, imposed on it from above, simply cannot modify.

However true the facts may be on which such considerations are based, there is some question if one can simply assume that, because the social and political order came first, the political leadership will firmly and permanently dominate military leadership. The political constitution, in contrast to the social and economic order, was in 1949 imposed more from outside and above, than established through democratic initiative. Taking this into consideration, the priority thesis is restricted in two important points.

First, the Federal Republic is only a part of Germany. In a divided Germany, the Federal Republic can only to a limited extent claim to represent the political will of the whole nation. Its creators have, therefore, purposely set it up on a provisional basis. The thesis of the priority of the economic and political supremacy over the military is only valid for this provisional state but not for a reunified Germany. As long as one holds fast to the postulate of a reunified Germany, the main task of building the German nation is still to come, and this problem will not be solved *before* the founding of an army but in the face of two German armies.

There is no denying that reunification does not seem to be close at hand. The Federal Republic seems to be developing into a semidefinite state. But for this reason, the problem of establishing a state arises again from another angle; the conception of a provisional state contained considerable limitations on national sovereignty, determined partly by still valid reserved rights of the Occupation Powers and partly by foresighted orientation toward a future supranational European order. These consisted not only of a limitation of national sovereignty in foreign policy but also of reservations on the part of the Occupation Powers concerning domestic national emergency measures. If the development of Western Germany is now moving towards a certain degree of completion, then new decisions will have to be taken in connection with these limitations. The dispute which has been going on for some time between the Government and the Opposition about emergency laws shows that these problems are beginning to intensify, and that this time they must be solved under German responsibility alone. This points up the second limitation of the priority thesis;

---

2) Ernst Forsthoff, "Die Bundesrepublik Deutschland: Umrisse einer Realanalyse", in: Merkur, vol. 14, September 1960, pp. 807—821.

it could be that the actual setting up of the state is still to come or is now beginning in the Federal Republic.

Under these circumstances, it appears certain that the *Bundeswehr* will play some role. The above-mentioned hypothesis of the priority of the economic character and stability of West German society has significantly excluded the possible consequences of rearmament[3]), and a recent constitutional study about the "Basic Law and Military Constitution" comes to the conclusion that the Basic Law becomes "a full-fledged and final constitution of a sovereign state" only by the inclusion of paragraphs concerning the armed forces. In addition, this study points out, the three elements of the Basic Law, liberal, social, and democratic principles, have been altered by the introduction of general conscription: The liberal principle has been curtailed, the social principle has been extended (in so far as the reponsibility, which hitherto rested exclusively with the state, is now supplemented by citizen responsibility), and the democratic principle has been consistently developed.

Under these circumstances, a critical analysis of the build-up of the *Bundeswehr* and its assimilation into the political and social order of the Federal Republic achieves greater significance. This all the more so, since the task of rearmament was unusually difficult. After the total collapse and complete occupation of Germany by the World War II powers, a policy of total disarmament and reorientation was pursued, combined with discrimination against German soldiers as "militarists". However much the details and the methods of this policy were criticized and rejected in Germany, large circles of the population generally accepted it. Because of the great disillusionment which followed the National Socialist delirium and the hope of a new and better, peaceful world, which would make a repetition of such world catastrophies as the two world wars impossible, the majority of Germans were ready to give up their own military forces. The beginning of the cold war showed that the hypothesis for these hopes was unrealistic. The occupying powers were forced to change their policy gradually towards German rearmament. In the summer of 1948, the Soviet Union took the initiative by setting up armed units under the cover name of *"Kasernierte Volkspolizei"* in the East German Zone of Occupation, while the Western Powers decided to do the same in Western Germany only hesitantly and under pressure of the experiences of the Korean War. The initial reaction of the Germans to this development was one of strong opposition. One must remember that this opposition existed in both parts of Germany; it merely started later in the Soviet Zone than in the West, because the Communist regime camouflaged the first phase of its rearmament policy even from the East Zone population. When this camouflage was abandoned in 1955, and the *"Kasernierte Volkspolizei"* was converted into the *"Nationale Volksarmee"*, a strong "pacifist" movement developed in East Germany also, even though—for obvious reasons—it made itself felt only indirectly.

The same movement began in West Germany as early as 1950-51, because democratic freedom permitted neither a camouflaging of rearmament nor

---

3) Ibid., p. 811

4) Wolfgang Martens, Grundgesetz und Wehrverfassung, Hamburg 1961, p. 206., pp. 124 ff.

an influencing of public opinion. As its main slogan, "*Ohne mich*" (count me out), suggests, this movement was mainly nonpolitical and of a spontaneously emotional character. It embraced nearly all levels of the population and even affected the government. The first Minister of the Interior of the Federal Republic, Gustav Heinemann, resigned on October 9, 1950, in protest against the policy of rearmament. Because of its comprehensive character, the movement was very heterogeneous. "*Ohne mich*" was the slogan of both pacifists and antimilitarists as well as of nationalists and former professional soldiers—some because they never wanted to serve in an army and fight again, others because they did not want to serve in an army under the given conditions, and perhaps have to fight. Thus it was that the movement resisted all efforts to organize it. There were organizations which supported one or another aspect of the movement—such as the Social Democratic Party, the Trade Unions, elements of the Evangelical Church, youth organizations on one side, and soldiers' and officers' associations on the other—but no organization of the movement itself. For this reason the movement faded away after a while; its last remnants today are the organizations of conscientious objectors.

The roots of this wave of popular opposition against rearmament policy were to be found in the fresh memory of the war inferno and of National Socialist militarism. The evil experiences of the past were in the minds not only of the German people and their political leaders but also of the Allied originators of German rearmament. They were aware that they had begun a "fateful gamble".[5])

All those concerned, therefore, agreed to devote particular attention to political control in the build-up of the new German armed forces in addition to the matter of military effectiveness. The problem of political control was in the foreground of German rearmament from the outset largely because of the military-political situation that placed the main burden—namely that of atomic defense preparedness, of the problem of deterrence and of the basic decisions connected with it—on the shoulders of the Americans. The first attempt to solve the problem of political control of the armed forces consisted of the plan for a "European Army", which envisaged the complete integration of national contingents under multinational command. This plan, born out of among other things, French fear of a reactivation of German militarism and furthered by the French Prime Minister Pleven, finally failed in 1954 through resistance of the French Parliament, which was not prepared to take the consequences for its fear, namely the renunciation of authority over its own armed forces. They reasonably conquered their fear of the Germans rather than agree to the undoubtedly premature experiment of an integration of the military forces of Europe without first having political integration.

In place of the unsuccessful Pleven Plan, an emergency solution was agreed upon in 1954, one that is still valid today. It involves the partial integration of German armed forces in NATO and WEU, combined with an attempt

5) Gordon A. Craig, NATO and the New German Army, October 24, 1955 (Center of International Studies, Princeton University, Memorandum No. 8), p. 2

to build up effective civilian democratic control of the military forces in Germany itself. As far as the international aspect is concerned, the NATO solution undoubtedly makes it possible to prevent any independent action of the *Bundeswehr.* All *Bundeswehr* units come under the command of the central NATO commands even in peacetime. The *Bundeswehr* has no general staff of its own and no self-sufficient armament industry; even the reserves of weapons, ammunition, equipment, etc., necessary for warfare are stored in the ratio of one third on German territory and two thirds in foreign supply bases. Left to itself, the *Bundeswehr* is therefore only capable of fighting for about a week, and even that is dependent on fuel supplies through pipelines that NATO members can control at any time.

The Plan for Military Reform

Hand in hand with the integration of the newly formed German armed forces into the North Atlantic defense system came a large-scale attempt to give them a new standing within the framework of the West German governmental and social order. The problem that had to be solved in this connection was formulated by Richard Jaeger, Chairman of the Defense Committee of the *Bundestag,* at the beginning of the build-up of the *Bundeswehr* in 1955, as follows: "Germany has had a good army for a long time. Today, we have the beginnings and the development of an undoubtedly good democracy. But in Germany, we have never simultaneously had a good army and a good democracy, as well as balanced relationship between the two as other democratic nations have had."[6]) Exactly this had to be achieved in the Federal Republic. In theory there were two methods by which it could be done. Stated in brief, they were: either isolation of the armed forces *from* society, or integration of the armed forces *into* society. Great Britain offers the best example of the first method. Until the second World War, Britain had a paid or professional army, which was clearly separated from the rest of the population and was under strict parliamentary control. Its connection with the population was achieved through citizens' high estimation of its fighting ability in the event of danger, which compensated for the otherwise relatively low estimation of the military profession. The second method, that of ingration, has been practiced most consistently in the Swiss militia system, where every citizen is also a soldier and acquires and maintains his military efficiency by repeated short military exercises. There are hardly any professional Swiss soldiers, and there is also no permanent military organization worth mentioning. Apart from geographical strategical differences—on the one hand an insular, on the other a continental location—the difference of the two solutions is also caused by the difference in political constitutions.

The Swiss system is based on the strongly plebiscite-character of Swiss democracy, while the British military system conforms to the predominantly representative nature of the British system of government. It is significant that the extension of the electoral franchise in Great Britain during the 19th century was followed by a reactivation of the old militia system.

---

6) Das Parlament, No. 27, July 6, 1955, p. 4.

All modern constitutions try in some way or other to find a middle way between these two extremes, but there is a general tendency to gravitate in one direction or the other. This was also the case in Germany. However, in Germany, the professional army was never an element of representative government but of the absolutism of the monarchy, while the democratic movement always favored the militia and adhered firmly to the militia in both its liberal and social variations. The liberals have never considered the importance of a professional army to the representative form of government which they favor. The reforms that generals Scharnhorst and Boyen carried out in Prussia during the years from 1808 to 1814 resulted in a professional army as a skeleton organization for those doing compulsory military service, and alongside it, but separate, a militia *("Landwehr")*. This was a compromise solution reflecting the still undecided struggle between a liberal democracy and a monarchic autocracy. When in the course of national unification the latter obtained the supremacy, the professional army, as a skeleton organization, became the only type of German armed forces. It was, however, a mixed system in which integrated elements of the militia system were used to impose feudalistic views of the Prussian professional army on the entire nation, immunizing it against democracy and revolution. Even under the Weimar Republic, the German democrats were unable to realize their dream of a militia, although this would have corresponded to the strong plebiscite-elements of the Weimar Constitution. But the Treaty of Versailles forced Germany to maintain a professional army, which then preserved the Prussian tradition and thus became the instrument of a dictatorship even before this dictatorship was set up.

The military development in the Federal Republic appears to have begun by a reversal of this procedure. The political constitution of the Federal Republic, contrary to the *Reichs* constitution of the Weimar Republic, almost completely excludes the plebiscite-components in favor of representative components. One could have expected that the type of armed forces would have been based on the isolation principle in accordance with the British prototype. But as the result of the foreign political situation, the NATO Treaties made it imperative to again introduce compulsory military service. The unfortunate experience with the *Reichswehr* as well as the traditional military thinking of German democracy, which here displayed great persistence, promoted a shift towards the Swiss principle of integration. However much the Christian Democrats and the Social Democrats differed on other questions connected with the policy of rearmament, they were completely unanimous in their desire of a close democratic-military integration to prevent a resurgence of a military state within the state.

The basic ideas and plans for a military reform were prepared by Dr. Adenauer's government in the years between 1950 and 1955. The leading personalities were Theodor Blank, a Christian Democratic leader from the Christian Trade Unionist movement who, in October, 1950, became head of what was called the *"Dienststelle Blank"*—office responsible for the preparation of rearmament—and a small circle of idealistic and democratically minded former officers, from among whom Graf Baudissin soon emerged as intellectual leader. Tackling the problem of military reform, these men started from the premise that an adjustment of military values to democratic values and principles of public order were more likely to promote than detract from military effectiveness. They believed that moral forces could be mobilized which would make some former methods of compulsion superfluous. They also believed that today's industrial and ideological struggles require more independent and self-responsible soldiers than the merely traditionally drilled soldier of the past. Finally, they hoped to overcome, through a more humane military code, the resentments, manifested in the powerful *"Ohne mich"* movement, the main roots of which were the degrading "sergeants' rule" of the former *Wehrmacht.*

Out of these considerations there emerged the much-disputed image of the *"Staatsbuerger in Uniform"* (citizen in uniform), the essence of which was defined by the reformers themselves in the following words: "The inner structure of the armed forces in a free society must be such that young soldiers can complete their military training without fundamental break with their civilian environments."[7] They wanted to achieve this objective through three reform measures: complete subjection of military life to the principle that governs the state based on law and order, democratization and demilitarization of the armed forces as far as possible, and education of soldiers towards independence and political activation in support of democracy against totalitarianism through a new form of *"Innere Fuehrung."*

As far as the principle of a state based on law and order is concerned, the reform plans envisaged a guarantee of most basic constitutional rights to armed forces personnel. In the *Bundeswehr,* as in all others armies, restrictions of basic rights for reasons of military discipline and political nonpartisanship are naturally inevitable (such as the freedom of assembly, the freedom to choose one's place of domicile, and the freedom to express one's opinions, etc.), but these restrictions are kept to the absolute possible minimum. The *Bundeswehr* soldier not only has active but also passive voting rights, although if he is a professional soldier it is unlikely that he will care to make use of the latter because of the disadvantage to his military career. In addition, the soldier has the right of association, although according to military regulations the right to strike is naturally excluded. He has, above all, legal protection against all military proceedings, which is probably unique. Even the sentence of detention as a disciplinary measure can occur only if ordered by a special disciplinary court, and the application of the general and military penal code for the *Bundeswehr* must be left to the competence of the civilian courts. In peacetime there are in principle no military courts in the Federal Republic. In addition, regulations for submitting complaints attempt, with a maximum application of legality, to solve the old problem of making possible an effective complaint against military superiors without endangering authority and discipline. However, this method is so complicated that its application by both soldiers and superiors appears to be very difficult.

---

7) See the official publication: Vom kuenftigen deutschen Soldaten: Gedanken und Planungen der Dienststelle Blank, Bonn 1955, p. 25.

This defect is greatly compensated for by the institution of the *"Wehrbeauftragter"*, which will be described below.

The second characteristic of the reform plans was the intension to democratize and demilitarize the military organization. This includes the reorganization of the relationship between soldiers and superiors to be based chiefly on the function and, therefore, military performance of individuals involved. The factor of rank—formerly of supreme importance—was to play a role only during duty hours. Moreover, military administration, including the recruiting organization, was to be staffed only by civilian officials, in opposition to the Prussian-German tradition. In this way, as in the transfer of power in penal cases to the civil law courts, an attempt was made to give the young conscripts the feeling that all questions of mustering, drafting, and possible punishment—of greatest importance to him—are subject to the judgment of "his own people". There was also the bold experiment of introducing democratic methods of free discussion and decision into all those spheres of military life where this was possible without endangering military efficiency, above all on duty in barracks and during instruction, etc. *(Innerer Dienst).*

The third characteristic of the reform plans was closely connected with this: the attempt to develop new principles of training, education, and political leadership in connection with the concept of *"Innere Fuehrung"* with the aim of having soldiers who think independently and act coresponsibly. This problem was tackled by following the idea of integration to the logical conclusion that the armed power of a democracy must not by its training methods undermine the human values which it has to defend in wartime. The superiors were advised to be not only military instructors but also character moulders of their soldiers. To promote this education, special *"Lebenskunde"* instruction was introduced, which, is given not by officers but by military chaplains. In addition, all members of the armed forces, officers as well as soldiers, were required to adopt a new attitude toward politics. The memory of "nonpolitically" trained *Reichswehr* officers failure to react against National Socialist totalitarianism and the renewed threat of Communist totalitarianism to democracy spurred reform. *Bundeswehr* members are required not only to accept unconditionally the "free and democratic fundamental order as envisaged in the Basic Law", but also to participate in political thinking and even in political responsibility. Instruction in *"Staatsbuergerlicher Unterricht"* (social studies) has been introduced in order to intensify the application of the new principles. The reformers recognized, of course, that educational training alone was not sufficient to bring their new ideas of *"Innere Fuehrung"* to realization. But they hoped that an extensive organizational democratization of the *Bundeswehr* would at the same time promote a general democratic "way of life". They were aware that the new armed forces neither should be, nor could be, a "School of the Nation" and stated this clearly. They realized that this could not replace the responsibility of civilian institutions such as the home, school, university, professional life, etc. But they did believe that the *Bundeswehr* could continue the process of education and make its own contribution by organizing military training as a "training of the citizen" as well. Thus, the idea of integration was carried to its extreme logical conclusion, even beyond the Swiss prototype. The *Bundeswehr* was not only to be a protection against the outside but it was also to fulfill a civil function internally. Would a conflict not arise from this? And could one expect the necessary superhuman strength from the military leadership to overcome, day-in, day-out, what was bound to be a conflict in themselves? The reformers emphatically denied the possibility of a conflict, for they were convinced that the military profession already contained "democratic values". They maintained that authority, discipline and obedience were also indispensable in a democracy; their cultivation by the *Bundeswehr* therefore represented a contribution towards training for civilian life, too. Obviously the original hypothesis of the reform was now reversed. From the idea of increasing military effectiveness by democratization and the introduction of civil elements into the armed forces, emerged the thought of stabilizing democracy by the addition of military values. It is significant for the ideology of the reformers that they neither grasped this reversal nor clarified the extent and limitation of the two ideas. Therefore, their theory of civilian-military integration contained a fundamental ambiguity which might well have made its realization much more difficult.

Political Control of the Bundeswehr

Concurrently with the internal military reform came the incorporation of the armed forces into the political system of the Federal Republic. It is characteristic of this incorporation that the changes in the constitution on which the military reform was based gave the principle of isolation considerably more emphasis than would have corresponded to the idea of integration. Integration undoubtedly presupposes a maximum amount of confidence between the civil and military elements of a society, so that the military ideally requires only a minimum of civilian control. But actually, the originators of the changes in the Basic Law—government as well as opposition—remembering the evil experiences of the past, were mainly concerned with introducing the maximum amount of civil or political control. In the government declaration about the "principles of military constitution and military policy" of June 27, 1956, Minister of Defense Blank said: "Parliamentary control is to be exercised more firmly than was formerly the case in Germany."

This determination to introduce strong civilian control has been expressed in two ways in the Basic Law: in the supremacy of political leadership within the executive, and in complex political control (in the narrower sense of the word) on the part of the legislative. The supremacy of political leadership is expressed in the creation of a purely civilian supreme command, which includes the right to appoint officers. In peacetime, the supreme command is in the hands of the Federal Minister of Defense; in wartime, in the hands of the Federal Chancellor. Neither may be officers. Furthermore, even in peacetime, the Minister is formally subordinate to the Federal Chancellor regarding fundamental questions of military policy, because, in accordance with the Basic Law, the latter determines "general policy". This arrangement is new in that according to German tradition the supreme command has, in principle, been the head of state. Today, however, the Federal President has only purely representative functions in military affairs and a certain share in decisions about war and peace. This change in the authority of the actual supreme command from the head of state to the executive ensures that the person with this function can be made subject to parliamentary control at all times. Indeed, this control has become doubly important because the executive increased considerably in power through the direct power of command over the *Bundeswehr;* this alone could seriously disturb the balance of power within the state.

The control functions formerly exercised by the Parliament were not sufficient to cancel out such a disruption of the balance of power, even less, because the parliamentary system of the Federal Republic acknowledges only the responsibility of the Federal Chancellor and the government as a whole and not the responsibility of individual ministers. In addition, the institution of the "constructive vote of no confidence" further restricts the responsibility of the Chancellor. Thus, the Federal Minister of Defense, who has at his disposal the strongest element of power within the state and must be regarded as the most important Minister in the Government, is doubly shielded from parliamentary control. In order to pierce this shield again and enable Parliament to have control over the armed forces, constitutional changes were made, and Parliament was endowed with a new, enlarged power of control. Firstly, it was stipulated that the annual budget of the Federal Government should clearly show the strength of the *Bundeswehr* and the basic outline of its organization. In addition, a specially privileged Defense Committee of the *Bundestag* was created, which: (1) is a permanent committee, i.e., it can function in the interim between legislative periods, (2) has the function of an investigation committee with all appertaining rights and (3) can function on its own initiative if a quarter of its members demand it. However, as the Defense Committee meets only behind closed doors and alone is competent for all questions of defense, the *Bundeswehr* is now the only national institution that cannot be subjected to a public parliamentary investigation.

The third arrangement which gives Parliament an increased power of control is the institution of the *"Wehrbeauftragter"* (Commissioner for the Armed Forces), something completely new in Germany. This post was created on the Swedish example, and the special functions of the *Wehrbeauftragter* are to supervise the maintenance of the basic rights in the *Bundeswehr.* In addition, the *Wehrbeauftragter* functions in general as an auxiliary of the *Bundestag* in the execution of its parliamentary control. For this purpose, the *Wehrbeauftragter* has a comprehensive right of inspection within the *Bundeswehr* and may demand official help from all governmental and local authorities. Above all, any member of the *Bundeswehr,* irrespective of his rank or position, has the right to apply directly to the *Wehrbeauftragter,* over the heads of all superior officers, in questions of basic rights and *"Innere Fuehrung".* Such an applicant may even demand that his name be kept secret if he considers it necessary. This institution may prove very beneficial. Even during the short time it has existed, it has already shown that it largely replaces the official complaint channels. It is also possible that the existence of this institution will counterbalance the fact that meetings of the Defense Committee are not public.

With these extensive control rights, distrust of the armed forces—which is naturally not directed against the loyalty of the soldiers but against the logic of military thinking—is expressed so clearly that the question arises whether it does not represent an inner contradiction to the equally clear demand for confidence contained in the military reform's trend to integrate. It must be admitted that such a contradiction could develop, and that it might lead to political conflict, but this is by no means inevitable. For even if the control originates from distrust, it can, if properly carried out and properly understood, also be the basis of confidence; this is, in fact, its only reasonable aim. Which of these two possibilities materializes will depend entirely on the practical developments and on the degree of mutual understanding and cooperation.

International connections which the Federal Republic has entered into with NATO and WEU will also play an important role. Though, on the one hand, these connections are an additional guarantee against independent military action, on the other hand they could also restrict the effectiveness of the Federal Republic's control mechanism. Basic decisions on strategy and military policy are made by the NATO Council in Paris or by SHAPE in Fontainebleau even in peacetime. In case of war, the supreme command would be entirely in the hands of NATO. Thus, the Basic Law's stipulation about the supreme command in times of war is largely fictitious. The same applies to the right of decision about war and peace, which according to the West German Constitution lies with Parliament. Also the control rights of the *Bundestag* in relation to the federal government are restricted; the latter is bound to the decisions of NATO and could possibly ignore the decisions of Parliament, citing ties with NATO. The significance of this is enhanced by the fact that the Federal Republic itself takes part in decisions of NATO. It remains to be seen how the system of checks and balances created by the Basic Law will function under these circumstances, but fears are unfounded that a future federal government could obtain enough freedom to act by playing off NATO against the *Bundestag*.

These remarks conclude the admittedly sketchy survey of the reform plans with which government and opposition have tried to set up a "good army in a good democracy". The essence and importance of these reform plans may best be defined by quoting a Frenchman, regarded as one of the best authorities on the Federal Republic's political system. He made the following comment in 1955: "At the moment it is obviously impossible to foretell what will remain of the ideas (of the reform) in a few years time. But doubtlessly we are witnessing one of the most earnest efforts that has ever been made to reappraise the problems of the armed forces in a democratic system."[8])

The Build-up of the Bundeswehr: Difficulties and Problems

Half a dozen years have passed since these words were written. Outlines which were then still shrouded in an uncertain future are beginning to

8) Alfred Grosser, Review Article in: Revue Francaise de Science politique, vol. 5 (1955), pp. 169 f.

become clearer. The physical build-up of the *Bundeswehr* is as good as completed. It has almost reached planned strength, the first lots of conscripts have completed their military training, the first officers trained solely by the *Bundeswehr* are beginning to be promoted, and the first two annual reports by the Commissioner for the Armed Forces have informed us at least roughly of the *Bundeswehr's* internal development and its problems.[9]) To repeat, this does not make a final judgment possible. It may, however, be justifiable to attempt a short survey of these reforms in the first stage of their implementation.

Inevitably, reform plans required modification when they were transferred from the "desks" of the planning offices to the reality of the barracks. But frictions that very soon arose were obviously caused not only by the usual discrepancy between theory and practice, but also and not least by the ambivalence inherent in these particular reform plans. Difficulties, obstacles and disagreements piled up so fast at first that the reform deadlocked as early as October, 1956, i.e., one year after rearmament started. The federal government had to explain that the short-term agreements which had been concluded with NATO for the build-up of the *Bundeswehr* (by 1959-60) could not be fulfilled. At the same time, Theodor Blank was replaced as Minister of Defense by Franz Josef Strauss, who had in the meantime become the chief critic of the weak points in his predecessor's policy, and who then continued and completed the build-up of the new armed forces under the motto "quality before quantity".

One of the more deep-seated difficulties in carrying out the reform was that although the reformers had to a large extent applied the Swiss principle of integration they had, for obvious technical reasons, refused to introduce the corresponding militia system in the *Bundeswehr.* It is true that the Federal Republic has general conscription, which is also the basis of militia forces, but the *Bundeswehr* is organized according to the traditional German cadre system, as are all other so-called "conscription" armies. This means that the armed forces consist of a permanent skeleton organization of professional soldiers and a "filling" of conscripts who are called up at regular intervals. The introduction of the cadre system was technically necessary under the conditions of modern warfare. The militia system can hardly be used outside Switzerland. But here, difficulties had to be expected in the application of the principle of integration, namely, in connection with professional soldiers, and these difficulties became greater with the change-over from Blank to Strauss.

Herr Blank's plan of a quick build-up would undoubtedly have led to a looser structure of the *Bundeswehr;* although it would have been a conscription army it would have had a more militia-like character. With the slowing down of the build-up and Strauss's motto "quality before quantity", the professional military view came considerably more to the fore, because a large number of long-service soldiers for the technical branches were needed. In this way, the number of professional soldiers was increased by a group of long-service volunteers ("Soldaten auf Zeit"), so that today the conscripts make up only about 40 percent of the total strength of the

9) Bundestagsdrucksache 1796, April 8, 1960, and Bundestagsdrucksache 2666, April 14, 1961.

Bundeswehr. This also means that only about a third of those annually liable for military service are actually drafted; the selection is carried out by drawing lots. Thus, general conscription has changed from being a responsibility of all citizens to being an administrative action for filling the gap between the supply of volunteers and the planned number of soldiers. Under pressure of circumstances and technical requirements, Herr Blank's militia-like army has become more of a professional army.

This tendency was underlined by the build-up of the officers' corps. To begin with, there was only one reservoir of professionally trained military leaders in Germany: the former officers of the Nazi *Wehrmacht.* They were by no means all National Socialists—many former officers were members of the resistance movement—but both government and Parliament realized that selection was difficult and re-employment not without danger. Under these circumstances, one could have put less emphasis on professional qualification and employed civilians from related professions, such as managers and senior employees from industry. This would have made more improvisation at the beginning necessary, but it would also have made it possible to carry out a stricter selection among the *Wehrmacht* officers. Moreover, this procedure would have been more in keeping with the aim of integrating the civilian and military elements. But even Herr Blank did not seem to consider this method suitable, and Herr Strauss even refused to consider it. Instead of recruiting civilians, it was decided to concentrate on subjecting former *Wehrmacht* officers to very careful scrutiny. The Parliament and the Government set up a *"Personalgutachterausschuss"* (Personnel Scrutiny Committee) of independent personalities. This committee had the task of checking the political and character qualifications of all officers with rank of colonel and above who were to be employed. Without the agreement of this Committee no officer could be appointed. In this way, a reasonable basis was found for excluding unsuitable elements from the officers' corps of the *Bundeswehr.* On the other hand, the professional aspect was also newly emphasized.

The relative emphasis on professional soldiers in the *Bundeswehr* inevitably presented impartial objections to the realization of the Blank-Baudissin integration program. The exclusive employment of former *Wehrmacht* officers also inevitably resulted in a certain amount of subjective resistance against the reform. This was not based, however, on fundamental political differences of opinion or on social bias. The loyalty of the officers' corps towards the democratic state is beyond all doubt today, and they no longer lay any claim to precedence as an elite. That does not mean that no old resentments remain from the period of the "defamation" after 1945 and from the disputes over the conspiracy of July 20, 1944 (attempt on Hitler's life by the former German resistance movement, in which there were many officers), which was criticized by many officers as "oath breaking" and "treasonable". However, criticism of what July 20, 1944, stands for is not always identical with a pro-Nazi attitude, but is often based on formalistic views or other misinterpretations of the duties of a soldier. Meanwhile, Minister of Defense Strauss and his staff have succeeded in making it official *Bundeswehr* policy to recognize and honor the participants of the July 20th plot. It has been done by intensified historical instruction, supported by the experience of a series of concentration camp trials, including the Eichmann trial.

At the same time, but only partly in connection with such tension, a dispute developed over the military reform, especially the new principles of the *"Innere Fuehrung"*, against which not only traditional and formal prejudices were used but also practical arguments of military effectiveness. The supporters of this opposition were found above all in the large group of those officers who after 1945 had successfully established themselves in civilian life. This success in civilian life in the decade from 1945-1955 played a great role for the first generation of *Bundeswehr* officers. Their outlook had been broadened and their attitude changed in many ways. But their relatively advanced age, which enabled them to serve only a short time, as well as the restlessness of the period of build-up, when it was not possible to consider introducing systematic re-education, restricted the decisive effect of their influence. The 1959 annual report of the Commissioner for the Armed Forces stated that the intellectual controversy about the reform was continuing undiminished, and the report for 1960 showed that the front line, to use a military term, ran approximately between middle- and high-ranking officers: brigade commanders and upwards showed more understanding for the reform and more readiness to apply its principles, while battalion and regimental commanders tended to emphasize the authoritative view and to protect their officers and non-commissioned officers in their relations with soldiers. The reason may be the fact that this latter group of commanders belong to the generation whose civilian upbringing took place mainly during the National Socialist era and whose military training took place during the war. Or the reason may be that they are the officers who carry the main burden in the practical application of the new principles.

This highlights a third difficulty in the application of the reform. There is evidence that its objectives tend to overtax the military and human capabilities of officers. The application of the new principles demands more of the officers as human beings as well as professionals than can be fairly expected in the average officer and N.C.O. Therefore, the officers and N.C. officers soon reacted with a feeling of personal insufficiency and rejected the reform or looked for a way out. This resulted in demands for a return to the "well-tried principles" of the *Reichswehr* and *Wehrmacht* and above all for a strengthening of the formal authority of the superiors. These difficulties were made even greater at the beginning by the complications which normally arise during a period of build-up: administrative inadequacies, insufficiency of equipment and training possibilities and, above all, a continuous fluctuation of personnel due to the division, reorganization, and increase of units. In one case, a company had four company commanders in nine months, another battery had ten battery commanders in three years. It is understandable that under these circumstances the resistance against the reform was strongest among the junior officers and that its implementation in general was erratic, depending entirely on the personal interest and capability of the unit commander. Unfortunately, no reliable documentation is yet available from which quantitative deductions can be made. If it is true that the new principles require above-average military leaders, then it is hardly wrong to assume that the realization of these principles leaves much to be desired in the average *Bundeswehr* unit.

Problems of Reorientation

These circumstances resulted in a realization by the Ministry of Defense that they had gone too far in some aspects of the reform. This awareness grew as the *Bundeswehr* turned to its actual military tasks upon completion of the build-up. An officer of the Federal Ministry of Defense, when asked by an American journalist, "Would your present system work in war?" replied with a clear "No."[10]) Those concerned obviously did not want to do a complete turnabout, but tried instead to find a middle way, making it possible to maintain the necessary authority without eliminating human dignity. The Commissioner for the Armed Forces also stated in his annual report for 1960 that a change of attitude regarding the "Citizen in Uniform" was beginning to develop, and that, therefore, "contrary to the overemphasis of the rights of individual freedom for each member of the armed forces as hitherto ... the special duties of the soldier and his connection to society and to the nation should now be emphasized equally."[11]) These statements, incidentally, are remarkable because their wording agrees in general with the views of Herr Blank and Graf Baudissin. Herr Blank and Graf Baudissin also had looked for a middle way between authority and human dignity and aimed at a balance between the rights and the duties of the soldier.

This obvious lack of clarity would seem to indicate that the Federal Defense Ministry itself has not yet found the right answer. Under the circumstances, one would expect a weakening of the principle of integration, i.e., a better adaptation of the internal structure of the *Bundeswehr* to its military tasks and a greater concentration of its activity on military necessities. In fact, some of the adjustments that have meanwhile been made appear to have this objective in view. For instance, new regulations have strengthened the formal authority of superiors, the civilian administration of the armed forces has been slightly curtailed, and the question of restricting civilian jurisdiction over the members of the armed forces is under discussion. Opposed to this, however, is a development sponsored by the Federal Defense Ministry for a *"psychologische Kampffuehrung"* (psychological warfare). This aims at remilitarizing the "education of the citizen" Herr Blank and Graf Baudissin had proposed that this should be a civilian task of secondary importance in the *Bundeswehr.* It has now been built up to a main task. The reason for this was the war of nerves, that has been carried on since 1957 by Moscow and East Berlin with increasing intensity against the Federal Republic in general and against the *Bundeswehr* in particular. In October 1958, Defense Minister Strauss pointed out that it was necessary to immunize the population, and in particular to "immunize the *Bundeswehr,* the troops, against Communist infiltration".[12])

---

10) S.L.A. Marshall, "The Prussians are out of Date", in: New York Herald Tribune, January 24, 1961.

11) Bundestagsdrucksache 2666, p. 42.

12) Bulletin der Bundesregierung, No. 190. October 14. 1958

From this point, the considerations of the Federal Ministry of Defense have in the meantime moved toward a comprehensive conception of psychological warfare. This takes its orientation from the teachings of Lenin and Mao Tse Tung and the experiences of the American army in Korea, and the French army in Indo-China and Algeria. The main and unwavering objective of world Communism is to strive for world domination, and Communist strategy, by its revolutionary nature, has abolished the difference between war and peace. With this premise in mind, it follows that the *Bundeswehr* now already finds itself at war, although as yet only in a psychological war in which it must defend itself with psychological weapons.[13]) The *"Innere Fuehrung"* is now also being embodied into this psychological warfare. According to the views of the competent authorities, the *"Innere Fuehrung"* should supply the *"psychologische Ruestung"* (psychological equipment) for the *Bundeswehr* soldier, above all through instruction about citizenship and other aspects of community life. In addition, it has the task of making the soldiers willing to fight by means of *"zeitgemaesse Menschenfuehrung"* (modern leadership). Also, the postulate of political responsibility is given a new interpretation here: According to the original conception, the soldier received this responsibility through citizenship rights granted him. The present concept makes it more an appeal to duty—namely, the duty of the citizen to function independently in the psychological warfare sense.

The Federal Defense Ministry has emphasized that all this is not for the purpose of sowing hate, of influencing the *Bundeswehr* soldier ideologically, or of stifling political opposition. On the contrary, they say that the purpose is to make the soldier aware of what he is asked to fight for by giving him a clear picture of his own free democratic society and the difference between it and totalitarianism. However, whether or not such a reasonable and commendable limitation can be upheld in the long run—if one proceeds on the assumption of being at war with an implacable enemy—must remain doubtful at least until the Federal Defense Ministry explains more clearly how it proposes to counter the dynamic logic inherent in such ideas. In any case, one thing is certain: the original idea of citizenship training by the *Bundeswehr* is now beginning to be modified. At the beginning, it may have been an end in itself, from which only an incidental strengthening of the military potential could be expected; now certainly, within the framework of psychological warfare, the tendency to reverse this relationship is developing. That this is apparently taking place without friction and without great difficulty is an additional indication of the original ambivalence of the Blank-Baudissin ideas.

The necessity of so comprehensive and intensive a psychological training as is demanded by the *Bundeswehr* may seem debatable. Even the Federal Ministry of Defense does not deny that the massive propaganda campaign from the East has had no serious results either among the population or

---

13) See Psychologie als Waffe: Einfuehrung in Wesen und Formen des psychologischen Kampfes, ed. by Bundesministerium fuer Verteidigung, Fuehrungsstab der Bundeswehr I, 1961 (Schriftenreihe Innere Fuehrung, series: Psychologische Waffen, No 1).—Cf. Taschenbuch fuer Wehrfragen 1960—61, vol. 4, Frankfurt/Main 1960, pp 190 ff., 195 ff.

in the *Bundeswehr.*[14]) Detailed investigations seem to have confirmed that in questions of policy concerning the armed forces, as in other matters, the population combines an understanding of what is needed with a realistic appraisal of what the future may hold.[15]) True, the population shows more fear of a future war than of Communist occupation of Germany. Nor is the public completely convinced that in the struggle against Communism the existence of the *Bundeswehr* is as important as the armed forces themselves believe. Presumably, this is one of the reasons for nervousness in the Federal Defense Ministry.

The attitude of conscripts is generally satisfactory. Competent authorities of the *Bundeswehr*[16]) unanimously stress this. The majority of conscripts recognize that conscription is necessary, without, however, being enthusiastic about military service. What attracts them most is the opportunity for many sports activities and the chance to increase their technical skills. But they are conscious of the fact that the main task of the *Bundeswehr* is the defense of home and fatherland, that is to say, of peace and freedom in the new democratic state. It is certainly true that their knowledge of the nature and function of this democratic state is in many ways still imperfect, and that their political understanding is often inadequate. But it is doubtful if one should conclude that these defects of intellectual education also indicate a lack of determination to defend the state, since similar defects are to be found in the "old" democracies. Investigations among the volunteers of the U.S. Marine Corps, for instance, have shown that only 50 percent of them understood the meaning of the 4th of July, that only a very few could differentiate between the Constitution, the Bill of Rights and the Declaration of Independence, and that only 10 percent could name the basic differences between Communism and a free system of government.[17]) Nevertheless, it would be obviously wrong to conclude that this indicates a lack in the will to fight, especially with regard to this elite corps in the United States.

Seen from the viewpoint of great military idealism, the attitude of Federal Republic citizens may not appear completely satisfactory. But it does not justify the fear that the Germans of 1962 would not fulfill their national duty less well in a future war, if it should unfortunately break out, than did their fathers of 1914 and 1939. One could say that the "count-me-out" movement of the beginning of the 1950s is now dead; on the other hand, the slight reserve in the attitude of the population and the conscripts towards the armed forces is definitely an encouraging sign that the citizens of the Federal Republic have remained immune against militarism and that they also correctly understand the limited importance of the military as

---

14) Minister Strauss, Interview in: Frankfurter Allgemeine Zeitung, October 19, 1960; Psychologie als Waffe, op. cit., S. 65

15) Gerhard Baumann, "Psychologische Rueckwirkungen in der Bevoelkerung der Bundesrepublik beim Aufbau einer Gesamtverteidigung," in: Wehrwissenschaftliche Rundschau, vol. 12, No. 3 (1962), pp. 123—139. — Cf. Umfragen: Ereignisse und Probleme der Zeit im Urteil der Bevoelkerung, vol. 3/4 (1959/60), ed. by DIVO-Institute, Frankfurt/Main 1962.

16) Major Gerd Schmueckle, "Die Jugend und das innere Gefuege des Heeres", in: Wehrkunde, vol. 6, No. 12 (December 1957), pp. 656—661; Annual Report of the Wehrbeauftragter 1959, p. cit. 1796, pp. 8 f.

17) Hanson W. Baldwin, "Troop Information", in: New York Times, January 11, 1962.

an instrument in the dispute with Communism. The same conscripts—and this applies to the majority of them—who accept the necessity of conscription at the same time reject military service as a career with the argument that it is not a "genuine" profession (in the sense of a mission).[18]) This surely shows a remarkable reversal in traditional values. This opinion of a military career increased in proportion to the measure in which those questioned had already settled down in a civilian profession, fortifying the hope that the original autonomy of West German society has not been basically disturbed.

Under these circumstances, the future development of the *Bundeswehr* will depend mainly on the interplay of civil and military power. Just how this will function in the long run cannot be said after such a short time. Thanks primarily to the forceful personality of the Defense Minister, however, the supremacy of politics within the executive appears ensured—so much so, in fact that occasionally the suspicion arises that Herr Strauss uses the machinery of the *Bundeswehr* for party-political purposes. In particular, it has been suggested that the instruction in "psychological warfare" has been used to influence conscripts in favor of the Christian Democratic Party. Parliamentary control, for its part, appears to be less firmly established. It even met with initial opposition on the part of some officers. Misunderstanding the meaning and purpose of this control, they maintained that they felt like *"Soldaten im Ghetto"* (soldiers in a ghetto). Although such sensitivity has largely disappeared, it should not be assumed that all misunderstandings have been eliminated. A more questionable aspect is this: how effectively can parliamentary control really function where political confrontation—after the same party has been in power for 13 years—tends to take place between government and opposition rather than between government and Parliament? In the dispute about equipping the *Bundeswehr* with missiles capable of carrying atomic warheads, the opposition was defeated although according to opinion polls, it was backed by two thirds of the population.[19]) And the reorientation of the internal reform appears to have been largely ignored by Parliament, even though the Commissioner for the Armed Forces drew attention to it in his annual report for 1960. However, because of the secrecy of the Defense Committee's meetings, it is not possible to make definite statements in connection with this question. In any case, it appears important under these circumstances that, apart from Parliament, other counterweights should come into being. In many "civilian" sectors of political life, the beginnings of such a development have already emerged. For instance, the law courts, in particular the Federal Constitutional Court; as well as the *Land* Governments; the *Bundeswehr* and the large pressure groups and top-level organizations have been able to limit governmental powers. But in questions of policy concerning the armed forces they are partly not competent and partly not fully in the picture. At times the press has proved to be an effective substitute; in particular the newsmagazine *Der Spiegel*, which is at present carrying on a sort of private war against Defense

---

18) Baumann, op. cit., p. 137.

19) Umfragen, op. cit., pp. 15 f.

Minister Strauss. However, this can only be considered a temporary and not completely harmless auxiliary, however indispensable a vigilant press may be as one more element of democratic politics.

This concludes the short survey of the build-up of the *Bundeswehr* and its assimilation into the existing national and social order of the Federal Republic. The survey by no means claims to be comprehensive or final. Nor can it determine whether or not the task of creating a "good army in a good democracy" has already been completely successful. But perhaps it has been able to show that, despite all difficulties and problems, there does not seem to be any danger of a new militarism in the Federal Republic. As far as this is concerned, the statement that Jack Baker, of the Anti-Defamation League, made two years ago is still valid today. He wrote: "The portents are good; there is no perceptible resurgence of militarism in West Germany in the year 1960. But if the *Bundeswehr* is indeed to be moulded into an instrument of international cooperation and freedom, if the ghosts of the past are to be exorcized, the hands of the military reformers of Germany must be sustained and strengthened."[20]

20) The ADL-Bulletin, December 1960.

Strength and Prospects of Communism in Germany

By Eduard Wald

"Whoever holds Germany holds Europe."
This statement was made by none other than Lenin himself. His attitude toward the labor movement in pre-1914 Germany vacillated between admiration and hatred; he admired the strong, big, and disciplined organization of the Social Democratic Party and of the trade unions while, on the other hand, this hatred was directed at their revisionist and, allegedly, opportunist antirevolutionary leaders. After the Bolshevist Revolution of 1917, he had no doubts, however, that Germany would follow the example of Russia's revolutionary rise; without such a development, he feared for the stability of the new Soviet State. Consequently, all efforts of the Russian Communists and of the "Communist International" founded in 1919 were aimed at support to be given to the German Communists and to the furthering of their prospective rise to power. The President of the "Communist International" and close assistant of Lenin, Gregorij Sinoniev, stated on September 1, 1923, with reference to Germany:
"The Communist Party considers the present period as being ripe for the seizing of power by the proletariat and, therefore, has the task of regarding itself as the future governing party and of making concrete preparations for the seizure of power."

(*"Jahrbuch fuer Politik - Wirtschaft - Arbeiterbewegung 1923-1924*— Yearbook for Politics - Economics - Labor Movement 1923-1924—; Publishing House of the Communist International, Carl Hoym, Hamburg)

In the same context, Sinoniev called attention to the fact that all sections of the Communist International "should be prepared to grant support to the German revolution". For Germany, he added, the "hour of the decisive battle has arrived".
All wishful thinking of this type came to nothing, however, due to the democratic attitude of the German workers. Nevertheless, after the death of Lenin when Stalin rose to power, Germany continued to be one of the main objectives of Communist strategy. Lenin's statement remained valid.

An inquiry into the present position and strength of Communism in Germany can only provide correct results if the years prior to Hitler's rise to power in 1933 are also considered for the sake of comparison. In those years, the Communist Party of Germany numbered approximately 400,000 members. In the German parliamentary elections (the *"Reichstag")* in November, 1932—at the climax of Germany's economic and political crisis—the Communists obtained, with almost 6 million votes, approximately 17 % of the total vote. It moved into parliament with 100 deputies. Its center of strength was in the big cities of the industrial areas, in particular, those in the Rhine-Ruhr region. In Berlin, it was the strongest political party for many years. Finally, the Communists even succeeded in surpassing the Social Democrats in a large number of industrial communities (the following list includes only the cities located within the territory of the present Federal Republic of Germany: Bochum, Bottrop, Dortmund, Duesseldorf, Duisburg, Essen, Gelsenkirchen, Hamborn, Cologne, Mannheim, Wuppertal).

In 1928, the German Communist Party thought its influence in the various big trade unions and in the Works Councils sufficiently strong to split the trade unions, up to that time under Social Democratic leadership, and for the establishment of strong Communist trade unions. This proved to be a miscalculation. The political activities of the Communists were of a nature which, together with their fanatic fight against all democratic institutions in the German State of those days, was bound to promote and speed Hitler's rise to power.

After the collapse of National Socialist Germany in May, 1945, the Communists once again believed themselves to be quite close to their goal: all Germany appeared to be ready to fall prey to them. The Western Powers were their allies. In the United States, in England and France as well as in Germany, this alliance had greatly boosted the prestige of the Soviets. Only a few people still believed in the possibility of a revival of a strong and influential Social Democratic Party as an effective barrier against the onrush of Communism. The sanctimonious and mendacious slogan of the Communists claiming the necessity of "antifascist and democratic unity" corresponded to the generally prevailing attitude and the wishes of a great many people. Also, memories of the struggle of the Soviets in 1917-18 for a peace "without annexations (i.e., without the seizure of foreign territories and without a forcible affiliation of foreign ethnic groups) and without contributions"—as stated by the "Decree on Peace", dated November 8, 1917, and signed by Lenin—came up again. In the German zone occupied by Russia—the present "German Democratic Republic"—the Communists carefully and methodically placed Communist functionaries, most of them trained in Moscow, in all key positions. In these positions, they developed and implemented a concept which not only provided for the rapid formation of political parties and trade unions under their leadership and supervision but also included plans for the systematic infiltration and disintegration of the three Western Zones of Germany existing at that time (the American, British, and French Zone). In those days, these three occupying powers definitely had no clear ideas, let alone identical ones, of what the future of Germany was to look like.

In the beginning, everything appeared to go well for the Communist plans. In the Western Zones, they were most generously asked to participate in the reconstruction of Germany's administration. Their representatives were socially acceptable. In the newly set up federal states of West Germany they supplied a total of 17 Cabinet Ministers. They were admitted to the editorial staffs and administering bodies of the newly licensed German newspapers. At first they were not prevented from taking active part in the reconstruction of the trade unions. Thus, in several trade unions, they could move right to the top level. They succeeded in obtaining key positions in many important enterprises. Cooperation between the trade unions in the Western Zones and those of the Soviet Zone, agreed upon and guaranteed by conferences and committees of various kinds, facilitated their work. At the same time, these arrangements complicated the efforts of the Social Democrats under Dr. Schumacher to push back the Communists and to delineate clearly existing differences of views and principles. Also, the economic hardships up to 1948-49 helped promote the objectives of the Communists.

There are no exact statistical data on the strength of the Communists in those days. They may be estimated to have had a total of 250,000-300,000 members within the territory of the present Federal Republic of Germany. The overwhelming majority of these members engaged in political activities. As a rule, wherever elections of a general nature took place in West Germany up to 1948, the proportion between the number of Communist party members and the number of votes cast for the Communist Party amounted to 1 : 8. It may be said, consequently, that if general elections in all of West Germany had taken place at that time, the Communist Party would have obtained a total of approximately 2.4 million votes.

Since that time, however, Communist influence has shown a continuous downward trend. What are the reasons for this development?

To start with, the Social Democratic Party, under its leader Dr. Schumacher, became stronger and engaged in a systematic fight against Communist and Soviet policies.

In 1948, the trade unions broke off relations with the Communist trade unions in the German Soviet Zone. They systematically pushed the Communists out of positions held until that time.

The behavior of the Russians toward the population in their own occupation zone and the brutal methods of the expulsion of the population from the former German Eastern territories, from Poland, Czechoslovakia, and the other East and Southeast European countries, resulted in an abrupt change of attitude toward the Soviets. A repercussion of this change of attitude was felt also by the Communists in West Germany. The detention of German war prisoners in Russia contributed, too, to these feelings.

With the start of the Marshall Plan, the basis for West German future prosperity and for an economic boom was laid which, in extent and length of duration, had never been experienced by the Weimar Republic in the years 1918-1933. This development also provided chance for the integration of the millions of expellees and refugees from the East. The Communists had hoped that these millions of dispossessed people would constitute social dynamite for a long time to come.

Last but not least, the brutal blockade of Berlin by the Soviets in the years 1948-49 also severely impaired the reputation of the Communists in Germany.

The first *Bundestag* elections of the Federal Republic of Germany took place in August, 1949. The Communists could freely participate in these elections as well as in the second *Bundestag* elections of September, 1953. On August 17, 1956, the German Communist Party was declared unconstitutional by the highest German court, the Federal Constitutional Court. Since that date, the influence exercised by the Communists in West Germany has no longer been clearly discernible from the results of general elections in the Federal Republic. The Communists tried, however, to regain access to Parliament through a back door with the help of a newly founded neutralist party, the *"Deutsche Friedens-Union"* (German Peace Union); but since the votes cast for this new party also came from other sides such as pacifists, opponents of atomic armament, church circles, and similar elements, only approximately 50 % of the election result obtained by the German Peace Union in the *Bundestag* elections of 1961 may be attributed to Communist voters.

The dwindling influence of the Communist Party in West Germany is clearly demonstrated by the results of the various elections. In the *Bundestag* elections of 1949, the Communists obtained 5.7 % of the votes cast, with a total of approximately 1,360,000 votes for their own party. Four years later, their total number of votes amounted only to 607,000, i.e., 2.2 %. In the *Bundestag* elections in 1961, the "German Peace Union" obtained the same number of votes which, however, only amounted to 1.9 % of the total votes cast. As stated above though, only approximately 300,000 of these may be estimated to have come from Communist voters.

An even more interesting picture is provided by the development in the industrial West German State of North Rhine-Westphalia. The heavy industry of the Rhine and Ruhr is located within this state which had always been, therefore, one of the main objects of Communist wishful thinking. In that same region, too, their seemingly unshakeable "strongholds" were found in the days prior to 1933. In the first elections in North Rhine-Westphalia in April, 1947, the Communists obtained 702,000 votes, i.e., 14 % of the total, a fact which caused great rejoicing. Ever since, however, their decline has been even more conspicuous in this specific area than in the entire Federal Republic: in the year 1949, they obtained 513,000 votes, i.e., 7.6 %; in 1953, only 228,000 votes i.e., 2.8 %; and in 1961, the "German Peace Union" had no more than 188,000 votes, i.e., 2 %.

It must be realized, of course, that the efforts of the Communists to gain influence with the help of parliamentary elections and to exercise that influence via the parliaments represent only one of many other fields of Communist activities. Actually, they only regard them as a minor sphere of work, and considerably more importance is being attributed to what they term the "transmission belt to the masses", that is, the trade unions, enterprises, organizations, and institutions for economic, social, cultural, and recreational purposes. In addition, there exist movements in favor of disarmament and against atomic weapons. In all of these sectors, it is far more difficult to arrive at a correct estimate of the Communist influence. Last but not least, this is due to the fact that the Communists have learned how to adjust and camouflage themselves effectively. As far as elections to trade union congresses and to the leading boards of the trade unions are concerned, their influence has decreased to a large extent though, and for the foreseeable future no serious danger is visible in that area. In fact, it is far smaller than the Communist influence in certain British trade unions where in the recent past it has caused considerable difficulties for democratic elements. Every two years, general elections to the Works Councils are held in the businesses of the Federal Republic of Germany; these Works Councils represent the interests of the employees vis-à-vis management. The Communists have been most eager to be successful in these elections in which all employees of the respective enterprises participate. In the recent past, however, they have also failed in that respect, not even triumphing in isolated cases as they still managed to do in some big concerns in 1956-57.

Generally speaking, it may be said that at the present time the influence of the Communists in the Federal Republic of Germany has reached an all-time low. The erection of the wall in Berlin by Ulbricht dealt a blow to them which will have long-lasting results. But this development was not only caused by the object lesson provided to people in West Germany by the conditions in the Soviet Zone. The "cells" of the Communists in West Germany trying to engage in political underground activities are also weak, having a total of not quite 3,000 members.

The economic boom situation contributed considerably to the increase in the standard of living in West Germany. This very fact disproved the Communist "pauperization theory"; their hopes for an economic crisis collapsed. All democratic parties in West Germany want Germany to remain a stable part of the free West. There are no concrete indications of a possible German seesaw policy between East and West. This is particularly true for the Social Democratic Party and for the trade unions. To sum it up in a few words: our situation today differs to a far-reaching extent from that existing prior to 1933. It offers far less chances to the Communists than at that time.

The picture would not be complete, however, if some existing concrete dangers were to be glossed over. What are these dangers?

People forget easily. That generation of democrats which had been compelled to engage in hard struggles with the Communists is slowly dying out. All political parties and trade unions complain about the growing number of persons whom prosperity has made indifferent and self-complacent, and they raise the question as to what this type of person will be apt to do in times of possible internal or external crisis. In other words: the continuous decrease of Communist influence is certainly not due primarily to the democratic activities of the non-Communist side.

There is something else, too. By holding the German Soviet Zone, the Communists are in possession of an instrument of power and of a starting position which they try again and again to put to use in the Federal Republic of Germany. In this way, they have succeeded to a considerable extent in counteracting and annulling the effects of the outlawing of the Communist Party in 1956. For years, they have been smuggling innumerable millions of propaganda pamphlets into the Federal Republic in all possible ways. The basic democratic attitude of the Federal Republic makes it impossible to effectively curtail activities of this type. Consequently, only provision of information and training and of civic democratic education remain the ultimate means of counteracting this permanent Communist danger.

The available ways and means as well as the funds used by the Communists for their efforts to destroy West Germany's democratic structure appear to be practically inexhaustible. The funds spent by them are estimated to amount to approximately 60 million DM and 50 million "East Marks" per year. Up to the present, these expenditures have not been effective. Will this always be the case, however?

With the help of the most extensive propaganda activities throughout the world, the Communists continuously try to prove that the Federal Republic of Germany is the "successor state of Hitler", and that militarism and Nazism are once again rearing their ugly heads. Similar to the megalomaniacal ways of Hitler's propaganda chief, Joseph Goebbels, the *Propaganda Minister* of the Communists in the Soviet Zone, Albert Norden, tries to talk people east and west of the Iron Curtain into believing: "We can assure you that militarists will never again march through the Brandenburg Gate, nor will millionaires move in. On the other hand, it is an absolutely unshakeable certainty that some day red flags will be flying in West Berlin, Hamburg, and in the Ruhr area."

A long-range program is being carried out. The Communists in the Federal Republic of Germany, depending on their own resources, will not be able to endanger seriously Germany's new democracy. However, stable democratic conditions in this part of Germany will be the most essential prerequisite to make the Soviets realize, some day in the future, that even with the help of their position in East Germany it will not be possible to overthrow democracy in West Germany.

Thus, it might be stated, as a modification of the remark by Lenin quoted above: "Whoever holds the Federal Republic of Germany will hold, in the long run, all of Germany." In order to bring this about though, the willingness to make sacrifices, ceaseless activity, farsightedness, and the perseverance of all democrats will be required.

How Enduring is the Present Democratic System?

By Peter D. G. Brown

Paradoxical as it may sound at first, the democratic system in Western Germany was born under comparatively favorable circumstances. After the Second World War, there was no antidemocratic regime to be overthrown in order to establish a democracy, for there was no existing regime in this country. The foundations on which the German people and their leaders had based their future hopes were totally destroyed. Since nearly everything tangible had been eradicated by what the Germans considered to be a disaster, there were no great obstacles within the country to prevent the victors from introducing their way of government. What many Germans once considered to be the greatest catastrophe in their history, the collapse of the Third Reich, may, in the long run, turn out to be their salvation.

The Federal German Constitution of 1949 was the third one ever to be written and ratified in Germany. The first one, written in 1871, was the work of Bismarck. The executive powers alloted in this Constitution were so strong that it could hardly be termed democratic. In the second one, dating from 1919, the main emphasis was on the legislative powers, thus making for a weak and unstable government. The Constitution of 1949, based to a great extent on British and American traditions, can be understood as an improved version of the Weimar Constitution (1919) to ensure a stable and smoothly operating government while still giving the people as much influence as possible.

The voters elect delegates to the *Bundestag* (parliament) who, in turn, elect the Federal Chancellor; he, then, is in charge of forming the cabinet and heading the government's executive powers. In order to prevent the impotence of the executive power following a no-confidence vote, a safety clause was written into the Constitution. It requires that the *Bundestag* must elect a successor to the Chancellor before his dismissal can take place. Another weakness of the Constitution of 1919 was that it permitted too many political parties in parliament, making coalitions of many small parties necessary. The effect, of course, was a much weaker government than if only one or two parties had formed it. The present German Constitution gives only those parties a seat in the *Bundestag* which have collected at least 5 % of the total number of votes.

The creation of the Federal German *Bundestag* in 1949 introduced a new era in German history. The signs were so encouraging that, with the return of full sovereignty to the Federal Republic in 1955, the Western Allies confidently hoped that the new German democratic system would be both workable and enduring. They thought that the democratic machinery which they had created and set into motion had brought about a change in the German people; that this nation, which within one generation had twice dragged the whole planet into chaos, had become a democratic and independent republic as well as a trustworthy ally. How true and lasting this really is remains to be seen. There is no doubt, however, that the German nation has undergone a multitude of changes and that the German population as a whole differs from that of a quarter of a century ago.

The most spectacular aspect of present-day Germany is its prosperity, its phenomenally successful economy. Although in a capitalistic economy a country's wealth (national income) can never be perfectly distributed among the whole population, there nevertheless are no conspicuous economic or social class differences in Germany today. There are a number of very rich people, but there are no really poor ones. Ideologically, Germany is one of the most unlikely countries in which Communism could become popular, due to the absence of fundamentally different and opposed social classes.

As mentioned above, while there are no major opposing social forces in Western Germany, there is, however, one division or split among the people which works in favor of the growth and development of democracy: the younger versus the older generation. This is much more than the ordinary age differences that normally appear in every society. The years immediately preceding the Second World War, the war itself, and its aftermath caused an almost surgical schism between the last two generations.

Although the older generation is ideologically divided among itself, the younger one stands rather firmly on many fundamental issues. This older generation includes those who grew up and were educated in the Kaiser's era as well as those who received education and re-education during Hitler's regime and who, almost without exception, could be termed his active or passive accomplices. In this same generation are also those who opposed Hitler's reign of terror, whether in thought or in deed. And lastly, there are those now actively employed in the present government as they were in the Third Reich, regarding themselves first as civil servants serving to the fullest extent of their capacity whatever government is in power, regardless of its morals or objectives. These latter are considered to be the most dangerous to the Federal Republic's democracy, not only because of their potential evil influence on the government from within and the fact that they are targets for adverse propaganda from without the country, but also because they tend to propagate a certain slave-to-the-state attitude which has proved disastrous to Germany more than once.

Many unusual circumstances contributed to the younger generation's break with tradition. They were educated for the most part after the war, all persons twenty-three or younger having started the first grade of school after 1945. They learned from teachers with denazification clearance and from books which had been carefully screened by the Allied authorities. In addition, the contemporary literature which they read during their formative years was predominantly American, French, and British, along with German language writers such as Bertholt Brecht, Franz Kafka, and Thomas

Mann,*)—all of whose books were banned during the Third Reich. The films they saw were mainly Hollywood productions, and much of their food, clothing and other consumer goods came from the United States. This generation grew up in a democratic system for which neither they nor their parents had fought. They knew that Germany had unconditionally surrendered in an all-out war which had left its mark of destruction and devastation everywhere.

They were surprised by all the aid and assistance the conquerors bestowed upon them. To learn the whole truth and to ascertain the causes of this terrible war and its consequences, they turned to their parents for denial or confirmation of what they had begun to suspect—Germany's guilt and responsibility. Although the older generation could verify most of the facts concerning the last war, they could not always offer causes and motives in their own defense that were convincing.

It cannot be said that all of the younger generation has condemned the older one. What is of prime importance is that this generation has to a large degree condemned and rejected the values which their parents and grandparents had so highly prized. They came to embrace new standards, first examining them carefully, for they had learned to take nothing at face value. These new principles of democracy which they have been acquiring are ones for which Americans died almost two hundred years ago—in the Federal Republic, they were placed in a neat package at the feet of a whole state.

It can and has been said that there is no guarantee that these basic values of liberty, equality, and justice will remain in the hearts of a people if they have not had an opportunity to demonstrate their willingness to forfeit their lives for them. On the other hand, every new American generation receives this sacred inheritance packaged and presented in the same way. The essential difference is that the individual American, regardless of the year in which he was born, is conscious of the fact that his ancestors fought and died to give him the freedom he enjoys. It is this national consciousness mixed with pride, admiration, and gratefulness that is missing.

Germany's masses have no popular heroes for the cause of democracy to look back on or live up to. The glorious German heroes of the past, the ideals and examples of former German generations, were either men of action or men of genius, famous either as conquerors and military leaders or as brilliant writers and philosophers. It has been one of the great tragedies in German history that the significant liberal thinkers and writers never joined forces with those who had the power to change Germany's *Schicksal* (fate). Although there certainly are fathers and heroes of German democracy, none of them lend themselves to mass popularity or appeal as do so many American figures such as George Washington, Paul Revere, Thomas Jefferson, Patrick Henry, Benjamin Franklin, Abraham Lincoln, or even David Crockett, to name just a few. German history boasts democratic forerunners, but their activity usually did not get far beyond writing books

*) Bertholt Brecht 1898—1956; Franz Kafka 1883—1924; Thomas Mann 1875—1955.

or giving speeches. As the German poet Hoelderlin*) once so aptly put it, "When will the books finally come to life?"

Former German idols such as Frederick the Great, whose Prussian discipline encouraged the patriarchal tradition and "father-complex" throughout Germany, thus enabling Hitler to have so many blindly obedient officials at his disposal, have diminished in popularity with the rise of the new German generation. As democracy goes up, democratic heroes and ideals become vital in order psychologically to secure this way of life in the minds and hearts of a whole people.

This has placed Konrad Adenauer's ruling Christian Democrats' CDU party in a somewhat embarrassing position. Not only is it unable to boast historical examples from his party's past—a past which dates back a mere 16 years—but it is also forced to recognize that a great number of Germany's truly democratic heroes, men who combined liberal thinking with positive action, are to be found among the former ranks of the opposition Social Democrats' SPD party with its 99 year history. Among these historical examples is Friedrich Ebert*), an ardent Social Democrat and the first *Reichspraesident* in the Weimar Republic, often considered to be a German Abraham Lincoln for his role in preserving the German union in the first few months after the First World War. The famous Friedrich Ebert Foundation, known throughout the world as an institution for democratic teaching and research, has educated over 25,000 German adults in the field of political science since the war and is supported by all the major political parties.

Along with a lack of popular democratic heroes is the lack of democratic symbols on which to hinge their dramatic sentimentalism. The young German generation does not know how to regard its national anthem, *Deutschland ueber Alles*. They find it hard to take it seriously and give it the respect due a national anthem. The same applies to the Federal German national holiday on the 17th of June, the "Day of German Unity". This is in commemoration of the 1953 uprising by Germans against Communist authority in East Germany. Most of the younger generation has long recognized the *de facto* existence of two German states. Their present prosperity and well-being means more to them than a utopian German unity. What West German truck driver can "get into the spirit" of the 17th of June as the Frenchman can on Bastille Day, the Indian on the 26th of January, or the Monagasque on the 19th of November, not to mention the American on the 4th of July?

The heroic attempt to assassinate Hitler in order to overthrow the entrenched tyranny on July 20, 1944, is another classic example of this public attitude. This day, too, commemorates the loss of lives for the cause of freedom. It seems that neither of these holidays instills German pride and confidence in a democratic heritage, because no matter how valiant these acts were, they ended in total failures. Freedom did not win in the end, at least not in the short run, but as a result of these courageous attempts, oppression by the police state became even more severe.

---

*) Friedrich Hoelderlin, 1770—1843

*) 1871—1925

One of the most welcome changes in the new German generation is the sharp decline of military values and militarism in general. New German officers of the *Bundeswehr* are more likely to be sneered at than envied when passing German high school or university students. The fact that many German children lost one or both of their parents in the war makes them even more pacifistically inclined. This decline and virtual disappearance of military enthusiasm in the newest German generation is of utmost significance.

After having seen documentary films, read books, and heard original recordings of and about the Third Reich, Germany's youth desires less than anything else the return of these conditions, or the start of another war. They are convinced that there can be no more conventional wars in Europe, there can only be one final atomic war. This attitude naturally has its drawbacks, as many of these young people would rather be "red than dead", thus possibly sacrificing the ideals of democracy for the expedient of Communism in order to save their own skins.

As has already been stated, there exists a sharp cleavage between the older and the younger generations, with the younger one slowly but consistently winning more power and support. The older generation personifies the German as we have known him prior to 1945. The new generation which holds the hope of a lasting German democracy closely resembles its equivalent age group in the United States. Although steadily growing, the present influence of the young on German politics is still limited. But since they lack the necessary experience and maturity, this is not altogether regrettable.

From the first days of the Federal Republic, all the major political parties (naturally founded by the older generation) have had the same general objectives:

a) to rebuild Western Germany into an economic power with prosperity for all;

b) to bring about a reunited Germany in peace and freedom;

c) to cooperate in the integration of Western Europe.

The first objective was realized with the help of American funds in a very few number of years; the second one has failed miserably; and the third one could be termed progressing slowly but surely.

Along with the rebuilding of Germany's economy came a closer cooperation with other countries of the Western world. Not only did the average German realize that his economy was being rebuilt with foreign aid, but Germany, which already had an influx of American soldiers soon became flooded with American consumer goods as well as products of our entertainment industry. Added to this comes the average German's desire and financial ability to spend his vacations outside of Germany and to travel to distant places. The effect of all these outside influences on the German people has been a sharp decline in their traditional nationalism. The German who owns a summer cottage on the Spanish coast, drives an Italian automobile, has his home furnished with Swedish furniture, consumes Dutch and Danish dairy products, smokes an English pipe, drinks

Scotch or Irish whisky, and enjoys French cigarettes, films, and literature, cannot help but feel one with the European subcontinent.

For nearly a decade, while the economy was steadily spiraling upwards, the governing CDU party became more and more identified with German democracy and the country's economic prosperity.

As long as everything was going well, the people continued to give the CDU the majority of their votes. CDU campaign slogans such as "Don't experiment! Keep voting for the CDU!" led the voters to believe that voting for any other party than the CDU would be a political experiment and would endanger the democratic and economic future of the nation. The German people, though, have learned through hard experience to become critical and are not too easily persuaded or convinced by mere threats or promises of politicians. As the recent elections*) have shown, the present trend is markedly towards a balanced, and away from a lop-sided two-party system. This is obviously a large step forward in the democratic development of the German people.

General interest and active participation in politics is to be found in more walks of life and on more intellectual levels than ever before. This by no means is to say that there is no indifference toward political problems past and present in the Federal Republic. Although documentary films and books on recent German history attract much public attention, there still is an appalling lack of interest and indifference toward certain basic issues among many individual Germans. This is unfortunately true in both the younger and the older generations.

One often finds remnants of an almost Islamic tendency to accept the inevitable, whatever it may be; politics is a realm to which only the chosen few, if anybody at all, has insight, and a dirty, thankless business at best, so their thinking goes. Hitler and National Socialism are things of the past, born of the unfairness of the Versailles Treaty and the ensuing economic disaster. Why not just forget about them and "let the dead bury the dead", they say. The reason for this attitude is an opportunistic egoism which is to be found among people in every nation, but it is especially disturbing to observe it in the Federal Republic.

The Federal Government has made a commendable effort in trying to combat this attitude of political indifference. But again, this is something that cannot be superimposed on the mature adult; the seeds must be planted in childhood, must be developed and nourished throughout a lifetime. How successful the Government has been in this respect cannot yet be fully ascertained; but from the initial signs, the Federal Republic of the 1980's will consist of many politically aware and active citizens.

Along with its prospering economy, Germany has had to share the free world's burden of giving assistance to the developing nations of the world. This responsibility has given positive and genuine feelings of world significance to the Federal Republic. It is gradually acquiring a consciousness

---

*) Bundestag elections in / State elections in North Rhine-Westphalia

	Bundestag 1957	Bundestag 1961	North Rhine-Westphalia 1958	North Rhine-Westphalia 1962
CDU/CSU	50.3 %	45.3 %	50.5 %	46.4 %
SPD	32.0 %	36.3 %	39.2 %	43.4 %

comparable to that of the "American Destiny" in the United States. The German people are finally realizing that the role of a great and influential country is to aid and not to conquer other nations. They are becoming increasingly aware of the fact that this form of greatness is more satifying and enduring than their former goals.

Another factor giving the Federal Republic's democracy an increased measure of durability is the fact that it identifies itself with the Western world, politically, economically, culturally, and ideologically. Although basically a sovereign State, the Federal Republic is neither able nor wants to free itself from these ties to the free world. Until the present day it has shown no signs of wanting to revert to a totalitarian system of government. This, however, cannot be presented as proof of the democratic system's reliability. As the whole population has been busy rebuilding Germany, the West German people were united in this common effort. The present democratic system has enabled them to achieve and even surpass this objective; there has been no political or economic disaster which could entice them to abolish democracy.

The German people are, for the time being, thus immune to extreme Rightist or Leftist infiltration and propaganda. The question remains to be answered, however, in which way the German people would react if the Federal Republic found itself faced, for example, with a major economic depression such as that which resulted in the fall of the Weimar Republic. A valid answer to this question would be to say that in twenty years from now the principles of democracy will be, in all probability, strongly enough implanted in the German people to withstand any major political or economic crisis.

For this to become a reality, Germany in the meantime will have to take on even more of Western democratic heritage. It will have to develop, recognize, and honor its own democratic heroes, will have to bridge the gap of the Third Reich and build on to its early democratic heritage, which started with the revolution and constitution of 1848 (not ratified by the German states and thus never effective) and continued up until the year of 1933 when German democracy annihilated itself. If ever Europe should become united, and German politicians are very optimistic about this, then Germany can organically assume the democratic heritage of the other European states, just as the Californians identify themselves with their "forefathers" who won independence from British rule on the Atlantic coast long before California joined the Union.

It would be a boost both to the democratic development and the polititcal party system if a party other than the CDU were to come to power at an early date. It is extremely dangerous for Germany to become dependent for long periods of time on one political party regardless of its efficacy. A change along these lines would cause the people to place more trust in a true democratic system; it would blow a fresh wind into the Government's various departments. At present, high officials have no fear of losing their positions, barring public exposure of those who had a serious Nazi record. It would rejuvenate the CDU as it would have to face the task of being the opposition for at least four years. And lastly, it would give the new governing party leaders the challenge of forming a Government and a chance to prove the desirability and effectiveness of their promises.

It would be foolhardy to conclude that Germany's democratic system in its present state is already "crisis-proof"; there are still too many intransigent people of the older generation in influential positions. Even in the youngest generation, there remain a number of unfavorable old traditions which have not yet died out, such as the anachronistic *"Studentenkorporationen"* (fraternities) among the university students.

If there is to be any hope for the Federal Republic, and in my mind there are many sound reasons for this, then it can only be placed in the generation which has not yet made itself publicly heard. It is, however, the task of their elders to make them conscious of the responsibility to which they are destined. It is up to the teachers and professors, the politicians, the businessmen, and the artists to keep broadening Germany's ideological and historical, political, economic, and cultural bases and horizons; to kindle in the young people a positive, creative, imaginative outlook without which they will be very ill-equipped to solve the problems facing the Federal Republic. It is destructive for critics, Germans as well as non-Germans, to take on a defeatist attitude about the future of Germany's democracy. It is easy to say that the Germans just cannot change. This attitude strongly resembles the national prejudices and chauvinistic tendencies of which the Germans themselves are so often accused.

At present, democracy in the Federal Republic is considered to be stable. But when the reigns of this republic are handed over to younger, energetic, and imaginative individuals, whose values and ideals are firmly imbedded in the democratic heritage of the free world, men and women who can draw hope and courage from the support and cooperation of other free nations, then German democracy can not only be depended upon to remain stable but will continue to grow.

Part IV German Issues in the Light of Press Reports, Scholarly Research, and Polls of Opinion

Reparation in the Federal Republic

By Hendrik G. van Dam

The term *Wiedergutmachung*, which might be translated by the term "reparation", covers the domestic action being taken to make good the misdeeds of the National Socialist regime, but does not cover the field of "reparations" in international law. Both houses of the Federal Parliament and the Federal Government have repeatedly declared reparation of the misdeeds of the National Socialists to be one of the most important and most urgent tasks before the German people and that this moral and judicial debt must be settled as fully and as rapidly as possible. In its last declaration of Government policy, made at the end of 1961, the Federal Government stated that there was every probability that reparation in this field would be completed during the life of the present legislature, and that a number of supplementary points and amendments to the existing provisions were to be introduced in the form of a law concerning the completion of this reparation to the victims of Nazi persecution.

In the Soviet Zone of Occupation in Germany there is no arrangement comparable with this reparation of National Socialist misdeeds; those who are recognized as persons who had suffered under the Nazi system enjoy only limited social assistance and certain advantages such as benefits under the accident insurance scheme if they are work-handicapped.

Restitution

The first measures for the reparation of National Socialist misdeeds were taken shortly after the war by the Western Occupation Forces. In 1947 and 1949, they issued ordinances on the restitution of sequestrated property (for instance, confiscated or alienated real estate, movable property, securities or bank accounts). Restitution under these provisions was more or less completed years ago; it covered the actual handing back of objects which still existed and could be returned, claims for compensation where objects could no longer be found or had been damaged, and claims against individuals and communities for having been deprived of the use of property. The total amount of restitution carried out under these provisions runs into thousands of millions of German marks, though actual statistics are not available.

Alienation of property outside the Federal Republic or Berlin does not in principle justify a claim under the restitution provisions unless the object concerned was subsequently brought into the area. This gap was partly filled by Ordinance No. 11 (1956) concerning compensation payments under the Equalization of Burdens Act. Under the terms of this Ordinance, victims of Nazism or their heirs are entitled to compensatory benefits for damage in respect of property alienated in the areas from which Germans were expelled.

The Federal Restitution Act of July 19, 1957, carried on the work begun under the Allies' restitution measures for settlement of the obligations incurred by the former German *Reich* and similar bodies (such as the NSDAP) in cases where restitution in kind is no longer possible. Over half a million claims have been filed under this Act, and of these more than half had been settled one way or the other by December 31, 1961, the date originally fixed for completion of the work. Under an agreement with the three Western Powers, the commitment for payments under this Act has been limited to 1,500 million DM. Disbursements up to and including December 31, 1961 totaled 1,189,725,000 DM.

The claims still outstanding mostly concern alienation of property outside the boundaries of the Federal Republic and Berlin. Under section 5 of the Federal Restitution Act, a claim may be submitted if it can be proved that the object was subsequently brought into the area within which the Act applies; these claims are dealt with by the Finance Directorate of Berlin. A large proportion of the outstanding cases concern claimants from Iron Curtain countries with which the Federal Government has no diplomatic relations, and under section 45 of the Act, no payment can be made to these claimants.

Section 32 of the Act guarantees that even if the maximum of 1,500 million DM is exceeded the first 20,000 DM of all claims approved will be paid in full, plus 50 % of all amounts above 40,000 DM. Should the total of 1,500 million DM prove insufficient for the remaining portion of the claim to be settled in full, this portion will also be paid subject to the necessary reduction. On the basis of present estimates, it appears that the relevant claims total some 2,700—2,900 million DM, of which some 2,000 million DM would come under the guaranteed payments. There is at present no firm entitlement to payment of this remaining portion of claims (as defined in paragraph 4 of section 32 of the Restitution Act).

An amendment to the Act is being prepared; it will finally settle the extent to which claims can be met. To enable elderly claimants to receive further sums while awaiting amendment of the Act, the Government on June 7, 1961 approved a "Directive for advance payments to persons with recognized claims under the Federal Restitution Act" (published in the Official Gazette of the Federal Republic No. 128 on July 7, 1961). Under the terms of this Directive, persons who have reached the age of 65 can apply for and receive advance payment of up to 75 % of the recognized claim up to a maximum payment of 100,000 DM. Other claimants will receive payments over and above the 50 % already paid only when the amendment has become law—which should be before the end of 1962.

Indemnification

Since 1953, the Federal Indemnification Act has been the mainspring of activity in the field of personal reparation. This piece of legislation developed out of the Reparation Act in the U.S. Zone of Occupation and since October 1, 1956, has been in force throughout the Federal Territory and in West Berlin, at first as a Federal Amending Act. The Third Amending Act of June 29, 1956, gave this legislation its present form with over 240 sections covering indemnification for loss of life, injury to body or health, loss of freedom (whether close arrest or other form of restriction on movement), damage to property (provided the circumstances do not justify a claim under the provisions relating to restitution) or damage to one's professional or economic activities. All persons who on December 31, 1952, were living in the Federal Republic or in West Berlin, or who had prior to this date emigrated from or been deported from the territory of the former German *Reich* (1937 boundaries) are entitled to claim for all such losses or damage. Emigrants expelled from the non-German areas (in particular Poland, Czechoslovakia, Hungary, and Rumania) and victims of Nazi persecution who were on October 1, 1953, stateless persons or refugees as defined in the Geneva Convention are also entitled to indemnification, subject to limitations of scope and extent. There are special clauses covering refugees who have suffered damage because of their nationality and in defiance of human rights.

2.8 Million Claims For Indemnification

The total number of people entitled to indemnification under the relevant Act is not yet clear. In the *Land* Statistical Office in Duesseldorf, where there is a Central Index of the victims of Nazi persecution, more than 1.8 million claimants are registered—and the number of claims filed is considerably higher. Statistics showed that on January 1, 1962, 2.8 million claims had been lodged with the responsible offices. Some 760,000 (or 27 %) of these had been put forward by residents and some 2,040,000 (or 73 %) by persons residing abroad. By December 31, 1961, decisions had been reached on some 1.9 million (or 68 %) of these 2.8 million claims. The *Laender* are individually responsible for applying the Act, and the progress made varies from *Land* to *Land,* as can be seen from the table below.

	Claims submitted	Decisions reached	(approx.) %
North-Rhine Westphalia	662,214	493,382	76
Rhineland-Palatinate	611,246	354,833	58
Berlin	444,567	241,682	55
Bavaria	319,799	258,143	81
Hesse	223,119	168,868	76
Lower Saxony	180,125	137,715	77
Baden-Wuerttemberg	163,464	134,648	83
Hamburg	113,923	63,907	56
Slesvig-Holstein	34,708	33,963	98
Saar	31,809	9,624	31
Bremen	14,600	11,915	82
	2,799,574	1,908,680	68

The authors of the Federal Indemnification Act originally put forward March 31, 1963 (end of the financial year 1962-63) as the final date for implementation of the Act. When the financial year was brought into line with the calender year, this date was moved forward to December 31, 1962. It is specifically laid down that all claims (apart from annuities falling due after this date) shall be settled by this date.

In most Indemnification Offices, the work will in the main have been completed in time, but it appears that at the end of the year some 15—20 % of the claims lodged will still be outstanding. This remainder will be unavoidable, even though the pace at which claims have been processed has been greatly increased in the last few years. In 1960 and 1961 alone, decisions were reached on more than 900,000 cases, or nearly one third of all claims lodged.

In several *Laender,* however, a percentage of the claims lodged will still be outstanding at the end of the year. These are mainly claims concerning injury to health, and damage to professional activities or to property. The delay is largely due to the difficulties and delays which face victims of Nazi persecution living abroad when they have to obtain medical certificates proving that their health has been injured and to the problems that arise when damage to professional activity or property has to be assessed. The problem of the medical certificates has recently been reduced greatly by sending medical officials from the Indemnification Offices to spend considerable periods at diplomatic or consular offices of the Federal Republic, particularly in the USA; these officials were able to make the requisite medical assessment on the spot.

There are also other reasons why, despite the increased speed with which the Act is being implemented, a number of cases will still be outstanding at the end of the year. The number of claims lodged just before the closing date of April 1, 1958—and the number of subsequent claims filed till quite recently and with legal justification for the delay—greatly exceeded all official expectations. On March 31, 1958, only 1,991,326 claims had been registered, but the total has since risen to 2.8 million. Consequently, the authorities were only at a comparatively late date in a position to see the full magnitude of the work to be done and to make the necessary arrangements. Since 1958, both the Indemnification Offices and the tribunals dealing with the matter have been strengthened, and the total number of officials and clerical staff working in the *Land* Indemnification Offices today has reached 4,000, to whom must be added the judges and clerical staff of the *Land* Courts, *Land* Courts of Appeal, and Federal Supreme Court. The role of these courts is shown by the fact that between October 1, 1958 and January 1, 1961, no less than 245,890 cases were submitted. For a proper appreciation of the situation, it should also be realized that in a number of still outstanding cases considerable advance payments have already been made to claimants. Of the remainder, an appreciable percentage of the claims are likely to be quite unfounded, for the offices dealing with the matter have reported that many of the claims either duplicate each other or come from people in Iron Curtain countries who are not covered by the Act. Of the 1.9 million cases in which a decision has already been reached, 504,700 claims (or 26—27 %) have been turned down. The proportion is smaller in respect of claims lodged by persons living abroad (21 %) than for claims submitted by residents within Germany (38 %).

11,500 Million DM Paid Out as Indemnification

The increased pace at which the Federal Indemnification Act has been implemented in the last two years has led to a notable increase in payments. By December 31, 1961, payments under the Federal Act totaled 10,817,997,000 DM; if to this sum we add the 738,183,000 DM paid out by the *Laender* under their own Indemnification Acts before the Federal Act came into force, the grand total by the end of 1961 was 11,556,180,000 DM. The breakdown of this total can be seen in the following table:

Up to December 31,	1956	2,393,791,000 DM
In	1957	1,641,695,000 DM
In	1958	1,549,677,000 DM
In	1959	1,669,912,000 DM
In	1960	2,059,856,000 DM
In	1961	2,241,249,000 DM
Up to December 31,	1961	11,556,180,000 DM

The sum of 2,241,249,000 DM paid out in 1961 was made up of current and overdue annuities totaling 1,130,585,000 DM and capital amounts of 1,110,664,000 DM. The ratio of annuities to total outlay will, of course, go on growing till payments consist entirely of these annuities paid to victims of Nazism. Of total outlay under the Federal Indemnification Act up till the end of 1961, more than 8,000 million DM (c. 75 %) were paid to persons not resident in Germany.

The latest figures for payments under the Federal Indemnification Act suggest that by the end of 1962 some 14,000 million DM will have been paid out as indemnification under the Federal Act and the earlier *Land* Indemnification Acts. This would mean that by the time all claims have been settled, further payments would total at least 3,000 million DM, so that total outlay will have risen to 17,000 million DM, apart from subsequent payment of annuities. This contrasts sharply with the estimate of total expenditure of 4,500 million DM made in connection with the Federal Amending Act and the figure of 8,500 million DM estimated at the time the Federal Indemnification Act was passed in its original form in 1956.

Proposed Amendment to the Federal Indemnification Act

As with the Federal Restitution Act, the Federal Government is preparing a bill amending and extending the Federal Indemnification Act. This will be a major element in the bill for the completion of reparation to the victims of Nazi persecution mentioned in the last declaration of policy by the Federal Government. The legislative organs have not yet had details of proposed amendments put before them, and it is improbable that the amendments to the Federal Indemnification Act—unlike those affecting the Federal Restitution Act—will be passed this year. The organizations representing the victims of Nazi persecution, in particular the Conference on Jewish Material Claims against Germany, have submitted to the Federal Government far-reaching proposals for the extension of the Federal Indemnification Act. So far no concrete statements have been put out by the Federal Government or the legislative organs concerning the character or scope of the amendments.

Reparation for Those Occupied in Public Service

The Act concerning the Reparation of Nazi Socialist Injustice to Persons in the Public Service, passed on May 11, 1951, and several times amended, the last amendment being that of August 18, 1961, is primarily concerned with reintegrating in the public service those forced out by the Nazis and with the payment of the salaries and benefits due to these people. Under the Act, a victim of Nazi injustice is entitled to the position in the public service which he would have reached had it not been for this injustice; payment of salaries and benefits is made from April 1, 1951, and to cover the period prior to this a sum amounting to one year's benefits is paid by way of indemnity. (Compensation for injury suffered prior to April 1, 1950, is covered by the Federal Indemnification Act.) Officials and clerical employees residing abroad are dealt with in a special Act dated March 18, 1952. Former servants of Jewish communities and institutions, or their heirs, are entitled to benefits under the terms of an implementing regulation under the Act dated July 6, 1956. Except for fresh or more extensive claims arising out of the latest amendments to the Act and for the benefits already being paid, reparation under this legislation can be regarded as more or less complete. Statistics of the total expenditure are not available. Including the amounts still to be paid in the years ahead, it is estimated that this expenditure will be not less than 1,500 million DM.

The Agreement with Israel

In addition to reparation of loss or damage suffered by individuals, general reparation agreements of a global character have been negotiated with various states. The most important of these is the agreement made in 1952 with Israel, in which the Federal Government undertook to pay Israel 3,000 million DM in reparations. The Federal Government's obligation was based on the argument that Israel had to accept considerable financial burdens in receiving and integrating Jews who had been uprooted in Europe as a result of Nazi Socialist persecution. Payments to the State of Israel are coupled with a payment of 450 million DM to the Conference of Jewish Material Claims against Germany. The Conference uses this money as a special fund through which it helps Jewish offices throughout the world to support, settle, and integrate Jewish victims of Nazism living outside Israel. Total payments under the agreement with Israel amount, therefore, to 3,450 million DM. The amount is to be paid in 14 annual installments, and Israel accepts performance by the delivery of goods. By the end of 1961, the sum transferred to Israel had reached a total of 2,400 million DM.

Agreements with Other States

The Federal Republic has reached agreements with 11 European countries under which it undertakes to pay lump sums to be used for payments to the surviving dependents of persons who lost their lives at the hands of the Nazis and for compensation to nationals of these States who suffered injury to health or were deprived of their freedom, yet are not entitled to the benefits of the Federal Indemnification Act. The agreements mainly affect people who suffered injury from measures taken by the Nazi Socialists, particularly in the period of military occupation during the war, but who have neither lived previously in Germany nor been stateless persons or refugees, as defined by the Geneva Convention at the time when the Federal Indemnification Act came into force. The distribution of the sums placed at the disposal of the various States has been left to their own governments. Under the agreements, France receives over 400 million DM, the Netherlands some 125 million DM, Greece 115 million DM, Austria over 100 million DM, Belgium 80 million DM, Norway 60 million DM, Italy 40 million DM, Luxemburg 18 million DM, Denmark 16 million DM, and Switzerland 10 million DM.

The Federal Government's "Special Funds"

The Federal Government has taken action to help particular groups of persons who have suffered injury. There is, for example, a fund of 50 million DM for persons not of Jewish faith persecuted on racial grounds; from it, assistance is given to groups or individuals. The fund is administered by the *Regierungspraesident* in Cologne.
One of the earliest of these Federal arrangements was made on behalf of the survivors of medical experiments. Under a decision taken by the Federal Government in 1951, victims of medical experiments carried out in concentration camps are entitled to a nonrecurring grant to cover the restoration of their health if the residence qualification or other grounds exclude them from benefits under the Federal Indemnification Act. This special fund is directly controlled by the Minister of Finance.

Within the last year, the Federal Government has reached an agreement with the United Nations High Commissioner for Refugees in which it agrees to give greater help than that available under the Federal Indemnification Act to persons who have suffered injury because of their nationality and who are refugees as defined in the Geneva Convention. Action under this agreement is the responsibility of the Federal Administrative Office in Cologne. In addition, a sum of 45 million DM has been placed at the disposal of the UN High Commissioner for further assistance measures to refugees and their surviving dependents.

Total Cost of Reparation Activities

The total cost to the Federal Republic of its endeavors to repair the damage caused by the injustices of the National Socialists is estimated to be more than 24,000 million DM. This includes 17,000 milion DM for indemnification under the Federal Indemnification Act and the earlier measures taken by the *Laender* themselves, nearly 2,000 million DM under the Federal Restitution Act, 1,500 million DM under the Act concerning Persons in the Public Service, nearly 3,500 million DM under the agreement with Israel, and under the heading of various other agreements, acts and special funds over 1,000 million DM. Of this total amount, some 16,000 million DM have been paid out by the end of 1961. This means that, apart from the proposed amendments to the relevant legislation and any extension of commitments, some 8,000 million DM remain to be paid in the next few years.

The Future

The figures cited show the reparation effort made by Germany in a comparatively favorable light and leave one wondering what lies behind all the criticisms and dissatisfaction which come from the victims of Nazism themselves and at times lead to outbursts of indignation. The reasons are various. We can discount crass ignorance and the determination to treat reparation with scepticism whatever happens; these factors are not without their importance, but they are not decisive.

We must from the start realize that what is being done in this field inevitably wears a different aspect when viewed from the angle of the individual with a claim and when looked at as part of a whole. The individual who presents a claim will inevitably experience many disappointments, because he has to deal with the whole indemnification machinery of the State with officials and clerical staff bound by regulations, with authorities, courts, last dates for submissions, appeal procedures, in short with the whole red tape of government offices. He finds it at times very trying, particularly when it all comes along years after the injustice he suffered. What to the judge, the lawyer, the civil servant is merely a matter of legal provisions or normal bureaucratic practice appears to the victim of Nazi crimes, who has probably lost close relatives and the essentials of life such as health, wealth, possessions, and job, almost as a personal affront.

This difference in approach can, it is true, be reduced by doing everything possible to make things easier for applicants, but it cannot be entirely avoided. Every State, every well-organized administration, whether in a country previously deprived of the rule of law or in a country that was occupied by German troops, will have its bureaucratic methods, must establish certain criteria, must use questionnaires and impose time limits when dealing with claims for indemnification. This is true not only of Germany, but also of Holland, France, Italy, and even Israel.

In view of the volume of work involved in implementing relevant legislation—the scale of the task emerges clearly from the statistics—difficulties have occurred in the Federal Republic which are not easy to overcome, no matter what the attitude of the individual official may be towards the problems raised by the whole operation. Of course, an official imbued with good will is preferable to a more awkward colleague, but what really matters is reliability and knowledge of the subject.

One of the greatest sources of dissatisfaction is the conflict between the victim seeking his right, feeling that he is absolutely entitled to full satisfaction of his claims, and the bureaucracy of the authorities, who must perforce call for proof of injury and evidence that this injury was in fact the result of persecution. Despite all the provisions intended to make allowances for difficulties in producing evidence, the procedure often creates a situation characterized by despair and bitterness. This applies in particular to claims arising from injury to health, which for many of the victims of Nazism is the only ground on which they can base their claims. It is of course extremely difficult after a lapse of ten or twenty years to produce medically and legally convincing proof of the relationship between gruesome and unjust persecution and the morbid state that is being investigated.

The situation is complicated by the fact that in these days of rapid advances in medical knowledge, an examination made today will lead to conclusions which differ from those drawn in the past, so that in practice we have a situation, repugnant to any democratic constitution, in which similar facts receive dissimilar treatment.

There is no need to multiply the examples of conflict between the individual applicant and an administration that must abide by the law. It is to be hoped that legislators will make every effort to obviate all possible cases of actual disparity of treatment.

A further source of criticism is to be found in the concepts underlying both the legislation on reparation and the reparation agreements reached with other countries, agreements which have in part determined the content of subsequent legislation in Germany. The agreements—the Bonn Conventions between the three Western Powers and the Federal Republic which put an end to the Occupation, and the Luxembourg Reparation Agreement between the Federal Republic on one side and the State of Israel and certain Jewish organizations on the other—limit the circle of possible claimants to specific groups. The legislation concerning reparation is an act by which Germany re-establishes law at home, and therefore applies to persons who have suffered injury and either live in Germany or have emigrated from Germany; the legislation also covers certain categories of persons specifically referred to in the international agreements who have come, owing to post-war circumstances, to have a legal relationship with Germany; one such category is that of Displaced Persons. Rights similar or equivalent to those of Displaced Persons were accorded to stateless persons and refugees living in countries West of the Iron Curtain, and to victims of persecution driven as "expellees" from certain areas; these persons were included in the Reparation Agreement by analogy with the Equalization of Burdens legislation, and were later added to the list of those who benefited under the indemnification measures. On the other hand, the law does not cover victims who were foreign nationals at the time they suffered injury and who are living in their own country. This meant that a victim of Nazi persecution who lived in France or Belgium or Holland but came from Germany was fully entitled to file his claims under the indemnification measures, while the Frenchman, Belgian or Dutchman who had suffered the same persecution had no rights under this legislation. It was this very unsatisfactory situation which led to the agreements with eleven European countries; as these agreements only cover the payment by Germany of lump sums, the countries concerned enjoy a large measure of discretion in the distribution of the available money.

In this way, inequality before the law is reduced, but not eliminated. There are, after all, a great many victims of Nazi persecution who are neither nationals of the eleven States nor covered by the legislation concerning reparation. To the lawyer, the difference in treatment may be understandable; the victims of arbitrary action commited by the State in war or in peace fail to understand why they should fare less well than others.

It is an open question, and one which cannot be decided on the basis of purely legal and ethical considerations, whether further legislation can remove these shortcomings by allowing new claims or by establishing a fund to cover hard cases.

The Federal Government has not been, and is not, an entirely free agent in the steps it has taken to establish the present legislation on indemnification. It is tied to treaties which have led to certain injustices, in particular, the provision that nothing shall be done to make the position in the South German *Laender* (former US Zone of Occupation) any less advantageous. This arrangement does not always help the victims of persecution, for it divides them permanently into four classes before the law, and works in particular to the disadvantage of those who were relatively young when they became victims of persecution under the Third Reich.

If we examine the problem objectively, without stressing budgetary considerations or the subjective reactions of the individual sufferer, we must conclude that the Federal Republic has shown good will in the matter of reparation and has made a considerable effort in terms both of outlay and of administrative effort. The operation of this effort, which is certainly intended to be a not unimportant element in Germany's foreign policy, is hindered by the complicated structure of the law, by the incomplete application of the underlying concept and by the greatly varying interpretation placed on the law by the courts, which is at times extremely narrow and unhelpful, at others quite surprisingly broad. This is most regrettable, as a higher level of indemnification and restitution would give grounds for a correspondingly positive reaction on the part of all concerned.

A quite peculiar situation has arisen in connection with the application of the Federal Restitution Act. The general attitude of the Federal Ministry of Finance in connection with particular difficulties over the production of evidence on the removal of confiscated objects to Western Germany or Berlin had created a situation which leads to unequal treatment of injured parties, who could not have expected the law to be applied in such a manner. A further result was that the limit of 1,500 million DM placed on the Federal Government's obligations lost its validity.

The legislation now being prepared must at least simplify existing provisions and make the position of all injured parties absolutely clear. Without this clarity, the whole action will never produce the desired success. A situation characterized by constant expectations and by illusions concerning the legal position and the legislative possibilities makes of reparation a subject of everlasting argument and reduces the impact which, for political reasons, it is intended to have.

The Prosecution of National-Socialist Crimes by the Public Prosecutors and Courts in the Territory of the German Federal Republic since 1945 *

The capture of Eichmann by the Israeli secret service aroused great public interest in the German prosecution of those persons whose crimes had not been prosecuted in the years from 1933 to 1945 for political reasons. Domestic and foreign press releases created the false impression that only since 1956 has the Federal Republic of Germany, under the pressure of world opinion, been seriously engaged in prosecuting national socialist crimes. The following compilation shows, however, that these crimes have been prosecuted vigorously ever since 1945, partly by the occupation authorities and partly by German authorities. In spite of the great difficulties which had to be overcome (see p. 300), most of the proceedings were completed by 1953 (for details see statistics p. 298).
Because the convictions for national socialist crimes are not shown as such in the court statistics, it was difficult to procure the necessary data. Only the special cooperation of the *Land* Judiciaries permitted this work to be subsequently undertaken.

The National Socialist Crimes

After taking control of the government in 1933, the national socialist rulers used not only every legal means to secure their power, to eliminate all actual and possible opposition, and to achieve their political goals, but soon resorted to illegal measures as well. Generally, these were camouflaged carefully. A number of these actions, though, could not be kept secret indefinitely. That is why, for example, the assassinations following the alleged Roehm-revolt in 1934 were declared "legal" by a special law (Law Concerning Measures of National Self-Defense of July 3, 1934, *Reich* Law Gazette p. 529). In the years that followed, the number of crimes committed for political reasons and not prosecuted, rose continually. These ranged from the maltreatment of political prisoners during interrogation, and the destruction of shops, homes, and synagogues in what was called the *"Kristallnacht"* (November 8-9, 1938), to the concentration camp atrocities and mass murders involved in the so-called "Final Solution of the Jewish Question".

Prosecution by the Former Occupying Powers

Following the occupation of the *Reich* by Allied troops, German courts were temporarily nonexistent. At this time, therefore, the prosecution of national socialist crimes was a matter solely for the occupying powers. In accordance with the *London Agreement of August 8, 1945,* "concerning the prosecution and punishment of principal war criminals of the European Axis", the *International Military Tribunal* convened in Nuremberg. The judgment of October 1, 1946, sentenced 19 of 22 defendants:
twelve to death (Bormann, Frank, Frick, Goering, Jodl, Kaltenbrunner, Keitel, v. Ribbentropp, Rosenberg, Sauckel, Seyss-Inquart, Streicher);
three to life imprisonment (Funk, Hess, Raeder);

*) Prepared by the Federal Ministry of Justice in cooperation with the *Land* Judiciaries, Bonn, 1961.

four to prison terms (Doenitz, v. Neurath, v. Schirach, Speer);
acquitted: three (Fritsche, v. Papen, Schacht).

On December 20, 1945, the Control Council in Germany passed *Law No. 10* (Control Council Gazette p. 50). As stated in its preamble, the Law was to "establish a uniform legal basis in Germany for the prosecution of war criminals and other similar offenders".

The implementation of this procedure fell upon the Allied authorities. Pursuant to Article III, Paragraph 1d of the said Law, the occupation authorities were entitled to declare the German courts only competent for pronouncing sentence on crimes *which had been committed by German citizens against other German citizens or against stateless persons.*

Under this law, a great many criminal proceedings were carried out in the individual Zones of Occupation:

a) In the American Zone, the military courts in Nuremberg and Dachau convicted 1,814 defendants, 450 of whom were sentenced to death;

b) In the British Zone, the British Military Tribunal and British Control Commission courts convicted 1,085 defendants, 340 of whom were sentenced to death;

c) In the French Zone, the military courts sentenced 2,107 defendants, 104 of whom were sentenced to death.

The Allied courts thus convicted a total of 5,025 persons charged with national socialist crimes, *806 of whom were sentenced to death.*

The prosecuting authorities and the courts in the Federal Republic may not again prosecute offenses which have already been prosecuted or investigated by the Allied authorities. This follows from *Part I, Article 3, Paragraph 3b* of the Convention on the Settlement of Matters Arising out of the War and the Occupation in the text published on *March 30, 1955* (Federal Law Gazette II p. 405).

As a result of this provision, German courts may not retry a number of persons for the above mentioned crimes. These individuals have attracted considerable public attention during the past few years, both in Germany and abroad. A few examples are the former Director of Public Prosecution at the German Supreme Court, Lautz; the former Vice-Minister *(Staatssekretaer)* Schlegelberger; the concentration camp physician Dr. Oberheuser; the SS officer Six; and the former Foreign Office counselor Veesenmeyer. All these persons had been sentenced by the American military court in Nuremberg to various terms of imprisonment but have since been released.

The total number of investigation proceedings instituted by the Allied authorities is not known but was probably greater than the above—mentioned number of convictions.

In foreign countries, too, a considerable number of German citizens have been tried for national socialist crimes. Some of the persons charged had been captured in the territories of the powers by whom they were later tried (mainly prisoners of war). Other defendants were handed over by the occupying powers to certain foreign countries. The legal basis for this was Article 4 of Control Council Law No. 10.

Complete data on the number of extraditions are not available. The existing material shows, however, that several thousand persons were probably handed over.

Renewed prosecution of persons previously tried abroad is possible in the Federal Republic. However, in determining the sentence passed on a conviction in the territory of the German State, the court must deduct punishment exacted abroad for the same crime (Paragraph 7 of the Penal Code). Sometimes the case has been dropped under Paragraph 153b, No. 3 of the Code of Criminal Procedure because the net German sentence, after setting-off the sentence served abroad, would have been negligible.

Prosecution by the German Authorities

I. **Under Control Council Law No. 10:**

The possibility provided by Article III, 1d of Control Council Law No. 10, of empowering German courts to prosecute national socialist crimes, was used by the Occupying Powers in different ways, as follows:

1. *In the American Zone,* authorizations were issued in individual cases.
2. *In the British Zone,* a general authorization to German courts to take the legal proceedings described above was issued by virtue of Military Government Ordinance No. 47 of August 30, 1946 (Military Government Gazette, p. 306).
3. *In the French Zone,* a general authorization was only issued on June 1, 1950, by virtue of Military Government Ordinance No. 154 (Allied High Commission Gazette, p. 44).

The above mentioned authorizations were withdrawn by virtue of British Military Government Ordinance No. 234 of August 31, 1951, (Allied High Commission Gazette, p. 1138), and by French Military Government Ordinance No. 171 of the same date (AHC Gazette, p. 1137). After that date individual authorizations were no longer issued in any zone. Thus, a conviction by a German court under Control Council Law No. 10 became virtually impossible. The Law itself was not repealed until May 30, 1956, through Article 2 of the First Law for Terminating the Occupation Law (Federal Law Gazette I, p. 437).

Statistical data for 1950 and 1951—the first two years after the establishment of the German Federal Republic—show that 730 persons (including 49 women) were sentenced by German courts empowered under Control Council Law No. 10, as follows:

	Total	1950	1951
Life imprisonment	6	5	1
Penitentiary terms	115	92	23
Prison terms	587	476	111
Fines	22	16	6
Number of persons sentenced	730	589	141

II. **Under German Law:**

Ever since 1945, German courts have tried national socialist crimes as far as they fell within their jurisdiction. Insofar as Control Council Law No. 10 could not be applied (because the case did not fall within its provisions or because authorization had not been granted), decisions were based on general German penal law.

The States of Bavaria, Bremen, Hesse, and Baden-Wuerttemberg issued substantially identical state laws concerning the Disciplining of National Socialist Crimes (Bavaria: Law No. 22 of May 29, 1946, Gazette of Laws and Ordinances p. 182; Baden-Wuerttemberg: Law No. 28 of May 31, 1946,

Government Gazette p. 171; Hesse: Law of May 29, 1946, Gazette of Laws and Ordinances p. 136; Bremen: Law of June 27, 1947, Law Gazette p. 267). The following data show that other German states, too, have conducted numerous proceedings. (In these figures, both those persons convicted under Control Council Law No 10, as well as those convicted under German law, are included).

These crimes, some of which had been committed directly by the supreme public authorities or had been supported by them—and which, in numerous cases had assumed the form of organized mass murder—confronted the German judiciary with many difficult and sometimes novel legal problems: e.g., with the question whether provisions of statutory law may be invalid when conflicting with rules of higher value, or the extent to which the fact that an action is performed in execution of an order or in the belief that it is a duty, exempts from punishment, or an error of interdiction excludes guilt, etc. Both scholars and courts have made a considerable effort to find answers to these questions. Indicative were often the rulings of the Federal Supreme Court, the judgments of which provided jurisprudence with a number of clearly directive precedents.

German public prosecutors have carefully investigated every suspicion of a national socialist crime. In those cases in which the investigations did not produce a sufficient basis for prosecution (e.g., due to lack of evidence, a statute of limitation, or inability to locate the accused), the prosecutors closed the proceedings. Formal charges were brought in over 12,000 cases (see column 2 in the following chart III 1). The outcome of these cases can be seen in columns 3 through 9.

III. **Statistical Tabulation**

1. Cases finally adjudicated from May 8, 1945 to March 15, 1961.

Land	Total Number of Persons Charged	Disposition of Charges						
		Charges Dismissed Without Trial	Defendants Sentenced	Defendants Acquitted	Charges Dismissed During Trial Total	Reasons: Statutory Limitation	Amnesty	Cases Terminated in Other Ways
1	2	3	4	5	6	7	8	9
Baden-Wuerttemberg	970	62	585	267	56	—	56	—
Bavaria	2 583	216	993	696	594	153	430	84
Berlin	403	15	205	159	24	10	6	—
Bremen	107	2	62	34	8	—	8	1
Hamburg	303	34	120	57	92	3	20	—
Hesse	2 025	23	941	745	291	—	173	25
Lower-Saxony	1 308	17	582	375	334	20	314	—
North-Rhine Westphalia	2 663	174	1 153	914	422	25	255	—
Rhineland-Palatinate	1 661	66	461	515	602	6	572	17
Saarland	347	36	142	154	15	2	7	—
Slesvig-Holstein	345	5	128	95	111	3	54	6
Total	12 715	650	5 372	4 011	2 549	222	1 895	133

2. Summary of the types of crimes.

Land	All Persons	Who Were Sentenced Persons Convicted of: Murder	Manslaughter	Other Punishable Offenses
1	2	3	4	5
Baden-Wuerttemberg	585	15	28	542
Bavaria	993	31	63	899
Berlin	205	6	—	199
Bremen	62	4	8	50
Hamburg	120	3	2	115
Hesse	941	29	18	894
Lower-Saxony	582	21	34	527
North-Rhine Westphalia	1153	18	67	1068
Rhineland-Palatinate	461	3	1	457
Saarland	142	—	—	142
Slesvig-Holstein	128	1	10	117
Total	5372	131	231	5010

3. Summary of the sentences passed.

Land	All Persons	Who Were Sentenced Persons Sentenced to: Death	Life Imprisonment	Prison Terms	Fines
1	2	3	4	5	6
Baden-Wuerttemberg	585	1	4	576	4
Bavaria	993	—	15	973	5
Berlin	205	3	4	196	2
Bremen	62	—	1	61	—
Hamburg	120	—	3	112	5
Hesse	941	3	12	902	24
Lower-Saxony	582	1	13	556	12
North-Rhine Westphalia	1153	3	14	1094	42
Rhineland-Palatinate	461	—	2	456	3
Saarland	142	—	—	130	12
Slesvig-Holstein	128	1	—	122	5
Total	5372	12	68	5178	114

IV. **Yearly Analysis**

The following is a breakdown by years of the 80 death or life imprisonment sentences which became final:

	1946	1947	1948	1949	1950	1951	1952	1953
	6	10	11	12	14	7	3	2
= %	7,5	12,5	13,75	15	17,5	8,75	3,75	2,5

	1954	1955	1956	1957	1958	1959	1960
= %	0	1,25	1,25	1,25	2,5	5	7,5

Thus 75 % of the most serious cases adjudicated until 1961 had already been adjudicated by the end of 1951. The percentage relationship in minor cases is similar. The total number of sentences has not been recorded on a yearly basis. However, in the Federal Ministry of Justice, 1,611 sentences, or approximately 30 % of the total number, are now on file. Following is a breakdown by years of these sentences:

	1945	1946	1947	1948	1949	1950	1951	1952
	3	73	278	487	396	117	45	60
= %	0,19	4,53	17,26	30,23	24,58	7,26	2,79	3,72

	1953	1954	1955	1956	1957	1958	1959	1960
	49	21	10	14	22	13	13	10
= %	3,04	1,30	0,62	0,87	1,37	0,81	0,81	0,62

Difficulties of the Prosecution

The fact that relatively few sentences were passed on national socialist crimes during the years of 1953 to 1958 has led to the assertion that the German Judiciary has failed to prosecute offenders with sufficient vigor. This, however, is incorrect. The true causes for the decrease in the number of persons sentenced in these years are as follows:

From 1945 through 1952, the Allied and German authorities sentenced a total of approximately 9,000 Germans for Nazi crimes. In addition, at least an equal number of accused could not be sentenced for various reasons (e.g., due to insufficient evidence for conviction). Hundreds of other Germans were sentenced in other countries.

A considerable number of persons accused of national socialist crimes had already died. Of the 14 participants in the First Wannsee Conference of January 20, 1942, where the "final solution of the Jewish problem" was discussed, only 4 are still alive: Eichmann; former *Reichsamtsleiter* Leibbrandt (proceedings stopped by a final decision of the Nuremberg-Fuerth *Land* Court of May 10, 1950); *SS-Gruppenfuehrer* Hofmann (sentenced by an American military court in 1948 to 25 years' imprisonment and released in 1954); and *SS-Oberfuehrer* Klopfer, against whom preliminary investigations by the public prosecutor's office in Ulm are at present pending. In 1948, Vice-Minister *(Staatssekretaer)* Buehler was sentenced to death in Poland; whether the sentence was executed is not known. *SS-Sturmbannfuehrer* Lange was captured by the Russians towards the end of the war and was reportedly shot in 1945. The other participants at the conference have died, among them former President of the People's Court of Justice *(Volksgerichtshof)* Freisler, who was killed in an air raid; and Eichmann's immediate superior, *SS-Gruppenfuehrer* Mueller, Director of Department IV of the *Reich* Security Main Office *(Leiter der Abteilung IV des*

Reichssicherheitshauptamts), who was killed in Berlin during the last days of the war. The following have also died: *SS-Gruppenfuehrer* Thomas, chief of *Einsatzgruppe* (Commando) C, who died in 1945 in Wuerzburg; *SS-Oberfuehrer* Dirlewanger, leader of a notorious *"Bewaehrungseinheit"* (unit composed of convicts released on probation), who died in Altshausen/Wuerttemberg in June, 1945; *SS-Oberfuehrer* Panzinger, who dropped dead while being arrested. Numerous other persons have evaded prosecution by committing suicide: Hitler; Himmler; Goebbels; *SS-Gruppenfuehrer* Globocnik, who was responsible for the murder of undisclosed numbers of Jews during Operation *"Reinhard";* and Rudolf Batz, commander of *"Einsatz"*-commando 2 of *"Einsatz"*-group A. Among those who committed suicide are also Karl Jager, commander of *"Einsatz"*-commando 3 of *"Einsatz"*-group A; *SS-Obersturmbannfuehrer* Puetz, who was responsible for the mass murders in Rowno and Lublin; Bothmann, commander of the *"Sonderkommando Chelmno",* responsible for the gassing of more than 300,000 persons; *SS-Hauptsturmfuehrer* Dannecker, Director of Jewish deportations in France, Bulgaria, and Italy; and former police officer Karl Simon, who is accused of murdering Jews at the Auschwitz concentration camp.

In 1953, hundreds of witnesses and many suspects were still being held as prisoners of war, particularly in Russia. Others, due to war and postwar circumstances, were scattered all over the world and frequently could not be located. This presented considerable problems in connection with collecting evidence. Furthermore, most of the documents necessary for conviction were in foreign hands and not available at the time to German authorities.

Shortly before the end of the war, or by taking advantage of the early postwar circumstances, some defendants had succeeded in assuming other names and thereby avoiding prosecution, at least temporarily. For examples Richard Baer, last commander of the concentration camp Auschwitz, was living under the name of Neumann; *SA-Obergruppenfuehrer* Blankenburg, responsible for euthanasia crimes, lived under the name of Bielecke in Stuttgart and has since died; *SS-Obergruppenfuehrer* Wilhelm Koppe, a senior police officer in Posen and Krakau charged with participation in the shootings of Jews, lived in Bonn under the name of Lohmann; *SS-Gruppenfuehrer* Katzmann, who took part in the murder of Jews in Galicia, lived under the name of Albrecht in Darmstadt until his death.

Other suspects escaped arrest by fleeing abroad. Among these were Eichmann, Alois Brunner, his colleague in the *Reich* Security Main Office, and the concentration camp physicians Mengele and Schumann. The Federal Government has continually attempted to bring these persons before the German judiciary. Investigations to track down Eichmann were begun in 1952 but remained fruitless. In 1953, preliminary investigations initiated by the public prosecutor in Berlin had to be suspended according to Paragraph 205 of the Code of Criminal Procedure, due to the defendant's absence. In 1956, the Director of Public Prosecutions in Frankfurt resumed the judicial inquiries on Eichmann, and on November 24, 1956, procured an arrest warrant for murder. By virtue of this arrest warrant Eichmann was on the German list of persons wanted by the police until August, 1960.

Mengele was reported to be in Argentina. A German request for extradition was granted, but Mengele could not be found. His present home is not known. Brunner is reported to be living in the Near East. An official confirmation of this rumor has not yet been obtained. The concentration camp physician Schumann is presently living in Ghana. The Federal Government has requested his extradition.

In the beginning of 1956, thousands of prisoners of war returned from Russia. Many persons among them were able to testify to national socialistic crimes committed in Polish and Russian territories. A small number of missing defendants also returned. Criminal proceedings were instituted immediately against these persons. Due to the above-mentioned difficulties, the collection of uncontestable evidence took a relatively long time. Gustav Sorge and Wilhelm Schubert, former guards at the concentration camp Sachsenhausen, received final sentences of life imprisonment at the Court of Assizes in Bonn on February 6, 1959; Horst Hempel and August Hohn, both former wardens, were convicted of concentration camp crimes by a sentence of the Duesseldorf Court of Assizes on October 15, 1960; Hempel received five years' and Hohn lifelong imprisonment (the judgment has not yet become final). Proceedings against the concentration camp physician Dr. Baumkoetter have not yet been concluded.

The Activity of the Central Agency for the Investigation of National Socialist Crimes Established by the State Judiciaries

While the return of German prisoners of war from Russia produced a great deal of evidence, the necessity for coordinating investigations was at the same time recognized. In 1958, therefore, the State Judiciaries established a Central Agency in Ludwigsburg for the investigation of national socialist crimes. This agency is mainly occupied with investigating those crimes which were committed outside the Federal German territory. These consist above all of crimes committed in connection with hostile acts against civilians, especially the activities of the so-called "*Einsatz*"-commandos and the atrocities carried out in concentration camps and similar camps outside Federal territory. Within the scope of this competence, the Central Agency has interrogated numerous witnesses and evaluated documents which were in the possession of foreign countries and had previously been unobtainable. This made it possible to ascertain the overall organizational setup of agencies responsible for the actions of the "*Einsatz*"-groups and "*Einsatz*"-commandos, as well as of other responsible individuals. A number of formal investigation proceedings are presently being prepared by the Central Agency, others are pending in the Public Prosecutors' offices and the courts. These proceedings are tabulated below on the basis of records in the Central Agency; the tabulation is arranged according to the area or organization within which the crime was committed. The figures in the tables represent the number of proceedings, and most proceedings involve several or even many accused persons.

Summary

of Cases Still Pending

(Status of March 10, 1961)

I. **Concentration Camps and Annexed Camps not in the Territory of the Federal Republic:**

1. Auschwitz and annexed camps	=	3
2. Buchenwald and annexed camps	=	8
3. Gross-Rosen and annexed camps	=	6
4. Mauthausen	=	4
5. Ravensbrueck	=	2
6. Sachsenhausen	=	8
7. Stutthof	=	7
8. Oranienburg	=	1
9. Unnamed concentration camp	=	1
Total		40

II. **Einsatz-Groups Commandos of the Reich Security Main Office:**

1. Einsatz-group A	=	32
2. Einsatz-group B	=	24
3. Einsatz-group C	=	27
4. Einsatz-group D	=	12
Total		95

III. **Poland:**

1. Extermination camps and Operation Reinhard	=	8
2. District of the "Commander of the Security Police in Cracow"	=	17
3. District of the "Commander of the Security Police in Lemberg"	=	30
4. District of the "Commander of the Security Police in Lublin"	=	11
5. District of the "Commander of the Security Police in Warsaw"	=	10
Total		76

IV. **Other Countries:**

Belgium	=	1
Bulgaria	=	1
Denmark	=	1
France	=	4
Greece	=	4
Italy	=	5
Yugoslavia (Serbia, Croatia, and Lower Styria)	=	6
Netherlands	=	3
Norway	=	3
Austria	=	7
Roumania	=	2
Czechoslovakia	=	9
Hungary	=	6
Total		52

V. **Reich Territory:** (including those territories annexed by the national socialistic regime up to 1942, with the exception of the "Reich-protectorate of Bohemia and Moravia")

1. Province of East Prussia	=	4
2. "Bialystok District"	=	20
3. "Reichsgau Danzig-West Prussia"	=	97
4. "Reichsgau Wartheland"	=	27
5. Province of Lower Silesia	=	3
6. Province of Upper Silesia	=	14
7. Land Saxony	=	4
8. Province of Pommerania	=	1
Total		170

VI. **Other Cases:**

(Reich Security Main Office, "Kristallnacht", Wannsee Conference, euthanasia, execution on board a ship, Wehrmacht units)	=	12
Total		445 cases

General Conclusions

The following may be gathered from the preceding facts and figures:

Since 1945, first the Occupying Powers and, thereafter, the German authorities have vigorously carried out the prosecution of national socialist crimes in the territory of the Federal Republic of Germany. By the end of 1953, most of the proceedings had been completed. There remained the prosecution of the offenders in some especially important groups of cases, which could not be completed at that time in view of difficulties in obtaining evidence and other circumstances. The establishment of a Central Agency permitted the investigations to be coordinated, so that now every essential phase has been covered. The number of convicted offenders exceeds 10,000 persons, 5,300 of whom were tried by German courts.

The number of suspects still identifiable today is estimated at 1,000. In the Federal Republic, there were 137 accused persons in custody on March 31, 1961. The number of criminals who fled abroad is estimated at no more than 150.

On the basis of the present status of the investigations, it may be assumed that most of the cases still pending will be completed within two to three years.

Anti-Semitism in the Federal Republic

Totalitarian Anti-Semitism *

Totalitarian anti-Semitism is by no means a specifically German phenomenon. Attempts to attribute it to such a questionable entity as "national character", which is all that remains of what was once called "national spirit", deal too lightly with the incomprehensible which must nevertheless be comprehended. Scientific consciousness must not be satisfied with expressing the enigma of anti-Semitic irrationalism by a formula which is irrational in itself. For this enigma demands its sociological explanation, and this is impossible in the context of national peculiarities. In fact, totalitarian anti-Semitism owes its German triumphs to a social and economic situation, rather than to the characteristics or conduct of a people; for the German people generated perhaps less radical hatred than those civilized countries which expelled or exterminated their Jews centuries ago. During the period covered by Massing, anti-Semitism was hardly less virulent in France—the France of the Dreyfus case and of Drumont.

Whoever wants to understand totalitarian anti-Semitism should not let himself be induced to explain it as a more or less natural necessity. It is true that retrospectively everything looks as if it were bound to happen the way it did and could not have been otherwise. Among the famous representatives of the German past, up to such outstanding personalities as Kant and Goethe, are only a few who were completely free from anti-Jewish sentiments. But only a fatalist would insist that anti-Semitism was universal and that its consequences were inevitable. Along with the symptom of the oncoming tragedy, countervailing signs can be found; and to say that what actually happened was inevitable from the beginning is to take too much for granted. In France, a few of the most courageous Dreyfusards, such as Emile Zola and Anatole France, included in their novels descriptions of Jews resembling the clichés whose consequences they fought. The study of history requires an appreciation of the inexplicable, of the diffuse, and of that which can be interpreted in many ways.

---

*) From the preface written by Dr. Max Horkheimer and Dr. Theodor Adorno, Directors of the Institut fuer Sozialforschung, Frankfort-on-Main, to the German edition of Paul W. Massing's *Rehearsal for Destruction.*

Nazism and Anti-Semitism in the Thirties*

By Eva Reichmann

Ladies and Gentlemen, feelings of disgust and envy, annoyance, aggressiveness, and hatred result from every crisis simultaneously with efforts to escape the consequences of the crisis, if possible or necessary at the expense of a weaker people. Weaker people include the newcomers who in some respect do not yet entirely fit into the community. These are "outsiders"; and, with the help of some twisting of history and some distortion of tangible truths, one can prove that basically they are not only "outsiders" but that they are still "foreigners". I have previously mentioned many political and social differences between the Jews and their neighbors. These differences were indeed constantly diminishing, but they were still noticeable. With these differences, not to mention the religious differences, the Jews were still just different enough to be thought of as "outsiders" when the differences were amplified with the necessary exaggerations and falsifications. And through their relatively heavier concentration in towns and cities, in trade and banking—concentrations which social romantics and reactionaries have always particularly criticized—the Jews were particularly susceptible to crises.

So when the struggle for employment and daily bread became unusually intense because of the world economic crisis and mass unemployment, the heretofore good willed bourgeois citizen felt fortunate in being given a reasonable excuse to rid himself not only of individual competitors but of a whole group of competitors. To achieve this end for the glory of the nation was the very function of Nazi anti-Semitism. And it accomplished this with such a virtuosity that its success, especially among the susceptible and unresisting narrow-minded bourgeois citizens, is understandable. A certain imbalance in their national consciousness, resulting from their late national unification, has always been a special characteristic of the Germans. Many examples could be given of fluctuation between feelings of national inferiority and national arrogance. Another factor contributing to this imbalance was the feeling after the end of World War I of having been "humiliated as a nation" by the military defeat, which caught the people completely unprepared, and by the peace treaty of Versailles. To the psychological need resulting from this situation, i. e., to exculpate themselves before themselves in one way or another, the doctrine of racial superiority of the "Aryan" Germans was the fitting response. Furthermore, the people suffered from the economic situation. They could

*) Excerpts from a lecture on the history of anti-Semitism in Germany given before the Friedrich-Ebert-Stiftung in Bonn on November 9, 1958. This lecture and others have been published by the Friedrich-Ebert-Stiftung e. V., 54 Koblenzer Strasse, Bonn, in a booklet under the title of *Die Reichskristallnacht — Der Antisemitismus in der deutschen Geschichte*.

not understand it any longer and they felt themselves helplessly subjected to its forces. They did not understand why grain in Argentina was dumped into the sea—they heard this constantly—while the unemployed in Germany had hardly enough to eat. From this chaos and from these doubts, they then escaped to a dogmatically founded ideal of a *"Fuehrer"*. From the freedom which they had not learned to use, they fled into another disorder, into blind obedience. And from the difficult commandment to love one's brother, even when he is "different" from oneself, they fled into a hatred of the Jewish scapegoat, a hatred developed by hypocritical propaganda into a powerful idol. The Jews were turned into a frightening antisymbol, featuring all imaginable hideousness, having no similarity any longer to the living Jewish neighbors whom they had known and with whom they had lived.

There was only one level of the population which resisted this demonically tempting propaganda in an admirable manner: the German workers. I think that this remarkable fact, which possibly is the only hopeful sign at the time of the mass downfall into Nazism, should be stressed again and again. It is my oppinion that at that time Social Democratic education passed its crucial test under most difficult conditions. Nothing shall be extenuated: I know that there were also inroads into the Social Democratic electorate. However, even in the general election of March, 1933, thus under most unfavorable conditions, 120 deputies of the Social Democratic Party were returned to the *Reichstag.*

Ladies and Gentlemen, mass psychology is a pessimistic science. I do not know who among you have read Le Bon, the classic of mass psychology, or some of the remarks about mass psychology in Hitler's *Mein Kampf,* which sound as if he had copied them from Le Bon. Hitler had probably not read anything by Le Bon, but he was intuitively aware of the pitiful things one can do with people by manipulating them into becoming a mob, thus weakening the sense of responsibility of the individuals. However, although this science of mass psychology generally leads to such pessimistic conclusions, the power of resistance among the German workers against the demonic arts of Nazi seduction is a most hopeful sign.

Outside this bulwark, however, the ground was instable. The German economy had gone completely out of control. The number of unemployed approached the six-million mark. How strongly anti-Semitism was related to the economic situation is evident from the parallelism of the election successes of anti-Semitism and Nazism with the rise and fall of the economic crisis. I have to combine the two terms of anti-Semitism and Nazism, although I am aware of the fact that they cannot be regarded as being absolutely identical. Between May and December, 1924, when due to the Dawes Plan the economic situation had improved, the number of anti-Semitic deputies dropped from 40 to 14. Between 1928 and 1930, with the outbreak of the world-wide economic crisis, the percentage of anti-Semitic voters for the first time went up from 3.4 to 18.3 % and, thereafter, constantly increased. When the first signs of an economic revival became noticeable, with a fading out of the world-wide economic crisis, the NSDAP lost more than two millions votes after an apparently irresistible growth. This drop from 37.4 to 33.1 percent of the voters was more serious for a dynamic party, living only by its successes, than is evident from the figures alone. The Jewish problem had remained constant throughout the whole period, however. Actually, one might even say that it had become less acute with the dismissal in 1929 of Rudold Hilferding, the last Jewish Cabinet Minister. The critical situation was reflected much more correctly by the performance in elections than by the so-called Jewish problem.

But what about genuine anti-Semitism, you will ask; what about that emotional anti-Semitism which did not need to be kindled by Nazi propaganda, and which by itself might have made Nazi propaganda possible? It did exist. It existed in all shades between slight feelings of something strange and outspoken aversion. It was particularly existent among the bourgeoisie, and, unfortunately, it was existent above all in academic circles. Only a fool would deny it. What I deny, however, is that that type of anti-Semitism which existed within the German people in quiet times, which one might call ideologically founded and deliberate anti-Semitism—as bad and harmful as it was—could ever explain the orgies of hatred which part of the people indulged in during the Nazi era and which eventually led to the night of pogrom, whose anniversary we observe today, and to the murder-factories in Treblinka and Auschwitz.

The remnants of the still existent group tensions between the non-Jewish majority and the Jewish minority in Germany can never be a satisfactory explanation. There had to come over the German people a widespread feeling of helplessness, a grave, vital crisis, and then there had to come a propaganda steam roller for frightened minds which shriekingly rose above any independent ideas, any impulse of love and fairness, even above plain decency, until faith was placed in what was told the people in this deluge of hatred. It is deplorable enough that eventually faith was placed in this, and the analysis of the spiritual condition in which it was believed gives poor comfort. Nevertheless—if I may be permitted to express my very personal opinion—it would appear to me still more disconsolate if from the analysis of the events I had gained the conviction that the terrible things which were done to the Jewish fellow citizens in the name of the German people had resulted from a decision duly reached in cool deliberations. To those who stay absolutely outside and on the side, it might be satisfying to impose on a whole nation the stigma of original political sin. Among my fellow sufferers there are those who are so deeply hurt that they are more inclined to adopt this explanation than to analyse the facts carefully. Nobody who knows what they suffered will blame them for preferring that course. And, next to a few hopeful signs in the postwar years, there were also many indications justifying pessimism rather than optimism. To those Jews, however, who know what they owe to the first half of their life and to a youth lived in the illusion of having a homeland, and who see now that decent people in all age groups in just this supposed homeland try to help banish the horrors of the past by scientific analysis and by grand efforts for the education of adults, to them it must mean comfort and satisfaction that the German people as a whole did not fail as wretchedly as the first glance seemed to indicate.

The SA were just as stupid *

"The Jews are our misfortune"—Trial of the desecrators of the Synagogue in Cologne

By Heinz Stuckmann

On Christmas Eve 1959 I was given a book as a present. It contains a photograph: very young men with unintelligent expressions goose-stepping along a street in brown uniforms and jackboots. They are carrying placards with the words: "The Jews are our misfortune." The picture dates from 1934.

On the morning of December 25, 1959, churchgoers of the Heart of Jesus parish in Cologne could read on their way home from Christmas Mass the words "Out with the Jews" on the wall of the Synagogue in the Roonstrasse. This demand was decorated with swastikas. The paint was fresh. While some argued for removing the writing immediately, others called the police. The police came. The very same day the culprits were detained for investigation in Cologne. They were two young men aged 25.

One was against "besmirching oneself", the other "against the Jews". The one who was against the Jews was not worried about "besmirching oneself". The one who objected to "besmirching oneself" had nothing against the Jews. In theory they had made a nice distinction. In practice they had been agitators together—with paint and brush. As a result they found themselves together in the dock, the clerk Paul-Josef Schoenen and the baker's assistant Arnold Strunk, last occupied as a laborer.

Schoenen did not like the monument to the victims of the *Gestapo* which stands in the gardens on Cologne's Hansa Ring. To be exact, he had nothing against it at first; he had even, so he said, laid flowers on the monument in 1954. Even today he had no fault to find with the first part of the inscription, "Here lie seven victims of the *Gestapo.*" But the second part made him angry; it ran: "This monument is a reminder of Germany's most shameful period, 1933—1945."

Schoenen: "After all, that is besmirching oneself. I would have accepted This is a memorial to the victims of the *Gestapo.*" The German people was not after all the *Gestapo* . . ."

The presiding judge, Dr. Metse, puts the question: "What then was the reason why the *Gestapo* made these victims?"

Schoenen: "A small group of Nazis . . ."

Judge: "Leading Nazis?"

---

*) From *Die Zeit,* 12 February, 1960.

Schoenen: "Yes—the . . . they were not all bad, as people say today. The whole period was not bad."

Judge: "Of course not. Every period has its good sides and its bad. But isn't this period branded first and foremost with the crimes of the National Socialists?"

Schoenen: "The whole German people accepted the NSDAP. They can't all have been criminals."

Strunk says: "I am an anti-Semite . . ." The judge would like to know why.

Strunk: "So that the German race shall not be destroyed."

Judge: "How could that happen?"

Strunk: "They mix with us and then we go under." There is laughter in the Court.

Strunk, on his own telling, disapproved the killing of the Jews by the Nazis. But they should "go back where they came from . . . Israel." He is sceptical of the presiding judge's explanation that there are few Jews who came to Germany from Israel. He does know that the State of Israel has only been in existence for ten years.

The judge probes further. He would like to throw light on the ideas in this muddled head, to find a motive. Strunk: "And the Jews after all are in the higher situations everywhere . . ."

Judge: "In the State?"

Strunk: "Yes."

Judge: "In business?"

Strunk: "In business, they are always so loud, especially when they have been drinking . . ."

Judge: "Hm—in that case their higher situation can only have been on top of the tall stools in front of the bar . . ."

Twixt Bubbly and Mass

Strunk decided "to do something about the Jews." The Synagogue seemed to him the right place and the night before Christmas the right time, "as it will cause more of a stir at that time."

Schoenen did not agree. He wanted to do something about the *Gestapo* monument, and Strunk was to help. "So I couldn't leave him in the lurch with his job."

On December, 24, 1959, the Christmas tree was decked out in the Schoenens' appartment—Schoenen senior was a wholesale dealer in office requisites. The Christmas presents were presented between 7 and 8 p. m., and Strunk was there too, for he had taken a room at the Schoenens'. Towards 9 o'clock, the two young men took the Schoenens' maid over to her sister, who was also working in Cologne. Then they drove on to Gereons Wall and went backwards through the gardens to the memorial. Strunk smeared over the offending words.

"But why Strunk?" inquires the presiding judge. "It was your idea, wasn't it?" Schoenen says that Strunk wanted to do the painting and he had let him do it. "But the action is mine. I'm the one responsible . . ."

Then they drive home to Schoenen's parents. Champagne is served. But time is short, for the two young men want to be at the Heart of Jesus Church for the Midnight Mass, and they wanted to visit the Synagogue first. It was already 11.30 p. m. when they brought the maid home; and on reaching the Synagogue they found it "still too unquiet". So they went to Mass first.

Next, they drove to Beethoven Street and parked the car. Strunk started off with paintbrush and pot, but was back a moment later. He had been disturbed. "Drop it," said Schoenen; but Strunk was off again already.

The Judge devoted a great deal of time and patience to clearing up the background. Again and again there is mention of Strunk's furnished room, known to his friends as the "Brown House". "Who visited you there?" asks Dr. Metse. "Oh—just friends . . ." It proves impossible to find out anything more about these friends. "Members of the *Deutsche Reichspartei?*"

"Yes—they have been there, too." Strunk had joined the DRP in 1958, with Schoenen, but "I had already interested myself in politics in 1957."

Judge: "In what way?"

Strunk: "I was studying Germany—I don't agree with many things as we see them today." For instance, he disapproved of the State doing so little for young people. "That's why we have so many rowdies . . . Young people today hang pin-up girls in their cupboards. Do you think that is nice?"

Judge: "And you hang up Horst Wessel instead . . ."

Strunk: "He is the man I seek to copy."

Judge: "And Adolf Hitler, too—he was hanging there."

Strunk: "But he is a collector's piece."

Judge: "Do you mean to say you bought the picture as a collector's piece?" The accused is not sure what a collector's piece is.

He had also bought a lot of books, very varied books: *Hitler as a General, The Nuremberg Trial, We Germans in the World, Karin Goering, Kersten's Machinegun Section, From the Kaiserhof to the Reich Chancellery, State without Law, Leading and following . . ., Members of the Waffen-SS Decorated with the Knight's Cross.*

It was not possible to discover what he had read of it all. Strunk: "Parts . . . one can't read everything at once." The collection was completed by a family picture of Goebbels and badges from the National-Socialist *Reichsparteitag.*

With Schoenen, too, it was not possible for the judge to obtain a clear picture of his political ideas. Schoenen said, "I am not necessarily a National Socialist; but I have a nationalist attitude." At last it comes out: Schoenen's ideal is the Bismarckian *Reich.* The attorney interrupts with a question: "What was this *Reich* of Bismarck's, Mr. Schoenen?" Schoenen: "A socialist monarchy." The judge repeated the question, but the answer was the same: Bismarck's *Reich* was a socialist monarchy. The lawyer follows up this line: "Was it perhaps a constitutional monarchy?" But evidently the accused was not familiar with the word.

A Hero Like Schlageter

The public prosecutor addresses the Court and calls for two years and three months prison for Strunk, one year and nine months for Schoenen. It is not their first sentence: a stolen automobile, fraud—and for Schoenen customs evasion into the bargain.

Schoenen is allowed to speak once more. "Perhaps it is right for us to be punished, and I accept the punishment. But then there should be punishment also for the people who decry our soldiers and the *Waffen-SS.*" He was speaking on behalf of Rudel and thought that the case of Dr. Heyde was worse than his own. Anyhow: "I stick to my appeal and my action. I think I may even, like Albert Leo Schlageter before me, go down in German history as a champion of the German soldier's honor . . ."

Outside in the corridor, we were waiting for the sentence. "A lot of nonsense," some were saying, "That's quite clear from the trial. Call it politics? It is just boundless stupidity." Someone else was telling of the S.A. in the days of the Weimar Republic and thought they were not one whit cleverer. "They were slinging around catchwords like "Slaves of capital" or "the Jewish cancer"; but none of them could say what the phrases really meant.

Someone else produced a quotation from Adolf Hitler: "If the Jews were alone in this world, they would suffocate in dirt and filth as they tried in their vicious struggles to get the upper hand and to be rid of their neighbor".

We wondered if there were really any difference between that nonsense and the nonsense we had heard in the trial.

Loss of Civic Rights for Two Years

Strunk was found guilty of damage to public property in two cases, one of them being intended to be a threat to the State and also coupled with violation of paragraphs 4 and 28 of the law on assembly, of damage to property in conjunction with insulting behavior in three cases and of violation of paragraphs 24 (1) and 26 (1) of the law on arms; he was given a total sentence of fourteen months.

Schoenen was found guilty of damaging public property, of being an accessory after damage to public property and of damage to property in four cases; he was given a total sentence of ten months imprisonment.

Both the accused were deprived of their civic rights for a period of two years.

* * *

And that was the end—the legal end—of an unhappy affair.

"For We'll Be in the Papers ..."*

A Swastika on the Church Wall—Two Youths Before the Judge

By Robert Strobel

The scene is a trial before a jury in Bonn, and before the court are two young daubers of swastikas, both from Urfeld, a village near the Federal Capital. The accused are huddled up, their faces are scarlet with excitement. They remind the onlooker of schoolboys who had been caught as they were up to serious mischief and who have been called to account. They stand in awe of the judge in his severe black robes.

The elder of the two accused, *Willi Roeder,* is the first to speak. He is 22 years old and works in a factory producing chemicals. Income 400 marks a month. This he has to hand over at home; but each weekend he gets 20 marks as pocket money, with which he goes the round of the taverns in his village and sometimes takes a drop more than is good for him. His father, a serious worker, had just built a small house for the family in which there are two younger sons.

The other accused, however, nineteen-year-old *Peter Berger,* has an unhappy family background. His father fell in the war. His mother had for years been keeping her three sons from her earnings in service. The eldest son is married, has one child, and is blind; the second is doing a spell of penal servitude. He had raped and killed a little girl. Peter, the accused, is the youngest of the family. His mother can no longer manage him. True, he gives her 200 marks out of the little more than 300 marks in his pay packet, but with the rest he has bought a Lloyd car. He also belongs to the *"Tango Club"* where, he says, they not only dance but drink freely.

The representative of the Youth Office felt it must be clear to anyone how much Peter needed the firm hand of a father. Obviously he had some while back fallen into bad company—and he was callous. On the day his brother was arrested for murder he went dancing. This showed that he had not reached a stage of development corresponding to his age.

The prosecutor disagreed, considering that such callousness was rather a sign of precociousness. Peter Berger's employer had praised the young man when speaking to the representative of the Youth Office, saying he was a very serious and industrious lacquerer.

The judge, an experienced man of middle age and like the prosecutor, who was about the same age, blessed with a sense of proportion, would like to know how the whole thing came about. Roeder, the older boy, gave the story—hesitatingly, but frankly, and without any glossing over. Nor did he try to put the blame on the younger boy. Quite the reverse: he exonerated him.

On the third of January, a Sunday, they had been drinking in Urfeld from early in the afternoon till one in the morning. Then he had an idea. "We've heard so much on the radio and in the papers of these fellows who painted

*) From *Die Zeit,* 15 January, 1960.

swastikas. Let's do the same." Berger agreed at once. They went home to the Roeders' house where, as the new building was still being busily painted, there was a pot of white paint. This Peter used to paint, on the outside of the church and on the cemetery wall, "Out with the Jews" in large letters—and he added a swastika. Berger said the reason he did it was that he was better at it. After all, he was a lacquerer.

The Judge: "What was actually your idea in doing it?"

Roeder: "I'd no particular idea."

An attempt by Roeder to put the blame on his drink was not accepted by the Judge. "You were merry, but not drunk." Roeder agreed. (Each of them had had about ten beers in ten hours.)

The Judge: "I suppose you've seen in the papers how much everyone disapproves of such daubings and that the punishment is severe?"

Roeder: "Yes, I have."

The Judge: "What were you aiming at in doing this?"

Roeder (pitifully): "Nothing."

The Judge: "In that case one doesn't do it. Are you Catholics?"

Yes, both of them.

The Judge: "Does your religion mean anything to you?"

They both declare that it does.

The Judge: "And then you don't hesitate to daub things on a House of God and in such a mean fashion?"

Embarrassed silence. It turns out that there is not one Jew in Urfeld.

The Judge asks the accused, "Have you ever met a Jew?"

"No."

"Were you not taught in school about what happened here in Germany under Hitler, especially the treatment meted out to the Jews?"

No, they had heard nothing about it. And they were believed. And so it turned out that they looked on their daubing as a lark: "We'll be in the papers." Adventure and a cheap desire to impress—such were their motives. Anti-Semitism or any other political feelings obviously played no part in it all.

Even the public prosecutor had to agree that neither of them was interested in what went on around them. None the less, he called for severe punishment. Newspaper reports had given them warning that such actions were not approved of. The presiding judge inquired if they had anything further to say before the court withdrew to consider their cases. Roeder replied quietly but firmly, "I'm sorry I did it. I would like to apologize." The presiding judge addressed Berger. "What about you?"

"I'd like to say the same."

The accused are scarlet as they hear the sentence, which was evidently more severe than they had expected. They would like to think it over to see whether they accept it: four months prison for one of them, three months for the other, and no probation.

I left the court with an uncomfortable feeling. The sentence was just, no doubt. But couldn't these two primitive youths have avoided being stamped for life if they had been told in time, while still at school, something of the horrors of Hitler's *Reich?* Perhaps they would have understood better that, after all that had occurred in the past, this sort of daubing cannot be looked on just as a lark . . .

The Warning of the Past—Desire, Method, and Courage to Overcome the Difficulties *

By Walter Jacobsen

A. The Most Recent Anti-Semitic Excesses—A Warning Signal

1. The Overt Development: Triggering Stimulus and Motivation

On the basis of all present reports, it seems obvious that the frequency of the anti-Semitic demonstrations has the character of a chain reaction resulting from "contagion". That is probably the most likely explanation. With respect to the triggering stimuli, a characteristic element is the immaturity of most of the perpetrators, which is not to be deduced from their age alone. Thoughtful individuals choose other ways of lending force to their political tendencies. In the case of immature individuals, the desire for recognition plays a *very* great contributory role. The *success* in gaining recognition that became apparent in this conjunction evokes emulation. Activity drives and actions intended to impress others hit upon an especially serviceable opportunity for satisfaction in the swastika and anti-Jewish slogans. The deterrent method seems to be the indispensable emergency measure against childish stunts of this kind. On the other hand, the only measures that are effective in the wider view are an appropriate education and the mental digestion of the past.

The characterization of these triggering stimuli does *not tell anything at all* about the basic anti-Semitic attitude, its intensity or its distribution.

We have mentioned the triggering stimuli affecting the individual (need for action and recognition, mutual contagion) on the one hand and the anti-Semitic *basic attitude* on the other, which is possibly, in fact, extant to a certain degree. The missing link between the two is the unanswered question as to the current *motivations* in the various individual cases. It is not sufficient even to calm the German domestic public, to say nothing of the outside world, if the eruptions of the drive for action and recognition that have suddenly occurred in such large numbers throughout the country are "explained" as rowdyism or boorishness. In the last analysis, there must in fact be some reasons why rowdyism is making use of *these* specific tactical symbols (swastika and "Out with the Jews") with such enthusiasm.

It can be presumed that each individual offender felt quite personally, that is, spontaneously, called upon to express his own conviction of solidarity and his craving for recognition in the same way. That does not preclude the possibility that, in addition, there was and still is coaching from ex-

*) From *Aus Politik und Zeitgeschichte*, a supplement to the weekly *Das Parlament*, July 6, 1960.

treme left-wing quarters on occasion. Yet *without a corresponding basic attitude* at least in potential form, most of the paint-pot forays probably were hardly possible.
Extreme right-wing organizations probably were not "guiding" these actions. It is true that it was probably a great satisfaction to them to discover what a "general" resonance is to be anticipated for a starting signal of this kind. They probably felt strengthened and encouraged. On the other hand, they were probably more aghast than anyone at now suddenly being so highly compromised in the eyes of the entire world.
The dubious role of the offenders affords a strong challenge to illuminate their *individual motivations* more precisely. The task is to uncover those "sympathy" relationships which *predispose* an unknown portion of our population to acts of this kind. It must be kept in mind that in fact only an insignificantly minor *portion* of those in sympathy (and of semidemocrats or antidemocrats) give way to demonstrations that are moreover of such an immature nature.

2. Analysis

It must unfortunately be feared that such motivations will be either inadequately revealed or mistakenly interpreted if the first and second interrogations of those who were caught are left to routine procedure in the police stations. In most instances, it cannot be expected of the police officers that they will be in a position to throw light on the often rather complicated psyche of delinquents at the most fruitful moment and in the best way in the preliminary investigation, and especially in the case of adolescents and of the mentally retarded, forensic and interrogation psychology has consistently succeeded in bringing shocking facts to light in this respect. It is my view that in such a delicate case, which is besides so serious from a political point of view, the nearest competent forensic psychologist should therefore be called in immediately upon the arrest of an offender whenever possible. Such psychologists can be provided or named by almost all university departments of psychology.
The things that could be accumulated in the way of primary psychological material by this means could be of great benefit for all future measures that must be carried out in order to combat right-wing extremism and anti-Semitism.

3. Foreign Countries

There are convinced—so to speak, "genuine"—anti-Semites in all countries. They believe in the conception of a world conspiracy of Jewry, or at least in its having a disintegrating function with respect to order and national sentiment. In other countries as in our own, the anti-Semites are generally, *but not exclusively,* associated with the parties of the extreme right. Individuals with set notions of this kind are often inclined to want to raise a clearly visible signal light. If these individuals in other countries gained the impression that a general anti-Semitic feeling of indignation against the Jews was beginning to form in Germany, then, as has already been said, one or another of them might feel moved to make a sort of demonstration of solidarity. It would even indicate that good understanding between men of like mind in various countries is maintained.

4. Genuine and Sham Anti-Semitism

Before 1914, anti-Semitism in Germany was not necessarily linked with parties of the ultra-right wing. During that time, it might be inculcated first in one political group and then in another, in accordance with the current need of supporters, demagogical talent, and unscrupulousness. Even in those days, the art of "manipulation" was understood. Since Goebbels' 12-year propaganda war, however, anti-Semitism is *the* privilege of the German *nationalists* and the right-wing extremists. *Any other* latent dislike of Jews that may, consciously or unconsciously, be extant among a large number of Germans would become uninteresting with protracted inactivity. It would be forgotten. That is especially true of that type of superficial anti-Semitism which is not even meant seriously and consists only in the unthinking use of anti-Jewish expressions.* At any rate, there will always be individuals who are particularly susceptible to those anti-Jewish slogans of clever demagogues which once more become manifest. In the case of such individuals, the "sounding board" for these slogans is ready-made, as it were. Proper education against both prejudice and the disposition to prejudice could to a certain extent protect those individuals who are only subject to dangers from *this* quarter (the *potential* anti-Semites) against excessive gullibility. However, *the actual* danger in our country stems from the "die-hards", that is, from all of those individuals who still adhere in whole or in part to the deities established and cultivated by *Nazism.*
At this point, the expression "die-hard" in the meaning intended here must be explained in more detail. The following could be numbered among the deities "established" by Nazism:
The unqualified principle of leadership.
The right of the "Nordic" race ("master race") to domination.
The "Myth of the Twentieth Century".
Providence as used by the never-erring dictator.
"Neurope" in accordance with Hitler's notions and under his leadership, etc.
Among those deities that were only "cultivated"—that is, the ones that were already in existence, but were then forcebred without limit—the following may be mentioned:
Exaggerated national self-confidence (partly an overcompensation of fears of inferiority).
Overevaluation of the "German character" and the German mission in the world.
The educational ideals of "discipline and order", obedience to authority, and self-sacrifice in the performance of duty, forced to the point of saying "You are nothing; Your nation is everything!"
Other traditional exaggerated ideas of superiority. The individuals who are meant by my expression, "The Die-Hards", in this connection are those who cannot forego any of these exaggerations and who feel compelled to preserve a significant remnant of loyalty to them, though they do not feel that they are permitted to make unduly loud use of them at the present time. Some of these individuals will not want to number themselves among

*) Actually, a distinction must also be drawn between irrational prejudices, which automatically dissolve into nothingness when they enter the conscious mind, and so-called "mental clichés", stereotypes, which do not even have to carry an emotional charge.

the "die-hards". This refusal applies especially to those who went only part of the way with Hitler with a large number of reservations. On the other hand, an individual of this kind, with his unconditional loyalty to duty and moral subjection was perhaps a more dependable support to the regime than were Hitler's dyed-in-the-wool revolutionary standard-bearers. For right-wing extremists, the anti-Semitic slogan is the one by means of which they most readily find dupes. To put it more precisely, it is the one with which they are most readily able to revive unconscious prejudices. Consequently, for them it is first and foremost a slogan and an instrument of publicity. Thus, it does not embody their true ultimate conception of their aims. The result is that it would not be possible to get the better of this evil at its very roots simply by combating anti-Semitism. In my opinion, the actual root of the evil is to be found in the remnant of Nazism that has not been overcome, in its underlying motives and in its variants. It will therefore be necessary to direct the main effort of all educative measures towards those individuals who have not yet accomplished a determined and *total* break with Nazism, authoritarianism, or mere *nationalism*. With respect to our people's younger generation, it is *primarily* the teachers and parents who have the most important key position in this educative process.

B. The Background

5. Nationalism and Authoritarianism

The fact is that it is not as though there were a clandestine, widespread, and possibly fanatical *anti-Semitism* using the swastika and nationalistic clichés and providing sustenance for extreme right-wing splinter groups. On the contrary, the background is one of a widespread nationalism that was of necessity furloughed from most people's minds, but was purposely kept alive in *some* groups. This nationalism is moreover an eclectic term containing many nuances. There are two reasons why it has a preference for utilizing, *among others* the anti-Semitic slogans. The first is because they are so convenient.* The second is that because the irrational is provocative, a guranteed publicity-getter, as centuries of experience have in fact consistently proved, the individuals whose support is being canvassed then offer their little finger by putting faith in race prejudice and certain anti-Jewish insinuations. In this way, the irrational emotion is rationalized subsequently. Such individuals are then partly under the spell of the antidemocratic demagogues. Within the past few days, an ecclesiastical magnifico rightly termed these semidemocrats the real danger to democracy. They could also be called pseudodemocrats. In many instances, they talk themselves into believing that they are good democrats, using the pattern, "as I understand democracy". None of them wants to hear anything of "digesting" or of genuine, complete rejection of the Third *Reich*. They want to put a heavy black line under it. They like to listen to those who assure them that every one of them and a major portion of the Hitler regime were justly entitled to moral rehabilitation. This extensive sector

*) This is confirmed by statistics: Of every hundred daubings in the Federal Republic recently, only 17 % were confined to purely anti-Semitic slogans; another 31 % contained a mixture of anti-Semitic and Nazi slogans; and the largest share of them, 52 %, embodied purely Nazi slogans. Consequently, the *Nazi* reaction is in fact far more in conformity with the disposition of the daubers than is the disliking for the small remnant of German Jews.

of the population represents fruitful soil for antidemocratic (i. e., authoritarian and nationalistic) tendencies. That means that it resists all democratic educative efforts by veiled but mounting counterpressure. It resembles a highly resistant foil sheet of low elasticity: The only means of opening a path is by perforating it. In similar fashion, the "die-hard" cases first require a dissolution of their psychological resistance, their irrational taboo, in order to enable them to engage in unreserved controversy with their own consciences.* This controversy is an indispensable premise for removing reservations against the present and relaxing the internal state of spasm. Then there will be willingness to re-examine the individual scale of values.

That sounds a little like psychoanalysis, but all falls within the scope of normal psychology and normal pedagogy.

6. "The Future is More Important Than The Past"

The sound tendency to self-preservation and self-development, which happens to prefer concentrating on the present and the future rather than the past, should not be overlooked either. The resistance to "digesting" is therefore not necessarily based on bad intent. If it were not realized that so many individuals are in all innocence prone in fact to heed such slogans once again, after they have proved to be ominous for our national existence and would be even more so in future—if one did not know the "political deception" of the Great Powers and the gullibility of the broad, "politically disinterested" masses—then it would perhaps not be necessary to expect *so* implacably from these "harmless" individuals a fundamental and honest coming-to-grips with the most recent German past, provided that they at least openly and unconditionally admit that horrible and irreparable things have been committed in Germany's name.

7. The Basic Attitude

In the case of many Germans, the antidemocratic, nationalistic basic attitude has the character of something inborn and hereditary that is consequently deep-rooted. It cannot be overcome from one day to the next by means, let us say, of mere rational "enlightenment", instruction or convincing reasons, nor can it be killed with silence, but overcome by a long-term educational program. Every second or third fellow citizen secretly (and in many cases unconsciously) harbors the longing for a vindicated, proud, and mighty Germany. He regards democracy as actually an emergency solution which, though it is not exactly bad, was introduced by force, which he believes should be accepted, but without having to commit himself to it unconditionally or even to cooperate in it. From this arises what is called "abstinence from state and politics", "with-out-me-attitude" or even "political indifference". It is a firm withdrawal into oneself, a compensation for the compulsory foregoing of former indeals of the community which many regret. In this respect they confuse untimeliness with general defamation.

---

*) This not wanting to accept as true (because what may not be, cannot be) revolts against an unbeautified presentation of history because of injured national pride, the self-justification against the admission of intentional complicity. This taboo arises from a collective as well as an individual root of interests.

Hitler's defeat was certainly not a sufficient reason suddenly to transform a majority of nationalistic Germans believing in authority into nothing but liberal and responsible-minded, well-intentioned apprentices of democracy. Apart from that, "re-education" reached many of their minds with an inherent bias. This was a result not *only* of the method and of the victor-and-vanquished situation, but probably to some extent of the "passive resistance" of the subjects, as well. In spite of all opportunistic conformism and lip service to democracy, a suppressed opposition of nationalistic character smouldering in the emotional sphere probably continued in existence more or less subliminally. Any attentive observer of political conversations could detect it. Of course, there is no desire for "experiments", surely none for extreme right-wing ones, but the residues from the Nazi period are still latently in existence. There is no point in closing one's eyes to the fact or soothing one's own mind with the thought of the small size and internal division of the extreme right-wing organizations. I refer to this fact as the "maternal soil" for nationalism and authoritarianism. It has *always* been extant in the German people. This is the maternal soil on which slogans like the following were always able to flourish:
"The German Nation is the World's salvation".
"The Black, White and Red march proudly ahead".
"Teutondom".
"A place in the sun".
"The others are at least equally to blame".
"Not *everything* that Hitler wanted was bad".
"How can one befoul one's own nest?"
"What is needed is a demonstration of force for the outside world".
"Strong leaders and a pledged community".
"Discipline and order", etc., etc.
Even today, they can be certain of enthusiastic applause from a very large number of fellow citizens. The following are factors that characterize the maternal soil on which nationalistic demagogues are able to harvest many fruits when the occasion is favorable:
Dislike of personal, joint political responsibility and of demands on personal judgment and conscience.
Widespread "Count-me-out" attitude and shifting of all responsibility to "the higher-ups".
Readiness to "say what the others say" in the face of superiors and the *cliques* to which one belongs.
Joy over *occasionally* possible nonconformity when something derogatory can be said about democracy, "the parties", or the Government (cautiously), or when utterances of this kind can be applauded.
Utilization of every occasion for self-vindication and self-confirmation, saying that oneself and Germany have actually always had the best intentions, oneself and Germany had actually met with unjust treatment, the others are "no better either", etc.
Nationalistic arrogance (the most efficient and reliable people in the whole world, the best soldiers and most loyal comrades, integrity, loyalty to duty; in addition, casually seeking an excuse: "Jews have of course done us a great deal of harm").
There are a number of other factors of a similar kind.

C. **Problems**

8. Education and Digesting of Current History

The only thing that could have a preventive effect in this respect is an education based on *special* considerations and measures. The fact is that the educational situation is unusual and perhaps completely new *in this form.* It is not likely to be possible to manage on the basis of old, accustomed educative measures alone. The educational situation is unusual in two respects:

A. In regard to youth.
B. In regard to teachers and parents.
A. The young people face two worlds of values, as it were:

The first is represented (expressly or tacitly) by those theachers and parents who are to be numbered among the "die-hards" according to the comprehensive definition given above; and the second, by the advocates of the free, highly exacting democratic way of life with the appeal to personal responsibility, conscience, truth, and justice. The young people notice and observe this schism in their two most competent educational forces (parents and teachers) very critically, but (naturally) *egoistically,* suitable soil for the creation of a nihilistic gang morality.

B. The parents, but most of all the teachers, are in many cases (of course, not all by a far cry) in a state of inner conflict of conscience which cannot be concealed from the pupils (or from their own children). Moreover, inner "change-over", a change in attitude of which they simply are not capable without helps of a quite special kind is expected of many teachers. This incapability expresses itself in the form of an *evasion of the issue.* The fact is that at one point or another, the process of enlightening, arguing, demonstrating, and all rationalizing efforts of any kind finally encounter that taboo which we have already discussed. Conceptions of value and dislikes that have become favorites in the course of an individual's entire life cannot be excised by rational means alone. A really convincing treatment of the subject matter of contemporary history can hardly be expected of these teachers.

In some cases, one will have to resign oneself to the fact that the change-over will not be successful. In some other cases, it will be possible to relax the spasm, not by persuading, enlightening, argumentation or in fact moralizing, but by stimulating the consciousness of such psychological processes involved in the fixation of certain value judgments and in its origin. In addition, the process of succumbing to unnoticed demagogic influences and the diversity of personal susceptibilities to tendencies, value judgments, prejudices, etc., would have to be presented in convincing manner with the result of rerecognition of one's own person. To put it concisely, "digesting the past" in these cases requires special *psychological* instructions and self-tests. It is necessary to find and give specialized training to suitable psychological assistants and to call them in for *collaboration* on extension courses dealing with the subject of "Contemporary History". The initial open-mindedness in regard to these problems would have to be gained at model scientific conventions.

If contemporary history is merely "gone over" in the schools because it happens to be required—just as though it were the Thirty Years' War, and thus distinctly remote—then it would almost be better to forego it entirely. Without a personal avowal by the teacher, he will often fail to reach his pupils' minds in the proper way. (Of course, the pupils sometimes save the situation *themselves.*) Admittedly, failures will always occur even with the best instruction, because the topics of current history have become a ticklish matter in the schools. The teacher must be prepared for such difficulties and should not let himself be discouraged.

It must nonetheless be mentioned that even in instances where teachers are not only capable but also have the good intent and a proper attitude, there is sometimes a lack of the courage to join the sometimes inescapable dispute with "die-hard" parents.

9. Complications Due To Communistic World Values

Some are of the opinion that there is even a third "realm of values" that is making itself felt in an irritating way: the Communist one. They say that the extensive "agitprop" activity cannot as a matter of fact be entirely without effect in the last analysis. This is probably a mistaken conclusion The Red "world of values", the doctrine of dialectical materialism *as such,* is not contagious and neither does it cause any split in personality or conscience, as do the two-value worlds just mentioned in the minds of an appreciable portion of the population. The "Red Peril", it is true, is great; but it is of an entirely different kind: It is not authoritative in the intellectual and ideological sense. Instead, it is primarily *demoralizing* and confusing in regard to foreign and power policy and moreover to quite elementary, personal areas. That means that there need be no anxiety that many Germans might be infected by the trains of thought contained in the Communist *dogmatic system,* but they actually might be intimidated, discouraged, confused (in some cases by crude promises that take into account their momentary, *e. g.,* on-the-job dissatisfaction and their political indifference), and perhaps even be misled into some sort of mistaken reactions. This is, therefore, a quite different type of susceptibility to which *teachers* in particular are probably exposed in relatively rare instances. The danger menacing from the "right" and at the present time only *latent* can be countered only by a very deep-going, timely personality training. That from the left, which is actual, can be met by untiringly unmasking the camouflaged enemy recognized as being a *common* foe together with his arts of deception, as well as by encouragement: voluntarily, that is by being really convinced, hardly anyone will capitulate to it.

10. Mental Reservations of Some Teachers

In the year 1945, almost all teachers, including practically all of the more or less convinced Nazis, had to be given assignments in the period that had just begun. It is true that political enlightenment courses were initiated immediately. They were intended to evoke a change in political views. This change probably was achieved in part, but still only up to a certain point; there were some who clung completely to their Nazi conceptions and sealed off their minds from the outside world ("The *Fuehrer* intended the best. It was traitors and incompetent men who caused his failure," or: "These or other excesses were certainly not to be approved, but the National Socialist philosophy was basically right."). There were others who allowed themselves to be persuaded of the unjust character of Nazi dictatorship only *in part* ("Squabbling parties are basically not better than a good authoritarian leadership, either. Hitler's dictatorship simply went a bit too far." or: "It may be that the traitors of the 20th of July were of the belief that the war could no longer be won, and that this is an extenuating circumstance, but they were *still* traitors.").

In short, reservations have remained in the minds of some teachers.
This fact, which was to have been expected, has become plainly apparent in the meantime. The reservations asserted themselves in irritating fashion when the portion of the teachers characterized above was compelled to take contemporary history or even to "digest the past". Everyone is aware how questionable any training in mental attitude in school usually remains if the teacher does not adhere to what he is expected to advocate with his entire conviction and his heart. The result is often just the opposite of what was intended.
Of course, all of this applies only to a *portion* of the teachers. The others can show records of the best instructional success in the subject of "contemporary history". They do not confine themselves to transmitting facts, but state a personal view and consciously precipitate "controversy". If this could be achieved in all cases and in equal intensity, then a good guarantee would be provided that there will not only cease to be any "die-hards" at some point in the foreseeable future, but good Germans and good "Europeans" will take their place.

11. Schizophrenia of National Consciousness

There is a widespread opinion to the effect that right-wing extremism no longer has any chance at all in our country, and that the only danger is that from Communism (for familiar reasons of infiltration). Taking it entirely literally, this opinion is probably correct, since Communism is really dangerous as an international power on the world stage of ideological conflict.
In a lesser direct sense, the right-wing extremism is basically even more dangerous. Still, in the last analysis, when we speak of the "Hitler in ourselves", we do not in fact mean that it is necessary to take precautions against a threatening new seizure of power like the one in the past. The extreme right-wing splinter groups actually have no chance of receiving an enormous influx of supporters. Rather, the catchword of the "Hitler in ourselves" refers to the *schizophrenia in our people,* and it is this which incorporates the great danger. Not only do we lack a traditional and undistorted concept of history which we are able to cling to, we have apparently been unable to prevent (as in Goethe's *Faust)* two souls developing in our breasts, the one that belies the other, and also our leading the coming generation as well into this conflict of conscience. From their parents, children learn differing truths and concepts of right and wrong, as well as concepts of freedom and the dignity of man, tolerance, and... democracy. So long as it is not cured, we cannot call ourselves "democrats", despite any perfect democratic constitution. And likewise, it is impossible for us to count on any unshakable trust from the outside world. Consequently, it is likely to be an ominous error for anyone to take comfort in the belief that the elements having an extreme right-wing attitude have

been victoriously driven from the field and that the only foe remaining is the one on the left; and it would be equally erroneous to go so far as to accept allies in propaganda against the left indiscriminately.

D. Possibilities and Difficulties

12. Predisposition of Present-Day Youth

Like young people in all epochs, those of the present day are "sceptical" and in opposition. As ever, a goodly proportion of wonderful idealism is back of this, as well as the resolution to shape one's own fate on his own responsibility and according to his own laws. This is also the reason for rejection of what is past and what has been "bungled". The result is that some of them do not care to hear anything about the past, although the majority probably do. *In any event, an absolutely new start is desired.* There could be excellent pedagogical work based on this mental attitude of the young people, who are aware of being personally unblemished by what has happened in the past. There are teachers who know how to do this, want to and venture to do so. Successes promptly became evident. (Spontaneous demonstrations of young people against anti-Jewish excesses; pilgrimages to Bergen-Belsen; personal action for restitution in the moral sense, etc. The exhibition by the Political Youth League in Berlin is an indication of this kind.)

Moreover, the question arises whether teachers should really strive for an "open" attitude toward the past that could be quickly attained. Recently, an educationalist took this position.

Perhaps it is really better if one does not free oneself so quickly and completely from this prejudice. It is unseemly if one only then feels a part of a nation when one presumedly has reason to be proud of the fact, because a compatriot wins a gold medal at the Olympic Games. The "Mark of Cain" is unfortunately obvious and clear. The estimation which we hope eventually to regain depends on how we as a people bear this Mark of Cain.

13. Inhibitions in Digesting the Past

"Digesting" is so complicated not only because of the resistance on the part of those older individuals who have as yet grasped nothing, learned nothing and do not care to do either of the two, but also because of the healthy self-confidence in young and old that will inevitably be injured. There is not only a natural resistance to the theory of "collective *guilt*" —with justification—but in addition, against the postulate of "collective shame"—without justification. For many individuals, this expectation is unfeasible. It is only outwardly and not inwardly that notice is taken of the fact that the Nazi regime:

A. Was basically so unprecedentedly corrupt *in reality*.
B. Was perhaps helped into the saddle by oneself, who thus became an unwitting, self-sacrificing helper of such a corrupt, conscienceless band.

This resistance stems from natural psychological roots, from the need for moral self-preservation and the maintenance of psychological equilibrium. Only in a few cases does robust unscrupulousness probably enter into the question, as well. On that account, some efforts to demonstrate without quarter the crimes of the Nazi period (hoping that the *shock* will take care of the rest) simply do not register. Perhaps this "psychological blindness and deafness" is even present in characters that are particularly sensitive and unstable, and therefore lacking in self-confidence. They are *in complete dependence* upon this protective armor in order to be able to hold up their heads. In other words, there is sufficient reason to assume that the presentation of simple contemporary historical facts to the younger generation is not adequate enough. There is the danger of expecting something of this generation which extends beyond its psychological ability. Obviously, psychological help of a special sort is needed here.

14. Who is Competent?

If in this respect mention is here made almost exclusively of that portion of our population for whom the *teachers* bear responsibility, then there are two reasons for this. In the first place, the teachers are now in the spotlight of general interest in this context. In some instances, they are made generally responsible for what has now happened, and in others, they are already revolting publicly against this "scapegoat role". Yet anything that is actually to be hoped for in the way of democratic education is after all concentrated upon the newly arising generation which did not itself consciously and actively experience the Third *Reich,* and for that very reason is especially accessible to unprejudiced judgments. The teachers actually have the key position in whatever may develop in our native country in the next few decades. In the second place, it would lead us much too far afield if we were now to analyse all other "forces of education" to find the part which they, of course, ought to take as well in this process of self-purification. In this respect, the role of parents merits particular attention for the simple reason that they so frequently appear as opponents of the teachers as soon as politics are mentioned.

15. What can be done?

In view of the situation of conflict and in fact of the state of mental spasm that affects a part of the teachers when they are expected to deal with "contemporary history", it seems necessary to consider very carefully the means by which this situation of conflict and this spastic state could perhaps be resolved and given a turn for the better.* The following are just a few initial thoughts:

It is understandable that no faith can be placed in "indoctrination", prescribed enlightenment, and instruction from the top down. In my opinion, it can be done only on the proven level of *discussion meetings.* However, these meetings would have to be given a quite special character.

At the meetings, every *older* participant who consciously experienced the Third *Reich* should be skillfully induced to make a *retrospective search for motives* in his own mind without moralizing pressure on the part of the meetings' directors. That period must be presented to the *younger* teaching staff in such a vivid manner that they are put in a position *to become completely at home in it* and *to experience* their older colleagues' motivation conflicts vicariously. Suitable helpful literature is available, although

*) It cannot be my task at this point to report on the numerous efforts already undertaken by the private and governmental agencies of education in order to combat anti-Semitism and extreme rightism, or even to evaluate them. I am dealing here only with supplementary and in fact somewhat "irregular" measures that seem to me to have become more inevitable than ever at the present time.

the coverage is only very sporadic.** By means of experiences, it is to be suggested to both categories that *even today,* and even in the "open hunting grounds" of democratic opinion forming, processes of political *mis*guidance are being carried on with great effect. It must be pointed out *how poorly people in general are prepared to counter them.* This is a consequence both of gaps in personality training still existing and of ignorance of the effect of demagogy and conformism upon the ostensibly "personal" formulation of opinion. *Autonomy in the formation of a political judgment* is therefore an additional problem of education that has not yet been surmounted.

Of course, it is true that in the area of the Federal Republic there are only a very few persons who are trained in social psychology and are suited to this work of "digesting", which is pedagogical, political, and psychoanalytical. Accordingly, a large staff for field work must first be created. Therefore, the beginning of this action would probably be the training of conference directors. They would then have the task of continuing this work in the *Laender* in direct conjunction with the teachers under the supervision of the Ministers of Education and Religious Affairs. The technical and jurisdictional prerequisites for the initiation of this type of psychologically founded educational extension operation are found in the Federal Republic.

For example, these discussion meetings would deal with the following points:

The fact that the German people became abnormally *susceptible to misguidance* in the political sphere between the two World Wars as a result of specific causes.

The fact that it was possible for extremistic demagogues to take very clever advantage of this susceptibility to misguidance, this general predisposition and disorientation, this hunger for new panaceas in the exigencies of that period, and this open-mindedness *without educated criticism.*

It ought to be demonstrated in what form this took place and to what old middle-class ideals, *what traditions, what conceptions of value,* etc., it was possible to appeal with particular success *at that time* in order to achieve a following. Then it should once more be thought through on a joint basis in detail. Of course, even in establishing the composition of such discussion groups it should be seen to that convinced "nonconformists" who are courageous enough to swim against the stream and to speak out are not left out. At meetings having political training as their aim, it has occa-

---

**) E.g., Wanda von Baeyer-Katte, *Das Zerstoerende in der Politik* (The Distructive Element in Politics), Quelle and Meyer, 1958; H. Wiesbrock, *"Ueber Ethnocharakterologie"* (Concerning Ethnocharacterology), *Koelner Zeitschrift fuer Soziologie und Sozialpsychologie* (The Cologne Periodical for Sociology and Social-psychology), 1957; and Wiesbrock's *"Schlagwort 'Vermassung', zugleich ein Beitrag zur Charakterologie unseres Zeitalters"* ("The Disappearance of Individualism", A Contribution to the Characterization of our Age), *Soziale Welt* (Social World), 1951; W. Metzger, *"Erziehung zum selbstaendigen Denken"* (Education for Individual Thinking), *Psychologische Rundschau* (Psychological Review), 1957; K. Sacherl, *"Zur Pathologie des politischen Denkens"* (The Pathology of Political Thinking), *Kongressbericht Psychologie* (Congress Report of Psychology), 1957; Walter Ehrenstein, *Daemon Masse* (The Demoniac Masses), Frankfurt: W. Kramer, 1952; *Ueberwindung von Vorurteilen* (Conquest of Prejudice) in the Series of the Friedrich-Ebert-Foundation, Hanover: Verlag fuer Literatur und Zeitgeschehen (Publisher of Literature and Current Events), 1960, and in the same series and by the same publisher two books in preparation: *Politische Urteilsbildung in der Demokratie* (The Forming of Political Opinion in a Democracy; Minutes of a Convention) and *Autoritarismus und Nationalismus* (Authoritarianism and Nationalism), Minutes of a Meeting of the Institute for Citizen-Education in the Rhineland.

sionally been possible to experience how harrowing and finally purifying a discussion can become when, as has happened, one participant for instance precipitated great applause with the exclamation: "My *Weltanschauung* is obedience!" Another participant aroused even more by saying: "For me, there is only *one* law and that is Germany!" In cases of this kind, it is up to the discussion leader to have sufficient pedagogical skill to be able to dull the menacing, demagogic edge of the absoluteness and one-sidedness inherent in such suggestive hypotheses. Then the discussion could turn to the general topic of the "natural history" of political deception and the hypnotic effect of various phrases. In this manner, certain research findings could be exploited for pedagogical purposes.

16. Experts

A number of sociologists and psychologists have turned their attention to this entire complex of problems. It would seem to me extremely beneficial if it were possible to stimulate some more of them to perform relevant research and then make available their observations in *this* field of research on motivation and social affairs. This could be done at discussion meetings of the kind mentioned above and primarily on the federal level. (Not long ago, it was possible to hold four pilot meetings of this kind.)

At study conferences among sociologists, psychologists, ethnologists, historians, and political figures consulting with practitioners from the pedagogical field, "crucial" problems of greater scope must later be taken up as well. The outside world consistently asserts, for instance, that the Germans are *different* from other people; that they have characteristics against which the rest of the world must be on its guard; and that there is good reason for distrusting Germany in spite of its reliable democratic constitution and government. No one has it in his power to refute this impression. The embarrassing occurrences at the present time are evaluated as unequivocal symptoms. No amount of euphemizing, of good will on the part of government leaders or of the police is of any help against it. If we want to make it really credible that this image that is created of "the German" is an emotional prejudice or even simply a mental cliché that has been set up for this purpose . . . or last harmless residues, then we cannot evade the necessity of performing thorough research work this time and incorporating its results into political education cautiously but quickly. Its main effort would then shift perceptibly from the transmission of knowledge concerning historical developments to the simple transmission of *findings* concerning processes of social psychology and basic premises of typology.

A "Political Psychology" section was established two years ago in the Federation of German Psychologists. It has already compiled a small catalogue of political psychology research topics that are waiting to be undertaken. Encouragement would be necessary in this respect: in practical terms, the allocation of funds for research assignments and conferences. The following are just a few key words on the subject matter of political psychology:

What is the background of the "fellow-traveler" attitude?

Of mass contagion?

Of the suggestive power of political slogans?

Of susceptibility to collective prejudices?
Of the "Count-me-out" complex?
Of the general lack of ordinary civil courage?
Of the inclination to authoritarian behavior?*
Of the problematical value of certain methods of public opinion survey?
Of so-called "class-consciousness" at the present time?
How much truth is there in the hypotheses of Packard and Dr. Dichter concerning the "manipulability" of human beings by means of modern subliminal publicity stimuli?

E. Summary

But let us return to the immediate occasion for these considerations. First in one place and then in another, the unconnected anti-Semitic manifestations are the most convenient and at the same time the most effectual methods for radical and opposition-minded bully-boys to try to satisfy their need for recognition. For this reason, they are also highly contagious. Genuine, clearly *conscious* hatred of Jews is not the motive in the minds of the perpetrators themselves, in general. The emerging emotion against the *concept* "Jew" is imposed artificially. (Tucholsky once said that if it did not exist, it would have had to be invented.) The same is true of the rationalization for the hating of Jews. Consequently, it is in general simply imagined and parroted, without personal experience and mostly without any personal object of hatred. On the other hand, the genuine factor is the *authoritarianism* and *nationalism,* the "Hitler in ourselves", and the opposition to the charge of complicity. It has without any doubt not been totally overcome in the German people as yet.

It is hard to say how many anti-Semites there are who are genuine, that is, inwardly convinced and believing in the world-wide conspiracy and the like.

By and large, the German people now want peace and quiet, and they want to enjoy their prosperity. These simple reasons are among the ones that have aroused indignation in the great majority over this new breach of the peace. In any event, the plainly audible disassociation of all agencies of public opinion from the trouble-makers has the effect of purifying the atmosphere. At the same time, it would perhaps be appropriate to expose the immature perpetrators to an even greater degree of ridicule and shame by pointing out their retarded puberty. This general excitement, which in fact will pass, must not by any means be the last of the matter. Last "brownshirt" reservations must still be eliminated. These are reservations located at an especially "deep" level and are in some instances unconscious. For this very reason, special methods are required in order to gain access to them. Four basic principles should be kept in mind: Freedom from the past; Honesty toward the recent past; Responsibility for the present; and the courage for a better future. If the Cologne incident should in this way precipitate countermeasures, then it would be another proof of the truth of Goethe's words: "I am a part of that power which always intends evil but constantly creates good."

---

*) Cf., Horkheimer and Adorno; *Das Gruppenexperiment* (The Group Experiment), Europaeische Verlagsanstalt, Frankfurt; *Die autoritaere Persoenlichkeit* (The Authoritarian Personality), Institute for Social Research, Frankfort; E. A. Saarbourg, *Frustration und Autoritarismus* (Frustration and Authoritarianism), Dissertation of the University of Cologne.

Reactions to Anti-Semitic Incidents *

By Peter Schoenbach

In the middle of January 1960, at the height of the wave of anti-Semitic incidents started by the smearings on the synagogue in Cologne on December 25, 1959, the *Institut fuer Sozialforschung* conducted a survey in Frankfort on the Main about the reactions of the Frankfort population to the anti-Semitic desecrations.

Sociology students interviewed a quota sample of 232 Frankfort adults. A schedule of 14 questions, mostly open-ended, was used. The core of the interview aimed at the opinions about the "justification", the clandestine support and the danger of these incidents, their causes and the roles of juveniles and adults in their perpetration, and finally the measures to be taken against them.

On the basis of his spontaneous comments each respondent was assigned to one of the following four groups:

Group I (19 %): Strong reactions against anti-Semitism
Group II (41 %): Mild reactions against anti-Semitism
Group III (24 %): No reactions for a against anti-Semitism
Group IV (16 %): Mild and strong anti-Semitism reactions.

Each respondent was independently classified by two judges. The percentage of identical classifications was 58 %; if groups II and III are combined, the percentage of agreement rises to 74 %. Discrepancies in classification were resolved through discussion of the judges with the survey director. The classification of the respondents into those four groups was not intended to yield a reliable representative distribution of the attitudes with respect to anti-Semitism; it was performed for comparison purposes. Hence, the percentages do not represent attitudes for or against anti-Semitism in Frankfort at large.

From what is known about the characteristics of the authoritarian personality and the theoretical and empirical work on cognitive dissonance, two contradictory hypotheses about the reactions of the anti-Semites to the desecrations could be deduced from the specific conflict situation of anti-Semitism in postwar Germany:

A. Most anti-Semites magnify the importance of the incidents.
B. Most anti-Semites diminish the importance of the incidents.

In a survey of American high school students conducted a few months after our study, Johan Galtung found that the anti-Semites among his

*) A summary from *Reaktionen auf die antisemitische Schmierwelle im Winter 1959—1960*, Frankfort, 1961. The author is social scientist at the Institut fuer Sozialforschung in Frankfort/M.

respondents tended to attribute some significance to the anti-Semitic incidents, whereas the philo-Semites minimized their importance. This result is compatible with hypothesis A rather than hypothesis B. Our own data, however, clearly support hypothesis B. The Frankfort anti-Semites tended more strongly than their opponents or the "middle groups" to belittle the incidents and to regard them as juvenile pranks without political significance.

The discrepancy between Galtung's and our results is probably a consequence of the different degrees of anxiety which the German and the American wave of incidents created among our adult respondents and Galtung's high school students, respectively. We incline to the following interpretation of the characteristic reactions in the four groups compared:

1. The young American anti-Semites had only vague notions of the Nazi terror against the Jews and did not entertain the thought that similar atrocities could occur in their own country. In this group, the anti-Semitic desecrations hardly elicited odious associations, thus there was no real barrier against perceiving them as social support for the own "critical" attitude towards the Jews. Many respondents, consciously or unconsciously, regarded the incidents under this perspective and hence tended to attribute to them importance and "respectability".
2. The American high school students with philo-Semitic attitudes certainly disapproved of the incidents, but they also did not perceive them as signs of a potential serious danger. They regarded the desecrations as "un-American", that is, primarily as embarrassing, and thus they also felt embarrassed by the publicity given to the incidents. Consequently they tended to minimize the importance of the anti-Semitic wave.
3. The adult anti-Semites in Germany were likely to be reminded by the incidents of the persecution of the Jews in the "Third *Reich*" and the charges against the Nazis. Many of them tried to ward off their disquieting associations and guilt feelings by magnifyng the psychological distance between the incidents and themselves. They achieved this by representing the incidents to themselves and to others as unpolitical pranks of hoodlums and foolish boys.
4. The German opponents of anti-Semitism who had seen the beginnings of the anti-Semitic persecutions and had learned with horror about their development were alarmed by the wave of anti-Semitic phenomena. Angered and frightened by the thought that these desecrations might be a new beginning of public defamations and persecutions of the Jews, they openly condemned the incidents and stressed their political significance.

Men and women reacted very similarly to the questions.

The tendency to repress or deny any linkage between the incidents and the past was strongest in the middle-age brackets. The older respondents showed a relatively strong tendency to attribute the incidents to Communist and other outside instigations. The youngest respondents were most ingenious in their judgments: many of them pointed to the harmful influences of the past, and the anti-Semites among them admitted to their attitude towards the Jews more easily than the older anti-Semites.

Rejection of anti-Semitism was much stronger in the highest social sub-group (upper middle) than among the other respondents. The highest rate of expressed anti-Semitism was found among the lower middle-class respondents between 18 and 30 years of age. Instances of repression and denial were most frequent among the lower middle-class respondents over 40.

The true character of the "Swastika rash" cannot be explained here. However, its effects led to the assumption that even anti-Semitic circles repudiated these incidents and did not seek to derive advantage from their political implications. Hence, it need not be apprehended that the sporadic, aggressive, radical manifestations against Jewry by some extremists will meet with much enthusiasm in broad sectors of the population—at least not under present political and economic conditions.

Under the Spell of Guilt and Indifference*

A Lecture by Eva Reichmann for Brotherhood Week in Bonn

Brotherhood Week, annually organized by the Society for Jewish-Christian Cooperation, has once again brought together tens of thousands of people of different religious beliefs, social origins, and various political convictions. For the most part, they were of the same opinion as the speaker. But what about millions of others who were admonished only from afar during this week? After this lecture was given in the auditorium of the University of Bonn, a professor said to the lecturer, "You are absolutely right with what you have said here. But it is always the same story. Those who are sitting here in this assemby hall hardly need to hear this, and those who really ought to hear it are not here." If Brotherhood Week should not remain a purely academic affair, only a matter of a minority, ways have to be found which lead to the rest of the people who still stand aloof.

* * *

The invitation also to add a word on the German situation of today which I have received along with men whom I admire as the best representatives of the new Germany, put me up against a task that was as difficult as it was intriguing. Who am I, I asked myself, that I could accept the responsibility for such a lecture? An Englishwoman I shall never fully become, although England has given me the right to live when my homeland denied me this. I am a former German Jew of British citizenship—a somewhat

*) From *Frankfurter Allgemeine Zeitung*, March 23, 1960.
Dr. Eva Gabriele Reichmann is Director of the Wiener Library's Department of Research in London. This institute, which is named after its founder and director, devotes itself to the study of contemporary history in Central Europe. In her book *Flucht in den Hass (Hostages of Civilization)*, which appeared in the Europaeische Verlagsanstalt, Frankfort, Dr. Reichmann explores the causes of the Jewish catastrophe during the Third Reich.

complicated phenomenon, before whose multifarious loyalties, which mutually overlap, I sometimes become uneasy, in the effort to balance them.

The German and Jewish element in me, which in happier times we called our "united duality", was then a double possession of whose complications I was hardly aware. After it had been split apart and destroyed, it never grew together again out of the fragments. But perhaps thanks to the anchorage on the British Isles and due to the new horizen opened to me among those friendly and modest people there, that part of me which belonged to a totality still felt itself a member after the undesired separation from the whole and I realized that the Jewish element is strongest in its tie to German Jewish history. Also that former German element, in its overcoming of the guilt-loaded relationship to the Jewish citizens, has also gained a new dimension through its contact with the English world.

The Hope for a Recovery

I should like to begin with an example of what I mean by this. It happened in the year 1942. The outcome of the war was completely unknown. There was a number of academic researchers gathered together in London through the stimulation of my highly respected teacher and professor of sociology, Morris Ginsberg, a Jew, in order to take stock of the nature of Germany. The lectures held in this workshop were later collected in a volume under the title, *The German Mind and Outlook.* The preface was written by the historian G. P. Gooch, President of the English Goethe Society. He wrote, "It is the purpose of this book to contribute to the understanding of this gifted, clever, industrious, disciplined, romantic, unsteady, excitable, and frightening nation, against whom we, for a second time in a generation, find ourselves at war. No other country in Europe makes such a thorough and unprejudiced study necessary as Germany, since despite a common bond of origin and language, an understanding of its peculiarity is made difficult by the deep-rooted differences in tradition and mental attitudes. Modern Germany has been mainly built upon the concept of power and the majesty of the state, whereas in England the concept of the rights and freedom of its citizens has been decisive. Herder called his homeland a country of obedience—a principle which neither friend nor foe has ever brought to bear in England or France."

And another associate on the same symposium, Professor Willoughby, ended his contribution on "Goethe in the Modern World" with these words: "We cannot suffer that the thoughts on that which Germany (through National Socialism) has become today make us through stirred-up emotions blind to that which Germany was and will be again. Goethe himself taught us how stupid snap judgments are, when he, at a time when Napoleon's star stood at its zenith, refused to hate the French in consideration of their great contributions to mankind. For us, too, who have loved Germany in the past, now is the great opportunity to proclaim our belief in the recovery of Germany.

The "recovery of Germany" after the "terrors and misery" of the present —all the discussions of this group of scholars rotated around this aspect. And not that alone. Without interruption their thoughts centered on this fact, the fears and hopes of my friends, who knew the conflict with the monsterousness of the abyss, not so much from learned treatises as from the pain of their own experience. We survivors of the catastrophe—and that is not meant to sound either pathetic or sentimental—have survived our own death. We all went through periods of deathly paralysis, and we do not know whether we shall fully overcome them. But as one says, we Jews are optimists. We grope step for step forward with great effort and begin to live again. And for those of us who have lived half of our lives in Germany, this means simultaneously a finding of a new position toward Germany. It was very difficult and for many impossible. But whoever felt courageous enough tried to think of the many unnamed and unknown helpers who lessened the fate of the unfortunate persecuted and sometimes saved their lives. We thought of the men and women of the Resistance Movement, of the battle of the Church, and the faithfulness of those who never stepped into the limelight of history.

Then came the end of the war with its horrible revelations, with the certainty that we would never see many of our dearest friends and relatives again. We did not till that time want to believe it, could not believe it. Even then a remnant of unbelieving resistance checked us against the dark finality of it all. But it remained inexorable. At the moment, I probably surrendered myself over to my completely unreal expectations. I believed that an outcry would sound throughout Germany, an outcry of outrage and emotional release at the same time. Never since the awakening of mankind to a consciousness of freedom and human rights, be it also of a different nature, were ever such unspeakable things committed in the name of a people that devotedly and enthusiastically contributed to this consciousness. I believe in the great emotion of the Greek tragedy, in catharsis, the rebirth. Since that time, experienced, expert politicians and social psychologists have taught me that a bewildered and hungry people in the middle of marching groups of refugees and ruins do not have the strength for such cathartic emotion.

The Stamp of Great Setbacks

Reconstruction, the founding of a state, and normalization followed. An almost vertiginous economic recovery resulted. Also—not a bit should be forgotten or belittled—a magnificent manifestation of a drastic turnabout on the part of the individual as well as of the people's representatives took place. The ever new words of warm human obligingness, clothing the addresses of the first President of the Federal Republic, Professor Theodor Heuss, broke through the hardest crust which covered the sorrowing heart of his listeners. The reparation program which the Chancellor with the aid of his party friends and opponents called into being, will always be recognized by the people of my intercourse not only because of the material results, but rather also as a symbol of good will and compensatory efforts. And much more. In spite of many hopeful beginnings, we have not assembled here today to rejoice over the results. We find ourselves rather under the stamp of great setbacks on the hard road to one another. Let us be quite open with each other. These were not unanticipated. They could only be found to be unexpected by those people who were only slightly familiar with the state of conditions in Germany. Whoever, like my co-workers at the Wiener Library in London, is accustomed to view the German scene with critical and alarmed eyes, could at no time be reassured and confident. There were always, alongside the signs of recovery, also some of a new danger. Yes, it is certainly not unjust to state that the signs of danger seemed to increase. To describe the happenings of the Christmas Eve of 1959 and the resulting smear-campaign as a new outbreak of anti-Semitism in Germany were to depict them inadequately.

What really happened could at the most be compared with the symptomatic development of latent germs of sickness that are still at hand. Inflammations break out because the unhealthy disposition was never fully healed. It hardly needs to be emphasized that this diagnosis of a chronic disposition is more serious than that of an acute attack. But the attack can only provide the occasion for a better treatment of the latent conditions. It would seem to me as if the almost unanimously shocked reaction of the German public, provided it can be brought under one name, has expressed it in this manner. As if the German people welcomed this demonstration that something undercurrent, repressed into the subconscious, had reappeared in the open and that it demanded imperiously their taking a position toward it. In Germany, so I am told, the people were disconcerted by the angry protests from abroad pertaining to the smearings.

Outside of Germany it was not supposed that the sentiments, which the bleeding swastika symbolizes, were entirely vanished. But people abroad had the right to hope that the representatives of these convictions and its symbol would not dare show themselves in the open, that they were outlawed. That suddenly something could arise like an appeal from the political underworld, by which one gave the other to understand in the jargon of criminals "You aren't alone— we're also here!" was received with great excitement abroad.

The Terribly Simple Facts of the Case

A new point of view is therefore demanded. This new attitude cannot avoid reference at least to a discussion of what has been committed by Germans under that disgraceful regime against Jewish and Christian citizens and also against equally innocent human beings living outside of Germany. The simple facts of the case are that a group of barbarous human beings swore to make quick dispatch of humanity in the name of a nation that was elevated through lies as the standard for mankind.

We humans are certainly a questionable society. A hybrid of animal and God, we are equally damned to stand in continuous battle with ourselves, "ever striving", as it were, to exceed ourselves. Poets, believers, and philosophers have contended for the secret of mankind from time immemorial. It was left to National Socialism to damage through their brutal methods the "temple of secrets", in which the human drama takes place. In that this doctrine set itself up as the perfecter of man to a powerful, youthful, prospective superman, National Socialism cut off the Hebraic, Christian, and Classical foundations of our civilization, which were developed with great efforts, and turned back to the primitive barrenness of prehistoric times. Love, consideration, sympathy, helpfulness as well as the achievements of the mind like wisdom of judgment and clarity of understanding were despised in favor of such primitive and early human characteristics as might, force, and the right of the stronger. Whoever does not recognize National Socialism to be the abolition of humanity, has not understood the nature of its diabolism.

These terribly simple facts of the case, of the inhumaneness appear to me not quite fully understood by the Germans of today. Otherwise, they would have had to free themselves of the muddy waters in which they threaten to drown through a gigantic process of purification and renunciation. There has been no lack of voices from their very midst which have tried to point out this necessity to them. Today, in Germany, there is an excellent intellectual *élite* which accepts no compromise in the condemnation of those mad deeds of the past.

But I am sometimes grasped by the fear that this *élite* does not speak for the people. Moreover, that much rather there are two Germanies, not however as in reality divided between East and West, and not between the enlightened and the unteachables. No, these unteachables disturb me less than you might suppose. There are not too many of them despite the signs of alarm and they need not as unteachables be taken so seriously, as much as I agree with Jacob Burckhardt that "the slightest demonstration" can be "a proof of power. One wants to see how much the powers that be will take". Their strength rests, however, not on the extremists, not on the shocked, shaken, humanly fully intact *élite* and also not on those who live behind the times. It rests, in a democratic state, on the unequally large stratum of the indifferent, on those who were never moved by the events and which they therefore, as the catchword says, could not overcome in themselves.

The nature of their character is probably typical for the majority in most nations. But—pardon me, if I err into the realm of the utopian—in Germany this indifference should not be, after what has happened. Germany should have experienced a revolution. I do not mean by that a bloody upheaval, although after a phase of unscrupulous despotism an overthrow of its own power would quite likely have proven to be the proper historical solution. But I do not want to make myself guilty of a wish that could only have caused more blood and tears to flow. What I mean is a revolution of the spirit, a radical re-evalution of moral and political standards.

I am acquainted with all counterarguments which one tends to set in opposition. The nation was deathly exhausted. The Allies made psychological errors. The denazification was abortive. One could not walk about his whole lifetime long in a penitential robe. The line has to be drawn somewhere. If only a line could finally be drawn somewhere! It should not be drawn at the prosecution of the criminals—please understand me correctly—but at the devastation of humanity, which made their criminal acts possible and was a direct result of them. It is still with us. And when we stop speaking about it, this would be only a further sign of how far beyond the span of its historical reign National Socialism has reached its goal.

It is this undiminshed, persistent devastation of human relations, which permits the great mass of the indifferent to sleep with a good conscience and to speak with probably honest regret about the "injustice" that unfortunately befell the Jews, and which they of course do not approve of. However, they do not seldom add, "but one has to admit that there really were too many Jewish physicians and lawyers and, finally, Hitler did provide the population with bread and work, and built the superhighways *(Autobahnen)*. One must confess that not everything was wrong with National Socialism." Whoever believes that he "has to admit" something in this insoluble causal chain of lame excuses and murder, sins against the victims of the gas chambers as well as the martyrs who died for the belief in a new Germany.

The Germans—and that is no sin—are, as one says, not talented for revolutions. If a revolutionary troop of men were ordered to take possession of a railway station they would, as it has also been pointed out, certainly first step up to the ticket office and buy platform tickets. Herder called his country a land of obedience. Nevertheless, there is an example in the German-Prussian tradition that could have been imitated. During the historically fateful turn of the nineteenth century, which introduced an era of freedom and social justice, the "revolution from the top", coupled with the names of Stein and Hardenberg, is a case in point.

It is surely a daring analogy, but you will understand what I mean when I say even this "revolution from the top" was lacking in the second German Republic. Not in the sense that wisdom was lacking at the top. I have already mentioned what sort of blessed effects of the leadership of the state were at hand. But by a revolution—even in a figurative sense—I understand something radical. The renunciation of the justiceless state of the Third *Reich* should have been more definite, decisive, and, as to facts and persons, more fundamental.

With this past there has not been a last uncompromising break. One carries it about, sometimes apolgetically, pleading for milder circumstances, sometimes even vindicatingly, but always as a piece of national history, for which one has to answer because in this period the nation had bravely fought, industriously labored, and greatly suffered. And, indeed, one must bear the responsibility for it. But not with a "Yes, but . . ."; rather with a "Never again!"

The Well-Meaning Caught in the Web

You probably know that in England it is a matter of honor to be a good loser, on the playground as well as in daily life. The Germans are poor losers. After the First World War, they disowned the military defeat and placed the responsibility on the democratic parties and the Jews. The result of all this we have already seen. This time the defeat is certainly not denied. But what one cannot and will not admit is that one lost oneself in National Socialism and that National Socialism in its unleashing of a war and in its death factories has lost the last nimbus of national idealism acceptable by decent men. It was evil and inhuman. But it is a part of that devilish industriousness that so many good men were deceived who gave this doctrine their wild, helpless patriotism, and did not realize that they were duped. Even worse, that these men were drawn into the web of criminal acts before they could defend themselves against them.

The Intellectual Revolution Can Be Made Up For

The assault on the individual conscience was at that time much too successful. Is it, however, necessary to preserve the stratagem of enmeshment in guilt beyond the defeat of this system by artificial means? Would it not be better to destroy its effect finally by recognizing in all clearness and honesty that one is a complete loser? Of course, civil courage is a part of it, but not to such a degree that it could not also be awakened in the average father or teacher. He would need only to be willing to yield his claim to infallibility. This claim to infallibility is, moreover, obsolete and inopportune. The relationship between the generations in Germany could be improved when fathers would step up before their children and teachers before their pupils and say, "I also took part in it all. Much appeared to be good and right. Later, I realized how much we were taken advantage of and because I have grown wiser through my own bad experience, I believe it to be my honest, holy duty to strengthen you against such temptations, so that what happened to us could not happen to you." I cannot understand why such a manly confession cannot be made. And if it were done by thousands and thousands of all classes and professions, then the ominous ban of the enmeshment of guilt would be broken. The Germans would then have executed their intellectual revolution, they would have achieved an objective perspective toward their own history.

The Enemy is the Tepidity

It does not concern anything less than humanity. It is not a matter of the Jews any more. What earlier was coined as a challenging catchword, that in reality anti-Semitism is not a Jewish, but a Christian question or better an anti-Semitic question, is in modern times proven beyond any doubt by sociological and psychological research. With the anti-Semites, it is simply a matter of the type, the misanthrope: intolerant, aggressive, fanatical, distrustful, loaded with prejudices to the degree of inability to think for himself, submissive and authoritarian, and incapable to deal with freedom, either with his own or that of his fellow men. He is a type which tends to radical nationalism.

Im our time of supranational communities, Nationalism has been transferred from Europe to the stage of the so-called "underdeveloped" nations. There its star is on the horizon, while its European task has been fulfilled. Nationalism consists—about the turn of that very century mentioned above—of the awakening of the individual to the consciousness of his language and location, of his freedom from the absolutism of princes and from religious intolerance. Nationalism was a creation of the Enlightenment. It went hand and hand with Liberalism and Pacifism. And tragically enough it was in Germany, the country in which Nationalism would one day degenerate at its worst, that its harbingers—Schiller, Herder, Schlegel, Humboldt—in their national vision of understanding between peoples and freedom of the nations of the world, dreamed of perfected harmony in a concert of free nations.

They had, we could say carefully weighing our words, the privilege to dream. There was still no German political life which was able to curb their obligation to *raison d'état* to a *sacro egoismo.* At that time they used the ineffectual opportunity honorably. I have often asked myself whether or not perhaps in our time the provisional lack of a complete, German political life offers to the German people a chance to outgrow itself. In the early postwar years, when the first German pioneers came over the English Channel and found understanding and encouragement here with us in the Wiener Library, it often seemed to me as if the conditions for a new orientation were ripe. Germany was defeated and broken, but "Europe" was on the lips of them all. Even if in the meantime the great expectations of those years have been ground up in the mill of political conflicts of interest, the hope need not be fully given up that even in our time a spiritual victory arises from out of this national tragedy.

In our century, Germany stands under the basilisk glance not from the West, but from the East. Fear and defense in this direction are much too much a part of our daily life that we could succeed to free ourselves from them. We are in the middle of a stormy event and cannot gain an adequate perspective of the whole. We can ourselves say that it is dangerous to stand by and let oneself be paralysed by one's own enemy. The basilisk glance is its strongest weapon. It is not good to stare steadfast in one direction. Under these conditions, the enemy at our backs could gather and strike us from behind. Thereby we have truly arrived at the meaning and background of this conference by way of a great detour. It would have been easier to proceed with a "scapegoat approach". But that would have been wrong, untruthful, and deceptive. The enemy with whom we have to deal is not to be identified with swastika-smearings and not with a political power on the other side of the frontier. The enemy is tepidity, the indifference from within.

According to the wisdom of a Chassidian book, the *Book of the Pious,* one should especially feel akin to three types of men: the judicious person, whom a madman dominates; the good man, who is subordinate to an evil man; the noble man, who is dependent on a wicked person. But for three others, one should have no sympathy: for the unthankful person; for the man who himself executes merciless viciousness; and for the man who stupidly incites his own disaster.

It seems to me as if there is a piece of advice from the Chassidian wisdom directed to the German nation and another to the world. To the Germans it says—since this can be done only by them—what should be done with those who even today "stupidly incite their own disaster?" To the world it says that it should think of the judicious, the good, and the noble, and that it should feel at one with them, and support them in their effort to free the indolent and unscrupulous from the laming weight of indifference.

The Eichmann Case *

By Juergen Tern

One of Hitler's most inhumane executioners has finally been brought to trial, fifteen years after the defeat of the National Socialist reign of terror. Adolf Eichmann, formerly a high-ranking functionary in the so-called *Reich's* Main Bureau for Security, behind whose romantically dolled-up emblem a perfect terror-machine of incomparably cold-blooded cruelty was hidden, has met his pursuers, and much more, his judges. The satisfaction that is widely felt about this, considering the mass murders, for which Eichmann is to blame, is nowhere free of great emotion. Here, in our country, the abhorrence of these acts by decent and judicious people is closely connected with shame and horror.

We cannot be fully satisfied to see in the prisoner just one of Hitler's slaughterers, to whom so many hundreds of thousands of Jews fell victim. For us, the affair cannot be done away with, in that his part of the outrages of the National Socialist government is portioned out. Eichmann, who officiated in the inner core of the SS as one of those mainly responsible for the bestial "final solution of the Jewish problem", his name, and what it symbolizes make clear to us again, that the German nation may not and cannot feel itself free from the responsibility for the horrible deeds that have been committed in its name.

It is not our place to ask the Israeli officials, who succeeded in seizing Eichmann, questions about the "how" and "why" of his imprisonment. We have no right to refer to juridical points of view. After all, that would serve to still the unrest of our conscience. A person who has brutally overridden the law and unscrupulously offended every natural right, has, in our opinion, lost every claim to support. In our country, we, who did not succeed in bringing Eichmann to trial, should have confidence in the Israeli administration of justice: there will be justice and not revenge. The government of the State of Israel is firm and morally strong enough to avoid every aspect of a sensational trial in the proposed proceedings.

But in the event that one of Israel's neighboring states should feel its rights of sovereignty infringed upon by the imprisonment of Eichmann, it would itself be to blame. The government of Israel on its part could argue, that a termination of the status of war with its neighboring states has not yet been achieved on the basis of international law. Their governments consistently and uncompromisingly refuse to sign a treaty of peace, though Israel has repeatedly declared itself prepared to negotiate for peace. A continuance of the status of war, according to international law, is demonstrated, for example, through the permanent closing of the Suez Canal

*) Editorial from *Frankfurter Allgemeine Zeitung*, May 27, 1960.

to Israeli ships or ships under a foreign flag but loaded with cargo destined for Israel, without any power or the usual channels up to now being able to effect a real armistice in this quarter. The legal hovering between war and peace makes Israel's quasi-militant status necessary.

The government of Israel feels obligated to avoid this state of affairs leading into a permanent and unilateral discrimination against its country and the delicate balance of powers, by and by, shifting to its disadvantage. This forces Israel to be equally well armed as her neighbors and prepared not to let the least provocation go unanswered, and finally not to shrink back from the war for survival. This militant mentality, which Israel sees itself forced to maintain, particularly since it is prepared to integrate itself into its oriental environment, but feels itself rejected in this effort, also explains the efficiency of the Information Service (which tracked down Eichmann). Also that determination is explained that does not shy away from the calculated risk of a so-called commando action as long as the Israeli *raison d'état* is in favor of it. This all is a part of the Maccabean existence of the modern Jewish state. The question arises whether and how far all that is tied to the powerful figure of Ben Gurion, who, as philosopher, settler, and tribune of the people, finds his way over crevices and through abysses.

The capture of Eichmann is obviously a part in that confused, difficult, and unfortunate chapter of the relations between Israel and Arabia, which we hope will one day improve through tireless patience. But for us Germans, the Eichmann Case is certainly a part of our own past. It is representative for each of those murders which have been committed in the name of a German government against an inconceivably large number of defenseless, Jewish fellow men out of pure maliciousness. As much as the hunt for Eichmann may occupy human curiosity, it is the dark past, because of which Eichmann tried for fifteen years to escape the arm of justice, that is important for us Germans.

It is not necessary to tell those of us who experienced and even suffered under the National Socialist regime what it meant particularly for the German and East European Jews, as well as for many citizens of Western Europe, that Eichmann, as superintendent of the so-called *Reich's* Main Bureau for Security, was given the job of realizing the "final solution of the Jewish problem". Only a remnant of this Jewish element of the population, which has lived with us for decades and centuries in a symbiotic relationship, one that was often dangerous for them but never before deadly, and from which the modern German nation has drawn a considerable part of its intellectual power, has survived Eichmann and his executioners.

The nation must guard itself against forgetting and repressing that horrible extremity. It should avoid self-pity and flagellation. It must find the courage to live in the awareness of the calamities that have been committed in its name. Since the end of the war, a new generation has grown up that was itself not involved in the disaster and that tries hard to understand the calamity. We have no right to conceal it from them. They just have to know about it. Otherwise, they will not be able to understand the outer situation and the inner condition of the nation, neither the mutilation of our state nor the dissension of the people. The misery of our existence did not begin in 1945, but in 1933.

Eichmann: Impact on Germany *

A Sense of Shame Is Widespread, But Few Feel Personal Guilt

By Sydney Gruson

Bonn, Germany, April 15—An elderly man, perhaps 60 and obviously the worse for too much beer, stood in one of Bonn's bus stations and shouted to the long queue:

"And you want to be Germans. This Eichmann, he killed 6,000,000 Jews and you dare to smile!"

Some people laughed at the man. Most paid him no attention.

The three soldiers in the jeep did not mind being stopped by the American reporter seeking reaction to the opening proceedings of the Eichmann trial. What did they think about it?

Said one: "No punishment can be made to fit his crime. We Germans are ashamed of ourselves."

Said another: "Orders are orders."

Said the third: "I have not thought about it much."

The television program the night before the trial began was entitled "On the Trial of the Hangman." It was a documentary on the life of Eichmann that spared viewers none of the horrors of the concentration camps and included the first showing of film taken of the mass executions of Jews in Eastern Europe by S. S. extermination units.

A Woman Cries

Two Americans, a Finn, a Swiss girl, and a German woman were watching. When it was over, the German woman was crying.

"I did not know, how could I know," she said over and over again.

There is, then, no single German attitude to the trial of Adolf Eichmann, the S. S. colonel charged with responsibility for the murder of millions as a key figure in Hitler's "final solution" of the Jewish question—the extermination of European Jewry.

Perhaps there is only one emotion that practically all Germans share about the trial, the wish that it was done and finished with. Eichmann's individual fate is of no concern except to a lunatic fringe that believes that the only thing Hitler did wrong was to lose the war and thus prevent completion of the "final solution."

Variety of Attitudes

The whole variety of attitudes and reactions evident among Germans were on display this week. The most important was the official position taken publicly by Chancellor Adenauer on behalf of the West German Govern-

*) From the New York Times International Edition, Monday, April 17, 1961.

ment and elaborated at great length by practically every important newspaper.

"We hope," Dr. Adenauer said, "that in this trial the full truth will come to light and that justice may be done."

He spoke of the "shame" felt by Germans after the war when they learned the full extent of the Nazi horrors and the "concern" that the people could never be cleansed of the "poison" of Nazism. He also expressed the belief that the "poison" had been completely removed. Many newspapers went further than Dr. Adenauer.

"Nobody can deny," said *Die Zeit,* West Germany's leading political and literary weekly, "that what Eichmann did took place in Germany and was done under a system created by Germans and applauded by Germans for a long time."

The *Frankfurter Allgemeine,* an influential and widely read daily, devoted one and a half pages to excerpts from documents showing the systematic preparations by the Nazis to exterminate the Jews. The documents, the paper said, "reflect the darkness of a history no German can deny, a burden we cannot shake off."

There was no effort by the country's leaders and the major moulders of public opinion to find excuses, to minimize the horrors or to escape a share of responsibility.

Otto Dibelius, Evangelical Bishop of Berlin, said all Germans shared Eichmann's guilt, and reminded his compatriots that the Nazi murderers were "from our midst, of our blood, our kind, our people." The Frankfort City Government issued as a pamphlet a collection of speeches and articles by Prof. Willy Hartner, vice-chancellor of Frankfort University, that stated unequivocally that anyone in their teens by 1938 knew about the Nazi terror.

For how many Germans did these voices speak? There is no certain way of knowing but, so far as a foreigner could judge, the feeling of shame is widespread throughout the country now that the full glare of the spotlight has been turned on the trial. There is less conviction that, as Bishop Dibelius indicated, there should be collective guilt as well as collective responsibility and shame.

Part of an Era

The voices that spoke out just before the opening of the trial represented, in the main, a generation that was part of the Nazi era. This is a deeply divided generation, made up of those like Prof. Hartner who believe that Germany's Nazi past must be faced up to in order to be lived down and those who find the past, and their part in it, too much for constant appraisal.

It is the youth of the country that can examine the past, and the Eichmann trial, with the least difficulty, for, as they say, "We were no part of it" and "We are not responsible for what our parents did."

If the first impact of the trial is being judged correctly it is having less effect on the youth than on their elders. The story of the horrors has been available for anyone to read or see or study. Those of the youth who are interested have read about it, seen the television shows and movies and studied the period. Those who did not care before do not seem to have changed.

Mood of Chastisement

At the moment, with the trial just beginning, there is a mood of chastisement that practically everyone seems willing to accept. There are, of course, exceptions. The *Deutsche Zeitung* of Cologne, for example, wrote the other day that the "wartime generation has suffered enough. They have borne so far the guilt of others, silently, although the majority of their fathers were also guiltless of the disaster of 1933."

"Look," said a German the other day in the midst of an argument about what made the Germans tick, "how long and how often do you want us to beat our breasts? Does it make you feel better if we repeat it every day that Nazism was evil, that, if you want, we were evil? What we are trying to tell you is that we know it, we understand it and that we are not now evil."

Only a Pair of Black Sheep?

Scandal of the Eichmann Discussion in Bremen*

"We certainly cannot supervise every program of the university extension service with municipal control." With this reply, Bremen's Minister for Internal Affairs, the Social Democrat Adolf Ehlers, esteemed in the Hanseatic city for his collected objectivity, answered the question raised as a result of the turbulent discussion of the Eichmann Trial by the extension service. It was asked why the Bureau for Constitutional Rights has neglected its duty in this case.

Indeed, not even the Bureau for Constitutional Rights could have foreseen that, exactly in this city, which is noted for the deliberation of its inhabitants, an aggressive outbreak of anti-Semitism could result in a public discussion of those humiliating events of our recent past that came to debate in connection with the Eichmann Trial.

Firstly, the rather large number of participants in this evening meeting on such a theme seemed to imply that a gratifyingly brisk desire to take issue with the past was at hand. Soon after the introductory lecture of Dr. Max Plaut, the Deputy Head of the Israeli Community in Bremen, it became clear that not all of the audience was prepared for an unprejudiced, objective discussion. The cue for the discrepancy was involuntarily given by the first speaker of the evening, the former Minister for Economy in Bremen, Herman Wolters. He, whose democratic affiliations are beyond reproach, did not even answer the piercing question of Dr. Plaut, "Who is responsible for Eichmann?", but spoke generally about the present state of anti-Semitism in the world.

In this way, the direction of the discussion was badly put underway from the beginning. Incorrigible radicalism determined the tone of the discussion from then on, whereby it was useful for them that the extension service had invited Dr. Plaut not only to speak but to lead the discussion as well. A less tolerant man would have nevertheless been perhaps able to steer

*) From *Die Zeit*, June 2, 1961.

course to a somewhat safer harbor. But, under these circumstances, the vessel that was loaded with anticomplexes, resentments, and absolute injudiciousness floated capsized on the waves of a so-called discussion.
It was explained that it was the Jews who must change, since world-wide anti-Semitism demonstrates that something is wrong with them. Other speakers complained that they could not bear to hear the name Eichmann any longer, after all there are "black sheep" in every country. Of course, the argument that through the loss of the war Germany had atoned enough for the sins of the past was not lacking. Dangerous folly of this sort were said in such a terrifyingly aggressive manner that the well-intending speakers of the evening hardly had a chance to push through the resistance with their arguments.
It was a humiliating performance and an evening that made it quite clear that Eichmann is not as foreign to our way of thinking as we sometimes like to believe.

I don't have an Answer *

I just had to write this to you. I can't help it! I must say aloud what I felt and feel when I read your report on the Eichmann Trial. I feel ashamed and nothing but wild, uncontrollable shame.
I am ashamed because I am a German and was once compelled to wear that uniform. An incredible accident of fate saved me from joining the commandos that were ordered to commit such atrocities. Horrified, I ask myself again and again what I would have done, if I had been ordered to perpetrate such crimes. Would I have had enough character or humaneness to swing my weapon around and shoot those who dragged children from their mothers and simply gunned them down? Would I have shown the same bad character to fire on wounded women and children who, with great effort and pain, had worked their way out of a mountain of corpses?
My God! It is terrible! I just don't know. I cannot say it. I can't give any sufficient excuse for it, anyway not a convincing one. The shame, however, the burning shame, which no one can extinguish, remains, since I once called these guys my "comrades". Of those who fired and of those who obeyed such orders, there are surely some who are still alive. Were they really commanded to be so brutal? Can they honestly be called "soldiers"? Were they at all ever soldiers who would perform such acts? Isn't there one of them who is still living that has committed such atrocities and would stand up, pound himself on the chest, and admit for the sake of our honor, "I was also one of them and committed myself to do these things!"
And Eichmann? Lay it all before him, piece for piece, act for act, since he didn't dirty his hands, he just gave the orders. He gave us the orders and we carried them out . . .

---

*) The author, Horst Poeschmann, is a former sergeant major in the *Luftwaffe* (former German air force) and now resides in Husum, Schleswig-Holstein. His letter appeared in Hamburg's *Die Welt*, May 17, 1961.

Could it Happen Again?*

By Franz Boehm

At a meeting held in Bonn University on March 13, 1960, in connection with the "Week of Brotherhood", Dr. Franz Boehm delivered an address of which the following is an extract:

The incidents which we have witnessed during Christmas week and afterwards have compelled us to wonder whether there is something seriously wrong in the Federal Republic. It is true that as a result of police enquiries these matters appear in a somewhat more harmless light. Nevertheless, we have to question ourselves, and there can be no doubt about the reply: there certainly is something wrong in our country; after what has happened, after the complete disorganization and demoralization through which our state and society have gone, this is bound to be so. Such things are not overcome in a mere fifteen years.

But I do not propose to talk about whether the condition of our public morality, our thinking, or our attitude harbors any serious risks for the Jews amongst us, or what we should do in the fields of education and self-searching so as to create in Germany a social and political atmosphere which makes it easy and pleasant for all upright people to live amongst us. I should like to draw your attention to an entirely different aspect. I am concerned with the conditions under which the existence of an anti-Semitic ideology can lead to such gigantic extermination operations as we have been horrified to see in the National Socialist state. Further, we must inquire whether such conditions, or rudiments of them, are to be found in the political and social life of our Federal Republic.

Unlimited Power as a Presupposition of Radical Terror

I should like to start with a statement which I do not think is open to dispute: I say that extermination operations such as the so-called "final solution" of Heydrich and Goering, and extermination camps such as Auschwitz, Treblinka, Sobibor and others are possible in a totalitarian state only and totally impossible in a democratic or constitutional state where the rule of law applies. Before such things can happen, there must be a crushing, strangulating concentration of political and social power in the hands of a small dictatorial group. A state which does not have at its disposal such an abundance of power cannot carry through final solutions nor

*) From *Bulletin des Presse- und Informationsamtes*, March 19, 1960.

establish extermination camps in its territory. Where the power of the state is only somewhat curbed and subject to effective controls by a constitution, even the most vicious type of anti-Semitism can never lead to the systematic extermination of Jews. In other words: radical terror presupposes radical and unlimited power.

The Coup d'état from Above

Let me add a second statement which can at least be proved as probably correct in theory and which is also confirmed by the experience of history: I say that no state whose constitution is based on the rule of law and which protects the liberty of the citizen through restrictions on the power of government, can be transformed unnoticeably and quietly into a totalitarian dictatorship. Such a change can only be brought about forcibly and by several stages, one of which will produce either a revolution from below or a *coup d'état* from above.

In our century, the *coup d'état* has become the customary method. If you want to win totalitarian power, you start by founding a radical conspiratorial party based on the principles of leadership, strict discipline, and subordination; if possible, you also build up some terrorist organization. Then you set out to create an internal political crisis. But you will try your best to avoid a direct revolutionary attack on the democracy you have undermined, because the forces of even a weakly led, poorly defended state in the middle of an economic or political crisis are still considerably stronger than those of an attacker forced to operate from below, from the streets so to speak.

Mussolini was the first to give a classical demonstration of this procedure, by which the totalitarian party leader begins with forming a parliamentary government—through the use of blackmail, it is true, but otherwise quite in the conventional manner—only to remove the constitution by a *coup d'état* and to set up a totalitarian one-party regime as soon as he has gained control of the normal machinery of government.

Hitler copied this procedure consciously and fairly exactly, except that he was much more radical in his *coup d'état* than Mussolini had been. It was Hitler, too, who invented the technical term for this sort of thing: he called it a lawful revolution, a lawful assumption of power.

In November, 1917, matters were a little more complicated for Lenin and Trotzki. A bourgeois revolution on the accepted eighteenth and nineteenth century pattern had already gone before, and the Bolshevik victory was due to the situation of dual power as Trotzki later described it very clearly. But when he set up the communist satellite states of Bulgaria, Rumania, Hungary, Poland, and Czechoslovakia, Stalin reverted very closely to the methods of Mussolini and Hitler. In all these countries, a kind of sham democracy was allowed to continue for a while under predominantly communist influence, and then there followed the totalitarian *coup d'état* from above. Finally, Soviet Russia tried the same in its German Zone of Occupation, with the interesting difference, however, that here they saved themselves the trouble of a sham-democratic intermediate stage and simply changed what was a mere zone of military occupation into a full-fledged

Soviet subsidiary, to which they transferred their military occupation rights; they then proceeded to call the administrative machinery they had thus set up a sovereign German state, never bothering to ask the Germans, to whom this area belonged and still belongs under international law, what they thought of it all.

Modernization of Revolutionary Techniques

You see, then, that revolutionary techniques have been considerably modernized in the course of time—so much so, in fact, that most of our ideas of what a revolution is have remained far behind the developments of reality. We all imagined a revolution to be something by which the entire established order of authority and administration is brought to a complete halt; we thought of uncontrolled hordes storming into the streets, occupying public buildings, disarming the police and the army, firing about blindly, and creating utter chaos and complete lawlessness.

We have always been terribly afraid of such chaos, of such wild hordes; they seemed to us the most horrible of all horrors. But now all that has changed. Today, a revolution is a carefully prepared job of staffwork in all its successive phases, executed by well-drilled professional revolutionaries with their supporters marching in disciplined columns—flags, torches, newsreels and all. The nation itself, the man in the street, is no longer needed in this process; he is not asked, and whether he likes it or not he is represented by a carefully selected and drilled guard of activists.

The Preconditions for the Total Assumption of Power

For all this to happen, a number of conditions must be fulfilled. In the first place, there must be grave dislocations in state and society. Secondly, the mass of malcontents must find resolute, ruthless leaders with political and organizational talents. The third condition is that nothing effective is done by the government, the political parties, the administration, the courts, the police, or the army to meet this danger, and that they passively watch the build-up of terror. In the fourth place, the revolutionary leaders must succeed in using their forces in such a way as to completely ruin normal social and political life; the nation will then become convinced that its government will not be able to restore order by constitutional means.

When this point is reached, it is pretty certain that one day the revolutionaries will be offered a share in the government. Once the revolutionary chief has become head of government, the remaining phases before the totalitarian assumption of power is completed will follow almost automatically; in particular, the *coup d'état* itself, by which the constitution is set aside and the last barriers and controls of authority are removed, will then be no more than a problem of organization—of staging as it were. It is, therefore, not all that easy to upset even a poorly defended democracy. Such an enterprise takes a lot of ingredients to be successful.

The Situation in the Federal Republic

If we look fairly and squarely at the present situation in the Federal Republic, I think we will find—without any frivolous self-delusion—that not one of these conditions exists at present. There can be no question of the existence of grave dislocations in state or society. Nor are there any signs of the Federal Parliament or the *Land* Diets lacking resolution, of inadequate government action, or of any weakness vis-à-vis subversive trends. Far and wide, we cannot discern any leader-types of sufficient political or organizational caliber. The only possibility is that there may be a group of people who are perhaps dreaming of becoming the new activist guard of a new leader and a new terrorist movement.

So far as the third condition is concerned, I think we can safely assume it to be highly improbable that our nation, our government, our politicians, and our civil servants will once again stand at attention and watch a bunch of activists, with or without a leader, rigging up some terrorist action. So far, the successful totalitarian revolutions have taken the unprepared society by surprise. But in 1960, society is no longer unprepared, and, in particular, we in Germany have gathered some experience. When the National Socialists began their work in Germany, none of us had a very high opinion left of democracy, the rule of law, the rights of man, the division of powers, or parliamentary control. We had been softened up and made sceptical by a century of socialist, romantic, and biological criticism of bourgeois society and capitalism; and as for the totalitarian state—well, we had not yet met it.

Meanwhile, however, we have met it, and that dreadful experience has reopened our eyes to the wisdom and experience stored up in our liberal constitution and our economic principles. The concept of totalitarianism has lost the bloom of its ideological youth. There are very few left who still believe that whatever good it might be able to do—at least historically—could justify even a fraction of all its filth and blood and horror and sorrow and vileness. On the other hand, the old established principles of the structure of state and society, which we had already thrown on the rubbish heap in the turmoil of our development hysteria, have regained some of their spiritual and practical authority—not, however, in the intellectual camp, where unfortunately some frightening concessions are still being made to the wiles of totalitarianism.

We therefore have every reason to expect that in any future clash with the totalitarian principle its aggressive drive will be far less virulent than in the years before 1933, and that the defending forces will be backed by more spiritual, moral, political, and social energy than in the days of Weimar.

Two Political Sins

I hope you will not think that I say this in order to provide grist for the mills of those amongst us who frivolously minimize the gravity of these matters. My purpose is to take up an idea at which I hinted two years ago in a speech in Munich. Then, I said—as I do now—that we needed the concurrence of two sins before the terrible extermination of Jews could become possible: the sin of harboring anti-Semitism and the sin of throwing away our liberties and helping a dictator to acquire unrestricted power. Had we not committed the latter, politically organized mass murder could never have happened. Conversely, had we not harbored any anti-Semitism, the terrorist crimes would have been directed not against the Jews, but against some other category of citizens, as for instance in the communist countries. It has been our unspeakable misfortune that in Germany—and nowhere else—these two sins have joined forces. The anti-Semitism ingredient transformed the gigantic totalitarian terror into a crime, low, filthy, diabolical and depraved in its very motive. In my previous speech, I did not deal any further with the specifically political sin of treachery to freedom and the adoration of power; I spoke only of the other sin, that of anti-Semitism, the sin of a spiteful and inhuman group prejudice; I then attempted to follow up the history of anti-Semitism and its modern manifestations.

Today, I shall try to discuss the other phenomenon, the German submission to totalitarian temptation. Why have we in Germany allowed not only the hatred of Jews, but also the hatred of political and civic freedom to grow so big within us? Is there any connection between these two forms of hatred?

So far as this last question is concerned, we can say with absolute certainty that if there was a connection, it definitely did not mean that we had willfully thrown away our freedom and set up a totalitarian state in order to give free rein to our hatred of the Jews and to exterminate them. The reasons were quite different ones. People wanted a dictatorship in order to make Germany into a fear-inspiring state, in order to tear up the Versailles Peace Treaty, perhaps also in order to gain *"Lebensraum"* in the East. Many of them—and they were the real National Socialists—wanted it because it was their ambition to belong to the ruling class of such a state so that they might oppress their fellow citizens, push them around, and keep them in fear and terror because all things humanitarian, democratic, liberal, literary, commercial, and civilian were anathema to them, because they could not understand the complicated, intricate workings of industrial society, and because they yearned for a wider field to satisfy their urge of activity, unhampered by considerations of law, morality, or any similar "sentimentalities".

Reasons for the Abandonment of Freedom

But I believe that the abandonment of freedom has deeper roots and that these have something to do with the daily life of industrialized society, and with a number of trends which exist in such a society. The more a nation revolts against the rhythm, the risks, and the complexity of this type of society and its computing machine characteristics, the more strongly it tends to incline toward totalitarianism. It was, I think, in the first place, the growing intensity of daily routine which made the idea of freedom obsolete for workers, employees, craftsmen, farmers, and members of the free professions and the middle classes in trade and industry. All these people began to wonder what the use of their civic and political freedom was if all they had achieved was to exchange subjection to feudal overlords, landowners, the privileged and the guilds, for subjection to some anonymous law of supply and demand, and if, under the whip of competition and through the lack of property, their state of servitude had become even worse than it had been before machines, large factories and the so-called free society and the free state had been invented.

Their argument runs approximately as follows: "If, as it seems, there is no genuine freedom for us in this world, then we prefer dependence on a strong state, which, at least, looks after all its subjects and allocates a share to each, to dependence on the laws of supply and demand which don't care for human beings and are indifferent to those who get left behind. If we are to be pushed around anyhow, then let us have appointed civil servants and party bosses rather than the rich who owe their power over us not to office, but to their moneybags, to chance, to the laws of inheritance and to the solidarity of their class."

Two great movements have risen against industrial society: the movement of the industrial workers and that of the middle classes. Both have produced political programs—radical ones and less radical ones. The radical ones encourage totalitarianism or at least set certain postulates which presuppose a totalitarian state. The workers' radical program is marked by a clearly rational character; it has a philosophical and scientific streak, whereas—at least in Germany—the radical programs of the middle classes show strong emotional and anti-intellectual trends. The socialism of Marx and Engels accepts the methods of industrial production and its dynamism; it only wants to eliminate the elements of exploitation and anarchy inherent in the market mechanism and its central institution: private property. The radical programs of the middle classes, on the other hand, revolt against industrialism as such and aim at some form of safe establishment for medium-sized enterprises with the repression and, if possible, the break-up of large concerns; their goal is a world of privileged small and medium-sized businesses, of local craftsmen and farmers—a world full of hostility to outsiders, intellectuals, and the great.

The central idea of Marxist socialism is the nationalization of the means of production. This necessarily calls for central direction of the whole economy by the state through governmental central planning. Such a gigantic state function makes a totalitarian state indispensable.

The Ahlwardt Movement

The middle-class anticapitalist movement never managed to produce such a central idea. It became bogged down in its negative attitudes without producing any economic or social program. There was not one thinker in its ranks, but only propagandists and drummer boys. The movement was at once decidedly anticapitalist, antidemocratic, antiliberal, antihumanitarian, antisocialist, anti-Christian, and anti-Semitic. To make up for all this, it was extremely nationalist. These, at least, were its features during the great and protracted economic crisis to which Germany fell victim shortly after the war of 1870, and which lasted until well into the nineties. The movement had come into the hands of a certain Ahlwardt who managed to secure quite a number of seats for it in the *Reichstag,* and for some time it flourished considerably. The main reason for this was that at election time both the right and the left assiduously wooed its supporters. By the way, the remnants of Nazidom may have a slender analogous chance in our day. You have no doubt all noticed that we politicians speak up with passion against anti-Semitism every time something like this swastika-daubing happens; but when you look more closely, you will see that we take some care to be ambiguous. Because when we have to decide on such things as the law concerning former nazi officials, quite some fatted calves are sacrificed to our prodigal sons.

Well, the same was true of the Ahlwardt movement in its time, though it was Mr. Ahlwardt who thought of the propaganda trick of making up for the lack of a positive program by putting up anti-Semitism as his central slogan. It was Mr. Ahlwardt who drew a clear distinction between the new type of German anti-Semitism and the old, religious kind, by basing it on the idea of race and extending to Christianity his reproaches against Jewish thought. By describing the Jews as members of a world-wide secret conspiracy, he could blame them for everything the broad masses disliked during those years of economic crisis: capitalism, the ideas of the French Revolution, liberalism, the concept of restricted and controlled state authority, rational socialism of the Marxist kind, humanitarianism, the intellectuals, foreigners, the churches, the press, the banks, and the stock exchange.

Only after anti-Semitism had ceased to be based on the idea of religious persecution (which had inspired its mainly conservative adherents) and had become a purely temporal and biological obsession, was it possible to make the slogan of anti-Semitism into a political mass slogan with revolutionary trimmings. As I have said, historically, this was linked with a radical middle-class movement.

As time went on, political anti-Semitism became separated from its specifically middle-class connection and found itself sociologically orphaned. The Ahlwardt movement had not succeeded, even in its finest hour, to capture the middle classes. It had always remained a sect and disappeared almost completely from the scene when, at the beginning of this century, the economy took a new upswing which continued until the outbreak of the First World War.

Hitler's Theory of Total Power

After the defeat of 1918, Hitler and the extreme National Socialists found this sort of political anti-Semitism based on racial theories; it was the legacy of Ahlwardt, by then long dead and forgotten. Hitler hardly changed his precursor's doctrine, but since as a demagogue he was of very different mettle and his make-up varied widely from that of Ahlwardt, he realized much more clearly how well anti-Jewish slogans were suited as an ideological foundation for the theory of total power and how useful they could be in a practical attack on the bourgeois state. Hitler based his theory of power on the concept of an elite—but the qualification for this elite was to be naked, unthinking brutality. So that the German nation could trample down all other nations in its way, it was necessary to put at the head of the German state those individuals who were best qualified and most eager to trample down their gentler, more decent, and more conscientious fellow citizens. Such murderous brutality, however, needed to be practiced, because only in practical competition was it possible to select the most virulent and those with the strongest elbows.

The best scope for bestiality was offered in the thuggery of political meetings and in the fight against the Jews. The defenseless Jews, who in themselves perform no specific, important function in the state or in society but are spread over all professions, were an ideal subject on which to demonstrate that vile quality which Hitler liked to call "toughness". To trample down the defenseless requires no more than to overcome natural inhibitions of conscience, and a resolute emancipation from all principles of morality and humanitarian feelings. Whoever committed the greatest brutalities against the Jews was fit for Hitler's "millennial *Reich*"—indeed, a diabolically rational and safe method of selection. Hitler himself said that he regarded it as his main mission to pass like a magnet over the German people, extracting from its ranks every bit of iron they contained. From these bits of iron he built up his elite and showed the world on what principles political action for the establishment and enforcement of total power must be founded.

This is where National Socialist and communist totalitarianism differ from one another. To National Socialism, totalitarianism was the final aim, the be-all and end-all of everything, an absolute value in itself. It was the only guarantee of national survival in the natural struggle for existence which, as Hitler never tired of saying, was a thoroughly amoral phenomenon. In the communist doctrine on the other hand, totalitarianism is no more than a means to an end. Its final goal is humanitarian, in that it aims at a society which is free from exploitation. This is where there is a crack in the communist doctrine, because to apply an inhuman method—indispensable throughout—in order to attain a lasting humanitarian state, is self-contradictory. The only result of such procedure can be to make the inhumanity of the means prevail over the humanitarian ends, finally and irrevocably destroying them.

There is, therefore, an inescapable link between the principle of freedom and the practical possibility of attaining a humanitarian state of affairs. Conversely, there is an inescapable link between the principle of the unlimited concentration of political power—of absolute subordination—and the ruin of any prospect for man to have dignified and fraternal dealings with man. Power corrupts, and absolute power corrupts absolutely.

The Misunderstood Idea of Freedom

In this context we must recall the remarkable misunderstanding to which the political and civic idea of freedom has been exposed in German philosophical tradition. Our philosophers and political thinkers have regarded the concept of freedom far more as a moral and religious one than as a social or political one. Socially and politically, freedom means that man shall have an objective margin for his actions. Such a concept of freedom does not in any way fail to realize that freedom is as much subject to abuse as are authority and force, and it realizes that in choosing between freedom and force we must decide whether we would rather accept an inescapable abuse of freedom or an inescapable abuse of force. We decide in favor of freedom because man, if he has no power worth mentioning over his equals, is much more effectively prevented from making abuse of his freedom, since he inescapably depends on his equally powerless fellow citizens, than is the possessor of uncontrolled power, against the excesses of whose insolence there is no remedy at all.

A society or state founded upon domination is full of intolerable temptation: the dependence of man on the individual discretion of man is the most dangerous of all human relationships. Where, on the other hand, man depends on the existence, the acting and planning of his fellow citizens in a society founded upon coordination, human relations rest upon the principle of equal chances for all; even when, as is regularly the case, the equality of chances cannot be safeguarded, the exploitation and enslavement of man by man is far more effectively restricted. Free societies live under the motto: "Lead us not into temptation. Lord, have mercy upon us sinners!"

Laws, Not Man, Shall Govern

How, then, is cooperation in society to be directed in a community based on coordination and equality before the law? Happily, there is a most effective and magnificent solution which can be applied, not to all, but to the most important social and political spheres of life: the indirect guidance of individual human behavior by the law—binding, calculated to last, and equal for all, such as, for instance, our system of private law. Laws, not man shall govern. This sort of opposition to authority goes back to Aristotle. It is one of the most splendid principles for the formation of social and political life. Consequently, all free constitutions tend toward the rule of law and away from the rule of discretion.

However, such a decision involves some sacrifice. Certain monumental projects cannot be realized, or at least not half as effectively realized, in a society based on freedom as they can in a totalitarian state. But then, nothing in this world is gratis.

Thus, we find that at bottom the struggle between domination and freedom is a struggle between two different kinds of men. In a free society, the type of man who will assert himself is not the same as in a totalitarian order. But much in the state and society depends on the sort of person who can rise to the top. Here, we have the fundamental difference between individuals and states or nations. In his actions, the individual follows his own inherent laws under which he is judged—good or evil go to his personal account. The behavior of a state or nation, on the other hand, is determined by that group of individuals which asserts itself in the struggle with other groups of individuals.

This means, however, that if we want anti-Semitism and bestiality to be deprived of any effective power amongst us, it will not be sufficient to educate others and ourselves to humanitarian principles and brotherly love; we must also see to it that those who have made these principles their own shall assert themselves politically in their state and society, and shall use their influence to mould these in such a way as to set real limits to any kind of force, to allow freedom its full scope, to honor the law, to improve it, and thus to remove not only the desire but also the facilities for torture, oppression, and man's degradation of his fellow man.

Therefore, in this week of brotherly love, we cannot content ourselves with an appeal to be harmless as doves; in political and social life we are forced to obey that other commandment also: Be ye wise as serpents!

Dr. Franz Boehm was born in Constance in 1895. He is professor of law at the University of Frankfort. Dr. Boehm is a member of the *Bundestag* (Christian Democratic Union). From 1945—46 he was minister of education in Hesse. 1952 he headed the German delegation that negotiated reparation agreements with Israel and the Jewish world organizations.

The "Psychopathology" of Nazidom *

Mr. Astor's Proposals for a Study Center

A proposal to establish a center of study of the "political psychopathology" of the Nazi era was put forward by the Editor of the London *Sunday Observer,* the Hon. David Astor, in an address delivered at a Warsaw Ghetto Memorial meeting in London on April 29, 1962. Such a center, Mr. Astor thinks, can be "based on the Parkes and the Wiener Libraries". Its terms of reference should be "the fate of the Jews as one example, albeit by far the worst, of a widespread human phenomenon, namely, man's capacity to destroy his fellow beings without rational motive."

Mr. Astor cites four reasons why research should not be confined to the persecution of Jewry:

"First, this wider view corresponds with the truth—there have been other exterminations, and mass exterminations are themselves related to all lesser killings.

"Second, to study the lesser examples together with the greater will make easier the investigation of the greater. If you understand the processes which produce a lynching, you are more likely to be able to fathom the processes which underlie the greater perversions of moral sense.

"Third, this wider study is more likely to prepare us and our children to detect future symptoms of this disease, in whatever form they may appear.

"Fourth—and perhaps the most fundamental reason for studying these atrocities as a latent possibility in all mankind—this approach brings us squarely up against our own difficulty in coming to terms with these facts. Unless we dare to study these events as something that was done by ordinary people like ourselves, we may continue to be paralyzed and remain unable to study them at all."

Mr. Astor rejects the "belief that inhumanity and perverted morality are something which belong particularly to one category of the human race, namely, the Germans." That belief, he says, is "as intellectually false and stultifying as anti-Semitism itself."

The "utmost importance" is to be attached to an understanding of "the fatal, fearful process of thought which makes people feel, not only justified, but that they have a duty to destroy others." If the events of the past have not hitherto been "studied academically to the extent that they so obviously deserve," it was because "we cannot quite believe that these

*) From *The Wiener Library Bulletin,* July 1962, No. 3.

events really happened. We know they happened, and yet they seem to us impossible, incredible."

And now, Mr. Astor continues, "we cannot tell what may next excite this process of mass psychology. Its next form may not be racial or religious, but political (as has happened before in times of revolution or civil war). The world situation of today is, as we all know, dominated by the rivalry of two ideologies. There are people on each side who believe that all the world's troubles stem from one small but powerful category of person (in one case, capitalists, in the other case, Communists); that this small category constitutes a threatening, secretive, world-wide conspiracy aiming primarily at their debasement or destruction; and that after the elimination of that category (whether it be the bourgeoisie or the Communists) all would be well.

"These strongly held views, which imply a 'devil' class among men, and the perverted moral attitudes which this produces, contain an emotional element that resembles the way of thinking we find in anti-Semitism. Whether civilization itself will be destroyed may depend on whether too many people in either ideological camp impose on to the actual political and economic rivalry this emotional fantasy view of the 'devilish' character of the other camp—and therefore cease to be able to see them as fellow human beings."

While this was "not the only possible cause of future manifestations of the pathological destructive process," nevertheless, Mr. Astor writes, "it is the largest and the most imminent," and it should be "as closely studied as the scourge of cancer."

War Letters of German Jews Who Fell in Battle*

An Introductory Word to the Republication of the Book by the German Minister of Defense, Franz Josef Strauss

The phenomenon of anti-Semitism strikes young Germans as being historical and very abstract. Therefore—as convincing as it might be—whatever must unfortunately still be said against anti-Semitism, affects them only theoretically. The young people need to be removed from the theoretical and confronted with the sources and realities. The anti-Semites held abstruse prejudices on the relationship of the Jews to soldiery. The young people look at the armed forces of Israel and behold one of the bravest and strongest armies of the present day. And now they can also study another historical source, namely, the war letters of German Jews who fell in battle during the First World War, which have been re-edited by the Ministry of Defense and brought out by the Seewald Publishing House in Stuttgart-Degerloch. (135 pages, DM 9.80, middle September.) The Minister of Defense has stated the reasons for this publication as being the expressed desire of the Armed Forces in a foreword, which itself belongs to the above-mentioned "theory", but is nevertheless a document of the times.

* * *

There are three reasons which have moved me to have this book republished. First of all, the desire to help put the picture of the Jewish citizen and soldier in Germany, that was infamously distorted by the Nazis, back in its right place.

I fully accept the reproach that I set myself an all too simple goal, since actually my intention here is quite modest alongside the great problem of anti-Semitism and its consequent horrors. However, in my opinion, clever observations on Judaism are of little use for people into whose heads a malicious propaganda machine has for years tried to pound inhumaneness in the form of racial hatred.

The planting of an inhumane hatred that would extend beyond the length of their lives and reign was the explicit intention of Hitler and his cohorts. The totalitarians devised early the method of actualizing feelings against individuals and groups of people with the ultimate aim of destroying human mercy, tearing the bonds of neighborly love, mocking the respect for human values, for the equality of guilt and responsibility before God, dissolving the bonds between men, and, finally, of ruling over them with iron-hard terror. All devices of propaganda were put into operation with the objective of robbing the victim of name, esteem, and honor.

---

*) From *Frankfurter Allgemeine Zeitung*, August 30, 1961.

In Good Faith in the Fatherland

Thus, the Jewish citizen was marked and listed. He was no longer a human being, no longer God's image. He was stamped as a subhuman being, a nonhuman being, marked with a branding iron similar to that which a meat inspector in a slaughterhouse uses. Man was degraded into a thing, an amusement piece for concentration camp guards, into raw material for the ultradimensional death machinery. The systematization by which each individual would be exterminated, was well thought out. All rights in the community were abolished, the right to be a human being among other human beings was objected to and denied.

With terrible precision, the process proceeded and in the end, it was all too easily forgotten how it had actually begun; namely, with the defacement of a concept of man through the aid of a principle radically opposite to the words: "God created man in His own image". Always and everywhere, it was and remained the intention of the totalitarians to demonstrate the full valuelessness and uselessness of a human life.

The war letters of German Jews who died in the war show us another situation. They present us with a generation of fellow Jewish citizens who, in their deportment, attitudes, and patriotism, were children of their age. At times for our feelings somewhat too pathetic, they were filled with pride and a belligerent enthusiasm for the national state, fired by a patriotism whose set goals strike us as strangely foreign and which can only be understood in its own historical setting.

One hundred thousand men of Jewish faith and origin wore the gray uniform of the German *Reich,* more than a third of them were decorated, 2,000 were officers, 1,200 military doctors and officials. On the battle field and with good faith in the fatherland, 12,000 Jewish soldiers fell. The youngest volunteer of the war, Josef Zippes, fourteen years old, was also a Jew as was one of the first recipients of the *Pour-Le-Mérite* in the German air corps, Wilhelm Frankl.

Frankl died during an air battle in 1917. Twenty years later, his name on the list of the *Pour-Le Mérite* holders was not to be found. It was eradicated, because Jews, according to the official view of the Hitler *Reich,* cannot be brave, they may not even have—as crazy as it sounds—died for Germany's sake. The names of those who died in battle, as the National Socialists wanted, had to disappear from all memorials. Himmler also let loose his terror on the Jewish veterans of the front lines, chased them across the border, had them thrown into concentration camps, Jewish camps, ghettos, and gas chambers, and without hesitation shot them down.

All this supports the argument that Hitler did to the Jewish veterans of the front nothing more or less than to millions of Jews wherever he could lay hands on them. But what should a thin volume of their war letters mean, especially for our recognition of the atrocities?

The Deceptive, Brutal Question

This question hits upon the second reason which encouraged me to have this volume republished. The horror of the mass murdering of the Jews and other peoples, the massive degree to which the criminals operated, evades human imagination and, thereby, sympathy. It is a part of the methods characteristic of modern totalitarian rule that their mad acts and lies rise to great dimensions—the Nazis never hesitated to boast publicly about it all—which not even the wildest phantasy can follow. It distorts the perspective of the observer. Yes, it could occur that as soon as he is incapable of seeing the insanity in the predicaments of the totalitarians, it is the murdered and not the murderer who is guilty. He may, blinded by the sight of such horrific homicide, make way for the brutal question: What must these people have done to deserve such punishment? To reach this effect, was a professed goal of Hitler.

Although it cannot satisfy me that the history of humanity can be almost exclusively measured on the yardstick of battles, I am aware of the depth of the furrows which the course of two great sacrifices on the battlefields have dug deep on the souls of today's living generations. With the publication of these war letters, I should like to direct a look at a section of the evil results that is conceivable by the human mind, and because I believe in the conviction of every person and nation that the thanklessness of the fatherland towards its frontline veterans has certain definite limitations, if by the concept ingratitude—which is sometimes used in a cheap sense—that which has been done to the German Jewish soldiers can at all be explained.

They believed, as they first began to perceive Hitler's terror, it to be a misunderstanding, a terrible error, which like all errors would be clarified. Actually, however, their fate had already been decided. But like other Germans, they were psychologically unprepared for the methods of the totalitarian politics and, therefore, unsuspecting and bewildered. They believed in and judged according to the usual moral standards—until they were taught a worse one.

Nothing, but nothing at all, could hinder the totalitarians from their cold-blooded plans, neither the sacrifice of those fallen in battle nor the proved love for the fatherland, nor the loyalty to the state, not even the political, economic or military expediences.

The open inexpediency of the governmental measures seems to me to be the characteristic of the totalitarian state form. The persecution of loyal people, the eradication of the names of those killed in battle on monuments, the refusal during the war to print special identification cards for handicapped Jewish veterans from the front, the transporting of Jewish victims at a time when the cars of *Reich's* railroad were not sufficient for the fighting troops—this all bears the stamp of irrationality and consistent madness. Hitler went so far as to say at one of his after dinner speeches that he would, in event of victory, "be rigorously of the viewpoint that he would destroy every city that harbored any Jews".

This is not a case, as many gullible persons believe, of a statement by a lunatic, but a systematic formulation by a totalitarian ruler who inaugurated new and horrible laws, who—in spite of nationalistic phrases—dealt anationalistically in a fully consistent manner, and made special troops of his conviction appear in their own country like foreign conquerors.

Of course, on the surface, Hitler seemed to annihilate one single nation, but others were to follow, political opponents and his own followers, even whole ranks of the hierarchy. Thus, this system desired to satisfy itself with the above-mentioned defacement of the concept of man, but cold-bloodedly goes a step further, in order to realize the opposite principle of the Augustinian thesis which reads, "initium ut esset, creatus est homo"—in order to have a beginning, man was created.

They Belong to the History of the Army

Not one of those German Jews who fell in battle, and whose letters have been collected in this volume, could have suspected that such a form of government would descend on Germany. They died for the homeland, their fatherland, and many in the hope of a better future for Germany and for the Jews in Germany. In my opinion, their fate, their death, their hope insolubly belong to the history of the German army. This is the third reason which occasioned my having this book brought out anew. It is necessary to understand the fate of the German Jewish soldiers, their loyalty to the homeland, their bravery in battle, all as a part of the tradition of the armed forces. To this belongs also the course of their suffering which the totalitarians, who set up camp in Germany for twelve years, prepared for them.

These war letters were published in 1935, a date which clearly indicates what was about then. Probably it was the last attempt to shake the conscience of the rulers in this way, to oppose the anti-Jewish propaganda, and to dull the so-called "Aryan paragraphs" of the forthcoming Nuremberg Laws.

Indeed, these war letters were an astounding proof for the patriotic standing of the German Jews and a crushing counterevidence against the Nazi propaganda, which tried to present the Jewish citizen as cowardly, corrupt, and traitorous by nature. Alone by the title of the book, the National Socialists felt disturbed. They demanded a change in the title because "it presented a desecration of the wisdom of the German nation". In the Nuremberg Laws, which appeared half a year later than the first edition of the war letters, all special regulations pertaining to the German Jewish veterans who were on the front, which Hindenburg put through in 1933, were dropped. From then on, the Jews in Germany were made victims of a system, were ostracized from the body social, and as human beings declassified.

Himmler, in whose hands the power of capture and liquidation lay, announced then to his troops that humanity weakens the backbone. Of course, there were exceptions in Germany, great acts of helpfulness, of brotherly love, of humanity. In this sense, the *Bundeswehr* seeks its way. The war letters of German Jewish soldiers who died during the war should therefore serve as a warning against evil, against racial-hatred, and against modern totalitarian forms of government, and as an example of love for the fatherland, greatness in suffering, and loyalty.

Not Interested in Poltics?*

By Walter Jaide**

Before one can draw a picture of the real facts of a matter—like the political attitude of present-day youth—one should first state how one has arrived at these results, that is to say, one must first discuss the scientific methods which have been employed, at least with the aid of a few indispensable preliminary remarks.

Firstly, no questionnaires were sent out and no school essays were gathered. There were no formal interviews in the form of a general poll of opinion. Rather, young people were thoroughly questioned, that is to say, they were drawn into an individual conversation that was moreover prepared, pliant, elastically directed, informative, and repetitive, and in which there was ample opportunity for open discussion.

Secondly, these explorative discussions with the young people were not only held on political questions, but also on important daily problems which interest them like religion and how to spend one's own free time. From this point of departure, a total picture of the actual attitude of each young person toward the class room, school, apprenticeship, the family, etc., could be dealt with. Otherwise, it would not be worthwhile to gain only a simple remark unqualified by a context. An illustrative example of this is the following case:

A rather passive, colorless pupil in the intermediate school complained in the discussion that he had to participate in a class trip to the Mosel River. There one had to walk, God knows where, sometimes up a mountain, then down the mountain, for absolutely no reason. He would have preferred to remain home. This student wrote the following in a school essay:

> I have great sympathy for people who have to emigrate from their fatherland, because they want to be free, and I would fight with all my strength that Germany would be united once again in freedom.

In that the following quotations are given, they have been continuously selected with respect to the credibility and honesty on the part of the individual pupil.

Thirdly, one cannot, of course, investigate a great number of pupils with such a monographic method, but one can select the young people carefully and strive for a good coverage, that is to say, to select students in a re-

*) From *Aus Politik und Zeitgeschichte* (Politics and Contemporary History), a supplement of the weekly *Das Parlament*, November 30, 1960. The following study on the political attitudes of today's youth in Lower Saxony, Bremen, and Hamburg and its results are printed here with the kind permission of the German Bureau of Youth Affairs.

**) The author, Dr. Walter Jaide, is a professor of sociology at the College of Education at Hanover, Germany.

presentative cross section: from both sexes, gifted as well as less gifted pupils, the shy and the talkative, those from towns, those from small, medium-sized, and large cities, pupils from primary, vocational, intermediate, and high schools. One can limit oneself to a not too broad an age group and to a definite locality, in order to cover the breadth of differing opinions within this classification.

This is what was done. About 550 young people born between 1941 and 1944 (i.e., 15 to 18 year-olds from Lower Saxony, Bremen, and Hamburg) were drawn into such discussions, or rather, were asked to take part in them between October 1958 to April 1960, at the request of the German Bureau of Youth Affairs in Bonn. And I can say, moreover, that these young people took an interest in the talks and provided information as if it were their own enterprise through open and willing participation, even collaborated.

Fourthly, in the frame of this investigation, reproductions of pictures and many catchwords were laid before the young participants. These devices were to free the examinees and examiners from the all too direct relationship present in an examination situation, to allow for as free a play of thought as possible for the young people, and to avoid any direct influence whatsoever. There were fourteen reproductions of pictures, as listed below.

1. "Boy with a beggar's bag", (Photo: "Family of Man" Exhibition*);
2. "Expulsion from the Warsaw Ghetto", (*Ibid.*);
3. "Bread" by Kaethe Kollwitz;
4. "Proclamation of the *Reich*" by Werner;
5. "Mother with a crying child" (Photo: *ibid.*);
6. "Prayer at Table" by Uhde;
7. "Nest egg" by Dieter;
8. "The Holy Family" by Correggio;
9. "Crucifix" by Ernst Barlach;
10. "Jazz Hall" (Photo: *ibid.*);
11. "Wanderers" (Photo);
12. "Look into the Valley" by Ludwig Thoma;
13. "Working Women" (Photo: *ibid.*);
14. "Workers by an Oil pump" (Photo: Esso Archives).

And in addition there were forty-one catchwords arranged in four groups.

1. Jesus; *The Holy Bible;* "The Ten Commandments"; Rome; Lourdes; Luther; Confirmation;
2. Bismarck; Hitler; Gandhi; Tito; The U. N.; Russia; Potsdam; Hiroshima; Berlin; 20th July, 1944; 17th June, 1953; Algeria;
3. 1st of May; Labor Unions; Five-day week; Home and car; Unemployment; School; Equality of the sexes; Nitrite poisoning; Brussels, 1958;
4. Henri Dunan (German Red Cross); Albert Schweitzer; Porsche; Fritz Walter*); Marina Vlady; Soraya; Hobbies; Hollywood; Trip to Italy; "Take it easy".

Presented with these pictures and catchwords, the young person was then asked to choose three pictures (according to theme—irrespective of the manner of presentation and reproduction) as well as one catchword out of

*) These pictures appeared in book form under the same title, published by the Metropolitan Museum of Art, New York.
*) A German football player.

each group of catchwords which he would like to discuss with the examiner. In this way, relatively uninhibited and informative discussions arose which either expanded dialogically, deepened exploratively or simply gave the young people an opportunity to express themselves. The questions were not about Hitler or Bismarck. Only he who had himself chosen such a catchword or picture uttered his opinion on that subject. Such revelations must more or less have the character of a natural, unmanipulated, serious, and personal response; and that was the main point here.

I must, however, refrain here from closer description of the problems and nature of the investigation. Nevertheless, I should like to make the methodological preference for oral and direct individual meetings between the young people and the examiners more understandable with the aid of linguistic and psychological arguments and experience.

In every poll of opinion (which is directed moreover not only towards mere contexts, but towards attitudes and motives as well), the linguistic formulation plays a very important role. If one, for example, would ask (as has happened) are you "interested" in "politics". Is there an "idea" for which you would be very "enthusiastic", one would have to take into consideration that such terminology not only has various meanings and value judgments, but that even the accompanying sound of an out-worn platitudinous voice will influence the answer considerably and uncontrollaby. Even the word "politics" is, of course, not free of prejudice and is regarded by many as a bone of party contention or as a belligerent sign of might and is, therefore, avoided. "To be able to change something", that is to say, to exert an influence on politics, is, in such terse formulations, understandably conceived of as a managerical operation taking place in a huge, mammoth organization beyond the radius of personal influence or responsibility—similar to a "social reformer". The selective casting of one's vote, as such, is not widely evaluated as a possibility for the individual to exert his will on the issues at hand. But on the other hand, we can broach upon the general, unconscious educational pretentions of pupils (Are you interested in . . .?) and thereby harvest many praiseworthy, but not very seriously meant *clichés,* or the rejections of the pupils directed against the much disliked school subject "history" and noncurrent political relationships. A questionnaire does not have any classification for the shaking of heads, shrugging of shoulders or a solicitous nodding of the head.

However, when such words pregnant with meaning like *"Reich"*, "nation", "Fatherland" or "We Germans" were used without commentary in the interview, answers were given that did not refer to the questions as such, but to a contemporary coinage and the resulting usage of language. Even questions testing the political knowledge of the influence, the mechanics, legal basis, and apparatus of legislation and administration, control and the judiciary were (of course) insufficiently answered.

Through all this, one still does not gain an adequate picture of the real interest of the young people in current events. In our investigation, a somewhat fruitful approach among others developed out of the preferences and commentaries made with reference to the (above-mentioned) pictures and catchwords.

Next, the selection as such and as made by the young people yielded a remarkable result: among the reproductions—aside from the particular interests of specific age groups (jazz, hiking groups)—exactly those were chosen which had a politically or socio-politically stimulating context.

Boy with a beggar's bag;
"Bread" by Kaethe Kollwitz;
The Warsaw Ghetto.

The hardly avoidable range in the impressiveness of the reproductions was certainly not decisive.

From among the catchwords of political import, the most problematical were equally well preferred.

Hitler;
20th July, 1944;
Hiroshima;
(furthermore, Algeria and Bismarck).

Even if one takes into consideration that a certain preliminary decision had already been made by the examiner in the selection of the pictures and catchwords presented, the attitude of the young people did not remain fully spontaneous; it cannot be denied that at least a third of these 550 young people did not at all beg the issue when answering the most exciting, unsolved, difficult political questions.

> No, why shouldn't we look at something depressing ("Bread" by Kollwitz)? We shouldn't shut our eyes to misery. Such things are not so well-known, but they exist. For this reason, they move us so powerfully. (m)*)
>
> Hitler killed innocent women and children, and similarly annihilated the Jews. One cannot often enough make reference to this fact, and we must see to it with all the means at our disposal that it will never again come to such a ridiculous war. (f)
>
> I do not at all understand this "without-me" type. This attitude is basically wrong. If all mankind would think in this way, there would be a concentration of power which could have unpleasant results. Democracy is only for those people who are mature enough for it. This cannot be said of Germany. Even the party system in Germany is not on the right road. Healthy opposition makes the soup of politics spicy. (m)

The often-cited dodging of problems, alienation, indifference or laziness do seem to characterize the attitude of the younger generation. But one should not characterize them this way; there is much too much that indicates the opposite. Actually, I am of the opinion (and in this connection it can unfortunately not be more fully grounded) that a generation of a new special sort will develop out of these seventeen-year-olds and bear another designation other than Schelsky's*) "sceptical generation".

Of course, noncommittal movie sentimentality or schoolboy industriousness may be mistaken for active political interest. However, this is contradicted by the responses of the young people to the above-mentioned topics as well as to the remaining subjects of the interview. These young people had a lot of information at their disposal and they demonstrated —aside from the very naive and the disinterested—a healthy, uninhibited

*) The sex of the interviewee will be hereafter identified with "m" for masculine and "f" for feminine.

*) Helmut Schelsky, professor of sociology at the University of Muenster. The German coinage is *skeptische Generation.*

sympathy for the represented misery and horribleness. In addition, they have certain acceptable but unconscious basic ideas and maxims, and make the effort to arrive at an unprejudiced and well-weighed judgment.

I should like to give a detailed presentation of our findings (on the basis of the information supplied by the young people) and, moreover, in relationship to four interrelated topics:

The Race Problem (i.e., the Jews);
Hitler and National Socialism;
Bismarck and Nationalism;
Democracy or Authoritarianism.

1. It is the first subtopic which I should like to deal with here, because it is exactly the picture of the Ghetto which was so often chosen and proved to be a rather fruitful subject of discussion. It allowed us to draw important conclusions from the political attitude of the young persons interviewed because the condemnation of Hitler draws its strongest arguments and emotional impact from the persecution of the Jews.

Only a minority of the young people remained indifferent to the "Jewish Problem" as shown in answers such as:

> . . . it is all the same to me . . . don't know any Jews . . . can understand why it isn't discussed in school . . . it took place too long ago and much too much has already been said about it . . . one should know about it, but it doesn't interest me.

The majority took a decided position and not with—please note, statistically demonstrated—passionate participation and indignation. They spoke of uncontrolled discrimination, extreme hatred, blind obedience, inhumane misuse of power, cruelty towards the defenseless, fright-toleration of injustice, as well as expiation and reparations.

> Didn't any one really know about it? That is the most tragic chapter in German history. Next to slavery, there is nothing nearly so bad. Such madness should never again be tolerated. We have dirtied our own hands. We shall have to bear this guilt for a long time and it cannot be made good by money. (m)

These great ills and crimes in the history of mankind—even for these young people—seem to be of continuous topical interest.

> Well, yes, the concentration camps were the greatest injustice that the German nation has ever saddled itself with. I find it terrible that even today the older generation says that they knew nothing about it all. They should admit their guilt . . . How many of them cooperated in order to get ahead? (f)

> The concentration camps were so well perfected that they were simply death machines. Something of this kind could only happen in a dictatorship. (m)

These young people have received their impressions and opinions through the newspapers, radio, youth forums, the instruction at school, *Night and Fog**), "Anne Frank", etc. They complained that they had not been taught about these matters in detail, because many grown-ups (parents and teachers) hush up the facts (out of a feeling of shame) or brush them aside with excuses.

---

*) German film on the Nazi reign of terror. Cf., "Mass Media" in Walter Stahl's *Education for Democracy in West Germany*, New York, 1961, especially p. 270 f.

Many of these young people—and this is probably typical of their generation—try spontaneously to incorporate the stimulating information into wider relationships, to compare them through retrospect and predictions, regarding their general significance and eternal value. Thus, with all their heart—be it out of religious, moral, humane, or political reasons—they condemn the persecution of the Jews in the rest of the world and, without being able to see the problem in its particulars and in proper perspective, protest against the racial discrimination in the United States, the Algerian policy of France, and moreover, against the *Apartheid* polity in the Union of South Africa. Without wanting to de-emphasize the bitter extent of the tragedy of the German Jews, they expect to see the problem of racial discrimination dealt with in all its depth, honestly, completely, and without tactical considerations. That is their right as young people and, in this respect, they are—thank God—as typical young people as there ever were.

> That is a great injustice in America. There, they are so proud of their Constitution and respect for the Rights of Man, but still such things happen there. (m)
>
> I believe that France has made a grave error by granting some countries their freedom on the one hand, but carrying on a many years' war against Algeria on the other. One day they will have to give in anyway, if they don't want to lose the respect of the world. (f)

Only a small group, in proceeding from this tendency to a many-sided perspective of the problem, falls into the danger of erring. Their members accept somewhat rashly the argument that the Germans under Hitler's dictatorship were ignorant of everything and should not bear the responsibility for it. Reparations should be made only within small bounds. They suppose that the Jews should be accused of complicity, should persecution of them arise again and again in the world—since the young people tend on their part to seek a balancing of accounts—and they say further that the Jews held unproportionally high positions of influence, possessed too much wealth, and held too much power in professional spheres. Despite this, they judge the annihilation of the Jews as inhumane, crazy or at least stupid. They also show no sympathy for Nazi biological theories.

> I should not like to discuss it further, because I have heard too many different things about it. One cannot make one man alone responsible for all that. I should like to say that we all should try to right this wrong. No one person alone has the right to judge over others. (f)

Only four out of 550—and it would speak against the credibility of this investigation if such exceptions did not appear—admitted having anti-Semitic attitudes.

> Jews are parasites. (m)
>
> That which was done in the Ghetto was right. One had to act against these people and, once and for all, make a clean bill of affairs. (m)
>
> Hitler had to kill the Jews because they were of a different opinion than his own and in wartime all people must be united. Reparations are not necessary. The Jews are not so badly off today. (m)

I do not believe that these four youths are the spokesmen of a secret, silent minority, or even of a larger group or body. They are exceptions and lone wolves; and it would not be natural if such were not also to be found. It is not from an underground, unhealed, and infected cell, that the personal political views of the young people are in danger, but much more blatantly from the happenings in the United States, Algeria, and in South Africa. In conformity with this, the recent swastika smearings are considered by the majority of the young people as the stupidities of lone wolves and as having no political bases.

> It was only through its treatment by radio and press that this individual case became so well-known and important. (m)

2. The decisive, believable, and not unskillful rejection of Hitler and National Socialism also prevails and draws its strongest argument from his annihilation of the Jews. Furthermore, Hitler, in their opinion—himself sick, extremistic, burning with hate, ecstatic, psychopathic—awakened in his hearers latent, murderous instincts and made use of them for his mad racial theories. The next important argument against him was his demonic greed for power, which resulted in an extravagant claim for "living space" and in a foolishly directed war. Why, it is (schoolboyishly?) asked, had the German people not read *Mein Kampf,* in which Hitler laid bare his aims and revealed his fanaticism? It is not understandable how this "devil" could have received votes, applause, and confidence—even devotion—from the German people.

> How could he draw an entire people into his web? How could one believe him everything? I find it hard to believe that nothing of his deeds trickled down to the masses. The mysterious disappearing of people could not have gone unnoticed. (f)

> The attitude of the grown-ups today is ridiculous. They should admit that they really took part and that they were deceived. (f)

> He demanded that one should continue fighting, although he knew that it was impossible to do so. Like a coward, he took his own life. And this man was supposed to be a model for and a leader of his people. I am astonished that so few people tried to put an end to the needless sacrifice of human life. They certainly did not know how they as individuals could fight against this. (m)

> Hitler was to blame for the war . . . intellectually speaking he was not much to brag about and earlier he was lazy and possessed rather confused political ideas . . . even more terrible than the war was his race-theory. His real goal was the power as such. He advocated disarmament in order to conquer Europe and achieve control of the world. Hitler's greed for power and hatred of the Jews were characteristic of him, and these intoxicated him. In a regular profession, he would not have progressed far. He spoke enthusiastically, not logically, but in metaphores, and he believed them himself to the very end. (m)

These young people show neither agnosticism nor defeatism, but ask clear questions and sum them up against tyranny, deprivation of rights, and mass murder.

With respect to this topic, there was a larger group than was the case with the race question which did not (at first) want to accept the theory that Hitler was the sole criminal, the absolute scoundrel. Because they felt themselves bound to the principle of historical objectivity and to the still incomplete research on the era, they wanted to pursue a broad and many-sided interpretation of the German catastrophy. A certain reservation on the part of the young people against the instruction of the grown-ups

("They don't tell us everything; we only hear of the negative aspects") plays a role as well as the praiseworthy tendency gradually to reach a well-weighed judgment. One should not hold this against the group because it is even rather difficult for a mature person to accept the idea that a whole nation could be deceived by a single criminal as a decisive factor in an entire epoch of history. However, some of these young people would like to see the historical events presented less seriously than they actually were.

This group as a whole strove to find other explanations and men responsible for the Nazi era and therefore took the following into consideration: the political and economic crises of Germany previous to 1933; the "inability" of the earlier governments; the reparation claims of the Allies; the misery resulting from the unemployment of five million men and women; the supposed "power" of the Jews; the frivolity of the reactionary, bourgeois classes, of big industry, and of the armed forces, all of whom believed in Hitler and wanted to make use of him for their own ends, but were themselves misused by him. These young people also take into account Hitler's agitatory talent (he "spoke" to the masses) and the susceptibility of the people to it.

> One should not make Hitler the scapegoat for everything. Almost every one voted for and followed him enthusiastically. They thought him to be the miracle-worker, the one who always succeeded, who relieved them of their responsibility. By means of his rhetorical powers he convinced the people of his supposed good intensions and they followed him blindly . . . my parents say that he also did some good: he built the *Autobahnen* and solved the problem of unemployment. Probably he gradually became insane just like Napoleon. (f)

Methods such as the apparently legal seizure of power, the influencing of public opinion by means of modern mass media are probably still beyond the comprehension of these young people.

> His speeches were fascinating; he knew how to appeal to the masses. In Germany, governmental failures were daily events. Suddenly success waxed on the horizon. The youth was filled with enthusiasm and was carried away with the combative spirit. Hitler arose out of the lowest social class and must have been moved by an immensely strong, inner power because he went on fighting long after his defeat at the *Feldherrenhalle**). (m)

> They were all in favor of it. He himself could not have anticipated what was to follow. The applause he received made a megalomaniac of him. (m)

> In *Mein Kampf,* Hitler wanted to warn everyone about his own demonic nature. (f)

From this standpoint, it is not a long way from the creation of a legend, which (in a crass and rather fairytale-like formulation) says that Hitler was:

> partly good, partly bad;
> theoretically sound, methodically bad;
> at first good, later on bad.

He also did much good: the abolishment of unemployment and punishment of sexual criminals, construction of the *Autobahnen* and *Volksempfaen-*

---

*) Refers to the *putsch* in Munich, 1923.

*ger**), establishment of the *Arbeitsdienst***), and the reinstatement of Germany in the esteem of the world. He was an "idealist" and had rather good ideas in the beginning. But later on, he made many errors, turned out to be basically evil, and became insane and a mass murderer. The balance between legal and illegal, moral and criminal, which characterized the Nazi system, is for these seventeen-year-olds difficult to understand.

There are only a few voices—and this is also a sign of the frankness of these young people—which acknowledge, even admire Hitler.

> I admire the man, his power to convince and his talent to organize. The German nation is a gregarious animal and must be treated as such. How easily he duped them all! (m)
>
> To think of all the Nazis achieved! What Hitler succeeded in doing can be achieved by no one today. The way he defeated Russia, will never be equaled by the Yanks. He provided every one with a job. If he had not done that to the Jews what he did, he would have been just terrific. (m)

Also the number of the indifferent, the absolutely insecure or naive is relatively small although not as much so as was the case with the racial question.

> Hitler? A leader like Adenauer or any other. These people make politics. (m)
>
> Well, today that is a part of general education, but I am not interested in it. Then, one was not able to change anything and now it is all over anyway. (f)

Those in the middle group (with respect to both sets of questions), and as long as they did not tend to invent such silly stories, had two things in common with those who rejected with conviction. Firstly, there is a thorough knowledge of the facts, which is commendable. Secondly, a quite explicit reserve towards the partial, unweighed, opinionated theories of armchair politics, the indiscriminative generalization about all political opponents, the mere acceptance of what they are taught and otherwise get to hear and, lastly, a reserve towards an expedient conforming to it. And this is promising for the type and genesis of their political views, which may also be only the temporary import of the convictions of some of them.

To this also belongs the aversion to pathetic and contrite overaccentuations and exaggerations as well as apodictic reprimands, which are contrary to the language of these young people's generation, which rather inclines toward understatement. Just this hesitating, neither indifferent nor belittling nor intellectualizing, with which they want to form their opinion, is so captivating. Their political emotions do not seem to have become shallow, but much rather to be healthfully tempered.

> We want to form an unbiassed judgment and have always to hear nothing but rejection. (m)
>
> No pilgrimage to Belsen. (f)
>
> One ought to be nonpolitical. My parents are not yet able to be so and for our teachers some things are just too embarassing, but the young people are able. (m)

---

*) A small radio planned for the domestic market as was the *Volkswagen*.

**) A governmental employment agency that supplied the jobless with work, comparable with Roosevelt's W.P.A.

They do not want to overcome the past through loquacious and humiliating self-accusation before the tribunal of world opinion. They are certainly willing to recognize something like "collective guilt" but either something so broad that it includes all possible complicity or *entre nous* in the quiet intimacy of their own *(sit venia verbo)* fatherland!

From these points of view, it can be seen how sensitive we Germans really are when we have to identify ourselves with our historical destiny as a people, and the political implications of this destiny in the present day. It has to be respected that these young people take pains at all with these problems, and one has to help them with great care.

In this lies the root of the falsely called neonationalism of this age group. As young people, they are ashamed of and objective toward the fact that we as Germans comprise a living and cultural community which shares a common destiny. Within this body, we must overcome our history in which even Hitler was simply not a foreign element; and moreover, we must be objectively modest, tolerant, and honest so that we ourselves can accept this yoke of fate before having to do so in the presence of the outside world.

Therefore, it is not a matter of nationalism, but of a feeling that there is a basic element of life called "people"—and moreover, as a fact as well as a value. This basis of life can be incorporated into larger political bodies, it can also be viewed critically, but it cannot be annulled or defamed. In this sense, it is a problem of greater import. Many a fact, many a value has been subjected to many various coinings and appelations (i.e., "national heritage", "nation", "*Reich*") in the course of history and especially in recent history, and many an educator has accustomed himself to employ terminology variously and to misuse such value judgments irresponsibly. The young people have sent us the bill for this carelessness; they suspect that even a misused value remains a value, and that repeated failure to fulfill a cause does not make this cause ineffectual. On the contrary, it will be recognized by its indestructable core, it will be preserved and come to light again in the present. The Swiss, for example, also have a national feeling today which has absolutely nothing to do with militarism or authoritarism. It is, of course, of great importance for the political viewpoints of this rising generation to fill that with actual, living, progressive meaning which may be understood to be a healthy feeling of patriotism. so that it cannot grow wild like an unfulfilled cause, as, however, can be read in the pamphlets of the neo-Nazi youth groups.

A great many German journalists have twice sinned against our national sense of shame, namely, through their coverage of adolescent rowdiness and of the swastika-smearings.

3. The so-called neonationalism has a second root which may even attribute it with chauvinistic nuances. I came upon this through the comments of my interlocutors on the reproduction of the "Proclamation of the *Reich*" at Versailles as well as the catchword "Bismarck". Both of these were not infrequently selected and even the picture was—remarkably enough—more often selected than the catchword—on the whole less often by pupils than by apprentices.

Amongst the adolescents who commented freely, there were few who rejected "Bismarck" or the "Proclamation of the *Reich*" in 1871, because he had been against the workers, the voice of the people in governmental affairs, he had the celebration of the unification of Germany officiated of all places on French soil, and because such pomp is old-fashioned.

> I find the ado about the Kaiser silly and the way the tin soldiers stand about all dolled-up. I am entirely for democracy, not at all for the Empire, etc. I don't like the ostentatiousness of decorations, etc. I think it's terrible. Older people still hang on all that sort of stuff, but they also participated in all of that. It's foreign to us. It is almost idolatry. Even we girls would have to stand at attention. (f)

> Enthusiasm reigned after the victorious war . . . It makes a somewhat pompous impression and thereby the magnitude of its achievement is expressed. This aspect has a funny effect today. Complete enthusiasm for the Emperor . . . This epoch was closed by the First World War. The embodiment of the nation was the great army . . . I think democracy is better for us . . . A monarchy is old-fashioned. (m)

An equally small number was partly in favor, and partly not in favor, of the idea of a monarchy. The establishment of national unity, Social Security, and the institution of civil marriage were juxtaposed by the young people against the wars, the outlawing of socialism, and the authoritarianism of Bismarck; they extolled the advantages of democracy. Democracy is less costly than splendid monarchy. More than half of those who chose Bismarck-Versailles, however, was strongly attracted to him, even regarded him as a Messiah. For them, Bismarck is the ideal leader, the Man, the genius, the savior, the successful hero in German history. His era is the *kairos,* the perfect, elevated, magnificent, brilliant, happiest epoch of our history, yes, for them Bismarck is even a Barbarossa, who must return to settle the present predicament as the Iron Chancellor; he would be better, even more elastic and simultaneouly more vital than Adenauer (not to mention the SPD*), and could also have coped with the case of Hitler and his intentions in a fitting way and who, even today, could and should lead an individual and authoritarian government.

> Since Bismarck's time, we have not had any of those successes which marked his reign. (f)

> I can easily imagine Bismarck as a dictator because he thought everything through so correctly. (m)

> I would rather have a Bismarck today. He would govern Germany better economically and politically than our present leaders. He could make good treaties. He could be very useful for us today by balancing East and West. (m)

> I admire the real Prussia, but only the genuine one of Bismarck, and not that bourgeois, Wilhelminian Prussia. (m)

The myth of the Great Man who makes history and is carried on by the tide of his successes, is, as we see, still in full swing. Further elements of this frame of reference are the "manfulness" ("he knew what he wanted, pushed it through, and had no fear of war") for which such concepts as stature, honor, chivalry, discipline, comradeship as well as an interest in sensational coverage of state proceedings, which smack of the Sunday pictorial section, are typical.

> Power attracts me; the imperial uniform, the courtly atmosphere, the pomp, and the role of the Kaiser. Much more, it is honor which im-

*) "SPD" is the German abbreviation for the *Sozialdemokratische Partei Deutschlands,* the Social Democratic Party of Germany.

presses me as being the actual power. I would support something like that. But reason tells us that a good democracy is worth everything. (m)

It is a pity that we do not have anything more of this. The institution of the Guards in England is an eye opener. Something of this kind should be retained, just like old castles and cities. More tradition should be preserved. But politics should not let itself be influenced by this factor. (f)

This regression to former historical glory makes a play on national state pride, on England and de Gaulle. Many attacked the alleged laxity in questions of the reunification and clear-cut political intentions in Germany.

Such differences of opinion should not be overrated. Of course, for the adolescents, the supposed clearness and character in the Germany of those times with its definite successes and results are more congenial than a bureaucratic and managerical democracy. On the contrary; they show a reasonable tolerance, especially in current questions of topical interest. Of course, the division of school subjects plays a role here. Epochs and personages of history, which have been described thoroughly, "expertly", "enthusiastically", gain in greater importance as fixed subject matter or glorified reminiscences than the still unsolved problems of contemporary times. Contrary to this is their burning interest in the latter. Probably, in the case of many adolescents, this is due to their reaction to the all too eager effort on the part of the teachers to re-educate them, which presents Hitler as well as Wilhelm II and Bismarck as cancerous growths in German history that have to be extracted. This generation shows a definite resistance toward this sort of exaggeration. In this respect, they demonstrate a remarkable sense for the inescapability, peculiarity, and dignity of national history. A renunciation of the past or of one's own national heritage is alien and incomprehensible to them. This keeps the thought of reunification alive. It is balanced by the idea of a united Europe. This generation does not live in the immediate shadow of the German collapse.

One should also appreciate the fact that such comments testify to a justifiable need for political responsibility, emotion, and education, which could, under certain circumstances, degenerate into a not inconsiderable degree of sentimental romanticism and resentment, should our all too bare, prudish, colorless, and symbolless political life not satisfy the need in an appropriate way.

On the other hand, it should not be forgotten that these young people might misunderstand and fundamentally misapply historical continuity through a fixation toward the past. The question arises whether a qualified minority could not regard the German past as a myth, whereby Bismarck's role toward the German liberalism of his time would be forgotten. A certain prejudice against current events and future political responsibility results from this and is expressed in the tendency toward a pliable democracy, a moderate autocracy, and a constitutional monarchy, all of which were weighed and discussed seriously by this group. These tendencies grow not out of the soil of the Nazi past, but more out of the soil of the dreams of a German-Bismarck restoration. And in Germany this is not so comletely innocuous, because, after the Treaty of Versailles (1919), expectations of this nature also drove a portion of the bourgeois to Hitler as the possible or desirable restorer of the old power and glory. In the case of these young people who still cling to Bismarck, that task of education with respect to national feelings has obviously been neglected. It has certainly not been adequately discussed and made known to them that even in a European or world family of peoples one's own national character and life remain a reality and that therein one may strive for their appropriate existence and honorable prestige. For this reason, many of these young people err into an anachronistic and hypertrophical interpretation of these matters.

4. The attitude toward democracy as a form of government and legal order was made clear through our investigations in opposition to the chosen catchwords and pictures of misery and to the obligatory antitheses of autocracy and democracy. The adolescents praised legal order, personal liberty, freedom of fear, private property, material prosperity, individual disposal of free time, voluntary membership in youth organizations, freedom of the press, as well as participation of the people in governmental affairs, free discussion of political decisions, and independant opposition toward the government.

They emphasized the mistakes, the egoism, the questionable intelligence and superiority of a dictator, and they realized that many measures require a longer time for decision and fulfillment than in a dictatorship, as well as the moderate punishment of crime and criminals.

> Better the small weaknesses of democracy than the great errors of dictatorship. (m)

The broad free play of daily needs and personal choice of profession were taken so self-evidently that there is no need for comment. The representatives of this opinion were confronted with as large a middle group with critically differentiated opinions. They complained that freedom is not broad enough (or too seldom limited) as, on the one hand, in the case of the outlawing of the Communist Party, the abolition of the splinter groups and independent candidates, and the whip system ("nothing may be written against the Jews . . . one may say nothing about the Nazis . . . nothing good may be reported about the 'German Democratic Republic'"), and on the other hand, witch-hunting, exaggerations in the press, idolatry of the moviestars, and the laying bare of family scandals. Further, they criticized the tone of party controversies, the pedestrian speed of legislative and executive action, the laxity of the administration of justice, as well as the pompous and politically indifferent character of the German economic miracle. Some even doubted that every one has his own opinion in a democracy and values it. A part of these views could be characterized with the phrase "not too tolitarian, but authoritarian". They originate from the same young people who, starting from the dicussion on Bismarck, tended towards a reasonable autocracy under the right man, the real ruler and strong leadership, to line up Bismarck, Adenauer, Eisenhower, and even Franco and Khrushchev in the category. Other young people, who would like to combine the advantages of democracy and autocracy, wanted to avoid the party conflicts, misuse of freedom, and laxity in the political sphere. The people must maintain its influence through legally guaranteed polling, but during the term of office, somewhat in the sense of executive democracy—the strong man must hold the helm firmly in his hands, and he and his associates should not be too young—somewhat between forty and fifty years of age or older.

> The Old Man (Adenauer) rules. He has done a good job. Who knows whether any one else could have pulled us out of the mess. (m)
> It is good for the state when there is an emperor, especially for tradition's sake. He provides a conservative attitude. With uninterrupted monarchy, one knows what one has. The Hohenzollern, the Guelphs, the Hohenstauffen have legal claims. The Guelphs would be the best. (m)
> Reasonable dictatorship is better than this democracy. (m)
> Versailles has its effects on the present day. A monarchist, like myself, can be enthusiastic about it. The English are also monarchists. (m)

The number of the determined adherents of a dictatorship was, however, very small.

> I believe that one man should rule, who can, however, listen to the opinions of the people; but the participation of the people in a government only causes confusion. Every one seeks his own advantages. It is better when one person says what is to be done. (m)

Above all, the battle-preparedness of a dictatorship in the danger of war (of an atomic war) was stressed. Also, a very small group consisting of the naive and the indifferent answered the question in the following manner:

> I really don't know what democracy or a dictatorship is. Are we now living under a dictatorship or in a democracy? (f)
> Different countries, different customs. (m)
> One really should know for whom one votes. (f)

If I may once again sum up what to my mind are the dangers, disturbances, and confusion of the political opinions and principles of our present-day youth, it is in this generation that the uncongenial emotionalism of overcoming the Hitler years, through a lax romanticization of the Bismarck era at school, the daily failures of the "others" (USA, Algeria, and South Africa) and in the respective successes and failures of the two great political blocs and systems which are quite avidly followed by the younger generation. In addition to this are the problems of the political activity in the current form of German democracy.

Furthermore, we have to deal with the question whether enough information and direction are offered to these young people who, with so much sensitivity, interest, weighing and discriminatory effort to form their own opinion, show so much desire to do so. To what degree are the actual political happenings made accessible to them? And further, what is the extent to which such are made public to adults, and, especially, to the adolescents? Most people do not seem to be satisfied by this. Only a few make reference to schoolroom instruction, radio broadcasts, and exhibitions. Under the sources referred to, newspapers, journals, as well as radio, rank before school instruction. (A teacher has said, "We get as far as Stresemann; they get to know about the rest through TV.") The lack of contemporary historical coverage must also be taken into account with reference to the great respect for Bismarck.

> I like to read political articles because they interest me. Afterwards, I compare the various newspapers because each writes differently. In this way, one learns a lot. But one does not always learn the truth.

> Therefore, one should also be able to read the foreign newspapers. One is sometimes astounded by the different viewpoints of the respective newspapers on the same subject. (Fifteen-year-old primary schoolboy.)

> I think that it is such a pity that one is not provided with the reasons and background information. In this connection, I think of the problems in the Near East. One hears so much about current events, but how they arise and what the real issues are can seldom be found out. And when we have reached this period in school, the topic is no longer current. We are still dealing with the Spartans. (Intermediate schoolgirl in the 9th class.)

Nevertheless I should like to admit to half of my interlocutors that they were, according to their age, sufficiently well-informed about the facts at hand. Other young people were of a different opinion. They got to hear enough about contemporary history, but there was no real interest at hand. One really ought to and must participate, read, and discuss more, but it just does not happen.

> I attend the political workshop only because of the teachers; otherwise I would be reproached. I don't understand anything because of the terminology. (f)

The knowledge offered differs in effectiveness according to the presentation and the type of listener. For the most of them, it is that too little rather than too much is presented. Even the didactic goals and methodical presentation of such education seems—according to the testimony of the young people—to be still in the early stages of trial and error. It does not suffice with a few sources, articles, and radio programs which disappear in the monstrous swell of publication. For these young people value, and miss most, the personal and open discussions with their teachers which have as their aim, the discovery of truth, and are not done for the sake of appearances or to satisfy the fads of the day. Of course, the broad effectiveness of instruction in contemporary affairs on the forming of political opinions and the ideas of this rising generation should not be overrated, as shown in the school subject, history. The question arises whether all this armchair discussion, aside from emotional resonance and factual interest, really leads to political participation, to responsibility, and willingness to make decisions. I cannot answer this question quantitatively because I have not gathered large numbers of examples as in accordance with the laws of the method which I have chosen. Therefore, I humbly beg for indulgence with my naive standards of measurement, such as: majority, moiety, minority, etc. This is, of course, unsatisfactory and must be made more precise through further inquiries, although I believe that the complexity of the private views of the adolescents is hard to count and much more difficult to evaluate and weigh. This would mean that one would possess not the actual views but only diluted divergences of opinion. I have, therefore, resorted to other forms of differentiating my monographic material, namely, by grouping and typing the young people examined. According to this we, of course, found the naive and the disinterested, from whom we have already heard many a voice.

> In school, we have never talked about democracy or any such nonsense. I don't know anything about such things. I usually don't understand what is written in the newspaper about it. (f)

There were also sceptics who did not offer any hope for the effect of higher levels of thought and principles as well as the responsibility of the individual in politics. The irony about the grown-ups and their lamentable politics originates from them.

> At first they were so very enthusiastic, but now they repent equally as thoroughly. (f)

But these three types do not—in my material—dominate the scene. Neither do they provide the tone nor represent the typical in this generation. There has certainly always been a number of devil-may-cares and heretics in all ages and times.

There is another group which appears. Within the frame of my investigation, it forms about a half of the total—which in this age group is thoroughly interested and well-informed—be it in more conservative or in a more progressive character. And within this group critallizes a small number of "seekers" who in this age group already bore the conciousness of becoming politically responsible and not being able to avoid it. Many of these were deeply uneasy and passionately rejected indifference, satiety, and scepticism, even if they were so experienced and taught by their closest educators. To a degree, they have quite definite aims: freedom and self-determination, disarmament and peace, Europe, World Federalism, and aid for underdeveloped countries.

> The most dangerous attitude is indifference. Every one must be politically up-to-date. I read every day. One just cannot let everything pass over one. Particularly more young people should concern themselves with politics so that a new generation will be there to take the place of the old. Democracy demands this of us because there are far too many old fogies. (f)

> One can't live without politics. Whoever wants peace and quiet must participate in politics. (f)

Most of these adolescents, however, refuse to join a political party, on the basis of their criticism of the activity of such parties, the whip system, the elimination of splinter political groups, and out of a fear of having to make a firm political decision, which would later prove premature. One should not accuse them of being unpolitical after one had blamed their predecessors for being "conformistic". Only the conventional organs stand open to them: training for community-living through group-living, the international workcamp, youth forums, student council work, participation in public discussions, and contacts with governmental representatives and newspapers. But will their receptibility and effectibility be preserved and permitted to develop? What other possibilities does our democracy offer them? This must be considered before judging the political preparedness of the youth.

A rather rich variation according to groups and types at hand within these age groups with regard to political views and responsibility. Conformism and scepticism do not seem to prevail any longer. One may place high political expectations in these young people.

Youth and Politics . . . Or Else the Soviets Will Win

Transcript of a West German Television Program
by Juergen Neven-du Mont Televised in the Spring of 1962

Ladies and Gentlemen,

Three years ago I questioned our pupils on their knowledge of Hitler's Germany and Ulbricht's Germany and unfortunately this questioning brought a rather shocking result to light. It had to be given the title "Hitler and Ulbricht—Nil Return". To refresh the memory, here are a few examples of the answers to the question: What do you know about Hitler and National Socialism?

"When Hitler drove through the streets, the people had to always raise their hands and shout Heil Hitler. If they didn't do that, then they were punished somehow."

"Hitler was a dictator."

"He sold pins, to, to . . . in order to seize power."

"Hitler always had a dog with him and he had a little black beard."

"He was the leader of the National Socialist Party and Stresemann was against him."

"He found work for the unemployed and ordered the *Autobahns* to be built."

"Under Hitler it was partly pretty good, because then there wasn't any murderers, like taxicab murderers which we have now or other murderers, murderers of women, they were immediately done away with."

One could laugh if the subject matter were not so serious. But it was taken completely seriously not only by the entire press but also by the Ministers for Cultural Affairs and the school authorities. And here on my desk you see numerous ordinances and study plans exclusively concerning political education and contemporary history. Just in the last three years the pupils and teachers have been schooled much more intensively than ever in political education. Let us take a look at how matters stand today. I have visited the graduating classes of fourteen *Volksschulen* (elementary or primary schools) and *Gymnasien* (nine-grade secondary schools) and have explained to the pupils my questions in great detail. Each of them has himself determined the amount of time he felt was necessary for him to think over the questions. Naturally our television interviews cannot possibly by representative. We have, therefore, asked the opinion research institute *INFRATEST* to make for us a representative poll comprising the entire area of the Federal Republic of Germany, the results of which I shall also give to you today. One last point which we must take into consideration is that the Bavarian pupils do not complete their school year until summer, while the pupils in all the other schools in the States of the Federal Republic finish at Easter time. So . . . my first question once again read: What do you know about Hitler and National Socialism; what are the principal characteristics of that epoch?

"Well, in my opinion, most important was that he was allowed to govern with unlimited power, the Enabling Act, and that he wanted to kill off all the Jews."

"I don't think National Socialism is so good, perhaps it would have been better if we hadn't had it at all, then perhaps the present situation wouldn't be like it is at the moment."

"I think what impressed me about the history of National Socialism is that the German people didn't realize that Hitler plunged them into misery and at many points, in my opinion, they could have seen that the situation would turn out like it is now."

"Hitler came to power because of the Enabling Act, in 1939."

What was the Enabling Act?

"He didn't need . . . what I mean is he could govern all by himself . . . no parliament."

"He built up a lot of railroad lines and big houses and streets. Then when he just didn't know what to do any more, he ran away."

Answers such as this last one I found actually only in schools in which I had the impression that National Socialism had not exactly been dealt with very intensively. Otherwise, quite substantial views and a considerable knowledge on National Socialism were to be found on the average. In the poll, the good sides of National Socialism were asked to be named. The elimination of unemployment was listed as first by 41 percent; 26 percent also mentioned the Autobahns. The bad sides of National Socialism: placed first by 51 percent was the persecution of the Jews; put in second place by 38 percent were war, criminal felonies, the dead. At any rate, the criminal felonies of National Socialism have made, if only by some degrees, a greater impression on the pupils than the Autobahns and the elimination of unemployment. Three years ago, just the opposite seemed true. At that time, also Anne Frank and Ludendorff were considered assassins. Then I asked: What do you know about the resistance against Hitler, which actions are familiar to you, which aims, what names?

"The churches, the military and also the Communists were against him."
"On the 20th of June(!), 1944, there was an assault by Hitler . . . I mean, on Hitler."

"I can't exactly mention any particular steps taken against Hitler. Certainly something was done. There were certainly groups coming together who saw what Hitler did wrong, above all, perhaps religious groups."

"Stauffenberg, and then von Thadden, who then got together and talked about everything and attempted an uprising, against Hitler, I mean, and . . ."

When was the uprising?

"That I don't know, I think on *'Kristallnacht'* (Crystal Night) or sometime. I've heard something about it, but I can't really permit myself to give an opinion on this."

Such views are not particularly surprising when one learns that to the *INFRATEST* question "Do you know who Stauffenberg was", 48 percent answered yes, 52 percent no. Then I was interested to find out what knowledge they had on the division of Germany. For after all, the National Socialists did lay the groundwork for this division. Today there exists the Federal Republic of Germany, the Soviet Zone in which is situated the divided city of Berlin, the German Eastern territories under Polish administration beyond the Oder and Neisse, and the northern part of East Prussia under Russian administration. What do our primary school pupils know about this? Which of you can tell me exactly the names of each part into which Germany is now divided? Only two out of 32 pupils raise their hands.

"After the war, in 1945, Germany was divided up into four zones of occupation—the American, English, French and Soviet zones of occupation. In 1949, the American, English, and French zones of occupation were turned into the Federal Republic. Part of the Soviet zone of occupation was turned into the GDR, the so-called GDR. The territories lying behind the Oder-Neisse Line are under Polish administration. Silesia and West Prussia belong to this. East Prussia was again divided. Poland has half of it and the Soviets half. Berlin was also divided up, also into four zones of occupation. West Berlin, East Berlin."

"First there's the Federal Republic and then there's Silesia, and Silesia was . . ."

Didn't you forget something situated between the Federal Republic and Silesia? Silesia doesn't directly border the Federal Republic. That you certainly know.

"Yes, Berlin lies between."

And where is Berlin situated. Isn't it situated within something else?

"Brandenburg."

"The Eastern part of Germany is called East Germany and is administrated by Russia."

Do *you* know of still another part? He named only one part. There are still more. What do you call that place where we ourselves are?

"Germany."

No, where we live, our State here?

"Bavaria."

And further, within what then is Bavaria?

Ladies and Gentlemen, what should one say to this? The result of the poll looks even worse. There, the question was asked: Into how many political territories has the whole of Germany of 1937 now been divided? Fifty-six percent named only the Federal Republic and the Soviet Zone; correctly naming all parts—zero. For the majority of our primary school pupils, the territories beyond the Oder-Neisse Line apparently do not exist at all any more. And we of the Federal Republic are supposed to be trying to avenge our lost territories! In any case, that's what the Communists maintain. I then asked for the principal characteristics of that doctrine which forms the fundamentals of world Communism. What do you know about Marxism/Leninism; what do you know about Communism?

"I'd say that the whole of Communism and Leninism, too, is based upon Marxism. Because Karl Marx himself wanted the workers to unite and to establish the so-called consumer cooperatives. And Lenin himself took that over and at the time of the Russian revolution he . . . it was his intention . . . that equal rights for everybody . . . that everyone should earn the same and that there wouldn't any longer be people of a higher class and therefore none of a lower one either. And the goal of Communism is a world revolution that puts the whole world in their power." "Well, I think you can compare Communism with National Socialism. Both have a dictatorical(!) government."

"The children are supposed to worship their rulers, like Stalin. The children didn't get anything to eat. They had . . . When they said something in favor of Christ, they were tormented and tortured till they then believed in Stalin."

"If you don't belong to an association then you're not allowed to study."

Which of you believe that the Communists one day will by all means succeed in obtaining their goal, world domination? Six out of 21 pupils put up their hands. And which of you believe that the West will be strong enough to resist the Communists? Out of 21 pupils 5 raise their hands.

"Well, I don't think Communism will conquer the whole world, because the Western Powers are much stronger in one respect, they are more united, and some countries and peoples, they are more informed about Communism."

"I also think that the West will win, the West just needs to stick closer together, not only in economic matters, but also in political matters, then I think Communism won't win."

"I think that Communism has a goal to become a world power and I also believe, I don't know in how many years, but I believe they'll accomplish it sometime or other. You see that now, they're always gaining more and more ground and I think they will accomplish it sometime or other, I don't know in how many years, but they will make it."

This last question was asked only during my own interviews. Unfortunately *INFRATEST* had already completed its poll. It appears to me, however, that also our result gives cause for thought, for after all more than one fourth of all the primary school pupils asked believe in the victory of Communism. However, the *INFRATEST* also asked for the main goals of Marxism/Leninism. Twenty percent named the classless society; furthermore, ten percent mentioned the abolition of capitalism; only three percent the world revolution; 37 percent said 'I don't know'. Thirty-seven percent —that's more than one third—knows nothing about Communism. Certainly a Communist dictatorship is only conceivable here if it comes from without. I now asked the pupils if they believed that it could come to a dictatorship in the Federal Republic without external pressure.

"No, because we are doing relatively well now and a dictatorship is only set up if the people are badly off. Besides, our government can't do just exactly as it pleases, because it is subordinate to the Constitutional Court which sees to it that the Basic Law is kept."

"I'm of the opinion that in Germany, in West Germany it can't come to a dictatorship, because things are going so well for us here, and if things are going so well for us, why then should another government come to power?"

But what might happen if sometime things went badly for us?

"Well, if things would go badly for us, somebody could then perhaps make use of that again, and then it really could perhaps come to a dictatorship."

"I'd say it could once again come to a dictatorship, when Dr. Adenauer dies and someone else comes to power, perhaps he could persuade the people."

"Well, I think it could, it could perhaps happen once more, but then there would have to again be a certain state of emergency and if that happens, I don't believe that we'd fall for that anymore, because our parents did accumulate a certain amount of experience from that time, and in that way many of the younger people have been informed, and that we could fall for such a thing again, that I don't believe."

INFRATEST: Can another dictatorship be prevented? Yes, 56 percent. No, 16 percent. Undecided, 28 percent. Altogether there are, therefore, 46 percent who don't believe that a dictatorship could be prevented or who are at least very uncertain as concerns this question. My next question was: Which advantages and possible disadvantages does the form of government under which you live offer you as citizens?

"Well, it's a great advantage that we live in a democracy, but I'd say democracy is still not an absolutely sure thing here. Just for one thing, that business about the television, when Federal Chancellor Adenauer wanted to decide that the second television program was to be carried through, there it was quite plain to see that this had nothing to do with democracy. And then, too, at the last election, that wasn't quite right either, there was some finagling going on there too."

What then was finagled?

"Mende promised a new government without Adenauer, only then would he unite with the CDU, and what do you see now, Adenauer is there again."

"I think in the Federal Republic I can freely express my opinion about politics and everything, whether that what the head of state does is right or not, that I couldn't do, for example, in Russia. And later, I can also participate in the voting, I can elect whom I'd really like to have as federal chancellor and everything. And of personal disadvantages, I don't see any, at the most, that in general with the East Zone . . . that we're still separated."

"The parliament first has to, when they want to issue a new law, they must first give it to the Constitutional Court of Law in Karlsruhe."

"Democracy comes from America and England and no law can be . . . you can't change a law in any way, you have to first submit it to the Constitutional Court."

"I consider it a big disadvantage that here with our democratic government the morals have sunk so greatly."

What makes you think that the morals have sunk?

"The young people aren't held together right, they run all around, and over there under Communism it's different. There everyone must, perhaps forced, join one of the youth clubs, not just any club, but the political . . ."

And you think that is better?

"Yes."

INFRATEST: Under our form of government do the advantages predominate? Yes, 72 percent. No, one percent. Don't know, 27 percent. Even though 27 percent—more than one fourth—aren't aware of the advantages of a democracy, the pupils do seem indeed to be quite alert, as their critical remarks show. Exactly for this reason I asked in addition: Is there anything in the Soviet Zone of occupation which seems to you to be better than in the Federal Republic?

"Personally, the East Zone could never appeal to me, that you see with the many refugees always coming over."

"I think that over there more is done for the young people, but that, of course, is only done so that they won't think about us over here any more, that perhaps things are going better for us . . . so that they won't think for themselves but only what the state wants them to think."

"In the Soviet Zone, a lot is done for the young people, for sports and everything, and I think we could use this, too, stadiums and sport things and gymnasiums . . . and I think they could do that here, it's only that there everyone knows that that's just only to get the youth, well, to get them for the government, that they . . . so that they really yell for the government and scream rah-rah; and if that would be done over here in the sense of a republic, then I think that would be real good."

I heard such answers very often. Our youngsters apparently feel left too much to themselves. They would certainly not be against it, if our democratic government occupied itself somewhat more with them and if it would present clearly to them its ideals. If the government paid more attention to the young people, then they might be more able to answer the question: Which of you are of the opinion that it is necessary for every single person to be concerned about politics. Eleven out of 17 pupils put up their hands. And who is of the opinion that it's not necessary? Only two out of 17 raised their hands.

"I'm against it, we've elected representatives who run the government for us."

"I think in a democracy everyone should take an interest in politics, because they do want to live in freedom and if no one is interested in politics and doesn't help to keep it free, then afterwards he can't complain if it turns out some other way than he wanted it to."

"I'd say politics are certainly important because anyone who concerns himself with politics ... we are after all in a country where everyone can freely express his opinion and, therefore, it's necessary that we know what's happening and what's right."

"Because everyone, before he goes to the polls, should know for whom he votes, so that another dictatorship doesn't arise."

INFRATEST: Should every single person make politics his concern? Yes, 58 percent. No, 22 percent. Don't know, 20 percent. Almost one half doesn't know or doesn't think that in a democracy every single person should make politics his concern. Many of the pupils showing in the interviews up to now that they had learned something were pupils from the 9th grade primary school classes, which now exist in some Federal States. In Berlin, there are even already ten-year primary schools and it is rewarding to see how these pupils react to political subjects.

"Our present form of government in the Federal Republic certainly does offer us advantages in any case, and if I may briefly enumerate. In the first place there's above all the freedom to express your opinion which seems very important to me, for instance, you can obtain information for yourself from all sources, you can listen to every radio station, to whatever one you like, and compile various information and by this means make a compromise and then from this form your own opinion."

"I think you can dedicate your life to the three first words of our national anthem: unity and right and freedom."

"I'd say a dictatorship could arise, for there are also, for example, examples which show that the interest in politics in the Federal Republic is very weak. Then on television, an example was also given, what a woman in Munich thought about Berlin. She, too, said: 'What's Berlin to me, the important thing is that I'm left in peace and quiet.' So, and if it ever came to a dictatorship, then naturally I would join the resistance against this dictatorship."

"Every single person is responsible for what happens in the state. And no one can say later, I didn't have any opinion, I am not responsible for the calamity that's happened. After Adolf Hitler, we saw plenty of that. All of a sudden no one had had anything to do with it, no one had shouted, yes shouted. And for this reason it's my opinion that everyone has to voice his opinion, then later he can't say I didn't have any opinion, I'm not guilty."

"We are a democracy and therefore everyone should participate in political affairs and do his share, express his opinion. For after all, the freedom to express your opinion is there for that purpose."

To be sure, for that purpose the freedom to express your opinion is indeed there. For these young people there is absolutely no doubt on this point. Ladies and Gentlemen, please don't say: Well, after all, in Berlin. It's not only Berlin, but above all it's the 10th-grade class. Perhaps one of these days it will also be introduced all over in the Federal Republic and then there, too, the political education will bear completely different fruit. Then the schools will have the pupils at their disposal for political education two years longer, and they will have more mature and open-minded pupils.

Now we come to the gymnasiasts (pupils of the nine-grade secondary school). To the question: Who can tell me exactly the names of the political parts into which Germany is now divided, only seven out of 24 pupils raise their hands.

"Germany of the 1937 borders is now divided into four parts, that is, the Federal Republic of Germany, the so-called GDR, then the Polish occupied Eastern territories and Northern East Prussia under Soviet administration, there is also the State of Berlin, divided into four sectors."

"The Federal Republic of Germany, the GDR, and a Polish occupied part in the South, Southeast."

"This territory falls into several parts, first there is East Prussia, then the present GDR, the so-called GDR, then Pomerania, the East . . . the borderland, then Silesia, and finally the Federal Republic."

Let us also this time take a look at the results of *INFRATEST*. Naming the Federal Republic and Soviet Zone only, 16 percent; correctly listing all parts, three percent. The result is scarcely better than that of the primary school pupils. I then asked a question concerning reunification. Are the pupils of the *Gymnasium* graduating class also in favor of reunification, even if economic, but above all, political disadvantages followed as a result?

"For the sake of reunification, the Federal Republic should put up with all the disadvantages resulting from it, with only one exception, and that is, that also the present area of the Federal Republic of Germany would, as a consequence, come under the Communist system of government."

"I'd be prepared to accept economic losses. But political losses I'd only accept under force."

"Well, I'd absolutely be in favor of a reunification bringing possible economic disadvantages, for these disadvantages, springing up for us as a consequence, we could in all probability overcome at a later time. As concerns a reunification bringing political disadvantages, I believe that we should accept this also, for the democracy now thriving among our people would surely overcome the possible Communist subversion which could perhaps occur."

"I would be in favor of a reunification in any case, even with political disadvantages and economic disadvantages, because I think when the German people are at last reunified—this has indeed been the goal aimed at for many years, decades even—then they'll also have within themselves the strength to fight against another type of political system and to assert themselves."

INFRATEST: Reunification under all circumstances? Fifty-four percent say yes. The other half apparently fears the political disadvantages more than the economic ones. Then came the question about the principal characteristics of the National Socialist epoch, about the importance of the Enabling Act, and about the resistance movement.

"The National Socialist government tried to or rather did succeed in completely destroying the constitutional state which previously had existed. Hitler strove for an absolute dictatorship and only his will counted in Germany. All the parties were dissolved and his police organizations saw to it that he alone had sole power. Over and above this, the worst chapter of the National Socialist epoch was undoubtedly the persecution of the Jews. Till now it has not occurred again, and it is to be hoped that it never will occur again, that so many human beings only because of their race were murdered."

"In my opinion all the problems resulted from an overevaluation of the Germanic race. The German people was to become a master race and therefore . . . and that caused the contempt for the Jewish race and for the supposedly inferior races, and that then led to the horrible persecution of the Jews, and that is certainly, in my opinion, the most terrible thing that happened during this time."

"The Enabling Act occurred in 1933 and it was . . . it was suggested by Franz von Papen that Hitler be nominated as Reich Chancellor."

"The Enabling Act in the year of 1933 was, according to my opinion, the first step towards Hitler's dictatorial rule. With this, a power was placed in his hands allowing him to completely disregard the will of the people or rather the parliament and to govern according to his own will and whims and fancies."

"The opposition against the 'brown' dictatorship was comprised of the following groups: the Socialist unions, the clergy, the officers, and the students, and others. Well-known names are, naturally, von Moltke, Stauffenberg, and there was the attempted assassination on the 20th of July, which though, was certainly not the only attempt on Hitler's life."

"One person I know of, too, is Rudolf Hess, who on his own initiative flew to England to make peace with the English."

"The aims of the resistance were, I think, first of all to do away with the totalitarian state and to create a constitutional state in its place."

"You can't really say that Stauffenberg wanted a direct democracy. I rather believe that Stauffenberg wanted to be a sort of second Hitler."

INFRATEST: Do you know who Stauffenberg was? Yes, 88 percent. No, 12 percent. Although there are still gaps in knowledge and partly rather wrong notions to be found, I really must say that the answers are much better than three years ago. Let's go on. When the question was asked: Who was of the opinion that it could come to a dictatorship in the Federal Republic without external pressure, seven out of thirteen pupils raised their hands.

"I don't think it is possible that it could come to a dictatorship in the Federal Republic, for the reason that we have a strong opposition in the *Bundestag* (Federal Parliament) and also a relatively strong third party."

"I don't think that without external force a dictatorship will develop in the Federal Republic; for one thing, because we have the warning example of the Third *Reich* before our eyes; second, because the political situation at the time when the Third *Reich* was founded . . . which helped to bring it about—just to mention the Versailles Treaty or the World Depression—does not exist in our case; and third, because our safeguards, like the Federal Constitutional Court, I think, are too big and too well installed, let us say."

"I think it would be possible that in Germany a dictatorship could again be established; all that is needed is a smart enough dictator."

"I am of the opinion it could happen to us every day now, that Germany once again comes under the regime of a dictatorial clique. It has always been this way with the German people that it has been readily inclined to submit to the power of a dictatorial rule, as you can see from the history, as it was under the reign of the *Kaiser* and as it was in the Third *Reich*. What I would do against it—that I don't know."

"If the danger really should threaten, then—well, I haven't thought about it very much yet, but I believe the worst thing to do would be to emigrate."

"If, in spite of all, it should come to the point that a dictatorship would be proclaimed here, I would first of all try to find out if I could somehow work against it from the inside; if that wouldn't be possible—and this is just my personal opinion—I would emigrate and work against Germany from abroad."

INFRATEST: Can one prevent a new dictatorship? Yes, 78 percent; No, 6 percent; Undecided, 16 percent. Of the high school pupils, a total of 20 percent believe that a dictatorship could not be prevented or are not sure about this question.

I also asked the pupils of the *Gymnasium* graduating class: What are the main goals of Marxism/Leninism? And I asked: What are, in your opinion, the advantages and the disadvantages in the Communist-dominated parts of the world?

"I think first of all one has to separate Marxism from Leninism. Marx wanted to carry through a revolution within the society, while Lenin tried to carry through a revolution with a cadre. But one or two ideas the two do have in common, that is the world revolution and the classless society. Only the methods of reaching these aims are a little different, but at the last party convention again some things were changed. One time they try it by peaceful coexistence and the next time by military means."

"Through a world revolution a classless society shall be created."

"This Marx occupied himself very much with the workers' movement, he said that in the production a surplus of value is created which falls to the employers and which the workers are being deprived of, and that in that way the workers are being exploited and that therefore the difference between employees and employers will always be very great and that a permanent struggle will be going on."

"The advantages in the Communist world are, I think, only to be found on paper. There, all men are supposed to be equal which, I think, is not true in reality. The disadvantages then are these, that what is promised on paper is not kept, but instead the people are treated very unequally, and that the basic laws—as far as any such laws exist there—are not observed, that the laws are freely interpreted and that jurisdiction is very bad."

"To begin with, I would like to point out the excellently developed system of medical care. There are indeed not enough doctors on hand, but the health control is well organized. And then I would by all means mention the opportunities of education. There, not only those knowing the right people and so on reach higher positions, but everyone who has the capabilities to learn a profession or a trade is trained, and that is done by the state. And also I should like to emphasize the organization of youth. Of course, it is all compulsory over there, but when you think of England, for instance, there the youth is also united in associations, and all is organized, and the youth has something to do."

Which of you think that the Communists will reach their goal of world domination in the foreseeable future? Three out of 25 raise their hands. And which of you think that the West will be strong enough to resist Communism? Ten out of 25 raise their hands.

"I think that the West will be strong enough to overcome Communism because, first, it has the more favorable position from the military point of view, and second, also on the economic side the system of free market economy is more favorable than that of planned economy, because in a free market economy everyone works for himself and not for such an anonymous body as, for instance, the state."

"Approaching this question primarily from the intellectual, rational point of view, I must say that up to now I have seen no sign that the Soviets did not reach their goals."

"I think we cannot stop Communism because our satiated . . . the satiated people can hardly offer resistance against such a strong ideology."

"I think the West really has the stuff to resist Communism. However, as long as the West acts according to Lenin's word that it would even sell the rope on which it will be hanged, the West surely will not win."

The number of those who think that a victory of Communism might be possible is smaller here than with the primary school pupils, but even this smaller number should give us cause to think. For us, political propaganda seems to have become a privilege of dictatorial regimes. Yet, there are great democracies who prove that you can make excellent publicity also for democratic ideas. Let us cast a glance at the *INFRATEST* now. Among the main goals of Marxism/Leninism the classless society was mentioned by 25 percent, the abolition of capitalism by 20 percent, the world revolution by 17 percent. Three percent said they didn't know. Remember: in the primary school, 37 percent said "Don't know."—Yet three years ago I could hardly find any pupils who knew something about Communism. Today, we get quite clear answers from the majority. Let us now hear what the pupils of the *Gymnasium* graduating class think about the advantages and the possible disadvantages of life under our own form of government.

"Our constitution grants the basic rights, and these basic rights guarantee my personal freedom in our . . . in the Federal Republic—to point out just one of the basic rights. This personal freedom guarantees me, for instance, the right to vote, the free choice of my profession; I can freely choose my religious confession—all this means that my personal freedom is not in the least restricted by our form of government."

"As a disadvantage of democracy in general, I would like to mention that very much is said but too little is done, and that all in all, according to my opinion, too little is done for the youth compared with Communism."

"I see hardly any disadvantages in our ... for the citizen in our form of government; except perhaps, when we make a comparison with the Communist regime, there they do more for the furtherance and education of youth; that's actually the only disadvantage I can see."

"I have lived under a dictatorship for 16 years, and I fully appreciate life in a democracy. I can fully develop my personality, and no restrictions whatever are imposed upon my intellectual development. I think the disadvantages of democracy, particularly in the Federal Republic, are that people care too much for their private little things—whether the slippers match the dressing gown, for instance—and that they don't care at all about what goes on in the East bloc and behind the Iron Curtain."

This last student is a refugee who came here only after August 13, 1961. Understandably, he did not wish to be recognized. His criticism holds certainly more truth for the average population here than for the pupils who answered the question of *INFRATEST*: do the advantages in our form of government outweigh the disadvantages, as follows: Yes, 91 percent; No, 0 percent; Don't know, 9 percent. A gratifying result. I would like to point out, however, that also many *Gymnasium* students are of the opinion that too little is done for the youth in our state. Last question: Is it really necessary that every single person concerns himself with politics? 19 out of 23 students raise their hands.

"If one wishes to preserve the form of government which one deems to be the only one possible to live under, then the individual is also bound to pay attention to its development, because otherwise others might do it to his disadvantage."

"I think it is everybody's duty to take an interest in politics, as we all live in one community; we depend on each other and every one of us has the right to vote and as soon as he relinquishes it also the right of criticism is lost."

"By all means, yes; for if our people would remain silent towards all political events, it would very quickly lose that what we have possessed for only a very short time and what is very precious, namely, democracy."

INFRATEST: Must every single citizen concern himself with politics? Yes, 79 percent; No, 13 percent; Don't know, 8 percent. Also not a bad result. All in all, the political education of the *Gymnasium* students has been considerably improved. That is also true of the methods and materials of instruction. A Berlin *Studienrat* (Gymnasium teacher) can give us an example.

"Following the suggestion of the *Landesschulrat* (superintendent of schools in the State of Berlin), the Berlin schools have provided rooms with collections for contemporary history and politics. The advantage of such a collection consists in giving the pupils direct access to the sources of information. You find here a good library and an extensive collection of maps which is always kept up-to-date according to the latest political developments. Furthermore, we work with tape recorders and films. Thus, the pupils get a direct impression of what is going on."

Such well-furnished collections are by no means the rule as yet, and it would be hoped that many more schools follow the Berlin example. But also in the primary schools such efforts have been made, as we were told by the Goettingen *Stadtschulrat* (superintendent of schools for the city of Goettingen) Max Buchheim.

"After we had visited my schools the last time, the results of your interviews made me think. I kept pondering, together with my teachers, what could we do to reach better results in this field. I have also conducted courses, continuation courses for training teachers, as we have them here in Lower Saxony, and we agreed that this work must be intensified. On the other hand, I heard the teachers' complaints: 'We simply do not have the time, considering the abundance of material, to sift and to classify what we would like to put to use in civics instruction.' "

So that was probably the reason why you published your 'Working Materials for Civics'?

"Exactly, yes. Because with that I will help the teacher to get this material readily available, without too much trouble, without too much preparational work, for there are also other subjects which he has to take care of. And I believe that due to my practical instructional experience, I have managed to give the teacher about what he needs for this subject."

Well, I see, Herr Buchheim, you have made extraordinary efforts to activate the schools and the teachers for political education. But for a moment, I would like to talk about the parents, too, if you don't mind, for the children are not only at school, they come from a home and there again they are under a very strong influence. Have you tackled that problem, too?

"Yes, in this connection certain difficulties can arise, as it may happen once in a while that children are influenced at home in quite a different way than at school. And there's the question: how can we reach a common level with the parents?"

That's what I mean.

"And therefore we have made an attempt—which I would say was successful; we have invited the parents to come to these lessons as "guest auditors", as silent listeners, and to hear which ideas the school tries to convey to the children and, on the other hand, what the children have to say and what they ask."

Has this had a positive effect on the parents?

"Oh yes; proof of how valuable this cooperation has been, was that the parents stayed in the school afterwards and discussed these questions with the teacher in a very intensive and very serious manner, and we think that in this way we have found a common denominator for the political education."

Herr Seifert, as the principal of a Berlin school you send your 14- to 15-year-old pupils directly out into life. Do you have enough teachers now who are able to teach political education?

"Much has changed for the better in this field, Herr du Mont. Many colleagues are very much interested in political instruction and attend courses. I myself have also attended such courses because I intended to coordinate my instruction plan as far as possible."

In front of the *Otto-Suhr-Institut* in Berlin cars are parked, most of which belong to teachers who every Wednesday attend courses of "Continual Teachers Training" here. The *Otto-Suhr-Institut* is part of Berlin's Free University.

"We have seen . . ." (lecturer's voice)

Here, Professor Richard Loewenthal lectures on totalitarian foreign policy, for example. His students are history, geography, and German teachers from high, vocational, elementary, and intermediate schools. The courses for the political training of Berlin teachers last a whole year.

". . . a totalitarian state aims at modeling the whole world according to its ideology and, therefore, at subjugating the whole world to its rule . . ." (lecturer)

The subject matter treated in the lectures is thoroughly discussed in seminars. Thus, the teachers are able to correct each other, at the same time learning to treat the various subjects in an interesting manner. In many Federal States, similar efforts have been made. Here is another example. The *Bundestag* in Bonn has been found to offer excellent object lessons of political education. Almost every week, teachers from all sorts of schools from all over the Federal Republic sit in the gallery, following the parliament's work with vivid interest. A discussion with *Bundestag* deputies belongs to the program of each seminar. Thus, every day, and all over the country, more and more teachers are brought into contact with politics and political issues. I remember that three years ago the Frankfort *Referent fuer Sozialkunde* (the official in charge of social studies at Frankfort's schools), *Schulrat* Hilligen, said to me that the schools did not take political education any more serious than, for example, the study of the hare. And now I was curious to hear what his answer would be today to the question: Is it still that way?

"It isn't. As a consequence of your TV broadcast at that time, but also, unfortunately, as a consequence of the swastika daubings, a flood of good publications, and also of very good ordinances and new instruction plans, has had the effect that today our pupils are informed on what happened in the past; and not only has their intellect grasped the facts, they have also understood them. However, I'm afraid that now the present and the future are being neglected in favor of the past. What has to be done if these young people want to live in peace and in freedom? What are the dangers that threaten peace and freedom? And on the other hand, what great chances are offered by our time? All these problems are still given too little space in our schools. I think we should now devote as much effort to the enlightenment of the future as we did to the explanation of the past."

To enlighten the future, we need teachers everywhere who do not try to shirk political instruction. Tests taken at random revealed, however, that in the grade diaries of some schools no entries had been made about the subjects discussed in the history and social studies lessons. Therefore, I asked the Minister of Cultural Affairs in the State of Hesse, Professor Schuette—who, exactly like his colleagues in the other Federal States, makes every effort to activate political education—whether he thought he had enough teachers in his State, for example, who are prepared to treat political topics with genuine individual attention.

"I can give you the following answer: actually every subject of educational value for political instruction by its very nature is bound to arouse the interest and genuine response both of the teacher as well as of the pupils. Otherwise, the subject is wrongly chosen."

But in some Federal States, I have found grade diaries in which, of all things, all entries for the history, social studies, and civics lessons were missing.

"I should say that these blank spaces are no longer typical of the situation. Let me give you an example. When I issued, in June 1959, an ordinance—much debated at the time—asking the teachers, especially of the thirteenth grade, to concentrate history and civics instruction during the last six months on the newest history since 1917, the result was that our State Organization for Civics was deluged with inquiries for suitable instructional material. And this should make it clear that most teachers, also if they do not know too much about these subjects right away, are at least willing to inform themselves and to take the task of political education seriously."

So you think that, all in all, you are on the right track in regards to political education?

"I am not that optimistic, but I think we are making headway, and the events of our time furnish us with material, so to speak. There is the Wall in Berlin—what does it mean to us, among other things? That we have to make the youth steadfast towards dictatorial regimes."

But an opinion poll at a pedagogic college showed that not even all young teachers will be able to reach such steadfastness with their future pupils. Just listen to this—which parts of East Prussia are under Russian and which are under Polish administration?

"Russia has East Prussia, Poland West Prussia. This means that Poland has got very little of it."

"I do know some names from the National Socialist period, but I could not tell which positions were actually held by these men."

"For me, the advantages of the form of government under which we live today are that I am able to freely choose my profession and my place of employment—as far as that is possible with teachers—and to create a personal sphere of my own, that is, to found a home and a family with which the State interferes as little possible. As I see it, the disadvantage is that we—and I include myself in this case—make too little use of the freedom offered to us, because that means work, and we are all more or less inclined to take it easy and to let others do the work."

"You can notice it here, at the Pedagogical Institute, too, that there are students who take no interest in politics, and who say that politics is a dirty business by its very nature, and that they would rather not have anything to do with it."

Those who are not even informed about Germany, who do not even know the leaders of the Third *Reich* themselves, certainly cannot enlighten their pupils either. And those who think that politics is a dirty business will never be qualified teachers. Of the about 50 pedagogical academies up to now only about two thirds have a professorship for political science; attendance of lectures on political themes is not obligatory, and many do not avail themselves of this opportunity. Here, one really wonders whether it would not be better to restrict the academic freedom a little for such students who want to become teachers. I had wished to speak also with the first Vice-President of the Permanent Conference of the Ministers of Culture and Education, Minister Schuetz of North-Rhine Westphalia, to hear something about further plans for the further improvement of political education. But much to my regret Minister Schuetz had no time for us. His ministry was the only one in Germany that refused to give us the permission to question pupils. The Acting President, Minister of Cultural Affairs Vogt of Lower Saxony, was readily prepared to answer our questions.

"Herr Neven-du Mont, I am really pleased with the result of your interviews this year. It shows that we are on the right track. In the meantime, many teachers have become much more qualified for their task of conveying political education. The pupils are open-minded and extremely interested, and they really wish to get objective information about democracy and politics. What remains to be done? We want to strengthen the sense of responsibility of the school administration, of the teachers, of the parents, and of the pupils. Besides conveying knowledge, we want to deepen the understanding for the values of the democratic way of life and to create school communities which embrace the teachers as well as the parents and the pupils."

The President of the Permanent Conference of the Ministers of Culture and Education surely means the overall result of our investigation when he says that he is pleased. And there is no doubt that the situation is much better now, in spite of the weaknesses and shortcomings that still exist. After all, one cannot expect a miracle within three years. Certainly, we should be grateful to each teacher and to everybody concerned with the schools in general who has devoted his energies to political education. And many have done this, for they are aware that we have to know and to use our democratic freedoms, that we all share the responsibility for what happens in our State. For the Soviets will win, if we do not know what we believe and what we love.

Juergen Neven-du Mont, chief reporter of the North German Television System has become known at home and abroad for his aggressive Nation-wide television interviews in the field of education for democracy.

The Youth Wants to Make Good the Sins of Their Fathers ...
...But the Old Prejudices Against the Jews Are Still Smoldering*

By Schalom Ben-Chorin

Even as one entered the hall, one was captivated by a remarkable sight. On the platform behind the speaker's lectern glittered a *Magén-David* (Star of David) of monumental size next to the five crosses set up for the Church Day celebration, so that the symbol of the Church and that of the Synagogue stood vis-à-vis.

The desire to change one's way of thinking and to re-educate oneself, to forget old prejudices and to see in the Jew a brother, could not be mistaken. What can one say when German students spontaneously sing Hebrew songs at such a celebration which they have learned on their travels in Israel and nuns from the Mary Convent in Darmstadt encircle the author of these words as an old friend and chant a Hebrew Psalm as a Canon ...? But that is by far not all. A young physician came over to me and asked me whether he might serve in a new settlement in the Israelian desert without compensation.

The limit was reached when President Kreyssig of the *"Aktion Suehnezeichen"* (Project Expiation) who, supported by his associate, Pastor von Hammerstein, spontaneously offered to establish a synagogue for the small Reformed Jewish Community under my leadership in Jerusalem and to send a group of specialists to Israel in order to realize this plan. These specialists would, of course, work voluntarily and without remuneration.

Student-chaplain Weckerling is organizing a travel group to Israel again and his colleague, Pastor Markquardt invited me from Israel to give a lecture at the Free University of Berlin and to a Bible hour where Hebrew songs were sung and the Israeli "Schalom", the greeting "welcome in peace", was customary.

Provost Dr. Heinrich Grueber, whose testimony in the Eichmann Trial remains unforgotten by us, asked me on the third day of the Church Convention, deeply moved, "Isn't this a sign?" Actually, this is a promising sign when 6,000 or more people even on the third day listened excitedly to the reports of Christian professors and the Jewish speaker, and while the Christian speakers unsparingly revealed the terrible blame of the Church for the hatred of the Jews. Not without justification was it noticed that the Jewish speakers were received by the audience with particular cordiality.

*) From *Sonntagsblatt*, July 30, 1961.

This enthusiasm took on even a humorous side. The author of these lines was often asked for his Hebrew autograph, which the eager collectors could probably not even read, and a lady from Marburg offered me a silver cup filled with spring water so that the visitor from Jerusalem could enjoy this precious drink.

But one should not overestimate these symptoms. I had an opportunity to speak with a theology student who works as a student-teacher at a South German high school. He told me that among the pupils and even the teachers themselves, the oldest anti-Semitic prejudices are to be found in a latent state. Therefore, it is especially important that one does not tire in the task as in the words of the "Teacher" (3:3): "There is a time to tear down". The time to tear down the walls of hate was considered to have come on this Church Day. The Rabbi, Dr. Geis, said in his report, "We first had to march through the Red Sea in order to get here." Really a sea of blood and tears.

Is it too late for a sign of reconciliation? Yes and no. Yes, since what has been done, cannot be made good. No human desire is able to bring the dead to life again. But, again, this hour is also the hour of grace, since the new generation will make good the sins of the fathers. And should we stand by and remain cold and inactive?

Is this not a sign of Jona, who was sent to Ninive in order to call the people to repent, but was himself of too little faith to believe in the possibility of genuine repentence? Perhaps he was even too arrogant to be able to believe that the foreigners, others, had the power to mend their ways. The experience of this Church Day tells us that we want to try it once again . . . for the sake of the youth, the future, and of peace.

Insulting German Soldiers is No Punishable Offense *

By E. Kern

The *Blaetter des Bielefelder Jugend-Kulturringes* (Bulletin of the Youth Culture Circle in Bielefeld) carried a cartoon recently showing a rooster wearing riding spurs, covered with decorations and medals, decked out with monocle and banners, stalking over a field of graves. Under this cartoon the following verse was printed:

Ick bin der General, und det jenuecht.
Und wer jejen mich is, der luecht.
Und ick ha trotz Stalingrad gesiecht.
Und bin heut och schon wida janz vajnuecht.

In free translation:

I am the General, and that's enough.
And he who opposes me, lies.
Despite Stalingrad I have been the victor,
And now I am already quite happy again.

Rightfully feeling indignant at this insult, the veterans organizations of Bielefeld—primarily the *Verband deutscher Soldaten, Kyffhaeuserbund, Marinekameradschaft of 1897, Bund der Wehrtechniker, Kameradschaft ehemaliger Angehoeriger des Infanterieregiments 19, Traditionsverband der Deutschen Afrikakorps, Notgemeinschaft ehemaliger RAD-Angehoeriger,* and the *Bund der Feuerwerker*—addressed an open letter to the Lord Mayor and protested against this defamation. The city council factions of the Christian Democrats (CDU) and Free Democrats (FDP) disassociated themselves from this publication of the Youth Culture Circle. Thereupon, the Bielefeld Youth Ring addressed an open letter to the Lord Mayor in which the veterans' organizations were called "fascist and militaristic" and their representatives to be "Neos", "Formers", and "Blood-and-soil Theorists."

Because of this obvious insult Colonel (Ret'd) Koensgen and Senior Assistant Headmaster Moeller, chairman of the local chapter of *Kyffhaeuserbund,* filed a complaint contending slander of the memory of soldiers killed in action.

Dr. Hopfener, Judge at the Bielefeld Low Court, has now turned down this complaint, court costs to be borne by the plaintiffs. The following excerpts are taken from the explanation of the court decision:

---

*) From *Deutsche Soldaten-Zeitung* (right radicalist), Munich, August, 1960.

"What the author of the cartoon and the publishers of the Bulletin wanted to say—and have said—is clearly evident from the cartoon itself and also from the contents of the Bulletin. They wanted to depict and ridicule the most evil advocates of Hitlerite militarism of whom, unfortunately, a rather large number were found among the officers and generals of the Nazi *Wehrmacht* and a substantial number of whom are also members of those organizations which are headed by the plaintiffs. Whoever frequently reads the publications of these organizations and is an observer not infected by militarism and the Nazi line, and who also occasionally attends their meetings, cannot fail to notice that, although these organizations wear a democratic disguise, there is glorified and cultivated in them the old militaristic and fascist spirit.

"There is nothing, absolutely nothing, in the cartoon which indicates that it was intended to slander those killed in action or insult the big mass of decent soldiers. Unfortunately, the cartoon depicts accurately a rather large number of bad officers and generals of the Nazi *Wehrmacht,* and this the plaintiffs will certainly not earnestly deny. If they do not consider themselves to belong to the bad representatives of militarism and Nazism, why do the plaintiffs don the shoe not meant for them?

"The monstrous charge made by the plaintiffs that the publishers of the Bulletin defiled the memory of those killed in action, is exactly the same method which the *'Stahlhelm'* and Goebbels used after 1933 . . .

"Through their general line evident from their publications and meetings, and especially through their letter to the Lord Mayor, the organizations represented by the plaintiffs have brought upon themselves at the very least the well justified suspicion that within them trends are predominant which cultivate the bad militaristic and fascist spirit. With the complaint about slander of those killed in action, contained in their letter, they have gravely insulted the publishers of the Bulletin . . .for it needs no explanation that the Youth Culture Circle has not only the right but even the duty to inform youth about the evil excesses of Hitlerite militarism . . .
"All these reasons led to the rejection of the private complaint."

This explanation deserves being noted by wide sectors of the German public. In view of the situation no one should be astonished that *"Welt der Arbeit",* the weekly of the German Federation of Trade Unions (DGB), in its issue of July 22, 1960, carried in a prominent place and with bold letters this banner line: "Herr Dr. Hopfener—we congratulate you!"

Part V West Germany's Relationship to the World

How Germans View America

By Helmut Hirsch

On the front page of a prominent German weekly there appears a cartoon showing a chubby little man with a nightcap. To the initiated this is *Michel.* He represents Germany just as Marianne stands for France. Sour-faced, *Michel* is carrying a huge load on his back marked *Verteidigungslasten*—the defense burden. The caption under the picture reads, "The package from the USA". It would be hard to suggest that the drawing (which evokes the bygone days when the surprise from overseas was a Care Package) is a pro-American joke. It definitely is not. Nevertheless, only a rather superficial reader could get the impression that the newspaper is anti-American. Some people might actually derive a certain satisfaction out of discovering, at a hasty glance, that the Germans have become again nasty. After all, whole industries thrive on the pleasure of detecting and despising the villain. Unfortunately, in world politics we can no longer afford the perspective of the Lone Ranger. "In the light of the crucial new relationship of the United States and Germany it is of great consequence what Americans think of Germany (and vice versa)," Norbert Muhlen wrote in his thoughtful survey, *Germany in American Eyes.** I quite agree. His parenthetical phrase is a parent of the present essay.
However, in contrast to my counterpart, I cannot, for lack of space, take up the history of the relationship under discussion. It is important to keep in mind, however that there is such a history. The German Liberals who, for example, in the 1830's fled from autocracy and, by buying and selling real estate, developed a section of Illinois at a profit of over 1,500 per cent, had visions of "the land flowing with milk and honey" which Germans of any persuasion seeking refuge from Hitlerism in the same state could no longer entertain. They had to be content with saving their skin and their freedom. Two of these exiles, Fritz T. Epstein (European Specialist at the Library of Congress) and Ernst Fraenkel (presently Dean at the Free University, Berlin) have each traced significant stretches of the "basic patterns of conflict and understanding" discernible in the relations between the two nations. The latter combines a searching introduction with an annotated collection of readings.
Our discussion of some contemporary images of America must be prefaced by further qualifications. In the first place, we all know too little of a considerable number of Germans—those living behind the Wall. Judging from the reversal in the West after World War II as well as from the apparent disposition of most of those who managed to escape the Red dictators, their domain may eventually turn out to be the biggest reservoir of pro-American sentiment.

*) Published by Atlantik-Bruecke, Hamburg 1959.

In the second place, we assume that the top journalists adequately express, and the leading analysts correctly assess, whatever trends there are in the Federal Republic. The available evidence, partly reproduced elsewhere in our book, tends to indicate that a majority of the German people, at that an increasing one, is on the American side. This does not mean that we should overlook the uncommitted minority and the relatively few right wing and left wing extremists who, to put it mildly, do not exactly sympathize with America. The *Reichsruf*, for example, a weekly of unreconstructed Third *Reichers* now in its eleventh year, has headlines such as "The American distrust and Bonn's subservience", criticizes the subsidized American food exports, and utters a more frequently heard view by blaming the inactivity of the American forces in Berlin for the very construction of the Communist Wall. The radical Socialist bimonthly, *Das Andere Deutschland*, which calls itself "an independent newspaper for a decidedly democratic policy" and claims to have been founded in 1925, in a single issue motivates the strengthening of the American army stationed in Germany with the continuing unemployment "in God's own country"; charges the U.S. Secretary of State with ignorance; considers German purchases of arms a mere device to support the dollar; and speaks of America's "cold annexation of Europe". Needless to say that the staff members of this paper have no connection whatever with the Social Democratic Party (S.P.D.) whose policy they, on the contrary, strongly reject. While the average *Bundesbuerger* who is not much of a politician pays little attention to these groups, their existence in a democracy, except where there is an anti-Semitic infection, is to be registered as a sign of health.

In the third place, for every aspect under observation, individual differences cannot easily be overestimated. The tables of opinion polls, listing time, place, age group, sex, and so on, bear this out to some extent. The impact of our military establishment is another case in point. Theodor White, in an article, "Germany—friend or foe" (Collier's Magazine, 1955), which after several years has lost nothing of its freshness, through a convincing story —three American officers during the maneuvers help one of their privates to pull his jeep out of the mud—underlines the educational significance of the presence of American troops on German soil. An unqualified success is Armed Forces Day. In 1961, in spite of inclement weather, it drew approximately 200,000 persons at Ramstein Air Base, 200,000 at Wiesbaden Air Base, 80,000 at Sembach Air Base, 60,000 at Bitburg Air Base, 40 000 at Hahn Air Base, and 10,000 at Rhein-Main Air Base, while German American Friendship Week at Tempelhof Air Base (Berlin) attracted over 40,000 people. Ten thousands of service men crowded together, however, cannot possibly be as many ambassadors of good will. In barrack areas some incidents are bound to occur, and "what they saw and heard of American soldiers" (as a monograph puts it) will be remembered by German civilians at least as vividly as the manifestations of good neighborliness. Conversely, those who have not seen enough Americans or have not seen them long enough—perhaps they mainly ran into that occasionally less impressive representative, the tourist—are likely to become prejudiced. On the basis of that sample, of which several hundred thousands per year touch Germany, Americans are often thought to be superficial. The same hardly happens when the American under inspection is one of the over

2,000 Fulbright Scholars or one of the almost 3,000 high school seniors who so far have come to Germany.
In the fourth place, as the Berlin crisis of 1961/62 has again demonstrated—frustration before the coming of American reinforcements and Vice-President Lyndon B. Johnson, enthusiasm upon their arrival, disappointment when details about a tunnel under the Wall were reported by Americans, concern over the liberation of Francis Powers, joy about the protection of rights in the air corridors, Robert Kennedy's visit, and so forth—feelings change with the tide of events. They may do so more rapidly in Germany than in cultures with a highly stable political history. What can be affirmed with a degree of reliability today, therefore, could be dated when it appears in print. To anticipate a future that does not match the present is, thus, advisable although the ups and downs of the past do not necessarily have to repeat themselves.
Lastly, our printed sources, obviously, differ as to their value, and it is not a simple matter to gauge their respective influence. Let us take one of the best-known German tabloids, the *Bild.* It boasts of almost four million readers. On August 21, 1961, in a conspicuous leading article, "Jubilation, flowers, and tears", it exclaimed: "The steps of the Americans are convincing. They are apt to absorb the disappointment of the last days". Then three times: "We are thankful for that". On October 9, 1961, the same paper complained: "Eight weeks of Ulbricht KZ (concentration camp)—*and we talk and talk*". The flowers were a little faded. Now let us open a certain learned publication. It appreciates American developments with an evenness, and insight, and a respect not always to be encountered among Americans themselves. Its content, on the other hand, reaches only an elite. Which of these two will, in the long run, carry more weight? To the present observer it is the academic voice, but that appraisal might merely betray his own professional bias.
In any event, our painting, with the multiplicity of its layers and the simplification, in places also the distortion, of its lines, resembles a Picasso rather than a Watteau. This all the more calls for a careful examination by all who, for one reason or another, take interest in Uncle Sam and his German relative.

The Amerika-Institut

Does it stem from a traditional bent of their mind or is it a reciprocal phenomenon common to intellectuals everywhere, that the Germans understand the Americans best on the level of research already referred to? This is evidenced by the voluminous yearbooks edited for the German Society of American Studies by a group of scholars from Frankfort-on-the-Main, Freiburg, Hamburg, Mannheim, Munich, New York, and Philadelphia. The usually trite formula, last but not least, this time is appropriate. American contributions to that organ, such as F. H. Tenbruck's analysis, *Mind and History in America* (1959), occupy a leading position. Next in importance as contributors are those Germans who have lived as *émigrés* in the United States or, as Hans Rothfels (Chicago-Tuebingen) did for a while and Dietrich Gerhard (formerly head of the Cologne America Institute, now at Goettingen University and a professor in St. Louis) still does, share their lives with two continents. Shuttling back and forth gives them the advantage of learning and teaching up-to-date facts from first hand experience. It has the disadvantage of fatiguing the eternal wanderer and of disrupting his activities. One of these is to act as a *Doktorvater.* In the not so short list of doctoral or, in some cases, master theses dealing with American topics those supervised by repatriates from America, apparently, excell in quality. As the older men retire their students take over, e.g., Waldemar Besson, who is teaching at Erlangen and of whom my bibliography includes a valuable item, and Hans Bernhard Graf von Schweinitz, who is working at an America desk in Bonn and provides us with a discriminating report cited in this essay. It is still too early to determine what that change of the guard signifies in terms of German concepts. Factual data are more readily accessible. Yearly newsletters put out by the *Deutsche Gesellschaft fuer Amerikastudien* already mentioned as well as by an European Association for American Studies reflect the undeniable progress made in recent years with regard to the creation of the new professorial chairs and assistantships, student enrollments, examinations, library holdings and cataloguing, financial aid, annual conferences, American visitors, and the like. Everyone of the eighteen German universities now offers one or the other form of American Studies. There were 57 established teaching positions for Americana in 1961, including 13 chairs.

Some basic problems regarding the institutes, however, are not as much in the limelight as they most likely would be in corresponding American circles. There are, it would seem, two or three schools of thought. One, no doubt, feels that the funds involved could be spent more efficiently if the American Studies were closely integrated with the traditional curricula of the German universities. Maintaining separate institutes, naturally, entails the various beneficial effects of any "splendid isolation" and—closer controls. Whether these, in turn, will eventually result in raising the study of our culture to the scope, ingenuity, and reputation of Slavic and other East European Studies in Germany remains to be seen.

Special mentioning deserves in that connection an American Studies Seminar held for the first time in the summer of 1961 at an adult education center in the Taunus Mountains. Here, thanks to the cooperation of the American Embassy and the cultural departments of the German federal states, four American instructors lectured to forty-two selected future educators from all parts of Germany. "While American literature has gained access to the German universities," an official leaflet explained, "American history and the social sciences occupy only a small place, which often has led to a one-sided picture of America. This is entirely understandable if one considers that such a picture is predominantly created by the reading of Steinbeck, Saroyan, O'Neill, and Faulkner." To offer a counterweight the seminar, without neglecting literature, emphasized history, sociology, political science, and education.

The opposite viewpoint, presumably welcomed by more than one European professor of *Anglistik* who has gone into *Amerikanistik,* has been expressed by no lesser an authority than Robert E. Spiller. According to him there is "no better tool" than the best literary works of art. He thinks that we should more frequently turn to them and less to the historians and sociologists when we wish to capture the meaning of American culture. This was asserted in a brilliant lecture, "the alchemy of literature", given in 1959, partly through the good offices of the *Amerika-Haeuser* in question, at the universities of Hamburg, Kiel, Freiburg, and Mainz. In another lecture, the same speaker took a middle-of-the-road position between "the *Gestalt* and the analytical approaches", the two chief competing formulae. It was at this occasion that he made before his German audience the flattering remark: "Probably no national group of scholars has so well considered and tested a tradition for the study of culture, whether as a whole or in its parts, as have the Germans." Perhaps one will reply that Great Britain, France, and Russia, as the homelands of Thomas Hamilton, Gustave de Beaumont, Alexis de Tocqueville, and Moisej Ostrogorski, have also a claim to such a title. It, nevertheless, remains true that, beginning with Margret Boveri's *Amerika-Fibel fuer erwachsene Deutsche* (1948) and, for the time being, ending with Herbert von Borch's *Amerika, die unfertige Gesellschaft,* serious writers in Germany lately have shown remarkable ability in producing a key for that intricate lock—the American character. In fact, returning to an earlier comparison, we may well wonder whether the readers of the last-mentioned author, to the extent that they grasp his beautifully phrased investigation, do not gain a clearer overall-knowledge of the era closing with President Kennedy's advent than do most Americans.

The Amerika-Haeuser

If the institutes try to enlighten every year hundreds of highly trained Germans, another set of centers, generally named *Amerika-Haeuser,* on the level of adult education, has primarily the task of informing millions of informal guests. The latest total attendance figure which has been released (for 1960), indeed, is over 3,000,000. Hedin Bronner, for several years director of the *Amerika-Haus* in Cologne and subsequently in charge of the one in Freiburg, tells us that a life-sized model of the "Pioneer", flown from Akron, Ohio, immediately following the successful launching of the original, within a week had been viewed by 6,000 *Amerika-Haus* visitors. In existence since 1946, operating after 1953 within the framework of the United States Information Agency, the twenty *Amerika-Haeuser* still in operation (to continue Bronner's testimony) "have acquired a new look as America's permanent cultural centers designed to provide dignified representation and to foster the deeper understandings which otherwise span geographical distances only with considerable difficulty. The libraries have been severely weeded to avoid wasteful competition with the German public libraries which now are well stocked."

The same authority assures us that the concerts offered free of charge by the *Amerika-Haeuser* "present the best available American artists, who perform American music to the extent that it is included in their normal repertoire." In order to check up on the assertion it might be indicated to consult the Cologne program for the time of the writing of the present lines (February 1962). It features the young American piano players Joseph Rollino and Paul Sheftel, playing works by Matthesen, Mozart, Diamond, Fauré, and Strawinsky; a lecture by the European "Dr Jazz", Dietrich Schulz-Koehn, with recorded illustrations on "The Negro in American jazz"; and in two neighboring cities a concert given by the symphony orchestra of the Seventh Army, featuring one day Marcello, Bach, Mozart, Dvorák, Creston, and the other Purcell, Schubert, Mozart, Copland, and Verdi. Anybody who has heard these young artists knows how warmly they are received, especially by German youth, and must regret the imminent disbanding of this orchestra.

As to the lectures, they are aptly said to be "few and exclusive, aimed at the highest level of interest and intelligence and designed to promote specific American ideals and concepts." In the month under our inspection, Cologne sponsors an "American Heritage Series—English Language Discussion" on the topic, "Election campaigns in Germany and America: Do they sway the voters?", with a Visiting Rockefeller Foundation Scholar as introductory speaker and a German Labor Union-run conference on automation. There is also a film evening on the Wall and a gathering of *Amerika-Fahrer* of whom more will be said below. The reunion is cosponsored by the local German-American Society. Lastly, seven artists from California show their work "to correct certain one-sided impressions" obtained from the exhibits of the better-known American painters—Pollock, de Kooning, Francis. Some exhibitions, notably in this and related fields (it should be added) were geared at a level of refinement more congenial to this or that of the almost one hundred other countries sharing with Germany a total of 218 American cultural centers.

Thanks to a recent booklet, *Zwei Voelker im Gespraech,* the general reader today is in a position to enjoy himself or herself several of the *Amerika-Haus* talks heard, between 1954 and 1961, in the Federal Republic. Interestingly enough the space in this collection is almost evenly divided between the social sciences and the arts, both terms taken in the broadest sense. To the latter belongs an inquiry into that essential tradition of American literature—its humor; a study of *"Moby Dick"* which, like the one preceding it, stresses the American affinity to the abstract; a portrait of Henry James' Americans abroad; a short but revealing piece on "Scott Fitzgerald and the American dream"; and a comparative analysis from which the achievements of Eugene O'Neill emerge with greater clarity. This, at any rate, is my assumption. Since no tests are taken, no papers are submitted, no oral examinations are administered on those premises there is no other method of measuring the mental image thus generated.

The first hundred pages of the "talk between two nations" (as one may translate the title) require less familiarity with the material than what has been reviewed. Of particular help should be an attempt made by Thornton Wilder whose works are about as popular in Germany as they are in his native land. He answers six questions most often asked of Americans traveling in Europe. Each of his points is so well taken, both from the historical and from the sociological and psychological viewpoints, that the public would have to be very obtuse to miss them. The same does not apply to Richard Hofstadter's address on "the land of Lincoln". He rightly points out that specific liberal traditions of Continental catholicism have had little influence in America. But what of it? How shall someone who never had on opportunity for comparing, say, a French Canadian and a Mid-Western priest profit from that statement?! Other facets of American culture, on the contrary, must strike the European precisely because of the difference they intimate. Justice Earl Warren, in speaking of the American legal system and the Supreme Court, provides for an admirable lesson in American humility by mentioning that of the eighteen lawgivers portrayed

on the murals of the highest American tribunal there figures only one American—John Marshall.
The most effective speeches on this rostrum, in all likelihood, are those made by native Germans who have spent enough time on the other side of the Atlantic. Golo Mann depicts the role of the American president, and Arnold Bergstraesser debates the common goals and problems of German and American foreign policy. Nobody, I believe, will ever forget his anecdote of the famous chancellor of the University of Chicago, Robert Maynard Hutchins, and the elevator boy. On VE-Day both, independently from each other, exclaimed: "The day of our test has arrived." The American genius for self-criticism could not have been better illustrated. I have, in addition to these, read the mimeographed transcripts of two American Studies Conferences. One, on "The reform impulse and the American Civil War", was jointly sponsored by several German organizations and the *Amerika-Haus* Cologne, the other, on "America in the 20th century", by the Cultural Office of the American Consulate General Duesseldorf, the Muenster school board, and the *Amerika-Haus* Essen. I also, among other things, attended a round-table discussion on the first year of the Kennedy administration held before a sympathetic, though not uncritical, capacity audience. In the light of these experiences I must concur with John J. McCloy, one-time High Commissioner for Germany, when in his preface to *Zwei Voelker im Gespraech* he calls the *Amerika-Haeuser* "one of the most important links in the development of close connections between the Federal Republic and the United States."

Yet, as was noted in the case of the America Institutes, one searches in vain for a more critical evaluation of the institution. This would require a comparison with the accomplishments of other cultural centers in Germany, foreign or German. The Bielefeld *"Bruecke"*, to cite an example, in recent years received 80 additions for its American section of 3,700 volumes, whose circulation amounts to 10 percent of the total circulation in that *Auslandsinstitut.* The British Council, on the other hand, donates every year 300 to 400 books and the French Embassy for years has been turning over NF 400.— to be used at the library's discretion. Bronner puts his finger on one perennial shortcoming when he explains: "The opening of an unusual exhibit or the presence of a distinguished artist gives the director of an *Amerika-Haus* a unique opportunity for cultural representation on behalf of the United States. Receptions given in conjunction with such events bring German community leaders into direct contact with Americans and afford the best possible forum for exchange of opinions on cultural matters. Sad to say, however, some public misunderstanding in the U. S. . . . has led to such curtailment of funds in recent years that this important aspect of the work can be only half done, even though many American officials overseas, not only *Amerika-Haus* directors, spend hundreds of dollars of their own salaries to help maintain the necessary front." The present conversion of almost half of the *Amerika-Haeuser* into binational centers, jointly financed and administered, may help to alleviate the situation. Some qualified observers regret that the objectives of the *Amerika-Haeuser* are not sufficiently well defined. It is confusing (so they argue) to connect propagandistic and informative tendencies. In fact, several centers figure as *Deutsch-Amerikanisches Institut.* Would it be presumptuous to propose that James B. Conant, who as former ambassador to Germany took such an active part in the life of the *Amerika-Haeuser,* be some day invited to survey their strong points and their weaknesses and then to assist us with a "down-to-earth report" comparable to the one we owe him on "The American High School today"?

The Amerika-Fahrer

Besides the solid learning transmitted through an America Institute and the wealth of information to be secured by frequent visits to an *Amerika-Haus* there is a third clearly observable avenue to America. This is a stay in the United States. Untold numbers of POW's still have interesting memories. Next come the private tourists. In 1961, 35,000 such visitors arrived from the Federal Republic, with only Great Britain and Canada sending stronger delegations. Strenuous efforts are being made by the newly created U.S. Travel Service to raise the numbers of tourists from everywhere further. There are several other categories of *Amerika-Fahrer.* Some 16,000 of these are said to have crossed the ocean since 1949. A large and, in terms of a lasting effect, particularly significant group of them consisted of secondary school students. At the end of the first decade after the operation of this program started over 3,000 male and female students between 16 and 18 years of age had already been sent over by the Federal Republic and West Berlin.

This has all the appearances of a thorough job. Screened by veteran organizations like the American Friends Service Committee, the American Field Service, the Georgia District of Kiwanis International, the International Christian Youth Exchange, the Michigan Council of Churches, and the National Catholic Welfare Conference (and/or their German partners), the German participants, first of all, must have a certain command of English. They, furthermore, are requested to have six years of secondary schooling, a good record in social and civic activities, and—ample knowledge of their own country. These prerequisites, if fulfilled, should go far to insure that our young visitors will get a maximum out of their one year in the States. Nor is this all. With the help of school partnerships bridging the continents and special clubs for returnees who, in their turn, help those who wish to follow in their footsteps, the preservation of the impressions obtained during the stay is institutionalized. For fairness' sake it must be added that a German newspaper recently reported how young German visitors, in the wake of a temporary disturbance in the American climate of opinion on Germany, were treated as "Nazis" and returned dissatisfied. The correspondent, unfortunately, alluded to the boomerang effect these regrettable incidents could have. Would it not have been wiser simply to express the expectation that future guests will be no less favorably impressed than those of their predecessors who later came back as immigrants?

There is as yet no overall examination of the American experience to which so many German teenagers were exposed. German leaders in the field regard it vital enough to ask for public funds with which to finance the trips of impecunious candidates. By contrast we now have a study of the German-American exchange of teachers for the period of 1952—1959. Of the 2,400 German educators who visited the United States, 105, in the seven years under study, were enabled to spend a whole year teaching in an American high school. Their carefully computed judgment of our country in general and of our school system in particular looks like a model of its kind. It certainly deserves to be translated and discussed by all who take pride in the American way of life and, for that reason, are eager to contrast and improve it. These Germans are not only well informed, in both theory and practice, about our principal problems. They also intelligently compare these with the corresponding German faults and merits.

It is not surprising that the teachers should have familiarized themselves with the conditions in our schools in a relatively short time. "With very few exceptions all were overwhelmed by the cordiality with which they were received and taken care of at the place where they worked and wherever they went (the account reads). Here the strongest superlative of European imagination does not approach reality. To some the proud passing around of the honored foreigner became burdensome, because time and energy did not suffice to accept all hospitality offered, and some were surprised about the discrepancy between this cordiality and the neighborly readiness to help on the one hand and, on the other, the extreme harshness toward those natives who trailed behind in their achievements or were disfavored by their background. As a total experience committed to memory, however, the gratitude remains for a thousand alleviations, amenities, and pleasures granted again and again to somebody who at first was a total stranger." True, this statement made in 1961 by the two padagogues, Gerhard Neumann and Gerhard Schellenberg, responsible for the report, is backed up by just a trifle over one hundred persons. But everyone of them (as long as he does not change his attitude and until he retires) will train one generation of German students after the other.

Since March 1961, we have an even more exact mirror of returnee opinion. The project in question was carried out by the Frankfort Divo Institute. It evaluated the Fulbright Program. The well-known program started operating in Germany in 1953 and by 1959 had processed 1,834 German grantees. On well over two hundred pages of a most careful text and tabled data a sample of 647 German respondents is closely scrutinized. "It includes grantees with a wide variety of U.S. experiences: some studied or taught or did research in colleges and universities, some worked and studied as interns or residents in hospitals; some taught in high schools." All spent at least one year and some several years abroad. What we hear of them approaches foolproof evidence of the present nature of German-American relations.

Of the innumerable telling facts gathered by the investigators, I select a few that I consider especially pertinent to this essay. "It was easier to gain confidence in the new environment," a student taking law in Germany and social sciences in the United States reported. "I was met at the railroad station by an American professor. This would not be possible in Germany." A German professor of botany who had a research appointment at Harvard University commented about his start: "The director of the institute introduced me to all colleagues. He showed me the working places and the working materials. I was therefore able to adjust quickly. The friendly support and the readiness to help which I experienced on the part of American colleagues was very beneficial." Anyone who has lived and worked on both sides of the Great Water will appreciate the implications of these seemingly trifling remarks. Their full meaning becomes clear when we learn that—partly because "only a few exchangees are no longer in touch with either their American school or friends"—ninety-eight percent of the returnees are used as experts on America by their fellow Germans. Sure enough, not all of the respondents were satisfied. Four percent in each of the two groups consulted (Juniors and Seniors) were "dissatisfied" or "very dissatisfied". The nature of their dissatisfaction is revealing. Some of it reflects deep-seated cultural contrasts. "A good *'Studienrat'* from Germany (one complaint runs) should not be placed at an American high school. He should be placed at a university instead if the exchange takes place on the same level. If somebody wishes to participate in the exchange program for private interests only, then a placement at an American high school is indeed to be recommended because there he can obtain the best insights into the American educational system. Normally an exchangee thinks, however, that he will be exchanged on the same level. Thus, it would be more advantageous for purposes of further education to see that he is placed at an American university." Here we see, among others, the German emphasis on status and strictly professional training. Some of the criticism takes an entirely different angle. No less than thirty-five respondents who felt "that their opinion had become somewhat more negative, pointed especially to the racial prejudice against Negroes, Jews, and immigrants." This condemnation is perhaps the nicest thing that comes out of present-day Germany and, although a cloud on American-German relations, will be welcomed by many an American opponent of discrimination.

The most diversified, and possibly the most momentous, of all these programs is one which so far has not been the subject of comprehensive research. It serves German professional leaders in practically every field. They are invited to tour the United States for a couple of weeks in order to get acquainted with their opposite numbers. As an illustration we refer to a study of five weeks undertaken in the fall of 1961 by a group of thirteen graduates in law *(Referendare)* from the Bonn area. After having taken part for several months in a preparatory workshop, the participants familiarized themselves with American law studies by being the guests of such institutions as Fisk University, Harvard University, the University of Chicago, and Vanderbilt University. In Chicago, they studied special courts—Narcotics Court, Woman's Court, Ordinance Violations Court, etc. In Washington, they were able to discuss the work of the Supreme Court with Associate Justice Harlan. In New York, the Standard Oil Company of N. J. and the German-American Chamber of Commerce enlightened them about the legal problems of their respective business. "One should with particular gratitude welcome that the Ministry of Justice of the *Land* North-Rhine Westphalia through its sponsoring and the other participating German and American authorities, industrial, and professional organizations through their partial financing of this study tour gave expression to the need for enriching the preparatory stage of young jurists by their actual acquaintance with foreign state, legal, and economic institutions.

The idea of taking effectively account of this possibility in the future by providing for the corresponding budgetary means within the framework of *Land* or federal jurisdiction is worth being strongly supported," wrote Dr. Raimund Wimmer in describing the venture for the *"Neue Juristische Wochenschrift"*.

Having had the privilege of aiding a goodly number of German "leaders" while they toured Chicago I am in a position to testify that most of them, apparently, went back with an image which, by and large, was as positive as it was accurate. Others, in general, voiced constructive criticism. The most recent visitor belonging to the leader group to whom I was able to talk, Count Schweinitz, offered these reflections: "One understands the intellectual position of the Americans best when he starts from the fact that their basic democratic rights are embodied in the Declaration of Independence. The document which sanctifies the freedom of the individual likewise sanctifies the separation of America from Europe. There is a close relationship between the basic rights and isolationism. This is reflected in the relations of the individual to society. In contrast to Europe, America is a country without neighbors. While the European is bound to look beyond the frontiers of his country, the American can develop his way of life in the interior of his land. His relationship to public life remains communal, that of the European is political. Part of this way of life is the technique of democracy. Only in more recent times the thought that American democracy might be endangered from without has spread. In many instances, however, we encounter the old idea that it is sufficient to know how one can best protect the democratic rights and not, what totalitarianism really means. Pragmatism takes the place of the basic principles involved. Here is a reason for concern. Communism, in fact, conducts the intellectual discussion with theoretical weapons which are completely alien to the practical scheme of reasoning familar to the Americans. Even the church is no exception to that. It, too, through "practical tasks", has long deviated from the quest for finding the truth and does not much distinguish itself from the multitude of social institutions." Relating his impressions to a broader frame of reference, the young German concludes: "Today it no longer suffices that the Americans themselves believe in the superiority of their style of living. Above all, the younger nations should be convinced of it. In their eyes the concepts of 'America' and of 'democracy' form an inseparable entity. Thus the American people becomes the spokesman of our common form of existence. Undoubtedly, it will have to pay for this fact with the loss of its former ease and many a conceptual pattern which has become dear to it."

General Amerika-Kunde

Germany's relations with the United States, as far as the general public is concerned, boil down to the personal relationship of millions of ordinary Germans with things reputedly or really American. Since that is an unmanagable subject for individual treatment, my paper at this point, unavoidably, becomes more impressionistic. Let us imagine, for a moment, that there is a German girl by the name of Gretchen. To be sure, it is not too plausible an assumption since nowadays that old-fashioned name is popular mostly with a limited group of German-Americans. Let us also

fancy that Gretchen lives in Duesseldorf, that is, in the heart of one of the most populated German *Laender.* (The story would at once be different if we selected, say, a South German village.) Had Gretchen in her infancy any urge to explore the mysteries of the New World, she could theoretically satisfy her curiosity by going to the local *Bruecke.* Formerly a British center, it has for some time now been a German institution dedicated to international matters. In 1961, 14,739 American books and 9,111 copies of American periodicals and newspapers were taken out of the Duesseldorf *Bruecke* library. But chances are good that, as long as she is a child, Gretchen will hardly venture to enter what is still felt to be the preserve of adults. The books primarily in demand, we are told, are novels, histories of literature, works on sociology and—jazz. In the same year, the *Bruecke* in question arranged for four lectures on American topics and 30 American motion pictures and documentaries attended by some 6,300 persons.
If, as is more likely to be the case, Gretchen uses the children's room in the main Public Library (whose departments for adults are extremely well provided with materials on America) she will find there just one book with general information regarding the United States, namely, the encyclopedic *Amerika-Buch fuer die Jugend.* The only copy of that fairly decent publication is visibly much in use. Gretchen may secure additional data from a few works of fiction, such as *Susanne in Amerika* by Marion Kellermann. Our hypothetical youngster may, of course, as well be one of the 130,000 German pupils who are lucky enough to have *Peter Pim in the U.S.A.* as their English language textbook. Though already dated in a few spots, it contains as fair and complete a description of Chicago as a patriotic resident of that area would wish to see. Nonetheless, of this secondary school text, one of several admitted by the German school authorities, a veteran expert, Paul Hartig, writing on "the presentation of the United States of America in the German English textbooks", raises this criticism: "Four representative poems by Whitman, Sandburg, Lazarus, and Longfellow are reproduced and seven songs with notes are offered. But that remains the only genuine primary contact with the United States in this book."

An equally thorough examination of German readings in literature for the use of secondary schools by Gerhard Linne yields, besides many positive results, the negative findings: "Nothing can be said on the basis of the collections of readings about the products of German writers living as exiles in America; in this respect any hint is absent." The reviewer also discovers no trace of the works of Theodore Dreiser and Upton Sinclair and wonders whether political considerations played a part in the omission. Nor is there a single line by John Dos Passos and, in the appropriate section, George Washington is mentioned only once in all of the 100 schoolbooks under review—when a German poet visits his grave!
An even more critical survey of twenty-one geography texts for secondary schools, undertaken by J. U. Samel, misses especially an adequate treatment of American social and human relations. Yet, Gretchen might be taught from one of the 1,300,000 copies of a richly illustrated geography pamphlet, *Die Vereinigten Staaten von Amerika,* in which case she would indirectly benefit by the historical introduction due to Professor Gerhard. As we would expect, he does not neglect social history. These copies were distributed to each of the 34,000 German schools, to church organizations,

labor unions, and every factory with more than fifty employees. The German information service which signs as the editor of the series where the two part brochure appeared received requests for hundreds of thousands of additional copies, and thousands of teachers (so we hear) have sent in samples of work by their students, based on that geography text. As to the history books, one of the two leading Germans in the international movement for the freeing of schoolbooks from national bias, Ott-Ernst Schueddekopf, thinks that, in regard to U.S. history, "basically, this presentation meets the demands which must be made with respect to form, scope, and content." In his report to the Third Atlantic Study Conference on Education held at Luxembourg in July 1960, he noted, however, "that not a single special book" has been compiled "on American history in the numerous collections of sources for the teaching of history." Incidentally, as Schueddekopf also noticed, one of the texts contains a longer quotation from Upton Sinclair's *Wallstreet.* In other words, if Gretchen has the ability to absorb this material, if her teacher cares to present it, and if he finds enough time to cover foreign areas—three "ifs" which are even more important than the existence of commendable textbooks—she could make the acquaintance of that writer in connection with her study of the great depression of 1929.

What about Brother Hans? Suppose he does not go to a school of higher learning. Would he still get some idea of a current American phenomenon like the John Birch Society? The question is difficult to answer. Hans' family might subscribe to the Socialist monthly, *Geist und Tat.* Unless he rejects its tendency altogether, he might read there an article on the subject written by the political émigré, Karl O. Paetel. Echoing from America earlier German tunes, he advises that one should stop in time *(das Handwerk legen)* the activities of the Americanist *"Fuehrer"*. Or Hans might read *Die Zeit,* a weekly that stands much more to the right. Here a political-minded young Berliner, Hans Gresmann, shrewdly suggests that "strengthening once more the prestige of the United States" may stem the tide of neo-McCarthyism which he, too, fears, could otherwise lead to incalculable consequences. Or again Hans may consult the moderately rightist weekly, *Rheinischer Merkur,* and, instead of a somewhat sensationalist story of Robert Welch, find a well-rounded portrait of Barry Goldwater and the conservative Renaissance due to Hans Steinitz, New York.

Television and radio stations (including a first rate educational program), legitimate and motion picture theaters, adult education courses and individual lectures, pocket books and illustrated weeklies, practically every section of an ordinary newspaper, hit songs and Negro spirituals, foods, fashions, and dances in a thousand ways strive to mould Hans' views on America. He may be impressed enough to buy German tobacco only after, through some phony device, it has been given an American pedigree. He could even belong to that greater part of the eighteen percent of the Germans who still profess their intention to emigrate and dream of going to America. He could also be indifferent, if not cool or hostile, towards us. Some of the periodicals which he would prefer in the latter case have been cited in the beginning of the essay.

If our brief discussion requires a summary it should probably be something like this: The German universities, by their offerings in American Studies, constantly create experts in the culture of our country. This work by some is said to be in need of certain reforms but, undoubted, deserves every support. The U.S. government, thanks to its special agencies, likewise is accomplishing a great deal in that direction. Here, too, there appears to be room for improvements and equally good reason for lending a helping hand. Over the years, multitudes of qualified Germans, during a protracted stay in our country, on the whole receive the very best preparation for building a firm and broad bridge, reaching from people to people. Stronger financial contributions for this useful work, it seems, are expected from the German partners. There is a considerable amount of mass-scale education regarding America, and much of it is to the point. German feelings, partly, no doubt, as a result of these media, are, in general, quite friendly. We need not fear that this friendship will suddenly vanish.

What has, in fact, all but disappeared is a naive philo-Americanism. It was a produce of questionable value, stemming from the conditions prevailing at the end of the war. Germany and America today are political, economic, and military partners. Fate does not extend to them a guarantee that their partnership is in any way ideal. It may some day become substantially less attractive than it right now is—and still would exist. It could also fall to pieces, although former President Theodore Heuss' assertion before Congress, "never in all future will German and American soldiers fight against each other" presently is beyond questioning. A good deal of bad luck, mutual suspicion, and downright stupidity would be required to bring about such an eventuality.

Representative Population Opinion Poll By Institut fuer Demoskopie Allensbach	Territory of the Federal Republic including West Berlin Population 16 years and over

QUESTION: "Do you actually like the Americans, or don't you like them particularly?"

	January 1957	December 1957	April 1961
I like them	37 %	40 %	51 %
I don't like them particularly	24 %	24 %	16 %
Undecided	18 %	20 %	17 %
No opinion	21 %	16 %	16 %
	100 %	100 %	100 %

Typical American Characteristics

According to the Opinion of Germans having met Americans

POSITIVE CHARACTERISTICS

0 10 20 30 40 50 60 70 80 90 100%

Carefree, don't unnecessarily complicate life for themselves	30	41
Modern, progressive	28	30
Americans are friendly, cordial, they get along well with all people	20	37
Good natured, warm hearted, always willing to help	19	38
Place personal freedom above everything else	26	29
Practical, not fussy	21	34
Natural, free and easy	18	34
Honest, straightforward, open	22	28
Self-assured, self-confident	16	33
Energetic, have a great spirit of enterprise	10	33
Diligent, hard workers	7	14

0 10 20 30 40 50 60 70 80 90 100%

NEGATIVE CHARACTERISTICS

0 10 20 30 40 50 60 70 80 90 100%

Characteristic	Especially typical of Americans	Also applicable for Americans
Love the tasteless, gaudy and cheap	19	27
Too much out to make money	10	23
Conformists	12	15
Too familiar, too quick to act as old friends, even with people whom they don't know	8	18
Pampered, spoiled, attach too much importance to luxury	7	14
Cannot adapt to another country	4	14
Not enough interest in intellectual things, lacking culture	4	12
The American young people are not moral enough, the American boys and girls are too loose in their relationship to one another	4	12
Braggarts, boast too much	6	9
Cannot behave, bad manners	6	9
Want to force the American way of life on everybody else		11
Arrogant, presumptious, know everything better	2	5
Ruthless, brutal	2	5

0 10 20 30 40 50 60 70 80 90 100%

JfD

EXPLANATION: The diagram shows how many Germans out of 100, having made the acquaintance of Americans in Germany, considered the individual traits to be:

especially typical of Americans

also applicable for Americans

Reprinted with the kind permission of *Institut fuer Demoskopie Allensbach*. The poll was made in the winter of 1961 - 62.

Germany in Europe

By Karlheinz Koppe

Since the establishment of the Federal Republic of Germany, the foreign policy of West Germany has been nearly identical to a European policy, that is, to a promotion of European unity. This European emphasis in the foreign policy of the free part of Germany is so pronounced that at times doubts have arisen as to the motives of the Federal Government. In the other Western countries, the impression has occasionally been received that the Federal Republic was pursuing European unification for quite egoistical reasons. In fact, the Federal Republic essentially owes its acceptance as an equal member of the free world to this policy; although other factors—for instance, the Soviet policy of expansion— have also contributed to this development. In Germany, the politicians advocating a European unification have had to defend themselves against the charge from nationalist quarters that they have promoted European unification in the interest of consolidating the West German segmentary state, that is, of reconciling themselves to the division of Germany.

If the European aspect of West German foreign policy is now less obvious, the causes for this are not to be found in any change in German policy. Instead, they are a consequence of the developments that have in the meantime set in. In the first place, it should be mentioned that the general freedom of movement in Western Europe which had been lost since the years prior to World War I and which has caused the disputed national problems such as frontier issues, nationality, etc., has virtually disappeared. In view of this almost imperceptible process of eliminating frontiers, the problem of European unification was bound to lose weight in public opinion. It should be pointed out in the second place that the process of European unification in the economic field has been initiated and is taking its course almost automatically, so that in this respect the pressure of public opinion is also diminishing. In addition to these two positive trends of development, however, there are also negative influences to be noted. The German question has in recent years, and above all as a result of the Berlin Crisis, undergone a grave development which has had a greater influence on public opinion than the problem of European cooperation, which had been regarded as a matter of course. However, the stronger the belief becomes that the only conceivable place for the German Federal Republic is on the side of the free European nations, the louder are the voices of those who perceive a danger for German reunification in any excessively close European cooperation, and the more intent is the registration of such voices in the other Western countries. A further complication is that the Federal

Republic's political desire for unification has not met with the same willingness on the part of other European governments, a circumstance which accounts for the reserve shown recently by the Federal Government.

A Historical Retrospect

It would be mistaken to infer from these preliminary remarks that the policy of European unification is no longer as important for the Federal Republic as it was during the first years of its existence. West Germany's European policy has not changed; it has merely adjusted itself to the changed rhythm of the process of European unification as such. The aims are no longer quite so far-reaching as before, but have on the other hand become more concrete. To be able to gauge completely the bearing of European unification upon the present policy of the Federal Government, a brief summary of the historical development of European unification is necessary. Hardly any continent has in the course of history been so conscious of its intellectual unity, and at the same time so politically rent, as Europe. What at first glance seems to be a contradiction, is explained by the continent's particular geographic and climatic situation and the resulting influences on the evolution of its peoples. The intellectual unity of the Europeans from the early Middle Ages down to the present time was imbued with the awareness of their cultural richness. The consequent intellectual tension was a cause and prerequisite for the achievements, of the Europeans throughout the world. Thesis and antithesis inspired the minds of explorers, researchers, and inventors. In Europe, collective action was never paramount as in other cultural regions. The creative spirit of the individual was always able to assert itself. Names like Galileo, Columbus, Newton, Leibniz, Pasteur, and Einstein testify to a development in intellectual history which was possible only on the basis of reciprocal stimulation among all Europeans.

Extreme developments were bound to occur in the process. They often assumed alarming dimensions, but without ever dominating the entire continent. It is usually not possible to make a clear distinction between mercantile spirit and religious zeal, ambition for power and sense of mission. Colonization can be separated from missionary activity just as little as the Spanish Inquisition from the Italian Renaissance or the devastating Thirty Years' War from German Humanism. Europe has always been conceived as an expression of intellectual and political multiplicity. Although to the outside world Europe has always manifested herself in the form of individual nations—Spain, Portugal, the Netherlands, Great Britain, France, Germany, Italy, Sweden, and whatever they may be called—it has presented a more uniform concept than have Africa and Asia or even the two Americas. For the peoples of other continents, Europeans are still firstly Europeans and only secondly Englishmen, Frenchmen, and Germans.

In Europe itself, this awareness was still predominant down to the close of the 19th century. Up to the year 1870, the European internecine wars were political conflicts that did not jeopardize intellectual cohesion, or did so only on a very small scale. No artist, philosopher, scientist, not even a merchant had to leave his host country because of its being at war with his own. Only the exaggerated growth of nationalism at the close of the 19th century led to the loss of European consciousness; the complete disappearance of the best European traditions and the isolation of the European peoples from one another created the atmosphere which enabled the two World Wars to take place. Yet, it was only World War II which demonstrated to the Europeans, once and for all, the senselessness of these actions. A half century of a self-destructive delusion led Europeans to realize that a consciousness of unity is essential to diversity of modes of living.

* * *

The two World Wars not only carried Europe to the brink of the abyss, but effected a new distribution of power in the world. America and Soviet Russia—both sustained by the European intellectual heritage—have assumed the role of leading world powers. Other nations on other continents enjoy an increasing share in progressive political, technological, economic, and social development. In addition to this is the controversy between those nations which advocate a free social system and those powers which are based on a totalitarian system of society. As a result of World War II, the dividing line between the two worlds runs through the middle of Europe, which through its history and way of life belongs to the free world. Europe will be able to maintain the validity of this claim only if it consolidates into a political and economic unit capable of action.

To bring about this political and economic unity has been the explicit goal of the free countries of Europe since the end of World War II. The idea of European unification is, however, as old as historical Europe itself. Since the time when the European peoples appeared on the scene of political history after the disintegration of the Roman Imperium, the efforts to realize the idea of uniting Europe have not ceased. Some historians consider that, up to the present day, it was Charlemagne's Empire that achieved this unity for the first and last time. Others hold the position that at the height of the Middle Ages the Holy Roman Empire was already very close to realizing the idea of a united Europe.

At the beginning of the 14th century, Dante dreamed of a unified occidental, Christian monarchy as the guardian of order in a society of states—a dream that had quite a concrete reason considering the advance of the Turks at that time. At almost the same time, a Frenchman, Pierre Du Bois, defined the foundations of a "Christian republic" in which the princes of the individual states bend to the decisions of an ecclesiastical council.

Further writings on the organization of Europe are known from the following centuries. However, the first person to arouse the interest of historians was the Duc de Sully, minister and friend of King Henry IV of France, through his work on *Economies Royales*. His thoughts could have been the basis for the first draft of a European constitution. At this early period, he pondered how best to combine the five elective monarchies, six hereditary monarchies, four sovereign republics, and numerous other sovereign territories existing at that time, a problem that is of no small importance in the Europe of our day as well. His deliberations led to a confederation under the supervision of a Council of Europe *(Conseil de l'Europe)*. This is the first time in history that mention was made of this term, which has meanwhile come to designate the Consultative Assembly of the free European states with its seat in Strasbourg. That was in the mid-17th century. A short time afterwards, in the year 1693 probably the most well-known of all early Americans, William Penn—the founder of Pennsylvania and author of the most tolerant, democratic, and pacifistic constitution the occident has ever known—wrote his *Essay towards the Present and Future Peace of Europe,* which also contains a proposal for a general European confederation of the princes.

The supreme authority of this federation was to be a parliament with the express right to compel every sovereign member state to comply with the common good. There is a minute description of the rules of procedure for the work of this parliament.

Probably the best-known of the historical essays on the organization of Europe was written by Abbé de Saint-Pierre, who was able to gather his knowledge of constitutional law as envoy of France at the peace congress of Utrecht in 1712. His project of *Perpetual Peace* appeared in the same year. Subsequently, it was expanded on several occasions and published as a summary—the later famous *Abrégé*—in 1729. Saint-Pierre sketches a regular treaty of union with precise allocation of competencies between union and member states and with a European senate as the supreme executive authority of the union. As coincidence would have it, the first congress of the European Movement after the war, in 1948, took place in the very city that Saint-Pierre had also suggested as the meeting place for the first congress of the union: The Hague.

This congress at The Hague in May, 1948, is the starting point for the modern European unity movement. Several hundred political leaders convened there in order at long last to realize the idea of European unification. However, the foundations had already been laid shortly after World War I by Count Richard Coudenhove-Kalergi, who founded his Pan-European Union in 1923. He received the particular support of the then German Foreign Minister, Gustav Stresemann, who labored together with his French colleague, Aristide Briand, to improve Franco-German relations as a basis for European unification. These efforts unfortunately met with little encouragement on the part of European governments. Later, Briand submitted to the British and German governments the proposal of at least forming an economic union as the first step towards later political unification. On September 5, 1929, at the meeting of the League of Nations, he suggested the establishment of a European union. However, the unsolved problems arising from World War I were already leading to the ominous developments of the thirties. Fascism and National Socialism were driving towards World War II, from which was to emerge a shattered Europe, whose Eastern part fell prey to the totalitarian rule of the Communist Soviet Union.

Cooperation in Europe

Already before the end of the War, on March 22, 1943, the British Prime Minister, Winston Churchill, presented his thoughts on a united Europe in a radio address to the world. However, it was only through his famous speech of September 19, 1946, in Zurich that public attention was drawn to these ideas—at the same time that various groups of European federalists, some of which had been formed within resistance movements and in concentration camps, were meeting for the first time in the little Swiss town of Hertenstein in order to work out a common program.

The numerous organizations and associations that had formed after the War then joined together, at the aforementioned congress in The Hague in May, 1948, to constitute the European Movement. From the political resolution of this congress, let us cite only those clauses that have become important with respect to the subsequent developments.

The Congress

—declares that the time has come for the peoples of Europe to relinquish certain sovereign rights in order that these be jointly exercised in the future for the coordination and development of their common resources;

—demands the convocation at the earliest possible time of a European Assembly which is to be elected from among their constituency or otherwise by the parliaments of the participating nations and which will recommend immediate measures suited to bringing about more and more the necessary unity of Europe in the economic and political fields;

—is of the view that such a union or federation must be open to all nations of Europe who live under a democratic system and would obligate themselves to respect a charter of human rights;

—proclaims that for the protection of the rights of the individual and the principles of liberty, the Assembly must propose the establishment of a court capable of imposing the sanctions necessary to bring about respect for the charter;

—declares that the only solution to the German problem, in the industrial as in the political sphere, is to be found in the European Federation.

Yet, even if they had pooled all their resources together, the European nations would have been too weak in 1948 to effectuate such an extensive project as the formation of a European federation, in addition to their own work of reconstruction. Therefore, the President of the United States of America should go down in history for having put into effect the plan of assistance for the European economy worked out by General Marshall, thereby providing the Europeans with the funds necessary for the reconstruction of their economy. A prerequisite for this was the establishment of a joint Organization for European Economic Cooperation (OEEC), which allocated "the credits and aid deliveries according to purely economic considerations, and not according to national ones; so that they also benefited the three Western occupation zones of Germany which still existed at that time. In addition, an international payments system, the European Payments Union, was established to liberate the individual countries from the hampering bilateral balance of trade in favor of a multilateral balance of payments.

It should, however, be mentioned here that it was not America alone that perceived the necessity for European cooperation and fostered it. The Soviet Union had also become aware of the significance of a unification of

Europe, but with the opposite reaction, that is, through the destruction of this work of peaceful reconstruction which stood in the way of its aim of world revolution. American assistance was originally intended for all of Europe, including those countries occupied by Red Army troops. By means of force and Communist *coups-d'état,* the Soviet Union was able to prevent the East European countries from taking the free course of development which characterized the recovery of the Western countries, including Western Germany, in the following years.

Nevertheless, for the first time in history, European unity was thus provided with a concrete basis, at least on the Western part of the continent. On May 5, 1949, almost a year after the Hague Congress convened, work was completed on the statute for the establishment of a Consultative Assembly of the European countries, called the Council of Europe. The Assembly convened for its first sitting in August and September, 1949. It has the right to communicate recommendations to a Committee of Ministers, which as a rule must decide on them unanimously. Resolutions passed in this way do not become operative until ratified by a certain number of member countries. They are applicable only in countries that have ratified the individual resolutions. Accordingly, the Council of Europe is the most limited and informal form of political cooperation. It has nevertheless accomplished noteworthy work in the 13 years since its establishment. In this connection, first mention is due to the European Convention of Human Rights, requested at the original Hague Congress, which is recognized by all member states and constitutes the basis of the democratic unification of Europe. It opens to all member countries the possibility of lodging complaint at an impartial court of justice if basic human rights are violated. Most member countries have moreover recognized the right of individual complaint, which grants each individual citizen the opportunity of lodging complaint with the European Court of Human Rights.

This convention is supplemented by the European Social Charter which took effect in 1961 and lays down common guiding principles for social policy, e. g., regarding strike laws, protection of minors, social welfare, and other matters. Both conventions make it especially apparent that European cooperation serves human beings first and foremost.

Among the other achievements of the Council of Europe are the abolition of compulsory visas and passport checks, and other measures to facilitate travel and border traffic. The resolutions on the equalization of European citizens in the fields of social and health insurance, on the mutual accreditation of the certificates and degrees of higher education, and on common regulations concerning the establishment of businesses in foreign countries, have also contributed in large measure to eliminating the existing national borders. What seemed not very many years ago to be a dream, is now reality. From the North Cape to Sicily, all free Europeans have the assurance in emergencies of being treated like any citizen of the country where they happen to be. Finally, it should be mentioned that the Consultative Assembly of the Council of Europe regularly observes and, though with some limitations, exercises parliamentary supervision over the activities of OEEC (which meanwhile has received other assignments, to be discussed later) and the work of almost all other European-level institutions.

The Integration of Europe

The Hague Congress of the European Movement was the climax in the history of the movement for European unification. It marked the end of the period of manifestoes and theoretical conceptions, and the beginning of the period of practical unification efforts. The perceptible result was the Council of Europe in Strasbourg. It was at first the object of all hopes, of which only a few came true. As a matter of fact it soon became clear that this same Council of Europe, which was regarded as the starting point for an ever closer merger of the European states, meant for some countries—particularly Great Britain—a final stage beyond which they were not willing to go.

The Council of Europe is the classic example of the cooperation of states without the transfer of sovereign rights to a joint institution. Such dissimilar countries as Belgium, France, Italy, Luxemburg, the Netherlands, Norway, Sweden, Denmark, Great Britain, Iceland, Ireland, Greece, Turkey, Austria, and the Federal Republic of Germany consult the Council on common problems. Since 1961, Switzerland, which is intent on preserving its neutrality, has participated conditionally in the work of the Council of Europe. It is all the more surprising that it has been possible to adopt a large number of conventions and carry them out in the member countries. The Consultative Assembly, in which 135 representatives (not counting the representatives of Switzerland, who do not take part in all sessions) convene several times a year, is an important forum of European public opinion. However, the Council of Europe and the Consultative Assembly are not suited for the solution of practical political and economic problems. Several attempts to develop the Council of Europe into a political union of the European peoples headed by joint federal authorities met with failure during the years 1949 to 1953.

Consequently, already during the first months after the establishment of the Council of Europe, plans appeared for a closer merger of those member countries who were willing to set out on the road to integration, that is, to transfer sovereign rights to superior authorities as had been demanded at the Hague Congress. Such a solution was made urgent by the strained economic situation in the Western European countries, the as yet unsettled German question, and already in the background, the menacing policy of the Soviet Union. These considerations culminated in the declaration of Robert Schuman, then French Foreign Minister, who on May 9, 1950, demanded the establishment of a European Coal and Steel Community, the outlines of which had been worked out by the French Planning Commissioner, Jean Monnet. Belgium, France, Italy, Luxemburg, the Netherlands, and the Federal Republic of Germany negotiated on the conclusion of a treaty which was signed on April 18, 1951, and took effect on July 23, 1952. This treaty inaugurated a common market for coal and steel in the six countries, that is, the customs barriers among the six countries were eliminated. The authorization for implementation and application of the treaty was delegated to a joint institution, the High Authority, which was independent of the national governments and subject to the supervision of a joint parliamentary assembly. In addition, a joint Court of Justice was instituted to which appeal may be made in case of dispute between the High Authority and governments or between the High Authority and entrepreneurs, and in case of doubts as to the proper interpretation of the treaty. Its verdicts are final. With the establishment of the Coal and Steel Community, the road to integration was taken for the first time, though only in one sector of the economy. In the preamble to this treaty, it is stated that "the signatory governments are determined by the establishment of an economic community to lay the foundation for a broader and more developed community among the peoples in place of the centuries-old rivalries and to create the institutional foundations capable of indicating the direction for a destiny now common to all." Yet, the objectives of the Coal and Steel Community, in contrast to the later trend, did not at first aim at the political merger of the member countries. It was intended to solve specific problems in the spirit of reconciliation and met with the full support of the Council of Europe for this purpose. Therefore, not only the sensational expansion in the basic industries of the Community, but also the solution of the Ruhr and Saar problems must be regarded as successes of this Community, the latter having ushered in the era of Franco-German understanding, which has meanwhile become a matter of course and has struck deep roots in both nations, east and west of the Rhine.

It was only when the political development failed to make progress in the Council of Europe that the plans to expand the Coal and Steel Community into a political community took shape. Here again, it was France who seized the initiative for the establishment of a European Defense Community in which the defense forces of the participating countries were to be combined under a joint supreme authority. The treaty was signed on May 27, 1952, shortly before the treaty of the European Coal and Steel Community took effect. The two communities were to be joined by a political statute, the working out of which was undertaken by the Common Parliamentary Assembly, which presented it to the foreign ministers of the six countries on March 10, 1953. The treaty project envisaged nearly perfect federal institutions, although at first they were to apply only to the limited economic field of coal and steel and for defense. As before, only a coordination was foreseen in the field of foreign policy, but development towards closer cooperation was not precluded. With regard to economy as a whole, the governments are simply obligated by the statute to employ all measures for the effecting of a progressive economic integration. During the winter of 1952-53, the European political community seemed to approach realization.

Although the Council of Europe had expressly approved and fostered the European Coal and Steel Community in the interest of the whole of Europe, many objections were raised in view of the six countries' efforts at political union. The controversy over whether an informal cooperation of all free European countries is preferable to the close integration of the six countries flared up in full intensity and has not even now died down. At that time, a special role was played by Great Britain, which had distinctly decided in favor of cooperation. The British attitude in turn gave impetus to those forces in France which opposed any unduly extensive political commitment in Europe on the part of France. The French parties of the center, harried by crises in foreign policy and economics, were unable to obtain a majority in favor of the treaty. On August 30, 1954, the French parliament, by a bare majority, struck the debate on the treaty for the European Defense Community from the agenda, which was tantamount to rejection. Thus, the effort to lay the contractual foundation stone for a political federation in Europe had for the time being failed.

(In order to solve at least the most urgent problem, that of making the economic strength of the Federal Republic of Germany available to the joint defense efforts, the Federal Republic was admitted to the Western European Union, which includes Great Britain along with the six countries of the Coal and Steel Community. In the so-called Paris Treaties of 1955, the Federal Republic was granted all the rights of a sovereign state. As a member of the Western European Union, the Federal Republic is a member of NATO.)

The Economic Approach

No failure occurred in the endeavor to bring about integration first in the economic field. In spite of disappointment over the failure of the European Defense Community as the starting point for the political community, the statesmen of the six countries began to look for ways and means of implementing economic integration. In the summer of 1955, the foreign ministers of the Six decided to draw up a treaty creating a European Common Market. By April, 1956, the treaties for the European Economic Community and the European Atomic Energy Community had been completed in outline. The two treaties were signed in Rome on March 25, 1957, and took effect on January 1, 1958.

The foundations of the European Economic Community are the elimination of all internal customs barriers, establishment of a common external tariff, freedom of movement for employees and capital, coordination of social policy, and elimination of all other barriers hampering economic freedom of movement. The establishment of the Common Market is foreseen in stages which may extend over a period of 12 years and can be increased to 15 years in case of emergency. However, the economic development that has taken place in the meantime has already led to a reduction of the projected intervals, so that the final realization of the Common Market may be expected in seven to eight years.

At the same time, the European Atomic Energy Community for joint research and application in the field of nuclear energy began its operation. This Community is intended to promote progress in the peaceful utilization of atomic energy, assure protection of the population's health, supply the member countries with nuclear fuel, and supervise its use. EURATOM, as the Community is called for short, has research institutes of its own in all six countries.

Commissions have been assigned to supervise and implement the Rome Treaties. That for the Common Market—of which the former Secretary of State in the German Foreign Office, Professor Hallstein is chairman—numbers nine members, and that for the Atomic Energy Community, five.

The Commissions may act on their own responsibility within the limits of the authority conferred on them in the treaties. The Council of Ministers decides only on special and vital matters, unanimously in important cases, but by simple majority as a rule. The treaty provides that at the close of the transitional period, all decisions will become operative by simple majority.

The Commissions and the Council of Ministers together constitute the executive, a gradual shift of emphasis being foreseen in favor of the Commissions. The executive is supervised by the European Parliament, whose competency also extends to the executive branch of the Coal and Steel Community. In the European Parliament, the national parliaments of the Federal Republic of Germany, France, and Italy are each represented by 36 delegates, Belgium and the Netherlands by 14 each, and Luxemburg by six. The Parliament discusses the reports of the executive organs, must be heard on certain matters, and may draw up recommendations. So far, the Parliament is not, however, entitled to either legislative authority or the power of the purse. It can lend emphasis to its views in so far as it may at any time force the two Commissions and the High Authority to resign by means of a vote of nonconfidence. In addition, the treaties provide for direct elections for the Parliament. The Parliament has already forwarded a pertinent draft to the Council of Ministers which, if it is adopted, must then be ratified by all six parliaments. The same Court of Justice which has jurisdiction for the Coal and Steel Community may be appealed to both by the European Institutions and by the governments in case of controversies. Finally, an Economic and Social Committee including representatives of the various groups engaged in economic and social activities will act as an advisory organ.

The treaties on the Common Market and the Atomic Energy Community took effect under quite dramatic circumstances. Shortly before the effective date, General de Gaulle had assumed the political leadership in France. In contrast to the fears that France might from the beginning invoke the escape clauses provided in the treaty, de Gaulle's Minister of Economic Affairs and Finance, Antoine Pinay, made every preparation to enable the European Economic Community to come into force according to schedule. The reform of the French currency provided the necessary basis.

Since then, the Common Market has proved its worth. Taking advantage of the international boom in business, the area of the Common Market registers by far the highest rate of industrial growth in the entire Western world. Since the trade and economies of the other European countries also profited from the expansion in the Common Market area, the danger of Western Europe splitting into two economic zones was less great than originally feared. The effort, particularly fostered by Great Britain to form a free trade area, embracing all of Western Europe, at the same time as the European Economic Community came into being, had already failed in 1958. In addition, the United States of America had intimated that it would acquiesce in a certain degree of economic discrimination by the six countries because it supports the political objectives of the Rome Treaties. However, America was not willing to accept purely economic agreements excluding it.

Since then, the negotiations on economic cooperation in Europe and within the Atlantic Community have been conducted on various levels. On the initiative of America, the OEEC was renamed Organization for Economic Cooperation and Development (OECD), in which in addition to the former OEEC states, the USA and Canada are also full members. On the other hand, under the leadership of Great Britain, Switzerland, Sweden, Austria, Denmark, Norway, and Portugal formed the European Free Trade Association (EFTA), which Finland also joined later under a treaty arrangement. Latest developments have already exceeded both initiatives. The economic successes of the Common Market of the Six have led all other interested countries to realize that a direct understanding with the European Economic Community is indispensable. As the first country, Great Britain itself submitted an application for full membership in the European Economic Community in the summer of 1961. Ireland and Denmark followed. The other European countries are working either for full membership, or, as in the case of the three neutral countries of Switzerland, Sweden, and Austria, for association with the Six, according to their respective situation.

America was not able to remain aloof from this development, which it had itself introduced in 1948 through the Marshall Plan. Early in 1962, it negotiated successfully with the European Economic Community on a reciprocal 20 percent reduction of customs tariffs. At the same time, the American President, John F. Kennedy, in a message to Congress, seized the initiative for a liberalization of economy and commerce that is revolutionary by American standards. Thus, prospects have been opened up which can lend impetus to the economy of the entire world and will have favorable political repercussions on the free world.

The Political Approach

The economic development originating in the Rome Treaties of the Six, with its world-wide consequences, far surpasses the hopes of EEC's founders. They wanted to establish a common market for economic reasons, hoping at the same time that such a common market would be the basis for a later political community. They were compelled to tread this path alone because at that time, the other European countries, headed by Great Britain, were not willing to follow them on the road to integration with political aims. However, these political objectives seem to be cast in doubt by the very success of economic integration. The Treaties of Rome are expressly open to all European countries for membership or association on the condition that they thereby intend to set out on the road to integration, i. e., not to make any changes in the structure of the Common Market. This is the specific right which Great Britain and the other European countries now wish to exercise. Even such weighty problems as agricultural policy and Great Britain's ties with the world-wide Commonwealth no longer present any fundamental obstacle, particularly since the Six, contrary to all expectation, achieved agreement in January, 1962, on their own future agricultural policy.

On the other hand, it is not conceivable that Great Britain will be willing to join a political community in the near future. Hence, there are voices within the Common Market opposing full membership for Great Britain and other countries in order to avoid jeopardizing the community's political development.

These political objectives have in the meantime been given an entirely different emphasis by the President of France. He has in mind a "Europe of the fatherlands" to be based on cooperation of the governments, foregoing joint integrating institutions. Compelled by the urgent need for close coordination in all fields of policy within the Community of the Six, the other five countries also assented to drafting a treaty on the establishment of a political union of the six countries at a conference of the six heads of government held at Bonn in the summer of 1961. Uppermost in the minds of all partners is the wish to create the nucleus of a political community of the six countries before the economic community is expanded to include other countries.

However, at present there still exists no agreement as to whether this nucleus will lead to a true political community or not. Even the President of France sees the necessity of a common European policy. Yet it is incomprehensible to him that France should one day submit itself to a set common European institution. His plan for European cooperation amounts to a close and insoluble alliance of the European governments. This formula is again unacceptable to the smaller European countries. They fear the strength of the large countries, especially West Germany and France, in such an alliance particularly if these two countries unite beforehand. To be sure, in such a union of nations even Belgium and the Netherlands would have the possibility of vetoing certain designs of the large partners. But since, in the final analysis, one cannot always say "no", in the long run, they would succumb to the pressure of the others and would only have equal rights for the sake of appearance. For this reason, just such countries as Holland and Belgium see their interests preserved only in an integrated community which has at its disposal institutions independent of national governments, liable to strict common parlamentarian control. Since such a European Community seems possible only at some future time, considering France's attitude, the small countries demand the participation of Great Britain in the political alliance to create a certain counterbalance to France—and also to West Germany.

This is a vicious circle whose solution depends on the inner political development of France in the next months—or perhaps years. Until then, it is important to strengthen the existing European Community economically and to bind it satisfactorily to the entire West. In both cases, a strong parliamentary current in favor of the European integration and opposed to the French propositions is to be established. In the Federal Republic of Germany in March 1962, seven leading personalities, among them former Foreign Minister Brentano and the well-known Social Democrat Dr. Mommer, have spoken out in the *"Aueler-Erklaerung"* (Aueler Declaration), named after the place of the meeting, against the French plan, and have influenced even the German Parliament. For the same reason, a group of European parliamentarians in France, under the leadership of Maurice Faure, has refused the confidence of the Pompidou government. Five ministers of the Mouvement Républicain Populaire, headed by Pierre Pflimlin and Maurice Schumann, have resigned in protest against de Gaulle's European policy. Therefore, the Parliaments have taken the initiative for the first time in European history, and in this way have also contributed to the acceleration of political unification in free Europe.

Public Opinion in Europe

It would be incorrect, however, to let the responsibility for the realization of the European unification rest exclusively with the French government, in particular, and the governments of the European states, in general. Public opinion in these countries plays a special role, too. Just as the policy of the administrations has changed in regard to European unification during the past years because of political changes, so has the people's attitude been subject to fluctuation. In the first years after the war, there was a general European enthusiasm in the Federal Republic of Germany. The same was true for Italy, Belgium, Luxembourg and the Netherlands. In contrast, public opinion in France and Great Britain was considerably more reserved. The high point of the enthusiasm was in 1953 when—as already mentioned—with the creation of a European Defense Community even the reality of a United States of Europe seemed to be within reach. The day on which these plans were shattered by the resistance of the French Parliament will go down in the history of the European Unification Movement as a "black day".

In these first years of European reconstruction, is was relatively easy to gain the interest and enthusiasm of public opinion for the goal of European unification. Conversely, it was very much more difficult to make clear to the people of the Federal Republic of Germany and the other countries that they would have to be content with the promotion of economic cooperation for some time. When the Common Market then became a reality, the interest in the problems of European unification became visibly lessened. An example illustrates the situation: In the year 1950, according to a survey of several large West German cities, up to 90 % of the population favored the unification of Europe; in the fall of 1961, an inquiry proved that 62 % of the population did not know what "EWG" *(Europaeische Wirtschaftsgemeinschaft*/European Economic Community) meant. This especially showed that the interior policy of individual countries is still essentially decided by economic and social successes and only secondarily by the foreign political development. Accordingly, even responsible statesmen and politicians advocated the concept that with EWG the deciding step toward European unification would already be accomplished. It was believed that the further development toward the political community would automatically and cogently result from the existence of the Common Market. In the parliaments of the individual countries, the question of a European political community was put aside for some time. Even the public stopped discussing a United Europe. Interest flamed up again only when the success of the Common Market and the strengthened foreign political pressure, which was expressed in the threat to Berlin by the Soviet Union, brought sharply into focus the necessity of political cooperation between the European countries. Although it will not be obvious for some time how this political union can be realized—because the interpretation of the French administration stands in bold opposition to the ideas of the other partners of the Common Market. A positive result of the Berlin Crisis is that, in contrast to the year 1953, public opinion in even France, Great Britain, the Scandinavian countries, Switzerland, and Austria sympathizes with the questions of European political unification.

The International European Movement

Special merit in this regard is due to the "European groups" *(Verbaende)*. The role of the European Movement at the founding of the Council of Europe has already been discussed elsewhere. Also the plan mentioned previously for a statute regarding the European Political Community, worked out in 1953, to a great extent goes back to the preparatory work of the "European groups". At times, they alone have borne the burden of propaganda for European unification, above all in the years after the destruction of the European Defense Community. At that time, they advocated the significance of the Common Market before the public and produced the tie between the activity of the European institutions and public opinion, thus filling informational gaps.

The work of these private groups is often underestimated. For this reason, it seems necessary to point out the origins and work of these organizations and groups. They can be divided into four large groups—composed of smaller ones for the setting of general European goals, with leanings toward political parties, with special assignments, and with problems of education. To the first group belong the *"Union Europaeischer Foederalisten"* (Union of European Federalists), which stands for the creation of a European federation on a nonpartisan basis, the "United European Movement" called into being in Great Britain by Churchill, and the "French Council for a United Europe". To the second group belong the "Nouvelles Equipes Internationales/NEI", a union of the Christian Democratic Party for the furtherance of European unification, the *"Sozialistische Bewegung fuer die Vereinigten Staaten von Europa"* (Socialist Movement for the United States of Europe), in which representatives of the Social Democratic Party work together, and likewise the European group of the *"Liberale Weltunion"* (Liberal World Union), a loose union of liberal and independent parties. In the third group, the *"Europaeische Liga fuer Wirtschaftliche Zusammenarbeit"* (European League for Economic Cooperation) is significant. This group has taken as its main assignment the furtherance of the economic unity in Europe. To the fourth and last group belong a large number of institutions, of which only the *"Europaeische Kulturzentrum"* (European Culture Center) in Geneva and the *"Europa Kolleg"* in Bruegge are to be mentioned.

With the great number of organizations which originated shortly after the war, danger existed that tasks would overlap and that confusion would result. For this reason, the representatives of these organizations in 1947 founded an "International Committee for the European Unification", from which, according to the first Congress in The Hague, the international European Movement, as the main organization of most of the active units for the European unification, evolved. The first president of the executive office was Duncan Sandys of Great Britain. Later, the Belgian Paul Henri Spaak stood at the head of the movement for several years. His successor was Robert Schuman of France, who resigned for reasons of health in 1961. Today, in his place, the young and dynamic president of France's Radical-Socialist Party, Maurice Faure, leads the work of the European Movement.

In succeeding years, many groups have changed their names, others have dissolved, new units have been added. The "Union of European Federalists" has undergone a particular development. After the failure of the European Defense Community, it divided into a radical and a moderate wing. While the radical group favored convening in a constitutional assembly of European peoples, the moderate group of the *Aktion Europaeischer Foederalisten* (Drive of European Federalists) supported economic integration as the first step toward a political community. Among the special organizations, the *Rat der Gemeinden Europas* (Council of the Communities of Europe) has obtained particular significance. Within it today are united over 40,000 groups which actively work for the spreading of the European unity idea.

Besides these organizations cooperating in the European Movement, so-called National Councils were formed in the individual countries, which have the task of coordinating the work of the European organizations in the individual countries. Today such National councils exist in Belgium, Germany, Denmark, Greece, Great Britain, Ireland, Italy, Luxembourg, the Netherlands, Norway, Austria, Sweden, Switzerland, and Turkey. For the European countries in which free opinion is impossible, primarily for the European states of the Communist bloc, so-called national committees were formed, which have given the exiled politicians of these countries the opportunity to cooperate in the work of the European movement. Such national committees in exile exist for Albania, Bulgaria, Estonia, Yugoslavia, Latvia, Lithuania, Poland, Rumania, Czechoslovakia, Hungary, and Spain.

Of the organizations which are not attached to the international European Movement, outside of the already mentioned radical group of the earlier *"Union Europaeischer Foederalisten"*, only the "Committee of Action for the United States of Europe" (Comité d'Action pour les Etats Unis de l'Europe), founded by Jean Monnet, is to be mentioned. In this committee leading personalities of the democratic parties and trade unions of the European countries come together to work out common opinions. The committee has, above all, succeeded in regard to the cooperation of various parties in the European Parliament of the Common Market. Finally, the "Paneuropa-Union" of Count Coudenhove-Kalergi, already founded in 1923, still exists, but unfortunately has not yet joined the European Movement, although its founder, along with Winston Churchill, Konrad Adenauer, Robert Schuman, Paul Henri Spaak, and the late Leon Blum and Alcide de Gaspari, is one of the honorary presidents of the European Movement.

The German Organizations of Europe

The construction and work of the European Organizations active in the Federal Republic of Germany resemble in broad outlines the international European Movement. As guiding organization, the *"Deutsche Rat der Europaeische Bewegung"* (German Council of the European Movement) has existed since 1949. Within it numerous parliamentarians cooperate with the representatives of the various units and groups. Its president is Professor Hans Furler, for many years president of the European Parliament.

Members of the executive committee include, among others, the president of the German *Bundestag,* Dr. Eugen Gerstenmaier, the foreign policy speaker of the Social Democratic Party in the Federal Republic of Germany, Fritz Erler, and the Cologne banker Baron Oppenheim, president of the *Europa-Union* of Germany, which is well the most important membership organization of the *Deutsche Rat der Europaeische Bewegung.*

The *Europa-Union,* the German branch of the international federalistic organization, bears the main burden of the European publicity work in the Federal Republic of Germany. It is a nonpartisan member organization with over 300 local groups in the entire Federal Republic of Germany and West Berlin. It is a private union of citizens who advocate the establishment of a United States of Europe. As their first tasks they hope to influence responsible political institutions—parliament, government—in order to further the European policy.

It wants to be, as its President Baron Oppenheim said at one time, "the permanent European conscience in German policy". The *Europa-Union* sees a further task in informing the large interest groups—trade unions and economic units—about the significance of the already existing European Community and the necessity of political union. It procures specialists for this purpose for lectures, pertinent literature, films and slides; and aids with the preparation and carrying out of events of its own local groups as well as for other organizations. An average of 200 events per month—discussions, lectures, and public demonstrations are, for such a group, a considerable achievement.

The political demands of the German *Europa-Union* are formulated by the chair, in close contact with leading European politicians, and are represented publicly in the annual congress. The economic bases are furnished by a *"Bildungswerk Europaeische Politik"* (Education Center of European Policy), founded by the *Europa-Union,* which also coordinates the work of several "Europe-Houses". These Europe-Houses are a sort of adult education institution in which all groups of the population have the opportunity to make themselves familiar with the problems of European unification. In these Europe-Houses, moreover, regular international meetings take place.

The *Europa-Union* attributes particular significance to the schools. It proceeds from the conviction that education toward the "European citizen" must begin in the school. It furthers the exchange of young people of various countries, and also of members of various professional groups—workers, employees of firms, civil servants, farmers, teachers, etc. In most cases, the *Europa-Union* can count on support from state and community authorities.

Publications of widely varied types, among them a newspaper of its own which appears semimonthly, give to those interested the possibility of becoming informed on all problems of European unification policy. A junior unit, the *"Junge Europaeische Foederalisten"* (Young European Federalists) has taken on the task of representing the European idea in the circles of numerous youth organizations at universities and institutions of higher learning, such as technical schools, conservatories, etc.

The German Citizen and Europe

At present, the official policy of the country and the efforts to influence public opinion still do not show the actual attitude of the population. Especially in view of the European policy, citizens in other countries, primarily in the United States of America, will ask to what extent the German population is really convinced of the necessity of a united Europe. Various symptoms of past economic development have caused an uneasy feeling on both sides of the Atlantic, that the average German, in the face of the economic and social achievements, might prefer the results of an emphatic German "national policy" instead of an arrangement which would channel German advantages into a common European advantage.

The German *Europa-Union* also shared this uneasiness and for this reason introduced in the spring of 1962, in cooperation with the well-known American motivation-researcher, Ernest Dichter, a comprehensive investigation of the conduct of the German population on the question of European cooperation. The results could, to some extent, give an indication of the psychological difficulties, still in opposition to the European concept, perhaps more so today than in the first postwar years. The investigation, resting on the results of modern socio-scientific and socio-psychological research, will in this way become an indispensible aid for future informational work of the German *Europa-Union* and, moreover, should also extend to the other European countries in cooperation with European organizations within them.

The investigation has shown that the average German thinks of the European concept in positive terms. One group of those interviewed expects personal advantages through economic and social development and also political security. Many were aware, moreover, of the weakness of a Germany standing alone. To many of those interviewed, the present situation summons a feeling of political inferiority, of being "sold out". One feels himself passed by and to be sure even more so, when one is convinced that German still has "something to offer" the world.

The German is conscious that the Iron Curtain has abolished the formerly central significance of his country but believes that a United Europe without Germany would be unthinkable. In some cases, a certain presumptuousness is connected with this view, but on the other hand, also the good will to place the economic potential of Germany unselfishly at the disposal of a United Europe.

It is also interesting that many prejudices about his own country and the neighboring European countries have changed. People have become more self-critical in Germany. They recognize its weaknesses and admit—even if unwillingly—that other peoples can point to the same accomplishments and—in the case of France and Italy—know how to live better. Again other prejudices have become entrenched through direct association with the other country. Thus, the French way of living is condemned as frivolous, which does not exclude that many interviewees gladly travel to France exactly because of the more informal French way of life. Also a majority of those interviewed is of the firm conviction that most social scandals occur in Italy. Here exist invisible barriers which must be put aside to smooth the way for a united Europe.

Other questions had extremely positive answers for the future. Sixty-three percent of the interviewees are ready to accept English as the common language in a United Europe, eighteen percent plead for French, and only fifteen percent are of the opinion that the German language could be elevated to the European language. A total of four percent would prefer an artificial language, such as Esperanto. Even resistance to intermarriages with foreigners has largely disappeared. Indeed, it is very interesting to see national groups receive priority. Swedes are most acceptable, followed by Dutch and English. French, and interestingly also Swiss, have the least chance to marry into Germany. Differences arise here, indeed, depending on whether older or younger people have been asked. Younger people do not make such great differences as older; prejudices have been largely already torn down by them.

A further question of this investigation attempted to fathom what the average German valued most highly himself. To the question, which country could most likely produce a revolutionizing technical invention, 87 % of those asked replied without hesitation that it could only be in Germany. The counterquestion was asked, in which country a production error could most likely occur that would cost the lives of hundreds of people. In general this question was met with a shrugging of the shoulders, and one was of the opinion that in any state and in any industry "something could go wrong" at some time. When this question was pursued further, the feeling of a European community showed itself as a bulwark against Communism, for 50 % of those asked gave the opinion that such an error would most likely occur first in the countries of the East Bloc.

Which conclusive deductions can be drawn from this first political motivation-research project in West Germany? Dr. Dichter himself has explained in a foreword to the publication of the results of the investigation: "A common Europe, toward which the Western democracies have been working for years, has not only a political and economic, but also a psychological aspect. It is, to be sure, only consistent to introduce a common currency, a common flag, and a uniform passport, but at the same time, that means a powerful inner conversion for the European nations. The Europeans have a strong feeling for national peculiarities. How is a whole to grow out of so many?—so they ask themselves apprehensively. Generally perceptible is the fear that one might lose his peculiar identity; it is as though one were to tear down with the national boundaries, a wall of security, if indeed illusory. Thus Europe has not only the wall in Berlin. Between the countries, in fact between various regions, exist walls of a sort, tempered by feelings. Many a Bavarian believes he has nothing in common with the Prussian; many a Parisian considers himself completely different from a man in Southern France.

The European community feeling certainly cannot and should not replace pride in a particular stock. But if we want to make a political reality of the geographical concept of Europe, then the feeling of unity of the Europeans must be placed before local pride. When we have once learned to say of a person, "he is a splendid man", before we think that he is a Frenchman, a Dutchman, or an Italian, we will have already come closer to the concept of the European, without which a United Europe cannot be created.

Hope and Outlook

Although the unification of Europe has not yet been carried to its conclusion, the measures initiated since 1948 have proved to be a motive force that makes any halt in the development seem impossible, aside from temporary interruptions. The economies of the European countries have been placed on an entirely new basis. Europe is already in a position to assume an increasing share in the defense burdens of the Atlantic Alliance and the free world. By this are meant not only the funds for military defense but the measures for the economic development of the Asian, African, and Latin American countries. The European Economic Community faces major tasks particularly in the area of assistance for underdeveloped countries. A large number of the African countries released from colonial rule are associated with the Common Market through ties with their former mother countries.

The old continent has risen to a new capacity for economic production which will contribute to proving the superiority of the free society in the eyes of those countries still in quest of an appropriate social system. This superiority is in turn the only hope for all those peoples who are unable to share in the free system, including the peoples of Eastern Europe and the eastern part of Germany. European unification has thus become the only conceivable policy for the liberation of Eastern Europe and consequently for the reunification of Germany.

By comparison to our fast-moving times, European unification is an extremely gradual process. What some firm supporters of European unity regard as a drawback can also be understood to be an advantage. The merging of the European countries is not being dictated from above, but is taking place on the basis of free decision by the peoples and their sovereign governments. Here the difference from events in Eastern Europe is obvious. There, too, a process of integration is taking place. The European countries of the Communist Bloc have joined to form a Council of Mutual Economic Aid (COMECON), which is intended to lead to closer economic cooperation in the so-called "countries of People's Democracy". However, this association serves only the interests of Moscow, which wants to make the Eastern European countries even more dependent on itself through a calculated division of effort. Yet, a community of peoples can only endure if it is imbued with the spirit of liberty.

The policy of European unification will not attain all prospective goals over night. It has already proved its worth. There will be signs of crisis in the future as in the past. Nonetheless, it will continue to be the only chance for the future of the European peoples and a security for the freedom of the world.

Germany and the Developing Countries

By Guenter Grunwald and Johannes Reinhold

A presentation of the relationship between the Federal Republic of Germany and the developing countries must be directed mainly at the structure and means of German aid activities. In this respect, it is less important to give statistical data than to make clear what determines the impulses and ideas governing German development aid and what kind of practical expression they find. For that reason, in addition to an account of the existing situation, a few preliminary remarks are in order. These remarks are even more indispensable due to the fact that Germany has had to clarify, to itself as to the rest of the world, its attitude towards its own past.

In the eyes of the world Germany is the country with the most pronounced racial prejudices. This point of view was amply confirmed by the years of Nationalist Socialist rule and by the subsequent discovery of inhuman atrocities. We believe, however, that we can say that progress is being made in the direction of unprejudiced thinking in Germany and that this change is reflected in the attitude toward the developing countries. Other races and peoples with different skin colors have become respected as partners and have come to be regarded as nothing out of the ordinary. Terms such as "sub-human", "inferior race", "alien blood", are today considered serious violations of the moral code acceptable in the Federal Republic. Expressions of superiority over less developed countries have been banned from discussions. Significant is the fact that Germany was the first country to replace the term "under-developed countries" with "developing countries".

It can be argued, of course, that here and there there are relapses and that incorrigible elements exist; but any process of change takes time since the process concerns men whose roots go far back into the history of their people, men who must come to terms with their own past as well as with their own generation.

A struggle similar to race prejudice took place once before—although it did not go so deep—in another political sector: within the area of the cherished German dreams of an empire, and this concerned the overcoming of colonialism.

Germany's Attitude Towards Colonialism

During the past 400 years, European colonial politics has developed colonies for the purpose of settlement, for enconomic reasons, and for the show of power and military influence. In the 19th and 20th centuries, the continually increasing expenditures required for the development of colonial areas, for their military protection, their administration, the ever-increasing criticism of colonial exploitation from humanitarian groups, growing trade competition and, in particular, the acquisition of technical and economic knowledge by the inhabitants of the colonial areas themselves, forced a gradual modification of European colonial policy.

Up to the 20th century, the military and administrative superiority of the European powers made it possible for them to secure their hold on colonies mostly with naval forces and small land-troop contingents and to rule with small administrative staffs. The humanitarian criticism of colonial policies, however, necessitated more administrative activities within the field of education and public health and also in the administration of justice. The European colonial powers had to take into account the increasing political emancipation of the colonial populations by according them self-administration or self-government. As a result of the two world wars, the national consciousness of the colonial populations also increased. In addition, socialist critics used the argument that colonialism was a form of imperialist monopolistic capitalism and thus contributed to the overthrow of European colonial rule. The ideologies of National Socialism, Socialism and Communism—all deriving from Europe—provided the required spiritual and intellectual weapons for the colonial nations.

Throughout the entire world, an evolution began, the different aspects of which are today identified by the terms "decolonization" and "developing countries."

The German *Reich,* which attained its national unity only in 1870, entered the field of colonization later than the other European countries. The growth of the German economy and population caused Bismarck, after considerable hesitation, to obtain colonies for Germany also. In 1884-85, he acquired, by a series of quick actions, areas in East and Southeast Africa, in Cameroun and Togo, in addition to a part of New Guinea and the Solomon Islands, as well as the so-called Bismarck Archipelago and the Marshall Islands in the South Pacific. Later on, in 1897, the Chinese coastal area around Tsingtau with Kiaochow was obtained on lease; in 1899 the Mariana Islands, Caroline Islands, Palau Islands, and the main part of the Samoan Islands by treaty; and in 1911, also through treaty, part of the French Congo.

Up to World War I, German colonial possessions amounted to approximately 3 million square kilometers with approximately 12.3 million inhabitants. The short dream of a German colonial empire was soon over, however. Through the Treaty of Versailles, Germany lost all her colonies to the West European victors of World War I. It was not willingly that Germany gave up all overseas territories but the military defeat of 1918 forced her to. Later on, especially during the Nazi era in Germany, thoughts of colonies once again came to the fore—incited by Hitler's plans to conquer the world.

When World War II ended with Germany's unconditional surrender, all thoughts of restoration of colonies ceased. There now came into being the conditions for unhampered cooperation with the young countries and the Federal Republic of Germany was provided with a good starting position, politically as well as psychologically, for its subsequent development policy. In those days, unfortunately, the idea of "aid to developing countries" was the hobby of a few idealists only. Nowadays, the necessity for such aid has become a basic theme of present political problems and plays a decisive role in the plans of even the most dispassionate statesmen.

German Public Opinion and the Developing Countries

Also a change has begun to take place in public opinion in the Federal Republic. As a public opinion poll conducted among a representative cross-section of the population indicated in 1961, 70 % of the people understand the term "development aid" correctly. That seems to indicate an above-average interest in the subject. But it is important to realize that proper understanding does not mean that the public is ready to support development aid, and that the phenomenon indicated by the public opinion poll has its basis in a number of sources.

In the first place, active public interest in developing countries is relatively new, dating back to approximately four years ago. After 1945, the Germans needed quite a while to consider their own problems and began, only after putting their own house in order, to consider world-wide problems and to grasp the idea of international responsibility. Because such shifts towards new historical-political concepts always take place with a display of emotion in Germany, it is no wonder that the developing countries had at the beginning, and to some extent still have today, the fascination of a new fashion. This fashion, however, takes various forms. To begin with, the lively interest in the countries of Asia, Africa, and Latin America is a reaction to the years of isolation from 1933 to 1945; with that goes the feeling, of course, of once again being in the swing of things. In addition, half-forgotten or suppressed ideas going back to the golden age of Christian missionary work are being revived; those who heard in their Sunday School days about the poor little negro children can begin once again from the same concept. And lastly, the most important source of this emotional stream is the fact that the world has become smaller thanks to the rapid spread of television and other mass-communication means. For Mr. Average Man, sitting before his television set, Nehru is nearer than the mayor of his home town and Conakry more familiar than Bonn.

Nevertheless, those citizens who understand the meaning of development aid are not automatically in favor of it. With respect to support of developing aid there is even a noticeable lack of enthusiasm. The reason for this is mainly the way some illustrated papers, in their efforts to increase circulation with sensational stories, show pictures of the jewel-bedecked wives of sovereigns and presidents and describe the extravagance of some rulers, their systems of nepotism and existing corruption. Such stories are accepted uncritically and spread by the public, thus strengthening the general impression that German development aid is either entirely superfluous or being directed into the wrong channels.

In addition, after the Belgrade Conference of the Neutral Countries, the more reliable West German press voiced some rather severe and bitter remarks about those developing countries which accept aid from the Federal Republic while at the same time dealing political blows to it. This unfavorable trend can only be counteracted if it becomes possible to turn discussions away from the sphere of the exotic and sensational and back to the sober and realistic aspects of the situation.

That presupposes, of course, clarification concerning motives and aims of German development aid and the making of a uniform, binding policy as the basis of action. Progress is already visible to the majority of those concerned and interested.

The Basic Motives of German Development Aid

It goes without saying that in view of the multitude of participating groups within a pluralist society, all working towards the same objective, one cannot speak of a uniform and rigidly defined motive. Various groups have different focal points. There do exist, however, several generally recognized basic motives. They stem from the principle of equality of mankind and the claim for the same social justice for all.

Naturally, these basic motives can be either partially or completely superceded by other considerations, or be governed by additional motives. Thus, within the field of government, the fact that Germany is divided and that there exists a Communist threat will necessarily add several tactical and pragmatic considerations to the basically recognized premise of equal dignity and rights. Within private and economic spheres, some modifications of the purely humanitarian motivation can also be observed; those for whom the just distribution of goods is intended will be the buyers of tomorrow. This thought is neither improper nor illegitimate, however, as long as it is not prompted exclusively by the greed for profit.

There is unanimity within the Federal Republic that in any inquiry into the motives of German development aid no attempt should be made to conceal the existing political and economic factors, because German development aid is not meant to be an "act of mercy" but, rather, a relationship among partners openly cooperating with each other under a system of mutual give and take. From this attitude there results the formulation of those principles valid for the development aid policy of the Federal Republic. They proceed from the realization that any development aid policy must be determined by the requirements of the developing countries themselves, i.e., aid can only be granted where it has been requested and is to be used in a way favorable to locally existing conditions. Since experience gained in an industrialized country cannot be transferred directly to developing countries, German aid can only provide the impulse for independent action or, according to the generally accepted idea, can only be aid to self-help. By its very nature, such assistance is against the setting up of conditions; due to basic principles it can neither be withheld from countries maintaining friendly relations with the "German Democratic Republic" regime nor from those countries whose economic, governmental, and constitutional setup do not correspond to the ideas of the Federal Republic. This fundamental idea will have to be adhered to within reasonable limits.

German Development Aid Measures in the Governmental Realm

On the basis of these motives and principles, various forms of development aid and ways of dealing with questions concerning the developing countries have come into existence in the Federal Republic. In accordance with the importance granted to all social groups within a democracy, development aid in the Federal Republic is being effected not only on the governmental level. Although the greatest part of funds required is being raised from official sources, sensible joint efforts between governmental and private agencies is gradually developing.

These two groups, however, definitely cannot be regarded as homogenous. To begin with, as far as the governmental level is concerned, it has to be divided into three groups: the Federal Government with its agencies, the West German states, and the communities. Of these, the most important partner is the Federal Government with its legislative and executive bodies. But here also there was no uniform picture during the first years of German development aid. Prior to the establishment of a special ministry for development aid, the *Bundesministerium fuer wirtschaftliche Zusammenarbeit* (Federal Ministry for Economic Cooperation), twelve ministries had to deal with questions of development aid and will probably have to do so for some time to come. For this reason, all necessary measures are being coordinated in interministerial steering committees. This entails not only a considerable amount of administrative effort but these committees are also, to some extent, subject to the promotion of their own self-interest.

Nevertheless, the increasing commitments of the Federal Republic in the field of development aid, having risen to 5 billion DM for 1961 and 1962, constitute a remarkable achievement, particularly in view of the fact that this does not include the considerable expenditure of more than one billion DM for education and training of trainees, university students, etc., within Germany. Private efforts cannot be estimated to their full extent.

The grants of the Federal Government take various forms. On the multilateral level, they consist of contributions to international organizations such as the Technical Aid Program of the United Nations, special organizations of the United Nations, and the development fund of the EEC, etc. Moreover, they are provided in the form of credits to the World Bank and in the taking over of debenture bonds as well as capital shares and by further participation in projects of the World Bank, the International Development Agency (IDA), the International Finance Corporation (IFC), and the European Investment Bank (EIB). In addition, capital aid has been given in the following forms: direct financing of projects from public funds, governmental promotion of private measures by way of investment counseling, the assumption of sureties and guarantees, export credits, tax reductions, etc. In individual cases grants meant to stabilize budgets and balance sheets, such as various trade policy measures in the form of long-term purchase contracts, tariff reductions and consumer tax reductions will be considered.

Besides the measures of capital aid, specialized technical aid, granted within the framework of cultural cooperation, is gaining in significance in the Federal Republic. Its most important function is education and training, with programs for trainees, university students, and executive employees. This is meant for persons who already hold leading positions in their own countries and who can pass on to others the knowledge acquired abroad. This program also includes the preparation and sending out of German professional experts to developing countries, as well as research into basic conditions and projects under consideration. Mostly, however, governmental aid in this area is being granted in the form of promotion of nongovernmental agencies active in the various fields. This system will be described in detail later.

The Federal Government has implemented its measures by use of several institutions outside its direct executive setup. They must be mentioned, because they permit a glance into the organizational forms of German development aid policy. In the sphere of capital aid, the most important institution is the *Kreditanstalt fuer Wiederaufbau und Entwicklung* (Reconstruction and Development Loan Corporation) which operates as the development aid bank on behalf of the Federal Government and processes all credits from public funds. Sureties and guarantees for export credits, finance credits, and debt conversion credits have been taken over by the *Deutsche Revisions- und Treuhand Ag.* (German Revision and Trusteeship Joint-Stock Company) and the *Hermes-Kreditversicherungs-Ag.* (Hermes Credit Insurance Joint-Stock Company), the Federal Government assuming responsibility for losses.

Administrative duties in the field of cultural cooperation and specialized assistance have been assigned to the *Bundesamt fuer gewerbliche Wirtschaft* (Federal Agency for Industry and Trade) which is under supervision of the Federal Ministry for Economics and to the *Deutsche Wirtschaftsfoerderungs- und Treuhandgesellschaft* (GAWI) (German Economy Promotion and Trusteeship Association) which, too, belongs to the Federation. The first-named agency cooperates in selecting German experts for the programs of the United Nations, while "GAWI" is concerned with the establishment of training shops and the sending of specialists to the developing countries as well as seeing to the carrying out of contracts.

A special role of the Federal Government in this field is played by the *Deutsche Stiftung fuer Entwicklungslaender* (German Foundation for Developing Countries). It was set up two years ago by deputies of all factions in the West German parliament and by the ministries concerned, and has to do with the organization of information courses for executives in various fields, preparatory courses for German experts, and documentation work. The special characteristic of this agency is seen in the fact that while it lies within the field of government, nongovernmental organizations are participating within the framework of an advisory council.

In addition to the activity of the Federal Government described so far, the various West German states also contribute to the carrying out of development aid. To begin with, everything having to do with cultural cooperation with the developing countries is part of the responsibility of the states because of the cultural stipulations of the constitution. Also, a large number of the German experts are state employees. In addition to this, at the present time several states are implementing the work with special development aid programs of their own with special emphasis on certain regions. These efforts, which are parallel to those of the Federal Government will, in the future, have to be improved through practical coordination.

The measures of the German cities on behalf of development aid must also be seen as part of governmental activities in this field. The city efforts are mostly concerned with training aid and the establishment of city partnerships.

Even after development aid is broken down into the main two categories of governmental and nongovernmental activity, there still exist two forms of organization which fall neither into one category nor the other: the political parties and the churches. It is true that the political parties determine indirectly the work of the legislative through their deputies and thus provide the framework for development policy and aid efforts. But the large parties of the Federal Republic have also founded working groups for development aid in which problems of the developing countries are considered from special political points of view. In this way, stimulating suggestions are offered on the governmental level as well as on the private one.

The two big churches also play an important part in development aid policy since, apart from their missionary activities, they have carried out exemplary educational and welfare aid projects in the developing countries. This was done long before the beginning of governmental work in this field. This work may be considered a model of its kind insofar as it has been carried out to the best advantage through the means of large monetary sums—both churches having made available more than 100 million DM—without any unnecessary bureaucratic interference. Quick aid in individual cases always presents a problem to the government but hardly ever to the churches.

A far more complex situation is to be found in the field of private endeavor with its various social groups.

Private German Development Aid

In Germany, the view is often publicly expressed that there are too many organizations and institutions in the field of private endeavor which concern themselves with questions of development aid. It is urged, therefore, that these efforts be coordinated for it is believed that the multitude of different agencies and activities is bound to lead to the squandering of means and energy. This is a false argument. It has promoted psychological resistance because of the apparent confusion within the organizations but exists only for those who have a relatively superficial knowledge of the facts. Democracy, however, derives its strength from the multifarious diversity of the initiative of its citizens. Dictatorial regimes also have a large number of organizations at their disposal as instruments of internal supervision and infiltration into the outside world, and they are all "coordinated". This does not mean, though, that there does not exist in them competition, bureaucratic red tape, waste, and differences of opinion. However, the manifold participation of nongovernmental organizations in a field of such important official activity as that of relations with the developing countries is not only an advantage for the democratic system but is in itself necessary and useful for the solutions of the problems in question.

The objective of nongovernmental organizations must be to promote cooperation with the developing countries beyond the possible governmental and economic contacts for the purpose of integration, as far as possible, of the social elements.

It is not possible in this article to enter details regarding all nongovernmental organizations concerned with the establishment of partnership relations with the countries of Asia, Africa and Latin America. Consequently, only the most important groups will be described.

The large business associations have created joint systems and committees for the preparation of policy regarding development aid questions for the different groups as well as for the dissemination of information for their members. While up to the present—according to the *Bundesverband der Deutschen Industrie* (Federation of German Industries)—the German efforts have been centered mainly around the granting of long-term credits, private investments, contributions to the international financial institutions, and technical aid, it has now been realized that the main task lies in the drawing up of a plan for the utilization of bilateral financial aid from public funds within the framework of a carefully thought out development policy. With respect to the organizing of financial aid, technical aid, and application of trade policy—the three pillars of development aid—German industry tries to cooperate closely with the Federal Government. Only by supplementing each other and coordinating public and private development aid can the greatest possible success be achieved—this is the opinion of the "Developing Countries" section of the Federation of German Industries.

The German trade union movement can justly claim that in the course of its historical development it has always been against colonialism. As an important partner in the International Confederation of Free Trade Unions (ICFTU), the *Deutscher Gewerkschaftsbund (DGB)* (German Trade Union Federation) developed useful focal points for trade union activities in Asia, Africa, and Latin America, and cooperated in several countries in the development of powerful and sovereign trade unions. In line with the old trade union principle of international solidarity, the German trade unions have for many years appropriated millions of DM for the solidarity fund of the International Confederation of Free Trade Unions in Brussels. This was earmarked for educational and training aid in the developing countries. Beyond this, the German trade unions have been making efforts to set up workshops for apprentices, vocational training institutions and to give technical aid in other ways, especially to the trade union organizations in the developing countries.

The German cooperatives also began very early—through their program "Help India"—with direct efforts on behalf of development aid. The importance of the cooperatives and trade unions in the developing countries cannot be overestimated since free cooperatives and strong unions constitute in many cases the only alternatives to totalitarian developments in Asia, Africa, and Latin America.

The universities and the large economic and social science research institutes in the Federal Republic are devoting increasing attention to the problems of developing countries. At the University of Heidelberg, for example, a special institute for developing countries, especially for those in the Indo-Asiatic area, was founded and another one at the University of Freiburg to deal with cultural questions. Similar institutes are planned as research projects at the Universities of Berlin, Hamburg, and Munich.

The large German research institutes are combined in the Association of the Union of Economic and Social Science Research Institutes. Of this association the following institutes are especially concerned with problems of the developing countries:

1) *Institut fuer Weltwirtschaft an der Universitaet Kiel* (Institute of World Economics at the University of Kiel)
2) *Hamburgisches Weltwirtschafts-Archiv* (Hamburg World Economics Archive)
3) *Deutsches Institut fuer Wirtschaftsforschung, Berlin* (German Institute for Economic Research, Berlin)
4) *Ifo-Institut Muenchen* (Institute for Economic Research, Munich)
5) *Forschungsstelle der Friedrich-Ebert-Stiftung, Bonn* (Research Center of the Friedrich Ebert Foundation, Bonn)
6) *Bremer Ausschuss fuer Wirtschaftsforschung* (Bremen Committee for Economic Research)
7) *Institut fuer Entwicklungslaender, Bonn* (Institute for Developing Countries, Bonn)
8) *Forschungsinstitut fuer internationale technische Zusammenarbeit an der Technischen Hochschule Aachen* (Research Institute for International Technical Cooperation at the Technical University, Aachen)
9) *Institut fuer Selbsthilfe und Sozialforschung, Koeln* (Institute for Self-Help and Social Research, Cologne)

The following—among others—are devoted to questions in the field of development aid:

1) *Gesellschaft fuer Generalstudien, Bonn* (Society for General Studies, Bonn)
2) *Gemeinschaft unabhaengiger beratender Ingenieurbueros, Bonn* (Association of Independent Consultant Engineers, Bonn)
3) *Verein Beratender Ingenieure e. V., Essen* (Union of Consultant Engineers, Essen)

The big scientific organizations such as the *Deutsche Forschungsgemeinschaft* (German Research Council), *Deutscher Wissenschaftsrat* (German Council for the Promotion of Science and Humanities), *Westdeutsche Rektorenkonferenz* (West German Rectors' Conference) and, on the side of industry, the *Stifterverband fuer die deutsche Wissenschaft* (Founders' Association for German Science), are also especially interested in the exchange of scientists with developing countries and in the granting of assistance to individuals and research projects.

Four years ago, the large cultural institutions in the Federal Republic formed the *Arbeitsgemeinschaft fuer internationalen Kulturaustausch* (International Cultural Exchange Alliance). Its most important members are:

Deutscher Akademischer Austauschdienst e. V., Bonn (German Academic Exchange Service). The Federal Government put this institution in charge of a scholarship program for university students from the developing countries. At the same time, it is responsible for the entire student exchange program and grants a large number of scholarships to Germans who wish to go to developing countries.

Goethe-Institut zur Pflege der deutschen Sprache (Goethe Institute for the Cultivation of the German Language). This institute maintains a large number of places abroad where German teachers give instruction in German. In the developing countries, this opportunity attracts more and more of those willing to learn, and the existing facilities, although already considerable, are sufficient to provide the required language instruction to only a fraction of the interested applicants. In addition, the Goethe Institute has, in the last two years, taken over the administration from the German Foreign Office of various cultural centers and cultural institutes, particularly in the developing countries.

Carl-Duisberg-Gesellschaft fuer Nachwuchsfoerderung e. V., Koeln (Carl Duisberg Society for the Support of Trainees). This is a society of the leading associations of German business and of the employers' and employees' groups. Its function is to assist in training students from the developing countries who hold university scholarships from the government in order to ensure the success of their studies. Help for other foreign trainees in German enterprises who do not have government scholarships for university studies is given by the 100 Foreigners' Circles of the Carl Duisberg Society.

Friedrich-Ebert-Stiftung e. V., Bonn (Friedrich Ebert Foundation). This foundation was founded in 1925 and is thus one of the oldest in Germany. Four years ago, it was instrumental in the establishment of the International Cultural Exchange Alliance. As far back as the Weimar Republic, the Friedrich Ebert Foundation was concerned with cooperation with the countries of Asia, Africa, and Latin America. After 1945, these efforts were resumed and intensified. In its residential college for adult education at Bergneustadt (80 kilometers from Bonn), the foundation has at its disposal an excellent home for lectures and seminars on questions of developing aid. In addition, it has set up a very active research center which has already published results from work on problems in the field of development aid. The Friedrich Ebert Foundation also grants scholarships to especially gifted university students from the developing countries and, during their stay in the Federal Republic, provides contacts in human relations as well as in their scientific work. In addition, the foundation endeavors to promote the education and training of junior executives from the developing countries, particularly in the fields of trade unions and cooperatives, adult education and administration, and mass-media specialists.

Institut fuer Auslandsbeziehungen, Stuttgart (Institute for Relations with Foreign Countries). It devotes special interest to the providing of books to developing countries and to contacts with Germans throughout the world.

Internationaler Arbeitskreis Sonnenberg, Braunschweig (Sonnenberg International Committee, Braunschweig). This institute maintains a large conference center in the Harz mountains and arranges meetings between young Germans and Europeans with young citizens of the developing countries. Among other things, it is concerned with the training of teachers concerned with questions relative to the partnership with developing countries.

Additional member organizations of the Cultural Exchange Alliance are: *Verband Deutscher Studentenschaften, Bonn* (Association of German Student Organizations)
Deutscher Kunstrat, Koeln (German Arts' Council, Cologne)
Deutscher Volkshochschulverband, Bonn (German Adult Education Association)
Deutsche Afrika-Gesellschaft, Bonn (German Africa Society)
Arbeitskreis der privaten Institutionen fuer internationale Begegnung und Bildungsarbeit, Koeln (Association of Private Institutions for International Meetings and Education Work, Cologne)
Deutscher Musikrat, Koeln (German Music Council, Cologne)
Deutsche Stiftung fuer Entwicklungslaender, Berlin (German Foundation for the Developing Countries)
The following institutions are also cooperating with the International Cultural Alliance because some of their leading executives are members:
Inter Nationes e. V., Bonn
Gemeinnuetzige Arbeitsgemeinschaft zur Foerderung der zwischenstaatlichen Beziehungen, Bonn (Nonprofit Association for the Promotion of *Intergovernmental Relations)*
Wirtschaftspolitische Gesellschaft von 1947, Frankfurt/Main (Society for Economic Politics of 1947, Frankfort)
Deutsche Orientstiftung, Hamburg (German Orient Foundation, Hamburg)
Alexander-von-Humboldt-Stiftung, Bonn (Alexander von Humboldt Foundation, Bonn)
Haus Rissen, Institut fuer Wirtschafts- und Sozialpolitik, bei Hamburg (House Rissen, Institute for Economic and Social Politics, near Hamburg)
Almost all German welfare institutions and agencies such as the German Caritas Association, the Inner Mission, the Workers' Welfare Association, the Jewish Welfare Committee, and the German Nondenominational Welfare Association deal with problems raised by developing aid. In part, organizations have been formed by Germans in developing countries, social work experts have been trained for development aid tasks, and these activities have been carried out in cooperation with private international organizations such as the international Catholic organizations, the Ecumenic Council in Geneva, and others.

The *Arbeitsgemeinschaft fuer Jugendpflege und Jugendfuersorge, Bonn* (Association for Youth Care and Youth Welfare, Bonn), which has as members the youth organizations as well as the welfare organizations and agencies of the West German states and communities, has made of itself—following a suggestion of its international association, the International Federation for Aid to Youth in Geneva—a clearing center for development aid projects dealing with the problems of hardships confronting juveniles in the developing countries.
Among the organizations on the state level a difference must be made between state associations—partly old foreign trade associations stemming from the traditional export trade and shipping companies—and the state societies whose activities are aimed at the promotion of cultural, political, and general human understanding.

Some of the state associations are: *Afrika-Verein Hamburg-Bremen e. V.* (Africa Association Hamburg-Bremen); *Nah- und Mittelost-Verein, Ham-*

burg (Near and Middle East Association, Hamburg); *Ostasiatischer Verein, Hamburg* (East Asiatic Association, Hamburg); *Ibero-Amerika-Verein, Hamburg* (Ibero-American Association, Hamburg) with the affiliated Ibero-American Foundation and the Ibero-American Physicians' Academy.

The state societies whose interests extend beyond purely economic matters include, among others: *Deutsche-Indische Gesellschaft e. V., Stuttgart* (German-Indian Society, Stuttgart); *Deutsche Afrika-Gesellschaft e. V., Bonn* (German-Africa Society, Bonn); *Deutsche-Tuerkische Gesellschaft e. V., Kiel* (German-Turkish Society, Kiel); *Deutsche Ghana Gesellschaft* (German Ghana Society), and a German-Togo Society, a German-Chinese Society, a German-Tunisian Society, a German-Brazilian Society, as well as several Ibero-American clubs, and African and Asian circles in various towns which frequently cooperate with local foreign country societies.

Within the last few years almost all students' organizations and youth associations in the Federal Republic have realized the seriousness of their responsibility towards the students and youth in the developing countries and have implemented their aid projects and exchange programs. Through study tours and conferences or practical cooperation in international organizations, their participation in developing aid questions has been intensified. Particularly active in this field have been the *Verband Deutscher Studentenschaften, Bonn* (Association of German Student Organizations), the *Internationale Studentenbund (ISSF),* (International Students' League) the student groups, the political students' organizations and, above all, the World University Service (WUS), Bonn, which years ago had already made special efforts in the support of students' centers, particularly with regard to welfare assistance measures on behalf of students in the developing countries.

Schools, students' organizations, and large German teachers' organizations have been active in recent years, sponsoring groups in Asia, Africa, and Latin America.

More Recent Tendencies in German Development Aid

Since the beginning of cooperation with developing countries, the Federal Republic has made various mistakes both at home and abroad. Basic experience has been gained, however, and this will decisively influence future dealings.

On the domestic front, the most important fact is the realization that in spite of the manifold system of the Federal Republic its development aid policy must be made uniform. This necessitates coordination of all measures both in public and private spheres. These first steps towards cooperation have been made with the German Foreign Office, the agency showing most understanding. It has even gone so far as to delegate governmental tasks to private agencies and is a by-product of the development aid policy which provides a new aspect for Germany in the positive sense.

But new directions can be perceived in the measures themselves. For a long time, the public attitude toward development aid was that it was nothing more than the transferring of sufficient amounts of money to the developing countries. Only gradually has some understanding of how to further progress in the developing countries come about. Considerable time elapsed into a bottomless pit as long as there was not personnel in the developing countries capable of putting aid to the best possible use. With that realization, education moved into the foreground and brought about a noticeable modification in the structure of German development aid.

Since the most important factor of development aid—as argued today—is to be seen in the preparation of the partner countries for systematic self-help, the assistance aimed directly at the individual, i. e., educational and welfare aid, takes priority over all financial and economic help.

The recognition of this basic principle will have consequences for future German development aid programs. More intensive programs dealing with education projects and training of executives for public positions, for administrative posts, for places in the economic, cultural and social life, as leading representatives in the elementary and vocational training schools as well as of adult education, especially within communities and villages, will be required. Particular attention will have to be paid to the development of mass media as a means of education.

Moreover, with respect to German development activities having to do with education which are supported by intergovernmental or private investments, it has been urged that these projects contain a definite proportion of funds and effort directed toward social welfare. That is, private business projects should be compelled to include education in their planning.

Generally speaking, it is believed that the necessary amount to be allotted to training and social aid measures within German development aid grants should, in the coming years, amount to one third of the total.

In this connection, the example of the American Peace Corps has set off lively discussions in the Federal Republic and promoted new ideas. The organizations participating in the International Cultural Exchange Alliance intend to send observers to the United States to study the training methods of the Peace Corps. In addition, in the effort to stimulate the interest of young Germans to work in the developing countries, a *Gespraechkreis Entwicklungshelfer* (Discussion Group of Development Helpers) was founded in which the important students' and youth organizations participate with large cultural organizations. The objective of this discussion group is to find, following the initiative set by the Americans, some method of action suited to German conditions.

Another change can also be seen. Thus far, the training of students and executives from the developing countries took place almost exclusively in the Federal Republic. In the future, the training of professional experts and executives through means of development aid will be done mainly within the developing countries themselves since the number of German instructors available for teaching posts in the developing countries is increasing. And the situation with regard to university students will probably change to some extent. At the present time, approximately 10 % of all students at German universities are foreigners, most of them from developing countries. Apart from the fact that German universities are overcrowded, it must be taken into consideration that the developing countries are building up their own centers of instruction. Consequently, studies in

Germany will be promoted only in special cases, for example, for highly qualified young scientists.

There appears to be yet another side to German aid activities: an awareness of the existence of European neighbors. This is a new thought, for despite the fact that there have been lively discussions and intensive cooperation in European institutions, the fact of belonging to the European family of nations was frequently somewhat shamefacedly left unmentioned by the Germans. They were afraid of gambling away the unique chance existing for a noncolonial power by a show of solidarity with former colonial powers. In the meantime, a cooler and more detached way of regarding the situation has come about. On the one hand, the pledge of allegiance to European partnership only makes more credible reservations on certain matters; on the other hand, the Africans and Asians have long ago realized that within a family there exist troubles for which not all members can be held simultaneously responsible. Thus, in the Federal Republic, the wish for European cooperation becomes more discernible in the field of development aid activities and extends also into the private domain. The somewhat one-sided bilateral development policy is supplemented by multilateral awareness. Within this increasing awareness, which regards development aid as a joint task, many promising contacts with American agencies are being strengthened, particularly with the big foundations.

The Federal Republic in the East-West Struggle

There is, of course, a political fact which frequently enforces, despite all inclinations towards European and international cooperation in development aid, bilateral thinking and action: the division of Germany.

In developing countries everywhere representatives of the free Federal Republic meet Germans who paint another picture of Germany and who seek to arouse confidence in the Eastern bloc. For this purpose these functionaries have at their disposal all the means which a totalitarian state has for its propaganda and self-promotion.And frequently aid from the eastern side is so spectacular in some aspects that the actually far greater aid from the Federal Republic is completely unknown to the general public. Because of this, the Federal Republic is compelled to regard its partnership with the developing countries from the point of view of a divided Germany. Although no one in the Federal Republic will go so far as to consider development aid as a new aspect of the Cold War, or to use it as a means of preventing recognition of the Pankow regime, the realization of these facts makes the soliciting of friendship for free Germany a legitimate activity within the German development aid policy.

Moreover, in this respect the Federal Republic has a special task. Many visitors from the developing countries have understood for the first time in this country, divided by the Iron Curtain, what the difference between the free world and the so-called "Communist camp" is.

The wall in Berlin represents more than an unnatural national border. It separates two worlds from one another in a way which Africans, Asiatics and Latin Americans see clearly and raises the question of future freedom in the entire world for all those who see it.

Germany's Eastern Policy, Yesterday and Tomorrow

By Immanuel Birnbaum

Of all the nations of the Western world, West Germany* has, at present, the worst relations with Eastern Europe. Even in Germany this is felt to be most unsatisfactory, for it contradicts the best traditions of German history. It also handicaps the possibility of a return to normal relations between German and all peoples of our ever-shrinking earth. To be sure, it has only slightly injured Germany's economic exchange with Eastern Europe.

The statement that the poor condition of the relationship between Germany and Eastern Europe contradicts Germany's tradition may surprise a foreigner, who remembers the horror which Germany's policy during the Hitler era brought to large sections of Europe. Of the millions who lost their lives under the Nazi occupation, especially in Poland, the Soviet Ukraine, Soviet Russia, and the Baltic countries, only a small number died in battle. The vast majority were sacrificed in Nazi prisons, in places of execution, and in concentration camps. This has meant a frightful moral handicap to Germany's relationships with its Eastern neighbors. Indeed, the Germans almost unanimously refuse to recognize a morally collective guilt of the entire people for these crimes. They cannot reject the fact, however, that the entire German population has been justly held responsible for the consequences of these crimes. Since, however, even leaders of Israel, the nation most plagued by Hitler, have openly recognized that West Germany has proven itself to be something other than Hitler's Germany, one can assume that this view will gradually prevail in Eastern Europe as well.

Light and Shadows of the Past

To be sure, the earlier history of Germany's relations with its Eastern neighbors has seen nationalistic antagonism again and again. There were, however, long centuries of peaceful compatibility. The German settlers who moved to Eastern Europe in the Middle Ages seldom arrived as warlike conquerors. For the most part they were peaceful citizens and peasants, who had been summoned to the land by Slavic princes and large landholders. The German Order of Knights in East Prussia was an exception. Indeed, the Order transferred, at the wish of the Polish dukes of Masovia, its entire citizenry there, in order to serve with the border patrol against the pagan Prussians and Lithuanians. The Order of Knights degen-

*) Federal Republic of West Germany *(Bundesrepublik).*

erated, however, after the pagan enemies of Christendom were converted. In the last century of its existence, it developed into a military state with a selfish policy which prospered in contrast to its Christian neighbors. The German Order of Knights was conquered by the allied Poles and Lithuanians about a century after this policy change. Their successors, the dukes of Prussia, became dependent on the king of Poland a century later.

The Brandenburg-Prussian and the Saxon prince-electors of the 17th and 18th centuries competed frequently with Habsburgs, French Bourbons, and other princes for the Polish throne. However, when the Saxons achieved temporary success, they utilized their rights to the throne in Warsaw not for German national purposes but to support their position in the circle of German princes.

The event which reopened German-Polish antagonism for some time to come was the participation of two German monarchies in the division of Poland at the end of the 18th century. Undoubtedly, one of these princes, the Prussian king Frederick the Great, had even provided the initiative for this policy of division. He was faced with the threat that the entire broad territory of the old Polish Republic could fall under the control of the Russian Czarina. In that event, the rising Russian power state would have advanced deep into middle Europe. Instead, he preferred to counterbalance Russia's expansion—at Poland's expense—with an expansion of his own state, more modest in area, into Polish territory, and at the same time to share with Austria the inheritance of the politically and socially backward Polish feudal states. Thereby he produced at the same time a certain solidarity of Prussian, Austrian, and Russian interests in Eastern Europe. From then on, all three participating powers felt pledged to cooperation through the common desire for maintenance of the territorial order, since they had created the division themselves.

One called this policy of Russo-Prussian solidarity, which extended itself even to a common attitude against the Western critics of Eastern European policy, the "old system" of Eastern power. In principle, this system governed the Eastern policy of Germany for most of the 19th century. Its most important advocate after Frederick the Great was the Prussian minister-president and German chancellor, Bismarck. His cooperation with Russia assured the peace between the two monarchies of Middle and Eastern Europe, of course at the expense of the smaller nations. which had come under the rule of these monarchies. When the Czar had to suppress a Polish rebellion in 1863, Bismarck gave him his support. Whenever other nations showed impulses of independence, whether in the Russian Czarist state or in the Austro-Hungarian monarchy, they received no encouragement from Germany. Bismarck exhorted even the German Baltics and the German-Austrians on various occasions to remain loyal to their rulers in Petersburg and Vienna.

In opposition to Germany's pro-Russian Eastern policy, predominant during the century between the division of Poland and the fall of Bismarck, another anti-Russian tendency always existed there—public opinion. It had already made itself apparent at the time of the division of Poland. Its most important advocate was, at that time, Johann Gottfried Herder, an East Prussian predecessor of Goethe. He warned the German government against laying aggressive hands on the national independence of the neighboring Polish peoples, because such power politics could lead to eventual division of Germany itself. Other freedom writers were also inspired by the opposition of the Polish nation against the conquerors of their land and by the belated attempt at a liberal reform of the Polish social constitution.

This enthusiasm for the Polish freedom battle flamed high when in 1830-31 an armed Polish uprising stirred again. At that time, German patriots' own hopes for the building of a free German unified state were disappointed with the battle for freedom against Napoleon. Thus, one saw in the Polish national movement a model for one's own land. The most important German poets of the time, August von Platen, Ludwig Uhland, Nikolaus Lenau, the Silesian Karl von Holtei, and many others sang inspired praises of Poland.

The anti-Russian enthusiasm in Poland did not remain a purely literary expression, however. When a liberal government in Prussia attempted a new foreign policy in the revolutionary year 1848, it envisaged a common war of liberation of the Western democracies against the Czarist state, the reactionary center. The Russian power was to be driven far back toward Eastern Europe, and Poland thereby restored. The plan failed due to Western opposition. The attempt had previously been made to win over the French cabinet. At the same time there were conflicts between the newly stiring Polish national movement and the German settlers in the Prussian-Polish boundary area. One of the advisers and collaborators of the king of Prussia, who was himself enthusiastic at the thought of German-Polish cooperation, General von Willisen, attempted an on-the-spot settlement. He suggested generous concessions to the Poles, because for the price of a few hundred square miles, he felt that this could perhaps bind the entire Polish nation permanently to the West.

However, the military element opposed the idealistic general. Already at the time of the Polish uprising of 1830-31, the later Field Marshall von Moltke, then at that just beginning his career, had explained that the Prussian state could never again give up its former Polish areas without losing its defense capacity in the East. This conception carried through in 1848 against an attempt at German-Polish compromise. Therefore, the pro-Russian course of Germany's Eastern policy remained victorious.

Only in 1900, when the conflicts between the policies of the three European empires of that time—Germany, Austria-Hungary and Russia—again became topical, through conflicts of interest in the Balkans and Western Asia, did the two factions of Germany's Eastern policy, pro- and anti-Russian, stir again. They penetrated the political factions and parties. There were conservatives who considered it a survival factor for Germany to stick with Russia through thick and thin. One such foreign-policy conservative, the historian and parliamentarian Otto Hoetzsch, did not change his opinion even when a communist dictator had taken the place of the Czar in the leadership of Russia. But another more universal-thinking conservative historian and politician, Hans Delbrueck, proclaimed at the same time that the greatest dangers for Germany and for Europe came from Russia. He recommended, therefore, a continuing cooperation with all anti-Russian powers in Eastern Europe, in particular with the smaller, freedom hungry nationalities in these countries. During and after World War I, it was evident that even in Catholic centers both tendencies were represented. One of the most active leaders of this party, Mathias Erzberger, belonged at that time to the advocates of a policy which wanted to build out of the Polish areas annexed to the Czarist power, and out of the Baltic states, new monarchies which would lean on Germany. This would build a protective wall against future Russian political expansion in Europe. However, in the same party, side by side with Erzberger, sat the delegate and later republican *Reichs* Chancellor Josef Wirt, who maintained that cooperation with Russia was the only possible German Eastern policy. He then became a strong backer of military cooperation between the Red Army of the Soviet Union and the German Army of the Weimar Republic.

Even among the liberals, who exercised influence chiefly through their great newspaper, both points of view were to be found. One of their tradition-rich papers, the Berlin *Vossische Zeitung,* long championed cooperation with Russia, because its leading men believed England to be Germany's most dangerous opponent. Other notable liberal papers as the *Berliner Tageblatt* and the *Frankfurter Zeitung* supported, conversely, the anti-Russian policy of cooperation with the "border peoples" living between the Germans and Russians. Likewise, the opinions of the Social Democrats were confused in regard to foreign policy. Representatives of the far left, such as Rosa Luxemburg, the Polish-born woman who was later to become a co-founder of the German Communist Party, as well as several very moderate parlamentarians of the furthest right wing of the party, stood for a separate peace with Russia during World War I. The leading foreign-policy makers of the party were inclined, conversely, to a pro-Polish policy, stemming from old anti-Russian feelings and sympathy with the West. This also corresponded to the inner political traditions of the German radical left, which had always defended a policy opposed to suppression of Poland within the German borders. One of the leading Social Democrats, Georg Ledebour, had been given the Polish-sounding nickname "Ledeburski" for sharing this opinion.

New Borders—New Antagonism

The 1919 Treaty of Versailles not only restored the old boundaries of the Polish Republic to the disadvantage of Germany, but in the supplementary decision over Upper Silesia (1921), gave regions back to Poland which had not belonged to Poland since the 14th century, giving rise to a national trauma in Germany. One sympathized strongly with the fate of some one million people of the German minority who were left behind in the new Polish borders. Too, the condition of the German ethnic groups in the other new national states east of the borders of the German *Reich* became a theme which stirred national sensitivities. The largest of these German ethnic groups was in Czechoslovakia. It could still force the admission of a few of its representatives into the Prague government. But it could not prevent the joining of the state founded by Masaryk and Benesch with the French alliance system nor the opposition of that state to every territorial order from Versailles.

The German sentiment, in regard to the Eastern nations of Europe, was again divided at that time. The immediate neighbors, especially the Poles and Czechs, appeared as profiteers and supporters of the Versailles Peace Treaty. Bolshevist Russia was, like Germany, hard hit by the territorial postwar order, which the Western powers had dictated. Soviet politicians, such as Foreign Minister Chicherin and the effective propagandist Radek, emphasized this common element of the Russian and German fate quite effectively at times. On the other hand, communist Moscow was obviously the main support for the attempt to undermine the young German republic. Its German partisans never once shied away from working tactically together with the most extreme representatives of the nationalistic German right wing.

In the German interior policy, a rather wide front surrendered first against the debilitation furthered by the East. In the foreign policy, on the other hand, one was torn back and forth. During the world economic conference of 1922, the democratic foreign minister Rathenau yielded, half unwillingly, to the attempt of Chicherin in Rapallo to sign a special protocol with the Soviets over the reciprocal renunciation of war compensations. That must have appeared to the West as a special German arrangement with the Russians. His successor, the liberal Gustav Stresemann, was induced three years later by the British ambassador D'Abernon to effect a contract in Locarno with Germany's Western neighbor over final recognition of the existing Western boundaries. However, only a common renunciation of hostile means of revising boundaries in the East was defined at that time between Germany, Poland, and Czechoslovakia. That had the effect in Warsaw and even in Moscow of a new mobilization of German foreign policy directed against the East. Stresemann supplemented both agreements, Rapallo and Locarno, shortly after (1926), with a more exacting and specific Berlin contract with the Soviets. He now believed he had effected a sort of balance between West and East.

Germany's smaller Eastern neighbors felt even more threatened by this cooperation of Berlin with the Western capitals and, concurrently with Moscow. Neither did they let themselves be calmed by the fact that the Weimar Republic at least tried for better economic cooperation with them and, for example, brought about a comprehensive agreement with Poland over the liquidation of economic consequences of the war. A provisionally signed contract of 1930 between Berlin and Warsaw, which was to end the import-export tax battle which had existed between Germany and Poland since the end of World War I, found no further acceptance in the German parliament, which at that time was already deprived of a democratic majority. The contract was characteristically put into use only by Hitler after his entrance into power by force.

Hitler Helps Stalin to Victory

The National Socialist Third *Reich* misused both traditions of Germany's Eastern policy, the pro-Polish and pro-Russian, in turn, through two great maneuvers of deceit. Having come to power, Hitler saw himself surrounded by a general mistrust in the West and East. This mistrust was perhaps nowhere greater than in Poland, whose authoritative man at that time, Marshal Pilsudski, discreetly inquired in Paris and London as to whether the dangers of this German regime were not to be avoided by a preventive war. When refused there, the Polish ruler temporarily attempted to negotiate directly with Hitler himself. Yet it went no further than a nonagression pact on both sides, like the one Poland had also concluded with the Soviet Union a short time before. When Hitler believed he had broken up the ring of hostility which surrounded him, he soon went further indeed. He tried to interest Poland in an alliance-tempered convergence against the Soviet Union, and presented to the successors of Pilsudski the prospect of gains in the East, primarily in the Ukraine, as the results of such an adventure. The Poles were to pay for this chance, indeed in advance, through a rearrangement in the Weichsel Corridor, which had separated East Prussia from the rest of Germany since 1919. Since the Warsaw government did not want to enter into such an agreement, and Hitler's self-confidence had been greatly increased in the meantime through the power-implemented annexation of Austria and the two successive strokes which had brought about the division of Czechoslovakia, the master of the Third *Reich* now began a new tactic. He turned from cooperation with Warsaw and approached Moscow.

In the agreement of August 23, 1939, Hitler's foreign minister Ribbentrop and Stalin's commissioner Molotov came to terms, publicly, on the point that they would take part in no power groupings against either of the two contracting states. In secret, they came to an understanding over a division of their spheres of interest in Eastern Europe, according to which West Poland would be left to Germany, East Poland, in return, together with the main part of the Baltic states and a part of Rumania, would be delivered into the hands of the Soviets. When Hitler soon after was taken up by his war in the West, Stalin immediately allowed himself a breach of this agreement, in which he also took Lithuania, which really lay on the other side of the demarcation line of the Moscow agreement. Neither side trusted the other a moment with regard to the observance of their promises. Stalin would have only too gladly maintained the agreement in its main definition still longer, because he did not want to enter the World War until the last moment. He then hoped to speak the decisive word at the conclusions of the peace. Hitler destroyed this hope for him, since he did not dare to enter a war against England as long as the Soviet power with its whole potential stood at his back. On the other hand, he underestimated this potential, because he saw only the foreground of the ideology of Soviet Communism, and not the reserve of national Russian will to resist against intrusion. Thus, he failed because of this insufficient insight into the relative power in Eastern Europe.

The counterblow by Stalin made possible through the unbroken resistance of Great Britain against Hitler and through the intervention of the United States in Africa and Europe, ended all German power politics in Eastern Europe forever. Far beyond all earlier borders of their influence, the Russians have been able to extend their power since 1945 up to the Elbe River and in many places still further into the heart of Germany. Herder's gloomy visions of a divided Germany, resulting from a German policy of division in its Eastern neighboring lands, has become a reality. Even the possibility of a choice in the Eastern policy of Germany between pro-Russianism and cooperation with border states is, for the present and the foreseeable future, not likely. All of Eastern Europe stands today under the predomination of Moscow.

Bonn Speaks with Moscow not with Warsaw

One consequence, which has grown out of the policy of the German *Bundesrepublik,* is that it maintains diplomatic relations only with Moscow and not with the capitals of other states of the Eastern bloc. The denial of such relations with Warsaw, Prague, Budapest or Bucharest, with Sofia or even with Peking, is founded on the principle that Bonn could not exchange permanent representation with countries which for their part have taken up relations with Moscow's German satellite state. This principle was first formulated by the then Secretary of State, Walter Hallstein, and has since then been called the "Hallstein Doctrine" in international politics. This doctrine was broken in regard to the Soviet Union when Chancellor Adenauer traveled to Moscow in 1956 and arranged the exchange of ambassadors with the Soviet government. This break of the Hallstein Doctrine was founded on the principle that the Moscow government would undertake, with the inter-Allied agreements of 1945, co-responsibility for the settlement of German reunification and for the four-power control over Berlin. Considering the influence of the Soviets on the question of Germany's destiny, present and future, one could not avoid diplomatic contact with them. On the contrary, the diplomatic relations already begun with Belgrade were again broken off from the German side a few years later, when the Yugoslavian government entered into relations with East Berlin.

Undeniably, the refusal of diplomatic relations with Czechoslovakia, the immediate border neighbor of the *Bundesrepublic,* and with Poland, the second largest nation of Eastern Europe and the most haunted sacrifice of the Hitler policy, appeared, with the concurrent normalization of diplomatic relations between Bonn and Moscow, to be almost a continuation of the pro-Russian course of the Bismarck era. In any case, this different treatment of Eastern European states through the policy of Bonn meant a certain contribution to the strengthening of the authority of Moscow in Eastern Europe. Hence, the question is often raised, both by the Germans and by Germany's Western allies, as to whether or not such a position reflects Western interests. Without a doubt it can be neither useful to a general West-East lessening of tension nor to a deteriorating of relations within the Eastern bloc.

Still other obstacles, in addition to the Hallstein Doctrine, stand in opposition to a reopening of normal political relations with Prague and Warsaw. To be sure, no territorial differences exist between Germany and Czechoslovakia. But at the end of the war, almost 3.5 million Germans, whose ancestors had been residents there for centuries, were expelled from the territory of the Czech republic, as a reply to Hitler's policy against the Czech nation, and to the support which this policy found with a considerable portion of the German speaking citizens of Czechoslovakia. The organizations of these expellees, which formed in the territory of the *Bundesrepublik,* desire for their people the right to return to their homeland. They demand this return under conditions which would secure for them again an existence as an organized minority. Prague will not allow itself to be drawn into discussion on this point, because it already gives the choice of returning there to any single German if he submits to the laws of communist Czechoslovakia. The groups of expellees are seeking to restrain Bonn from recognizing the Prague Government without new agreements over this question. Just how large the number is of Germans formerly living in Czechoslovakia who would seriously make use of a "right to return" is another question. Most of these Germans from Bohemia, Moravia, and Slavic lands are prospering today in the *Bundesrepublik.* The favorable market of the last twelve years and the prevailing full employment have made possible their assimilation in the West German economy under very favorable conditions.

Indeed, the sympathies for the Communist regime of Czechoslovakia are slight in Germany, also for the reason that since 1945 Prague has shown itself, aside from East Berlin, to be the most obedient of all Moscow's political puppets in Eastern and Middle Europe. A greater sympathy in Germany, as in the entire West, is enjoyed by the Polish People's Democracy, since it showed itself in 1956, under the leadership of Wladyslaw Gomulka, to be a relatively independent structure within the circle of Soviet satellites. The semiliberal policy toward culture and religion to which Poland has adhered since that time, the protection of economic freedom offered its peasants—quite different from the communist-ruled part of Germany or Czechoslovakia—all this has awakened at least a certain respect for the Polish Gomulka regime. Even many Germans, in reflection of Poland's suffering, feel themselves obligated to renew ties with Warsaw.

The German-Polish Border Is Not Settled by Stalin's Dictates

Attempts toward such a renewal of ties have been undertaken, even though not officially. They have been dismissed, meanwhile, because Poland has tightened the conditions for such a renewal as time goes on. As late as 1959, Warsaw seemed prepared to renounce the regulation of international law of the border question, with an agreement over the exchange of diplomatic representation with Bonn. Even in the period between the two World Wars, normal relationships between Germany and Poland had existed, although a final acknowledgement of the German-Polish border had been refused by Germany at the time. The provisional border supervision, which was fixed between Poland and Germany at the end of the war by the Soviet government, far exceeded the territorial claims ever made by a Polish government from Germany. In the records of the inter-Allied conferences of Yalta and Potsdam in the year 1945, the representatives of the United States and the United Kingdom were in agreement with Stalin that Russia should keep the Northern sector of East Prussia, and that Poland should receive considerable compensations for its war damages at Germany's cost. The final settlement of the Polish-German border, however, was at that time explicitly reserved for a German peace treaty.

Then, in the next years, Poland declared the districts, which had been placed under its administration provisionally by the inter-Allied arrangements, as territory of its republic through acts of public law. In the meantime, it also integrated their economy extensively into the economy of the Polish people. In the widest circles in Germany, it has long since been clear that territorial compensation for Poland through German territory must be accepted as the Allies promised it to Poland. This acceptance does not go so far, however, that one is prepared to simply accept the 1945 dictate of Stalin. The provisional border settlement is in itself arbitrary and impractical. It divides old cities, such as Frankfort on the Oder or Goerlitz, from which one sector has remained on one side, the second on the other. At the mouth of the Oder River, the provisional border even exceeds the claims for Poland which Stalin made at the end of the war. There, it runs West of the Oder. Therefore, all of the larger German parties advocate the interpretation that so far the old German Eastern border, as it existed in 1937, has not yet been changed through valid acts of international law. One must one day continue from this legal standpoint, if one wants to fix the final German-Polish border by negotiations in which Germany is also to share.

The whole problem is not a question of topical policy. At present the German *Bundesrepublik* is really not a border neighbor of Poland. Between free Germany and Poland lies Moscow's German satellite state, which naturally has obediently accepted all of Stalin's dictates. Neither does the reviewing of the German-Polish border question make any sense at the moment, nor would it have any value for the lasting formation of German-Polish relations nor even for the East-West relaxation of tensions if Germany were at present to declare of its own accord that it would put up with the Stalin border dictate forever. The Poles are not at all so seriously frightened in the present situation by the propaganda slogan, "Danger of a German Border Revision," which is, to be sure, frequently proclaimed publicly. For the renunciation of such a border revision, they would, therefore not offer any equivalent. The acceptance of a one-sided dictate would be worth much less than free agreements on the future border reached through negotiations under German cooperation and under German concessions as sketched previously by the Allies in 1945.

When the Western peoples were trying to win West Germany for the defense alliance against Communism after the war, one of the strongest arguments in favor of American policy for the German public was the fact that Washington and London were to some extent defending German rights against Moscow in the border question and would defend them further. The speech which Secretary of State James Byrnes gave in 1946 in Stuttgart made a lasting impression in Germany. It was confirmed especially through the later publications over the negotiations of Yalta and Potsdam. The Western Powers in 1945 obligated Germany to pay large reparations as compensation for crimes of the Hitler regime in Poland. They did not obligate themselves, however, to regard as definitive the boundary dictates of Stalin.

Prague and Warsaw Cannot Be United from the Eastern Bloc

Even without normal diplomatic relations, the relations between Germany and the smaller states of Eastern Europe are improving. In fact, there is an active commercial exchange between the *Bundesrepublik* and most of these lands. An exchange of newspaper reporters is in effect, translations here and there of literary and scientific books from the other side are made, scholars and artists are invited to lectures and guest performances. All this is still increasing considerably. The mutual distrust, which, on one side, is still looking for followers of Hitler, and on the other side sees only the protagonists of the expulsion policy of the last war years, could not be completely subdued so easily. But perhaps it could be considerably lessened. The hope that a German-Polish and a German-Czech compromise would loosen capitals such as Warsaw and Prague from the Eastern bloc and would lead them back into their historic relations with the West is naturally illusional. The leading Communists today in Czechoslovakia and Poland can never give up their dependence upon Moscow for the very reason that without this dependence, their own inner political position would not be secured. German-Polish and German-Czech easing of tensions, therefore, cannot lead to the weakening of the cohesion of the Eastern bloc in the foreseeable future. Such an approach between Germany and the peoples of Eastern Europe would only contribute to the general tensions between East and West.

The decisive Eastern partner for a policy to ease tensions remains for Germany, as for the entire West, the Soviet Union. Germany will no longer have direct areas of friction as soon as Moscow renounces its intervention in inner-German affairs. The point on which the German population still sensitively feels such intervention is Berlin. A settlement on the former German capital which would be tolerable for the free segment of the population and which would not hinder relations between Berlin and the *Bundesrepublik* could also, bring about a substantial unburdening for German-Soviet relations. If Soviet policy were to refrain from intervention in Berlin only in order to strengthen the functioning of its German satellite, it would indeed be no improvement for the relations between Germany and its Eastern neighbors. It would, under such circumstances, even be a change for the worse.

German Unification—A Goal of the Future

Developments of the last years have made clear to the German public that it cannot rely on the disappearance of this German satellite regime of Moscow's in the foreseeable future. Thus, German renunification, based on the disappearance from Germany of this servant of foreign interests, is not presently an attainable German policy goal. That does not mean, however, that the German people will renounce this goal as a future possibility. If economic and other daily tasks draw all attention to themselves, the idea of unification can be temporarily put aside. The goal of reunification can even be deferred consciously if other tasks of foreign policy are to be solved first, for instance, the completion of the Western international community.

It can certainly be said that the conception of assembling all men of the same language, culture, and political tradition does not mean as much in the 20th century as it did in the 19th. It was, in one and the same country therefore, not necessary to convince the German people that they should give up the idea of the *Anschluss* of the German-speaking Austrians, when it became clear that the overwhelming majority of Austria's inhabitants wanted to have nothing more to do with the plan after the experiences of the Hitler era. But the reuniting of *Bundesrepublik* Germans with those east of the Elbe has an entirely different moral and political basis. The Germans living today under the rule of Moscow's agent, Ulbricht, want this reunification. Were it otherwise, their tyrannical masters would allow them free expression of their beliefs. This they have never yet dared.

Reunification of Germany remains in the long run, therefore, a goal of Germany's Eastern policy. Everyone knows that this goal cannot be reached by means of force. Since reunification cannot be forced, it must one day be bought. Today, the partners for such a transaction, specifically the rulers of the Soviet Union, are not ready to negotiate. But at one time that was different, and it can be different one day again.

When at the end of 1949, I, as a newspaper correspondent, lost my right to stay in Poland from one day to the next, a Pole of high position said to me: "Our allies, the Russians, now want to negotiate over the reunification of Germany. They have something to gain thereby, for they do not yet have the same nuclear weapons as the Americans. Through such a reunification they hope to prevent the joining of West Germany in a military alliance with the West. Should Germany be reunited, Poland would then be the Western border country of the Eastern bloc. Therefore, for the present, we cannot use Western observers like yourself here."

Today, the Soviets believe that negotiations over German reunification are no longer necessary. But their position of power can also change again. The Eastern policy of Germany could then, supported by its allies, display stronger activity. It could attempt to bring about the reunification by peaceful means. For the preservation of its citizens' freedom and of world peace must and will remain the primary goal of all future German policy.

It can certainly be said that the conception of assembling all men at the [illegible]

Appendix

Selected Bibliographies

I A State and Society

Ludwig Bergsträsser: *Geschichte der Politischen Parteien in Deutschland:* Muenchen 1960.

Rupert Breitling: *Die Verbaende in der Bundesrepublik:* Meisenheim 1955.

James B. Conant: *Germany and Freedom:* Cambridge, Mass. 1958.

Karl W. Deutsch und Levis J. Edinger: *Germany Rejoins the Powers:* Stanford, Cal. 1959.

Theodor Eschenburg: *Staat und Gesellschaft in Deutschland:* Stuttgart 1956.

Theodor Eschenburg: *Herrschaft der Verbaende?:* Stuttgart 1956.

Erwin Faul (Hrsg.): *Wahlen und Waehler in Westdeutschland:* Villingen 1960.

John Ford Golay: *The Foundation of the Federal Republik of Germany:* Chicago 1958.

Alfred Grosser: *La Democratie de Bonn:* Paris 1958. Uebersetzung: *Die Bonner Demokratie — Deutschland von draußen gesehen:* Duesseldorf 1960.

Andreas Haman: *Das Grundgesetz — ein Kommentar fuer Wissenschaft und Praxis:* Neuwied — Berlin 1960.

Arnold J. Heidenheimer: *The Governments of Germany:* New York 1961.

Arnold J. Heidenheimer: *Adenauer and the CDU:* Den Haag 1960.

Richard Hiscoks: *Democracy in Western Germany:* New York, London and Toronto 1957.

U. W. Kitzinger: *German Electoral Politics. A Study of the 1957 Campaign:* Oxford 1960.

Max G. Lange, G. Schulz u. a.: *Parteien in der Bundesrepublik:* Stuttgart, Duesseldorf 1955.

Rudolf Walter Leonhard: *X mal Deutschland:* München 1961.

Joseph Rovan: *Allemagne:* Paris 1955.

Joseph Rovan: *Le Catholicisme Politique en Allemagne:* Paris 1960.

I B Development of Domestic Policy

Fritz René Allemann: *Bonn ist nicht Weimar:* Koeln 1956.

Wilhelm Cornides: *Die Weltmaechte und Deutschland:* Tuebingen 1961.

Theodor Eschenburg: *Staat und Gesellschaft in Deutschland:* Stuttgart 1956.

Theodor Eschenburg: *Herrschaft der Verbaende?:* Stuttgart 1956.

Wolfgang Treue: *Deutsche Parteiprogramme 1861—1961:* Goettingen 1961.

Paul Weymar: *Konrad Adenauer:* Muenchen 1955.

Alfred Rapp: *Bonn auf der Waage:* Stuttgart 1959.

Carlo Schmid: *Politik und Geist:* Stuttgart 1961.

Eugen Gerstenmaier: *Reden und Aufsaetze:* Stuttgart 1961.

Ruediger Altmann: *Das Erbe Adenauers:* Stuttgart 1960.

III A Have the Germans Changed

1 Theodor W. Adorno: *Das politische Bewußtsein der Heimkehrer aus Kriegsgefangenschaft.* Unveroeffentlichte Studie des Instituts fuer Sozialforschung: Frankfurt/M. 1958.

2 Theodor W. Adorno: *"Was bedeutet Aufarbeitung?"* In Gesellschaft, Staat, Erziehung: Wiesbaden 1960.

3 Franziska Baumgarten: *Demokratie und Charakter:* Zuerich 1944.

4 W. v. Baeyer-Katte: *Das Zerstoerende in der Politik — Eine Psychologie der politischen Grundeinstellungen:* Heidelberg 1958.

5 Walter Beck: *"Sozialpsychologie"*. Im Kongressbericht 1947 des Berufsverbandes Deutscher Psychologen: Bonn 1948.

6 Walter Beck: *"Sozialpsychologie"*. Im Kongressbericht 1949 des Berufsverbandes Deutscher Psychologen: Muenchen 1950.

7 Adolf Daeumling: *"Angst und Sog als psychisches Phaenomen im politischen Leben"*. Festschrift der Hochschule fuer politische Wissenschaft: Muenchen 1960.

8 DIVO-Institut: *Umfragen. Ereignisse und Probleme der Zeit im Urteil der Bevoelkerung,* Band 2: Frankfurt 1959.

9 Walter Ehrenstein: *Daemon Masse:* Frankfurt/M. 1953.

10 Willi Eichler: *"Die Ueberwindung der Nazi-Gesinnung"*. In Geist und Tat: Frankfurt/M. 1960.

11 Paul Feldkeller: *"Psycho-Politik". Zur Demokratisierung, politischen Erziehung und Saeuberung:* Berlin 1947.

12 Friedrich-Ebert-Stiftung: *Politische Urteilsbildung in der Demokratie:* Hannover 1960.

13 Friedrich-Ebert-Stiftung: *Ueberwindung von Vorurteilen:* Hannover 1960.

14 Juergen Habermas u. a.: *Student und Politik:* Neuwied 1961.

15 Willy Hellpach: *Gesinnung, Gewissen und Gesittung der Wissenschaftlichkeit als positive Werte im oeffentlichen Leben:* Frankfurt/M. 1947.

16 Willy Hellpach: *Deutsche Physiognomik:* Berlin 1949.

17 Willy Hellpach: *Der deutsche Charakter:* Berlin 1949.

18 Max Horkheimer: *"Zur Psychologie des Totalitaeren"*. In Offene Welt, 1954.

19 Institut fuer staatsbuergerliche Erziehung in Rheinland-Pfalz: *"Autoritarismus und Nationalismus"*. Protokoll einer Expertenkonferenz: Mainz 1961.

20 Walter Jacobsen: *"Psychologie in der Politik"*. Im Kongressbericht 1949 des Berufsverbandes Deutscher Psychologen: Muenchen 1950.

21 Walter Jacobsen: *"Der neue Beamtentyp"*. In Deutsches Verwaltungsblatt: Detmold 1951.

[22] Walter Jacobsen: *"Lauter Vorurteile!"* In Schriftenreihe der Bundeszentrale fuer Heimatdienst, Heft 18/1957: Bonn 1957.

[23] Walter Jacobsen: *"Die Vergangenheit mahnt!"* In Beilage der Wochenzeitung "Das Parlament": Bonn 1960.

[24] Walter Jacobsen: *"Beitrag der Psychologie zu Bemuehungen um politische Bildung"*. Kongressbericht der Internationalen Gesellschaft fuer angewandte Psychologie: London 1955, und in: Psychologische Rundschau: Goettingen 1956.

[25] Walter Jacobsen: *"Vom Widerstand der Seele"*. In Geist und Tat: Frankfurt/M. 1961.

[26] Walter Jacobsen: *"Die grosse Abrechnung und das neue Deutschland"*. In Geist und Tat: Frankfurt/M. 1961.

[27] Walter Jaide: *"An Politik nicht interessiert?"* In Beilage der Wochenzeitung "Das Parlament": Bonn 1960.

[28] Paul Massing: *Zur Vorgeschichte des Antisemitismus:* Frankfurt/M. 1959.

[29] Wolfgang Metzger: *"Erziehung zum selbstaendigen Denken"*. In Psychologische Rundschau: Goettingen 1957.

[30] E. P. Neumann und Elisabeth Noelle: *Antworten — Politik im Kraftfeld der oeffentlichen Meinung:* Allensbach 1954.

[31] E. Noelle und P. Neumann: *Jahrbuch der oeffentlichen Meinung, 1947—55:* Allensbach 1956.

[32] Christoph Oehler: *Das Politische Bewusstsein der Studierenden und die Chancen politischer Bildung:* Frankfurt/M. 1960.

[33] Max Picard: *Hitler in uns selbst:* Zuerich 1946.

[34] Otto Plessner: *Die verspaetete Nation:* Stuttgart 1959.

[35] Friedrich Pollock: *Das Gruppenexperiment:* Frankfurt/M. 1955.

[36] Eva Reichmann: *Flucht in den Hass:* Frankfurt/M. 1958.

[37] E. Reigrotzki: *Soziale Verflechtungen in der Bundesrepublik:* Tuebingen 1956.

[38] David Riesmann: *Die einsame Masse:* Darmstadt 1956.

[39] E. A. Saarbourgh: *Frustration und Autoritarismus:* Koeln 1959.

[40] A. Sachse: *"Das Problem der unbewaeltigten Vergangenheit"*. In Freiburger Rundbrief Nr. 45—48/1959: Freiburg/B.

[41] Peter Schoenbach: 3. *Sonderheft des Instituts fuer Sozialforschung:* Frankfurt/M. 1961.

[42] H. Schelsky: *Die skeptische Generation:* Duesseldorf 1957.

[43] K. S. Sodhi und R. Bergius: *Nationale Vorurteile:* Berlin 1955.

[44] Verband Deutscher Studentenschaften: *Erziehungswesen und Judentum:* Muenchen 1960.

[45] Heinz Wiesbrock: *"Ueber Ethnocharakterologie"*. In Koelner Zeitschrift fuer Soziologie und Sozialpsychologie: Koeln 1957.

[46] Heinr. E. Wolf: *"Sozialpsychologische Untersuchung der Vorurteile gegen Neger und Juden bei Ober- und Volksschuelern"*. In Koelner Zeitschrift fuer Soziologie und Sozialpsychologie: Koeln 1959.

III B2 Extrem Rightism

Fritz René Allemann: *Bonn ist nicht Weimar:* Koeln 1956.

Hugo C. Backhaus: *Volk ohne Fuehrung:* Goettingen 1955.

Walter Baron: *"Deutscher Spaetsommer"*. In Deutsche Rundschau 70 (1947).

Ludwig Bergsträsser: *Geschichte der politischen Parteien in Deutschland:* Muenchen 1955.

Otto Buesch: *"Geschichte und Gestalt der SRP"*. In Rechtsradikalismus im Nachkriegsdeutschland. Studien ueber die Sozialistische Reichspartei: Berlin und Frankfurt/M. 1957.

Lucius D. Clay: *Entscheidung in Deutschland:* Frankfurt/M. 1950.

Feinde der Demokratie. Presseschau, Kommentare und Informationen aus gewerkschaftlicher Sicht. Hrsg. vom Landesbezirksvorstand Niedersachsen des DGB (Hannover) zweimonatlich 1950—1959. (Seitdem in Duesseldorf unter dem Titel *Fuer die Demokratie.*)

Justus Fuerstenau: *Die Entnazifizierung in der deutschen Nachkriegspolitik.* Dissertation: Frankfurt/M. 1955 (manuscript).

Justus Fuerstenau: *"Entnazifizierung"*. In Staatslexikon. Hrsg. von der Goerresgesellschaft. Freiburg.

Hans Grimm: *Die Erzbischofschrift. Antwort eines Deutschen:* Goettingen 1950.

Hans Grimm: *Warum, woher, aber wohin? Vor, unter, nach der geschichtlichen Erscheinung Hitler:* Lippoldsberg 1954.

Friedrich Grimm: *Unrecht im Rechtsstaat. Tatsachen und Dokumente zur politischen Justiz, dargestellt am Fall Naumann:* Tuebingen 1957.

Alfred Grosser: *La démocratie de Bonn:* Paris 1958. Dt. Ausgabe Duesseldorf 1960.

Die große Hetze. Der niedersaechsische Ministersturz. Ein Tatsachenbericht zum Fall Schlueter: Goettingen 1958.

Jahrbuch der oeffentlichen Meinung 1947—1955. Hrsg. von Noelle u. Neumann: Allensbach 1956.

Peter Kleist: *Auch Du warst dabei:* Heidelberg 1952. Neuaufl. Goettingen 1959.

Arno Kloenne: *"Jugendarbeit rechtsaußen"*. In Polit. Studien. Heft 101, September 1958.

Rudolf Kraemer: *"Terror der Anstaendigen?"* In Die Wandlung (1947).

Julius Lippert: *Laechle . . . und verbirg die Traenen. Erlebnisse und Bemerkungen eines deutschen "Kriegsverbrechers":* Leoni 1955.

Werner Naumann: *Nau Nau gefaehrdet das Empire?:* Goettingen 1953.

Erich Peter Neumann und Elisabeth Noelle: *Antworten:* Allensbach 1954.

Hans Ulrich Rudel: *Aus Krieg und Frieden. Aus den Jahren 1945—1952:* Goettingen 1953.

Beate Ruhm von Oppen: *Documents on Germany under Occupation. 1945—1954:* London 1955.

Hans Schlange-Schoeningen: *Im Schatten des Hungers. Dokumentarisches zur Ernaehrungspolitik und Ernaehrungswirtschaft in den Jahren 1945—1949:* Hamburg, Berlin 1955.

Otto Strasser: *Hitler und ich:* Konstanz 1948.

Wolfgang Treue: *Deutsche Parteiprogramme. 1861—1954.* Goettingen 1956.

Das Urteil des Bundesverfassungsgerichts vom 29. Oktober 1952 betr. Feststellung der Verfassungswidrigkeit der Sozialistischen Reichspartei: Tuebingen 1952.

... und morgen die ganze Welt. Der Neofaschismus und die Neofaschisten beleuchtet vom Bund Deutscher Jugend: Frankfurt/M. 1952.

Fried Wesemann: *"Die Totengraeber sind unter uns".* In Frankfurter Rundschau 9. 6. 1953 bis 13. 6. 1953 (5 Folgen).

J. Emlyn Williams: *"Wohin fuehrt der Weg?"* In Das ist Germany. Hrsg. von Arthur Settel: Frankfurt/M. 1950.

III B5 Militarism

Historical Foundations:

Gordon A. Craig: *The Politics of the Prussian Army, 1640—1945:* Oxford 1955.

Harold J. Gordon: *The Reichswehr and the German Republic 1919—1926:* Princeton, N. J., 1957.

Gerhard Ritter: *Staatskunst und Kriegshandwerk: Das Problem des "Militarismus" in Deutschland:* Muenchen, Bd. I, 2. Aufl. 1959, Bd. II, 1960.

Wolfgang Sauer: *"Die Reichswehr".* In Karl Dietrich Bracher: *Die Auflösung der Weimarer Republik,* 3. Aufl.: Villingen/Schwarzwald 1960.

Wolfgang Sauer: *"Die Mobilmachung der Gewalt".* In Karl Dietrich Bracher,

Wolfgang Sauer, Gerhard Schulz, *Die nationalsozialistische Machtergreifung:* Koeln und Opladen 1960.

Since 1945:

A. Official Documents:

Dienststelle Blank: *Vom kuenftigen deutschen Soldaten: Gedanken und Planungen der Dienststelle Blank:* Bonn 1955.

Bundesministerium fuer Verteidigung, Fuehrungsstab der Bundeswehr: *Handbuch fuer Innere Fuehrung: Hilfen zur Klaerung der Begriffe.*

Bundesministerium fuer Verteidigung, Fuehrungsstab der Bundeswehr, Schriftenreihe Innere Fuehrung, Reihe: Bolschewismus, Reihe: Bundesrepublik/Freie Welt, Reihe: Erziehung, Reihe: Soldatische Ordnung, Reihe: Psychologische Waffen.

Der Wehrbeauftragte des Deutschen Bundestages, *Jahresbericht 1959,* Deutscher Bundestag, Drucksache 1796, 8. April 1960.

Der Wehrbeauftragte des Deutschen Bundestages, *Jahresbericht 1960,* Deutscher Bundestag, Drucksache 2666, 14. April 1961.

Hans Edgar Jahn, Kurt Neher und Herbert Pfeill, Hrsg., *Taschenbuch fuer Wehrfragen 1960/61,* 4. Jg.: Frankfurt/M. 1960.

B. Monographies and Studies:

Fritz René Allemann: *"Die Nemesis der Ohnmacht: Wiederbewaffnung als politische Aufgabe"*. In Der Monat, 7. Jg., Mai 1955, S. 99—105.

Eberhard Barth: *"Die Stellung der Streitkraefte im Staat"*. In Zeitschrift fuer Politik, I (1954), S. 159 ff.

Gerhard Baumann: *"Psychologische Rueckwirkungen in der Bevoelkerung der Bundesrepublik beim Aufbau einer Gesamtverteidigung"*. In Wehrwissenschaftliche Rundschau, 12. Jg. (1962), S. 123—139.

Arnold Bergstraesser u. a.: *Von den Grundrechten des Soldaten:* Muenchen 1957.

Gordon A. Craig: *NATO and the New German Army,* Center of International Studies, Princeton University, Memorandum No. 8, 24. Oktob. 1955.

Der deutsche Soldat in der Armee von morgen: Wehrverfassung, Wehrsystem, Inneres Gefuege: Muenchen 1954 (= Veroeffentlichungen des Instituts fuer Staatslehre und Politik e. V., Mainz).

Horst Ehmke: *"Militaerischer Oberbefehl und parlamentarische Kontrolle"*. In Zeitschrift fuer Politik, I (1954), S. 337 ff.

Rolf Elble: *Vom kuenftigen deutschen Offizier: Aktuelle Gedanken zum Offiziersberuf:* Bonn 1956.

Richard Jaeger: *"Die Staatsbuerger in Uniform"*. In Festschrift fuer Willibalt Apelt (1958), S. 122 ff.

Heinz Karst: *"Staatsbuerger in Uniform"*. In Wehrkunde, 3. Jg. (1954), Heft 5.

Otto Marcks: *Die Bundeswehr im Aufbau:* Bonn 1957.

Wolfgang Martens: *Grundgesetz und Wehrverfassung:* Hamburg 1961.

Hans Meier-Welcker: *Deutsches Heerwesen im Wandel der Zeit:* Arolsen 1954.

Ulrich Scheuner: *"Der Soldat und die Politik"*. In Neue Zeitschrift fuer Wehrrecht, 1959, S. 81 ff.

Ulrich Scheuner: *"Staatsrechtliche Probleme einer Verteidigung der Bundesrepublik"*. In Wehrwissenschaftliche Rundschau, 12. Jg. (1962), S. 196—207.

Hans Speier: *German Rearmament and Atomic War: The Views of German Military and Political Leaders:* New York 1957 (The RAND Corporation No. 5291).

III B6 Communism

Ossip K. Flechtheim: *Die KPD in der Weimarer Republik:* Offenbach 1948.

Hans Kluth: *Die KPD in der Bundesrepublik — Ihre politische Taetigkeit und Organisation 1945—1956:* Koeln und Opladen 1959.

Hermann Weber: *Von Rosa Luxemburg zu Walter Ulbricht:* Hanover 1961.

The Outlawing of the Communist Party of Germany—Sentence of the Federal Constitutional Court of August 17, 1956; Karlsruhe, 1956.

Treason and the Endangering of the State—Sentences of the Federal Constitutional Court; Karlsruhe, 1957.

"*Versprochen - gebrochen*" published by the Federal Executive Board of the German Trade Union Federation, Duesseldorf 1961.

Periodical: "*Fuer die Democratie — Informationen — Kommentar — Presseschau*": published by the Federal Executive Board of the German Trade Union Federation, Duesseldorf.

V A The Relationship of Germans to America

Waldemar Besson: *Die politische Terminologie des Praesidenten Franklin D. Roosevelt: eine Studie ueber den Zusammenhang von Sprache und Politik.* Tuebinger Studien zur Geschichte und Politik, ed. by Hans Rothfels, Theodor Eschenburg and Werner Markert: Tuebingen 1955.

Herbert von Borch: *Amerika — Die unfertige Gesellschaft:* Muenchen 1961.

Hedin Bronner: "*The Amerika-Haus—Germany's window to the United States*", *The American-German Review:* for promoting cultural relations between the United States and German-speaking peoples, Vol. XXIV (Feb.—March 1960), pp. 4—6, 36.

Das Schueleraustauschprogramm zwischen den Vereinigten Staaten von Amerika und der Bundesrepublik Deutschland: durchgefuehrt von privaten amerikanischen Organisationen, n.p., n.d. (1959?).

Deutschland und die Vereinigten Staaten: Empfehlungen der 2. amerikanisch-deutschen Historikerkonferenz ueber die Behandlung der amerikanisch-deutschen Beziehungen vom 18. Jahrhundert bis 1941, Braunschweig, 23. bis 31. August 1955, reprint from *Internationales Jahrbuch fuer Geschichtsunterricht,* 1956.

Divo, Marktforschung/Meinungsforschung/Sozialforschung: *A German appraisal of the Fulbright Program:* A study among the German participants of the cultural exchange between the Federal Republic and USA: Frankfurt/M. 1961.

Georg Eckert und Otto-Ernst Schueddekopf: *Die USA im deutschen Schulbuch.* Schriftenreihe des Internationalen Schulbuchinstituts, Vol. III: Braunschweig 1958.

Ernst Fraenkel: *Amerika im Spiegel des deutschen politischen Denkens: Aeusserungen deutscher Staatsmaenner und Staatsdenker ueber Staat und Gesellschaft in den Vereinigten Staaten von Amerika:* Koeln und Opladen 1959.

Dietrich Gerhard: "*Zur Struktur des akademischen Unterrichts in den Vereinigten Staaten*": ein Vergleich mit den deutschen Universitaeten, reprint from Studium Berolinense, Gedenkschrift der Westdeutschen Rektorenkonferenz und der Freien Universitaet Berlin zur 150. Wiederkehr des Gruendungsjahres der Friedrich-Wilhelm-Universitaet zu Berlin: Berlin 1960.

Institut fuer Demoskopie Allensbach: *Amerikaner in Deutschland:* Eine Leitstudie ueber die Urteile der Bevoelkerung im Heidelberger Raum und in Bayern, durchgefuehrt im Auftrage des Inwood Institute, Upper Montclair, New York, USA (1960/61).

Norbert Muhlen: "*America in German Eyes*", *Meet Germany,* eight rev. ed., published by Atlantik-Bruecke, Hamburg-Wellingsbuettel, June 1961, pp. 112—117.

Gerhard Neumann und Gerhard Schellenberg: *Begegnung mit dem Erziehungswesen der USA:* Erfahrungsbericht ueber den deutsch-amerikanischen Lehreraustausch 1952—1959: Muenchen 1961.

Dieter Oberndoerfer: *Von der Einsamkeit des Menschen in der modernen amerikanischen Gesellschaft,* Freiburger Studien zur Politik und Soziologie, ed. by Arnold Bergstraesser and Heinrich Popitz: Freiburg 1958.

Sigmund Skard: *American Studies in Europe:* Their History and Present Organization, 2 Vols., University of Pennsylvania, Philadelphia, Pa., 1958.

Transatlantic understanding in the schools of the NATO countries: report of the 3rd Atlantic Study Conference on Education organized by the Atlantic Treaty Association, Secretariat, London, n.d. (1960).

Zwei Voelker im Gespraech: Aus der Vortragsarbeit der Amerikahaeuser in Deutschland: Sammlung "res novae", Veroeffentlichungen zu Politik, Wirtschaft, Soziologie und Geschichte, Vol. 11: Frankfurt/M. 1961.

V C Germany and the Development Countries

Deutsche Afrika-Gesellschaft: *Deutschland und die Entwicklungslaender.* Tagungsprotokoll: Bad Godesberg 1959.

Fritz Baade: *"Das Interesse der alten Industrielaender an der Industrialisierung der Entwicklungslaender"*. In Offene Welt, 1957, Nr. 49, S. 263.

Richard F. Behrendt: *"Eine freiheitliche Entwicklungspolitik fuer materiell zurueckgebliebene Laender"*. In Ordo (Jahrbuch fuer die Ordnung von Wirtschaft und Gesellschaft), 1956, Bd. VIII.

Klaus Billerbeck: *Deutscher Beitrag fuer Entwicklunglaender:* Hamburg: Weltarchiv 1958.

Winfried Boell: *"Entwicklungspartnerschaft — eine neue Herausforderung der politischen Bildungsarbeit"*. In Deutsche Jugend, J. 7, 1959, H. 9.

Bulletin des Presse- und Informationsamtes der Bundesregierung: *"Entwicklungshilfe in neuer Sicht"* (Interview mit Bundeswirtschaftsminister Erhard). In Bulletin Nr. 14, S. 123 (1959).

Bulletin des Presse- und Informationsamtes der Bundesregierung: *"Kontakte zu jungen Voelkern"*. In Bulletin Nr. 234, S. 2401 (1959).

Dieter Danckwortt: *Erfahrungen und Anregungen zur Betreuung auslaendischer Studenten:* Bonn: Auswaertiges Amt, Selbstverlag 1959.

Diskussionskreis Entwicklungshilfe der CDU/CSU-Fraktion des Deutschen Bundestages: *Die Entwicklungslaender und unsere Hilfe:* Bonn 1961.

Ludwig Erhard: *"Wir helfen wie uns geholfen wurde"*. In Indo-Asia, J. 1, 1959, H. 2, S. 111.

Friedrich-Ebert-Stiftung: *Beitraege zur Entwicklungslaenderdiskussion:* Hannover 1961.

Friedrich-Ebert-Stiftung: *Wirtschaft und Entwicklungshilfe:* Hannover 1961.

Gernot Gather: *"Die dritte Kraft — Aufbruch der farbigen Welt"*. In Offene Welt, 1955, Nr. 39, S. 5.

Günther Harkort: *"Deutsche Technische Hilfe fuer die Entwicklungslaender"*. In Germany, 1959, Nr. 13.

Hilfe fuer Entwicklungslaender: *"Was der deutsche Steuerzahler aufbringt"*. In Hilfe fuer Entwicklungslaender (heute: „Entwicklungslaender"), J. 1, 1959, H. 1, S. 29.

Deutsches Industrie-Institut: *"Die Bedeutung der privaten Entwicklungshilfe"*. In Unternehmerrundbrief d. DI, Nr. 4, 1956.

Hellmut Kalbitzer: *Entwicklungslaender und Weltmaechte:* Frankfurt/M. 1961.

Clodwig Kapferer: *"Die unterentwickelten Gebiete: eine internationale Verpflichtung"*. In Wirtschaftsdienst, J. 35, 1955, Nr. 1.

Adolph Kummernuss: *Entwicklungshilfe — Entwicklungsgeschaeft?:* Heilbronn 1959.

Heinrich Luebke: *"Bekaempfung des Hungers in der Welt"*. Antrittsrede des Bundespraesidenten am 15. 9. 1959. In Hilfe fuer Entwicklungslaender, J. 1 (heute: "Entwicklungslaender"), 1959, H. 1.

Klaus Mehnert: *Asien, Moskau und Wir:* Stuttgart 1956.

Tibor Mende: *Die dritten Maechte, Der Westen und die Entwicklungslaender:* Koeln 1959.

Alfred Nau: *"Entwicklungshilfe — nicht nur in Geld zu leisten"*. In Sueddeutsche Zeitung, 30. 6. 61, Nr. 155.

Walter Scheel: *"Afrika spricht mit"*. In Christ und Welt, J. 12, 1959, Nr. 10.

Percey E. Schramm: *Deutschland und Uebersee:* Braunschweig—Berlin—Hamburg 1950.

Rudolf Vogel: *"Deutsche Hilfeleistung fuer Entwicklungslaender"*. In Die politische Meinung, J. 4, 1959, H. 39.

II. Bibliographien

Carl-Duisburg-Gesellschaft: *Entwicklungshilfe — Entwicklungslaender. Ein Verzeichnis von Publikationen in der Bundesrepublik Deutschland und Westberlin:* Koeln 1950—1959.

Friedrich-Ebert-Stiftung: *Literatur ueber Entwicklungslaender I. Eine Zusammenstellung des wichtigsten Schrifttums deutscher, englischer und franzoesischer Sprache 1950—1959:* Hannover 1961.

Literatur ueber Entwicklungslaender II. Eine Zusammenstellung des wichtigsten Schrifttums russischer Sprache 1950—1959: Hannover 1961.

Biographies of the Authors

FRITZ RENE ALLEMANN, a Swiss journalist, born in Basel on March 12, 1910, has done newspaper work in various capacities all since 1928. He has studied history, sociology and economics at the University of Basel (1930-32) and political science at the Berlin *Hochschule fuer Politik*. After two years of travels in South America (1934-36) he became assistant literary editor of the *National-Zeitung* in Basel. In 1942, he went to London as a correspondent for the Zurich newspaper *Die Tat* with which he has remained ever since, consecutively as Paris correspondent, foreign editor and, from 1949 onwards, as its main representative in Germany. In 1960, he was called to Berlin to become editor-in-chief of the leading German monthly *Der Monat* with which he had collaborated for many years. His book *Bonn ist nicht Weimar* (1956) has been the first comprehensive study devoted to the Federal Republic of Germany and to the prospects of German democracy. Some other books have been the fruits of extensive travels to the Balkans and the Middle East: *Nationen im Werden* (1955) (Emergent Nations) and *Die arabische Revolution* (1958) (The Arabic Revolution). His latest publication *Die Revolution der Baerte* (1961) is a study of Castro's Cuba. At present he is preparing a collection of his political essays on Germany and a volume devoted to Switzerland.

KURT BECKER, 42, joined the editorial staff of *Die Welt,* a newspaper published daily in Hamburg in 1946, soon after it had been founded by the British Occupation Forces. He is now one of the political editors of the now German-controlled paper. His main fields of interest are interior politics, German foreign policy and defense problems.

A native of Hamburg, he was a reserve officer during World War II, served in France, Africa and Russia, was interned in an American prisoner of war camp and released at the end of 1945.

In 1948, at the invitation of the British Foreign Office, Herr Becker spent some time studying in England and in 1957 visited the United States as a guest of the State Department.

IMMANUEL BIRNBAUM, born 1894 in Koenigsberg, East Prussia, at present the foreign political editor of the *Sueddeutsche Zeitung,* a daily newspaper in Munich, has been active in newspaper circles since 1919, beginning as political editor in Bremen and Breslau. From 1927 to 1952 he served as foreign correspondent in Warsaw, Stockholm and Vienna. He has traveled widely through East and West Europe, Asia and America.

Among his publications are *Die dritte polnische Republik* (The Third Polish Republic), Stockholm, 1945, and *Kleine Geschichte der Sowjetunion,* (Short History of the Soviet Union), Frankfort, 1959. He studied at the Freiburg, Koenigsberg and Munich universities.

PETER D. G. BROWN, free-lance writer, is presently employed by the Columbia Broadcasting System. He was born in Alton, Illinois. Mr. Brown has lived in Europe for the past thirteen years, having attended schools in the United States, Germany, and the Netherlands. His two main fields of interest are political affairs and literature.

For the past decade he has lived in Bonn, closely observing the development of the young German democracy. This winter he will move to New York City to devote himself exclusively to literary interests.

DR. HENDRIK GEORGE VAN DAM, born 1906 in Berlin, serves as Secretary General of the Central Council of Jews in Germany. He writes editorials for the *Allgemeine Wochenzeitung der Juden in Deutschland* and has published various articles and books on the question of damages and reparation, as well as publishing in other fields.

Dr. van Dam, the son of the *Hofantiquar* of Kaiser Wilhelm II, studied law and history in Heidelberg, Munich, Berlin and Basel. He was suspended from law practice in 1933 as a result of National Socialist persecution, left Germany for Holland and Switzerland and was deprived of German citizenship in 1934. He received his doctorate in Basel with a thesis on problems of the misuse of economic power. Later he worked as a journalist in Holland. With the invasion of Holland by German troops, he fled to England in 1940, where he was at first interned.

In May 1945, Dr. van Dam served in the reorganization of the German law system in Oldenburg. From 1946 to 1950 he was justice and department director in Hamburg and Bremen for the Jewish Relief Unit.

He prepared, in 1950, a memorandum for the Israeli Government advocating direct reparations negotiations with the Federal Republic.
Also, in that year he was elected secretary general of the Central Council of Jews in Germany, which had been founded shortly before.

Dr. van Dam has concerned himself since 1946 with problems of reparation laws and practice. In 1947 he lectured on "Law protection against Incitement of Racial Hatred" at the first Jewish Laywers Congress in Detmold. He took part in the reparations negotiations between the Federal Republic, Israel and Jewish organizations.

DR. MICHAEL FREUND, born 1902, is professor of political science and history at Kiel University. In answer to the American Secretary of State's question, "What is Germany," Dr. Freund published an 800 page *Deutsche Geschichte* (German History) in 1960. Since 1952 he has also been occupied with the publication of *Geschichte des Zweiten Weltkrieges in Dokumenten* (History of World War II in Documents), of which three volumes have so far appeared. He was also one of the editors of *Gegenwart* and now frequently contributes to the *Frankfurter Allgemeine Zeitung.*

He studied history in Munich and took his doctorate with Hermann Oncken with a thesis, later published in book form, on *Die Idee der Toleranz im England der Grossen Revolution* (The Idea of Tolerance in the England of the Great Revolution). From this topic, he went on to do research on the political philosophical history of England, working mainly in the library of the British Museum. This research produced two books, one on Oliver Cromwell, 1932, and later a history of the great English revolution. In 1951 the first volume of *Anatomie einer Revolution* (Anatomy of a Revolution), was published.

On his trip home from England, Dr. Freund spent three months in Paris writing *Georges Sorel, Der revolutionaere Konservatismus* (Georges Sorel, The Revolutionary Conservatism), Frankfort, 1932. In 1934, he began publishing a series, *Weltgeschichte der Gegenwart in Dokumenten* (Contemporary World History in Documents), which he continued to publish until this new method of studying contemporary history was forbidden by the National Socialists.

DR. GUENTHER GRUNWALD, born 1924 in Duesseldorf, has been director of the Friedrich-Ebert Foundation in Bonn since 1956 and this year was appointed to the Board of Trustees of the *Volkswagen* Foundation. He is also a member of various other European organizations.
He studied history, Germanics, geography and political science at Cologne University, following his release from an American prisoner of war camp, and received his doctorate in 1951.
Dr. Grunwald then worked as a trainee at the Henkel Company. In 1952 he was appointed executive in the foreign department of the German Trade Union Federation in Duesseldorf and, in 1954, became director of the foreign department.

DR. HELMUT HIRSCH, born 1907 in Wuppertal, is engaged in research and lecturing since his return from America to the Rhineland and has recently done a study on the American administration of the Saarland. He has published two books on the Saar question, one on European labor, has contributed to the Encyclopedia Britannica and several scientific journals.
He studied at Munich, Berlin, Bonn, Cologne and Leipzig Universities, before leaving Germany during the National Socialist years. He became Paris representative of the anti-Nazi weekly, *Westland,* and later staff member of the bi-monthly *Ordo.* After the fall of France he was granted an emergency visa to the United States and in 1942 resumed his studies at the University of Chicago, where in 1945 he received his Ph. D. He taught at Roosevelt University, becoming associate professor of European History before his return to Germany.

DR. WALTER JACOBSEN, psychological adviser in the *Bundeszentrale fuer Heimatdienst* (Federal Organization for Civics) in Bonn, until his retirement, changed fields from businessman to psychologist in 1928 at the age of 33. He wrote his doctoral thesis on *Individualitaet und soziale Rolle* (Individuality and Social Character) under William Stern and worked in German social guidance until his dismissal by the Nazis.
For several years he lived in Stockholm, serving as scientific director of an institute for practical psychology. Later, while working as an industrial psychologist he turned more and more to political education problems, in the *Bund Freies Hamburg* (Organization of Free Hamburg) founded in 1932.

MANFRED JENKE, born 1931, is political editor of the North German Radio Network in Hamburg. He directs its foreign news coverage. He is director of the Commission for Political Education of the German Youth Associations.
He believes that the best place to observe the rise and fall of rightism in the postwar years was Hanover, capital city of Lower Saxony. The results of his observations are published in *Verschwoerung von Rechts?* (Conspiracy from the Right?), Berlin, 1961, in which Herr Jenke, 31, shows the balance of postwar German conservative radicalism. He lived in Hanover from 1945 to 1961, where as a journalist, first on a daily paper, later on the labor paper *Welt der Arbeit,* and finally for a radio station, he was able to observe the activities of neo-Nazi and rightist parties, groups and organizations.
A member of the Social Democratic Party, Herr Jenke has visited nearly all European countries; in 1953 he traveled to South Africa, in 1957 to North Africa.
He is married and the father of two children.

DR. HANS HELMUTH KNUETTER, born 1934 in Stralsund, is a scientific research assistant at the Seminar for Political Science of Bonn University.

From 1954 to 1959, he studied history, sociology and political science at Berlin Free University and Bonn University, where he received his doctorate in 1960.

KARLHEINZ KOPPE, born 1929 in Breslau (Silesia) has published the newspaper *Europa Union / Europaeische Zeitung fuer Politik, Wirtschaft und Kultur* (Europe Union / European Newspaper for Politics, Economics and Culture), for many years and is now after having participated in the beginnings of the European Union Movement Assistant Secretary General of the *Europa Union* and Secretary General of the *Aktion Europaeischer Foederalisten* (Association of European Federalists). Following the occupation of his native city, Breslau, by the Poles he fled by foot to the West in the winter of 1944—45, at the age of 15, a decisive experience for him. His journalistic and public relations career began in Berlin in 1948, where he experienced the Berlin Blockade.
He studied law and economics in Paris and Bonn, lived several years in France, England and North Africa, and has spent some time in most other European countries.

DR. WOLFGANG KRALEWSKI, born 1931 to a Polish-German family, has worked for the *Institut fuer Politische Wissenschaften* (Institute for Political Science) in Heidelberg since 1959 and has a research contract on organizational problems of the federal government. He is a member of the faculty at Heidelberg University. Dr. Kralewski also is director of the *Deutsche Vereinigung fuer Politische Wissenschaft* (German Union for Political Science) and works together with agencies and institutes occupied with problems of international relations and world Communism.

He studied political science, history, sociology and public law from 1953 to 1959 at Berlin Free University and Heidelberg University. He received his doctorate in 1959 from Professor Sternberger with a thesis on the Opposition in the German *Bundestag,* published in 1962. He was named by the university chancellor to the executive board of the student government.

ERICH LUETH, born 1902 in Hamburg, has for many years been active in establishing better relations between Germany and Jewish communities, both in Germany and abroad. A few years ago, the American Palestine Committee invited him to the United States where he gave over one hundred lectures on the problem of reconciliation between Germans and Jews.

He called together German youth in 1957 to make a Pilgrimage to the mass graves at the Bergen-Belsen concentration camps. Thousands of pupils and young people took part.

He has published reports on his five trips to Israel and has delivered the message of the new Germany, "We miss you!", to Jewish emigrants in England, Scandinavia, the United States, Switzerland and South Africa.

In 1950 he urged the boycott of films by the Nazi film director Veit Harlan. Following a seven-year legal struggle, the Constitutional Court, declaring the priority of freedom of opinion, lifted the boycott. Soon thereafter Herr Lueth addressed an appeal to the survivors of the Jewish persecution: "We beg Israel for peace", and requested an olive tree donation.

As a journalist, he founded the *Hamburger Jungdemokraten.* During the Weimar Republic he was for some years a member of the Hamburg Parliament. In 1933, as a member of the democratic *Hamburger Anzeiger,* he was forced to resign and served in business and industry.

During the war, interned in an American prisoner of war camp, he edited a prisoners' newspaper and produced a camp radio broadcast. In 1946 he took over the direction of the press office of the Hamburg *Senat* (City Government).

DR. OEC. PUBL. NORBERT MUHLEN, was born in Bavaria. He is an American newspaperman and author who lives in New York. Among his books are *The Survivors, The Incredible Krupps, The Return of Germany: A Tale of Two Countries, The Magician: The Life and Loans of Dr. Hjalmar Horace Greeley Schacht.* He writes a syndicated column for over 150 U.S. daily newspapers, frequently contributes to many American magazines, and serves as U.S. correspondent of leading German and Swiss weeklies.

Dr. Muhlen studied at the University of Munich. He lived and worked in England, Italy, Switzerland, France, before immigrating to the United States. He left Germany for political reasons in May, 1933. He toured Germany fifteen times since the end of the war.

HERMANN PROEBST, born 1904 in Munich, is the editor-in-chief of the daily *Sueddeutsche Zeitung.* He has translated American books and written two in German: a biography of The Elder William Pitt, *Earl of Chatham, Begruender der britischen Macht* (Earl of Chatham, Founder of British Power), and *Die Brueder* (The Brothers), biographical essays on the 18th century.

He studied history and Germanics at the universities of Munich, Cologne and Berlin, and attended the Institute for Newspaper Science in Cologne and the College for Politics in Berlin, as well as studying in England and America.

In 1929 he began in radio, working for the Berlin radio network in the news department and becoming director of this department in 1935. For political reasons he was shunted to the art department and in 1936 dismissed.

In 1938, after having done free-lance writing, he was sent to the Balkans as correspondent and, in 1946, became political reporter for the *Rheinische Zeitung* in Cologne. He then, from 1947 to 1949, was director of the Press and Information Service of the Bavarian State Cabinet, before going to the *Sueddeutsche Zeitung* as chief editor for domestic politics.

DR. ALFRED RAPP, born 1903 in Karlsruhe, is the Bonn bureau chief for the *Frankfurter Allgemeine Zeitung*. He has published two books on Germany: *Bonn auf der Waage* (Bonn on the Scales), a balance of the first ten years of the Federal Republic; and *Glanz und Elend eines Jahrtausends* (A Thousand Years of Glory and Distress), a summary of the German past.

He studied history in Heidelberg, Munich, Berlin and Freiburg, and worked for the Baden state government as a specialist in parliamentary history. At 26, he entered the field of journalism, working on the editorial staff of papers in Mannheim and Dresden. When the Mannheim newspaper collapsed under National Socialism, he worked for a time as a free-lance journalist. During the final war years, as a soldier, he crossed into Switzerland and was at first interned. There he directed the film distribution department of the YMCA refugee homes in Switzerland. Following his return to Germany, Dr. Rapp served as economic reporter in Frankfort for several newspapers and then became Bonn correspondent for the *Frankfurter Allgemeine Zeitung*.

JOHANNES REINHOLD, born 1925 in Hildesheim, is assistant director of the Friedrich Ebert Foundation in Bonn. He attended schools in Hildesheim, Koenigsberg and Hamburg. From 1943 to 1946, he served with the navy after which he studied protestant theology and law in Mainz and Bonn from 1957 to 1958. He was director of the German National Union of Students in 1951—52 and was a member of the city council in Bonn from 1957 to 1961.

DR. HANS ROTHFELS, born 1891 in Kassel, is professor emeritus of modern German history at Tuebingen University and edits the *Vierteljahreshefte fuer Zeitgeschichte* (German Quarterly for Contemporary History). He is a director of the Association of German Historians and a member of the American Historical Association and the Goettingen Academy of Science. He holds the title of *Ritter des Ordens Pour le Mérite (Friedensklasse)* and Doctor of Law.

Among his publications are theses on the history of Bismarck, social and foreign policy, national problems, German resistance, and modern history observations.

Dr. Rothfels was professor of German history in Koenigsberg from 1926 to 1934. In 1939—40, he was appointed research fellow in St. John's College,

DR. THEO SOMMER, born 1930 in Constance, is a political editor of the Hamburg weekly newspaper *Die Zeit,* and writes mainly about foreign affairs and defense problems but has frequently commented on the German domestic scene. He has traveled extensively abroad; in 1960 he participated in Henry Kissinger's international Summer Seminar at Harvard University. Dr. Sommer is the author of *Deutschland und Japan zwischen den Maechten, 1935—40* (Germany and Japan Between the Powers, 1935—40). He is a member of the Deutsche Gesellschaft fuer Auswaertige Politik and of the London Institute for Strategic Studies.

He studied history, international relations and political science—first in Sweden, then for two years in the United States (Manchester College, North Manchester, Indiana, and University of Chicago), and finally in Tuebingen, where he took his Ph. D. He is married to a Greek bacteriologist. They have two sons.

DR. BERNHARD VOGEL, born 1932 in Goettingen, is an assistant and lecturer at the Institute for Political Science at Heidelberg University and is writing a study on the control function of the German *Bundestag.* During the federal elections in 1961 he and other members of the team studied the election battle and the conduct of the parties and the voters. He is editor of a scientific yearbook. Dr. Vogel has been particularly interested in problems of adult education, especially political education.

He studied sociology, political economy, history and political science in Munich and Heidelberg under Alfred Weber, Alexander Ruestow, Carl Joachim Friedrich and Dolf Sternberger and received his doctorate in 1960 with a communal political dissertation.

EDUARD WALD, born 1905 in Kiel, has been associated with the German labor unions since 1950. In his function of fighting antidemocratic tendencies he serves as chief editor of the information services *Feinde der Demokratie* (Enemies of Democracy), later renamed *Fuer die Demokratie* (For Democracy).

Herr Wald, as journalist and politician, has concerned himself since 1928 with building an active resistance movement against National Socialism and Stalinism. From 1933—36 he was working illegally in Germany. He was imprisoned from 1936—45.

Oxford University, England. From 1940 to 1946, he held a guest professorship at Brown University and in 1946 went, as professor of modern history, to the University of Chicago. He returned to Germany in 1961 to accept a professorship in Modern History in Tuebingen, where he became professor emeritus in 1949.

DR. WOLFGANG SAUER, born 1920 in Berlin, has been research member of the Institute for Political Science at the Free University in Berlin since 1951. He has coauthored with Karl Dietrich Bracher and Gerhard Schulz *Die nationalsozialistische Machtergreifung* (The National Socialist Seizure of Power: A Study of the Building of the Totalitarian Power System in Germany 1933—34), Cologne and Opladen 1960. To be published soon: *Militaer- und Zivilgewalt in der Revolution—Die November-Revolution und das Buendnis Ebert-Groener, 1918* (Military and Civil Power in the Revolution: The November Revolution and the Ebert-Groener Alliance, 1918).

Dr. Sauer studied history, philosophy, German literature and geography from 1938 to 1941 and from 1949 to 1950. He served in the armed forces from 1941 to 1945, was independently employed from 1946 to 1948 and received his doctorate in 1956.

DR. KURT L. SHELL, born 1920 in Vienna, research associate of the Institute of Political Science of Berlin Free University, is working on a project dealing with the reaction of political leadership, mass media and population to the Berlin crisis. He has written a book, *The Transformation of Austrian Socialism,* New York, 1962, and several articles, among them *"Industrial Democracy and the British Labor Movement",* Political Science Quarterly, December 1957; *"Die Berliner Wahl vom 7. Dezember 1958"* (The Berlin Elections of December 7, 1958) (with Nils Diedrich), Zeitschrift fuer Politik, Fall 1960; *"The Crisis of Modern Socialism",* World Politics, January 1957.

He was forced to emigrate from Austria in 1938. He first spent two years in England and then emigrated to the United States. From 1942 to 1946, he served in the U.S. Army, first in the infantry, later in Intelligence, the last eight months in the Group Control Council in Vienna.

In 1955, he received his doctorate in political science at Columbia University. From 1950 to 1956, he was an instructor of political science at Columbia and then went to Harpur College, State University of New York, as assistant professor. In 1958-59, he was Fulbright lecturer at the Paedagogische Hochschule in Berlin.

Members of Atlantik-Brücke

President:

Dr. Gotthard Baron Falkenhausen	Personally Responsible Partner in the Banking House of Burkhardt & Co., Essen

Vice-President:

Prof. Dr. Arnold Bergstraesser	University of Freiburg

Vice-President:

Erik Blumenfeld, MdB	Personally Responsible Partner in the Firm Blumenfeld & Co., Hamburg
Prof. Dr. Paul Baumann	President, Chemische Werke Huels AG., Marl
Heinrich Baron Berenberg-Gossler	Personally Responsible Partner in the Banking House of Joh. Berenberg, Gossler & Co., Hamburg
Dr. Kurt Birrenbach, MdB	Chairman of the Board, Thyssen-AG. fuer Beteiligungen, Duesseldorf
Dr. Hans C. Boden	Chairman of the Board, Allgemeine Electricitaets-Gesellschaft (AEG), Frankfort/Main
Dr. Hans Karl von Borries	Montagnola (Tessin)
Dr. Max Brauer, MdB	Buergermeister a. D., Hamburg
Dr. Rudolf Brinckmann	Personally Responsible Partner in the Banking House of Brinckmann, Wirtz & Co., Hamburg
Prof. Dr. Arthur Burkhard	President, Wuerttembergische Metallwarenfabrik, Geislingen
Prof. Dr. Constantin von Dietze	University of Freiburg, President of the General Synod of the Evangelical Protestant Church of Germany
Dr. Marion Countess Doenhoff	Journalist, Hamburg
Dr. Klaus Dohrn	Personally Responsible Partner in the Banking House of Berliner Handelsges., Frankfort/Main
Ernst Friedlaender	Writer, Siena/Italy
Dr. Otto A. Friedrich	President, Phoenix Gummiwerke AG., Hamburg-Harburg
Gerhard Geyer	Chairman of the Board, Esso AG., Hamburg
Dr. Kurt Hansen	President, Farbenfabriken Bayer AG., Leverkusen
Karl Haus	Personally Responsible Partner in the Banking House of Sal. Oppenheim jr. & Cie., Cologne
Dr. Konrad Henkel	Personally Responsible Partner in the Firm Henkel & Cie. GmbH., Duesseldorf

Dr. Guenter Henle	Personally Responsible Partner in the Firm Kloeckner & Co., Duisburg
Prof. Dr. Max Horkheimer	University of Frankfort
Dr. Hermann Jannsen	Member of the Managing Board, Frankfurter Bank, Frankfort/Main
Dr. Fritz Koenecke	President (ret.) Daimler-Benz AG., Stuttgart
Prof. Dr. Helmut Kuhn	University of Munich
Dr. W. Alexander Menne, MdB	Member of the Managing Board, Farbwerke Hoechst AG., Frankfort/Main
Dr. Friedrich Carl Baron Oppenheim	Senior Partner in the Banking House of Sal. Oppenheim jr. & Cie., Cologne
Herbert Pavel	Personally Responsible Partner in the Firm Rheinnadel-Gruppe, Aachen
Dr. Wolfgang Pohle	Generalbevollmaechtigter, Friedrich Flick KG., Duesseldorf
Dr. Hans Reuter	Chairman of the Board, DEMAG AG., Duisburg
Dipl.-Ing. Klaus Scheufelen	Personally Responsible Partner in the Firm Scheufelen-Papierfabriken, Oberlenningen/Wuerttemberg
Prof. Dr. Karl Schiller	Senator of Economics, Berlin
Fabian von Schlabrendorff	Lawyer, Wiesbaden
Dr. Guenther Schlicht †	President, Deutsche Erdoel-AG., Hamburg
Dr. Ernst Schneider	Personally Responsible Partner in the Firm AGFECO Kohlensaeure-Werke GmbH., Duesseldorf
Curt E. Schwab	Personally Responsible Partner in the Banking House Ott, Stuttgart
Dr. Kurt Sieveking	Lawyer, Buergermeister a. D., Hamburg
Dr. Hans Guenther Sohl	President, August-Thyssen-Huette AG., Duisburg
Dr. Gerd Tacke	Member of the Managing Board, Siemens & Halske AG. and Siemens-Schuckert-Werke AG., Munich
Werner Traber	Member of the Managing Board, Hamburg-Amerika Linie (Hapag), Hamburg
Dr. Hans Christoph Baron Tucher	Member of the Managing Board, Bayerische Vereinsbank, Munich
Franz Heinrich Ulrich	Member of the Managing Board, Deutsche Bank AG., Duesseldorf
Dr. Ernst Hellmut Vits	President, Vereinigte Glanzstoff-Fabriken AG., Wuppertal
Prof. Dr. Carl Friedrich Baron Weizsaecker	University of Hamburg
Dr. Hermann Winkhaus	President, Mannesmann AG., Duesseldorf
Casimir Prince Wittgenstein	Member of the Managing Board, Metallgesellschaft AG., Frankfort/Main
Otto Wolff von Amerongen	Personally Responsible Partner in the Firm Otto Wolff, Cologne